Kant's "Tugendlehre"

Kant's "Tugendlehre"

A Comprehensive Commentary

Edited by
Andreas Trampota, Oliver Sensen
and Jens Timmermann

De Gruyter

ISBN 978-3-11-020261-8
e-ISBN 978-3-11-022987-5

Library of Congress Cataloging-in-Publication Data
A CIP catalog record for this book has been applied for at the Library of Congress.

Bibliographic information published by the Deutsche Nationalbibliothek
The Deutsche Nationalbibliothek lists this publication in the Deutsche
Nationalbibliografie; detailed bibliographic data are available in the Internet
at http://dnb.dnb.de.

© 2013 Walter de Gruyter GmbH, Berlin/Boston

Cover illustration: Hans Veit Friedrich Schnorr von Carolsfeld.
Bildnis des Immanuel Kant. Kupferstich-Kabinett Dresden.
Foto: Herbert-Otto Boswank/Photo-Design

Printing: Hubert & Co. GmbH & Co. KG, Göttingen

⊗ Printed on acid free paper

Printed in Germany

www.degruyter.com

Acknowledgements

This book is the product of an international research project funded by the Deutsche Forschungsgemeinschaft (German Research Foundation, DFG). By providing financial support for three colloquia on Kant's *Tugendlehre* in Munich in the years 2008 and 2009, the DFG created a lively forum for the contributors to this volume to exchange and discuss their ideas. We are very grateful to the DFG for its support.

18 scholars from Germany, Italy, Britain, and the United States collaborated closely to write a seamless commentary on the *Tugendlehre*. The international character of the project accounts for the fact that a third of the papers in this volume were written in German. We are grateful to all contributors for their valuable contributions to our common research project, pursued over an extended period of time.

We should like to thank Gertrud Grünkorn, Christoph Schirmer and Andreas Brandmair at De Gruyter for their constant encouragement and patient support during the publishing process. Moreover, thanks are due to colleagues and staff at the Munich Hochschule für Philosophie (Munich School of Philosophy), where the three workshops took place. We would also like to thank the following individuals for their contribution to the success of the project: Markus Dirr for organizing the three workshops in a highly efficient as well as laid-back (i. e. Bavarian) way, and for his foundational editorial work on the volume; Ruben Schneider for dedicated editorial assistance during the early stages of the project; Kathryn Sensen for her accomplished translation of Manfred Baum's contribution; Eva Schestag for her translation of Andrea Esser's paper; Leonard Randall for his help with editing Andrea Esser's paper; Henrik Grawe for judiciously compiling the index of names and subjects; and Lukas Wallacher who, as research assistant to Andreas Trampota, did the greatest part of the editorial work during the final and most crucial stage in a highly competent manner, persistently with great commitment and diligence.

Contents

VIII Contents

Abbreviations

AA	Akademie-Ausgabe *Academy Edition*
Anm.	Anmerkung *Note*
Anth	Anthropologie in pragmatischer Hinsicht *Anthropology from a Pragmatic Point of View*
BDG	Der einzig mögliche Beweisgrund zu einer Demonstration des Daseins Gottes *The Only Possible Argument in Support of a Demonstration of the Existence of God*
Br	Briefe *Correspondence*
EEKU	Erste Einleitung in die 'Kritik der Urteilskraft' *First Introduction to the 'Critique of the Power of Judgment'*
GMS	Grundlegung zur Metaphysik der Sitten *Groundwork of the Metaphysics of Morals*
GSE	Beobachtungen über das Gefühl des Schönen und Erhabenen *Observations on the Feeling of the Beautiful and Sublime*
HN	Handschriftlicher Nachlass *Notes and Fragments*
IaG	Idee zu einer allgemeinen Geschichte in weltbürgerlicher Absicht *Idea for a Universal History with a Cosmopolitan Aim*
KpV	Kritik der praktischen Vernunft *Critique of Practical Reason*
KrV	Kritik der reinen Vernunft *Critique of Pure Reason*
KU	Kritik der Urteilskraft *Critique of the Power of Judgment*
Log	Logik *Lectures on Logic*

LBl   Lose Blätter
               Loose Sheets
MAN   Metaphysische Anfangsgründe der Naturwissenschaften
               Metaphysical Foundations of Natural Science
MpVT   Über das Mißlingen aller philosophischen Versuche in der
               Theodizee
               On the Miscarriage of all Philosophical Trials in Theodicy
MS   Die Metaphysik der Sitten
               The Metaphysics of Morals
n   *Note*
V-NR/   Naturrecht Feyerabend
   Feyerabend *Natural Law Feyerabend*
OP   Opus Postumum
Päd   Pädagogik
               Lectures on Pedagogy
PG   Physische Geographie
               Physical Geography
Refl   Reflexion
               Note/Fragment
RGV   Die Religion innerhalb der Grenzen der bloßen Vernunft
               Religion within the Boundaries of Mere Reason
RL   Metaphysische Anfangsgründe der Rechtslehre
               Metaphysical First Principles of the Doctrine of Right
SF   Der Streit der Fakultäten
               The Conflict of the Faculties
TG   Träume eines Geistersehers, erläutert durch die Träume der
               Metaphysik
               Dreams of a Spirit-Seer Elucidated by Dreams of Metaphysics
TL   Metaphysische Anfangsgründe der Tugendlehre
               Metaphysical First Principles of the Doctrine of Virtue
VAMS   Vorarbeit zur ‚Metaphysik der Sitten‘
               Drafts for ‘The Metaphysics of Morals’
V-Anth/   Vorlesungen Wintersemester 1784/1785 Mrongovius
   Mron   *Anthropology Lectures, winter semester 1784/1785, Mrongo-*
               vius
V-Anth/   Vorlesungen Wintersemester 1772/1773 Parow
   Parow   *Anthropology Lectures, winter semester 1772/1773, Parow*
VARL   Vorarbeit zur ‚Rechtslehre‘
               Drafts for the ‘Doctrine of Right’

VATL	Vorarbeit zur ‚Tugendlehre'
	Drafts for the 'Doctrine of Virtue'
VAZeF	Vorarbeiten zu ‚Zum ewigen Frieden'
	Drafts for 'Toward Perpetual Peace'
V-Lo/	Logik Philippi
Philippi	*Logic Lectures Philippi*
V-Mo/	Moralphilosophie Collins
Collins	*Moral Philosophy Lectures Collins*
V-Mo/	Immanuel Kant: Vorlesung zur Moralphilosophie (ed. by
Kaehler	Werner Stark, Berlin/New York 2004)
(Stark)	*Moral Philosophy Lectures Kaehler*
V-Mo/	Moral Mrongovius
Mron	*Moral Philosophy Lectures Mrongovius*
V-Mo/	Moral Mrongovius II
Mron II	*Moral Philosophy Lectures Mrongovius, Second Set of Notes*
V-MP/	Kant Metaphysik Dohna
Dohna	*Metaphysics Lectures Dohna*
V-MP/	Metaphysik Herder
Herder	*Metaphysics Lectures Herder*
V-MP/	Metaphysik Mrongovius
Mron	*Metaphysics Lectures Mrongovius*
V-MP/	Metaphysik von Schön, Ontologie
Schön	*Metaphysics Lectures von Schön*
V-MP/	Metaphysik Volckmann
Volckmann	*Metaphysics Lectures Volckmann*
V-MP-K3E/	Ergänzungen Kant Metaphysik K3 (Arnoldt)
Arnoldt	*Metaphysics Lectures Arnoldt*
V-MP-L1/	Kant Metaphysik L1 (Pölitz)
Pölitz	*Metaphysics Lectures Pölitz*
V-MP-L2/	Kant Metaphysik L2 (Pölitz, Original)
Pölitz	*Metaphysics Lectures Pölitz (Original)*
V-MS/	Die Metaphysik der Sitten Vigilantius
Vigil	*Metaphysics of Morals Lectures Vigiliantius*
VNAEF	Verkündigung des nahen Abschlusses eines Traktats zum
	ewigen Frieden in der Philosophie
	Proclamation of the Imminent Conclusion of a Treaty of Perpetual Peace in Philosophy
V-PP/	Praktische Philosophie Herder
Herder	*Practical Philosophy Lectures Herder*

V-PP/	Praktische Philosophie Powalski
Powalski	*Practical Philosophy Lectures Powalski*
VRML	Über ein vermeintes Recht, aus Menschenliebe zu lügen
	On a Supposed Right to Lie from Philanthropy
VT	Von einem neuerdings erhobenen vornehmen Ton in der Philosophie
	On a New Superior Tone in Philosophy
ZeF	Zum ewigen Frieden
	Toward Perpetual Peace

1. All abbreviations referring to Kant's writings are those suggested by the editors of *Kant-Studien*. They are used throughout this book, usually followed by (1.) volume, (2.) page, and frequently (3.) line number(s) of the standard German edition of Kant's Works known as the 'Academy Edition' (*Kants gesammelte Schriften*, ed. by the Royal Prussian Academy of Sciences, Berlin: Walter de Gruyter, 1900 ff.):

   abbreviation volume: (example: Päd 9:488.30–37)
   page.line(s)
   abbreviation volume: (example: TL 6:430.37–431.1)
   page.line–page.line
   abbreviation volume: (example: KpV 5:73.18–34, 154.5–8 ...)
   page.line,page.line ...

   The exception is 'V-Mo/Kaehler(Stark)', where references do not contain a volume number because this edition is not part of the Academy Edition.

2. Occasionally, this standard form is slightly modified by the statement of, for instance, a particular section (example: KU §59, 5:351 f.) or the number of a 'Reflection', one of the handwritten notes of Kant, (example: Refl 3585 HN 17:73.15 ff.) before the volume number, in place of the line number(s) or in addition to it.

3. References to the *Critique of Pure Reason*, however, follow the A (first edition), B (second edition) convention (example: KrV A721 f./ B749 f.).

4. All references refer to the German original, even when the quotation is from an English translation, since the page numbers of the Academy Edition can be found in the margins of most English translations.

5. Unless otherwise indicated, the English translations are taken from *The Cambridge Edition of the Works of Immanuel Kant* (ed. by Paul Guyer and Allen Wood). If not, the reference will be followed by

'trans. X.Y.', stating the initials of the respective translator (usually the author of the text).

6. References to Kant's works, referring to the 'primary sources,' are all given in brackets in the main text. However, very long references have been moved to the footnotes.

7. All other (secondary) sources are generally stated in the footnotes in a standard short format (example: Atwell, 1986, p. 133), referring to the bibliographical details listed at the end of each particular contribution.

8. Words and phrases from foreign languages are usually italicized unless they are references to the German original given in square brackets in the context of an English translation.

9. In references the year of publication is usually given in round brackets. In the case of historical texts only the year of publication of the original is given in round brackets, that of any later edition which may have been used in square brackets.

Introduction

Kant's *Tugendlehre*, the second part of his *Metaphysics of Morals* (1797), is an essential part of Kant's moral philosophy. It is nowadays acclaimed as 'the book that contains Kant's ethics' (Manfred Baum) and as the 'final form of Kant's moral philosophy' (Allen Wood). The present volume contains the first comprehensive commentary on this important work. In it, eighteen experts comment on the entire text of Kant's *Tugendlehre* and on the general introduction to the *Metaphysics of Morals*.

The *Tugendlehre* is of central importance because it gives a fuller picture of Kant's moral philosophy than the foundational works: the *Groundwork of the Metaphysics of Morals* (1785) and the *Critique of Practical Reason* (1788). Traditionally, Kant's ethics has been criticized for its apparent formalism and rigorism. It was widely believed that the Categorical Imperative—the command: *"act only in accordance with that maxim through which you can at the same time will that it become a universal law"* (GMS 4:421.18–20)—exhausted his ethics. On the one hand, critics objected that a merely formal law is empty and cannot yield any concrete duties. On the other hand, Kant was criticized for the inflexibility of a system that does not allow for any exception to the rule not to lie. If the *Tugendlehre* received any attention at all, it was mainly to illustrate Kant's old-fashioned opinions about sexual morality, narcotics and the consumption of alcohol. The theory of the *Groundwork* was considered underdeveloped; the views of the *Tugendlehre* were thought to be the confused musings of an old man.

But the *Tugendlehre* helps us gain a more nuanced view of Kant's ethics. In contrast to the alleged formalism of his ethics, Kant emphasizes the importance of particular human ends, of virtue, and of sensibility. For instance, in the *Tugendlehre* Kant emphasizes the need of reason to provide a "moral end" (TL 6:381.2) and states its supreme principle as: "act in accordance with a maxim of *ends* that it can be a universal law for everyone to have" (TL 6:395.15 f.). Ends therefore play a crucial role in Kant's moral philosophy. Moreover, virtue is already mentioned in the book's title, and Kant calls wide ethical duties "duties of virtue" (TL 6:391.27). Contrary to the charge of formalism, Kant also emphasizes the role of feelings when he says that no human being "is entirely without moral feeling, for were he completely lacking in receptivity to it he would be morally dead" (TL 6:400.9–11). Furthermore, against the image of Kant's ethics as a matter of cold, rational calculation, the *Tugendlehre* pays close attention to friendships and the virtues of social interaction (cf. TL 6:468–474). After each discussion of a concrete duty, Kant raises casuistical questions that belie the myth of an overly rigorous system.

What is the significance of Kant's concern with these matters? Does the *Tugendlehre* radically alter Kant's moral philosophy, leading to a full and final statement of his views? Or does the *Tugendlehre* bring out elements that are particularly relevant to a *human* morality, but do not change the ultimate foundation of an ethical theory valid for all rational beings? This volume addresses such questions in the course of commenting on the whole text of the *Tugendlehre*.

Chapters 1–5 concern Kant's general approach in the *Metaphysics of Morals* as a whole. **Chapter 1** explores some related issues raised in the introductory sections at the beginning of the work as well as the "Preface" to the *Tugendlehre* (MS 6:205–209, 214–218 and TL 6:375–378). Günter Zöller first examines the status of the two parts of the *Metaphysics of Morals* as containing the metaphysical principles for the subsequent individual disciplines in his system; the scholarly (rather than popular) nature of any kind of metaphysics; Kant's contention that his critical philosophy lies at the foundation of the first and only true system of philosophy; and his claim to originality with regard to the constructive character of mathematical presentation. In the second section Zöller turns to Kant's "Introduction" to the *Metaphysics of Morals* and its arguments for the unconditional necessity of such a metaphysical discipline. He focuses on the disanalogy between the metaphysics of nature and the metaphysics of morals; the place of prudence in the doctrine of morals; the relationship between a metaphysics of morals and anthropology; the role of a moral anthropology; and the identity of practical philosophy and moral philosophy. In his third section Zöller examines Kant's preface to the *Tugendlehre*, which is where we find Kant's affirmation of the—explicit or implicit—metaphysical nature of any ethical theory; his criticisms of eudaemonist ethical theories; and the distinction between pathological and moral pleasure.

In **Chapter 2** Thomas Höwing discusses the first section of the "Introduction" to the *Metaphysics of Morals* (MS 6:211–214), which is of interest not only with regard to Kant's conception of a metaphysics of morals but also with a view to his moral philosophy as a whole. In this section, Kant clarifies his conception of the capacities of the human mind employed in action under moral laws. Moreover, he introduces his novel and much discussed distinction between the will (*Wille*) and the faculty of choice (*Willkür*) and, toward the end, the distinction between ethical and juridical laws, which raises questions about the thematic unity of the section. Höwing's contribution is intended as a continuous commentary on the text that can be used as a critical guide. He sets out to explicate interpretative difficulties raised by Kant's discussions of the desiderative faculty, practical pleasure, and rational desire. Moreover, he intends to shed new light on important aspects of Kant's theory of the practical faculties of the human mind that—unlike the distinction between *Wille* and *Willkür*—have received comparatively little attention, such as Kant's definition of the faculty of desire as a faculty "to do or to refrain from doing as one pleases" (MS 6:213.16 f.) and his distinction between wishing and choosing.

Chapter 3 chiefly relates to architectonic concerns discussed in two introductory sections that relate to the division of the *Metaphysics of Morals* (MS 6:218–221 and RL 6:239–242) as well as two further parts of the text that concern the division of the *Tugendlehre* and of ethics (TL 6:388–394 and TL 6:410–413). Bernd Ludwig pays close attention to the distinction between 'legality' and 'morality' as applied to actions, as opposed to right and ethics as parts of a single metaphysics of morals; the various ways the distinction between 'inner' and 'outer' can be drawn with regard to duties; and in particular the distinction—not consistently applied, but philosophically necessary—between (directly or indirectly) ethical duties and duties of virtue. According to Ludwig, by 1797 Kant assumes that there are inner duties of right that are strict but ethical in the sense that they cannot be externally enforced; to be distinguished from duties of virtue, which concern ends that are also at the same time duties. He notes that the latter, curiously, are not put to use in the main body of the *Tugendlehre*. The *Doctrine of Right* discusses external duties of right to others; the *Doctrine of Virtue* external duties to oneself and all internal duties. Other topics covered in this contribution include the primacy of duty vis-à-vis right, which is construed as not just epistemic and semantic but also as practical and metaphysical.

In **Chapter 4** Steffi Schadow turns to Kant's distinction between right and ethics (MS 6:218–221 and TL 6:390 f.). According to Kant, ethical as well as juridical laws are laws of freedom. As such they can be recognized by rational beings as unconditionally binding. The decisive difference between right and ethics consists in the way that obligations are required in their respective realms of legislation. A subject can be externally coerced to act according to juridical laws by means of the use of

force. As long as the action accords with duty it is 'legal,' irrespective of
the agent's motive. By contrast, ethical laws require that the agent do his
duty from a moral disposition. That is why the necessitation of an ethically adequate—i. e. morally valuable—action can only be effected by the
obligated subject himself. Unlike juridical legislation, ethical legislation
cannot be 'external.' Ethics is not just concerned with actions but also
with their underlying 'inner' motivations. As Kant says in the "Introduction" to the *Tugendlehre*, duties that result from ethical legislation are
wide duties because enacting corresponding maxims is a matter of judgment according to rules of prudence, rather than morality. By contrast,
juridical duties do not permit of any kind of latitude—they do not command dispositions but specific actions. These issues are examined in detail.

In **Chapter 5** Manfred Baum comments on the preliminary concepts
of the metaphysics of morals (MS 6:221–228). These concepts are common to both parts of the *Metaphysics of Morals*, the *Doctrine of Right* and
the *Doctrine of Virtue*. Baum explains Kant's use of fundamental terms
such as freedom, obligation, law, imperative, the permissible and impermissible, duty, and moral feeling, as well as will (*Wille*) and choice (*Willkür*). Baum also addresses Kant's relation to his predecessors, such as
Wolff, Baumgarten, and Achenwall. He concludes with Kant's response
to Reinhold's charge that—on Kant's account of freedom—responsibility
for immoral action is impossible. Baum explains in which sense, according to Kant, will and choice can be said to be free. The will gives the
moral law and is identical with pure practical reason. It is free in the
sense that it is not determined by natural laws. By contrast, choice is
shown to be the ability to choose between two maxims.

Chapters 6–8 cover the "Introduction" to the *Doctrine of Virtue*.
Chapter 6 analyzes the central conception of an end that it is also a
duty (TL 6:379–393). Andreas Trampota points out that this concept
does not appear in any of Kant's previous writings. Trampota defines
the concept, and tries to give an account of what prompted Kant to introduce the concept at precisely this point in his practical philosophy.
What made this move necessary? For this purpose, Trampota reminds
us of what Kant says about the concept of an end in the *Groundwork*.
He also discusses the alleged inconsistency of Kant's theory of ends.
Trampota's reconstruction suggests the following conclusion: The two
obligatory ends—one's own perfection and the happiness of others—
are introduced by Kant as the matter required for choice because they
are the material aspect of internal freedom for finite rational beings.

The two required—not natural—ends are wide duties, since they merely demand the adoption of general rules that tell us that we should have certain types of ends while giving judgment a certain latitude in the determination of particular actions that follow from these maxims in specific situations.

In **Chapter 7** Lara Denis focuses on Kant's account of virtue (TL 6:394–398). Kant characterizes virtue in five interrelated ways: as strength, as self-constraint, as moral disposition, as volitional conformity to duty, and as its own end and reward. Denis explores each characterization and the questions raised by it in turn, and spells out the connections between them. What emerges is a rich picture of Kantian virtue: It is a vigorous and pervasive realization of the inner freedom of a human being. A pure, unwavering fundamental commitment to the moral law is expressed not only through one's resistance to the influence of inclinations contrary to morality, but also through one's protection, cultivation, and employment of feelings, predispositions, and other aspects of sensibility conducive to the fulfillment of duty, and thereby also to moral self-realization. Denis concludes by suggesting some ways in which Kant's account of duties of virtue enhances our understanding of Kantian virtue: by indicating key elements of the direction, structure, and content of a human life governed by morality.

Chapter 8 addresses the relationship between virtue and sensibility (TL 6:399–409). Ina Goy addresses two questions: First, are there pure a priori elements of sensibility which play a—subordinate—role in grounding virtue? Second, to what extend does it take a strong will to be virtuous given our sensibility? Regarding the first question Kant discusses four a priori elements as conditions of sensibility for human beings to be receptive to the concept of duty: moral feeling, conscience, love of human beings, and respect. A strong will is needed in two respects. On the one hand, it takes a strong will to determine oneself to action in accordance with the moral law; on the other, a strong will is needed to resist inclination. Goy also discusses Kant's critique of an Aristotelian account of virtue as the 'golden mean.' For Kant the difference between virtue and vice is a matter of principle, not of degree. There are different duties of virtue but only one ground of obligation that serves as their foundation.

Chapters 9–13 address Kant's treatment of the topic of duties to oneself. In **Chapter 9** Jens Timmermann analyzes the alleged antinomy that threatens to undermine the very possibility of such duties at the beginning of this part of the *Tugendlehre* (TL 6:417–420). The thesis gives voice to a common objection. It is argued that the concept of a duty to oneself contains a contradiction because it cannot be one and the same self that is both—actively—obligating and—passively—being obligated. If that were the case, the argument continues, an agent would be able to release himself from an obligation to himself, and as a consequence there would be no obligation at all. By contrast, the antithesis establishes that there are duties to oneself because (Kant argues) all other types of duty—which are not in dispute—depend on there being duties to oneself. Accordingly, the thesis is rejected. While the structure of the antinomy itself is unconventional, the resolution follows a familiar pattern: the distinction between the self that obligates and the self that is being obligated is shown to be possible only on the basis of Kant's transcendental idealism. Ultimately, a duty to oneself can be shown to apply to us as phenomenal beings, bound by our noumenal selves. Timmermann emphasizes that duties to oneself in the thin, formal sense required here are not to be confused with any of the substantive duties to oneself that are the subject of later chapters. This contribution seeks to explain the exact structure of Kant's argument as well as its philosophical implications.

In **Chapter 10** Mark Timmons turns our attention to concrete duties to oneself in Kant's *Tugendlehre,* particularly his attempts to establish duties regarding suicide and other forms of self-mutilation, masturbation, and intemperance in the consumption of food and drink (TL 6:421– 428). In reconstructing Kant's arguments concerning suicide and intemperance, Timmons appeals to the idea of moral harm—such actions either permanently or temporarily cause harm to or hinder those rational capacities that partly constitute one's humanity and are for this reason violations of a duty to oneself. In connection with Kant's remarks about masturbation, he argues that Kant fails to provide a plausible argument in the passages in question, but that in his lectures on education he does appeal to the (alleged) harms, both prudential and moral, in condemning masturbation. So, this particular batch of duties can be understood as involving actions whose wrongness is explained in terms of their causal effects on one's humanity. Timmons concludes that Kant's arguments meet with mixed success, depending on the plausibility of the causal claims upon which they rest.

In **Chapter 11** Stefano Bacin explores the duties a human being has toward himself merely as a moral being: lying, avarice, and false humility (TL 6:428–437). These duties mark one of Kant's important innovations in the field of moral philosophy. They concern prohibitions, not the advancement of positive ends, and are conventionally—see e.g. Baumgarten and Meier—treated as duties to others, not duties to oneself.

In the case of lying it is clear why Kant considers it a violation of a duty to one's moral self. As such, neither the harm done to another nor the independent value of truth suffice to establish that lying is a vice. What is problematic is the liar's lack of truthfulness. Bacin distinguishes two separate arguments in Kant's text. The first concerns untruthfulness as a violation of the capacity to speak; the second interprets untruthfulness as a manifestation of a deeper, underlying insincerity. Bacin then sets out to show that Kant's actual ethical argument against lying as a violation of a duty to oneself rests on the second consideration: Every lie involves an 'inner' lie, which is why it is so insidious. Reflections on avarice and false humility conclude the paper.

In **Chapter 12** Andrea Esser examines the inner court of conscience, moral self-knowledge, and the proper object of obligation (TL 6:437–444). Contrary to some recent interpreters, she tries to show that conscience plays a minor role in Kant's moral philosophy. By limiting its function Kant seeks to prevent according conscience the status of an unverifiable authority that could challenge the supremacy of practical reason. Conscience is marginal. It is neither foundational, nor substantially guiding, nor systematically important. Yet Kant's conception of conscience, as expounded in his published writings, has been criticised by Hegel and Hermann Cohen, and not without cause: The subjective certainty conveyed by a 'good' or 'clear' conscience—that one's actions or maxims are in complete conformity with one's own moral principles, and that one has sincerely put all aspects of one's own actions to the test—can be morally perilous because it suggests that it is legitimate to withdraw from the process of critical self-assessment. Note, however, that the verdict of conscience is distinct from the duty of moral self-knowledge that Kant reviews in the two sections that follow. Finally, Esser turns to Kant's 'episodic' reflections on the concept of duty, which reveal that in Kant's critical ethics human beings can have duties only to persons they encounter in experience, i.e. to other human beings. Inanimate and animate nature, as well as God, become matters of duty only indirectly, when they serve to support obligations based on a duty to one's own self.

In **Chapter 13**, the final contribution dealing with duties to oneself, Thomas Hill focuses on the imperfect duties a human being has toward himself (TL 6:444–447). First, for background, his commentary briefly raises questions about Kant's ideas of ethical duties, duties to oneself, and imperfect duties. For example, in what sense is 'the human being as such' an 'end'? What does Kant's classification of duties as duties to oneself imply about their object, source, and appropriate sanctions? Second, Hill comments more specifically on the duty to develop and increase one's natural perfection. Kant's qualification that this is done "for a pragmatic purpose" (TL 6:444.15 f.) may suggest an instrumental requirement just to promote one's interests, and his description of the duty as "to be a useful member of the world" (TL 6:446.1) may suggest that it is basically a duty to others; but neither can be right. The duty is based not on self-interest or the welfare of others but rather on the worth of humanity in one's own person. Like the duty to avoid servility, it partially concerns how one is prepared to relate to others, but it remains a duty to oneself. Third, the essay discusses the duty to increase one's moral perfection. Moral purity would be an invariable and wholehearted will to do what is right from duty, but moral perfection includes this and something more: the complete attainment of one's moral end with regard to oneself. One must strive to attain virtue, which is a special strength of moral will that requires time and practice to develop. Because of the fragility of human nature and the "unfathomable" depths of the human heart (cf. TL 6:447.1), the duty to increase one's moral perfection is imperfect; but it does not allow the same kinds of latitude as the imperfect duties of beneficence and cultivation of one's natural powers.

Chapters 14–16 concern Kant's discussion of duties toward others. **Chapter 14** examines Kant's account of duties of love (TL 6:448–461). Dieter Schönecker first distinguishes between the duty of love and the feeling of love, and relates them to the feeling and the duty of respect. He argues that the feeling of respect always accompanies the duty of respect, while feeling and duty are not so united in the case of love. Furthermore, the duties of love and respect can be considered separately, but not the feelings of love and respect. But there is an accessory connection between the duties of love and respect, in such a way that performing a duty of beneficence should be checked by a duty of respect. For instance, one should not humiliate another when making a gift. Schönecker then raises the following questions: What is the maxim of the duty of love? Is there a duty to be benevolent toward oneself? And are there different degrees of benevolence?

In **Chapter 15** Oliver Sensen comments on the sections on duties to others that arise from respect (TL 6:462–468), by means of raising three questions. First, what is the justification for the requirement to respect others? Second, why does Kant think that there are merely three vices of disrespect—arrogance, defamation, and ridicule—but not others such as murder or deception? Third, why are these three particular vices the vices of disrespect? These three problems, Sensen argues, can be solved as follows. As to the first question, Kant conceives of the respect owed to others as a maxim one should have of not exalting oneself above others. This is commanded by the Categorical Imperative, which requires that one's maxim could be adopted by all others. If a maxim passes this test, one does not exalt oneself above others in acting on it. Second, the reason why Kant does not include murder, deception etc. under vices of disrespect is that such actions are already ruled out by the demands of Kant's juridical framework. Here, in his ethics, Kant is concerned with the inner maxims of the agent. Finally, Kant puts forth the three vices of arrogance, defamation, and ridicule, since they represent the three ways one can exalt oneself above others: One can regard oneself as more important than another, one can make this maxim public, and one can in addition take pleasure in doing so.

Chapter 16 analyzes the two forms of friendship discussed by Kant (TL 6:468–475): friendship as the union of two persons through equal love and respect, and being a friend to human beings as such. Marcia Baron first explains the duty to be a friend to human beings as such and relates it to the duty of beneficence. She then considers in which sense love and respect have to be equal for a friendship between two persons to exist. Does, for instance, A's love have to be equal to B's love, or also A's love and A's respect? Baron argues that the two persons must have equal love and respect for each other, but that it is not clear that one person must to the same degree have love and respect. The tension between love and respect, Baron argues, is a facet of our 'unsocial sociability' that makes us want to share our thoughts, but also makes us wary to do so. Furthermore, Baron critically examines in which sense friendship is a duty, and whether one needs to be cautious in accepting favors from a friend.

Finally, **Chapters 17 and 18** discuss the 'Doctrine of Method.' In **Chapter 17** Bernd Dörflinger explores the first two sections (TL 6:477–485), which concern two forms of the practice and application of moral concepts. In the 'Ethical Didactic' (Section 1) Kant talks about how virtue can be taught, particularly to students. It therefore constitutes a guideline for instruction in the theory of ethics. The 'Ethical Ascetic' (Section 2), by contrast, is a guideline for performing moral duties; it concerns the taming of inclinations, which will promote action from duty. Dörflinger wonders whether Kant's suggestions are in conflict with his commitment to autonomy when he intimates that virtue must be taught, and that another person may play a role in someone's becoming virtuous. Finally, in commenting on Kant's distinctions between a moral and a religious catechism, as well as on Kant's rejection of a monkish ascetic, Dörflinger relates Kant's educational views to his philosophy of religion.

Chapter 18 examines the conclusion of the 'Doctrine of Method' (TL 6:486–491) and Kant's claim that religion as the doctrine of duties to God lies beyond the bounds of pure moral philosophy. Friedo Ricken argues that the concluding part justifies the claim that the *Metaphysics of Morals* is complete without a section on duties toward God, which was part of Wolff's and Baumgarten's systems. Ricken brings out Kant's distinction between a direct duty *to* God and an indirect duty *with regard to* God. To have a direct duty to God, Kant argues, presupposes divine revelation, and its precepts would therefore have to be known empirically. As such, duties one owes to God are not part of a pure and a priori metaphysics of morals. But, second, there can be duties with regard to God, since duties toward other human beings can be regarded as God's commands in order to strengthen the moral incentive. Kant rejects the objection that one owes respect to God as a judge administering justice. God as judge is merely a personification of the substance of justice.

Idee und Notwendigkeit einer Metaphysik der Sitten (MS 6:205–209, 214–218 und TL 6:375–378)

Günter Zöller

Die drei zu präsentierenden Partien des Kantischen Textes (unterschieden als A, B, und C) werden abschnittsweise vorgestellt und dabei jeweils mit thematischen Titeln versehen.

A. Vorrede zur *Metaphysik der Sitten* (MS 6:205.1–209.16)

Die Vorrede war ursprünglich Teil der ersten Auflage der separat publizierten Rechtslehre (*Die Metaphysik der Sitten in zwey Theilen. Metaphysische Anfangsgründe der Rechtlehre*; 1797). In der zweiten Auflage der Rechtslehre (*Die Metaphysik der Sitten. Erster Theil, Metaphysische Anfangsgründe der Rechtlehre*; 1798) entfiel der letzte Satz der Vorrede, der die baldige Lieferung der „metaphysische[n] Anfangsgründe der Tugendlehre" (MS 6:209.15) in Aussicht gestellt hatte, die inzwischen erfolgt war.

1. Metaphysische Anfangsgründe statt Metaphysik (MS 6:205.1–206.3)

Zu Beginn der Vorrede charakterisiert Kant das Werk, das sie eröffnet, „die Metaphysik der **Sitten**" (MS 6:205.3), als das auf die „Kritik der praktischen Vernunft" (MS 6:205.2) folgende „System" (MS 6:205.2), das er sogleich auch als in „metaphysische Anfangsgründe" (MS 6:205.3) der Rechtslehre und der Tugendlehre gegliedert ausweist und dabei die Korrespondenz mit den bereits gelieferten metaphysischen Anfangsgründen der Naturwissenschaft herausstellt, die in Ausführung der Analogie als das der Kritik der reinen (spekulativen) Vernunft zugehörige ‚System' zu kennzeichnen wären. Den von Kant gebrauchten Titeln für die verschiedenen korrelierten und verglichenen philosophi-

schen Projekte korrespondieren die gleichlautend betitelten, von Kant
publizierten Werke. Doch verweist Kant nicht eigentlich auf die eigenen
Werke als im Druck vorliegende Schriften, sondern zitiert mit deren
Titelformulierungen die unterschiedlichen sachlichen Aufgabenstellungen
seines umfassenden, über lange Jahre weg verwirklichten Projekts eines
Systems der Philosophie, das mit dem vorliegenden Werk, der *Metaphysik
der Sitten*, zum Abschluss kommt. Im Hinblick auf die der Vorrede folgende Einleitung zu diesem Werk stellt Kant überdies die Präsentation
und Illustration der systematischen Form von jedem seiner beiden Teile
in Aussicht.

Für die Rechtslehre, die den ersten Systemteil der Metaphysik der
Sitten bildet, würde sich – nach dem zuvor Gesagten – der Sachtitel der
„Metaphysik des Rechts" (MS 6:205.10) zur Benennung anbieten.
Doch Kant verweist auf den Umstand, dass der Begriff des Rechts zwar
ein „reiner" (MS 206.11) ist, der insofern unabhängig von Erfahrung
gelten soll, aber zugleich ein Begriff, der die „Anwendung auf in der
Erfahrung vorkommende Fälle" (MS 6:229.11 f.) einschließt. Als rein-
empirisch gedoppelter, nämlich originär erfahrungsfreier und applikativ
erfahrungsbezogener Begriff, involviert der Begriff des Rechts ein „me-
taphysisches System" (MS 6:205.13), dessen Einteilung nicht a
priori erfolgt, sondern empirisch – im Rückgriff auf die empirische
Vielfalt von rechtlich relevanten Fällen. Die für die systematische Entfaltung des Begriffs des Rechts erforderliche Bezugnahme auf Erfahrung
macht nun aber die für ein „System[] der Vernunft" (MS 6:206.15 f.)
definitorisch geforderte Vollständigkeit der Einteilung des Systems unmöglich. Allenfalls kann in der Rechtslehre die Annäherung an das architektonische Ideal vollständiger systematischer Einteilung dadurch
versucht werden, dass die empirischen Spezifikationen des Rechtsbegriffs
nicht in das System selbst integriert, sondern ihm extern zugeordnet und
als Beispiele in Anmerkungen platziert werden. Dann ist der dem ersten,
das Recht betreffenden Teil der Metaphysik der Sitten angemessene
Sachtitel der von „metaphysische[n] Anfangsgründe[n] der
Rechtslehre" (MS 6:205.21 f.), mit dem die erforderliche Beschränkung des systematischen Kerns auf das Apriorische ebenso wie die Er-
gänzungsbedürftigkeit des apriorischen Systems, das nur erst die Prinzipien liefert, um das Aposteriorische im Hinblick auf deren mögliche
Anwendung angezeigt ist. Damit ergibt sich die architektonische Zweiteilung der Rechtslehre in das System des Rechts (im Singular) und in die
außersystematische, episodisch-exemplarische Behandlung der Rechte (im
Plural). Kant selbst vergleicht die Beschränkung des streng gefassten

Rechtssystems auf das System des Rechts unter Ausschluss der Rechte mit einer analogen Restriktion im Fall der metaphysischen Anfangsgründe der Naturwissenschaft, deren systematische Erörterung auf den singularischen Begriff der Materie als des Beweglichen im Raume beschränkt war unter Absehen von spezifisch unterschiedenen pluralen Ausprägungen der Materie.

2. Die Unpopularität der Metaphysik
(MS 6:206.4–34)

Auch die sich nun anschließenden apologetischen Äußerungen Kants zum wissenschaftlichen Charakter des Systems der Vernunftkritik sowie der im Anschluss daran auszuführenden systematischen Metaphysik (der Natur wie der Sitten) dienen der methodischen Vorabklärung und Vororientierung. Kant konzediert der zeitgenössischen Popularphilosophie in Gestalt ihres Hauptrepräsentanten Christian Garve ganz generell das aufklärerische Erfordernis der allgemeinen Mitteilbarkeit philosophischer Lehren mittels anschaulicher Darstellung („Popularität" (MS 6:206.15)), um dem konzeptuellen Obskurantismus vorzubeugen. Einzig die systematische Vernunftkritik mit ihrer konstitutiven Unterscheidung von Sinnlichkeit und Vernunft und ihrer Präsentation formeller Metaphysik nimmt er von der Forderung allgemeinverständlicher Philosophie aus, konzediert aber auch die Möglichkeit, die Ergebnisse solcher Metaphysik in anderer, populärer Form einem breiteren Publikum zugänglich zu machen. Die Unmöglichkeit, die systematische Vernunftkritik als solche populär darzustellen, begründet Kant damit, dass die zunächst einmal unkritische, dogmatisch auftretende Vernunft nur durch schulmäßige Genauigkeit („scholastische Pünktlichkeit" (MS 6:206.25)) zur Selbsterkenntnis gebracht und darin erhalten werden kann. Den Unterschied von wissenschaftlicher und populärer Darstellung fasst Kant sprachlich als Differenz von Schulsprache und Volkssprache.

3. Der Anfang mit der kritischen Philosophie
(MS 6:206.35–207.29)

Kants nächste apologetische Vorwegerklärung gilt dem scheinbar arroganten Anspruch der kritischen Philosophie, den (eigentlichen) Beginn von Philosophie zu markieren. Kant begegnet dem möglichen Vorwurf

mit der Frage, ob es denn wirklich viele Philosophien geben könnte oder
nicht vielmehr nur eine. Zwar gibt es viele Formen des Philosophierens
und damit des Rückgangs auf die ersten Vernunftgründe sowie des
Versuchs, im Ausgang von solchen Prinzipien jeweils ein System der
Philosophie zu errichten. Kant konzediert sogar das Verdienst der früheren philosophischen Versuche für seine eigene Bemühung um die
systematische Philosophie. Doch der Umstand, daß die Vernunft – objektiv betrachtet – wesentlich *eine* ist, begründet, so Kant, auch, dass es
nur *ein*, im Verhältnis zur Vernunft und ihrer Einheit „wahres" (MS
6:207.9) System der Vernunft aus Prinzipien geben kann, ungeachtet der
gegensätzlichen Ansichten, die das einheitliche Prinzip eines philosophischen Systems erhalten haben mag. Objektiv und formal betrachtet
gibt es in philosophischen Dingen jeweils immer nur ein einziges System
– und jeweils ein einziges, höchstes Prinzip, wie Kants eigenes ethisches
Prinzip der Tugend, und damit eine einzige Tugendlehre. Doch gilt – wie
auch in den analogen Fällen der neuesten chemischen und medizinischen
Systeme, die Kant zitiert (Lavoisier, Brown) –, dass die früheren, inzwischen als falsch erwiesenen Prinzipien ihren Verdienst um die Anbahnung
der späteren, überlegenen Einsicht behalten.

Aus dem Umstand, dass es objektiv betrachtet nur ein wahres philosophisches System geben kann, folgert Kant, dass jeder, der das eigene
philosophische System nicht als das erste und einzige (wahre) System der
Philosophie überhaupt ankündigt, mehr als die eine, eigene Philosophie
als wahr zulässt und sich in einen Widerspruch verwickelt. Damit ist auch
der Anspruch der kritischen Philosophie, erstmals das eine wahre System
der Philosophie zu liefern, gerechtfertigt und der etwaige Vorwurf intellektueller Arroganz gegen die kantische Philosophie entkräftet.

4. Ein falscher Vorwurf
(MS 6:207.30 – 208.18)

Als nächstes stellt sich Kant bei Gelegenheit der Vorrede dem in der
Rezension einer mathematischen Dissertation in den *Tübinger gelehrten
Anzeigen* aus dem Jahr 1795 gegen ihn erhobenen Vorwurf, die als eigene
Entdeckung der kritischen Philosophie ausgegebene „Definition der
Philosophie überhaupt" (MS 6:207.34 f.) mittels ihrer Unterscheidung
von der Mathematik sei bereits Jahrzehnte vor Kant zu finden. In der
Kritik der reinen Vernunft hatte Kant die philosophische Erkenntnis als
Vernunfterkenntnis *aus Begriffen* und die mathematische Erkenntnis als

Vernunfterkenntnis *aus der Konstruktion der Begriffe* (vgl. KrV A713/ B741) bestimmt. Der Tübinger Rezensent hatte auf ein mathematisches Werk von C. A. Hausen aus dem Jahre 1734 verwiesen, das „die gleichsam durch den Verstand gemachte Darstellung" (MS 6:208.12f.) („intellectualis quaedam constructio" (MS 6:208.35)) erörtert.[1] Kant betont in seiner Erwiderung auf den Vorwurf der Unoriginalität zunächst den Unterschied zwischen der historisch verbürgten, aber noch ganz allgemeinen Ausdrucksweise von verstandesmäßiger Darstellung und seinem eigenen viel spezifischeren Konzept der Darstellung eines gegebenen Begriffs in der Anschauung a priori, durch die allererst die Mathematik grundsätzlich von der Philosophie, die ihre Begriffe nicht in der Anschauung a priori darzustellen vermag, unterschieden wird. Sodann bestreitet Kant, dass Hausen selbst die Deutung der Rede von der „gleichsam durch den Verstand gemachten Darstellung" (MS 6:208.12 f.) als Vorwegnahme von Kants kritischer Raumlehre akzeptiert hätte. Dagegen sprechen, so Kant, die weitreichenden philosophischen Implikationen der Kantischen Auffassung vom Raum als Anschauung a priori. Für Kant reduziert sich deshalb der Sinn der vom Tübinger Rezensenten zitierten Wendung auf die illustrative Funktion des Raumes für die sinnliche Darstellung eines Begriffs, bei der von den Ungenauigkeiten des einzelnen räumlichen Bildes abgesehen und nur auf die regelgemäße Ausführung der geometrischen Operation geachtet wird.

5. Wer zuletzt lacht ...
(MS 6:208.19–209.16)

Schließlich distanziert sich Kant noch von dem missbräuchlichen Export des technischen Vokabulars der Vernunftkritik aus der engeren Sphäre der systematischen Philosophie, in der es unverzichtbar ist, in die weitere Sphäre des allgemeinen Gedankenaustauschs, in der philosophische Fach- und Fremdwörter überflüssig sind und geradezu einen „Unfug" (MS 6:208.20) darstellen. Im übrigen prophezeit Kant, dass die kritische Philosophie, nachdem sie über lange Zeit wegen ihrer Unpopularität und ihrer Pedanterie verlacht worden sein wird, über die unkritischen und insofern ignoranten konkurrierenden Systeme, die sich endlich als unhaltbar erweisen werden, das Lachen haben wird. Er beruft sich für diese Prognose auf eine Äußerung von Lord Shaftesbury, der es geradezu für

---

1   Siehe dazu die sachliche Erläuterung zu MS 6:207.30–208.18 unter: 6:521 f.

ein Kriterium der Wahrheit einer Lehre hält, wieviel Belachtwerden sie aushält.[2]

B. Einleitung in die *Metaphysik der Sitten*

II. Von der Idee und der Notwendigkeit einer Metaphysik der Sitten (MS 6:214.31–218.8)

1. Idee und Notwendigkeit einer Metaphysik der Natur (MS 6:214.34–215.15)

Kant begründet die Idee und Notwendigkeit einer Metaphysik der Sitten im Ausgang vom Kontrastfall der Naturwissenschaft, die zwar im Fall der Physik ebenfalls über einen metaphysischen Teil („metaphysische[] Naturwissenschaft" (MS 6:215.2)) verfügt, der die allgemeine Gesetzlichkeit der Gegenstände der äußeren Sinne verbürgt, die aber in der Aufstellung spezieller Naturgesetze ganz empirisch verfährt und sich dabei auf die Tragfähigkeit der äußeren Erfahrung für die Entdeckung von Gesetzen verlässt, die ihrerseits streng allgemein und notwendig gelten sollen. Ähnliches gilt für den Fall der Chemie, die ebenfalls von Erfahrung unmittelbar zur Aufstellung allgemeiner Gesetze der Vereinigung und Trennung der Materien fortschreitet und die dabei – anders als die Physik – nicht einmal auf spezifische apriorische Prinzipien, die unabhängig von Erfahrung aufzustellen wären, rekurriert.

2. Die Disanalogie zwischen einer Metaphysik der Natur und einer Metaphysik der Sitten (MS 6:215.16–23)

Im Gegensatz zu dem mit deren apriorischer Gültigkeit zusammenbestehenden empirischen Ursprung der naturwissenschaftlichen Gesetze sind die Sittengesetze, ihrem Begriff nach, nur dann als Gesetze anzusehen, wenn sie a priori begründet und in ihrer Notwendigkeit eingesehen werden können. Jeder Versuch, moralische Grundsätze auf Erfahrung zu

---

2 Siehe dazu die sachliche Erläuterung zu MS 6:208.32–209.7 unter: 6:522.

gründen, führt kognitiv zum Irrtum und praktisch zu Gefährdung im Hinblick auf die Sittlichkeit.

3. Die Sittenlehre ist nicht bloß Glückseligkeitslehre (MS 6:215.24–216.6)

Den begründenden Rekurs auf apriorische Prinzipien ganz aufzugeben, würde voraussetzen, dass sich die Sittenlehre auf „Glückseligkeitslehre" (MS 6:215.24) reduzieren ließe und damit auf rein empirische Quellen und Regeln des Verhaltens auf der Grundlage natürlicher Triebe, für die Vernunft weder notwendig noch hinreichend wäre. Die durch Induktion im Ausgang von Erfahrung ermittelten Verhaltensregeln des eudämonistischen Klugheitskalküls wären aber immer nur von komparativer oder genereller (im Unterschied zu absoluter und universeller) Allgemeinheit.

4. Die Rolle der Klugheit in den Lehren der Sittlichkeit (MS 6:216.7–27)

Doch die sittlichen Vorschriften gebieten apodiktisch und universell: unangesehen der partikularen Neigungen und für jede Person – und nicht aufgrund einer zufälligen empirischen Konstitution, sondern aufgrund der Freiheit und praktischen Vernunft, die der Person zukommt. Die gesetzlichen Vorschriften der Sittlichkeit gründen so weder in introspektiver oder behavioraler Selbstbeobachtung noch in wie auch immer bewährter Erfahrung mit dem Gang der Dinge in der empirischen Welt. Vielmehr gründen sie im Vernunftgebot für das Handeln, ohne Rücksicht auf Vorteil und ohne dass es für das geforderte Handeln ein Beispiel in der Erfahrung geben müsste. Zwar gestattet die sittlich gebietende Vernunft die Verfolgung des eigenen Vorteils im Rahmen der Moral und favorisiert sogar das Einbringen von Überlegungen der Klugheit in die Befolgung ihrer Gebote, weil dadurch die Wahrscheinlichkeit des Verstoßes gegen die Gebote abnimmt. Doch besitzen die prudentiellen Erwägungen nie selbst den Charakter von Geboten, sondern fungieren nur als Empfehlungen („Rathschläge" (MS 6:216.23)), die gegenteilige, moralwidrige Handlungsmotivationen aufwiegen und so das Übergewicht der apriorischen, rein-vernünftigen Handlungsgründe sichern helfen.

5. Das Verhältnis von Metaphysik der Sitten und Anthropologie
(MS 6:216.28–217.8)

Die praktische Philosophie oder Sittenlehre, die weder als eudämonistisches Kalkül noch als rein prudentielle Pragmatik Bestand haben kann, setzt deshalb „ein System der Erkenntniß a priori aus bloßen Begriffen" (MS 6:216.28 f.) oder eine „Metaphysik" (MS 6:216.29) als notwendig voraus, die im Unterschied zur theoretischen Metaphysik nicht die (äußere) Natur zum Gegenstand hat, sondern die Freiheit der Willkür und darum den Titel einer „Metaphysik der Sitten" (MS 6:216.30 f.) trägt. Eine Metaphysik der Sitten zu haben, ist kein bloß kognitives fachphilosophisches Projekt, sondern ein sittliches Gebot („Pflicht" (MS 6:216.32)) im Hinblick auf die Kultivierung der zunächst unbewußt („auf dunkle Art" (MS 6:216.33) in jedem Menschen präsenten Vorstellung apriorischer Handlungsprinzipien.

6. Die Rolle der moralischen Anthropologie
(MS 6:217.9–27)

Analog zum Parallelfall der Metaphysik der Natur, die über Prinzipien der Anwendung der obersten Naturgrundsätze auf Gegenstände der Erfahrung verfügt, muss die Metaphysik der Sitten auf die empirische Menschennatur angewandt werden können und dabei auf Erfahrung rekurrieren. Doch betrifft der Rekurs der Metaphysik der Sitten auf die Erfahrung nur die Konsequenzen der streng allgemeinen Moralprinzipen, ohne an deren nicht-empirischem, rein apriorischem Ursprung etwas zu ändern. Die Metaphysik der Sitten erlaubt so zwar die Anwendung auf Anthropologie, aber nicht die Begründung auf ihr.

Kant erwägt, dass die Metaphysik der Sitten in der Architektonik der praktischen Philosophie ihr Gegenstück an der moralischen Anthropologie haben könnte, die sich mit den subjektiven, individuellen wie sozialen Umständen der Ausführung der moralischen Gesetze beschäftigen würde und die dabei die faktische Entstehung, Verbreitung und Bekräftigung der metaphysisch begründeten Moralprinzipien im Kontext von Pädagogik und Bildung leisten würde. Zwar bedarf es einer solchen praktischen Anthropologie, doch darf diese weder der Metaphysik der Sitten vorhergehen noch dürfen die beiden Hauptteile der praktischen Philosophie vermischt und verwechselt werden. Kant insistiert auf der Notwendigkeit, das praktische Gesetz rein vorzustellen und auch keine

andere als moralische Motivationsgründe („Triebfedern" (MS 6:217.22))
zuzulassen, weil nur so der in der Vernunft als solcher gründende streng
allgemeine Charakter der Moralprinzipien für die Beurteilung wie für die
Befolgung aufrechterhalten werden kann.

7. Die Identität von praktischer Philosophie und Moralphilosophie (MS 6:217.28–218.8)

Die zuvor in die Metaphysik der Sitten und die moralische Anthropologie
geteilte praktische Philosophie integriert Kant sodann in die Oberein-
teilung der Philosophie in theoretische Philosophie und praktische Philosophie, mit der Maßgabe, dass letztere gänzlich mit der Moralphilosophie zusammenfällt. Auschlaggebend für die Grundeinteilung der
Philosophie in die theoretische und die praktische ist der exklusive Begriff
des Praktischen als dessen, was nach Freiheitsgesetzen möglich ist. Kant
verweist hierzu auf seine einschlägigen früheren Ausführungen in der
Einleitung zur *Kritik der Urteilskraft* und erinnert insbesondere daran,
dass alles Praktische, das nach Naturgesetzen – statt nach Freiheitsgesetzen – möglich ist, nämlich das Technisch-Praktische, in seinem prä-
skriptiven Charakter völlig von der theoretischen Erkenntnis („Theorie"
(MS 6:217.34)) abhängt und deshalb nicht zur praktischen Philosophie
gerechnet werden darf, die damit ausschließlich das Moralisch-Praktische
umfaßt.

Den freien Willkürgebrauch im Hinblick auf das Technisch-Praktische fasst Kant – wiederum im Rückgriff auf die *Kritik der Urteilskraft* –
als „Kunst" (MS 6:217.32). Wollte man den freien Willkürgebrauch im
Hinblick auf das Moralisch-Praktische wegen seines Gegensatzes zur
Natur als des Gegenstandes der theoretischen Philosophie ebenfalls als
„Kunst" (MS 6:218.3) kennzeichnen, müsste man unter dieser Kunst
des moralischen Freiheitsgebrauchs eine „göttliche Kunst" (MS
6:218.5 f.) verstehen, die es Menschen – kontrafaktisch – erlauben
würde, das von der Vernunft Vorgeschriebene allein aufgrund der Vorschrift komplett zu verwirklichen.

C. Vorrede zu den
Metaphysischen Anfangsgründen der Tugendlehre
(TL 6:375.1–378.31)

1. Ob die Tugendlehre metaphysische Anfangsgründe erfordert
(TL 6:375.1–14 und 375.17–30)

Kant formuliert zunächst die allgemeine architektonische Regel, dass es zu jedem genuinen Gegenstand der Philosophie als des Systems reinbegrifflicher Vernunfterkenntnis ein System reiner, nicht-sinnlicher Vernunftbegriffe und also eine Metaphysik geben muss. Damit stellt sich die Frage, ob auch für die praktische Philosophie, insofern sie Lehre von partikularen moralischen Pflichten ist, und speziell für deren (neben der Rechtslehre) anderen Teil, die Tugendlehre oder Ethik, metaphysische Prinzipien („Anfangsgründe" (TL 6:375.7 f.)) erforderlich sind, die den Status der Ethik als einer Wissenschaft sichern, die ihre Erkenntnisse im sachlichen Zusammenhang oder systematisch präsentiert und nicht bloß unzusammenhängend oder fragmentarisch. Im Fall der erfahrungs- und anschauungsfrei zu entwickelnden Rechtslehre steht das Erfordernis metaphysischer Anfangsgründe und damit einer reinen Rechtslehre deshalb außer Frage, weil diese nur die formalen Bedingungen der Einschränkung des äußeren freien Willkürgebrauchs betrifft und damit von aller Materie der Willkür oder allem Zweck absieht. Im Fall der Rechtslehre ist die Pflichtenlehre deshalb bloße Wissenslehre.

Die zugehörige Anmerkung unterscheidet den Experten der praktischen Philosophie („der praktischen Philosophie Kundiger" (TL 6:375.17)) vom dem, der sich nach Maßgabe der praktischen Philosophie zum Handeln bestimmt („praktischer Philosoph" (TL 6:375.18)) und der im Fall einer Tugendpflicht – anders als bei der Bestimmung einer Rechtspflicht, die genaue Berechnung erlaubt und erfordert – auch ohne subtile metaphysische Erwägungen auskommt. Ausschlaggebend für die Tugendpflicht ist nämlich nicht nur das – im Prinzip leicht zu ermittelnde – Wissen, was jeweils Pflicht ist, sondern vor allem die ethische Motivation, die darin besteht, dass die gewusste Pflicht als solche zugleich Handlungsgrund („Triebfeder der Handlungen" (TL 6:375.29)) ist. Im praktischen Philosophen verbinden sich so Erkenntnis der Pflicht („Wissen" (TL 6:375.29)) und der Grundsatz, aufgrund der Pflichterkenntnis zu handeln („Weisheitsprincip" (TL 6:375.29 f.)).

2. Die Tugendlehre erfordert metaphysische Anfangsgründe
(TL 6:375.15–376.22)

Dagegen scheint eine Ethik oder Tugendlehre schon von ihrer Idee her nicht mit metaphysischen Prinzipien vereinbar, wenn es darum geht, den von allen sinnlichen Antrieben gereinigten Pflichtbegriff zur hinreichenden Triebfeder zu machen. Wie sollte es auch möglich sein, die Neigung zum moralischen Fehlverhalten (Laster) allein durch metaphysische Begriffe zu überwinden, deren Abstraktionsgrad („Speculation") zu erreichen überdies immer nur wenige fähig sind. Doch trotz dieser grundsätzlichen Bedenken insistiert Kant auf dem Nutzen der Erforschung der ethischen Grundprinzipien, die in die Obliegenheit der Philosophie fällt und ohne die Gewissheit („Sicherheit") und Genuität („Lauterkeit") in der Ethik unmöglich wären. Auch der Rekurs auf ein vorgebliches Gefühl für das moralisch Richtige kann nicht von der Notwendigkeit der spezifisch metaphysischen, von allem Anteil der Sinnlichkeit gereinigten Herleitung einer Tugendpflicht dispensieren, die näherhin im vernünftigen Verfahren besteht, sich in jedem Fall danach zu fragen, ob das dem eigenen Handeln zugrundeliegende subjektive Handlungsprinzip („Maxime" (TL 6:376.18)) widerspruchsfrei zum allgemeinen Gesetz gemacht werden könnte. Wenn diese Beurteilungsregel nur wieder auf ein Gefühl (der Sympathie für alle anderen Menschen) zurückginge, dann wäre auch die daraus erwachsene Pflicht letztlich nicht Resultat der Vernunft, sondern Ausdruck von blindem, instinktivem Trieb.

3. Jedes moralische Prinzip ist, wenn auch unbewusste Metaphysik
(TL 6:376.23–33)

Doch es gibt, entgegen allem Anschein, kein moralisches Prinzip, das sich auf ein Gefühl, welcher Art auch immer, stützt. Vielmehr gründet ein genuines moralisches Prinzip immer in, wenn auch unbewusster („dunkel gedachte[r]" (TL 6:376.25)) Metaphysik, die in jedem Menschen als Disposition seiner Vernunft vorliegt. Kant verweist zum Beleg dieser Behauptung auf die Praxis des Lehrers, der seinen Zögling über das Vernunftgebot der Sittlichkeit („Pflichtimperativ" (TL 6:376.27)) und seinen Gebrauch bei der moralischen Beurteilung von Handlungen so unterrichtet, daß er ihn befragt und selbständig antworten lässt („sokratisch [...] katechisiren" (TL 6:276.28)). Nicht der Vortragsstil, wohl aber der Gedankengehalt dessen, was der Tugendlehrer lehrt, muss metaphysisch dimensioniert sein, d. h. zurückgehen auf jene ersten Prinzipien, ohne die weder Gewißheit („Sicherheit" (TL 6:376.32)) noch Reinigkeit und auch keine motivierende Kraft in der Ethik möglich sind.

4. Keine Ethik ohne Metaphysik
(TL 6:376.34–377.12)

Jeder andere Anfang als der mit metaphysischen Prinzipien – sei es der Rekurs auf ein pathologisches, ein rein sinnliches oder ein eigenes moralisches Gefühl –, involviert die Bestimmung der Pflichten im Ausgang von einem Zweck als der Materie des Willens statt von der Gesetzlichkeit als der Form des Willens. In einem solchen Fall gäbe es dann aber keine metaphysischen Prinzipien oder Anfangsgründe der Tugendlehre sondern nur physische, gefühlsbasierte Anfänge. Doch bedeutete dies den Ruin der Ethik. Immer bleibt ausschlaggebend, durch welche Motivationsgründe („Triebfedern" (TL 6:377.6)) man zur Pflichtbefolgung veranlasst wird. Deshalb erinnert Kant alle Philosophen, die glauben, in der Tugendlehre ohne Metaphysik auskommen zu können, an ihre Pflicht zu einer metaphysischen Begründung der Ethik, die allein im Rekurs auf erste Vernunftgründe des Tugendhandelns und nicht im Rückgriff auf angebliche außervernünftige Einsichten erfolgen kann.

5. Kritik des Neo-Eudämonismus
(TL 6:377.13–378.7)

Zum Schluss der Vorrede bringt Kant zunächst seine Verwunderung darüber zum Ausdruck, dass es in jüngerer Zeit – nach der von Kant selbst unternommenen Grundlegung der Moralphilosophie aus reiner (praktischer) Vernunft – zu einem Wiedererstarken des moralischen Eudämonismus in Gestalt einer angeblich nicht empirischen, sondern moralisch zu verstehenden Glückseligkeit kommen konnte. Kant hält schon den Begriff einer moralischen Glückseligkeit für widersprüchlich („Unding" (TL 6:377.18)). Er konzediert, dass der durch das Bewußtsein der Pflichterfüllung entstehende „Zustande der Seelenruhe und Zufriedenheit" (TL 6:377.20 f.), in dem sich die Tugend sozusagen selbst belohnt, durchaus „Glückseligkeit" (TL 6:377.21) genannt werden könnte. Doch der Vertreter des Eudämonismus geht weiter und macht die bewirkte Glückseligkeit zum Beweggrund für das tugendhafte Verhalten, als bestimmte die Pflicht nicht selbst und unmittelbar den Willen des Tugendhaften, sondern tue dies nur vermittelt durch die Aussicht auf Glückseligkeit. Doch da die fragliche Form der Glückseligkeit nur als eine nachträgliche Belohnung („Tugendlohn" (TL 6:377.27)) dem Bewusstsein der Pflichterfüllung folgt, bleibt es bei der Präzedenz der letzteren. Das Bewußtsein der moralischen Verpflichtung muss der Erwägung oder Berücksichtigung der Glückseligkeit, die aus der Befolgung der Pflicht entspringt, vorangehen. Der Vertreter des Eudämonismus, der dieses Abfolgeverhältnis nicht beachtet, bleibt in einem Zirkelschluss befangen: die begründete Aussicht auf Glückseligkeit setzt Befolgung der Pflicht voraus, und letzte wiederum hat die Aussicht auf Glückseligkeit zur Voraussetzung. Kant benennt den Widerspruch in diesem Raisonnement, der darin besteht, einerseits rein moralisch, ohne Rücksicht auf die bewirkte Glückseligkeit, handeln zu sollen, und andererseits die Befolgung einer Pflicht von der zu erwartenden Glückseligkeit abhängig zu machen und also aus einem nicht moralischen, sondern pathologischen Grund zu handeln.

6. Der Unterschied von pathologischer und moralischer Lust
(TL 6:378.8 – 18)

Kant verweist auf seinen Beitrag in der *Berlinischen Monatsschrift* zur Unterscheidung der Lust in pathologische und moralische Lust. Er nennt dort wie hier die Lust pathologisch, die der Befolgung des Gesetzes vorangehen muss, damit ihm gemäß gehandelt wird. Das Verhalten bewegt sich dann ganz in der natürlichen Ordnung der Dinge („Naturordnung" (TL 6:378.13)), während es bei der Lust, die dem Gesetz und seiner Befolgung allererst folgt, um die „sittliche[n] Ordnung" (TL 6:378.14) geht. Den Austausch der Glückseligkeit gegen die Freiheit im Prinzip der Moral – der Eudämonie für die Eleutheronomie – bezeichnet Kant als den „sanfte[n] Tod" (TL 6:378.18) oder die „Euthanasie" (TL 6:378.18) von jeglicher Moral.

7. Die Unverständlichkeit des moralischen Freiheitsbegriffs
(TL 6:378.19–31)

Abschließend benennt Kant noch die Ursache der falschen Ansichten über das Moralprinzip. Die moralischen Gesetze resultieren aus dem kategorischen Imperativ, der aber trotz seines unbedingt verpflichtenden Charakters denen, die nicht metaphysisch, sondern nur physisch („physiologische Erklärungen" (TL 6:378.21)) orientiert sind, unverständlich bleibt.

Das Verhältnis der Vermögen des menschlichen Gemüts zu den Sittengesetzen (MS 6:211–214)

Thomas Höwing

Im ersten Abschnitt der Einleitung in die *Metaphysik der Sitten* präsentiert Kant eine Theorie der „Vermögen des menschlichen Gemüths" (MS 6:211.4), die beim Handeln unter moralischen Gesetzen zum Einsatz kommen. Dabei werden Fragen beantwortet, die wir heute der Handlungstheorie oder der Moralpsychologie zuordnen würden: Welche Gemütsvermögen werden beim rationalen Handeln ausgeübt und wie hängen die Begriffe dieser Vermögen miteinander zusammen? Welche Rolle spielen Lust- und Unlustzustände beim rationalen Handeln? Und schließlich: Was bedeutet es, dass der Mensch das Vermögen hat, frei zu handeln? Allerdings liefert der Abschnitt keine allgemeine Handlungstheorie, sondern erörtert die Vermögen des menschlichen Gemüts, wie der Titel ankündigt, lediglich im „Verhältniß [...] zu den Sittengesetzen" (MS 6:211.4 f.). So führt Kant im letzten Absatz die Unterscheidung zwischen juridischen und ethischen Gesetzen ein, indem er zwischen zwei Aspekten der Ausübung der freien menschlichen Willkür unterscheidet.

Der Schwerpunkt dieses Beitrags liegt auf Kants Theorie des rationalen Begehrungsvermögens und seinen Ausführungen zur praktischen Lust. Dabei folge ich Kants Gliederung des Abschnitts. Im ersten Teil gehe ich auf Kants Definitionen des Begehrungsvermögens und des Lebens ein (Absatz 1). Im zweiten Teil erläutere ich dann die wichtigsten Definitionen und Aussagen Kants zur praktischen Rolle von Lust- und Unlustzuständen (Absätze 2–5). Der dritte und ausführlichste Teil behandelt Kants Theorie des rationalen Begehrungsvermögens (Absatz 6). Hier möchte ich den Blick auf die Interpretationsprobleme lenken, die sich vor allem aus Kants Definition des Vermögens nach Belieben zu tun oder zu lassen und seiner Unterscheidung zwischen Willkür und Wunsch ergeben. Im vierten Teil folgt ein kurzer Überblick über Kants Ausführungen zur Freiheit der menschlichen Willkür und zur Unterscheidung zwischen juridischen und ethischen Gesetzen (Absätze 7–8). Am Schluss thematisiere ich die Frage, wie wir Kants Formulierung im Titel des

Abschnitts verstehen sollen und welche Rückschlüsse sich daraus für die
Bestimmung von Thema und Ziel des Abschnitts ergeben.

1. Begehrungsvermögen und Leben (Absatz 1)

1.1 Begehrungsvermögen

„Begehrungsvermögen ist das Vermögen durch seine Vorstellungen
Ursache der Gegenstände dieser Vorstellungen zu sein" (MS 6:211.6 f.).
Die Schulphilosophen hatten sowohl das Begehren als auch Lust- und
Unlustzustände aus dem Zusammenspiel verschiedener Erkenntnisvermögen erklärt.[1] Für Kant hingegen stellt das Begehrungsvermögen –
neben dem Erkenntnisvermögen und dem Gefühl der Lust und Unlust –
ein Grundvermögen dar, dessen Funktion von keinem anderen Gemütsvermögen abgeleitet werden kann.[2] Das spezifische Merkmal des
Begehrungsvermögens besteht Kant zufolge in der besonderen *kausalen
Rolle* der Vorstellung: Ein Wesen kann begehren, wenn die Tatsache, dass
es einen Gegenstand vorstellt, dazu führen kann, dass das Wesen den
vorgestellten Gegenstand realisiert.[3] Dies bedeutet natürlich nicht
zwangsläufig, dass ein solches Wesen Gegenstände durch *bloßes* Vorstellen
realisieren kann. Kant geht vielmehr davon aus, dass die Menschen in der
Regel weitere Vermögen – er selbst spricht von „mechanischen", d. h.
„nicht psychologischen" Kräften (KU 5:177.38 f., Anm.) – einsetzen
müssen, um vorgestellte Gegenstände zu realisieren. Man könnte das
Begehrungsvermögen folglich als ein Vermögen ,höherer Ordnung' bezeichnen, welches stets zusammen mit anderen mechanischen oder ,ein-
fachen' Vermögen ausgeübt wird. Das Begehrungsvermögen ist das Vermögen eines Wesens, seine einfachen Vermögen so auszuüben, dass durch

---

1   Dies sollte dem Nachweis dienen, dass alle Vermögen der Seele auf eine einzige
    vorstellende Kraft reduziert werden können. (Vgl. Wolff, *Deutsche Metaphysik*
    §§ 878 ff.; Baumgarten, *Metaphysica*, § 655, AA 15:41; § 667, AA 15:46;
    Baum, 2006, S. 126 ff.)
2   Vgl. KU 5:177; EEKU 20:205 f.; V-MP-L1/Pölitz 28:262.
3   Vgl. KpV 5:9.20 ff., Anm.; EEKU 20:206; vgl. HN 20:445; V-MP/Mron
    29:893 f.; V-MP-K3E/Arnoldt 29:1012 f. J. S. Beck kommentiert Kants Defi-
    nition auf folgende Weise: „Eine Vorstellung stellt erstens Etwas vor; wenn ihr
    aber zweitens noch obenein die Causalität zukommt, ihr eignes Object hervor zu
    bringen, dann ist sie ein Begehren" (Beck, 1798, S. 4).

die Ausübung dieser einfachen Vermögen ein vorgestelltes Ziel realisiert wird.[4]

In seiner Definition des Begehrungsvermögens grenzt sich Kant in zwei weiteren Punkten von den Philosophen der Leibnizschen Tradition ab. Während letztere das Ziel des Begehrens darin sahen, *Vorstellungen* hervorzubringen,[5] besteht Kant zufolge das Begehren darin, *Gegenstände* von Vorstellungen zu realisieren. Diese Neuerung hat Kant den Einwand eingebracht, dass seine Definition des Begehrungsvermögens von einem Idealisten, (der die Existenz vorstellungsunabhängiger Gegenstände abstreitet), nicht akzeptiert werden kann.[6] Der Ausdruck „Gegenstände dieser Vorstellungen" (MS 6:211.7) in der Definition des Begehrungsvermögens hat allerdings eine weite Bedeutung: Er umfasst sowohl die Gegenstände, die durch sinnliche Empfindungen unwillkürliche Reaktionen hervorrufen, als auch die beim freien Handeln eingeplanten Mittel und selbstgesetzten Zwecke. (Vgl. RL 6:246; TL 6:381.4–6, 384.33 f.) Zweitens begreift Kant das Begehrungsvermögen, im Unterschied zu den Schulphilosophen, auch nicht als ein *Strebevermögen*.[7] Für Kant liegt eine Bestrebung (lat. *conatus* oder *nisus*) nur dann vor, wenn eine Kraft durch eine Gegenkraft daran gehindert wird, ihre volle Wirkung zu entfalten.[8] Das Begehrungsvermögen ist Kant zufolge nun nicht das Vermögen, die Realisierung eines vorgestellten Gegenstandes wider ein entgegenstehendes Hindernis bloß anzustreben. Kants Verwendung des Ausdrucks „Ursache" (MS 6:211.7) in der Definition legt vielmehr die Ansicht nahe, dass wir das Begehrungsvermögen dann und nur dann ausüben, wenn die Vorstellung des Gegenstandes auch tatsächlich dazu führt, dass

---

4   Es ist bemerkenswert, dass Kant seiner Definition des Begehrungsvermögens keine Definition des ‚Verabscheuungsvermögens' an die Seite stellt. Kant scheint mit Baumgarten darin übereinzustimmen, dass wir einen Gegenstand genau dann verabscheuen, wenn wir sein ‚Gegenteil' begehren, d.h. wenn wir uns darum bemühen, dass dieser Gegenstand *nicht* existiert. (Vgl. MAN 4:544.28 ff.; Baumgarten, *Metaphysica*, § 663, AA 15:45; 28:587.21 f.)

5   Vgl. Baumgarten, *Metaphysica*, § 663, AA 15:45; Wolff, *Psychologia Rationalis*, § 495.

6   Vgl. Bouterwek, 1797, S. 266; zu Kants Antwort vgl.: RL 6:356 f.; HN 20:445–447.

7   Vgl. Baumgarten, *Metaphysica*, § 663, AA 15:45; Wolff, *Psychologia Rationalis*, § 495.

8   Vgl. Refl 3585 HN 17:73.15 ff.; V-MP/Volckmann 28:434; V-MP/Schön 28:515; V-MP-L2/Pölitz 28:565; V-MP/Dohna 28:640 f. Kant verwendet den Ausdruck „Bestrebung" auch für Wünsche und Sehnsüchte. (Vgl. z.B. HAGEN 21, XLIII; RL 6:356.23)

wir den vorgestellten Gegenstand ‚verursachen' bzw. erfolgreich realisieren. Hieraus würde sich allerdings ein Widerspruch in Kants Konzeption des Begehrungsvermögens ergeben. Denn für Kant stellen, wie wir sehen werden, auch bloße Wünsche und erfolglose Versuche Ausübungen des Begehrungsvermögens dar. Auf dieses Problem werde ich bei der Diskussion von Kants Definition des Wunsches daher noch näher eingehen.[9]

1.2 Leben

„Das Vermögen eines Wesens, seinen Vorstellungen gemäß zu handeln, heißt das Leben" (MS 6:211.7–9).[10] Unter „handeln" versteht Kant hier nicht nur ein Handeln nach Absichten, sondern überhaupt alle Veränderungen, die ein Wesen bei sich selbst und in der Welt herbeiführen kann.[11] Das Kennzeichen eines lebendigen Wesens besteht also darin, dass es sich selbst und die Welt „seinen Vorstellungen gemäß" verändern kann. Hieraus ergibt sich die Frage, ob sich Kants Begriff des Lebens überhaupt von seinem Begriff des Begehrungsvermögens unterscheidet. Für eine Identität der beiden Begriffe spricht, dass Kant die Auffassung vertritt, dass nur solche Wesen leben, die auch begehren können, d. h. nur Menschen und Tiere, aber keine Pflanzen.[12] Der Wortlaut der beiden Definitionen im vorliegenden Abschnitt könnte allerdings auch auf einen Unterschied hindeuten. Während das Begehrungsvermögen im Vermögen besteht, „durch seine Vorstellungen" zu handeln, besteht das Leben im Vermögen, „seinen Vorstellungen gemäß zu handeln". Der Unterschied in den Formulierungen legt nahe, das Leben als einen *normativen* Aspekt des Begehren-Könnens anzusehen. Wenn ein Wesen Ursache von vorgestellten Gegenständen werden kann, dann kann es auch *nach Maßgabe von* Vorstellungen handeln, d. h. es ist

---

9 Vgl. Abschnitt 3.2 dieses Beitrags.
10 Zu Kants Begriff des Lebens vgl. auch: MAN 4:544; KpV 5:9.19 f., Anm.; VNAEF 8:413.
11 Vgl. Gerhardt, 1986; Willaschek, 1992, S. 35 ff.
12 Vgl. TL 6:443; KU 5:374 f.; TG 2:330 f. – An einigen Stellen setzt Kant die Begriffe ‚Leben' und ‚Begehrungsvermögen' sogar gleich. (Vgl. Refl 1034 HN 15:465; Refl 1048 HN 15:469; Refl 1050 HN 15:469) An anderen Stellen scheint er aber auch Denken (vgl. MAN 4:544), Erkennen (vgl. KU 5:219.4, 222.24) und Fühlen (vgl. Anth 7:231.23 f.; KU 5:204.8; TL 6:400.9–15) als Instanzen des menschlichen Lebens anzusehen.

in der Lage, seine Bewegungen aufgrund von vorgestellten Erfolgsbedingungen selbst zu organisieren.[13]

2. Begehrungsvermögen und Gefühl der Lust und Unlust (Absätze 2–5)

2.1 Gefühl der Lust und Unlust

In den Absätzen 2 bis 5 erörtert Kant die Rolle, die das Gefühl der Lust und Unlust beim menschlichen Begehren spielen kann. Gefühl und Sinn sind für Kant eigentlich nicht ‚Vermögen‘, die aktiv ausgeübt werden, sondern ‚Fähigkeiten‘ bzw. ‚Empfänglichkeiten‘, die wesentlich *passiv* sind.[14] Beide sinnlichen Fähigkeiten beziehen sich ferner lediglich auf die *subjektiven Aspekte* von Vorstellungen. Allerdings unterscheiden sich Gefühl und Sinn auch. Obwohl die Empfindungen des inneren und äußeren Sinns und ihre zeitliche bzw. raumzeitliche Anordnung subjektiv sind, können sie auf den Gegenstand als *Erscheinung* bezogen werden. Dies ist Kant zufolge bei Lust oder Unlust nicht möglich. Wenn wir in der Wahrnehmung oder im Denken einen Gegenstand vorstellen und als „Wirkung" (MS 6:212.35, Anm.) dieser Vorstellung Lust oder Unlust empfinden, dann gibt uns dies weder über den vorgestellten Gegenstand noch über uns selbst Aufschluss.[15] Es ist allerdings fraglich, ob aus Kants Abgrenzung des Fühlens vom Erkennen auch folgt, dass die verschiedenen Formen von Lust und Unlust keine spezifischen intentionalen Gehalte haben.[16]

---

13 So können wir uns die Organisation des tierischen Verhaltens nur erklären, wenn wir annehmen, dass auch Tiere leben. (Vgl. KU 5:464, Anm.; V-MP-L2/Pölitz 28:594.17 ff.) Zum Leben als einer Art von Selbstorganisation: Vgl. die aufschlussreichen Ausführungen von Beck, 1798, S. 5 ff.

14 Vgl. MS 6:211.19, 211.29, Anm., 212.34, Anm. Den Ausdruck ‚Fähigkeit‘ benutzt Kant oft, um die Passivität von Sinnlichkeit oder Gefühl herauszustellen (vgl. KrV A19/B33; KrV A94; KpV 5:80.16; KU 5:177.17); vgl. auch Baumgarten, *Metaphysica*, § 216, HN 17:72 sowie V-MP/Herder 28:27; V-MP/Volckmann 28:434; V-MP/Dohna 28:640.

15 Zum Unterschied von Gefühl und Sinn: Vgl. TL 6:400.5–9; KU 5:188 ff.; 205 f.; Anth 7:153; EEKU 20:221 f.

16 So spricht Kant etwa davon, dass das moralische Gesetz beim Menschen ein Gefühl der „*Achtung* für sein eigenes Wesen" (TL 6:403.1) erzeugt. (Vgl. TL 6:435.23–25, 454.32–455.1, 456.20 ff.) Zur Intentionalität von Lust und

Kant zufolge ist nun jede Ausübung des Begehrungsvermögens, also alles „Begehren oder Verabscheuen" (MS 6:211.10),[17] mit der Empfindung von Lust oder Unlust verbunden. Allerdings gilt dies nicht umgekehrt: Dem Geschmacksurteil liegt eine „contemplative Lust" (MS 6:212.16) an der Form der Vorstellung des Gegenstandes zugrunde, die, wie Kant in der *Kritik der Urteilskraft* ausführt, nicht zur Folge hat, dass wir den Gegenstand realisieren wollen. (Vgl. KU 5:204 ff.) Allerdings hat die kontemplative Lust auch einen indirekten moralischen Wert, denn sie bereitet uns darauf vor, „etwas auch ohne Absicht auf Nutzen zu lieben" (TL 6:443.7 f.). Da aus dieser Verbindung Kant zufolge auch Pflichten resultieren, wird die Fähigkeit zur Wertschätzung des Schönen in einem episodischen Abschnitt der *Tugendlehre* von Kant noch einmal thematisiert.[18]

2.2 Praktische Lust

Kant unterscheidet nun zwei Formen einer für das Begehren relevanten *praktischen Lust*. Während die Schulphilosophen davon ausgingen, dass die praktische Lust immer eine Ursache des menschlichen Begehrens darstellt,[19] kann sie für Kant auch als dessen Wirkung auftreten. In beiden Fällen handelt es sich um ein kausales Verhältnis zwischen zwei Eigenschaften einer Vorstellung, oder genauer: um ein kausales Verhältnis zwischen dem subjektiven Aspekt einer Vorstellung (*Lust*) und der kausalen Rolle einer Vorstellung (*Begehren*). Dass die Lust dem Begehren als Ursache vorhergeht, lässt sich also auf folgende Weise erklären: Die Tatsache, dass die Vorstellung der Existenz eines Gegenstandes mit dem subjektiven Lust-Aspekt verbunden ist, führt hier dazu, dass der Vorstellung des Gegenstandes die für das Begehren charakteristische kausale Rolle zukommt. Im Fall der nachfolgenden Lust verhält es sich genau umgekehrt: Hier kommt der Vorstellung eines Gegenstandes zunächst die für das Begehren charakteristische kausale Rolle zu, und dies hat dann zur Folge, dass mit der Vorstellung der Existenz eines Gegenstandes der subjektive Lust-Aspekt verbunden ist.

Unlust im Kontext von Kants Handlungstheorie: Vgl. Grenberg, 2001, S. 159 ff./169 ff.

17 Vgl. Fußnote 4 dieses Beitrags.
18 Vgl. MS 6:212.20; TL 6:442 f.; KU § 42, 5:298 ff.; KU § 59, 5:351 ff.
19 Vgl. Baumgarten, *Metaphysica*, § 667, AA 15:46; Wolff, *Deutsche Metaphysik*, §§ 878 f. Siehe auch Baum, 2006, S. 126 ff.

Da diese Beschreibung sehr abstrakt ist, lohnt es sich, auf die beiden Fälle genauer einzugehen. Im Fall der vorhergehenden Lust führt die Lust, die mit der Vorstellung der Existenz eines Gegenstandes verbunden ist, dazu, dass wir den Gegenstand begehren. Kant nennt die Ausübung des Begehrungsvermögens in diesem Fall eine „Begierde" im engen Sinn, die dann zur „Neigung" wird, wenn wir den lustvollen Gegenstand öfter und aus Gewohnheit begehren.[20] Kants Beschreibung der vorausgehenden Lust ist allerdings nicht so eindeutig, wie seine Formulierungen nahelegen. Der *Anthropologie* zufolge steht am Anfang jeder Begierde nicht Lust, sondern zunächst *Schmerz*, d.h. die Tendenz, „meinen Zustand zu verlassen (aus ihm herauszugehen)" (Anth 7:231.2 f.).[21] Allerdings schließt dies nicht aus, dass jeder sinnlichen Begierde Lust in einem ganz bestimmten Sinn vorausgeht. Denn um durch meine Handlung in einen lustvolleren Zustand zu gelangen, muss ich in der Regel eine Vorstellung davon haben, welcher neue Zustand gemessen an meinem gegenwärtigen Zustand lustvoller ist. Die Lust geht also der sinnlichen Begierde mindestens in dem Sinn voraus, daß es die *Erwartung* einer zukünftigen Lust ist, die dazu führt, dass ich einen Gegenstand oder Sachverhalt realisieren will. (Vgl. KpV 5:22.14–17, 23.4, 23.14 f., 23.30 f.) Im vorliegenden Abschnitt scheint Kant allerdings etwas anderes zu behaupten. Er behauptet nämlich nicht, dass der sinnlichen Begierde nur die Erwartung von Lust vorausgeht, sondern, daß ihr eine *tatsächliche* Lust an der Vorstellung der Existenz des Gegenstandes als Ursache vorausgeht. Eine mögliche Lösung dieses Problems besteht vielleicht in der Annahme, dass wir uns Kant zufolge nur dann von der Realisierung eines Gegenstandes Lust versprechen, wenn uns der Gegenstand in der Vergangenheit schon einmal tatsächlich Lust bereitet hat. Die Erwartung einer zukünftigen Lust setzt in der Regel eine Erinnerung an eine in der Vergangenheit tatsächlich empfundene Lust voraus.[22]

Im Fall der nachfolgenden Lust denkt Kant an das Gefühl, das beim Handeln unter moralischen Gesetzen eine wichtige Rolle spielt. Beim Handeln aus moralischen Motiven soll nicht die Erwartung einer zu-

---

20 Vgl. MS 6:212.20–23; RGV 6:28 f. (auch die dortige Anm.); Anth 7:251.5. Zu den unterschiedlichen Bedeutungen von ‚Neigung': Vgl. Allison, 1990, S. 108.
21 Vgl. Brandt/Stark, 1997, XLII–XLV.
22 Die Frage, in welchem Sinn dem Begehren tatsächliche Lust vorausgeht, ist allerdings umstritten. (Vgl. Reath, 1989a, S. 46 ff.; Willaschek, 1992, S. 61 f.; Kerstein, 2002, S. 29; Scarano, 2002, S. 139; Johnson, 2005, S. 51 ff.; Reath, 2006, S. 57 f.)

künftigen Lust an einem Gegenstand, sondern die Vorstellung des moralischen Gesetzes der maßgebliche Grund für die Entscheidung sein, einen Gegenstand zu realisieren bzw. eine Handlung auszuführen. Das Lustgefühl tritt Kant zufolge in diesem Fall lediglich als *Wirkung* des Begehrens auf bzw. folgt auf eine „vorhergehende Bestimmung des Begehrungsvermögens" (MS 6:212.28 f.). Nun stellt die Lust für Kant in zwei Bedeutungen eine Wirkung beim Handeln unter moralischen Gesetzen dar: In der Einleitung zur *Tugendlehre* spricht Kant einerseits davon, dass sich Selbstzufriedenheit oder Gewissensbisse einstellen, *nachdem* wir eine Handlung tatsächlich ausgeführt haben. (Vgl. TL 6:377.18–22, 401.15 f., 440) Grundlegender ist allerdings die Rolle, die die Lust bei der moralischen Motivation, und damit *vor* der eigentlichen Ausführung der Handlung (‚Tat'), spielt. Die Vorstellung, dass eine mögliche Handlung mit dem moralischen Gesetz übereinstimmt, bewirkt beim Handelnden ein Gefühl der Lust und führt dazu, dass er an der Ausführung der moralischen Handlung auch subjektiv ein Interesse nimmt. (Vgl. TL 6:399.21–27) Nun betont Kant auch im vorliegenden Abschnitt den Zusammenhang, der zwischen der nachfolgenden Lust und dem „Vernunftinteresse" (MS 6:212.30) besteht, das wir an der Ausführung einer moralischen Handlung nehmen. Daher liegt die Annahme nahe, dass Kant hier nur über die Lust in der zweiten Bedeutung spricht. Die nachfolgende Lust folgt zwar „auf eine vorhergehende Bestimmung des Begehrungsvermögens", tritt aber noch *vor* der Ausführung der eigentlichen Handlung auf.[23]

An dieser Stelle möchte ich nur auf drei weitere Interpretationsprobleme hinweisen, die mit Kants Beschreibung der nachfolgenden Lust verbunden sind. Erstens stellt sich die Frage, an welches Gefühl Kant bei der nachfolgenden Lust genau denkt. Während er nämlich noch in der *Kritik der praktischen Vernunft* das moralische Gefühl mit dem Gefühl der Achtung vor dem Sittengesetz identifiziert, (vgl. KpV 5:75.16–19; GMS 4:401, Anm.) unterscheidet er in der Einleitung zur *Tugendlehre* mit dem moralischen Gefühl, dem Gewissen, der Menschenliebe und der Achtung gleich vier „Gemüthsanlagen" (TL 6:399.11), die Voraussetzung dafür

---

23   Die Unterscheidung der beiden Arten der praktischen Lust im vorliegenden Absatz scheint also Kants Unterscheidung zwischen pathologischer und moralischer Lust zu entsprechen. (Vgl. TL 6:378.8 ff., 399.25–27; VT 8:395.27–37, Anm. und, der Sache nach, schon GMS 4:401.25–28, Anm.; vgl. auch VATL 23:373, 375) Diese Unterscheidung wird allerdings etwas anders formuliert: Während die pathologische Lust der Befolgung eines Gesetzes vorhergeht, stellt die moralische Lust eine Wirkung der Vorstellung des moralischen Gesetzes dar.

sind, dass wir durch Pflichtbegriffe affiziert werden können.[24] Zweitens lässt sich fragen, warum das nachfolgende Gefühl überhaupt eine Form von Lust und nicht vielmehr auch eine Form von *Unlust* sein soll. So behauptet Kant noch in der *Kritik der praktischen Vernunft*, dass sich das Gefühl der Achtung vor dem Sittengesetz weder eindeutig als Lust noch als Unlust charakterisieren lässt.[25] Das dritte und vielleicht interessanteste Interpretationsproblem besteht in der Frage, welche Konsequenzen sich aus der Aussage, dass die moralische Lust lediglich als Wirkung auf das Begehren folgt, für Kants Theorie der moralischen Motivation ergeben. Die Rolle des moralischen Gefühls bei der Motivation ist ein allgemeiner Streitpunkt in der Kant-Forschung. Einige Interpreten vertreten die Auffassung, dass für Kant das moralische Gefühl gar keine konstitutive Rolle bei der moralischen Motivation spielt, sondern lediglich aus der Tatsache resultiert, dass die Anerkennung des moralischen Gesetzes schon *allein* zur moralischen Motivation ausreicht.[26] Andere gehen davon aus, dass das moralische Gefühl für Kant eine *zusätzliche* Bedingung darstellt, die zu der Vorstellung einer gesetzeskonformen Handlung hinzukommen muss, damit wir zur Ausführung der moralischen Handlung motiviert werden.[27] Kants Ausführungen zur nachfolgenden Lust im vorliegenden Abschnitt scheinen nun *prima facie* die erste Position zu unterstützen: Die Lust ergibt sich Kant zufolge als eine Wirkung aus der Tatsache, dass wir den Gegenstand begehren, und dies bedeutet letztlich, dass die Vorstellung einer gesetzeskonformen Handlung schon unabhängig vom moralischen Gefühl einen kausalen Einfluss auf das Handeln des Menschen hat.[28]

2.3 Interesse

Bis zu diesem Punkt präsentiert Kant eine *kausale* Theorie des Begehrens und der praktischen Lust. Das Begehren besteht in der kausalen Rolle einer Vorstellung, und die praktische Lust ist beim Menschen ihrerseits

---

24 Vgl. TL 6:399–403. Siehe auch Beck, 1960, S. 224 f.; Schönecker, 2010, und den Beitrag von Ina Goy in diesem Band.
25 Vgl. KpV 5:77 f.; vgl. Beck, 1960, S. 225.
26 Vgl. Reath, 1989b.
27 Vgl. McCarty, 1993.
28 Allerdings setzt dies voraus, dass die kausale Kraft, die der Vorstellung *qua* Bestimmung des Begehrungsvermögens zukommt, *hinreichend* ist, um zur Handlung zu motivieren. McCarty bestreitet dies: Vgl. McCarty, 1993, S. 427 f.

entweder Ursache oder Wirkung dieses Begehrens. Die Definition des
Interesses macht nun deutlich, dass diese kausale Beschreibung für Kant
nicht im Widerspruch steht zu der Tatsache, dass für das Verhältnis von
Lust und Begehren auch rationale Überlegungen des handelnden Subjekts
relevant sind. Als ‚Interesse' bezeichnet Kant die Verbindung zwischen
der Lust und dem Begehrungsvermögen, „sofern diese Verknüpfung
durch den Verstand nach einer allgemeinen Regel (allenfalls auch nur für
das Subject) gültig zu sein geurtheilt wird" (MS 6:212.24–26). Kant
nennt demnach das kausale Verhältnis zwischen Lust und Begehren bei
einem handelnden Subjekt ein ‚Interesse', wenn dieses Verhältnis auch
Gegenstand eines *Urteils* dieses Subjekts ist. In diesem Urteil bestimmt
das handelnde Subjekt aufgrund einer allgemeinen Regel, dass Lust und
Begehren mindestens bei ihm selbst auf eine der beiden möglichen
Weisen kausal miteinander verknüpft sind.

   Ich werde nicht versuchen, in diesem Rahmen eine Interpretation
dieser schwierigen Definition vorzulegen.[29] Statt dessen möchte ich nur
auf zwei Probleme von Kants Definition des Interesses hinweisen. Das
erste Problem betrifft die Frage, an welche Urteile und allgemeinen Regeln Kant in seiner Definition des Interesses denkt. Nimmt man Kants
Ausführungen zum Interesse in der *Grundlegung* und der *Kritik der
praktischen Vernunft* hinzu, so liegt die Annahme nahe, dass es sich um
praktische Urteile handelt, in denen wir aufgrund von *praktischen Prinzipien* erkennen, dass wir eine bestimmte Handlung ausführen wollen
bzw. ausführen sollen.[30] Wenn dies stimmt, so geht aus Kants Definition
des Interesses hervor, dass in praktischen Urteilen auch das Verhältnis von
Lust und Begehren mindestens implizit thematisiert wird. Nun ist es
natürlich plausibel, dass praktische Urteile zumindest das Begehren thematisieren, denn schließlich bestimmen wir in solchen Urteilen, dass wir
eine Handlung ausführen wollen bzw. ausführen sollen. Es stellt sich
allerdings die Frage, in welcher Weise praktische Urteile auch die mit dem
Begehren kausal verbundene Lust thematisieren. In der *Kritik der
Urteilskraft* nennt Kant die Urteile, in denen wir bestimmen, dass mit
einer unserer Vorstellungen Lust verbunden ist, ästhetische Urteile. (Vgl.
KU 5:203 f.; EEKU 20:224 f.) Kants Definition des Interesses setzt
folglich voraus, dass es eine Art „ästhetisch-practisches Urtheil" (EEKU

---

29 Vgl. hierzu: Grenberg, 2001, S. 164 ff.
30 Vgl. vor allem GMS 4:413 f., Anm.; KpV 5:79, 90. Zu Kants Begriff des
    Interesses im Kontext seiner Handlungstheorie: Vgl. auch GMS 4:401, Anm.,
    459 f., Anm.; KU 5:204 ff.

20:232.1) gibt, d.h. ein praktisches Urteil, das zugleich ein ästhetisches Urteil ist. In einem solchen Urteil bestimmen wir, dass wir eine bestimmte Handlung ausführen wollen *und* dass dieses Handeln-Wollen auf eine der beiden möglichen Weisen mit einem Gefühl der Lust verbunden ist.

Im Fall der vorhergehenden Lust und dem korrespondierenden „Interesse der Neigung" (MS 6:212.27) leuchtet es vielleicht ein, dass das praktische Urteil zugleich ein ästhetisches Urteil ist. In diesem Fall urteilt das handelnde Subjekt, dass es eine bestimmte Handlung ausführen will, weil es durch die Anwendung allgemeiner Regeln erkennt, dass ein *lustvoller* Gegenstand durch diese Handlung realisiert wird. In einem solchen Urteil wird folglich zumindest implizit auch die Verknüpfung von Lust und Begehren thematisiert. Die Erwartung einer zukünftigen Lust wird von einer Person als Grund dafür angesehen, eine bestimmte Handlung ausführen zu wollen. Die Anwendung von Kants Definition auf den Fall der nachfolgenden Lust und auf das dieser Lust korrespondierende „Vernunftinteresse" (MS 6:212.30) führt jedoch zu Schwierigkeiten. In diesem Fall handelt es sich bei dem praktischen Urteil um ein *moralisches* Urteil, in welchem wir erkennen, dass wir eine bestimmte Handlung ausführen sollen, weil diese Handlung durch das moralische Gesetz geboten ist. Folgen wir nun Kants Definition des Interesses, so bestimmen wir in einem solchen Urteil darüber hinaus, dass die Vorstellung der gesetzeskonformen Handlung ein Gefühl der Lust zur Folge hat. Nun scheint allerdings die Vorstellung einer gesetzeskonformen Handlung nichts anderes zu sein als ein moralisches Urteil, d.h. ein Urteil, in dem wir erkennen, dass eine Handlung durch das moralische Gesetz geboten ist. Aus Kants Definition des Interesses ergibt sich in diesem Fall also die Konsequenz, dass wir in einem moralischen Urteil bestimmen, dass dieses moralische Urteil *selbst* ein Gefühl der Lust zur Folge hat. Es ist allerdings nicht einfach zu sehen, wie diese beiden Aussagen in einem einzigen Urteil verbunden werden können: Wie ist es möglich, in einem Urteil zugleich die Wirkung dieses Urteils auf das Gefühl des Urteilenden zu bestimmen?[31] Zu dieser Schwierigkeit kommt

---

31 Dieses Problem lässt sich umgehen, wenn man, wie Grenberg, 2001, mehrere Urteilsakte unterscheidet (164 ff.). – Ein ähnliches Problem stellt sich in Kants Theorie des Geschmacksurteils. Nach Kant folgt hier die Lust auf die Beurteilung des Gegenstandes (vgl. KU 5:218), das Geschmacksurteil macht jedoch zugleich eine Aussage über diese Lust, d.h. über ihre allgemeine Mitteilbarkeit (vgl. KU 5:213 f.; EEKU 20:229; vgl. hierzu Ginsborg, 1991).

hinzu, dass die dem moralischen Urteil zugrundeliegende allgemeine Regel – also das moralische Gesetz – *prima facie* keine Aussage über den Gefühlszustand der Person macht, an die sie sich richtet.[32]

Selbst wenn es eine Erklärung dafür gibt, auf welche Weise wir in unseren praktischen Urteilen im Rückgriff auf allgemeine Regeln auch das kausale Verhältnis von Lust und Begehren thematisieren, so bleibt ein zweites Problem von Kants Definition des Interesses. Dieses Problem betrifft die Frage, welcher Zusammenhang bei einem Interesse zwischen dem tatsächlichen inneren Zustand einer Person und dem Urteil über diesen Zustand besteht. Ist die kausale Verknüpfung von Lust und Begehren bei einem Interesse bloß der Gegenstand eines (ästhetisch-)praktischen Urteils oder stellt sich die Verknüpfung bei einer Person auch tatsächlich ein, sofern die Person ein (ästhetisch-)praktisches Urteil fällt? Hier bieten sich zwei alternative Lesarten an. Gehen wir vom Muster theoretischer Urteile aus, so liegt zunächst folgende Auffassung nahe: Wenn wir urteilen, dass Lust und Begehren bei uns in einer bestimmten kausalen Ordnung vorkommen, folgt daraus nicht, dass diese Verbindung bei uns auch tatsächlich besteht. Ein Urteil *über* ein Interesse muss weder dazu führen noch voraussetzen, dass wir selbst ein tatsächliches Interesse an der Ausführung der Handlung haben. Dieser Lesart zufolge liegt ein Interesse also nur dann vor, wenn das Subjekt ein Urteil über ein Interesse fällt und sich *darüber hinaus* auch tatsächlich in dem relevanten Gemütszustand befindet.[33] Wenn wir allerdings annehmen, dass das Urteil, von dem Kant in seiner Definition des Interesses spricht, kein theoretisches, sondern ein praktisches bzw. sogar ein ästhetisch-praktisches Urteil ist, so lässt sich vielleicht auch eine andere Lesart vertreten: Bei der kausalen Verbindung von Lust und Begehren handelt es sich um ein Interesse, sofern diese Verbindung selbst ein Aspekt des praktischen Urteils einer Person ist. Dieser Lesart zufolge sind das praktische Urteil und das Interesse *identisch*. Praktisch urteilen bedeutet nichts anderes als die Ausführung einer Handlung mit Bewusstsein auf die eine oder andere

---

32 Kant drückt sich allerdings zuweilen so aus. So schreibt er rückblickend in der ersten Einleitung in die *Kritik der Urteilskraft*, dass „wir […] in der Crit. d. pract. V., daß die Vorstellung einer allgemeinen Gesetzmäßigkeit des Wollens zugleich willenbestimmend und dadurch auch das Gefühl der Achtung erweckend seyn müsse, als ein in unsern moralischen Urtheilen und zwar a priori enthaltenes Gesetz, bemerkten […]" (EEKU 20:229.31 ff.).

33 Eine ähnliche Auffassung scheint auch Grenberg zu vertreten (vgl. Grenberg, 2001, vor allem S. 166 f.), die zugleich betont, dass es sich bei dem Urteil über das Interesse um ein praktisches Urteil handelt.

Weise affektiv wertzuschätzen. Wenn dies stimmt, dann unterscheiden sich praktische Urteile von theoretischen Urteilen über ein Interesse in einem wichtigen Punkt. Während sich die Person in einem theoretischen Urteil über ein Interesse lediglich eine bestimmte Einstellung zuschreibt, handelt es sich bei einem praktischen Urteil um die praktische Einstellung bzw. das Interesse selbst.

3. Das rationale Begehrungsvermögen (Absatz 6)

3.1 Vermögen nach Belieben zu tun oder zu lassen

Der sechste Absatz thematisiert das rationale Begehrungsvermögen des Menschen. Kant definiert zunächst den Begriff des Vermögens nach Belieben zu tun oder zu lassen (im Folgenden abgekürzt: *VBTL*): „Das Begehrungsvermögen nach Begriffen, sofern der Bestimmungsgrund desselben zur Handlung in ihm selbst, nicht in dem Objecte angetroffen wird, heißt ein Vermögen nach Belieben zu thun oder zu lassen" (MS 6:213.14–17). Der Begriff des *VBTL* wird von Kant durch zwei Merkmale bestimmt: Ein Wesen verfügt über ein *VBTL*, wenn es erstens „nach Begriffen" begehren kann und wenn zweitens der Bestimmungsgrund des Begehrungsvermögens zur Handlung nicht im Objekt, sondern im Begehrungsvermögen selbst liegt. Diese Definition ist aus mindestens drei Gründen schwierig zu verstehen: (1.) In Bezug auf das erste Merkmal stellt sich zunächst die Frage, welche Art von Rationalität ein Wesen beim Begehren einsetzt, wenn es über ein „Begehrungsvermögen nach Begriffen" verfügt. Dies könnte bedeuten, dass ein solches Wesen die begehrten Gegenstände im Unterschied zu anderen Wesen auch durch Begriffe vorstellen kann. Es könnte aber auch mehr bedeuten, nämlich dass das Wesen auch auf andere Weise handeln kann, weil es bei seinem Begehren schon Regeln der technisch-praktischen oder auch der moralisch-praktischen Vernunft anwendet. (2.) Auch das zweite Merkmal wirft ein Problem auf, denn es scheint trivialerweise auf jedes Begehrungsvermögen zuzutreffen. Denn die Bestimmungsgründe eines Begehrungsvermögens sind niemals die Gegenstände selbst, sondern immer *Vorstellungen* von Gegenständen, und diese liegen als „innre Bestimmungen unseres Gemüths" (KrV A197/B242) im begehrenden Subjekt. (Vgl. KrV A275/B331) Wenn die Bestimmungsgründe im wörtlichen Sinn in den Objekten selbst liegen würden, so würde es sich gar nicht um Begehren, sondern um „mechanische Causalität" (KpV 5:96.29) handeln. (Vgl.

KpV 5:96.19 ff.) (3.) Die dritte Frage betrifft die Verknüpfung der beiden Merkmale durch den Ausdruck „sofern" (MS 6:213.14). Dieser Ausdruck kann entweder *einschränkend* (‚unter der Bedingung, dass') oder *explikativ* (‚unter der Rücksicht, dass in diesem Fall') gelesen werden. Der einschränkenden Lesart zufolge verfügt ein Wesen über ein *VBTL*, wenn es nach Begriffen begehren kann und wenn *darüber hinaus* der Bestimmungsgrund seines Begehrungsvermögens nicht im Objekt, sondern im Begehrungsvermögen selbst liegt. Der explikativen Lesart zufolge stellt jedes Begehrungsvermögen nach Begriffen ein *VBTL* dar, weil bei einem Begehrungsvermögen nach Begriffen der Bestimmungsgrund immer im Begehrungsvermögen selbst liegt.

Die Definition ist also schwierig, und ich möchte daher zumindest die erste Frage etwas ausführlicher diskutieren und anschließend andeuten, wie die beiden anderen Fragen beantwortet werden könnten. Das erste Merkmal des *VBTL* lässt sich so erklären: Bei einem *VBTL* sind die Vorstellungen, die zur Realisierung von Gegenständen führen, *Begriffe* dieser Gegenstände. Dies legt zunächst die folgende Lesart nahe: Ein Wesen kann genau dann „nach Begriffen" begehren, wenn es sich auf die begehrten Gegenstände durch Begriffe beziehen kann, (vgl. MS 6:211.24 f., Anm.) oder einfacher ausgedrückt: wenn es *erkennen* kann, welche Gegenstände es begehrt. Allerdings ist diese Erklärung des Begehrungsvermögens nach Begriffen zu schwach. Wir können uns Kant zufolge auch ein Wesen denken, das zwar alles erkennt, was es begehrt, aber trotzdem nur nach *sinnlichen* Vorstellungen bzw. aus Instinkt handeln kann. (Vgl. GMS 4:395) Aus der Tatsache, dass ein Wesen die begehrten Gegenstände durch Begriffe erkennen kann, folgt also nicht, dass den Begriffen *als solchen* auch eine kausale Rolle beim Handeln dieses Wesens zukommt.

Um zu erklären, was ein Begehrungsvermögen nach Begriffen ist, scheint es daher angemessener vom Zweckbegriff auszugehen. Kant definiert in der *Kritik der Urteilskraft* ‚Zweck' als „Gegenstand eines Begriffs, sofern dieser als die Ursache von jenem [...] angesehen wird" (KU 5:220.1–3). Begriffe von Zwecken übernehmen dieser Definition zufolge die gesuchte kausale Rolle. Denn sie führen beim rationalen Begehren dazu, dass der ihnen korrespondierende Gegenstand verursacht wird. Folglich liegt es nahe, den Ausdruck „Begehrungsvermögen nach Begriffen" so zu verstehen, dass es sich um ein Begehrungsvermögen handelt, dessen Ausübung Begriffe von Zwecken zugrunde liegen.[34]

---

34 Vgl. Willaschek, 1992, S. 49 ff.; Baum, 2005, S. 37 f.

Obwohl Kants Ausführungen in der *Kritik der Urteilskraft* diese Lesart durchaus unterstützen, (vgl. KU 5:220.15–17) ist sie im Kontext der *Metaphysik der Sitten* nicht unproblematisch. Kant legt nämlich in der Einleitung zur *Tugendlehre* eine etwas andere Definition von ‚Zweck‘ vor als noch in der *Kritik der Urteilskraft*. Hier bestimmt Kant ‚Zweck‘ als „G e g e n s t a n d der freien Willkür [...]" (TL 6:384.33) und deutet damit an, dass ein Wesen nur dann Zwecke haben kann, wenn es über eine freie Willkür verfügt. (Vgl. TL 6:385.3 f.) Wenn dies stimmt, dann führt die vorgestellte Lesart zu einer merkwürdigen Konsequenz: Wenn das Begehrungsvermögen nach Begriffen nichts anderes ist als das Vermögen Zwecke zu haben und das Vermögen Zwecke zu haben nichts anderes als eine freie Willkür, so ist ein Begehrungsvermögen nach Begriffen eine freie Willkür. Nun definiert Kant im vorliegenden Absatz die Willkür als eine besondere Form des *VBTL* und damit auch als eine besondere Form des Begehrungsvermögens nach Begriffen.[35] Folglich ließe sich die Annahme der Freiheit der Willkür schon analytisch aus dem *Begriff* der Willkür ableiten, und Kants Begriff einer nicht-freien ‚tierischen‘ Willkür wäre logisch widersprüchlich.[36]

Doch selbst wenn wir annehmen, dass ein *VBTL*-Wesen nach Begriffen von Zwecken handeln kann, stellt sich immer noch die Frage, was es überhaupt bedeuten könnte, dass den Begriffen eine kausale Rolle beim Begehren zukommt. Wodurch unterscheiden sich Wesen, die nach Begriffen handeln können, von Wesen, die nur nach sinnlichen Vorstellungen handeln können? Eine mögliche Antwort auf diese Frage ergibt sich aus Kants Ausführungen in der zweiten Einleitung in die *Kritik der Urteilskraft*. Dort beschreibt Kant den Willen ebenfalls als eine Ursache, die „nach Begriffen" (KU 5:172) wirkt und erklärt auch etwas genauer, was dies bedeutet. Kant zufolge gibt es zwei Arten von Begriffen – die Naturbegriffe und den Freiheitsbegriff –, aus denen zwei unterschiedliche praktische Prinzipien abgeleitet werden können: technisch-praktische und moralisch-praktische Prinzipien. Dies legt folgende Erklärung des

---

35 Vgl. Abschnitt 3.2 meines Beitrags.
36 Vgl. MS 6:213.30–32 und Fußnote 61 dieses Beitrags. Um diesem Einwand zu entgehen, bietet sich eine Unterscheidung an zwischen dem Vermögen nach Zweckbegriffen zu handeln und dem Vermögen sich selbst Zwecke zu setzen. Nur das letztere Vermögen scheint die Freiheit der Willkür vorauszusetzen. Allerdings scheint aus der Definition von ‚Zweck‘ in der *Tugendlehre* auch zu folgen, dass ein Wesen nur dann nach Begriffen von Zwecken handeln kann, wenn es sich diese auch selbst setzen kann, d. h. wenn es über eine freie Willkür verfügt.

Ausdrucks „Begehrungsvermögen nach Begriffen" nahe: Ein Wesen kann genau dann nach Begriffen begehren, wenn es aus Begriffen praktische Regeln bzw. Prinzipien ableiten kann, an denen es sein Handeln orientiert. Ein Mensch kann folglich nach Begriffen handeln, weil er sein Handeln an hypothetischen und kategorischen Imperativen orientieren kann, die sich aus den Naturbegriffen oder dem Freiheitsbegriff ergeben. Nun erklärt diese Deutung zwar, was es heißen könnte, dass ein Wesen nach Begriffen begehren kann. Allerdings ergibt sich hier ebenfalls die Frage, ob mit einem bloßen Begehrungsvermögen nach Begriffen schon das Vermögen verbunden ist, sein Handeln an kategorischen Imperativen zu orientieren und in diesem Sinne frei zu handeln. Folglich führt auch diese Erklärung zu der Konsequenz, dass ein Begehrungsvermögen nach Begriffen nichts anderes wäre als eine freie Willkür. Darüber hinaus würde diese Interpretation aber auch zu der merkwürdig klingenden Folgerung führen, dass ein Wesen Handlungen *nach Belieben* ausführen oder unterlassen kann, sofern es unter dem Anspruch *kategorischer* Imperative handeln kann. Dies scheint Kants Auffassung eines kategorischen Imperativs entgegenzustehen, der, wie Kant an anderer Stelle betont, „dem Willen *kein Belieben* in Ansehung des Gegentheils frei läßt" (GMS 4:420.9 f., kursiv T.H.).

Um besser einschätzen zu können, in welchem Sinn das *VBTL* ein rationales Begehrungsvermögen darstellt, ist es daher wichtig zu verstehen, was es überhaupt bedeutet, dass ein Wesen Handlungen „nach Belieben" ausführen oder unterlassen kann. Für Alexander Gottlieb Baumgarten beinhaltet das „Belieben" (lat. *lubitus*) diejenigen Vorstellungen eines Wesens, durch die bestimmt ist, warum ein Wesen so und nicht anders handelt, also z.B. Lust, sinnliche Triebfedern oder rationale Beweggründe.[37] Ein Wesen verfügt daher Baumgarten zufolge über ein ‚Vermögen nach Belieben zu begehren und zu verabscheuen', wenn es die Wahl einer Handlungsalternative von seinen sinnlichen Antrieben oder rationalen Präferenzen („Belieben") abhängig machen kann.[38] Dieses Vermögen stellt folglich eine beschränkte Art von *Wahlfreiheit* dar, die darin besteht, in Abhängigkeit von den eigenen Antrieben oder Präferenzen unter Handlungsalternativen auswählen zu können. Voraussetzung für das Vorliegen dieses Vermögens ist natürlich, dass das Verhalten

---

37 Vgl. Baumgarten, *Metaphysica*, § 712, HN 17:134; Wolff, *Psychologia Empirica*, § 938; *Deutsche Metaphysik*, §§ 518 f.

38 Baumgarten, *Metaphysica*, § 712, HN 17:134.

des Wesens nicht durch andere äußere oder innere Faktoren determiniert ist, d. h. dass sich Tun und Lassen in seiner Gewalt befinden.[39]

Im Unterschied zu Baumgarten bestimmt Kant das *VBTL* nun zwar als ein „Begehrungsvermögen nach Begriffen" und damit als eine Art von praktischer Rationalität. Gleichwohl legt der Zusammenhang, der Baumgarten zufolge zwischen dem Belieben und der Handlungswahl besteht, eine Antwort auf die Frage nahe, um welche Art von Rationalität es sich hier handelt. Kant zufolge ist ein Wesen, das über ein *VBTL* verfügt, in der Lage, seine eigenen Antriebe oder Präferenzen als *Gründe* für die Wahl einer Handlungsalternative anzusehen. Ein *VBTL* stellt folglich in einem eingeschränkten Sinn ein Vermögen der rationalen Wahl dar. Dieses Vermögen besteht darin, in Abhängigkeit von vorliegenden Absichten („nach Belieben") Handlungsalternativen auszuwählen und dabei vernünftige Überlegung einzusetzen.[40] Wenn dies stimmt, dann lässt sich die Frage, was ein Begehrungsvermögen nach Begriffen ist, auf folgende Weise beantworten: Um in Abhängigkeit von bestehenden Absichten unter verschiedenen Handlungsalternativen rational auswählen zu können, muss ein Wesen nicht nur erkennen können, was es begehrt. Es muss darüber hinaus auch aufgrund von praktischen Prinzipien entscheiden können, welche Handlungsalternative den begehrten Gegenstand realisiert. Die praktischen Prinzipien, die das *VBTL*-Wesen bei dieser rationalen Handlungswahl einsetzt, vermitteln folglich nur zwischen bestehenden Absichten und der Wahl einer Handlungsalternative. Dies deutet darauf hin, dass es sich bei diesen praktischen Prinzipien noch nicht um moralisch-praktische, sondern lediglich um technisch-praktische Prinzipien handelt. Denn die praktische Vorschrift, in der eine Handlung „als Mittel zu einer andern Absicht geboten" (GMS 4:416) wird, ist für Kant ein hypothetischer Imperativ und damit ein technisch-praktisches Prinzip. Ein *VBTL*-Wesen verfügt also über ein Begehrungsvermögen nach Begriffen, sofern es (a) erkennen kann, was es begehrt, und (b) aus dieser Erkenntnis hypothetische Imperative ableiten kann, die bestimmen, welche Handlungsalternative es wählen soll, um den begehrten Gegenstand zu realisieren.

---

39 Vgl. Baumgarten, *Metaphysica,* § 712, HN 17:134, §§ 708 ff., HN 17:132 ff.
40 Vgl. Baum, 2005, S. 37 f.; Herman 2007, S. 237–241.

In diesem Rahmen kann ich diese Deutung nicht ausführlich diskutieren.[41] Ich möchte nur noch darauf hinweisen, dass sie auch eine Beantwortung der beiden anderen eingangs erwähnten Fragen zu Kants Definition des *VBTL* möglich macht. Die Frage, in welchem Sinn der Bestimmungsgrund zur Handlung bei einem *VBTL* nicht im Objekt, sondern im Begehrungsvermögen selbst liegt, könnte dann auf folgende Weise beantwortet werden: Kant zufolge liegt ein *VBTL* vor, wenn beim Begehren prinzipiengeleitete Überlegung als ein *subjekt-abhängiger* Faktor zwischen der Vorstellung des begehrten Gegenstandes und der Wahl der Handlung vermittelt. Dass bei einem *VBTL* der „Bestimmungsgrund [...] zur Handlung" (MS 6:213.14 f.) nicht im Objekt liegt, bedeutet also nur, dass wir in diesem Fall die Wahl der Handlung nicht vollständig durch die Vorstellung eines begehrten Objekts erklären können. Dabei ist nicht ausschlaggebend, dass das *VBTL*-Wesen das Objekt auch durch Begriffe und nicht nur sinnlich vorstellt; entscheidend ist die Tatsache, dass es aus seiner Erkenntnis des Objekts Prinzipien ableiten kann, die bestimmen, welche Handlung es wählen soll („Begehrungsvermögen nach Begriffen"). Folglich liegt es nahe, den Ausdruck „sofern", der die beiden Merkmale in der Definition des *VBTL* verbindet, nicht einschränkend, sondern explikativ zu verstehen. Wenn ein Wesen über ein Begehrungsvermögen nach Begriffen verfügt, dann liegt der Bestimmungsgrund zur Handlung nicht im Objekt, sondern im begehrenden Subjekt selbst. Denn das Subjekt entscheidet in diesem Fall selbst aufgrund von vernünftiger Überlegung, welche Handlungsalternative es in Abhängigkeit von einer vorliegenden Absicht wählt, um den begehrten Gegenstand zu realisieren.[42]

3.2 Willkür und Wunsch

Kant definiert ‚Willkür' und ‚Wunsch' als Formen des *VBTL:* „Sofern es [das *VBTL*, T.H.] mit dem Bewußtsein des Vermögens seiner Handlung zur Hervorbringung des Objects verbunden ist, heißt es Willkür; ist es aber damit nicht verbunden, so heißt der Actus desselben ein Wunsch." (MS 6:213.17–19) Die Unterscheidung zwischen Willkür und Wunsch bezieht sich auf die Einschätzung, die ein – im Sinn der Definition des

41 Zu dieser Deutung passt jedenfalls, dass Kant die Ausdrücke „Belieben" bzw. „beliebig" häufig verwendet, um hypothetische Imperative zu charakterisieren. (Vgl. KrV A823/B851; GMS 4:420.9 f., 427.33 f.; KpV 5:26.39 f., Anm.)
42 Für eine einschränkende Lesart: Vgl. Herman, 2007, S. 237 f.

VBTL – rational handelndes Wesen in Bezug auf die Erfolgsaussichten seines Handelns hat. Wenn das rational handelnde Wesen davon ausgeht, dass seine Handlung den vorgestellten Gegenstand realisieren wird, dann verfügt dieses Wesen über eine Willkür. Im Fall des Wunsches hat es hingegen nicht die Überzeugung, dass sein Handeln dazu führt, dass der vorgestellte Gegenstand realisiert wird. Willkür und Wunsch unterscheiden sich noch in einem weiteren Sinn: Während die Willkür ein Vermögen darstellt, handelt es sich bei dem Wunsch lediglich um den „Actus" (MS 6.213.19), d. h. um die Ausübung eines Vermögens.[43]

Hier möchte ich ebenfalls drei Interpretationsfragen vorstellen, die sich aus Kants Definition des Wunsches ergeben. Die *erste* Frage betrifft Kants Charakterisierung des Wunsches: Was bedeutet es, dass beim Wunsch im Unterschied zur Willkür ein Erfolgsbewusstsein fehlt? Kant zufolge gibt es zwar eine Art von Wunsch, bei welchem wir der Überzeugung sind, dass wir den Gegenstand nicht realisieren können. Ein „l e e r e r (müßiger) Wunsch" richtet sich auf Gegenstände, „zu deren Herbeischaffung das Subject sich selbst unvermögend fühlt" (Anth 7:251.7–9) – also etwa darauf, „das Geschehene ungeschehen zu machen" (KU 5:178.17 f., Anm.). Allerdings scheint dies nicht für alle Wünsche zu gelten. Kant spricht auch dann von Wünschen, wenn wir unentschieden lassen, ob wir unsere Absichten durch eigenes Handeln verwirklichen können oder nicht. So sollen wir auf den ewigen Frieden hinwirken, selbst wenn der kriegslose Zustand „auch immer ein frommer Wunsch bliebe" (RL 6:354.34–355.1). In diesem Fall sind wir, wie Kant am Ende der *Rechtslehre* ausführt, aber nicht von der Vergeblichkeit unserer politischen Bemühungen überzeugt, sondern in dieser Frage bloß unentschieden.[44] Dies legt die Annahme nahe, dass Kants Definition des

---

43 Es ist allerdings nicht ganz klar, welches Vermögen beim Wunsch ausgeübt wird. In der ersten Ausgabe der *Rechtslehre* heißt es, der Wunsch sei ein „Actus derselben", d. h. ein Actus der Willkür. (Vgl. Natorp, *Lesarten*, 6:529) Dies scheint allerdings ein Widerspruch zu sein, denn in diesem Fall wäre der Wunsch zugleich mit dem Erfolgsbewusstsein verbunden und nicht verbunden. Daher wird in den meisten Ausgaben „Actus desselben" gedruckt, so dass der Wunsch eine Ausübung des *VBTL*, des Begehrungsvermögens nach Begriffen oder einfach des Begehrungsvermögens darstellt. (Vgl. Natorp, *Lesarten*, AA 6:529) In jedem Fall ist der Wunsch eine Ausübung einer Form des Begehrungsvermögens. (Vgl. hierzu auch KU 5:177 f., Anm.; siehe auch Fußnote 54 dieses Beitrags).

44 Vgl. RL 6:354.12–19. Dass wir Kant zufolge bei Wünschen in Bezug auf Erfolg oder Misserfolg auch unentschieden sein können, legt auch die Bemerkung Kants nahe, dass wir durch Wünsche bzw. die sich daraus ergebenden Versuche erst

Wunsches in der *Metaphysik der Sitten* zwei Arten von Wünschen zulässt: Ein Wunsch liegt vor, (a) wenn wir glauben, dass unser Handeln keinen Erfolg haben wird oder (b) wenn wir in dieser Frage unentschieden sind.

Zweitens stellt sich die Frage, ob aus Kants Bestimmung des Wunsches folgt, dass wir nichts unternehmen, wenn wir etwas wünschen. Nun behauptet Kant zwar an einigen Stellen, dass bloße Wünsche „thatleer" (TL 6:441.29) und von der Willkür bzw. dem Willen abzugrenzen sind.[45] In der *Anthropologie* definiert er den Wunsch sogar als „[d]as Begehren ohne Kraftanwendung zu Hervorbringung des Objects" (Anth 7:251.6 f.). Allerdings erkennt Kant an anderen Stellen an, dass Wünsche mindestens zu Versuchen führen können – und zwar selbst dann, wenn der Wünschende genau weiß, dass seine Bemühungen nicht erfolgreich sein werden.[46] In einigen Fällen haben Wünsche für Kant sogar die Realisierung des begehrten Gegenstandes zur Folge. So enthält das aufrichtige Gebet „einen Wunsch, der, wenn er ernstlich (thätig) ist, seinen Gegenstand (ein Gott wohlgefälliger Mensch zu werden) selbst hervorbringt" (RGV 6:195.34 f., Anm.). Kants Begriff des Wunsches in der *Metaphysik der Sitten* impliziert also nicht, dass wir nichts unternehmen, wenn wir etwas wünschen. Vielmehr umfasst der Begriff sowohl (a) bloße bzw. ‚tatleere' Wünsche als auch (b) Versuche, die ihrerseits faktisch erfolglos oder erfolgreich sein können.[47]

Aus diesen Überlegungen ergibt sich *drittens* die Frage, warum ein Wunsch in jedem Fall eine Ausübung des Begehrungsvermögens sein soll. Folgen wir Kants Definition des Wunsches in der *Metaphysik der Sitten*, so stellen alle Wünsche, also auch tatleere Wünsche und erfolglose Versuche, Ausübungen des Begehrungsvermögens dar.[48] Nun hatte ich bei der Diskussion von Kants Definition des Begehrungsvermögens schon

---

unsere Kräfte kennenlernen. (Vgl. KU 5:178.34 ff., Anm.; V-MP-L1/Pölitz 28:254.6–12).

45 Vgl. GMS 4:394.23 f.; TL 6:430.30. Die Sehnsucht – auch eine Art von Wunsch (vgl. Anth 7:251.9–11) – ist „zwar *thatleer*, aber doch nicht *folgeleer*" (RL 6:356.21).

46 Beispiele hierfür sind „Gebete um Abwendung großer und, so viel man einsieht, unvermeidlicher Übel und manche abergläubische Mittel zu Erreichung natürlicherweise unmöglicher Zwecke" (KU 5:178.28–30, Anm.).

47 Hier stellt sich die Frage, ob Kant zufolge ein Zusammenhang zwischen der Erfolgseinschätzung und der Tat bzw. Tatlosigkeit bei Wünschen besteht. Kant geht jedenfalls nicht einfach davon aus, dass leere Wünsche immer tatleer bleiben oder dass auf Wünsche, bei denen wir in Bezug auf Erfolg oder Misserfolg unentschieden sind, immer Versuche folgen.

48 Vgl. Fußnote 43 dieses Beitrags.

darauf hingewiesen, dass diese Definition den Schluss nahelegt, dass wir das Begehrungsvermögen nur dann ausüben, wenn wir den vorgestellten Gegenstand auch realisieren.[49] Wenn dies stimmt, dann steht Kants Begriff des Wunsches in einem Widerspruch zu seiner Definition des Begehrungsvermögens. Denn weder bei tatleeren Wünschen noch bei erfolglosen Versuchen realisieren wir den vorgestellten Gegenstand. Einen ähnlichen Einwand haben schon Kants Zeitgenossen formuliert. „Wir begehren", schreibt August Wilhelm Rehberg, „viele Dinge, von denen wir selbst wissen, daß wir nicht Ursache ihrer Wirklichkeit sein können".[50] Der von Rehberg angeführte Fall stellt ein eindrucksvolles Gegenbeispiel gegen Kants Definition des Begehrungsvermögens dar. In diesem Fall ist es nämlich nicht nur wahrscheinlich, dass wir aufgrund unseres Wissens nichts unternehmen werden, um den Gegenstand zu realisieren; darüber hinaus ist auch faktisch ausgeschlossen, dass wir, selbst wenn wir einen Versuch unternehmen sollten, den vorgestellten Gegenstand realisieren können.

Kant hat seine Definition des Begehrungsvermögens an mehreren Stellen auf ähnliche Weise verteidigt.[51] Kant zufolge üben wir auch bei Wünschen unser Begehrungsvermögen aus – und zwar selbst dann, wenn wir mit Recht keinen Erfolg von einer Handlung erwarten können. Denn, so Kant in einer Anmerkung zur Einleitung in die *Kritik der Urteilskraft*, auch in diesem Fall kommt der Vorstellung des Gegenstandes eine kausale Rolle zu. Diese kausale Rolle wird für Kant zum einen daran „sichtbar", dass starke Sehnsüchte nicht ohne psychische Folgen für den Menschen bleiben und „das Herz ausdehnen und welk machen" (KU 5:178.23–25, Anm.). Zum anderen zeigt sich die kausale Rolle der Vorstellung bei Wünschen gerade darin, dass diese selbst dann noch zu Versuchen führen können, wenn wir von der Vergeblichkeit unserer Bemühungen restlos überzeugt sind. Dass wir in den meisten Fällen die kausale Rolle der Vorstellung in unseren tatleeren Wünschen nicht bemerken, liegt wohl daran, dass, wie Kant an einer anderen Stelle ausführt, sich die Vorstellung des ersehnten Gegenstandes und das Bewusstsein unserer Erfolglosigkeit zueinander wie Kraft und Gegenkraft verhalten,

---

49 Vgl. Abs. 1.1 dieses Beitrags.
50 Rehberg, 1788, S. 186; ähnliche Einwände finden sich bei Bouterwek, 1797, S. 266, sowie in der Greifswalder Rezension der ersten Auflage der *Rechtslehre* (vgl. Rezension der *Rechtslehre*, 1797, S. 137 f. und Kants Reaktion darauf in HAGEN 21, XLIIf.)
51 Vgl. KU 5:177 f., Anm.; EEKU 20:230 f., Anm.; RL 6:356 f.; HAGEN 21.

die sich gegenseitig ausgleichen.[52] Die Tatsache, dass die Vorstellungen auch bei derartigen Wünschen eine kausale Rolle haben, ist für Kant nun Indiz dafür, dass auch hier die „Causalbeziehung der Vorstellungen auf ihre Objecte" (KU 5:178.30 f., Anm.) gegeben ist und daher eine Begehrung vorliegt. – Spätestens an dieser Stelle stellt sich jedoch die Frage, warum die im Wunsch enthaltene Vorstellung auch dann eine kausale Beziehung zum Gegenstand haben soll, wenn diese, wie in dem von Rehberg genannten Fall, gar nicht dazu führen *kann*, dass der Gegenstand realisiert wird. Kants Antwort scheint nur zu erklären, warum Wünsche manchmal ‚tatleer' bleiben. Die Vorstellungen haben auch in diesem Fall eine kausale Kraft, die sich nur aufgrund eines ‚kognitiven Hindernisses' (d. h. des Bewusstseins unserer Erfolglosigkeit) nicht entfalten kann. Diese Erklärung zeigt noch nicht, warum Rehbergs Fall eine Ausübung des Begehrungsvermögens darstellt. Selbst wenn das kognitive Hindernis beseitigt wäre, würde die Vorstellung in Rehbergs Fall allenfalls zu erfolglosen Versuchen und nicht zu einer Realisierung des Gegenstandes führen.

Zwar kann ich dieses Problem hier nicht in der gebotenen Ausführlichkeit weiter verfolgen, ich möchte aber dennoch darauf hinweisen, dass es meines Erachtens eine mögliche Lösung gibt. Zunächst zeigt Kants Antwort deutlich, dass er nicht die Auffassung vertrat, dass wir das Begehrungsvermögen nur dann ausüben, wenn wir den Gegenstand tatsächlich realisieren. Folgen wir den Ausführungen Kants, so stellt die kausale Rolle, die einer Vorstellung *qua* Begehren zukommt, nur eine notwendige Bedingung dafür dar, dass wir den begehrten Gegenstand realisieren. Damit wir den vorgestellten Gegenstand erfolgreich realisieren, müssen weitere Bedingungen erfüllt sein. So darf z. B. die kausale Kraft der Vorstellung nicht durch kognitive ‚Gegenkräfte', etwa durch einen Zweifel am Erfolg der Handlung, an ihrer Entfaltung gehindert werden. Darüber hinaus müssen die ‚einfachen' Vermögen bzw. die ‚mechanischen' Kräfte, die der Mensch bei seinem Handeln einsetzen kann, auch dazu geeignet sein, den begehrten Gegenstand zu realisieren. Wenn wir einmal von Kants schwer verständlicher Behauptung absehen, dass auch bei leeren Wünschen eine kausale Beziehung der Vorstellungen zu ihren Objekten vorliegt, so können wir Kants Antwort auch deutlich schwächer lesen: Kant weist darauf hin, dass der Vorstellung des Gegenstandes auch bei Wünschen, bei denen es in der Regel nicht zur Tat kommt, eine kausale Kraft zukommt und dass es sich daher auch in

---

52 Vgl. HAGEN 21, XLIII, Z. 16–21.

diesen Fällen um eine Ausübung des Begehrungsvermögens handelt. Mit diesen Überlegungen verschwindet das sachliche Problem eines Widerspruchs in Kants Konzeption des menschlichen Begehrens. Für Kant stellen auch tatleere Wünsche und erfolglose Versuche Ausübungen des Begehrungsvermögens dar, denn nicht jede Ausübung des Begehrungsvermögens muss zur Realisierung des Gegenstandes führen.

Allerdings beantworten diese Überlegungen noch nicht die Frage, warum Kant seinen Begriff des Begehrungsvermögens nur über die Möglichkeit *definiert*, dieses Vermögen erfolgreich auszuüben, d. h. als „das Vermögen durch seine Vorstellungen *Ursache* der Gegenstände dieser Vorstellungen zu sein" (MS 6:211.6 f., kursiv T.H.). Vielleicht kann in dieser Frage die Beobachtung helfen, dass das Begehrungsvermögen nicht das einzige praktische Vermögen darstellt, dessen Begriff Kant auf diese Weise definiert. Bei seiner Definition des Begriffs der Freiheit der Willkür verfährt Kant nämlich auf ähnliche Weise. Auch in diesem Fall bemerkt Kant, dass der Begriff der Freiheit der Willkür nicht durch die Möglichkeit *definiert* werden kann, vom moralischen Gesetz abzuweichen, gesteht aber zu, dass wir – unerklärlicherweise – auch dann unsere Freiheit ausüben, wenn wir vom moralischen Gesetz abweichen. (Vgl. MS 6:226 f.) In beiden Fällen definiert Kant folglich den Begriff eines Vermögens durch die Möglichkeit der ‚erfolgreichen‘ Ausübung dieses Vermögens, gesteht aber zu, dass das Vermögen auch ‚ohne Erfolg‘ ausgeübt werden kann. Dies deutet darauf hin, dass Kants Definitionen eine allgemeine Theorie der Explikation von Vermögensbegriffen zu Grunde liegt: Wenn wir erklären wollen, worin ein bestimmtes praktisches Vermögen wesentlich besteht, dann verweisen wir auf die *erfolgreiche* Ausübung dieses Vermögens unter idealen Bedingungen.[53] Dieses naheliegende Vorgehen bei der Explikation eines Vermögensbegriffs schließt jedoch nicht aus, dass es Ausübungen des Vermögens gibt, die nicht erfolgreich sind.[54]

---

53 Vgl. insbes. Kants Bemerkungen zur Definition des Freiheitsbegriffs (MS 6:227.2 – 9). und hierzu Allison, 1990, S. 135 f., und Herman 2007, S. 247 ff.

54 Aus diesen Überlegungen ergibt sich eine Strategie zur Beantwortung der Frage, warum Kant den Wunsch tatsächlich ohne Widerspruch als eine Ausübung der *Willkür* (d. h. als einen „Actus derselben") auffassen kann (vgl. Fußnote 43 dieses Beitrags). Diese Antwort würde davon ausgehen, dass Kant den Begriff der Willkür definiert, indem er lediglich auf die *erfolgreiche* Ausübung dieses Vermögens verweist. Wir üben die Willkür *qua* Willkür erfolgreich aus, wenn wir nicht bloß wünschen, d. h. wenn wir uns sicher sind, dass die Handlungsalternative, für die wir uns entschieden haben, den begehrten Gegenstand auch

3.3 Wille

Kant definiert den Willen als „[d]as Begehrungsvermögen, dessen innerer Bestimmungsgrund, folglich selbst das Belieben in der Vernunft des Subjects angetroffen wird" (MS 6:213.20–22). Anschließend unterscheidet er mit dem Willen und der Willkür zwei Rücksichten, unter denen das menschliche Begehrungsvermögen betrachtet werden kann: „Der Wille ist also das Begehrungsvermögen, nicht sowohl (wie die Willkür) in Beziehung auf die Handlung, als vielmehr auf den Bestimmungsgrund der Willkür zur Handlung betrachtet, und hat selber vor sich eigentlich keinen Bestimmungsgrund, sondern ist, sofern sie die Willkür bestimmen kann, die praktische Vernunft selbst." (MS 6:213.22–26) Obwohl sich schon in Kants früheren moralphilosophischen Werken der Sache nach ein Unterschied zwischen Wille und Willkür nachweisen lässt, gebraucht Kant für beide Aspekte des rationalen Begehrungsvermögens dort auch den Ausdruck ‚Wille‘.[55] Ausdrücklich trifft Kant die Unterscheidung zwischen Wille und Willkür erst in diesem und im vierten Abschnitt der Einleitung zur *Metaphysik der Sitten*.[56] Vor allem die Stelle im vierten Abschnitt sowie Kants *Vorarbeiten* zur *Metaphysik der Sitten* deuten darauf hin, dass Kant diese Unterscheidung in die *Metaphysik der Sitten* einführt, um sich von der Behauptung Carl Leonhard Reinholds abzugrenzen, dass die Freiheit in der Wahlmöglichkeit zwischen guten und bösen Handlungen besteht.[57]

Kants Definition des Willens und die Unterscheidung zwischen Wille und Willkür werden in der Forschungsliteratur vor allem im Hinblick auf Kants Theorie von Freiheit und Autonomie thematisiert.[58] Hier möchte ich allerdings nur auf eine Interpretationsfrage hinweisen, die Kants Definition des Willens und indirekt auch seine Unterscheidung zwischen Wille und Willkür im vorliegenden Abschnitt betrifft: Um welche Art von praktischer Rationalität verfügt ein handelndes Wesen, wenn es einen Willen hat? Kants Formulierungen sind in diesem Punkt erstaunlich vage. Bei einem Willen liegt der innere Bestimmungsgrund des Begehrungsvermögens „in der Vernunft des Subjects" (MS 6:213.21), und der

---

realisiert. Der Wunsch ließe sich folglich ohne Widerspruch als eine ‚erfolglose‘ Ausübung der Willkür auffassen.

55 Vgl. hierzu Beck, 1960, S. 176 ff., S. 202 f.; Beck, [2]2002; Willaschek, 1992, S. 51 ff., S. 200 ff.; vgl. auch GMS 4:412 f., 427; KpV 5:15.9 ff., 89.25 f.
56 Vgl. MS 6:226 f.; OP 21:470 f.; VAMS 23:248 f.; VATL 23:378 f., 383 f.
57 Vgl. zu diesem Thema: Bojanowski, 2007; Zöller, 2005.
58 Vgl. Meerbote, 1982; Hudson 1994; Allison, 1990, S. 129 ff.; Baum, 2005.

Wille ist daher „die praktische Vernunft selbst" (MS 6:213.26). Im vierten Abschnitt bemerkt Kant, dass der Wille das Vermögen ist, das die „Gesetze" (MS 6:226.4) für die Maximen der Willkür gibt. Kant identifiziert den Willen also nicht ausdrücklich mit der *reinen* praktischen Vernunft und auch nicht mit dem Vermögen der *moralischen* Gesetzgebung. Aus diesem Grund liegt die Annahme nahe, dass der Wille für Kant nicht nur in der moralisch-praktischen, sondern auch in der technisch-praktischen Vernunft besteht.[59]

Natürlich kann ich die Argumente für und wider eine solche Deutung hier nicht in der gebotenen Ausführlichkeit diskutieren. Ich möchte nur darauf hinweisen, dass sich im Text auch Anhaltspunkte für die These finden lassen, dass der Wille *nur* in der moralisch-praktischen Vernunft besteht. Dazu müssen wir zunächst berücksichtigen, dass für Kant nicht nur der Wille, sondern auch die Willkür eine Art von praktischer Rationalität darstellt. Kant zufolge ist die Willkür nämlich eine besondere Form des *VBTL* und damit ein „Begehrungsvermögen nach Begriffen" (MS 6:213.14). Es ist nun bemerkenswert, dass der Wortlaut von Kants Definition des Willens explizit auf seine Definition des *VBTL* verweist. Der Wille ist Kant zufolge „[d]as Begehrungsvermögen, dessen innerer Bestimmungsgrund, folglich selbst das Belieben in der Vernunft des Subjects angetroffen wird" (MS 6:213.20–23). Ein handelndes Wesen verfügt also über einen Willen, (a) wenn der Bestimmungsgrund seines Begehrungsvermögens ein *innerer* Bestimmungsgrund ist und (b) wenn dieser innere Bestimmungsgrund (und „folglich selbst das Belieben") in der Vernunft des Subjekts angetroffen wird. Zunächst zum ersten Merkmal, das dem Willen in dieser Definition zugeschrieben wird: Es liegt nahe, den Ausdruck „innerer Bestimmungsgrund" im Rückgriff auf Kants Definition des *VBTL* zu verstehen. Ein innerer Bestimmungsgrund des Begehrungsvermögens liegt vor, wenn der Bestimmungsgrund des Begehrungsvermögens im Begehrungsvermögen selbst und „nicht in dem Objecte angetroffen wird" (MS 6:213.15 f.). In meiner Diskussion von Kants Definition des *VBTL* habe ich vorgeschlagen, dies auf folgende Weise zu verstehen: Der Bestimmungsgrund des Begehrungsvermögens liegt im Subjekt und nicht im Objekt, wenn das begehrende Subjekt selbst entscheidet, welche Handlungsalternative es in Abhängigkeit von einer bestehenden Absicht („nach Belieben") wählt. Dies legt die Annahme nahe, dass Kant zufolge das erste Merkmal des Willens (d. h. die ‚innere Bestimmbarkeit' des Begehrungsvermögens) eigentlich genau

---

59 Vgl. Meerbote, 1982, S. 70 ff.; Hudson 1994, S. 185 f.; Allison, 1990, S. 130.

dann gegeben ist, wenn das handelnde Wesen über ein *VBTL* verfügt. Denn in diesem Fall kann das Wesen selbst entscheiden, welche Handlung es wählt.

Allerdings scheint dies nur eine notwendige Bedingung dafür zu sein, dass ein handelndes Subjekt über einen Willen verfügt. Bei einem Willen wird nämlich darüber hinaus der „innere[] Bestimmungsgrund, folglich selbst das Belieben in der Vernunft des Subjects angetroffen" (MS 6:213.20 f.). Wenn wir hier unter „Belieben" die Absicht verstehen, die der rationalen Handlungswahl zugrunde liegt, dann können wir das spezifische Merkmal eines Willens auf folgende Weise beschreiben: Ein Wesen, das einen Willen hat, ist in der Lage, aufgrund von vernünftiger Überlegung *selbst die Absicht* („selbst das Belieben") zu bestimmen, die jeder weiteren Handlungswahl zugrunde liegt. Es gibt also auch einen Unterschied zwischen einem *VBTL* und einem Willen. Während das *VBTL* nur darin besteht, anhand von bereits vorliegenden Absichten eine rationale Handlungswahl zu treffen, stellt der Wille zusätzlich das Vermögen dar, allein aufgrund von vernünftiger Überlegung Absichten zu bilden, die dann der rationalen Handlungswahl zugrunde liegen. Wenn dies stimmt, so liegt tatsächlich die Annahme nahe, Kants Unterscheidung zwischen Wille und Willkür als eine Unterscheidung zwischen zwei speziellen Formen von praktischer Rationalität anzusehen. Während die Willkür (als eine besondere Form des *VBTL*) darin besteht, anhand von technisch-praktischen Prinzipien bzw. hypothetischen Imperativen Handlungsalternativen auszuwählen, besteht der Wille darin, anhand von moralisch-praktischen Prinzipien bzw. kategorischen Imperativen zu bestimmen, welche Absichten der Mensch als ein Vernunftwesen überhaupt haben kann. Hierzu passt die schon zitierte Bemerkung Kants, dass der kategorische Imperativ „dem Willen [und das heißt hier: der Willkür, T.H.] kein Belieben in Ansehung des Gegentheils frei läßt" (GMS 4:420.9 f.). Die praktische Überlegung, die auf den Willen zurück geht, legt anhand von kategorischen Imperativen die Absicht bzw. das Belieben fest, und der Willkür bleibt es überlassen, nach diesem Belieben zu handeln.

4. Die Freiheit der menschlichen Willkür und die Unterscheidung zwischen juridischen und ethischen Gesetzen (Absätze 7–8)

4.1 Die Freiheit der menschlichen Willkür

Im siebten Absatz entwickelt Kant seinen Begriff der Freiheit als einer Eigenschaft der menschlichen Willkür.[60] Kant zufolge unterliegt die menschliche Willkür zwar dem Einfluss sinnlicher Antriebe, kann aber durch reine Vernunft bzw. rein aus Willen bestimmt werden und ist daher frei.[61] Dies ist nun nicht so zu verstehen, als werde die menschliche Willkür sowohl durch sinnliche Antriebe als auch durch reine Vernunft bestimmt. So macht Kant in der *Rechtslehre* am Beispiel des Verbrechers deutlich, dass die Übertretung des Gesetzes nicht so erklärt werden kann, dass das Handeln des Verbrechers allein durch sinnliche Antriebe und nicht durch Vernunft bestimmt wird. Denn daraus würde folgen, dass unmoralische Handlungen nicht frei wären und nicht zugerechnet werden könnten. Daher muss selbst das Verbrechen „aus einer Maxime des Verbrechers (sich eine solche Unthat zur Regel zu machen)" (RL 6:321.28 f., Anm.) und damit aus der Freiheit des Verbrechers erklärt werden. (Vgl. RGV 6:28 ff.) Wie dies damit vereinbar ist, dass die Freiheit der menschlichen Willkür in ihrer Bestimmbarkeit durch reine Vernunft besteht, stellt für Kant hingegen ein Frage dar, die nicht beantwortet werden kann.[62]

Kant unterscheidet nun einen negativen und einen positiven Begriff der Freiheit der menschlichen Willkür. (Vgl. GMS 4:446 f.) Im negativen

---

60 Im Folgenden gebe ich nur einen kurzen Überblick über die Definitionen der Absätze 7 und 8. Zu Kants Theorie der Freiheit: Vgl. den Beitrag von Manfred Baum in diesem Band. Zur Unterscheidung zwischen juridischen und ethischen Gesetzen: Vgl. den Beitrag von Steffi Schadow in diesem Band.

61 Vgl. MS 6:213.29 ff.; KrV A534/B562, A802/B830. Der Gegenbegriff ‚tierische Willkür' (vgl. MS 6:213.30–32) bezieht sich nicht einfach auf die Willkür der Tiere. Denn die Willkür ist ein ‚Begehrungsvermögen nach Begriffen', und vieles spricht dafür, dass Kant zufolge Tiere gar keine Begriffe haben. (Vgl. z.B. AA 2:59 f.; Log 9:64 f.) Der Ausdruck scheint in diesem Abschnitt bloß ein Kontrastbegriff zu sein. Ein vernünftiges Lebewesen, das *nur* über technisch-praktische Vernunft verfügen würde, würde nur über eine ‚thierische Willkür' verfügen, weil es bei der rationalen Handlungswahl immer von seinen Neigungen ausgehen müsste. (Vgl. Beck, 1798, S. 21)

62 Vgl. MS 6:226 f. Siehe auch den Beitrag von Manfred Baum in diesem Band.

Sinn besteht die Freiheit der menschlichen Willkür in der „Unabhän-
gigkeit ihrer Bestimmung durch sinnliche Antriebe" (MS 6:213.36 f.).
Im positiven Sinn besteht die Freiheit der menschlichen Willkür in dem
„Vermögen der reinen Vernunft für sich selbst praktisch zu sein" (MS
6:213.37–214.1). Kants Unterscheidung zwischen einem positiven und
einem negativen Freiheitsbegriff führt zu der Frage, warum die positive
Freiheit nur eine Eigenschaft der Willkür und nicht mindestens *auch* eine
Eigenschaft des Willens sein soll. Schließlich hatte Kant ja kurz zuvor
festgehalten, dass der Wille nichts anderes ist als „die praktische Vernunft
selbst", „sofern sie die Willkür bestimmen kann". (MS 6:213.25 f.) Der
Begriff der positiven Freiheit scheint sich daher zumindest auf das *Ver-
hältnis* zu beziehen, das zwischen Wille und Willkür besteht, wenn die
Willkür durch reine praktische Vernunft, (und damit durch den reinen
Willen), bestimmt werden kann.[63] In der Passage im vierten Abschnitt der
Einleitung in die *Metaphysik der Sitten* betont Kant allerdings, dass nur
die Willkür, und nicht der Wille, frei oder unfrei genannt werden kann.
(Vgl. MS 6:226.4–11)

Was es nun genau heißt, dass reine Vernunft für sich selbst praktisch
werden kann, erläutert Kant in einer sehr gedrängten Formulierung am
Ende des siebten Absatzes.[64] Die reine Vernunft kann nur praktisch
werden, indem sie die Universalisierbarkeit der Handlungsmaxime, d. h.
ihre „Tauglichkeit [...] zum allgemeinen Gesetze" (MS 6:214.3 f.), zur
Bedingung des menschlichen Wollens und Handelns macht. Denn erstens ist die Vernunft das „Vermögen der Principien" bzw. ein „gesetzge-
bendes Vermögen". (MS 6:214.5 f.) Daher kann sie nur praktisch werden, indem sie das Handeln des Menschen durch ein allgemeines Gesetz
bestimmt. Zweitens kann sie nur die *Form* eines Gesetzes selbst, d. h. die
Gesetzesfähigkeit der Maxime, „zum obersten Gesetze und Bestimmungsgrunde der Willkür" (MS 6:214.9) machen. Denn die Gesetzgebung der reinen Vernunft muss von Erfahrung unabhängig sein und kann
daher keine Aussage über das Objekt der menschlichen Willkür, d. h.
über die „Materie des Gesetzes" (MS 6:214.7), voraussetzen. Da die
Menschen nicht notwendig nach diesem obersten Gesetz handeln wollen,
gebietet die reine Vernunft das moralische Gesetz in Form eines *Sollens,*
d. h. „als Imperativ des Verbots oder Gebots" (MS 6:214.11 f.). (Vgl. MS
6:222 f.; GMS 4:413)

---

63 Vgl. Allison, 1990, S. 129–133; Beck, 1960, S. 177 ff., S. 198 ff.; Beck, ²2002,
    S. 60 f.
64 Zum Folgenden vgl. KpV 5:27 ff. (§§ 4ff.).

4.2 Juridische und ethische Gesetze

Bereits aus Kants Erklärung, dass die Vernunft die Universalisierbarkeit der Maxime „zum obersten Gesetze und Bestimmungsgrunde der Willkür" (MS 6:214.8 f.) macht, scheint sich eine Differenzierung zu ergeben zwischen zwei Arten der moralischen Gesetzgebung. Kant zufolge fordern *juridische Gesetze* lediglich vom Menschen, dass er eine bestimmte äußere Handlung ausführen soll – unabhängig davon, welches Motiv seiner Handlung zugrunde liegt. Demgegenüber bezieht sich die Forderung der *ethischen Gesetze* auch auf den Bestimmungsgrund der Handlung. Die Übereinstimmung der Handlung mit dem Gesetz soll hier selbst das Motiv der Handlung sein. (Vgl. MS 6:214.13–19, 218 ff.) Menschliches Handeln kann daher auf zwei unterschiedliche Weisen den Sittengesetzen entsprechen: Stimmt die Handlung mit den juridischen Gesetzen überein, so ist sie legal. Stimmt die Handlung dagegen mit den ethischen Gesetzen überein, so ist sie moralisch. (Vgl. MS 6:214.17–19, 219.12 ff., 225.31 ff.)

Nun fordern eigentlich alle moralischen Gesetze, „als reine praktische Vernunftgesetze für die freie Willkür überhaupt" (MS 6:214.28 f.), dass die Übereinstimmung mit diesen Gesetzen zugleich die Bestimmungsgründe unserer Handlungen sind. Aus diesem Grund können alle juridischen Gesetze auch als ethische Gesetze betrachtet werden. Denn auch diese Gesetze soll der Mensch *aus Pflicht* befolgen. Allerdings sind umgekehrt nicht alle moralischen Gesetze auch juridische Gesetze. Denn nicht alle moralischen Gesetze fordern, dass der Mensch eine ‚äußere Handlung' ausführt. Kants Aussage, dass sich die ethischen Gesetze auf die „Freiheit sowohl im äußern als innern Gebrauch der Willkür" (MS 6:214.21) beziehen, ist daher nicht misszuverstehen. Nicht alle ethischen Gesetze beziehen sich auch auf die äußere Freiheit des Menschen, sondern nur diejenigen ethischen Gesetze, die zugleich als juridische Gesetze betrachtet werden können.

5. Titel und Thema des Abschnitts

Die Unterscheidung zwischen ethischen und juridischen Gesetzen führt zu der Frage, wie diese Unterscheidung eigentlich mit Kants Ausführungen zur Freiheit der menschlichen Willkür und seiner Theorie der Vermögen des menschlichen Gemüts in den vorhergehenden Absätzen zusammenhängt. Diese Frage berührt das Problem der thematischen

Einheit des ersten Abschnitts der Einleitung in die *Metaphysik der Sitten*, auf das ich zum Schluss dieses Beitrags eingehen möchte. Aufschlussreich für diese Frage ist die Formulierung im Titel des Abschnitts. Dieser zufolge besteht das Ziel des Abschnitts darin, das *Verhältnis* zu bestimmen, in welchem die Vermögen des menschlichen Gemüts zu den Sittengesetzen stehen. (Vgl. MS 6:211.4 f.) Dies deutet darauf hin, dass es Kant in diesem Abschnitt nicht einfach darum geht, mit seiner Theorie der menschlichen Gemütsvermögen die (moral-)psychologischen Voraussetzungen seiner reifen Ethik bzw. Rechtsphilosophie zu artikulieren. Im Zentrum des Abschnitts scheint vielmehr eine Theorie zu stehen, die das *normative Verhältnis* bestimmt, in welchem das allgemeine moralische Gesetz in seinen zwei Varianten zur spezifisch menschlichen Willkür steht.

Doch gehen wir der Reihe nach vor. Im Titel des Abschnitts spricht Kant zwar im Plural von den „Vermögen des menschlichen Gemüths" (MS 6:211.4), allerdings werden in dem Abschnitt nicht alle drei Grundvermögen (also Erkenntnisvermögen, Gefühl der Lust und Unlust und Begehrungsvermögen) im gleichen Sinn behandelt. Kant sieht es nämlich als eines der wesentlichen Ergebnisse seiner kritischen Philosophie an, dass sich die autonome Ausübung jedes der drei Grundvermögen an jeweils eigenen normativen Prinzipien orientiert, die von den drei oberen Erkenntnisvermögen (also Verstand, Urteilskraft und Vernunft) hervorgebracht werden. (Vgl. KU 5:177 f., 196 f.; EEKU 20:245 f.) Das Hauptinteresse Kants im vorliegenden Abschnitt liegt deutlich auf dem menschlichen Begehrungsvermögen und den apriorischen Prinzipien der reinen praktischen Vernunft. Die anderen beiden Vermögen des menschlichen Gemüts werden hingegen nicht unter der Rücksicht thematisiert, dass sie eigenen apriorischen Prinzipien unterliegen.

Im positiven Begriff der Freiheit scheint Kant nun das Verhältnis zu bestimmen, in welchem das menschliche Begehrungsvermögen zum Prinzip der reinen praktischen Vernunft steht. Die reine praktische Vernunft stellt die Ausübung der freien menschlichen Willkür im moralischen Gesetz unter die Bedingung der Universalisierbarkeit der Handlungsmaxime. Da die menschliche Willkür nicht schon von sich aus mit dieser Bedingung übereinstimmt, ist das Verhältnis, in welchem sie zum moralischen Gesetz steht, ein normatives Verhältnis der *Nötigung*; das moralische Gesetz gilt für Menschen als ein „Imperativ des Verbots oder Gebots" (MS 6:214.11 f.). In diesem normativen Verhältnis wird allerdings nicht allein das menschliche Begehrungsvermögen, sondern auch das Erkenntnisvermögen und das Gefühl der Lust und Unlust beansprucht. Denn erstens ist das moralische Gesetz ein Produkt des *Erkenntnisvermögens*, d. h. der reinen praktischen Vernunft. (Vgl. EEKU 20:206 f.) Um die Empfänglichkeit für die moralische Forderung zu gewährleisten, müssen wir zweitens voraussetzen, dass sich praktische Lust nicht nur als Ursache, sondern auch als Wirkung des menschlichen Begehrens einstellen kann. So erklärt sich vielleicht, dass Kant im Titel von den „Vermögen des menschlichen Gemüths" (MS 6:211.4) im Plural spricht. Die drei Vermögen des menschlichen Gemüts müssen in einer festgelegten Weise *interagieren* können, damit die Ausübung der menschlichen Willkür überhaupt unter der Forderung eines moralischen Imperativs stehen kann. (Vgl. EEKU 20:206 f.)

Nun kündigt der Titel des Abschnitts auch an, dass die menschlichen Gemütsvermögen in ein Verhältnis zu „den Sittengesetzen" (MS 6:211.5) (ebenfalls Plural) gesetzt werden. Erst im achten Absatz, im Rahmen seiner Unterscheidung von zwei Arten von „Gesetze[n] der Freiheit" (MS 6:214.13), scheint Kant an seine Formulierung im Titel anzuknüpfen. Nun folgt in einem ersten Sinn aus der Unterscheidung zwischen juridischen und ethischen Gesetzen, dass die Ausübung der menschlichen Willkür auf zwei Weisen mit den Sittengesetzen übereinstimmen kann. Unter dieser Rücksicht unterscheidet der letzte Absatz mit Legalität und Moralität also zwei mögliche Verhältnisse der Übereinstimmung menschlicher Handlungen mit dem moralischen Imperativ. In einem noch grundlegenderen Sinn *ergibt* sich die Unterscheidung zwischen juridischen und ethischen Gesetzen für Kant allerdings erst, wenn wir analysieren, was es heißt, dass sich das moralische Gesetz als ein Imperativ auf die spezifisch menschliche Willkür bezieht. Denn beim Menschen können wir den bloß äußeren Gebrauch seiner freien Willkür von dem äußeren sowohl als inneren Gebrauch seiner freien Willkür unterscheiden. Aus diesem Grund gilt der moralische Imperativ für den Menschen *als* Menschen in zwei Varianten: als juridisches Gesetz und als ethisches Gesetz. (Vgl. TL 6:406.29–33; KpV 5:8.12–24) Hieraus scheint sich eine mögliche Antwort auf die Frage zu ergeben, warum Kant im vorliegenden Abschnitt neben seiner Theorie der Gemütsvermögen auch die Unterscheidung zwischen juridischen und ethischen Gesetzen thematisiert. Die Unterscheidung ist im vorliegenden Abschnitt Teil einer Antwort auf die Frage, was es heißt, dass das moralische Gesetz ein normatives Prinzip für das Handeln des Menschen *als* Menschen darstellt.[65]

---

65 Für wertvolle Anregungen danke ich Claudia Blöser, Hannes Ole Matthiessen, Dieter Schönecker, Marcus Willaschek, Hong Zhou und Günter Zöller. Für

Literaturverzeichnis

Allison, Henry E. (1990), *Kant's Theory of Freedom*, Cambridge: Cambridge University Press.

Baum, Manfred (2005), „Freiheit und Verbindlichkeit in Kants Moralphilosophie", in: *Jahrbuch für Recht und Ethik*, Bd. 13, S. 31–43.

Baum, Manfred (2006), „Gefühl, Begehren und Wollen in Kants praktischer Philosophie", in: *Jahrbuch für Recht und Ethik*, Bd. 14, S. 125–139.

Baumgarten, Alexander Gottlieb (1757): *Metaphysica*, Halle. (Wiederabgedruckt in: *Kants gesammelte Schriften*, Bd. 15, Preußische Akademie der Wissenschaften (Hrsg.), Berlin/Leipzig: Walter de Gruyter [1923], S. 5–54; Bd. 17, Berlin/Leipzig: Walter de Gruyter [1926], S. 5–226.)

Beck, Jacob Sigismund (1798), *Commentar über Kants Metaphysik der Sitten. Erster Theil welcher die metaphysischen Principien des Naturrechts enthält*, Halle: Rengersche Buchhandlung. (Nachdruck: *Aetas Kantiana*, Bd. 19, Bruxelles: Culture et Civilisation [1970].)

Beck, Lewis White (1960), *A Commentary on 'Kant's Critique of Practical Reason'*, Chicago/London: The University of Chicago Press.

Beck, Lewis White (^{2}2002), „Kant's Two Conceptions of the Will in their Political Context", in: Hoke Robinson (Hrsg.), Selected *Essays on Kant*, Rochester/New York: University of Rochester Press, S. 57–68. (Ursprünglich in: *Annales de philosophie politique*, Bd. 4 (1962), S. 119–137.)

Bojanowski, Jürgen (2007), „Kant und das Problem der Zurechenbarkeit", in: *Zeitschrift für philosophische Forschung*, Bd. 61, S. 207–228.

Bouterwek, Friedrich (1797), Rezension der *Metaphysik der Sitten*, in: *Göttingische Anzeigen von gelehrten Sachen*, 28. Stück, 18. Februar 1797, S. 265–276.

Brandt, Reinhard/Stark, Werner (1997), „Einleitung", in: *Kants gesammelte Schriften*, Bd. 25, Berlin-Brandenburgische Akademie der Wissenschaften (Hrsg.), Berlin: Walter de Gruyter, S. VII–CLI.

Gerhardt, Volker (1986), „Handlung als Verhältnis von Ursache und Wirkung. Zur Entwicklung des Handlungsbegriffs bei Kant", in: Gerold Prauss (Hrsg.), *Handlungstheorie und Transzendentalphilosophie*, Frankfurt/M.: Klostermann, S. 98–131.

Ginsborg, Hannah (1991), „On the Key to Kant's Critique of Taste", in: *Pacific Philosophical Quarterly*, Bd. 72, S. 290–313.

Grenberg, Jeanine M. (2001), „Feeling, Desire and Interest in Kant's Theory of Action", in: *Kant-Studien*, Bd. 92, S. 153–179.

Herman, Barbara (2007), „The Will and Its Objects", in: dies., *Moral Literacy*, Cambridge/MA: Harvard University Press, S. 230–253.

Hudson, Hud (1991), „Wille, Willkür, and the Imputability of Moral Actions", in: *Kant-Studien*, Bd. 82, S. 179–196.

---

zahlreiche Verbesserungsvorschläge danke ich auch den Teilnehmerinnen und Teilnehmern der Kolloquien von Marcus Willaschek und Günter Zöller sowie den Teilnehmerinnen und Teilnehmern der drei Konferenzen des DFG-Netzwerks zur *Tugendlehre*.

Johnson, Andrew B. (2005), „Kant's Empirical Hedonism", in: *Pacific Philosophical Quarterly*, Bd. 86, S. 50–63.
Kant, Immanuel [²1998], „›HAGEN 21‹. Ein Kant-Autograph zur Greifswalder Rezension der Rechtslehre", in: Werner Stark, „Anhang zur Einleitung", in: Immanuel Kant, *Metaphysische Anfangsgründe der Rechtslehre. Metaphysik der Sitten. Erster Teil*, Bernd Ludwig (Hrsg.), Hamburg: Meiner, S. XLI–XLVI.
Kerstein, Samuel J. (2002), *Kant's Search for the Supreme Principle of Morality*, Cambridge: Cambridge University Press.
McCarty, Richard (1993), „Kantian Moral Motivation and the Feeling of Respect", in: *Journal of the History of Philosophy*, Bd. 31, S. 421–435.
Meerbote, Ralf (1982), „'Wille' and 'Willkür' in Kant's Theory of Action", in: Moltke S. Gram (Hrsg.), *Interpreting Kant*, Iowa: University of Iowa Press, S. 69–84.
Natorp, Paul (1907/14), „Lesarten", in: *Kants gesammelte Schriften*, Bd. 6, Preußische Akademie der Wissenschaften (Hrsg.), Berlin: Walter de Gruyter, S. 526–547.
Reath, Andrews (1989a), „Hedonism, Heteronomy, and Kant's Principle of Happiness", in: *Pacific Philosophical Quarterly*, Bd. 70, S. 42–72. (Wiederabgedruckt in: Reath (2006), S. 33–66.)
Reath, Andrews (1989b), „Kant's Theory of Moral Sensibility: Respect for the Moral Law and the Influence of Inclination", in: *Kant-Studien*, Bd. 80, S. 284–302. (Wiederabgedruckt in: Reath (2006), S. 8–32.)
Reath, Andrews (2006), *Agency and Autonomy in Kant's Moral Theory*, Oxford/New York: Oxford University Press.
Rehberg, August Wilhelm (1788), Rezension der *Kritik der praktischen Vernunft*, in: Rüdiger Bittner/Konrad Cramer (Hrsg.), *Materialien zu Kants ‚Kritik der praktischen Vernunft'*, Frankfurt/M.: Suhrkamp 1975, S. 179–196.
Rezension der *Rechtslehre* (1797), in: *Neueste Critische Nachrichten*, J. G. P. Möller (Hrsg.), 18. Stück, Greifswald 6. Mai 1797, S. 137–141; 19. Stück, S. 147–150.
Scarano, Nico (2002), „Moralisches Handeln. Zum dritten Hauptstück von Kants Kritik der praktischen Vernunft (71–89)", in: Otfried Höffe (Hrsg.), *Immanuel Kant. Kritik der praktischen Vernunft*, Berlin: Akademie Verlag, S. 135–152. (Klassiker Auslegen, Bd. 26.)
Schönecker, Dieter (2010): „Kant über Menschenliebe als moralische Gemütsanlage", in: *Archiv für Geschichte der Philosophie*, Bd. 92, S. 133–175 (unter Mitarbeit von Alexander Cotter, Magdalena Eckes, Sebastian Maly).
Willaschek, Marcus (1992), *Praktische Vernunft. Handlungstheorie und Moralbegründung bei Kant*, Stuttgart/Weimar: Metzler.
Wolff, Christian (1738), *Psychologia Empirica*, Frankfurt/Leipzig. (Nachdruck: Hildesheim: Olms [1968].)
Wolff, Christian (1740), *Psychologia Rationalis*, Frankfurt/Leipzig. (Nachdruck: Hildesheim: Olms [1972].)
Wolff, Christian (1751), *Vernünfftige Gedancken von Gott, der Welt und der Seele des Menschen, auch allen Dingen überhaupt* (Deutsche Metaphysik), Halle. (Nachdruck: Hildesheim: Olms [1983].)

Zöller, Günter (2005), „Von Reinhold zu Kant. Zur Grundlegung der Moralphilosophie zwischen Vernunft und Willkür", in: *Archivio di Filosofia*,
Bd. 73, S. 73–91.

Die Einteilungen der *Metaphysik der Sitten* im Allgemeinen und die der *Tugendlehre* im Besonderen (MS 6:218–221 und RL 6:239–242 und TL 6:388–394, 410–413)

Bernd Ludwig

I. Von der Einteilung einer Metaphysik der Sitten (MS 6:218–221)

Neben der Bereitstellung der begrifflichen und metaphysischen Voraussetzungen der Sittenlehre als Ganzer enthält die „Einleitung in die Metaphysik der Sitten" auch einen Abschnitt, der die bereits in der Vorrede angekündigte Zweiteilung der Schrift in Anfangsgründe der Rechts- und der Tugendlehre begründet. Aufgabe einer solchen „Deduction der Eintheilung eines Systems" (MS 6:218.26, Anm.; vgl. KrV A 290) ist es, dichotomische Vollständigkeit und Stetigkeit in der „Reihe der Untereintheilungen" (MS 6:218.28 f., Anm.) sicherzustellen. Der hier exponierte Begriff ist der einer Gesetzgebung, der das *genus proximum* für rechtliche und ethische Gesetzgebung bildet:[1] Jede Gesetzgebung besteht nun aus den beiden „Stücke[n]" (MS 6:218.13) Gesetz und Triebfeder, wobei allein die Triebfeder die *differentia specifica* der beiden genannten Gesetzgebungen ausmacht.[2] Während das erste Stück einer Gesetzge-

---

1   Dieses fundamentale Lehrstück finden wir bei Kant erstmals in der *Metaphysik der Sitten* von 1797. Jede Erörterung, die für Einteilungsfragen auf frühere Schriften zurückgreift, riskiert damit, mögliche Fortentwicklungen der Kantischen Auffassungen zu übergehen (wir werden unten sehen, dass es solche gibt).

2   Im Text MS 6:218.17 f. ist vermutlich ein irrtümlicher Einschub („mithin ist das zweyte Stück dieses: dass das Gesetz die Pflicht zur Triebfeder macht") zu streichen, weil er dem Wortlaut nach das Spezifikum der *ethischen* Gesetzgebung (siehe unten) zum Bestandteil *einer jeden* Gesetzgebung erklärt und damit die zentrale Unterscheidung torpediert. Ließe man ihn stehen, dann müsste man annehmen, er solle – an dieser frühen Stelle allerdings unmotiviert und auf irritierende Weise – zum Ausdruck bringen, dass in *jeder* Gesetzgebung *zumindest* die Idee der Pflicht eine Triebfeder ist. *In der Sache* wäre das dann vollständig mit

bung, das Gesetz selbst, die *objektive* praktische Notwendigkeit einer Handlung, d. h. deren „Verbindlichkeit" (MS 6:218.21) und damit den Pflichtcharakter statuiert (also *e suppositione* ein *moralisches*, kein Naturgesetz ist, *tertium non datur* (vgl. MS 6:221.19–29)), verbindet die Triebfeder einen *subjektiven* Bestimmungsgrund der Willkür mit der Vorstellung des Gesetzes. Ersteres als solches ist ein „bloßes theoretisches Erkenntniß" (MS 6:218.20; vgl. 411.24 ff.), insofern mir etwa die Einsicht möglich ist, dass Hans sich durch ein Versprechen Grete gegenüber verpflichtet hat, ohne dass dies mit irgendeinem subjektiven Bestimmungsgrund *meinerseits* verbunden wäre, wohingegen das Bewusstsein, dass *ich* aufgrund meines Versprechens eine Pflicht gegenüber Grete *habe*, also etwas tun *soll*, das Bewusstsein eines subjektiven Bestimmungsgrundes einschließt, ich also nicht nur ein *Gesetz* (theoretisch) erkenne, sondern *mir* zudem bewusst bin, das Subjekt einer einschlägigen Gesetz*gebung* zu sein. (Vgl. TL 6:375.13 f.)[3]

Die Unterscheidung von rechtlicher und ethischer Gesetzgebung wird nun von Kant ausdrücklich von Seiten der *ethischen* Gesetzgebung bestimmt: Eine Gesetzgebung, die „eine Handlung zur Pflicht und diese Pflicht zugleich zur Triebfeder macht, ist ethisch" (MS 6:219.2 f.), jede andere rechtlich. Rechtlich ist demzufolge jede Gesetzgebung, die „auch [!] eine andere Triebfeder als die Idee der Pflicht selbst zuläßt" (MS 6:219.5; vgl. auch TL 6:394.25). Kurz: Rechtspflichten sind alle diejenigen Pflichten, denen man Genüge tun *kann*, ohne sie *aus Pflicht* zu befolgen. Die bei der rechtlichen Gesetzgebung somit über die der Idee der Pflicht hinaus[4] möglichen Triebfedern können nur – *tertium non*

---

der nachfolgenden Unterscheidung von ethischer und rechtlicher Gesetzgebung vereinbar: Diese bezieht sich – wie wir gleich sehen werden – *expressis verbis ausschließlich* auf die Möglichkeit/Unmöglichkeit *anderer* Triebfedern als der der Pflicht.

3 Diese Unterscheidung ist uns freilich beim positiven Recht wohl vertraut: Gesetzestexte belehren mich (theoretisch) über die (objektiven) rechtlichen Bestimmungen im Ausland. Allein der dortige Aufenthalt (bzw. dortige Rechtsgeschäfte oder auch die Änderung meiner Staatsbürgerschaft) kann mir (subjektiv) Bestimmungsgründe liefern, mein Verhalten (praktisch) an ihnen *als Gesetzen* auszurichten: Von der Angst vor Strafe über Ehrsucht und Vaterlandsliebe bis hin zu einem reinen Pflichtbewusstsein.

4 Die in der Literatur recht verbreitete Unterstellung, Kant zufolge verbinde die rechtliche Gesetzgebung *als rechtliche* ausschließlich pathologische Triebfedern mit dem Gesetz (hier bloß exemplarisch Wood, 2002, S. 8), widerspricht nicht nur dem generellen Duktus der Kantischen Formulierungen im Einteilungsabschnitt (vgl. etwa MS 6:220.3: Wenn die pathologische Triebfedern der juridi-

datur – den „pathologischen" (MS 6:219.7), d.h. sinnlichen Bestimmungsgründen der Willkür entnommen werden. Folglich kann die
ethische Gesetzgebung unter Hinzunahme dieser Einsicht auch als diejenige definiert werden, die sinnliche Neigungen und Abneigungen als
Triebfedern *ausschließt.*

Indem Kant nun (vgl. MS 6:219.2 ff. und 225.31 ff.) die Übereinstimmung einer Handlung mit der rechtlichen Gesetzgebung „Legalität" und die mit der ethischen Gesetzgebung „Moralität" bzw. „Sittlichkeit" nennt (MS 6:219.14 ff.)[5], führt er eine Terminologie an, die
bezüglich des Adjektivs ‚moralisch' zu einer heillosen Begriffsverwirrung
eingeladen hat. Daher lohnt es sich, hier kurz darauf hinzuweisen: Bei
Kant ist das Adjektiv ‚moralisch' (wie auch ‚sittlich') primär ein *Gesetzesprädikat* und als dieses komplementär zu ‚natürlich': „Die Gesetze der
Freiheit heißen im Unterschiede von Naturgesetzen moralisch" (MS
6:214.14), und: „unbedingte praktische Gesetze, welche moralisch
heißen", gründen sich auf dem „(in praktischer Rücksicht) positiven
Begriffe der Freiheit" (MS 6:221.19 f.). In demselben Sinne stehen die
Gesetze der *Sittlichkeit* denen der Natur gegenüber (vgl. MS
6:214.31 ff.). In diesem ersten Sinne sind *alle Gesetzgebungen* naturgemäß
moralisch (bzw. sittlich), denn nur moralische Gesetze führen objektive
praktische Notwendigkeit mit sich. Kant verwendet das *Adjektiv* ‚moralisch' in der *Metaphysik der Sitten*[6] ausnahmslos in diesem Sinne. Seine
Rede von ‚Moralität' und ‚Sittlichkeit' von Handlungen im Unterschied
zu deren ‚Legalität' lädt nun aber offenkundig zur Bildung der evalua-
tiven *Handlungsprädikate* ‚moralisch' und ‚sittlich' ein, die dann selbst-
redend wesentlich Bezug auf den subjektiven *Bestimmungsgrund* nehmen.

---

schen weggelassen(!) werden, ist die Idee der Pflicht hinreichend; vgl. MS
6:219.27: „muss" statt „darf" o.ä.; vgl. MS 6:220.21: „auch" statt „nur"; usw.),
sondern sie beruht auf einem elementaren *logischen Fehler*, denn sie hebt ohne
jede Not die Vollständigkeit der Einteilung ethisch/rechtlich auf (jede *philosophische* Einteilung muss dichotomisch sein, s. Log 9:147); siehe auch oben
Fußnote 2 und unten Fußnote 26 dieses Beitrags.

5　Zitate, welche nicht unmittelbar belegt sind, werden durch den darauffolgenden
　　Stellennachweis mit abgedeckt.

6　Eine Prüfung aller anderen kritischen Druckschriften ergibt – soweit ich sehe –
　　denselben Befund. – Ähnliches gilt, nebenbei bemerkt, z.B. auch für ‚auto*nom*'/
　　‚hetero*nom*': Es ist bei Kant selbst ausschließlich ein Prädikatpaar für *Gesetzge-
　　bungen*, niemals aber für Handlungen (im Sinne etwa von ‚selbstbestimmt'/
　　‚fremdbestimmt'): Auch der Verbrecher ist im Moment der Tat auto*nom*, denn
　　diese ist ja nur ein Verbrechen, insofern sie die Übertretung des durch die eigene
　　Vernunft gegebenen (Sitten-)*Gesetzes* ist.

Folglich sind *diese* nun nicht mehr komplementär zu ‚natürlich‘, sondern vielmehr zu ‚bloß-legal‘ bzw. ‚bloß-rechtmäßig‘, sodass die Termini in *dieser* (*nicht*-kantischen!) Verwendung eindeutig *in specie* ethische Konnotationen gewinnen, denn für die – in *diesem* zweiten Wortsinne – ‚moralische‘ Dimension des Handelns ist eine äußere Gesetzgebung ja *e suppositione* blind.

Verwendet man nun das Handlungs- und das Gesetzesprädikat ‚moralisch‘ ungeschieden nebeneinander her, dann (aber eben auch *nur* dann) kann es als zweifelhaft erscheinen, dass die Gesetze der rechtlichen Gesetzgebung überhaupt ‚moralische‘ sein können (denn: ‚moralisch‘ scheint ja ‚ethisch‘ zu implizieren). Und dann scheint sogar die bloße Tatsache, dass Recht und Ethik unterschieden sind, bereits dazu zu nötigen, das Recht von Sittlichkeit und Moral zu trennen, (denn ‚nicht ethisch‘ impliziert ja vermeintlich auch *e contrapositione* ‚nicht moralisch‘). Kants ausdrückliche Deklaration, dass Recht und Ethik beide Teile *einer* Metaphysik der Sitten sind, wird auf diese fragwürdige Weise natürlich fragwürdig.[7] Hier ist jetzt nur festzuhalten, dass Kants Unterscheidung von Legalität und Moralität (bzw. Sittlichkeit) von *Handlungen* keinerlei Bedeutung für die Frage hat, ob Recht und Ethik beide gleichermaßen Teile der *Moral* sind, in der es nicht um *natürliche*, sondern um *moralische Gesetze* geht – und das sind sie bei Kant ausweislich der uns überlieferten Texte seit den 1770er Jahren. Und 1797 sind sie es schon deshalb, weil *alle Verbindlichkeit* sich hier unmissverständlich dem *einen* Sittengesetz verdankt (vgl. MS 6:222.1 ff., 225.1 ff.).[8] Rechtliche und ethische Gesetzgebung unterscheiden sich allein darin, dass sie die (objektive) „Verbindlichkeit so zu handeln" mit partiell unterschiedlichen (subjektiven) „Bestimmungsgr[ü]nde[n] der Willkür" (MS 6:218.21 f.)

---

7   Die hiermit verbundenen Fragen nach der Abhängigkeit der Rechtslehre von Prinzip der Moral/Sittlichkeit werden weitgehend im obigen Sinne bei Seel, 2009, behandelt, worauf hier verwiesen sei, da die Grundlagen der Rechtslehre im Besonderen hier nicht Thema sind.

8   Die positiven Gesetze der rechtlichen Gesetzgebung sind daher nur verbindlich infolge einer Autorisierung ihres jeweiligen Gesetzgebers durch ein natürliches (sc. Vernunft-)Gesetz (MS 6:224.34). – Die Rechtslehre begründet demgemäß sowohl die moralisch-praktische Notwendigkeit einer solchen Autorisierung (wesentlich im Privatrecht) als auch deren Reichweite (insbesondere im Öffentlichen Recht).

verbinden, und demzufolge die jeweiligen *Motive* der Gesetzes*befolgung* in unterschiedlicher Weise *bewerten*.[9]

Die nächsten Schwierigkeiten aufgrund terminologischer Tücken warten im nachfolgenden Absatz: „Die Pflichten nach der rechtlichen Gesetzgebung können nur äußere Pflichten sein, weil diese Gesetzgebung nicht verlangt, dass die Idee dieser Pflicht, welche innerlich ist, für sich selbst Bestimmungsgrund [...] sei." (MS 6:219.17–20) Von den hier entscheidenden Termini ‚außen‘ und ‚innen‘ macht Kant in unterschiedlichsten Kontexten und in den unterschiedlichsten Bedeutungen Gebrauch. Auf die gefährliche aber gleichwohl „nicht zu vermeidende" Mehrdeutigkeit etwa des „außer uns" macht auch Kant selbst mitunter (siehe etwa KrV A 373) aufmerksam: Damit nämlich bezeichnen wir sowohl das, was als Ding an sich selbst von uns unterschieden existiert, als auch das, was empirisch äußerlich im Raume anzutreffen ist.

---

9   Die Frage nach einer möglichen ethischen Begründung ‚des Rechts‘ oder einer ethischen Grundlegung einzelner Rechtsnormen ist in Kantischer Begrifflichkeit also schlicht unverständlich, da alle einschlägigen Begründungs- und/oder Geltungsfragen (die Fragen also nach ‚objektiver praktischer Notwendigkeit‘, d. h. nach der Verbindlichkeit von *Gesetzen*) bereits beantwortet sein müssen, bevor die Unterscheidung von rechtlicher und ethischer Gesetz*gebung* (die Frage nach den möglichen subjektiven *Bestimmungsgründen*) sich überhaupt stellt. Wenn M. Baum etwa schreibt: „Die kantische Lehre von der Autonomie der reinen praktischen Vernunft ist [...] eine dezidiert ethische Lehre von der positiven Freiheit des menschlichen Willens, die in seiner Rechtslehre kein Gegenstück haben kann." (Baum, 2007, S. 226), dann ist das keine Kritik einer vermeintlichen ‚ethischen‘ Rechtsbegründung, sondern vielmehr ein zu dieser komplementäres Missverständnis: Die *Kritik der praktischen Vernunft* zeigt auf, dass wir frei sind, ohne dafür die Unterscheidung der Gesetzgebungen in Anschlag zu bringen (und zwar ganz unabhängig davon, ob Kant 1787 über diese Unterscheidung bereits verfügte oder nicht). Zwar ist dort das *Bewusstsein der Pflicht* (d. h., das Faktum, dass „reine Vernunft wirklich praktisch ist" (KpV 5:3.11)) die *ratio cognoscendi* unserer Freiheit, doch *die Freiheit selbst* ist die *ratio essendi* der Verbindlichkeit: Wir *wissen*, dass wir frei sind, weil wir uns dessen bewusst sind, dass wir *unabhängig von unseren jeweils gegebenen Neigungen* pflichtgemäß handeln *sollen* und darum auch *können*. Und das heißt freilich, dass wir uns als Subjekte einer Gesetzgebung erkennen, die die Idee der Pflicht selbst zur Triebfeder macht. Ob diese Gesetzgebung aber eine *in specie ethische* ist, eine solche also, die *alle anderen* Triebfedern *ausschließt*, spielt für die Hauptaufgabe dieser Schrift („blos dar[zu]thun, dass es reine praktische Vernunft gebe" (KpV 5:3.5 f.)) überhaupt keine Rolle. Recht und Ethik haben als die beiden Abteilungen der Moral vielmehr eine *gemeinsame* Wurzel: Die Freiheit. (Vgl. Text zu Fußnote 26 dieses Beitrags)

,Innen' und ,außen' stehen ganz allgemein für eines jener vier Paare von Reflexionsbegriffen, mittels deren das Verhältnis „in welchem die Begriffe in einem Gemüthszustande zu einander gehören können" (KrV A 261), bestimmbar ist. In jeweils spezifischer Bedeutung treten sie bei Kant dann unter anderem auf (1) in der Unterscheidung von innerem (Selbst-) und äußerem (Fremd-)Zwang, (2) in der Unterscheidung von innerem und äußerem Sinn, (3) in der Unterscheidung von Seele und äußeren körperlichen Dingen, (4) in der Bedeutung räumlicher Positionierung relativ zu einer Grenze, und schließlich (5) in der Unterscheidung von (innerem) Selbstbezug und (äußerer) Fremdbeziehung. Für das Folgende soll diese rhapsodische Auflistung genügen, und insbesondere kann die Frage, in welcher Beziehung die fraglichen Bedeutungsdimensionen zueinander (und zu den Reflexionsbegriffen) stehen, ausgeblendet werden.

Im vorliegenden Falle lässt sich die spezifische Bedeutung von ,außen' und ,innen' rückwärts erschließen: Innere Pflichten beziehen sich auf innere Handlungen, und das tun sie, indem sie *direkt* vorschreiben, dass eine *bestimmte* Triebfeder die Willkür bestimmt (in diesem Falle wäre das dann die Triebfeder der Pflicht). Das Gebot, ein Versprechen zu halten, ist eine äußere Pflicht, das Gebot, es *aus Pflicht* zu halten, ist eine innere Pflicht (vgl. MS 6:220.21–24). Somit ist das ,die Pflicht zur Triebfeder machen' eine innere Handlung. Beschlösse man für sich, Verträge fortan *immer* (d.h., auch wenn man gerade überhaupt keine unmittelbare Neigung dazu verspürte) *aus kalkuliertem Eigennutz* zu halten, wäre auch dies in demselben Sinne eine innere Handlung. Der hier einschlägige Aspekt ist demnach nicht etwa,[10] dass innere Pflichten *deshalb* innere sind, weil sie nur *aus Pflicht* befolgt werden können, sondern vielmehr sind die *ethischen* Pflichten insofern *innere*, als ich mich *nur selbst* zu einer Pflichtbefolgung *aus Pflicht* bestimmen kann (wie ich mich auch *nur selbst* zur beständigen Pflichterfüllung *aus Eigennutz* bestimmen könnte (vgl. TL 6:394.20 f.)). Damit ist nämlich bereits klar, dass Kant behaupten kann, dass „die ethische Gesetzgebung keine äußere (selbst nicht die eines göttlichen Willens) sein" (MS 6:219.27 f.) kann. ,Außen' und ,innen' bezeichnen hier also in erster Linie zunächst (notwendigen) Selbst- versus (möglichen) Fremdzwang (1). Dies bestätigen auch Be-

---

10 Zu einem solchen Resultat kommt etwa von der Pfordten, 2009, S. 30 f., und identifiziert die innen/außen-Unterscheidung dann mit der von Verstandes- und Sinnenwelt.

merkungen wie „dieser Zwang mag nun ein äußerer oder ein Selbstzwang sein" (TL 6:379.16 f.).[11]

Die Pflichten der rechtlichen Gesetzgebung können also – umgekehrt – nur jene Aspekte menschlichen Handelns betreffen, auf die (auch) *andere* (seien es nun Götter oder Menschen) Einfluss nehmen können. Das geschieht, wie oben bereits bemerkt, allein vermittels der „pathologischen Bestimmungsgründe[] der Willkür" (MS 6:219.7 f.): Andere Menschen (und nur noch um diese geht es bei Kant fortan) können dazu Übel als Sanktionen androhen (und Glücksgüter als Belohnungen verheißen). Aber die *Austeilung* von Übeln *als* Sanktionen setzt u. a. voraus, dass das ggf. zu sanktionierende Handeln dem Sanktionierenden tatsächlich epistemisch *zugänglich* ist. Man kann schließlich niemandem etwas für den Fall *androhen*, dass er etwas Bestimmtes tut, wenn man nicht auch *post festum beurteilen* kann, ob er es denn getan hat oder nicht.[12] Damit kommt eine zweite Bedeutungsdimension (2) ins Spiel, denn nur über den *äußeren* Sinn können Menschen in der einschlägigen Weise von Menschen affiziert werden: Pflichten der *rechtlichen* Gesetzgebung können sich demnach grundsätzlich nur auf jene Aspekte menschlicher Handlungen beziehen, die (auch) in dem gemeinsam geteilten Raum erscheinen. Alles, was ausschließlich zum *inneren* Sinn gehört, ist epistemisch gleichsam privat und damit kein möglicher Gegenstand einer äußeren Gesetzgebung. Damit wird schließlich auch die obige Bedeutungsdimension (3) zumindest berührt.

In der Einleitung in die *Tugendlehre* bringt Kant die hier explizierten Unterschiede dann auf die knappe Formel: „Die Ethik giebt nicht Gesetze für die Handlungen (denn das thut das *Ius*), sondern nur für die Maximen der Handlungen." (TL 6:388.32 f.) Nimmt man die Definition der Maxime hinzu: „Die Regel des Handelnden, die er sich selbst aus subjectiven Gründen zum Princip macht, heißt seine Maxime" (MS 6:225.2 f.), dann erkennt man, dass die *Befolgung* der ethischen Gesetzgebung im oben exponierten Sinne eine *Selbst*-Gesetz*gebung* im doppelten Wortsinne ist: Nicht nur in Hinblick auf das Gesetz, d. h. als *Auto*-

---

11 Vgl. auch: „[...] in der Ethik dieses als das Gesetz d e i n e s e i g e n e n W i l l e n s gedacht wird, nicht des Willens überhaupt, der auch der Wille anderer sein könnte: wo es alsdann eine Rechtspflicht abgeben würde [...]." (TL 6:389.3 – 6; vgl. ferner TL 6:380.1 ff., 381.15 ff.)

12 Das ist freilich im 18. Jahrhundert keiner eigenen Betonung wert, weil es zum Standardargument etwa in den Debatten um die Kirchenpolitik gehört, dass nur der *äußere* religiöse Kult einer öffentlichen Beurteilung fähig ist. (Vgl. RGV 6:126 f.)

nomie (das gilt auch für die rechtliche *als* eine moralische), sondern auch in Hinblick auf den Bestimmungsgrund: Wenn die Idee der Pflicht tatsächlich die Triebfeder ist, dann ist es zusätzlich ein Fall von *Autokratie* (vgl. TL 6:383.24; vgl. auch VAMS 23:397; V-Lo/Philippi 27:496).

Vor unserer Folie der „Einleitung in die Metaphysik der Sitten" bedarf obige Ethik/Jus-Formel jedoch noch einer weiteren Erörterung, denn hier heißt es: „Hieraus ist zu ersehen, daß alle Pflichten blos darum, weil sie Pflichten sind, mit zur Ethik gehören; aber ihre Gesetzgebung ist darum nicht allemal in der Ethik enthalten, sondern von vielen derselben außerhalb derselben." (MS 6:219.31–34) Erinnert man sich an das Kriterium der dichotomischen Einteilung in ethische und rechtliche Gesetzgebung, dann folgt allein aus dem *Pflicht*-Charakter der Rechtspflicht, dass *jede* Rechtspflicht mit einer ethischen Pflicht verknüpft ist, ja im Grunde eine solche direkt *einschließt*, denn die ethische *Gesetzgebung* unterscheidet sich im Falle von *äußeren* Pflichten von der rechtlichen ja *ausschließlich* darin, dass sie keine „andere Triebfeder als die Idee der Pflicht selbst zuläßt" (MS 6:219.5). Das impliziert freilich nicht, dass jede Norm, die in Gestalt einer Rechtsnorm daherkommt, bereits aus Pflicht befolgt werden müsste. Es geht hier zunächst nur um den *begrifflichen* Zusammenhang: *Wenn* eine Norm eine *objektive* praktische Notwendigkeit vorstellt (und sich damit überhaupt erst zum ,ersten Stück' *irgendeiner* Gesetzgebung qualifiziert), *dann* ist sie *e suppositione* immer auch allein um der Pflicht willen, d. h. *aus* Pflicht zu erfüllen. Das ist gleichsam der ‚Witz' der Kantischen *Identifikation* von Pflichten mit *kategorischen* Geboten. (Vgl. MS 6:222.3 f. mit 222.31 f.) Insofern nimmt die ethische Gesetzgebung

> das Gesetz *(pacta sunt servanda)* und die diesem correspondierende Pflicht aus der Rechtslehre als gegeben an. Also nicht in der Ethik, sondern im *Ius* liegt die Gesetzgebung, daß angenommene Versprechen gehalten werden müssen. Die Ethik lehrt hernach nur[!], daß, wenn die Triebfeder, welche die juridische Gesetzgebung mit jener Pflicht verbindet, nämlich der äußere Zwang,[13] auch weggelassen[!] wird, die Idee der Pflicht allein[!] schon zur Triebfeder hinreichend sei. (MS 6:219.36–220.5)[14]

---

13 Hier ist die *Triebfeder* also der *Zwang* (bzw. dessen *Androhung*) und der subjektive *Bestimmungsgrund* wäre demnach die durch die Zwangsandrohung erzeugte *Abneigung* gegen die Gesetzesübertretung (ganz im Sinne von MS 6:218.15 f.). Analog wäre in der ethischen Gesetzgebung das Gesetz bzw. die Pflicht die Triebfeder und die Achtung vor dem Gesetz der Bestimmungsgrund für die Befolgung (siehe aber auch andere Verwendungsweisen der Ausdrücke, etwa: MS 6:219.6 ff.; KpV 5:72 u. ö.)

Später wird Kant dies noch einmal herausstellen:

> Obzwar die Angemessenheit der Handlungen zum Rechte (ein rechtlicher Mensch zu sein) nichts Verdienstliches ist, so ist doch die der Maxime solcher Handlungen, als Pflichten, d. i. die **Achtung** fürs Recht, verdienstlich. [...] Eben dieselbe Bewandtniß hat es auch mit dem allgemeinen ethischen Gebote: ‚Handle pflichtmäßig aus Pflicht.‘ Diese Gesinnung in sich zu gründen und zu beleben ist so wie die vorige verdienstlich: weil sie über das Pflichtgesetz der Handlungen hinaus geht und das Gesetz an sich zugleich zur Triebfeder macht. (TL 6:390.30–391.7)

Umgekehrt werden die so genannten „indirect-ethischen" (MS 6:221.3 f.) Pflichten (wieder) zu rechtlichen, indem die (ethische) Bedingung, dass eine gegebene *äußere* Pflicht *ausschließlich aus Pflicht* vollzogen werde, fallengelassen wird. Es gibt, wie hier noch einmal deutlich wird, 1797 keinen Raum für eine Unterscheidung von rechtlicher und ethischer *Verbindlichkeit*. Es ist *objektiv* praktisch notwendig, ein Versprechen zu halten. (Punkt!) Weil diese Notwendigkeit im vorliegenden Falle *auch* mit einer äußeren Triebfeder als *subjektivem* Bestimmungsgrund verbunden werden *kann* (vgl. MS 6:220.27–29), erhält die rechtliche Gesetzgebung gleichsam die Namenshoheit (*sc.* „*Ius*" (MS 6:220.1)).[15] Allerdings ist ein entsprechender Schritt nicht bei *allen* ethischen Pflichten möglich, denn nicht alle haben bestimmte äußere Handlungen zum Gegenstand. Pflichten, die ausschließlich einer ethischen Gesetzgebung (also keiner äußeren Triebfedern) fähig sind, nennt Kant „direct-ethische" (MS 6:221.1). Er erwähnt hier in der Einleitung „z. B. die gegen sich selbst" (MS 6:220.33) und setzt diese speziell gegen solche ab, die die Ethik mit dem Recht „gemein" (MS 6:220.34) hat (die also Pflichten *gegen andere* sind, s. u.). Wir werden sehen, dass es in der Tugendlehre auch direkt-ethische Pflichten *gegen andere* gibt:

---

14 In einer Notiz heißt es suggestiv: „Das Gesetz der *execution* ist jederzeit juridisch wenn gleich die Maxime der *intention* ethisch ist" (VATL 23:382.3 f.).

15 Irritation könnte allenfalls die *Formulierung* erzeugen, dass die ethische Gesetzgebung die Idee der Pflicht „in ihr Gesetz mit einschließt" (MS 6:219.25, vgl. auch 219.4), d. h., jeweils ein anderes (weil bestimmungsreicheres) *Gesetz* als die rechtliche (und damit *eo ipso* eine andere *Verbindlichkeit*) enthält. Aus dem Kontext geht jedoch hervor, dass „einschließt" hier im Sinne des „verknüpft" von MS 6:218.17 bzw. „verbunden" von 218.23 gebraucht ist. Es ist gerade der Dreh- und Angelpunkt der von Kant 1797 vorgestellten Konstruktion, dass es nur *eine Art der Verbindlichkeit* (objektiv-praktische Notwendigkeit) gibt, diese aber mit *zwei Arten von Triebfedern* (subjektive Beweggründe) verbunden werden kann (vgl. MS 6:220.15–18): Folglich gibt es *zwei Arten der Verpflichtung* (MS 6:220.34; vgl. auch TL 6:392.28 und 468.6).

Denn alle *weiten* Pflichten, d.h., solche, die einen *Zweck* vorschreiben, sind ausschließlich einer ethischen Gesetzgebung fähig.

Bislang sind die spezifischen innen/außen-Unterscheidungen im Sinne von (4) und (5) noch nicht in Erscheinung getreten. Diese spielen etwa in der Rechtslehre eine Rolle. Die erste (4) z.B. bei der Erörterung der Frage, was ein „äußer[er] Gegenstand [d]er Willkür" (MS 6:246.5) ist. Wichtiger für den hiesigen Kontext ist der Gebrauch von innen/außen im Sinne von Selbst- und Fremdbezug (5), denn diese Bedeutung ist einschlägig für die Unterscheidung von ‚inneren' und ‚äußeren' *Recht*spflichten, die der Sache nach noch in den Themenkontext der „Eintheilung einer Metaphysik der Sitten" gehört. Damit lässt sich die paradoxe Anmutung des Begriffs der ‚inneren Rechtspflicht' eliminieren und es wird zusätzlich Klarheit über die Gesamt-Architektonik der *Metaphysik der Sitten* und insbesondere über den Zusammenhang von Recht-(spflicht) und Zwangsbefugnis gewonnen: Eine innere Rechtspflicht ist eine äußere Pflicht gegen *sich selbst,* und eine äußere Rechtspflicht ist eine äußere Pflicht gegen *andere.*[16] Das ist bei terminlogischer Einsetzung auf den ersten Blick sprachlich zumutungsreich (‚innere äußere Pflicht' bzw. ‚äußere äußere Pflicht'), aber gleichwohl dank der unterschiedlichen Bedeutungsdimensionen der aufgereihten Adjektive in der Sache völlig klar: Der Begriff der inneren Rechtspflicht begegnet uns in der *Metaphysik der Sitten* erstmals im Zuge der Erörterung der ersten Ulpianschen Formel. (Vgl. RL 6:236.24 f.) Kant hatte das *„honeste vive"* („Mache Dich anderen nicht zum bloßen Mittel, sondern sei für sie zugleich Zweck." (RL 6:236.24–28)) noch bis 1794 stets als „Princip der Ethic" (V-MS/ Vigil 27:527.12 f.) (bzw. ethischer Pflichten) bezeichnet. In der *Metaphysik der Sitten* fungiert es dann als Prinzip von (inneren[17])

---

16 Für diese Unterscheidung siehe etwa VATL 23:395.2 ff. und die Metaphysik der Sitten-Vorlesung von 1793/94 (Vigilantius), dort u.a. V-MS/Vigil 27:592.23 f. – Die Vorlesung ist als Interpretationshilfe für die Schrift von 1797 mitunter hilfreich, weil sie den Stoff mit klärenden Beispielen anreichert. Sie ist allerdings insofern mit Vorsicht zu genießen, als Kant noch nicht überall bei den Positionen (bzw. bei der konzeptionellen Klarheit) der Schrift von 1797 angekommen zu sein scheint, was u.a. für einige Details der Unterscheidung von Recht und Ethik (siehe unten zum *„honeste vive"* (RL 6:236.24)) sowie für die Lehre vom äußeren Mein und Dein offensichtlich ist, hier aber nicht eigens zu Thema werden kann.

17 *„Neminem laede"* ist das Prinzip der *äußeren* Rechtspflichten. Das dritte Prinzip, *„suum quique tribuere",* ergibt sich dann direkt aus der Kombination der ersten beiden: Niemandem Unrecht tun, ohne dabei zugleich das Recht der Menschheit in der eigenen Person zu verleugnen, ist (sofern man nicht jede Gemeinschaft mit

*Recht*spflichten, und das ist, wenn man die (1797 ja erstmals dargelegte) Lehre von den zwei „Stücke[n]" (MS 6:218.13) einer Gesetzgebung für die Unterscheidung von Rechtspflichten und ethischen Pflichten heranzieht, nur konsequent: Ich muss es ja durchaus nicht *aus Pflicht* vermeiden, mich zum bloßen Mittel für andere (etwa durch Prostitution) zu machen, um der Rechtspflicht des „*honeste vive*" genüge zu tun (vielleicht fürchte ich ja nur die soziale Diskriminierung). Solange ich mich *de facto* nicht zum Mittel mache, habe ich dieser Pflicht *als Rechtspflicht* bereits genüge getan. Da diese Pflicht ferner eine solche Verbindlichkeit ist, die nicht aus einem Recht *anderer Personen* hervorgeht, sondern allein aus dem Recht der Menschheit in *meiner eigenen* Person, ist deren Übertretung naturgemäß keine Läsion anderer und daher auch nicht mit Zwangsbefugnissen auf deren Seite verbunden: Wenn ich einmal in Versuchung sein sollte, mich zum bloßen Mittel zu machen (weil mich die nachteiligen Folgen nicht schrecken), dann muss ich mich (als *homo phaenomenon*) allenfalls selbst (*qua homo noumenon*) zur Befolgung dieser Pflicht gegen mich selbst zwingen (siehe unten Abschnitte II und III). Aber dann gewinnt das „*honeste vive*" für mich freilich den Status einer *indirekt*-ethischen Pflicht (was *begrifflich* voraussetzt, das es *auch* eine Rechtspflicht ist).[18] Es gleicht in *dieser* Hinsicht dann einer solchen äußeren Rechtspflicht, bei der im Einzelfall der Fremdzwang auszubleiben droht.

Es wäre also im hier vorgestellten Theorierahmen von 1797 ein elementarer *begrifflicher* Fehler, wenn man Rechtspflichten bei Kant bereits qua Rechtspflichten mit (Fremd-)Zwangspflichten identifizierte. Nur die *äußeren Recht*spflichten, also diejenigen Pflichten, die eine *äußere* Verbindlichkeit *gegenüber anderen* beinhalten (die also gleichsam in *zweifachem* Wortsinne *äußere* Pflichten sind), werden von Kant überhaupt auf die Frage nach der Möglichkeit des Fremdzwangs hin untersucht, denn der Begriff des *Rechts*, um den es in den *Metaphysischen Anfangsgründen der Rechtslehre* geht, bezieht sich *e suppositione* nur *indirekt* („correspondirend[]" (RL 6:230.7)) auf die Rechtspflichten selbst,

---

anderen vermeiden kann) nur in einem die jeweiligen Rechtssphären bestimmenden *status civilis* möglich.

18 Vgl.: „Obzwar die Angemessenheit der Handlungen zum Rechte (ein rechtlicher Mensch zu sein) nichts Verdienstliches ist, so ist doch die der Maxime solcher Handlungen, als Pflichten, d. i. die **Achtung** fürs Recht, v e r d i e n s t l i c h. Denn der Mensch macht sich dadurch das Recht der Menschheit, oder auch der Menschen zum Zweck [...]" (TL 6:390.30–33) – also die Erfüllung seiner *inneren* „oder auch" seiner *äußeren* Rechtspflichten.

und zwar nur auf die Rechtspflichten *anderer.* In § B der „Einleitung in
die Rechtslehre" heißt es unter der Überschrift „Was ist Recht?":

> Der Begriff des Rechts, sofern er sich auf eine *ihm correspondirende Ver-*
> *bindlichkeit* bezieht, [...] betrifft e r s t l i c h *nur das äußere und zwar prakti-*
> *sche Verhältniß einer Person gegen eine andere,* sofern ihre Handlungen als
> Facta aufeinander (unmittelbar oder mittelbar) Einfluß haben können. (RL
> 6:230.7 – 11, kursiv B.L.)

Der folgende Gedanke aus der Metaphysik der Sitten-Vorlesung von
1793 scheint also auch noch für die Schrift gleichen Namens von 1797 zu
gelten:

> Soviel nun die scientiam juris oder wissenschaftliche Kenntniß der rechtli-
> chen Pflichten, welche eine äußere rechtliche Verbindlichkeit enthalten,
> betrifft, so gehört diese insoweit zum jure naturae speciell, als sie das Recht
> der Menschen gegen einander betrifft, dagegen nur zur Moral das jus gehört,
> so Rechte und Pflichten in meiner eigenen Person ausmacht. (V-MS/Vigil
> 27:587.8 – 13)

Nehmen wir diesen Gedanken in der Gestalt an, dass für das *ius naturae*
„speciell" (lies: die Rechtslehre) nur die äußeren Rechtspflichten eine
Rolle spielen, und die inneren Rechtspflichten (zusammen mit den
ethischen Pflichten) ‚nur' in der „Moral" (lies hier: Ethik/Tugendlehre)
abgehandelt werden, dann verstehen wir problemlos, dass Kant zumindest einige von den Pflichten, die er 1793 ausdrücklich zu den inneren
Rechtspflichten zählte (Selbsterhaltung, Verbot, sich zum bloßen Mittel
zu machen), 1797 *dem Inhalte nach* als *vollkommene* (siehe dazu unten
Abschnitt III) Pflichten gegen sich selbst am Anfang der Tugendlehre
behandelt – wo sie dann freilich als *ethische,* und zwar als *indirekt*-ethische
Pflichten anzusehen wären. (Vgl. TL 6:390.33 f.) Angesichts der Tatsache, dass die inneren Rechtspflichten in der Rechtslehre keinen eigenen
systematischen Ort haben[19] (vgl. unten Abschnitt II b)), ist das zumindest
eine mögliche und – soweit ich sehe – auch die einzige konsistente[20]

---

19 Selbst beim angeborenen Recht geht es nur darum, äußere Verbindlichkeiten
    „von sich" *abzulehnen* (RL 6:238.18). Es gibt keine Andeutung, dass Kant hier
    angeborene innere Recht*spflichten* mitführt. – In einigen Lehrstücken der
    Rechtslehre kommt das Recht der Menschheit in der eigenen Person freilich in
    seiner limitativen Funktion für die *eigene* Rechtsausübung zum Zuge: Explizit
    etwa im Eherecht (RL 6:278.9), im Strafrecht (RL 6:333.16 f., 362.36) und im
    Kirchenrecht (RL 6:327.36).
20 Diese Deutung hat nur den bescheidenen Makel, dass Kant die vollkommenen
    Pflichten gegen sich selbst in der Tugendlehre nicht *ausdrücklich* als innere

Auslegung der Kant vor Augen stehenden Systematik. Fasst man alle bisherigen Befunde auf diese Weise zusammen, so stellt es sich so dar, dass der Fokus des ersten Teils (*Rechtslehre*) des Buches *Die Metaphysik der Sitten* allein auf den *äußeren* Pflichten *gegen andere* liegt, und alle anderen Pflichten *dem Inhalte nach* im zweiten Teil (*Tugendlehre*) abgehandelt werden: die *äußeren* Pflichten *gegen sich selbst* und sämtliche *inneren*.

II. Die Einteilung der Metaphysik der Sitten überhaupt (RL 6:239–242)

Die „Eintheilung der Metaphysik der Sitten überhaupt" steht in der Druckschrift von 1797 hinter der „Einleitung in die Rechtslehre". Sie ist dort zumindest angesichts des Titels offenkundig fehlplaziert (man wird sie am Ende der „Einleitung in die Metaphysik der Sitten" erwarten), und sie bildet zudem eine zusammenhanglose Zusammenstellung von insgesamt *fünf* unterschiedlichen Einteilungen, die auf *drei* Unterabschnitte (I–III) verteilt sind.[21] *Zwei* der Einteilungen wiederum betreffen dem Inhalte nach gar nicht die *Metaphysik der Sitten* sondern allein die *Rechtslehre* und werden darum hier nur erwähnt:

a) Der III. Unterabschnitt (RL 6:241 f.) stellt eine viergliedrige Einteilung der möglichen *rechtlichen* Verhältnisse des Menschen zu Wesen, die Rechte bzw. Pflichten haben bzw. nicht haben vor.[22] Ein *ethisches* Pendant zu dieser Einteilung findet sich in der Einleitung in die Tugendlehre (siehe dazu unten Abschnitt IV).

b) Der allerletzte Absatz (RL 6:242.12–19 – durch einen Seitenwechsel und zusätzlich drei Sternchen vom Vorigen abgeteilt) leitet mit der „Eintheilung des Naturrechts" (RL 6:242.12) unmittelbar zur Zweiteilung der Rechtslehre in Privat- und öffentliches Recht über.

c) Direkt voran geht die Tafel „Von der Eintheilung der **Moral**, als eines **Systems** der Pflichten überhaupt" (RL 6:242.3 f.), die einfach die vorgefundene Architektonik der *Metaphysik der Sitten* abbildet (wobei allerdings – offenkundig durch ein technisches Versehen – die Einteilung

---

Rechtspflichten bzw. indirekt-ethische Pflichten *bezeichnet*. Aber die (neuen?) Termini kommen ohnehin nur an der hier diskutierten Stelle vor.

21 Den tumultuarischen Zustand dieses Abschnittes hat detailliert schon Parma dargelegt: vgl. Parma, 2000, S. 54 ff.

22 In RL 6:241.15 der Tafel muss statt des „uns" ein „wir" stehen.

in Elementar- und Methodenlehre an die oberste Stelle gerutscht ist[23]). Festzuhalten ist hier nur, dass die Architektonik einer „wissenschaftlichen Sittenlehre" (RL 6:242.10) Kant zufolge dieselbe sein soll, wie die der vorliegenden Metaphysischen Anfangsgründe.

d) Eingeleitet wird der gesamte Abschnitt mit einer Einteilung in „Rechtspflichten (*officia iuris*)" und „Tugendpflichten (*officia virtutis s[ive] ethica*)" (RL 6:239.4 ff.), die auf das (oben bereits erörterte) Kriterium der *Möglichkeit* einer äußeren Gesetzgebung zurückgreift. Damit wird der dezidiert *nicht*-dichotomischen Einteilung in ‚Rechtspflichten' und ‚ethische Pflichten'[24] nun die strikt dichotomische von Rechts- und Tugendpflichten zur Seite gestellt.[25] Und es wird als das besondere Charakteristikum der Tugendpflichten angeführt, dass sie dazu verbinden, „sich [...] einen Zweck vorzusetzen" (RL 6:239.9): „[N]icht alle ethischen Pflichten sind darum Tugendpflichten. [...] Nur ein Zweck, der zugleich Pflicht ist, kann **Tugendpflicht** genannt werden." (TL 6:383.9–14). Wie wir unten sehen werden, sichert die grundsätzliche Innerlichkeit von derartigen Zwecksetzungen jene Dichotomie der Einteilung in Rechts- und Tugendpflichten, welche das ‚entweder-oder' im ersten Satz (vgl. RL 6:239.4 f.) betont. Es ist an dieser Stelle nur wichtig, darauf zu achten, dass diese Aufteilung *nicht* – wie man anlässlich der davor stehenden Überschrift aber durchaus erwarten könnte – mit der „Eintheilung der Metaphysik der Sitten" in Rechts- und Tugend*lehre* zusammenfällt (das wird sich unten in Abschnitt III bestätigen).

Eine nicht in notwendigem Zusammenhang mit dieser Einteilung stehende Anmerkung schließt sich an (vgl. RL 6:239.13 ff.): Spätestens seit Ciceros *De Officiis* wird die „Sittenlehre (Moral)" die Lehre „von den Pflichten", nicht jedoch Lehre von den *Rechten* genannt. Kant liefert dafür eine Erklärung, für die er sein Lehrstück von der epistemischen Priorität des Verbindlichkeitsbewusstseins gegenüber der Freiheitszuschreibung heranzieht, d. h., die Lehre vom „Factum der [reinen prak-

---

23 Siehe unten unter IV. Dazu auch Parma, 2000, S. 55.
24 Alle Rechtspflichten sind *auch* (indirekt-)ethische Pflichten (s. o.).
25 Diese Unterscheidung wurde freilich bereits zuvor (MS 6:220.6–17) *benutzt*, fällt dort aber aus dem Gesamtkontext der „Einleitung in die Metaphysik der Sitten" (MS 6:211–228) insofern heraus, als Kant überhaupt nur in diesem einen Absatz (und dort gleich fünfmal) den Wortstamm ‚tugend' benutzt, das semantische Feld also kurzfristig wechselt. Ob sich dies möglicherweise der äußeren Textgenese (Einfügung eines heterogenen Absatzes o. ä.) verdankt, muss hier offen bleiben.

tischen, B.L.] Vernunft" (KpV 5:31.24) aus der *Kritik der praktischen Vernunft:* Nur insofern wir uns des unleugbaren kategorischen Sollens bewusst sind, wissen wir, dass wir können, also dass wir *frei* und unsere Handlungen somit einer Zurechnung fähig sind. Mit einem Wort: dass wir *Personen* sind. (Vgl. dazu MS 6:221.14–18, 223.24–31) Unsere *Rechte* gegenüber anderen bestehen nun gerade (wie sich oben in Abschnitt I bereits gezeigt hat) darin, dass diese ihrerseits als *Personen* uns gegenüber äußere Recht*spflichten* haben, d. h.: „correspondirende Verbindlichkeit[en]" (RL 6:230.7). Insofern kann der Begriff des Rechts „nachher" aus dem der Pflicht (und damit letztendlich aus dem „moralischen Imperativ") „entwickelt werden" (RL 6:239.18 ff.). Für Kant ist der Pflichtbegriff also epistemisch, semantisch und (*sit venia verbo!*) praktisch-ontologisch primär. Im § E der Rechtslehre wird dieser Befund dann später noch einmal unmissverständlich wiederholt: Das strikte Recht „gründet sich [...] auf dem Bewußtsein der Verbindlichkeit eines jeden nach dem Gesetze" (RL 6:232.17 ff.).[26]

---

26   Erst im § E, mit dem Überschritt zum Begriff des „**strikte[n]** Recht[s]" (RL 6:232.2), „dem nicht Ethisches beigemischt ist" (RL 6:232.13 f.), wird von der Pflicht *als Triebfeder* dezidiert *abstrahiert*. Das *strikte* Recht (das *als Recht* „mit der Befugnis zu zwingen verbunden" ist (RL 6:231.23); vgl. unten Fußnote 33 dieses Beitrags) reduziert sich somit auf ein System reziproker Zwangsbefugnisse. Die indirekt-ethische Gesetzgebung der Rechtspflichten wird damit aber nicht etwa *aufgehoben*, sie bleibt vielmehr *normenlogisch vorausgesetzt* („Bewußtsein der Verbindlichkeit" (RL 6:232.18)) und wird im Folgenden nur *ausgeblendet*. – Es kann daher bei Kant überhaupt keine Rede davon sein, dass „iuridical laws do *not* require obedience for their own sake", oder dass „these laws cannot *require* someone to do something" (so aber z. B. Willaschek, 2002, S. 70 und 79): Es ist das Rechtsgesetz, „welches mir [a] *eine Verbindlichkeit auferlegt*, aber [b] ganz und gar nicht erwartet, noch weniger fordert, dass ich ganz [allein, B.L.] *um dieser Verbindlichkeit willen* meine Freiheit [...] selbst einschränken solle." (RL 6:231.12 f., kursiv B.L.) Ganz ausdrücklich fordern (*sc.* „require") Rechtsgesetze hier [a] die *Befolgung um ihrer selbst willen* (um wessen willen auch sonst? – „Verbindlichkeit ist die Nothwendigkeit einer freien Handlung unter einem kategorischen [!] Imperativ der Vernunft." (MS 6:222.3)), allerdings fordern sie [b] *ausdrücklich nicht* (und als Gesetze einer *äußeren* Gesetzgebung *können* sie dergleichen *e suppositione* nicht, s. o.), eine *Befolgung um bestimmter subjektiver Beweggründe willen* – genau so wenig, wie etwa die unfreundliche Ansage ‚Geld her!' von mir neben meinem Geld auch gleich noch bestimmte Beweggründe für dessen Herausgabe ‚fordert' (etwa: ‚... aber gefälligst nur aus Respekt vor meiner tollen Pistole und bloß nicht aus Mitleid mit mir armen Wicht!'). Kant wertet hier also die Einsicht aus, dass der *äußere* Gehorsam gegenüber einer Forderung *nicht* beinhaltet, dass das, worauf die *Autorität* der *Forderung* beruht (sei dies nun

e) Der zweite Unterabschnitt stellt eine viergliedrige Tafel der Pflichten vor, die die letzteren gemäß ihrer Gegenstände klassifiziert (vgl. RL 6:240). Wir finden hier die beiden oben im I. Abschnitt betrachteten Innen/Außen-Unterscheidungen als Gliederungsprinzipien wieder. Selbst- und Fremdbezug werden dabei direkt übernommen („gegen sich selbst" resp. „gegen Andere"). Die Unterscheidung von Pflichten der inneren (ethischen) und der äußeren (rechtlichen) Gesetzgebung ist jedoch ersetzt durch die von unvollkommenen und vollkommenen Pflichten, wobei die unvollkommenen jene sind, die zu Zwecken verbinden. Entsprechend (siehe oben unter d)) werden die ethischen Pflichten hier Tugendpflichten genannt. In der Sache ergibt sich also nichts wesentlich Neues, und da Kant hier keinen direkten Zusammenhang dieser Tafel mit der *Gliederung* seiner *Metaphysik der Sitten* in zwei Teile herstellt,[27] sind auch keine diesbezüglichen Inkongruenzen zu beklagen: Die Rechtslehre wird wesentlich mit dem „Recht der Menschen" im nordöstlichen Quadranten befasst sein.

Voraussetzung für das so exponierte Pflichtartengeviert ist, dass „der Mensch nach der Eigenschaft seines Freiheitsvermögens" als *homo noumenon* vorgestellt wird (RL 6:239.23 ff.). Dieser Gedanke wird dann in den §§ 1–4 der Tugendlehre inhaltlich ausgeführt.

III. Einleitung in die Tugendlehre VI–VIII (TL 6:388–394)

In den Abschnitten VI–VIII der „Einleitung zur Tugendlehre" wird im Wesentlichen ein Bestimmungsmerkmal der ethischen Pflichten erörtert: Ihre ‚Unvollkommenheit' bzw. ihre ‚Weite' (mit den Gegenbegriffen ‚vollkommen' und ‚eng'). Die Erörterungen sind insofern ein wenig undurchsichtig, als Kant *erstens* die genannten Unterscheidungen nicht deutlich voneinander absetzt und *zweitens* nicht explizit macht, wie sich die Unterscheidung von Rechts- und Tugend*pflichten* zu der Einteilung

---

nackte Gewalt oder eben das Bewusstsein der Verbindlichkeit), in die *Motive* für den *Gehorsam* eingegangen sind.

27 Angesichts der Tatsache, dass auch die anderen Einteilungen sich wenig nach dem Titel des gesamten Abschnitts richten, sollte man nicht ausgerechnet hier nun darauf bestehen. Dies tut jedoch Parma und ist daher genötigt, entwicklungsgeschichtlich nachzulegen. (Vgl. Parma, 2000, S. 55) Der Eigenwert seiner Überlegungen wird allerdings dadurch, dass sie *hier* m. E. entbehrlich sind, nicht geschmälert.

in Rechts- und Tugend*lehre* verhält. *In der Sache* bieten die Grundgedanken allerdings ein erfreulich klares Gerüst.

a) ‚Ethik‘ vs. ‚Tugendlehre‘

Kant merkt in der Einleitung lapidar an, dass „jetzt das System der allgemeinen Pflichtenlehre in das der Rechtslehre (*ius*), welche äußerer Gesetze fähig ist, und der Tugendlehre (*Ethica*) eingetheilt wird, die deren nicht fähig ist; wobei es denn auch sein Bewenden haben mag" (RL 6:379.9–12). Eine Unterscheidung der Extensionen von ‚Tugendlehre‘ und ‚Ethik‘ ist hier offenkundig nicht intendiert, was auch aus der bereits oben in Abschnitt II d) zitierten Formel von „Tugendpflichten (*officia virtutis s[ive] ethica*)" (RL 6:239.5 f.) hervorging. Im Fortgang der Einleitung wird die „Ethik" (TL 6:381.16) dann (ganz wie zuvor die „ethische Gesetzgebung" (RL 6:219.27)) als eine Lehre vom „Selbstzwang nach (moralischen) Gesetzen" charakterisiert, die – und dies geht nun über die oben bereits erörterten Charakterisierungen hinaus – „eine Lehre der Zwecke" und damit eine „Tugendlehre" (TL 6:381.16–25) sei. Tugend wiederum ist „das Vermögen und der überlegte Vorsatz einem starken, aber ungerechten Gegner Widerstand zu thun" (TL 6:380.13 f.), und dies gelingt als Selbstzwang nur durch das Sich-selbst-Vorschreiben eines Zwecks. So

> correspondirt aller ethischen Verbindlichkeit der Tugendbegriff, aber nicht alle ethische Pflichten sind darum Tugendpflichten. Diejenige nämlich sind es nicht, welche nicht sowohl[28] einen gewissen Zweck (Materie, Object der Willkür), als blos das Förmliche der sittlichen Willensbestimmung (z. B. daß die pflichtmäßige Handlung auch aus Pflicht geschehen müsse) betreffen. Nur ein Zweck, der zugleich Pflicht ist, kann **Tugendpflicht** genannt werden. (TL 6:383.8–14)

Hiernach betreffen alle ethischen Pflichten die Tugend, aber nur die direkt-ethischen sind *in specie* Tugendpflichten, insofern sich deren Verbindlichkeit auf einen *besonderen* („gewissen") Zweck bezieht, während die indirekt-ethischen nur auf den ‚förmlichen‘ Zweck zielen, das Pflichtmäßige um seiner selbst willen zu tun. Die Tugendpflichten bilden also eine Teilklasse der ethischen Pflichten, denn „nicht jede Tugendverpflichtung (*obligatio ethica*) [ist] eine Tugendpflicht (*officium ethicum s[ive] virtutis*)" (TL 6:410.23 f.). Nimmt man diese Erörterungen

---

28 Lies: „nicht etwa", siehe unten Fußnote 36 dieses Beitrags.

beim Wort, dann ist die Einteilung in Rechts*pflichten* und Tu-
gend*pflichten* tatsächlich streng dichotomisch, solange nämlich unter den
Rechtspflichten sowohl die äußeren als auch die inneren Rechtspflichten
verstanden werden (welche letzteren indirekt-ethische Pflichten sind).
Dann wird die „Ei n t h e i l u n g der Ethik nur auf Tugendpflichten gehen"
(TL 6:410.32 f.), also auf die direkt-ethischen Pflichten, und das Buch
Tugendlehre enthielte demnach nicht nur die Tugend*pflichten* (*sc. officia*),
sondern *alle* Tugend*verpflichtungen* (*sc. obligationes*).

   Das ist freilich nur dann möglich, wenn man die Unterscheidung von
Rechts- und Tugend*pflichten* nicht mit der zwischen Rechts- und Tugend*lehre* und damit zwischen Zwangspflichten und solchen Pflichten,
mit denen kein (Fremd-)Zwang verbunden ist, gleichsetzt (denn die inneren Rechtspflichten sind ja keine Zwangspflichten im einschlägigen
Sinne). Die in dieser Hinsicht möglicherweise irritierende Passage RL
6:239.4 ff. wurde oben (in Abschnitt II d)) bereits erwähnt und auf TL
6:383 findet sich eine ähnliche: „Die Tugendpflicht ist von der
Rechtspflicht wesentlich darin unterschieden: daß zu dieser ein äußerer
Zwang moralisch-möglich ist, jene aber auf dem freien Selbstzwange allein beruht." (TL 6:383.18 ff.)[29] Hier stellt es sich so dar, als sei alles *das*
Tugendpflicht, was nicht zu den Zwangspflichten gehört, d. h., nicht in
der Rechts*lehre* behandelt wurde. ‚Tugendpflicht' wäre hier also eher im
obigen, weiteren Sinne von „Tugend*verpflichtung*" (TL 6:410.23, kursiv
B.L.) zu verstehen.[30]

   Von diesen zwei Irritationen abgesehen wird ‚Tugendpflicht' in der
Metaphysik der Sitten aber durchweg umfangsgleich mit ‚direkt-ethische
Pflicht' gebraucht. In der Sache geht es dabei um eine Terminologie für
die Abgrenzung jener ethischen Pflichten, die einen besonderen („gewissen" (TL 6:383.11)) Zweck vorschreiben (und deshalb gar keiner
äußeren Gesetzgebung fähig sind), von denjenigen, die auf den bloß

---

29   Sie weicht allerdings von der früheren Passage ab, als Kant hier (unexpliziert) von
     „*moralisch*-möglich" spricht. Insofern könnte man auch behaupten, dass diese
     Stelle nur *suggeriert*, was die andere *behauptet*.

30   Diese weite Verwendung finden wir bei Kant ausdrücklich (noch) 1793: „Was
     die Tugendpflichten anlangt so würden sie so wohl *officia Ethices ethica* als *officia
     ethices iuridica* enthalten d. i. die Tugendpflichten würden die Beobachtung aller
     Pflichten sie mögen nun von vollkommener oder unvollkommener Verbind-
     lichkeit seyn in sich enthalten nämlich die Beobachtung derselben als moralische
     Gesinnung in Erfüllung seiner Pflicht überhaupt." (VATL 23:395.6–11) Hier
     fehlt Kant offensichtlich (noch?) seine o. g. terminologische Unterscheidung von
     Tugend*pflicht* und Tugend*verpflichtung*.

‚förmlichen' Zweck der Pflichtbefolgung aus Pflicht zielen. Folglich hat die *Tugendlehre* ihren Namen 1797 nicht von den Tugend*pflichten*, sondern von der Tugend*verpflichtung* (vgl. RL 6:220.32 ff.).[31] Das *Buch* dieses Titels wiederum enthält dann freilich *nur noch diejenigen* der ethischen Pflichten, die nicht schon *dem Inhalte nach* als *äußere* Rechtspflichten (und damit *via* „Handle pflichtmäßig aus Pflicht" auch als Materie *indirekt*-ethischer Pflichten) in der *Rechtslehre* abgehandelt wurden.

b) ‚Vollkommen'/‚unvollkommen' – ‚weit'/‚eng'

Diese beiden Unterscheidungen werden in der *Metaphysik der Sitten* weitgehend austauschbar verwandt. Ob Kant gleichwohl an einem Bedeutungsunterschied festhält, ist nicht leicht auszumachen. Eine Orientierung an den schulphilosophischen Vorlagen wird zur Klärung nicht weiterhelfen, da Kant sich schon in der *Grundlegung* vorbehalten hat, diese Unterscheidungen auf eigenwillige Weise zu verwenden. (Vgl. GMS 4:421.31–38, Anm.)

Der primäre Sinn der ersten Unterscheidung bestand bei Kant zumindest zwischenzeitlich darin, dass das Zuwiderhandeln gegen vollkommene Pflichten sich selbst widerspricht (vgl. 27:496), und vollkommene Pflicht damit „nicht auf die Bedingung eingeschränkt ist, eine andere Pflicht nicht zu übertreten" (HN 19:297.21 f.).[32] Die zweite Unterscheidung (‚weit'/‚eng') betrifft hingegen primär die Frage, ob es einen „Spielraum (*latitudo*)" (TL 6:390.6 f.) bei der Pflichterfüllung gibt. Der Zusammenhang dieser Unterscheidung mit der vorigen wird in der folgenden Passage angedeutet:

> Es wird aber unter einer weiten Pflicht nicht eine Erlaubniß zu Ausnahmen von der Maxime der Handlungen, sondern nur die der Einschränkung einer Pflichtmaxime durch die andere (z. B. die allgemeine Nächstenliebe durch die Elternliebe) verstanden, wodurch in der That das Feld für die Tugendpraxis erweitert wird. – Je weiter die Pflicht, je unvollkommener also die Verbindlichkeit des Menschen zur Handlung ist, je näher er gleichwohl die Maxime der Observanz derselben (in seiner Gesinnung) der e n g e n Pflicht

---

31 Bei Alves, 2010, führt das Übersehen dieses Unterschieds (und, damit einhergehend, auch desjenigen von inneren und äußeren Rechtspflichten) zu unnötigen und letztlich unlösbaren Verwicklungen.

32 Anders als im Falle von Handlungen ergeben sich die hier einschlägigen *Gebote* der Tugend also nicht daraus, dass irgendwelche korrespondierenden Unterlassungen *verboten* sind.

(des Rechts) bringt, desto vollkommener ist seine Tugendhandlung. (TL 6:390.9–17)

Ein Spielraum bei der Pflichterfüllung verdankt sich also nicht etwa partikularen Ausnahmen (etwa um der Neigung willen – wie es noch die *Grundlegung* behauptete, siehe oben), sondern der Tatsache, dass sich einzelne Pflichtmaximen *gegenseitig* einschränken können – und das setzt freilich voraus, dass das Zuwiderhandeln gegen jede einzelne von ihnen sich nicht geradewegs ‚widerspricht‘ (*sc. notwendig* unter einer Maxime steht, die einer allgemeinen Gesetzgebung nicht fähig ist). Unvollkommenheit impliziert naturgemäß Weite – und unter der Voraussetzung, dass ‚Spielräume‘ nicht durch Ausnahmen erzeugt werden, gilt nun also auch die Umkehrung.

c)

Bringt man die beiden Erörterungen unter a) und b) zusammen, dann sind zumindest alle *direkt*-ethischen Pflichten, insofern sie einen Zweck gebieten, unvollkommene und damit weite Pflichten: „Die ethischen Pflichten sind von w e i t e r, dagegen die Rechtspflichten von e n g e r Verbindlichkeit." (TL 6:390.2 f.) Wie oben in Abschnitt I bereits herausgestellt, gibt die Ethik – im Unterschied zum *Ius* – Gesetze für Maximen, nicht für Handlungen. Und eine solche Gesetzgebung ist für Kant nur vermittels des Vorschreibens von Zwecken möglich:

> Der Begriff eines Z w e c k s, der zugleich Pflicht ist, welcher der Ethik eigenthümlich zugehört, ist es allein, der ein Gesetz für die Maximen der Handlungen begründet, indem der subjective Zweck (den jedermann hat) dem objectiven (den sich jedermann dazu machen soll) untergeordnet wird. (TL 6:389.12 ff.)

Da die äußere Gesetzgebung nur *äußere Handlungen* ge- oder verbieten kann (siehe oben Abschnitt I), kann sie die objektiv-praktische Möglichkeit der *Maximen* ebendieser Handlungen nur *restringieren*, d. h., sie der „einschränkenden Bedingung der Habilität zu einer allgemeinen Gesetzgebung, als formalem Prinzip der Handlungen" (TL 6:389.28 f.) unterwerfen.[33] Eine *Gesetzgebung* im vollen Wortsinne ergibt sich für

---

33 Vgl. *Rechtslehre*, § C: „Eine jede Handlung ist r e c h t, die *oder nach deren Maxime die Freiheit der Willkür eines jeden* mit jedermanns Freiheit nach einem allgemeinen Gesetze zusammen bestehen kann.'" (RL 6:230.29 ff., kursiv B. L.). Das allgemeine Rechtsgesetz lautet dementsprechend: „[...] handle äußerlich so,

Maximen daher nur im Falle von *Zweck*-Geboten. Da solche nun aber die *Mittel* der Realisierung nicht direkt vorschreiben, erlauben sie „der Befolgung (Observanz) einen Spielraum (*latitudo*)" (TL 6:390.6 f.).

Die Zwecke, mit denen die Ethik Gesetze für Maximen gibt, sind nur zwei: eigene Vollkommenheit (vgl. TL 6:391.29–393.10) und fremde Glückseligkeit (vgl. TL 6:393.11–394.12). Hiermit wird nicht zuletzt ein inhaltlicher Anschluss an die Ethiken der Wolffschen Schule wiederhergestellt, auch und gerade, weil Kant darauf besteht, dass die Moral nicht aus einer Lehre der Vervollkommnung und/oder der Glückseligkeit hervorgeht, sondern aus dem Bewusstsein der Verpflichtung allein.

d)

Kant fasst das Schema der Tugendpflichten noch in einer Tafel zusammen (TL 6:398), die bzgl. ihrer Enteilungskriterien allerdings nicht kohärent ist: Während „[i]nnere" Tugendpflicht (eigene Vollkommenheit) und „[ä]ußere" (fremde Glückseligkeit) in der oberen Hälfte („Das Materiale der Tugendpflicht" betreffend) Selbst- und Fremd*bezug* thematisieren (siehe oben Abschnitt I unter (5)), weisen „Moralität" und „Legalität" in der unteren Hälfte („Das Formale der Tugendpflicht" betreffend) darauf hin, dass es hier bei ‚innen' und ‚außen' eher um so etwas wie Selbst- versus Fremd*bestimmung* (siehe oben Abschnitt I unter (1)) geht: Mache ich mir fremde Glückseligkeit und eigene Vollkommenheit um des Gesetzes willen zum Zweck, handelt es sich um (ethische) Moralität. Sind sie aus anderen, d. i. pathologischen, Beweggründen meine Zwecke (man denke etwa an ein ‚Helfersyndrom', bzw. an ‚krankhaften Perfektionismus'), dann ist es bloße (ethische) Legalität (vgl. TL 6:393.4 ff.).

---

daß der freie Gebrauch deiner Willkür mit der Freiheit von jedermann nach einem allgemeinen Gesetze zusammen bestehen könne" (RL 6:231.10 ff.). Weil „die Vernunft sagt […], daß sie [*sc.* die Freiheit, B.L.] in ihrer Idee darauf eingeschränkt s e i und von andern auch thätlich eingeschränkt werden dürfe" (RL 6:231.15 ff.), ist es „nach dem Satze des Widerspruchs klar", dass *im Begriff der Freiheit* die (moralische) Möglichkeit des äußeren Zwangs enthalten ist. Dem in diesem Sinne „*analytisch*[en]" „oberste[n] Princip der Rechtslehre" (TL 6:396.2 f.) steht das der Tugendlehre: „[H]andle nach einer Maxime der Z w e c k e, die zu haben für jedermann ein allgemeines Gesetz sein kann" (TL 6:395.15 f.) als ein „synthetisch[es]" (TL 6:396.3) gegenüber, weil es noch einen „Zweck, den es zur P f l i c h t macht" (TL 6:396.14) mit dem „Begriff der äußeren Freiheit" (TL 6:396.12 f.) verknüpft.

Kants *Tugendlehre* macht es den Menschen nicht leicht – und ihren Lesern mitunter auch nicht.

e)

Die Elementarlehre der Tugendlehre ist in ihrem ersten „Theil" (TL 6:417.2), der die „Pflichten des Menschen gegen sich selbst" (TL 6:417.23) enthält, in zwei ‚Bücher' eingeteilt, die sich den vollkommenen (§§ 5 ff.) und den unvollkommenen (§§ 19 ff.) Pflichten gegen sich selbst widmen. Die ethischen Pflichten gegen andere (§§ 23 ff.) im zweiten Teil wiederum kennen eine solche Unterteilung nicht.

Projiziert man nun die bislang erörterten Distinktionen auf die *Metaphysik der Sitten* als ganze, so wird man im zweiten Teil der ethischen Elementarlehre die Lehre von den unvollkommenen ethischen Pflichten gegen andere (4) vorfinden. In den beiden Büchern vom ersten Teil dieser Elementarlehre werden die vollkommenen, indirekt-ethischen Pflichten gegen sich selbst, d. i., die inneren Rechtspflichten (2) und die unvollkommenen, direkt-ethischen Pflichten gegen sich selbst (3) abgehandelt. Die vollkommenen Pflichten gegen andere, die äußeren Rechtspflichten (1), hingegen fehlen, denn sie waren ja bereits Gegenstand der *Rechtslehre* (und sind durch das allgemeine ethische Gebot (vgl. TL 6:391.3 f.) freilich *auch* als indirekt-ethische Pflichten *implicite* Teil einer *Tugendlehre*, der Lehre von den Tugend*verpflichtungen*). Das deckt sich mit den Betrachtungen oben in den Abschnitten I und II e.

Die Ausgestaltung dieser (durch die neue Lehre von der Gesetzgebung systematisch strukturierten) Architektonik ist Kant offensichtlich nur zum Teil gelungen. Dass die beiden grundlegenden Tugendzwecke, die eigene Vollkommenheit und die fremde Glückseligkeit, im Haupttext nicht einmal erwähnt werden, obgleich sie die Lehre von den unvollkommenen Pflichten gleichsam aufspannen sollen, ist nur ein äußerliches Indiz, und dasselbe gilt für die dort nicht erwähnte Unterscheidung von direkt-ethischen und indirekt-ethischen Pflichten.

IV. Vorbegriffe zur Einteilung der Tugendlehre und Einteilung der Ethik (TL 6:410–413)

a)

Am Ende der Einleitung in die Tugendlehre (TL 6:413) stehen zwei Einteilungstafeln. Die erste der beiden greift thematisch noch einmal das Verhältnis von Verpflichtendem und Verpflichtetem auf, welches bereits eine irritierend platzierte (siehe oben, II a) Tafel im dritten Abschnitt der „Eintheilung der Metaphysik der Sitten überhaupt" (RL 6:241) mit Blick auf das Recht zum Gegenstand gemacht hatte. Auch hier liefert die Tafel nun kein Gliederungsprinzip der Schrift, sondern steht gleichsam im Vorfeld derselben: Die Ethik widmet sich – wie ein Blick auf die „Tafel der Eintheilung der Ethik" (TL 6:492) zeigt – in den zwei Teilen ihrer Elementarlehre den Pflichten „des Menschen gegen den Menschen" und zwar den Pflichten „gegen sich selbst" und „gegen andere Menschen". Pflichten gegen „nicht-menschliche" d.h., „untermenschliche" bzw. „übermenschliche Wesen" werden jedoch nicht erörtert. Das ist insofern bemerkenswert, als in den Ethik-Kompendien der Wolffschen Schule zumindest die Pflichten gegen Gott ein prominenter Gegenstand waren und als solche entsprechend auch in Kants Moral-Vorlesungen stets erörtert wurden (vgl. etwa V-Mo/Kaehler(Stark) 115 ff.; V-MS/Vigil 27:712.27 ff.). Und in Bezug auf „untermenschliche" Weltwesen andererseits gibt es in den Vorlesungen zumindest die Pflicht, „ohne Noth brauchbare Objecte der Natur [nicht] zu zerstören" (V-MS/Vigil 27:709.30 f.).[34]

b)

Die zweite Einteilungstafel stellt „das o b j e k t i v e Verhältnis der ethischen Gesetze zu den Pflichten überhaupt in einem System d e r F o r m n a c h" (TL 6:412.17 f.) vor und repräsentiert – wie sich gleich zeigen wird – tatsächlich in etwa die Makro-Struktur des Haupttextes. Da Kant betont, die Einteilung gemäß dieser zweiten Tafel müsse als „Grundriss des

---

34 Pflichten der Menschen gegenüber Tieren gibt es freilich nicht: „[...] Dankbarkeit für lang geleistete Dienste eines alten Pferdes oder Hundes (gleich als ob sie Hausgenossen wären) gehört i n d i r e c t zur Pflicht des Menschen, nämlich i n Ansehung dieser Thiere, d i r e c t aber betrachtet ist sie immer nur Pflicht des Menschen g e g e n sich selbst." (TL 6:443.22–25)

Ganzen" (TL 6:413.16) vor einer Einteilung gemäß der ersten Tafel vorhergehen, sollte man die Erörterungen der Pflichten gegen nichtmenschliche Wesen also in einem dritten und einem vierten Teil der Elementarlehre erwarten. Wenn Sie da nicht stehen, hat Kant sie entweder bloß versäumt – oder ganz bewusst dort nicht mehr behandelt: Genau dies ist zumindest mit den Pflichten gegen Gott der Fall, denn sie sind, als jenseits einer „rein-philosophischen Ethik" (TL 6:488.1) liegend, in den „Beschluss" (TL 6:486–491) verwiesen.

In der „Anmerkung" (TL 6:411 f.) zu den „Vorbegriffe[n] zur Einteheilung der Tugendlehre" (TL 6:410.2) weist Kant auf die Besonderheit hin, dass die Tugendlehre im Unterschied zur Rechtslehre in eine Elementar- und eine Methodenlehre eingeteilt werden müsse.[35] Der Text scheint dies *prima facie* damit zu begründen (vgl. TL 6:411.4–17), dass die unvollkommenen Pflichten der Ethik einen „Spielraum[]" (TL 6:411.10) (vgl. dazu bereits RL 6:233.21 ff. und ähnlich TL 6:375.20 f.) vorgeben, den auszufüllen es der *Urteilskraft* bedarf. Allerdings beweist *dieses* Erfordernis nun aber *expressis verbis* (vgl. TL 6:411.17–23) nicht etwa die Notwendigkeit einer („systematisch[en]" (TL 6:411.21)) *Methodenlehre*, sondern vielmehr die einer (bloß-„fragmentarisch[en]") „Casuistik" – und diese wiederum ist sowohl der zweiten Tafel zufolge als auch *de facto* ganz offenkundig nicht in der infrage stehenden Methodenlehre, sondern bereits in der Elementarlehre angesiedelt: In Gestalt ‚kasuistischer Fragen', „gleich den Scholien zum System" (TL 6:411.21 f.) nämlich (der obigen Begründung zum Trotz dann allerdings *auch* bei den *vollkommenen* Pflichten). Im Anschluss (TL 6:411.24 ff.) wird dann auch mit einem „Dagegen: nicht sowohl […] als vielmehr"[36] ausdrücklich darauf hingewiesen, dass es *gerade nicht* etwa die (soeben thematisierte) Übung der *Urteilskraft*, sondern vielmehr die Übung der *Vernunft* „in der Theorie [der] Pflichten sowohl als in der Praxis"

---

35 Aufgrund dieser Erörterungen ist klar, dass die Tafel 242.4 ff. drucktechnisch verunglückt ist (siehe oben unter II).

36 Das bei Kant häufige ‚nicht sowohl … als vielmehr' steht durchweg für den Gegensatz zwischen dem, was man zunächst erwarten könnte und dem, was tatsächlich der Fall ist. Demgemäß hätte der Text in TL 6:411.4 eigentlich mit einer Formulierung der Art einsetzen müssen: ‚Die Ursache *scheint zunächst* die zu sein: …', denn es zeigt sich ja sogleich, dass man durch die ‚Weite' der Tugendpflichten nicht etwa zu einer separaten Methodenlehre, sondern stattdessen zu einer Kasuistik *innerhalb* der Elementarlehre genötigt wird. Kant stellt dementsprechend seine *eigene, zutreffende* Erklärung für die Notwendigkeit einer Methodenlehre dann in TL 6:411.24 ff. mit einem „Dagegen: […]" vor.

(TL 6:411.25 f.) ist, um die es in der Methodenlehre gehen soll. Und für *diese* Übung spielt nun aber die ‚Weite‘ der ethischen Verbindlichkeit nicht die geringste Rolle: Sie wird weder in den folgenden Erörterungen (TL 6:411.24–413), noch in der Methodenlehre (TL 6:477 f.) selbst erwähnt. Dort erfolgt einerseits die Übung „in der Theorie [der] Pflichten“ „erotematisch[]“ (erfragend), bzw. „katechetisch[]“ (TL 6:411.29–32) (wenn Gelerntes wiederholt wird – oder auch *in specie* dialogisch-sokratisch, sofern etwas aus der natürlichen Vernunft entwickelt wird). Die Übung „in der Praxis“ andererseits, die Kultivierung nicht nur der Tugend*begriffe*, sondern auch des Tugend*vermögens* ist „[a] sceti[sch]“ (TL 6:411.36). Mit Dogmatik und Kasuistik in der Elementarlehre, sowie Katechetik und Asketik in der Methodenlehre ist die Ethik ‚formal‘ also vollständig. Auch lässt sich die in TL 6:412.6–11 angedeutete Gliederung der *Elementarlehre* nach der „Verschiedenheit der Subjecte, wogegen dem Menschen eine Verbindlichkeit obliegt“ (TL 6:412.7 f.) problemlos nachvollziehen – freilich mit der oben genannten Einschränkung dass nur zwei (gegen sich selbst / gegen andere Menschen) der vier möglichen Pflichtklassen behandelt werden (die gegen ‚unter-‘ und ‚übermenschliche‘ Wesen dort aber fehlen).

Wenn Kant hingegen schreibt, dass die *Methodenlehre* „nach Verschiedenheit der Zwecke, welche zu haben [...] die Vernunft [dem Menschen, B.L.] auferlegt, und der Empfänglichkeit für dieselbe[n] in verschiedene Capitel zerfällt“ (TL 6:412.8 ff.), dann hat er dabei ganz offensichtlich nicht jenen Text vor dem geistigen Auge, den wir heute lesen: Hierin steht Einschlägiges nämlich nicht etwa in der Methodenlehre, sondern wird – bereits vor dieser Ankündigung selbst – allenfalls in der überbordenden Einleitung (siehe dort Abschnitte IV, V, VIII bzw. XII) vorgetragen. Dass die ‚Zwecke die zugleich Pflicht sind‘ es überhaupt nicht in den Haupttext geschafft haben (wie oben in Abschnitt III schon bemerkt), weist nachdrücklich in dieselbe Richtung.[37]

---

37 Die Architektonik einer Tugendlehre stellt sich in Einleitung und Haupttext unterschiedlich dar, so dass man davon ausgehen muss, dass Kant eine Zusammenarbeitung beider Teile am Ende nicht mehr gelungen ist. Dass die Einleitung und der Haupttext als solche jeweils ‚aus einem Guss‘ sind, ist auch mehr als fraglich. Siehe dazu Ludwig, 1990, S. XVII–XXIV und Parma, 2000.

Literaturverzeichnis

Alves, Julius (2010), „Vollkommene Tugendpflichten. Zur Systematik der Pflichten in Kants Metaphysik der Sitten", in: *Zeitschrift für philosophische Forschung,* Bd. 64, S. 521–546.

Baum, Manfred (2007), „Recht und Ethik in Kants praktischer Philosophie", in: Jürgen Stolzenberg (Hrsg.), *Kant in der Gegenwart,* Berlin/New York: Walter de Gruyter, S. 213–226.

Kant, Immanuel [2004], *Vorlesung zur Moralphilosophie* (Nachschrift Kaehler), Werner Stark (Hrsg.), Berlin/New York: Walter de Gruyter.

Ludwig, Bernd (1990), „Einleitung", in: Immanuel Kant, *Metaphysische Anfangsgründe der Tugendlehre,* Bernd Ludwig (Hrsg.), Hamburg: Meiner, S. I–XXVIII.

Parma, Vinicio (2000), „Es war einmal *eine Metaphysik der Sitten...*", in: *Kant-Studien,* Bd. 91 (Sonderheft), S. 42–65.

Seel, Gerhard (2009), „How Does Kant Justify the Universal Objective Validity of the Law of Right?", in: *International Journal of Philosophical Studies,* Bd. 17, S. 71–94.

Timmons, Mark (Hrsg.) (2002), *Kant's 'Metaphysics of Morals': Interpretative Essays,* Oxford: Oxford University Press.

von der Pfordten, Dietmar (2009), „Kants Rechtsbegriff", in: ders. (Hrsg.), *Menschenwürde, Recht und Staat bei Kant,* Paderborn: Mentis, S. 27–40.

Willaschek, Marcus (2002), „Which Imperatives for Right? On the Non-Prescriptive Character of Juridical Laws in Kant's 'Metaphysics of Morals'", in: Timmons (Hrsg.) (2002), S. 65–88.

Wood, Alan (2002), „The final Form of Kant's practical Philosophy", in: Timmons (Hrsg.) (2002), S. 1–22.

Recht und Ethik in Kants *Metaphysik der Sitten* (MS 6:218–221 und TL 6:390 f.)

Steffi Schadow

1. Einleitung: Stellung und Funktion des Textabschnittes in der *Metaphysik der Sitten*

Im ersten Abschnitt der „Einleitung in die Metaphysik der Sitten" (MS 6:211.1–214.30) hatte Kant das begriffliche Instrumentarium für sein Verständnis des Menschen als eines freien, durch Vernunft bestimmbaren endlichen Naturwesens bereitgestellt. Bereits am Ende dieses ersten Abschnittes und im zweiten Abschnitt geht es ihm dann um die für die *Metaphysik der Sitten* grundlegende Thematik einer von der Metaphysik der Natur unterschiedenen Lehre der Sittlichkeit. Kant knüpft anschließend im Abschnitt „Von der Eintheilung einer Metaphysik der Sitten" (MS 6:218.10–221.3) an den Gedanken von der Metaphysik der Sitten als „System der Freiheit" (MS 6:218.4) an, wenn er den Begriff der Gesetzgebung für die Handlungen einer freien Willkür zum Gegenstand der Untersuchung macht. Mit den darauf folgenden Unterscheidungen zwischen juridischer und ethischer Gesetzgebung sowie zwischen Rechts- und Tugendpflichten enthält dieser kurze dritte Abschnitt der „Einleitung" (MS 6:218.9–221.3) bereits das Programm der *Metaphysik der Sitten*. Dem kurzen Abschnitt über die Rechts- und Tugendpflichten korrespondiert dabei Abschnitt VII der „Einleitung zur Tugendlehre" (TL 6:390.1–391.25), in dem Kant die ethischen Pflichten genauer als „weite[]" (TL 6:390.2) Pflichten, die Rechtspflichten hingegen als Pflichten „von enger Verbindlichkeit" (TL 6:390.3) ausweist.

2. Inhalt und Aufbau der Textabschnitte

Der kurze Abschnitt „Von der Eintheilung einer Metaphysik der Sitten"
(MS 6:218.10–221.3) enthält vier thematische Schwerpunkte und eine
Zusammenfassung. Er beginnt mit einer definitorischen Erläuterung zur
Gesetzgebung im Allgemeinen:

> Zu aller Gesetzgebung (sie mag nun innere oder äußere Handlungen und
> diese entweder *a priori* durch bloße Vernunft, oder durch die Willkür eines
> andern vorschreiben) gehören zwei Stücke: **erstlich** ein G e s e t z, welches die
> Handlung, die geschehen soll, o b j e c t i v als nothwendig vorstellt, d. i.
> welches die Handlung zur Pflicht macht, **zweitens** eine Triebfeder, welche
> den Bestimmungsgrund der Willkür zu dieser Handlung s u b j e c t i v mit der
> Vorstellung des Gesetzes verknüpft [...]. (MS 6:218.11–17)

Dieser Einführung zufolge hat eine jede Gesetzgebung einen objektiv-
normativen und einen subjektiv-motivationalen Aspekt. So schreibt eine
Gesetzgebung Gesetze vor, deren Befolgung für das dieser Gesetzgebung
unterworfene Subjekt Pflicht ist; dies ist der objektiv-normative Aspekt.
Diese Gesetze können erstens Gesetze für den inneren oder äußeren
Willkürgebrauch sein. Zweitens können ihre Vorschriften entweder auf
die „bloße Vernunft" (MS 6:218.12) oder aber auf eine fremde Willkür
zurückgehen.[1] Ein subjektiv-motivationaler Aspekt kommt einer Gesetzgebung zudem insofern zu, als sie berücksichtigt, inwiefern die objektiv erkannte Forderung des Gesetzes „s u b j e c t i v" (MS 6:218.17) auf
die Willkür des einzelnen Subjektes bezogen wird. Die subjektive ‚Verknüpfung' des „Bestimmungsgrund[es] der Willkür" (MS 6:218.16) mit
der objektiven Norm bezeichnet Kant als „Triebfeder" (MS 6:218.15 f.).
Ausgehend von dieser grundlegenden Definition widmet sich Kant der

---

1   Der von Kant in der Definition der Gesetzgebung eingebrachte Einschub „sie
    mag nun innere oder äußere Handlungen und *diese* entweder a priori durch
    bloße Vernunft, oder durch die Willkür eines andern vorschreiben" (MS
    6:218.11–13, kursiv S.S., Herv. des Originals getilgt) lässt verschiedene Lesarten
    zu. So kann „diese" (MS 6:218.12) auf „innere oder äußere Handlungen" (MS
    6:218.11) (d. h. auf beide Handlungstypen) bezogen sein. Das würde aber u. a.
    heißen, dass eine Gesetzgebung innere Handlungen durch eine dem Subjekt
    externe Willkür vorschreiben kann. Einer anderen möglichen Lesart zufolge
    bezieht sich „diese" ausschließlich auf „äußere Handlungen". Diese Lesart im-
    pliziert, dass allein äußere Handlungen Gegenstände apriorischer Vernunftvor-
    schriften sein können. Beide Lesarten sind problematisch. Daher schlage ich
    zugunsten der Konsistenz des kantischen Textes eine Lösung vor, bei der auf eine
    eindeutige Zuordnung von „diese" verzichtet wird und die die beiden Unter-
    scheidungen einfach der Reihe nach nennt.

Unterscheidung zwischen juridischer und ethischer Gesetzgebung. (Vgl. MS 6:218.24 f., 219.1–11) Eine Gesetzgebung, die zur Bedingung macht, dass die Vorstellung der Pflicht selbst die „Triebfeder" (MS 6:219.3) der Handlung ist, bezeichnet er als *ethisch*. Ist es nach Vorgabe der Gesetzgebung hingegen ausreichend, dass die Handlung, unabhängig von den ihr zugrunde liegenden Beweggründen, gesetzmäßig ist, so handelt es sich um eine *juridische Gesetzgebung*. Sie stellt nicht zur Bedingung, dass die Triebfeder bereits im Gesetz ‚eingeschlossen' ist und lässt „auch eine andere Triebfeder als die Idee der Pflicht selbst zu [...]" (MS 6:219:5). Da eine jede Gesetzgebung nötigenden (und nicht ‚anlockenden') Charakter hat, muss eine solche von der Idee der Pflicht unterschiedene Triebfeder Kant zufolge als eine „Abneigung[]" (MS 6:219.8) gegenüber den negativen Folgen der Nichtbefolgung der Pflicht verstanden werden. Es handelt sich bei ihr um ein Motiv, durch das eine Handlung äußerlich erzwungen werden kann. (Vgl. MS 6:220.2–5)

Gegenstand des dritten Themenschwerpunktes (MS 6:219.17–30) sind die einer Gesetzgebung zugehörigen *Pflichten*. Während die Pflichten einer juridischen Gesetzgebung nur „äußere" (MS 6:219.17) Pflichten sein können, ist die ethische Gesetzgebung auf Pflichten festgelegt, die „innerlich" (MS 6:219.19) sind und also nur unter der Bedingung der Wirksamkeit eines inneren Bestimmungsgrundes der Willkür erfüllt werden. Kant begründet diese Charakterisierung von Rechtspflichten als äußeren und Tugendpflichten als inneren Pflichten[2] damit, dass eine Rechtspflicht keine bestimmte Triebfeder zu ihrer Erfüllung benötigt und das Gebot der Rechtsgesetzgebung nur auf äußerlich erzwingbare *Handlungen* geht, nicht aber auf die *Bestimmungsgründe* des Handelns. (Vgl. MS 6:219.17–21) Im Gegensatz dazu wird eine ethische

---

2   Kant gebraucht ‚äußere Pflichten' schon an dieser Stelle synonym mit ‚Rechtspflichten' und ‚innere Pflichten' gleichbedeutend mit ‚Tugendpflichten', ohne dass er diese Terminologie eigens einführt. ‚Äußere Pflichten' sind dabei die Pflichten einer rechtlichen, ‚innere Pflichten' die Pflichten einer ethischen Gesetzgebung. Zudem operiert Kant v.a. in der *Tugendlehre* mit dem Begriff der ethischen Pflicht, den er ebenso gleichbedeutend mit dem der Tugendpflicht verwendet. (Vgl. z.B. TL 6:383.9 f.) Vom Begriff der Tugendpflicht bzw. ethischen Pflicht ist schließlich noch der Begriff der Tugendverpflichtung zu unterscheiden. Die „Tugendverpflichtung" (TL 6:410.27) besteht dem formalen Prinzip der Ethik zufolge darin, seine Pflicht aus Pflicht zu erfüllen; sie beinhaltet damit die ethische Gesinnung. (Vgl. TL 6:410.27–30) Es gibt nach Kant „nur Eine Tugendverpflichtung, aber viel Tugendpflichten" (TL 6:410.27 f.), nämlich so viele, wie es „Objecte giebt, die für uns Zwecke sind, welche zu haben zugleich Pflicht ist" (TL 6:410.28 f.).

Pflicht dann und nur dann erfüllt, wenn nicht eine beliebige Triebfeder hinter der Handlung steht, sondern die innere Idee der Pflicht selbst. Die von der ethischen Gesetzgebung ausgehenden Pflichten beziehen sich daher auf die „innere[n] Handlungen" (MS 6:219.22) und betreffen die innere Freiheit der Willkür. Aus dieser Beschreibung geht hervor, dass sich die Merkmale ‚innerlich' und ‚äußerlich' nicht aus den Pflichten als solchen ergeben, sondern aus der Rücksicht, die die Gesetzgebung auf die Triebfeder nimmt.

Im vierten thematischen Abschnitt (MS 6:219.31–220.18) leitet Kant aus der Aufteilung der Verbindlichkeiten in innere und äußere Pflichten Folgerungen für die Gegenstandsbereiche von Ethik und Recht ab.[3] So sind die ihnen eigenen Gesetzgebungen nicht etwa dadurch unterschieden, dass ihnen jeweils bestimmte Pflichten entsprechen, die sich wechselseitig ausschließen. Das sie unterscheidende Merkmal liegt im Gegenteil in der Art und Weise, auf die beide Gesetzgebungen die Erfüllung einer Pflicht *einfordern*.[4] So kann eine Rechtspflicht auch Gegenstand der ethischen Gesetzgebung werden, nämlich dann, wenn der Grund ihrer Befolgung die Vorstellung der Pflicht selbst ist. Denn „die Ethik lehrt [...] nur, daß, wenn die Triebfeder [...], nämlich der äußere Zwang, auch weggelassen wird, die Idee der Pflicht allein schon zur Triebfeder hinreichend sei" (MS 6:220.2–5).

Damit ist der letzte Abschnitt (MS 6:220.19–221.3) eingeleitet, der eine Zusammenfassung aller vorherigen Textstücke darstellt. „Die ethische Gesetzgebung [...] ist diejenige, welche nicht äußerlich sein kann; die juridische ist, welche auch äußerlich sein kann." (MS 6:220.19–21) Die grundlegende Unterscheidung zwischen Recht und Ethik besteht damit in der Art und Weise, wie in beiden Bereichen der Moral Verbindlichkeiten eingefordert werden. Eine andere fundamentale Differenz deutet Kant hier nur noch an, nämlich diejenige, dass die Ethik „ihre besondern Pflichten" (MS 6:220.32 f.) hat. Er wendet sich diesem Punkt

---

3   Mit ‚Ethik' und ‚Recht' sind hier und im Folgenden Kants Verwendungsweise dieser Termini entsprechend ‚Tugendlehre' und ‚Rechtslehre' gemeint. Die ‚Moral' als ‚Sittenlehre' umfasst beide Bereiche: Recht und Ethik. Siehe dazu unten (3.1).

4   Kants Formulierung lautet hier: „Die Ethik hat [...] mit dem Rechte Pflichten, aber nur nicht die Art der Verpflichtung gemein" (MS 6:220.32–34). Die besondere „Art der Verpflichtung" (MS 6:220.34), die von der Ethik ausgeht, bezeichnet Kant in der *Tugendlehre* als „Tugendverpflichtung" (z. B. TL 6:410.27). Das „allgemeine[] ethische[] Gebot[]" (TL 6:391.3 f.), das sie enthält, lautet: „Handle pflichtmäßig aus Pflicht." (TL 6:391.4)

explizit in der *Tugendlehre* zu, wo die ethischen Pflichten einer genaueren Analyse unterzogen werden.

Im Abschnitt VII der „Einleitung zur Tugendlehre" (TL 6:390.1– 391.25) greift Kant die Unterscheidung zwischen Rechts- und Tugendpflichten aus der „Einleitung in die Metaphysik der Sitten" (vgl. MS 6:219.17–30) erneut auf und präzisiert dabei insbesondere die Definition der ethischen Pflicht. Ausgehend von der explizit im vorhergehenden Abschnitt (TL 6:388.31–389.32) und implizit auch schon im soeben erörterten Abschnitt der „Einleitung in die Metaphysik der Sitten" exponierten These, dass die ethische Gesetzgebung auf die (inneren) Grundsätze des Handelns, die juridische aber auf die (beobachtbaren, äußeren) Handlungen geht, entwickelt Kant den Begriff der Tugendpflicht als einer „weite[n]" (TL 6:390.2) Pflicht, die sich von der Rechtspflicht durch den „Spielraum (*latitudo*)" (TL 6:390.6 f.) unterscheidet, den sie der freien Willkür bei ihrer Erfüllung überlässt. Das Merkmal ihrer ,Weite' besteht jedoch, wie Kant sofort klarstellt, nicht darin, dass sie „eine Erlaubniß zu Ausnahmen von der Maxime der Handlungen" (TL 6:390.10 f.) enthält, sondern in dem Umstand, dass durch die Pflicht nicht hinreichend bestimmt wird, durch welche Handlungen die Pflicht *in concreto* erfüllt wird. Tugendhaft und nicht nur moralisch richtig verhält sich jemand erst dann, wenn er nicht nur pflichtmäßig, sondern darüber hinaus auch ,aus Pflicht' handelt. Eine solche Gesinnung ist „verdienstlich" (TL 6:390.32 f.).

Die ethische Pflichterfüllung geht nach Kant mit dem Gefühl einer „moralischen Lust" (TL 6:391.12) einher. Als Verdienst am Wohl anderer Menschen kann sich eine solche „ethische[] Belohnung" (TL 6:391.10) dabei zum einen als ein „süße[s] Verdienst" (TL 6:391.19) erweisen, nämlich dann, wenn durch die verdienstvolle Handlung ein von allen Menschen anerkannter Tugendzweck befördert wird. Ein „saure[s] Verdienst" (TL 6:391.21) ist es hingegen dann, wenn durch die Maxime das Wohl anderer Menschen zwar befördert wird, diese jedoch unwissend über ihr „wahres Wohl" (TL 6:391.22) sind.

3. Textkommentar und Interpretationsfragen

3.1 „Gesetze der Freiheit"

Kant schickt seiner Einführung zweier Arten der Gesetzgebung und der damit verbundenen Unterscheidung zwischen Recht und Ethik ein kurzes Textstück über die „Gesetze der Freiheit" (MS 6:214.13) voran, die er dort bereits in „juridisch[e]" (MS 6:214.15) und „ethisch[e]" (MS 6:214.17) Gesetze unterteilt. Dieser Überlegung zufolge haben Recht und Ethik und die ihnen entsprechenden Arten der ‚Gesetzgebung' miteinander gemein, dass ihre Gesetze ‚moralische Gesetze' und als solche, „zum Unterschiede von Naturgesetzen" (MS 6:214.13), Typen von „Gesetze[n] der Freiheit" (MS 6:214.13) sind. Sie haben *einen* ‚Gesetzgeber': die reine praktische Vernunft. Und sie haben *einen* Adressaten: das vernunftbegabte Subjekt.

Kant verleiht dieser Bedeutung der moralischen Konstitution des Adressaten einer ‚moralischen Gesetzgebung' u. a. dadurch Ausdruck, dass er das Textstück über die Freiheitsgesetze an das Ende des Abschnitts „Von dem Verhältniß der Vermögen des menschlichen Gemüths zu den Sittengesetzen" stellt (vgl. MS 6:214.13–30). Den in diesem Abschnitt entwickelten Begriffsdefinitionen gemäß verfügt der Mensch als Teil der lebendigen Natur über die grundlegende Fähigkeit, Handlungen nach eigenen Vorstellungen zu verursachen und das heißt: Urheber seiner ihm deshalb zurechenbaren Handlungen zu sein. (Vgl. MS 6:213.14–26) Die moralischen Gesetze gelten daher, wie Kant ausführlich in seinen moralphilosophischen ‚Grundlegungsschriften' gezeigt hatte, für Wesen, die Vernunft und einen Willen haben.[5]

Ein ‚praktisches Gesetz' versteht Kant als einen objektiven Grundsatz, für den ein sinnliches und zugleich vernünftiges, für dieses Gesetz aufmerksames Subjekt empfänglich ist. Bereits in der *Grundlegung* und in der *Kritik der praktischen Vernunft* hatte er das Verhältnis, in dem der

---

5　So z. B. in KpV 5:32.7–15: „Dieses Princip der Sittlichkeit nun, eben um der Allgemeinheit der Gesetzgebung willen […], erklärt die Vernunft zugleich zu einem Gesetz für alle vernünftige Wesen, so fern sie überhaupt einen Willen, d. i. ein Vermögen haben, ihre Causalität durch die Vorstellung von Regeln zu bestimmen, mithin so fern sie der Handlungen nach Grundsätzen, folglich auch nach praktischen Principien *a priori* […] fähig sind." In der *Metaphysik der Sitten* führt Kant diesen Gedanken fort: „Sie [die Lehren der Sittlichkeit, S.S.] gebieten für jedermann, ohne Rücksicht auf seine Neigungen zu nehmen: blos weil und sofern er frei ist und praktische Vernunft hat." (MS 6:216.6–8)

Wille eines endlichen Vernunftwesens zum Gesetz steht, als „Abhängigkeit" (KpV 5:32.24) und „Verbindlichkeit" (KpV 5:32.24) bezeichnet. Des Weiteren ist die Nötigung, die das sinnlich affizierbare Wesen durch das Gesetz erfährt, „Pflicht" (KpV 5:32.26). Das Gesetz stellt sich dem Menschen aufgrund seiner Endlichkeit im Modus eines Gebotes dar; es ist ein „Imperativ" (KpV 5:32.22), der aufgrund der Unbedingtheit, mit der das Gesetz fordert, ein *kategorischer* Imperativ ist.[6] Das von ihm ausgehende Sollen, so Kant schon in der Auflösung der dritten Antinomie in der *Kritik der reinen Vernunft*, „drückt eine Art von Notwendigkeit und Verknüpfung mit Gründen aus, die in der ganzen Natur sonst nicht vorkommt" (KrV A547/B575).

Nun hat Kant an der zitierten Stelle aus der *Kritik der reinen Vernunft* noch nicht spezifisch *moralisches* Handeln im Sinn, wenn er vom Gebotensein einer vernünftigen Regel spricht. Dort sollte erst einmal gezeigt werden, dass Menschen *überhaupt* in der Lage sind, Gründen zu folgen, die nicht oder zumindest nicht allein durch ihre Sinnlichkeit vorgegeben werden, sondern rationale Gründe sind, die sich ein vernunftbegabtes Subjekt selbst vorlegt.[7] Der präskriptive Charakter von Geboten bzw. Imperativen besteht damit darin, dass sie Handlungen vorschreiben, weil sie *rational* sind.[8]

---

6 Dementsprechend heißt es in der Einleitung zur *Metaphysik der Sitten*: „Gesetz (ein moralisch praktisches) ist ein Satz, der einen kategorischen Imperativ (Gebot) enthält." (MS 6:227.10 f.; vgl. hierzu z. B. auch: MS 6:214.4–12 und VAMS 23:245.19–23)

7 „Diejenige [Willkür] aber, welche unabhängig von sinnlichen Antrieben, mithin durch Bewegursachen, welche nur von der Vernunft vorgestellet werden, bestimmet werden kann, heißt die freie Willkür (arbitrium liberum) […]." (KrV A802/B830) Dass die Gründe des Handelns nicht durch die Sinnlichkeit *vorgegeben* werden sollen, heißt natürlich nicht, dass Neigungen in ihnen nicht vorkommen. Sie können sogar aus Neigungen hervorgehen, und dennoch kann man eine Handlung, die diesen als Gründen folgt, rational nennen. Worum es Kant geht, ist zu zeigen, dass in überlegten Handlungen zwischen die Affektion und die Handlung ein vermittelndes Moment treten muss; diese Rolle erfüllt die Vernunft bzw. der Wille als ‚praktische Vernunft'. (Vgl. zu diesem Punkt KrV A803/B831, wo es heißt, dass „nicht bloß das, was reizt, d. i. die Sinne *unmittelbar* affiziert, die menschliche Willkür […] bestimmt." (Kursiv S.S.)) Allison hat diese weite Bedeutung praktischer Freiheit im Blick, wenn er schreibt: „Thus, even desire-based or, as Kant later termed it, 'heteronomous' action involves the self-determination of the subject and, therefore, a 'moment' of spontaneity" (Allison, 1990, S. 39).

8 Vgl. hierzu: Willaschek, 2005, S. 197.

Noch bevor Kant weitere Unterscheidungen trifft, stellt er den kategorischen Imperativ in der „Einleitung in die Rechtslehre" als allgemeines Prinzip der Moral vor: „Wir kennen unsere eigene Freiheit [...]
nur durch den moralischen Imperativ, welcher ein pflichtgebietender
Satz ist, aus welchem nachher das Vermögen, andere zu verpflichten, d. i.
der Begriff des Rechts, entwickelt werden kann." (RL 6:239.16–21)[9]
Und, wie es im Abschnitt „Von der Idee und der Nothwendigkeit einer
Metaphysik der Sitten" heißt: Die „Lehren der Sittlichkeit [...] gebieten
für jedermann [...]: blos weil und sofern er frei ist und praktische Vernunft hat." (MS 6:216.7–9) Praktische Vernunft schließlich ist ein
Vermögen, das moralischen Wesen als Rechtssubjekten und als Trägern
genuin ethischer Gesinnungen gleichermaßen zukommt.

   Zusammengefasst heißt das: Nach Freiheitsgesetzen handeln heißt,
nach Gesetzen zu handeln, die der vernünftigen Einsicht zugänglich sind.
Ethische *und* juridische Gesetze versteht Kant als *praktische Vernunftgesetze*, die a priori gelten und von jedem Vernunftwesen als unbedingt
geboten eingesehen werden können.[10] (Vgl. MS 6:215.16–18) Damit
erstreckt sich der Bereich der Moral (verstanden als „System der allgemeinen Pflichtenlehre" (TL 6:379.9) bzw. als „Sittenlehre" (TL
6:387.6)) für Kant sowohl über die Ethik als auch über das Recht.[11]

---

 9 Den Zusammenhang von moralischem Bewusstsein und moralischer Verpflich-
    tung hat Kant in der Formulierung auf den Punkt gebracht, das Sittengesetz sei
    die *„ratio cognoscendi"* (KpV 5:4.32) der Freiheit, die Freiheit hingegen die *„ratio
    essendi"* (KpV 5:4.31) des Sittengesetzes. (Vgl. z. B. auch: VAMS 23:245.27–31,
    246.30–33)

10 „Die Verbindlichkeit ist eine moralische, mithin nach Gesetzen der Freiheit er-
    folgte Nöthigung, gleich einer Nöthigung unserer Willkür als freie Willkür. Es
    wird also bey jeder Verbindlichkeit 1) die Willkür genöthigt, 2) durch Gesetze
    der Freiheit, d. i. ihnen gemäß zu handeln." (V-MS/Vigil 27:508.3–7) Zur
    Kritik der (vorkantischen) Auffassung, Rechtspflichten hätten stärkeren Ver-
    pflichtungscharakter als Tugendpflichten, siehe Kersting, 1997, S. 112.

11 Dass das Recht nach Kant ebenso wie die Ethik unter die Moral und deren
    allgemeines Prinzip, den kategorischen Imperativ, gehört, lässt sich auch an Kants
    Definition des Rechts nachvollziehen. Dieser zufolge ist das Recht ein „reiner
    praktischer Vernunftbegriff der Willkür unter Freiheitsgesetzen" (RL
    6:249.22); ihm ist es „um praktische Bestimmung der Willkür nach Gesetzen der
    Freiheit zu thun" (RL 6:249.19 f.). Nur weil die Freiheitsgesetze Grundlage
    der rechtlichen Gesetzgebung bzw. der Rechtsgesetze sind, ist auch äußeres, le-
    gales Handeln frei (= freiheitsbestimmtes Handeln). Beide Prinzipien, sowohl
    das Rechtsprinzip als auch das Tugendprinzip, sind Gesetze der Kausalität aus
    Freiheit. (Vgl. VAMS 23:381.19; siehe zu diesem Punkt z. B. Geismann, 2006,
    S. 31 f.) Zudem hatte Kant die Ethik in der *Grundlegung* zwar in Abgrenzung zur

Für den Bereich des Rechts ergibt sich aus seiner Zugehörigkeit zur Moral die nicht unerhebliche Folge, dass die mit ihm befassten Rechtsnormen gerade *nicht* den Charakter von *bloßem* äußerem Zwang haben. Als zugehörig zu einer moralischen Gesetzgebung beruht ihre Verbindlichkeit, wie die der ethischen Gesetze auch, auf ihrer vernünftigen Einsehbarkeit für alle vernunftbegabten Wesen. Auf diese Weise stellen sie sich ihnen als aus der Perspektive der Vernunft berechtigte moralische Regeln dar, auf deren Einhaltung sich jeder Mensch als vernünftiges Wesen selbst verpflichtet und nach denen er sich freiwillig in seinen Handlungen richten würde, ständen nicht sinnliche Antriebe einer solchen Übereinstimmung von Einsicht, Wollen und Handeln entgegen. Rechtsnormen haben den Charakter äußerer Erzwingbarkeit und enthalten gleichzeitig die innere Idee der Pflicht. Nur aufgrund dieser Voraussetzung sind die von der Rechtsgesetzgebung ausgehenden Gebote gültige Gesetze mit echtem Verpflichtungscharakter und nicht unberechtigte Forderungen in Form von bloßer Gewalt.

Kant führt zur Erklärung seiner Unterscheidung von juridischen und ethischen Gesetzen weitere Begriffspaare an, die ihrerseits erläuterungsbedürftig sind. Dabei ist es der Gegensatz von ‚Innen' und ‚Außen', der jeweils im Zentrum der Argumentation steht. So gehen die juridischen Gesetze nur auf „äußere Handlungen" (MS 6:214.14). Stimmen diese mit dem Gesetz überein, so spricht Kant von ihrer „Legalität" (MS 6:214.18; vgl. auch MS 6:219.12–14). Als Freiheitsgesetze, die nicht

Physik als „Sittenlehre" (GMS 4:387.16) bezeichnet; er nimmt diese Beschränkung der allgemeinen Sittenlehre (verstanden als *philosophia moralis* (TL 6:379.3 f.)) auf die Ethik in der *Metaphysik der Sitten* jedoch zurück. Das „System der allgemeinen Pflichtenlehre" (TL 6:379.9) teilt sich dieser revidierten Auffassung zufolge in Rechts- und Tugendlehre. (Vgl. TL 6:379.3–12) – Die Frage, ob das Recht nach Kant unter das allgemeine Prinzip der Moral fällt oder nicht, hat in der Forschung kontroverse Diskussionen ausgelöst. Dabei haben sich zwei Hauptpositionen herausgebildet. Die „traditionelle" These (so die Bezeichnung in Willaschek, 2009, z.B. S. 49 f.), das Recht gehöre unter die Moral und der kategorische Imperativ liefere dementsprechend das Begründungsprinzip für das Rechtsgesetz, wird von Guyer, 2002, Kersting, 1984, Ludwig, 1988, Oberer, 1997, Seel, 2009 und Tretter, 1997 vertreten. Ebbinghaus, 1958/1988, 1960/1988, Geismann, 2006, Pogge, 2002, Ripstein, 2004, Willaschek, 1997, 2009 und Wood, 2002 argumentieren gegen eine solche Verbindung von Rechtsgesetz und kategorischem Imperativ. Ihrer Ansicht nach ist Kants Rechtslehre unabhängig von seiner Moralphilosophie und gehört daher eigentlich gar nicht in die *Metaphysik der Sitten* (zum letzten Punkt siehe v.a. Willaschek, 1997). Einen Überblick über die mehr als 50-jährige Debatte gibt Seel, 2009, S. 72 f.

allein auf „äußere Handlungen" (MS 6:214.14 f.) bezogen sind, sondern auch die „Bestimmungsgründe der Handlungen" (MS 6:214.16) in ihre Forderung mit einschließen, sind die ethischen Gesetze hingegen genuin ‚innerlich'. (Vgl. MS 6:214.28 f.) Sie setzen nicht nur den „äußer[e]n" (MS 6:214.21), sondern auch den „inner[e]n" (MS 6:214.21) Gebrauch der freien Willkür voraus. Damit zusammenhängend kommt einer Handlung das Merkmal der *Moralität* genau dann zu, wenn auch der Bestimmungsgrund zu dieser Handlung mit dem Gesetz übereinstimmt. (Vgl. MS 6:214.14–19, 219.12–16)

3.2 Gesetz und Triebfeder

Wie bereits erwähnt, stellt sich ein praktisches Gesetz einem endlichen Vernunftwesen im Modus des Imperativs dar. Diesem Sachverhalt entspricht des Weiteren, dass sich Menschen aufgrund ihrer auch sinnlichen Natur die von ihnen als verbindlich eingesehenen Gründe in ihrem Handeln nicht notwendig derart zu eigen machen, dass sie dieses hinreichend leiten. Als der Moralität und des Handelns überhaupt fähige Wesen benötigen Menschen einen *Antrieb*, durch den der „Bestimmungsgrund der Willkür zu dieser Handlung s u b j e c t i v mit der Vorstellung des Gesetzes verknüpft" (MS 6:218.16 f.) wird. Kant bezeichnet dieses bewegende Moment in menschlichen Handlungen (seien sie Gegenstand der Moral oder nicht) als „Triebfeder" (z. B. MS 6:218.15 f.; VAMS 23:389.8).

Der Begriff der Triebfeder gehört, ebenso wie der Begriff des Gesetzes, zu den zentralen Theorieelementen in Kants Moralphilosophie. Bereits in der Zeit vor der Veröffentlichung der *Grundlegung* hatte Kant einen objektiven und einen subjektiven Faktor in der moralischen Gesetzgebung unterschieden. Als objektiven Faktor bezeichnet er die Norm, auch „Richtschnur" (V-Mo/Kaehler(Stark) 56.2) bzw. Prinzip der „Diiudication" (V-Mo/Kaehler(Stark) 56.3) genannt. Der subjektive Faktor hingegen ist die „Triebfeder" (V-Mo/Kaehler(Stark) 68.15); sie ist das Prinzip der „Execution" (V-Mo/Kaehler(Stark) 68.13) einer Handlung und damit ein „principium des Antriebes" (V-Mo/Kaehler(Stark) 57.7).

Unter der ‚Triebfeder' versteht Kant also schon früh den subjektiv bewegenden Aspekt einer Handlung.[12] Der Frage, wie die Pflichtidee

---

12 Kant hat den Begriff der Triebfeder („ELATER[..] ANIMI" (z.B. HN 15:46.23)) vermutlich von Baumgarten übernommen. (Vgl. zu dieser Vermutung Käubler,

Triebfeder und damit die bewegende Ursache einer Handlung sein kann, hat Kant in der *Kritik der praktischen Vernunft* ein ausführliches Kapitel gewidmet. (Vgl. KpV 5:71–89) Er geht dort der Frage nach der Wirkung eines praktischen Gesetzes auf das Gemüt eines endlichen Vernunftwesens nach und erörtert in diesem Zusammenhang die Funktion der Triebfeder des moralischen Gefühls der Achtung im moralischen Handeln. Ebenso wie der Begriff der Maxime und der des Interesses, so führt Kant dort aus, findet der Begriff der Triebfeder „nur auf endliche Wesen" (KpV 5:79.28 f.) Anwendung. Diesen Wesen, die aufgrund ihrer sinnlichen Natur immer auch Absichten haben, die mit ihrer vernünftigen Einsicht konfligieren, eignet ein „Bedürfnis, irgend wodurch zur Thätigkeit angetrieben zu werden, weil ein inneres Hinderniß derselben entgegensteht" (KpV 5:79.32 f.). Daher folgt aus der (moralischen) Einsicht die Handlung nicht notwendigerweise; es bedarf eines *Antriebs*, damit die Einsicht durch die adäquate Willenseinstellung begleitet wird und aus dieser die (moralische) Handlung hervorgeht.[13]

1917, S. 16, sowie Schwaiger, 1999, S. 161 f.) Dieser hatte die Triebfeder als „causa[] impulsiva[]" (HN 15:46.22 f.) und damit als bewegende Ursache des Handelns bezeichnet. Unabhängig von Baumgartens Verwendung des Begriffs „ELATER[..] ANIMI" als „causa[] impulsiva[]" wird *elater* auch im Allgemeinen im Lateinischen mit *causa impulsiva* wiedergegeben. (Vgl. Käubler, 1917, S. 7) – Kants synonyme Verwendung von ‚*elater animi*' („Triebfeder[] des Gemüths" (HN 15:46.34)) und ‚*causa impulsiva*' zeigt sich indirekt an vielen Stellen in den Nachschriften der Ethik-Vorlesung, so z.B. in der Kaehler-Nachschrift, wo es heißt: „Eine pathologische Necessitation ist, wo die Triebfeder aus den Sinnen und aus dem Gefühl des Angenehmen und Unangenehmen hergenommen sind [...]. Also die caus[]ae impulsivae, so fern sie vom Guten hergenommen sind, sind aus dem Verstande [...]." (V-Mo/Kaehler(Stark) 30.3–9) In einer späten Nachschrift von Kants Metaphysik-Vorlesung (*Metaphysik Dohna*, 1792/93) heißt es sogar wörtlich: „Elateres animi – Triebfedern des Gemüths heißen die causae impulsivae der Willkür." (V-MP/Dohna 28:677.16 f.) Mit Blick auf diese Begriffsgeschichte ist Becks Ausdrucksweise treffend, wenn er die Triebfeder (nach kantischem Verständnis) als „dynamischen" und „konativen" Faktor im Handeln bezeichnet. (Vgl. Beck, 1960, S. 216) – Zur systematischen Entwicklung einer Triebfederntheorie in Bezug auf moralisches Handeln im kantischen Werk siehe Schadow, 2012, Kap. 4–5.

13 Dieser Interpretation liegt ein Verständnis von praktischem Handeln bei Kant zugrunde, demzufolge Motive und Handlungen als gleichzeitig ablaufende Ereignisse verstanden werden. Nach Rohs ist dies eine Voraussetzung dafür, dass es Freiheit gibt bzw. dass sich die Bestimmung durch Motive und freies Handeln nicht ausschließen. Das sieht Rohs darin begründet, dass Freiheit in einem „Anfangen" (Rohs, 1986, S. 232 f.) besteht, dieser Anfang aber nicht gewährleistet ist, wenn die Motive der freien Handlung schon vorausgehen: „Die Motive

Zusammengefasst heißt das: Eine Gesetzgebung, die bestimmte Handlungen zu Pflichten macht und diese als geboten vorschreibt, enthält als System der Pflichten für eine freie und zugleich endliche Willkür („arbitrium sensitivum [...] liberum" (KrV A534/B562))[14] immer zweierlei: Zum einen ein Gesetz, das die Handlung als notwendig vorschreibt, zum anderen eine Triebfeder, die zur Handlung antreibt. Die moralische Gesetzgebung (sei sie juridisch oder ethisch) erschöpft sich nicht in der Nennung des Pflichtgehalts, sondern sie verbindet die gebotene Handlung mit dem Antrieb. Erst wenn, wie Kant schreibt, „die Verbindlichkeit so zu handeln mit einem Bestimmungsgrunde der Willkür [...] im Subjecte verbunden" (MS 6:218.21–23) wird und damit zur zunächst nur „theoretische[n]" (MS 6:218.20) Einsicht ein handlungswirksames (praktisches) Motiv hinzukommt, ist Pflichterfüllung gewährleistet. Die Form des *Antriebs* ist dabei definiert durch die Form des *Zwangs*, den die Gesetzgebung vorsieht und der seinerseits den Geltungsmodus ihrer Gesetze definiert.

3.3 Pflicht und Zwang

Bevor Kants im Anschluss an die allgemeine Definition zur Gesetzgebung thematisierte Unterscheidung zwischen juridischer und ethischer Gesetzgebung einer genaueren Analyse unterzogen werden kann, muss auf einen weiteren für das Verständnis der „Eintheilung einer Metaphysik der Sitten" wichtigen Begriff eingegangen werden, den Kant selbst in seine Argumentation einflicht: den Begriff des Zwangs. Kant ist der Ansicht, dass die Handlungen einer freien und dabei endlichen Willkür immer auch unter dem Aspekt der Nötigung betrachtet werden müssen. Hilfreich für ein Verständnis dieses Gedankengangs ist eine Stelle aus Kants *Vorlesung zur Moralphilosophie*, in der er – im Gegensatz zur Argumentation in der *Metaphysik der Sitten* – den Begriff des Zwangs erklärend einführt, *bevor* er zwischen „Jure" (V-Mo/Kaehler(Stark) 51.17) und „Ethic" (V-Mo/Kaehler(Stark) 51.17) unterscheidet:

> Der Zwang ist also nicht eine Nothwendigkeit sondern eine Nöthigung zur Handlung. Das Wesen aber, was genöthiget wird, muß ein solches seyn,

---

selbst würden den Anfang verhindern." (Ebd.) Es ist daher irreführend, zu sagen, dass sich im Handlungsvollzug etwas zwischen das Motiv und die Handlung stellt: „Das Motiv ist der Handlung stets gleich nah." (Ebd.)

14 Vgl. hierzu z. B. auch MS 6:213.32–35 sowie bereits V-Mo/Kaehler(Stark) 45.25 f.

welches diese Handlung ohne Nöthigung nicht thun würde, ja auch noch GegenGründe dawieder hätte. [...] Der Zwang ist demnach eine Nöthigung einer ungern geschehenen Handlung. (V-Mo/Kaehler(Stark) 45.8 – 14)

Das heißt: *Alle* Handlungen eines endlichen, mit einer freien Willkür begabten Wesens müssen, sofern sie Gegenstand der moralischen Gesetzgebung und damit Erfüllungen von Pflichten sind, als ‚erzwungen' vorgestellt werden. Kant hat diesen Zusammenhang von objektivem Gebotensein eines praktischen Gesetzes für ein endliches Vernunftwesen, Nötigung, Pflicht und Zwang in der *Kritik der praktischen Vernunft* an einer Stelle erläutert, die aufgrund ihrer argumentativen Dichte ausführlich wiedergegeben werden soll:

> Im ersteren Falle [d. h. in Bezug auf den Menschen, S.S.] aber hat das Gesetz die Form eines Imperativs, weil man an jenem zwar als vernünftigem Wesen einen reinen, aber als mit Bedürfnissen und sinnlichen Bewegursachen afficirtem Wesen keinen heiligen Willen, d. i. einen solchen, der keiner dem moralischen Gesetz widerstreitenden Maximen fähig wäre, voraussetzen kann. Das moralische Gesetz ist daher bei jenen ein Imperativ, der kategorisch gebietet, weil das Gesetz unbedingt ist; das Verhältnis eines solchen Willens zu diesem Gesetze ist Abhängigkeit, unter dem Namen der Verbindlichkeit, welche eine Nöthigung, obzwar durch bloße Vernunft und deren objectives Gesetz, zu einer Handlung bedeutet, die darum Pflicht heißt, weil eine pathologisch afficirte (obgleich dadurch nicht bestimmte, mithin auch immer freie) Willkür einen Wunsch bei sich führt, der aus subjectiven Ursachen entspringt, daher auch dem reinen objectiven Bestimmungsgrunde oft entgegen sein kann und also eines Widerstandes der praktischen Vernunft, der ein innerer, aber intellectueller Zwang genannt werden kann, als moralischer Nöthigung bedarf. (KpV 5:32.17 – 31)

Menschen müssen sich also, weil *subjektive*, in ihrer sinnlichen Natur liegende Gründe der Pflichtvorstellung meistenteils entgegenstehen, auch *subjektiv* zu Handlungen zwingen, die durch die Idee der Pflicht als notwendig vorgeschrieben werden. Jener „subjective Zwang" (V-Mo/Kaehler(Stark) 45.6) ist einer Definition aus der *Vorlesung zur Moralphilosophie* zufolge „die Nöthigung einer Person durch das, was in seinem Subject die gröste nöthigende und bewegende Krafft hat" (V-Mo/Kaehler (Stark) 45.7 f.). Das bewegende im Gegensatz zum einsehenden Moment in menschlichen Handlungen bezeichnet Kant, wie bereits erläutert, auch als ‚Triebfeder' des Handelns.

3.4 Recht und Ethik

Zwang ist die Nötigung zu einer Handlung, die ein endliches Wesen nur ungern tut. Da Menschen solche endlichen Wesen sind, müssen die Handlungen, zu denen sie als freie und der Moralität fähige Subjekte verbunden sind, erzwungen werden. Pflichterfüllung ist daher ohne Zwang nicht möglich, denn Pflicht heißt: „Nöthigung (Zwang) der freien Willkür durchs Gesetz" (TL 6:379.15 f.).[15] Im Gegensatz zur heutigen Verwendungsweise von ‚Zwang' verfügt Kant jedoch über einen Zwangsbegriff, der nicht auf die Nötigung durch die Willkür eines anderen beschränkt ist. Es gibt im Gegenteil auch einen Zwang, der von dem gezwungenen Subjekt selbst ausgeht. Ob die Pflichterfüllung aus einem solchen „Selbstzwang" (z. B. TL 6:380.35; KpV 5:83.32–84.1) oder aus „äußere[m] Zwang[]" (z. B. MS 6:220.4; RL 6:232.21 f.) hervorgeht, hängt dabei von der Art der Handlung ab, die erzwungen werden soll. Kant schreibt dazu in seiner „Eintheilung einer Metaphysik der Sitten":

> Die Pflichten nach der rechtlichen Gesetzgebung können nur äußere Pflichten sein, weil diese Gesetzgebung nicht verlangt, daß die Idee dieser Pflicht, welche innerlich ist, für sich selbst Bestimmungsgrund der Willkür des Handelnden sei, und, da sie doch einer für Gesetze schicklichen Triebfeder bedarf, nur äußere mit dem Gesetze verbinden kann. Die ethische Gesetzgebung dagegen macht zwar auch innere Handlungen zu Pflichten, aber nicht etwa mit Ausschließung der äußeren, sondern geht auf alles, was Pflicht ist, überhaupt. (MS 6:219.17–24)

Das heißt: Rechtsgesetze fordern keine Übereinstimmung von „Bestimmungsgrund der Willkür" (MS 6:219.19) und Gesetz. Eine Rechtspflicht ist erfüllt, wenn die Handlung äußerlich mit dem Gesetz übereinstimmt. In seiner Definition des Rechtsgesetzes fasst Kant diesen Gedanken folgendermaßen zusammen: „Also ist das allgemeine Rechtsgesetz: handle äußerlich so, daß der freie Gebrauch deiner Willkür mit der Freiheit von jedermann nach einem allgemeinen Gesetze zusammen bestehen könne [...]" (RL 6:231.10–12). Mit dieser Beschränkung der Rechtsgesetze auf äußeres Handeln kommt es im Recht gerade nicht darauf an, dass das Gesetz selbst der Grund ist, der zu der Handlung bewegt. Die juridische Gesetzgebung lässt im Gegenteil auch Antriebe zu, die sich extern zur

---

15 „Alle Obligation ist eine Art von Zwang [...]." (V-Mo/Kaehler(Stark) 48.14)

Pflicht verhalten.[16] Daraus, dass Rechtsgesetze allein auf (äußere) Handlungen Anwendung haben und die einer Handlung zugrunde liegende Gesinnung nicht Gegenstand der von ihnen ausgehenden Forderungen ist, folgt, dass die nötigende Instanz hier ein ‚äußeres‘, vom genötigten Subjekt verschiedenes Subjekt ist. Es ist in diesem Falle „die Willkür eines andern" (MS 6:218.12 f.), durch die die Befolgung einer Rechtspflicht (von außen, durch Androhung von Strafe) erzwungen wird.[17] Recht ist nach Kant die „Möglichkeit der Verknüpfung des allgemeinen wechselseitigen Zwanges mit jedermanns Freiheit" (RL 6:232.10 f.).

Während also im Recht Gesetzgeber und unterworfenes Subjekt von einander unterschieden sind, ist es in der Ethik ein und dasselbe Subjekt, das einerseits (sich selbst) das Gesetz vorgibt und andererseits diesem Gesetz verbunden ist. Ein solches Subjekt kann daher „Pflichten gegen sich selbst" (TL 6:417.3) haben. Als vernünftiges und zudem mit innerer Freiheit begabtes Subjekt ist der Mensch das „verpflichtende" (MS 6:417.7), als affizierbares, aber durch Vernunftgesetze in seinen Handlungen bestimmbares Subjekt ist er das „verpflichtete[]" (TL 6:417.7) „Ich" (TL 6:417.7). Diese Übereinstimmung von gesetzgebender und ausführender, unterworfener Instanz in einem einzigen Subjekt bedeutet genauer, dass die Nötigung zur Gesetzesbefolgung nur vom unterworfenen Subjekt selbst ausgehen kann.

Die Form der Nötigung in der Ethik steht außerdem in Verbindung zu der besonderen Bedeutung, die dem motivationalen Aspekt in der ethischen Gesetzgebung zukommt. Weil die Tugendgesetze die Pflichterfüllung aus der moralischen Gesinnung erfordern[18], ist die Nötigung zu einer moralisch wertvollen Handlung *nur durch das verpflichtete Subjekt selbst* möglich. Kant spricht in dieser Hinsicht vom „Selbstzwang" (TL

---

16 In diesem Zusammenhang präzisiert Kant den Gegenstand der Rechtslehre folgendermaßen: „Wenn die Absicht nicht ist Tugend zu lehren, sondern nur, was r e c h t sei, vorzutragen, so darf und soll man selbst nicht jenes Rechtsgesetz als Triebfeder der Handlung vorstellig machen." (RL 6:231.19–21)

17 Weil die Befolgung einer Rechtspflicht keine Frage der Gesinnung ist, ist sie, wie Kant an anderer Stelle darlegt, selbst für ein (vernunftbegabtes) „Volk von Teufeln" (ZeF 8:366.16) möglich. Denn in einer Staatsverfassung geht es nur darum, die widerstrebenden „Privatgesinnungen [...] auf[zu]halten, [so] daß in ihrem öffentlichen Verhalten der Erfolg eben derselbe ist, als ob sie keine solche böse Gesinnungen hätten" (ZeF 8:366.20–23).

18 Entsprechend dem „allgemeinen ethischen Gebote" (TL 6:391:3 f.) besteht die ‚moralische Gesinnung‘ darin, es sich zum Grundsatz zu machen, „pflichtmäßig aus Pflicht" (TL 6:391:4) zu handeln.

6:380.35), durch den sich das autonome, aber endliche Subjekt die moralische Gesinnung selbst vorschreibt und der dieser Gesinnung entsprechenden Handlung entgegen allen selbstsüchtigen Neigungen den Vorzug gibt. Während im Recht eine äußere Instanz die Durchsetzung des Rechts zwischen Rechtssubjekten erzwingen darf, ist es in der Ethik ein und dasselbe Subjekt, das sich durch die Vorstellung der Pflicht gezwungen fühlt und gleichzeitig zu ihrer Erfüllung zwingt.[19] Denn: „Ein Anderer kann mich zwar zwingen etwas zu thun, was nicht mein Zweck (sondern nur Mittel zum Zweck eines Anderen) ist, aber nicht dazu, daß ich es mir zum Zweck mache [...]." (TL 6:381.30–33)

Wie sich gezeigt hat, sind ethische und juridische Gesetze gleichermaßen Freiheitsgesetze und als solche praktische Vernunftgesetze mit apriorischer, unbedingter Gültigkeit für endliche Vernunftwesen. Daher erklärt bereits die Kaehler-Nachschrift von Kants *Vorlesung über Moralphilosophie*, der „Unterscheid vom Jure und der Ethic besteh[e] nicht in der Art der Verbindlichkeit, sondern in den BewegungsGründen, den Verbindlichkeiten ein Gnüge zu thun" (V-Mo/Kaehler(Stark) 51.16–19). In der „Einleitung in die Metaphysik der Sitten" nimmt Kant diesen Gedanken in seiner Unterscheidung zwischen juridischer und ethischer Gesetzgebung wieder auf:

> Alle Gesetzgebung also [...] kann doch in Ansehung der Triebfedern unterschieden sein. Diejenige, welche eine Handlung zur Pflicht und diese Pflicht zugleich zur Triebfeder macht, ist ethisch. Diejenige aber, welche das Letztere nicht im Gesetze mit einschließt, mithin auch eine andere Triebfeder als die Idee der Pflicht selbst zuläßt, ist juridisch. (MS 6:218.24 f.–219.1–6)

Mit Blick auf die vorangegangen Analysen zur Rolle der Triebfeder und des Zwangs im moralischen Handeln einer freien und dabei endlichen Willkür heißt das nun Folgendes: Als endliches Wesen verfügt der Mensch zwar über moralische Einsicht, muss zur dieser Einsicht gemäßen Handlung aber durch eine ‚Triebfeder' bewegt werden. Die von einem

---

19 Dies ist Kant zufolge auch der Grund, weshalb Menschen „Pflichten gegen sich selbst" (TL 6:417.3) haben können: Verpflichtetes und verpflichtendes Subjekt werden in ein und demselben Menschen gedacht, der einerseits als Naturwesen, andererseits als mit innerer Freiheit begabtes Vernunftwesen verstanden wird. (Vgl. TL 6:418.14–23) Die durch die Gesetzgebung vorgegebenen Vorschriften gehen daher in der Ethik nicht auf den Willen eines anderen Subjektes zurück, sondern sind rein vernünftige Vorschriften, deren Urheber das autonome Subjekt selbst ist. Eine solche ethische Gesetzgebung schreibt (innere) Handlungen „*a priori* durch bloße Vernunft" (MS 6:218.12) vor.

moralischen Gesetz vorgeschriebenen Handlungen begreift er als Pflichten, deren Erfüllung entweder von außen (durch andere, insbesondere durch eine öffentliche Gewalt) oder von innen (durch das vernunftbegabte Subjekt selbst) erzwungen wird.[20] Hinter einer jeden moralischen Handlung steht daher zum einen, als kognitiver Faktor, ein Gesetz, und zum anderen, als konativer Faktor im Handeln, eine Triebfeder. Dabei erkennt jemand etwas als Gesetz einer ethischen Gesetzgebung, wenn er dieses Gesetz selbst als zwingenden Beweggrund anerkennt. Seine Handlung entspricht den Forderungen dieser ethischen Gesetzgebung deshalb genau dann (und nur dann), wenn die erkannte Pflicht selbst die Triebfeder dieser Handlung ist.

Im Gegensatz dazu wird ein Gesetz der juridischen Gesetzgebung zwar als unbedingt nötigend wahrgenommen, die gesetzmäßige Handlung muss jedoch nicht durch die Vorstellung der Nötigung selbst motiviert sein. Daher basiert das Recht „zwar auf dem Bewußtsein der Verbindlichkeit eines jeden nach dem Gesetze" (RL 6:232.18 f.), es darf sich aber, wenn es um die Willensbestimmung geht, nicht „auf dieses Bewußtsein als Triebfeder […] berufen" (RL 6:232.20). Eine Handlung entspricht den Forderungen einer juridischen Gesetzgebung diesen Voraussetzungen entsprechend bereits dann, wenn sie als äußere Handlung mit dem Gesetz übereinstimmt. Das schließt nicht aus, dass auch Rechtspflichten prinzipiell aus dem Beweggrund der Pflicht erfüllt werden können. Die Handlung wird in diesem Fall zum Gegenstand der Ethik. Kant zeigt dies am Beispiel des Versprechens: „[S]ein Versprechen zu halten, […] [ist] eine Rechtspflicht, zu deren Leistung man gezwungen werden kann." (MS 6:220.11–13) Dennoch kann die „Leistung der Treue" (MS 6:220.8) eine „tugendhafte Handlung" (MS 6:220.13) sein, nämlich dann, wenn sie sich der Möglichkeit des äußeren Zwangs entzieht. (Vgl. MS 6:220.14) Dies ist z. B. dann der Fall, wenn jemand die „Leistung der Treue" (MS 6:220.8) erbringt, wenn er sich unbeobachtet wähnt und daher nicht befürchten muss, des Versprechensbruchs überführt zu werden.[21]

---

20 Vgl. zum letzten Punkt z. B. TL 6:379.15–17.
21 Es handelt sich hierbei um ein abgewandeltes Beispiel Kants, das er, wenn auch in einem anderen Kontext und mit anderer Funktion, in der *Grundlegung* anführt. (Vgl. KpV 5:27.21–36, 28.1–3)

3.5 Der Gegensatz von ‚Innen‘ und ‚Außen‘

Wie sich gezeigt hat, unterscheiden sich Rechtsgesetzgebung und Tugendgesetzgebung dem Text der *Metaphysik der Sitten* zufolge darin, dass die Befolgung von Tugendpflichten auf eine bestimmte Triebfeder, nämlich das Bewusstsein der Pflicht, angewiesen ist, während Rechtspflichten auch dann als erfüllt gelten, wenn die Handlung durch ein anderes Motiv als das der Pflicht selbst motiviert ist. Gleichwohl hebt auch die juridische Gesetzgebung auf Triebfedern ab (weil es sonst gar nicht zur Handlung kommt), die Triebfedern dürfen aber ihrem Inhalt nach beliebig sein. Im Gegensatz dazu ist es in einer ethischen Gesetzgebung das Gesetz selbst, das als Triebfeder gefordert wird. Das Gesetz ist damit notwendige und hinreichende Triebfeder eines Handelns, dem insofern moralischer Wert zukommt.[22]

Aufgrund der vorangegangenen Analysen ist es nun möglich, den Gegensatz von ‚Innen‘ und ‚Außen‘, der Kants Argumentation zur „Eintheilung einer Metaphysik der Sitten" durchzieht, genauer zu erläutern. In der „Einleitung zur Tugendlehre" schreibt Kant:

> Daß die Ethik Pflichten enthalte, zu deren Beobachtung man von andern nicht (physisch) gezwungen werden kann, ist blos die Folge daraus, daß sie eine Lehre der Zwecke ist, weil dazu (sie zu haben) ein Zwang sich selbst widerspricht. (TL 6:381.20–24)

---

22 Vgl. dazu: Willaschek, 1997, S. 213 f. Dass das Gesetz die Triebfeder ethischen Handelns sein muss, ist eine verkürzte Redeweise. Gemeint ist, dass die *Vorstellung* bzw. das *Bewusstsein* des Sittengesetzes zur Handlung motivieren muss, damit diese moralisch wertvoll ist. Dies legt zum einen eine Formulierung aus der *Grundlegung* nahe, der zufolge Moralität darin besteht, dass „nichts anders als die Vorstellung des Gesetzes an sich selbst" (GMS 4:401.11 f.) den Willen bestimmt. (Vgl. auch GMS 4:410.26 f.) Und auch an Stellen in der *Kritik der praktischen Vernunft* und in der *Metaphysik der Sitten* weist Kant konkret die „Vorstellung des Gesetzes" als moralische Triebfeder aus. (Vgl. KpV 5:151.15–17; TL 6:397.16 f.) Zum anderen muss das, was zur Handlung ‚antreibt‘, etwas sein, das dem Willen nicht als externe Ursache aufgezwungen wird, sondern ein solcher Antrieb muss durch das *Bewusstsein* desjenigen Subjektes begleitet und verursacht sein, das die Handlung ausübt. Handelt jemand im *Bewusstsein* des Sittengesetzes, so ist seine Handlung ihm selbst als moralische Handlung zurechenbar und frei. (Vgl. zu diesem Argument Beck, 1960, S. 208 f.) – Diesen Gedanken legt auch Kants Bezeichnung des moralischen Gesetzes als „*ratio cognoscendi*" (KpV 5:4.32) der Freiheit nahe, nach der das moralische Gesetz die Art und Weise bezeichnet, sich seiner Freiheit *bewusst* zu werden. (Vgl. KpV 5:4.28–37)

Da die Ethik nach der Moralität der Handlungen fragt, es ihr daher um die Grundsätze des Handelns (um Maximen, nicht bloß um beobachtbare Handlungen) geht[23] und diese Grundsätze weder beobachtbar sind[24] noch von außen (d. h. durch die Willkür eines andern) erzwungen werden können, so muss der Beweggrund zu dieser Handlung ein ‚innerer‘ sein, dessen propositionaler Gehalt das allgemeine moralische Gesetz ist. Während Rechtsgesetze gegenüber dem Beweggrund einer Handlung gleichgültig sind, sind es in der Ethik gerade jene „Gründe der Gesinnung" (V-Mo/Kaehler(Stark) 51.7 f.), die über die Qualität einer Handlung entscheiden und dieser zusätzlich zu ihrer Legalität auch Moralität verleihen. Wie gezeigt wurde, bezeichnet Kant diese subjektiven Bestimmungsgründe, die zudem das bewegende Element im menschlichen Handeln sind, auch als „Triebfeder[n]" (TL 6:380.3). Sie machen, wie er des Weiteren ausführt, einen bedeutenden Teil der „innere[n] Willensbestimmung" (TL 6:380.3) aus.

Dies ist nun die Begründung für Kants These, „[d]ie ethische Gesetzgebung [...] [sei] diejenige, welche nicht äußerlich sein [...] [könne]" (MS 6:220.19 f.).[25] Denn sie gibt, so Kants programmatische Wendung in der „Einleitung zur Tugendlehre", „nicht [die] Gesetze für die Handlungen [...], sondern nur für die Maximen der Handlungen" (TL 6:388.32 f.) und damit für „jene innere[n] Principien [...], die man nicht sieht" (GMS 4:407.15 f.). Kant bezeichnet die Tugend daher auch als „Stärke der Maxime des Menschen in Befolgung seiner Pflicht" (TL 6:394.15 f.) bzw. als „moralische Stärke des Willens" (TL 6:405.11) und „Stärke des Vorsatzes" (TL 6:390.22 f.).[26] Das heißt: Pflichten werden nach Forderung einer ethischen Gesetzgebung nur dann erfüllt,

---

23　Vgl. auch GMS 4:407.14–16.

24　„[...] die Maximen kann man nicht beobachten, sogar nicht allemal in sich selbst [...]." (RGV 6:20.27 f.)

25　Die Ethik unterscheidet sie sich vom Recht gerade darin, dass sie „den Selbstzwang nach (moralischen) Gesetzen in ihrem Begriffe mit sich führt" (TL 6:381.16 f.).

26　„Es ist nicht genug gesetzmäßig zu handeln (*legalitas actionis*) sondern diese Gesetzmäßigkeit muß überdem auch der Zweck der Handlung mithin für sich allein die Triebfeder derselben seyn (*moralitas*). Diese Qualität der Gesinnung (der Grund der Maxime) ist die Tugend (*ethica rectitudo*) hier wird der Wille über die Gesetze der Willkühr welche blos ihre Freyheit betreffen erweitert und die Nöthigung des Subjects durch das Gesetz im Allgemeinen über die Neigung als das Glückseeligkeitsprincip erhoben, welches Aufopferung und Wiederstand kostet dazu die Stärke des Vorsatzes die Tugend heißt." (VARL 23:258.13–21)

wenn eine bestimmte Eigenschaft des Willens vorliegt.[27] Tugend heißt, dass sich jemand aus eigenem Antrieb („nach einem Princip der innern Freiheit" (TL 6:394.22)) und das heißt aufgrund seiner Vorstellung der Pflicht pflichtgemäß verhält. Wie Kant insbesondere im „Ersten Abschnitt" der *Grundlegung* ausführt, ist die Handlung in diesem Falle nicht nur pflichtgemäß; sie wird „aus Pflicht" (GMS 4:397.13) ausgeführt und hat allein deshalb moralischen Wert. (Vgl. GMS 4:397.11– 401.16)[28]

Ich fasse zusammen: Eine moralische Gesetzgebung ist ‚innerlich', wenn sie die Rechtmäßigkeit einer Handlung aus guter Gesinnung erfordert. Sie ist ‚äußerlich', wenn es die Rechtmäßigkeit der Handlung ohne Rücksicht auf die dieser zugrunde liegenden Triebfedern ist, die sie zur Pflicht macht. Innerhalb einer solchen Gesetzgebung, die „auch äußerlich sein kann" (MS 6:220.21), können die entsprechenden Handlungen auch durch eine fremde Willkür erzwungen werden (‚äußerer Zwang'). Fordert eine Gesetzgebung wie die ethische hingegen, dass ich mir die Pflicht zum Zweck meines Handelns mache, so kann sie „nicht äußerlich sein" (MS 6:220.20), sondern setzt voraus, dass die ihr entsprechenden Handlungen ‚innerlich' erzwungen werden (‚Selbstzwang'). Es ist in diesem Falle ein „innerer, [...] intellektueller Zwang" (KpV 5:32.30), durch den sich das autonome Subjekt selbst nötigt und auf diese Weise moralisch wertvoll handelt. Diesen Voraussetzungen entsprechend kann die Erfüllung von Tugendpflichten nur dadurch gewährleistet werden, dass ein vernunftbegabtes Subjekt sich selbst zur Erfüllung dieser Pflichten zwingt. (Vgl. z.B. TL 6:395.5–8) Während Tugendpflichten in den Bereich der Ethik gehören, weil diese allein Gesetze für die Maximen der Handlungen vorschreibt und sich damit auf die Selbstverpflichtung des Einzelnen beruft, können Rechtspflichten

---

27 Diese Eigenschaft des Willens besteht darin, es sich zum Grundsatz zu machen, seine Pflicht aus Pflicht zu tun. Die „Beschaffenheit [...] des Willens" (TL 6:407.15), aus diesem Grundsatz zu handeln, bezeichnet Kant schließlich als „Tugend" (TL 6:407.11).

28 Moralität bedeutet daher sogar *mehr* als Pflichterfüllung: Eine Pflicht wird um ihrer selbst willen erfüllt, d.h. *weil sie Pflicht ist.* Der vernünftig eingesehene Grund für die Handlung ist selbst das Motiv, sie ausführen. Kant bezeichnet dieses Motiv als ‚Gefühl der Achtung'. Ob eine Handlung „aus Pflicht" (GMS 4:397.13) und damit „aus Achtung fürs Gesetz" (GMS 4:400.18 f.) oder aus einem anderen Motiv ausgeführt wird, ist entscheidend dafür, ob ihr Moralität oder Legalität zukommt. (Vgl. dazu GMS 4:397–401, 407 und KpV 5:81.10–19)

sowohl Gegenstand der inneren als auch der äußeren Gesetzgebung sein. So kann ich mir zwar „[d]as Rechthandeln [...] zur Maxime [...] machen" (RL 6:231.8 f.) – ich *muss* es aber nach Vorgabe der juridischen Gesetzgebung nicht. Dies ist allein „eine Forderung, die die Ethik an mich thut" (RL 6:231.9).[29]

3.6 ‚Enge' und ‚weite' Pflichten

Seine Unterscheidung zwischen Recht und Ethik führt Kant in der „Einleitung zur Tugendlehre" fort, wenn er die ethischen Pflichten (Tugendpflichten) dort als „Pflichten [...] von w e i t e r, dagegen die Rechtspflichten [als Pflichten, S.S.] von e n g e r Verbindlichkeit" (TL 6:390.2 f.) ausweist.[30] Ethische Pflichten sind ‚weite' Pflichten, weil sie die Maximen der Handlungen und nicht die Handlungen selbst betreffen und damit bei ihrer Befolgung ein „Spielraum (*latitudo*) für die freie Willkür" (TL 6:390.6 f.) bleibt. Kant räumt sofort das Missverständnis aus, dass man „unter einer weiten Pflicht [...] eine Erlaubnis zu Ausnahmen von der Maxime der Handlungen" (TL 6:390.9–11) zu verstehen habe.[31] Der „Spielraum" (TL 6:390.6 f.) betrifft vielmehr die

---

29 „Ä u ß e r e P f l i c h t e n sind die der L e i s t u n g e n [...] Innere Pflichten sind die der G e s i n n u n g e n." (VATL 23:251.7 f.)

30 Kant bezeichnet die „e n g e n" (TL 6:390.16) Pflichten auch als „vollkommene[]" (TL 6:390.17), die „weiten" (TL 6:390.9) Pflichten auch als „unvollkommene[] Pflichten" (TL 6:390.18). Seine mit dieser Unterscheidung vorgestellte These, „[d]ie unvollkommenen Pflichten s[eien] [...] allein Tugendpflichten" (TL 6:390.18), wird jedoch schon im Aufbau der „Ethischen Elementarlehre", deren erstes Buch den „vollkommenen Pflichten gegen sich selbst" (TL 6:421.5) gewidmet ist, fraglich. (Vgl. dazu Ludwig, 1990, S. XX–XXIV) Höffe, 2004, S. 266 bezeichnet die in der „Ethische[n] Elementarlehre" behandelten vollkommenen Pflichten gegen sich selbst als „Mischpflichten", weil diese die Merkmale vollkommener und unvollkommener Pflichten gleichermaßen erfüllen: Vollkommene Pflichten sind sie durch ihren Bezug auf äußere Handlungen, unvollkommene Pflichten bzw. Tugendpflichten sind sie durch den Selbstbezug, die sie als Gebote der Selbsterhaltung aufweisen.

31 Anlass zu diesem Missverständnis hatte bereits Kants Formulierung dieser Unterscheidung zwischen vollkommenen (engen) und unvollkommenen (weiten) Pflichten in der *Grundlegung* gegeben. Kant bezeichnet die vollkommenen Pflichten hier als diejenigen, „die keine Ausnahme zum Vortheil der Neigung verstatte[n]" (GMS 4:421.34 f.). Diese Charakterisierung suggeriert, dass die unvollkommenen Pflichten weniger streng (‚weit') sind und Ausnahmen zugunsten der Neigungen erlauben. Mit Blick auf Kants erneute Diskussion der

„Einschränkung einer Pflichtmaxime durch die andere [...]" (TL 6:390.11 f.) und damit nicht die Gesinnung oder den Pflichtcharakter der Tugendpflichten, sondern die *Ausübung* der Maximen und also die *Handlungen*.[32] Diese müssen unbestimmt bleiben, weil die Befolgung der Maximen eine Frage der Urteilskraft nach Klugheitsregeln und nicht nach Regeln der Sittlichkeit ist.[33] Wie Kant in den Vorarbeiten zur *Tugendlehre* ausführt, hat der „physische[] Effekt" (VATL 23:394.16 f.) des Zweckes, der durch das Gesetz zur Pflicht gemacht wird, „immer empirische Bedingungen an sich" (VATL 23:394.17) und erfordert daher „eine Überlegung in Ansehung technisch-practischer Imperative" (VATL 23:394.17 f.). Die ethischen Pflichten sind daher, weil sie die Maximen betreffen und keine eindeutig bestimmbaren Handlungen vorgeben, ‚unvollkommen'. (Vgl. z. B. TL 390.14 f.)

Unterscheidung der beiden Arten von Pflichten in der *Tugendlehre* interpretiert z. B. Stratton–Lake diese missverständliche Stelle in der *Grundlegung* wohlwollend dahingehend, dass sich unvollkommene und vollkommene Pflichten nicht in ihrer deontischen Stärke unterscheiden, sondern darin, welchen Gegenstand sie betreffen (nämlich entweder die Maximen und oder die Handlungen). (Vgl. Stratton–Lake, 2008, S. 108)

32 Voraussetzung ist, dass die Maxime während der Ausübung nicht verändert wird. (Vgl. VATL 23:391.30 f.)

33 „Daher [kann] der, welcher die Grundsätze der Tugend befolgt, zwar in der Ausübung im Mehr oder Weniger, als die Klugheit vorschreibt, einen F e h l e r (*peccatum*) begehen, aber nicht darin, daß er diesen G r u n d s ä t z e n mit Strenge anhänglich ist, ein L a s t e r (*vitium*) ausüben, [...]." (TL 6:433.27 – 30) Besonders prägnant äußert sich Kant zu diesem Punkt außerdem in den Vorarbeiten zur *Tugendlehre*: „Geht dieses Gesetz bestimmt und unmittelbar auf die Handlung so daß die Art wie? und der Grad wie viel? in ihr ausgeübt werden soll im Gesetz bestimmt ist so ist die Verbindlichkeit vollkommen (*obligatio perfecta*) und das Gesetz ist *stricte obligans* es bleibt uns keine Wahl übrig weder für ausnahmen wenn das Gesetz in seiner allgemeinheit gültig ist noch für das Maas der Befolgung desselben. *Gebietet aber das Gesetz nur nicht unmittelbar die Handlung sondern nur die* M a x i m e *der Handlung läßt es dem Urtheil des Subjects frey die Art wie und das Maas in welchem Grad das Gebotene ausgeübt werden solle* nur daß so viel als uns unter den gegebenen Bedingungen möglich ist davon zu thun nothwendig sey so ist die Verbindlichkeit unvollkommen und das Gesetz nicht von enger sondern nur weiter Verbindlichkeit *late obligans*." (VATL 23:394.1 – 13, kursiv teilw. S.S.) Zum „Spielraum" (TL 6:390.6 f.) weiter Pflichten in der *Metaphysik der Sitten* siehe auch: TL 6:393.4 – 10, 446.4 – 8. Zur Rolle der Urteilskraft in der Ausübung tugendhafter Maximen siehe KpV 5:67 – 71 und TL 6:411.10 – 17.

Eine weitere Begründung für die Weite ethischer Pflichten liegt in einer Eigenschaft dieser Pflichten selbst. Eine ethische Pflicht kann – streng genommen – nie ganz erfüllt werden, weil

a) man sich ethischer Pflichten nicht durch einzelne, eindeutig bestimmte Handlungen entledigen kann und

b) man seine eigene Gesinnung nie genau kennt (vgl. z. B. RGV 6:51.15 f., TL 6:392.30–33).

Da selbst dem handelnden Subjekt die eigene Gesinnung nie vollständig durchsichtig ist und sich Maximen genauso wenig „beobachten" (RGV 6:20.27 f.) lassen wie der intelligible Charakter (vgl. KrV A551/B579, Anm.), ist das Gebot des Sittengesetzes nur sinnvoll zu verstehen als Gebot des *Strebens* nach ‚Reinheit‘ der Maxime und Gesinnung, nicht aber nach der völligen Angemessenheit der Maxime zum Gesetz. Kants wiederholte Charakterisierung der Tugend als „moralische Gesinnung im Kampfe" (z. B. KpV 5:84.33 f.) ist in diesem Sinne zu verstehen, weil dem Menschen aufgrund seiner Sinnlichkeit und Unvollkommenheit immer nur eine Annäherung, nicht aber eine vollständige Übereinstimmung mit der Forderung des Sittengesetzes möglich ist.[34]

Schließlich ergibt sich das Merkmal der Weite einer ethischen Pflicht auch aus Kants Verständnis der Tugendlehre als einer objektiven Zwecklehre. So sind nach ethischer Gesetzgebung nicht Handlungen, sondern Zwecke geboten, die die für die Pflichterfüllung erforderlichen Handlungen ihrerseits noch nicht eindeutig festlegen.[35] Daher ist der „Spielraum" (TL 6:390.6 f.), den die ethischen Pflichten bei ihrer Befolgung lassen und der sie zu „we i t e [n]" (TL 6:390.2) Pflichten macht, eine Folge davon, dass Zwecke als Pflichten geboten sind.[36] Die Definition von Rechtspflichten als Pflichten von „e n g e r Verbindlichkeit"

---

34 Tugend und nicht Heiligkeit ist der „moralische[] Zustand" des Menschen. (Vgl. KpV 5:84.32–34) Mit Rücksicht darauf sind innere Pflichten bereits dann erfüllt, „wenn man die ernstliche Gesinnung hegt obgleich unvermögend sie zu vollführen" (VATL 23:251.13 f.).

35 Die Zwecke, die zu haben nach Kant Pflicht ist, sind eigene Vollkommenheit und fremde Glückseligkeit. (Vgl. z. B. TL 6:391–394) Aus diesen beiden formalen Zwecken resultieren eine Vielzahl von Zwecken, die Pflichten sind und damit eine Vielzahl von Tugenden, die der Mensch erwerben soll.

36 Kants Charakterisierung der ethischen Pflichten als ‚weite‘ Pflichten hat weit reichende Konsequenzen für den Aufbau seiner *Tugendlehre*. Da sie, im Gegensatz zur *Rechtslehre*, keine „b l o ß e Wi s s e n s l e h r e" (TL 6:375.14) ist, enthält sie neben einer ‚Elementarlehre‘ auch eine ‚Methodenlehre‘, die von der Anwendung von Maximen auf Einzelfälle handelt. (Vgl. TL 6:411.1–17)

(TL 6:390.3) folgt schließlich negativ aus der Tatsache, dass ihre Befolgung keinen „Spielraum" (TL 6:390.6 f.) lässt und ihn auch nicht zulässt. Gefordert sind einzelne (eindeutig bestimmte) Handlungen, die zugrunde liegende Gesinnung mag sein, welche sie wolle. Kant nennt die Pflichten einer juridischen Gesetzgebung daher auch ‚streng' im Sinne von ‚präzise'. (Vgl. TL 6:411.7)[37]

Eine Rechtspflicht zu befolgen heißt nach Kant außerdem, das zu tun, was man schuldet und was durch einen anderen, äußeren Willen erzwingbar ist. Jemand, der eine Rechtspflicht befolgt, tut seine Schuldigkeit, seine Handlung ist deshalb allein jedoch noch nicht lobenswert bzw. verdienstlich. (Vgl. RL 6:227.30–32, TL 6:390.30 f.) Im Gegensatz zum Recht fordert die Ethik mehr, sie geht über die Erfüllung von ‚messbaren' Schuldigkeiten hinaus.[38] Da sie Gesetze „nur für die M a x i m e n der Handlungen" (TL 6:388.33) vorgibt und es ihr nicht (allein) um die Handlungen, sondern um die Gesinnungen geht[39], entzieht sich der Gegenstand der ethischen Verpflichtung dem, was von außen erzwungen werden kann.[40] Eine Handlung, die der Befolgung einer ethi-

---

37 In Anlehnung an diesen Sprachgebrauch lassen sich unvollkommene Pflichten auch als ‚unpräzise' (im Sinne von: ungenauen) Pflichten verstehen, weil sie nicht angeben, wie die Pflicht in concreto erfüllt werden soll.

38 Im Recht hingegen ist es möglich, die mit der Erfüllung einer Pflicht zu erbringende ‚Leistung' auf der „Waage der Gerechtigkeit" genau ‚abzumessen'. (Vgl. TL 6:375.22–24)

39 Dass die Ethik mit der Ausrichtung ihrer Pflichten auf die den Handlungen zugrunde liegenden Gesinnungen ‚mehr' fordert, heißt jedoch nicht, dass das Rechtsgesetz einen weniger starken Verpflichtungscharakter hat als die Tugendgesetze. Zwar ist Kant zur Zeit der *Metaphysik der Sitten* nicht mehr der Ansicht, Recht und Ethik seien durch „das starke Gesetz der Schuldigkeit und das schwächere der Gütigkeit" (TG 2:335.4 f.) unterschieden, so dass Rechtspflichten einen stärkeren Verpflichtungscharakter aufweisen als Tugendpflichten. (Vgl. hierzu Kersting, 1997, S. 108 f.) Er definiert die Rechtspflichten jedoch als Pflichten „von e n g e r Verbindlichkeit" (TL 6:390.3), die inhaltlich genau bestimmt sind und – im Gegensatz zu den Tugendpflichten – keinen Deutungsspielraum enthalten.

40 „Was jemand pflichtmäßig m e h r thut, als wozu er nach dem Gesetze gezwungen werden kann, ist v e r d i e n s t l i c h (*meritum*); was er nur gerade dem letzteren a n g e m e s s e n thut, ist S c h u l d i g k e i t (*debitum*); was er endlich w e n i g e r thut, als die letztere fordert, ist moralische V e r s c h u l d u n g (*demeritum*)." (MS 6:227.30–34) Im Gegensatz zu rechtlichen Unterlassungen führt die Pflichtverletzung in der Ethik aber nicht zur Strafe; es bleibt lediglich das ethische Verdienst aus. Außerdem macht sich jemand moralisch schuldig erst dann, wenn die ethische Unterlassung tatsächlich auf einen bewusst gefassten Handlungs-

schen Pflicht dient, ist nicht nur moralisch richtig, sondern moralisch wertvoll, weil hier das Gesetz selbst das Motiv der Handlung ist.[41] Eine Person, die in dieser Hinsicht in Übereinstimmung mit einer bestimmten Tugendpflicht handelt, verhält sich *tugendhaft*. Sie macht es sich zum Prinzip, ihre Pflicht ‚aus Pflicht' zu erfüllen. Die Kultur einer solchen ethischen Gesinnung bezeichnet Kant als „verdienstlich" (TL 6:391.5). Mit ihr geht eine „moralische[] Lust" (TL 6:392.12) einher, die ihrerseits „über die bloße Zufriedenheit mit sich selbst [...] hinaus geht und von der man rühmt, daß die Tugend in diesem Bewußtsein ihr eigner Lohn sei" (TL 6:392.13–15, vgl. auch TL 6:396.32–34).[42]

Tugend ist nach Kant eine Eigenschaft des Willens (verstanden als Vermögen der Gesetzgebung) (vgl. TL 6:407.11–17), die in einem ständig befassten Vorgang moralisch-praktischer Deliberation erworben werden muss. (Vgl. TL 6:397.14 f.) Sie ist „eine Wirkung überlegter, fester und immer mehr geläuterter Grundsätze" (TL 6:383.36 f.). Tugendhaft sein bedeutet demnach, immer wieder „Stärke" zu beweisen angesichts des Vorsatzes, seine Pflicht zu befolgen. (Vgl. TL 6:405.15 f.) Dieser Vorstellung zufolge wird die Tugend (verstanden als Disposition) durch immer neue Tugendhandlungen verwirklicht. Je mehr Tugendpflichten jemand aus Pflicht erfüllt und sich damit der von der ethischen Gesetzgebung ausgehenden „Tugendverpflichtung" (TL 410.27) annimmt, desto vollkommener wird seine tugendhafte Gesinnung sein.[43]

---

grundsatz zurückgeht. Nicht jede moralisch wertlose Handlung ist daher zugleich ein Fall von moralischer Verschuldung. (Vgl. dazu TL 6:390.19–22)

41 Zu der Frage, inwiefern selbst die Richtigkeit einer moralischen Handlung bei Kant durch Motive gestützt wird, siehe Timmons, 2002.

42 Kants früher Unterscheidung zwischen ‚antreibenden' und ‚vergeltenden Belohnungen' zufolge handelt es sich bei der „ethischen Belohnung" (TL 6:391.10) um eine ‚vergeltende Belohnung': „Ein Praemium ist vom mercede zu unterscheiden. Die praemia sind entweder auctorantia oder remunerantia. Auctorantia sind solche Belohnungen, wo die Handlungen BewegungsGründe sind, wo man die Handlung blos wegen der verheissenen Belohnung thut; remunerantia sind solche Belohnungen, wo die Handlungen nicht BewegungsGründe sind, sondern die Handlung blos aus guter Gesinnung, aus reiner Moralitaet geschiht. Die ersten sind antreibende und die andern vergeltende Belohnungen. Demnach können die praemia auctorantia nicht moralia, die praemia remunerantia aber können moralia seyn" (V-Mo/Kaehler(Stark) 80.20–29).

43 Dieser Text geht auf einen Vortrag zurück, den ich im Juli 2008 auf einer Konferenz des DFG-Netzwerkes zu Kants Tugendlehre gehalten habe. Ich danke den Teilnehmern der Konferenz und Georg Mohr für wertvolle Diskussionen und Hinweise.

Literaturverzeichnis

Allison, Henry E. (1990), *Kant's Theory of Freedom*, Cambridge: Cambridge University Press.

Baumgarten, Alexander Gottlieb (1757): *Metaphysica*, Halle. (Wiederabgedruckt in: *Kants gesammelte Schriften*, Bd. 17, Preußische Akademie der Wissenschaften (Hrsg.), Berlin/Leipzig [1926]: Walter de Gruyter, S. 5–226; Bd. 15, Berlin/Leipzig [1923]: Walter de Gruyter, S. 5–54.)

Beck, Lewis White (1960), *A Commentary on Kant's 'Critique of Practical Reason'*, Chicago/London: University of Chicago Press.

Ebbinghaus, Julius (1958) [1988], „Die Idee des Rechtes", in: ders., *Gesammelte Schriften*, Bd. 2: *Philosophie der Freiheit. Praktische Philosophie 1955–1972*, Georg Geismann/Hariolf Oberer (Hrsg.), Bonn: Bouvier, S. 141–198.

Ebbinghaus, Julius (1960) [1988], „Kants Rechtslehre und die Rechtsphilosophie des Neukantianismus", in: ders., *Gesammelte Schriften*, Bd. 2: *Philosophie der Freiheit. Praktische Philosophie 1955–1972*, Georg Geismann/Hariolf Oberer (Hrsg.), Bonn: Bouvier, S. 231–248.

Geismann, Georg (2006), „Recht und Moral in der Philosophie Kants", in: *Jahrbuch für Recht und Ethik*, Bd. 14, S. 3–124.

Gregor, Mary (1990), „Kants System der Pflichten in der ‚Metaphysik der Sitten'", in: Immanuel Kant, *Metaphysische Anfangsgründe der Tugendlehre*, Bernd Ludwig (Hrsg.), Hamburg: Meiner, S. XXIX–LXV.

Guyer, Paul (2002), „Kant's Deductions of the Principles of Right", in: Timmons (Hrsg.) (2002), S. 23–64.

Höffe, Otfried (2004), „Kant über Recht und Moral", in: Karl Ameriks/Dieter Sturma (Hrsg.), *Kants Ethik*, Paderborn: Mentis, S. 249–268.

Käubler, Bruno (1917), *Der Begriff der Triebfeder in Kants Ethik*, Universität Weida, Diss.

Kersting, Wolfgang (1984), *Wohlgeordnete Freiheit. Immanuel Kants Rechts- und Staatsphilosophie*, Berlin/New York: Walter de Gruyter.

Kersting, Wolfgang (1997), „‚Das starke Gesetz der Schuldigkeit und das schwächere der Gütigkeit'" in: ders., *Recht, Gerechtigkeit und demokratische Tugend. Abhandlungen zur praktischen Philosophie der Gegenwart*, Frankfurt/M.: Suhrkamp, S. 74–120.

Ludwig, Bernd (1988), *Kants Rechtslehre*, Hamburg: Meiner.

Ludwig, Bernd (1990), „Einleitung", in: Immanuel Kant, *Metaphysische Anfangsgründe der Tugendlehre*, Bernd Ludwig (Hrsg.), Hamburg: Meiner, S. XIII–XXVIII.

Oberer, Hariolf (1997), „Sittengesetz und Rechtsgesetze a priori", in: ders. (Hrsg.), *Kant. Analysen, Probleme, Kritik*, Bd. 3, Würzburg: Könighausen & Neumann, S. 157–200.

Pogge, Thomas W. (2002), „Is Kant's Rechtslehre a 'Comprehensive Liberalism'?", in: Timmons (Hrsg.) (2002), S. 133–158.

Ripstein, Arthur (2004), „Authority and Coercion", in: *Philosophy and Public Affairs*, Bd. 32, Nr. 2, S. 2–35.

Rohs, Peter (1986), „Gedanken zu einer Handlungstheorie auf transzendental-philosophischer Grundlage", in: Gerold Prauss (Hrsg.), *Handlungstheorie und Transzendentalphilosophie*, Frankfurt/M.: Klostermann, S. 219–245.

Schadow, Steffi (2009), *Moral und Motivation bei Kant*, Frankfurt/M., Johann Wolfgang Goethe-Universität, Diss.

Schwaiger, Clemens (1999), *Kategorische und andere Imperative. Zur Entwicklung von Kants praktischer Philosophie bis 1785*, Stuttgart-Bad Cannstatt: Fromann Holzboog.

Seel, Gerhard (2009), „How Does Kant Justify the Universal Objective Validity of the Law of Right?", in: *International Journal of Philosophical Studies*, Bd. 17, S. 71–94.

Stratton–Lake, Philip (2008), „Being Virtuous and the Virtues: Two Aspects of Kant's 'Doctrine of Virtue'", in: Monika Betzler (Hrsg.), *Kant's Ethics of Virtue*, Berlin/New York: Walter de Gruyter, S. 101–121.

Timmons, Mark (Hrsg.) (2002), *Kant's 'Metaphysics of Morals': Interpretative Essays*, Oxford: Oxford University Press.

Timmons, Mark (2002), „Motive and Rightness in Kant's Ethical System", in: Timmons (Hrsg.) (2002), S. 255–288.

Tretter, Friedrich (1997), „Freie Willkür, Freiheit, Recht und Rechtsgültigkeit bei Kant", in: Hariolf Oberer (Hrsg.), *Kant. Analysen, Probleme, Kritik*, Bd. 3, Würzburg: Königshausen & Neumann, S. 151–251.

Willaschek, Marcus (1997), „Why the 'Doctrine of Right' does not belong in the 'Metaphysics of Morals'. On some Basic Distinctions in Kant's Moral Philosophy", in: *Jahrbuch für Recht und Ethik*, Bd. 5, S. 205–227.

Willaschek, Marcus (2005), „Recht ohne Ethik?", in: Volker Gerhardt (Hrsg.), *Kant im Streit der Fakultäten*, Berlin/New York: Walter de Gruyter, S. 188–204.

Willaschek, Marcus (2009), „Right and Coercion: Can Kant's Conception of Right be Derived from his Moral Theory?", in: *International Journal of Philosophical Studies*, Bd. 17, S. 49–70.

Wood, Allen (2002), „The Final Form of Kant's Practical Philosophy", in: Timmons (Hrsg.) (2002), S. 1–21.

Prior Concepts of the Metaphysics of Morals (MS 6:221–228)

Manfred Baum[1]

After Kant has treated the idea and the necessity as well as the divisions of the *Metaphysics of Morals*, he produces in section IV of the "Introduction" (MS 6:211–228) the "prior concepts [Vorbegriffe]" (MS 6:221.5, trans. K.S.[2]) that belong to it, along with their definitions, in a sequence of which the principle of selection and of order can be recognized only with difficulty. His discussion is introduced by treatments of freedom and moral laws and interrupted by the introduction of the "supreme principle of the doctrine of morals" (MS 6:226.1) and of a new definition of the concepts of freedom of will (*Wille*) and choice (*Willkür*). One can recognize Kant's intention to introduce only such fundamental concepts as are "common to the metaphysics of morals in both its parts" (MS 6:222.1 f., trans. K.S.), thus which belong to the doctrine of right and to the doctrine of virtue.

The subtitle of this section, "*Philosophia practica universalis*" (MS 6:221.6), is apparently taken from Christian Wolff's work of the same name[3], to which Baumgarten had already referred in his *Initia Philosophiae Practicae Primae*[4]. Kant repeatedly made Baumgarten's *Initia* the basis of his lectures on moral philosophy.

Kant referred already in the "Preface" to the *Groundwork of the Metaphysics of Morals* (1785) to "the celebrated Wolff's" (GMS 4:390.20) propaedeutic to his moral philosophy, in order to distinguish it from his own metaphysics of morals and its groundwork. There he had oriented himself by Baumgarten's version of the Wolffian enterprise. "[T]he authors [!]" (GMS 4:391.3) of this "*universal practical philosophy*" (GMS 4:390.21 f.), Kant complained in 1785, "form their concept of *obligation*, which is anything but moral" (GMS 4:391.10–12); and so Kant, in his own "*Philosophia practica universalis*" of 1797, for his part begins the ser-

---

1 Translated by Kathryn Sensen.
2 ‚K.S.' is short for ‚Kathryn Sensen'.
3 Cf. Wolff, 1738–1739.
4 Cf. Baumgarten, 1760.

ies of concepts that are common to both parts of his metaphysics of morals with a new definition of "[o]*bligation*" (MS 6:222.3). This concept, as well as the related concepts of the imperative, of the permissible and impermissible and of duty, are introduced already in the second paragraph of our section IV, before each is then given its own definition in turn (paragraphs 4–7).

The starting point and fundamental concept of the metaphysics of morals is the concept of freedom. Kant's moral philosophy is distinguished from all previous moral-philosophic enterprises in the realm of natural right and ethics by the fact that it interprets the doctrine of morals as a whole as a doctrine of the laws of freedom and the duties that correspond to them. Thus we read in the Vigilantius lecture notes (1793/94): "[…] Professor Kant […] calls […] all moral laws (i. e., those that lay down the condition under which something should happen, as opposed to *leges naturae, physicae*, which merely state the condition under which a thing does happen) *leges libertatis*, laws of freedom, and he includes among them the […] *leges justi et honesti* (*ethicae*)" (V-MS/Vigil 27:523.35–524.1).

The concept of freedom is according to Kant a concept of pure reason that belongs to theoretical and practical philosophy. For merely theoretical or speculative philosophy it is "transcendent," insofar as it goes beyond all possible experience, in which—as is the case for all ideas or concepts of pure reason—"no instance corresponding to it" (MS 6:221.8 f.) can be given. That freedom in the sense of the idea of reason cannot be ascribed to any object of inner or outer experience follows for Kant from the fact that the possibility of experience for its part is based on the determination by natural laws, on the predetermination, of all objective events by preceding causes, by which these events are made necessary. That holds especially for all inner and outer actions of a human being that can be experienced. But because, according to the *Critique of Pure Reason*, all cognition (*Erkenntnis*) possible to us is either empirical or pure cognition of objects of possible experience, freedom is already for that reason no object of theoretical cognition possible to us; for the freedom of an acting cause would stand in contradiction to the conditions of its possible experience, which are valid a priori. Nonetheless, in the attribution of a voluntary (*willkürlich*) action that we reproach, we make use of freedom as a "regulative principle of reason" (KrV A554/B582), as the *Critique of Pure Reason* says, in that we presuppose that acting reason is "in its causality not subject to any conditions of appearance or of the temporal series" (KrV A556/B584), thus in the negative sense "free, i. e., […] it could be the sensibly unconditioned condition of appearances" (KrV

A557/B585). Freedom cannot, in this kind of theoretical explanation of a voluntary action, "hold as a constitutive but solely as a regulative and, indeed, merely negative principle of speculative reason" (MS 6:221.11–13), i.e., it can be thought without contradiction as a kind of causality independent of time.

In contrast, the practical use of reason certifies the "reality" of the concept of freedom, insofar as "practical principles, as laws, prove a causality of pure reason to determine choice independently of any empirical conditions (of sensibility generally)" (MS 6:221.14–16, trans. K.S.). Freedom then means here a causality of pure practical reason that consists in this, that reason gives choice "laws"[5] and thereby subjects to itself the maxims of choice and the outer and inner actions in accordance with these maxims (cf. MS 6:214.2). Since now, as was said in section I, the will can be seen as practical reason itself (cf. MS 6:213.22–26), the proof of the causality of pure practical reason in its lawgiving is tantamount to the evidence of a "pure will in us" (MS 6:221.17).

One thereby gains a "positive concept of freedom" (MS 6:221.19, trans. K.S.), as Kant says, which at the same time implies the negative concept already familiar from the *Critique of Pure Reason.* For the causality of pure practical reason in its determination of choice is "independent [] of any empirical conditions," and since these are circumscribed by "sensibility generally" (MS 6:221.15 f.), this independence means not only a freedom from natural inclinations of the faculty of desire, but also from all feelings, including the so-called moral feelings. The positive element in this concept of freedom consists in the fact that pure practical reason determines choice through laws and thereby refers indeed not directly to actions, but to maxims for these actions as subjective grounds of determination for its actions. Therefore pure practical reason has causality and positive freedom only in the sense that it, through its lawgiving for maxims (of outer and inner actions), prescribes for them a norm (with regard to their form).

Here too Kant avoids ascribing positive or negative freedom to the pure will, not even "from a practical point of view" (MS 6:221.19). The grounds for this will become apparent later. But he says that the "moral concepts and laws have their source" (MS 6:221.17 f.) in the pure will. By means of these moral concepts and laws, pure reason has, "from a practical point of view," positive freedom, i.e., causality in the

---

5 Quotations for which the reference is not given immediately are covered by the following reference.

determination, that is to say in the necessitation, of choice. One should note that Kant speaks in the plural about moral concepts and particularly about moral laws (cf. MS 6:221.15). The concepts are those of right and of virtue and the concepts derived from them. The laws cannot mean "the supreme principle of the doctrine of morals" (MS 6:226.1) alone, but rather it together with the "universal law of right" (MS 6:231.10), the "supreme principle of the doctrine of virtue" (TL 6:395.15) and the moral laws that can be derived from them.

The second paragraph concerns these moral laws, about which Kant says that they are "based" on "this [...] positive concept of freedom" (MS 6:221.19 f., trans. K.S.). The moral laws, as unconditional practical laws, have their source a priori in the causality of pure reason qua lawgiver for human action. In this sense one can say that pure reason becomes practical, not in that it determines itself to actions, but rather in that it prescribes for the faculty of choice laws for its outer and inner acting that stem from reason, and therein is positively free, i.e., not in being simply independent of feelings and desires, but rather in that it performs its own (necessary) 'action' of lawgiving. Moral laws are not as such imperatives, i.e., commands or prohibitions of outer or inner actions, but only imperatives for us "whose choice is sensibly affected and so does not of itself conform to the pure will but often opposes it" (MS 6:221.21 f.). If pure practical reason as pure will commands or forbids actions of our choice, this happens through categorical imperatives, i.e., through such imperatives as command or forbid unconditionally in the sense that they presuppose no end of choice which should be realized by its actions as a means. Because the prohibition of any action can be understood as a command for its omission, one can say in general that categorical imperatives are unconditional commands, while technical imperatives command only under the condition that a purpose will be attained through the commanded action, as is the case for "precepts of art" (MS 6:221.24) or user instructions, which are not laws and certainly not moral laws. Actions that accord with a categorical imperative as a practical law are permissible or morally possible, while actions that do not accord with it are impermissible or morally impossible.

Among the permissible or morally possible actions, some are morally necessary, namely those whose "opposite" (MS 6:221.27), i.e., whose omission, is morally impossible or impermissible. Conversely those omissions (of actions) are morally necessary whose performance is morally impossible or impermissible. Thus the morally necessary actions are a subset of permissible or morally possible actions, namely those that are made "obligatory" (MS 6:221.28) by the practical law or the categorical imperative. Such an obligation makes the action commanded by law into a "duty" (MS 6:221.28). The observance or transgression 'of a duty' thus results from the agreement or disagreement of a person's action with a practical law that holds for him, and from the obligation grounded in it to act in a certain way.

Now Kant defines moral feeling (in the sense of the faculty of feeling) as "the susceptibility to feel pleasure or displeasure merely from being aware that our actions are consistent with or contrary to the law of duty" (TL 6:399.19–21). Consequently the observance or transgression of a law of duty by a human action is "indeed connected" in the agent himself (and where applicable in other human beings) "with a pleasure or displeasure of a distinctive kind (that of moral *feeling*)" (MS 6:221.29 f., trans. K.S.). But Kant insists that "in practical laws of reason we take no account of" (MS 6:221.36) these feelings. He cites two grounds for this:

(1) these feelings do not concern "the *basis* of practical laws," for this lies in pure practical reason, but rather they concern only "the subjective *effect* in the mind [Gemüth] when our choice is determined by those" (MS 6:221.31–33, trans. K.S.) practical laws. The determination of choice through practical laws is thus seen by Kant as a process of mind (*Gemütsvorgang*). But this psychological fact, according to Kant, says nothing about the origin and the validity of these laws; he thereby distances himself from the psychologism of Wolff and his school as well as from British moral-sense philosophy. For the psychological facts that are spoken of here show only that the subjective effect in the mind of the actor "can differ from one subject to another" (MS 6:221.35 f.). But with that the rug is pulled out from a grounding of the validity of moral-practical laws as such, i. e., as universal and necessary norms in a moral philosophy as metaphysics of morals.

(2) A consideration of that effect in the mind of the agent is somewhat superfluous. For this subjective and real effect can "objectively, i. e., in the judgment of reason" neither "add to [nor, M.B.] detract from" the "validity or influence" (MS 6:221.33–35, trans. K.S.) of those moral-practical laws on our choice. The "aesthetic prior concepts [[ä]sthetische Vorbegriffe] of the mind's receptivity to concepts of duty as such," (TL 6:399.2 f., trans. K.S.), to which moral feeling belongs and which Kant himself treats in the "Introduction" (section XII (TL 6:399.1–403.6)), contribute nothing to the grounding and justification of moral laws and duties. In addition, Kant's choice of the words "con-

cepts of duty as such" and 'law of duty' already indicate that the so-called 'moral feelings' represent no distinguishing mark of ethics or doctrine of virtue, but rather are generally connected with "observance or transgression" of "duty" and with "the determination of our choice through those" (MS 6:221.28–33, trans. K.S.) moral laws, thus also with the duty of right and the laws of right. But because all duties as such, i. e., "just because they are duties, belong to ethics" (MS 6:219.31 f.), so it is appropriate that Kant treats the "aesthetic prior concepts" in the "Introduction to the Doctrine of Virtue."

Kant does not justify the selection of concepts that should be common to both parts of the metaphysics of morals, the doctrine of right and ethics, and their sequence. But one should not overlook that these concepts for the most part are contained in Baumgarten's *Initia philosophiae practicae primae* and Achenwall's *Ius naturae*[6] as well as his *Prolegomena iuris naturalis*[7]. The claim that these concepts are common to the doctrine of right and ethics obliges the interpreter to understand them in such a way that their definitions can apply to both parts of moral philosophy, although Kant occasionally makes comments which can only hold for the doctrine of right. That may have its ground in the fact that the "Introduction to the Metaphysics of Morals" was published in the first volume of the complete *Metaphysics of Morals*, which contains the "Metaphysical First Principles of the Doctrine of Right." The list begins, as already noted, with obligation and its definition. There Kant apparently presupposes that the concept of free action or of the "*act of free choice*" (MS 6:218.32 f.) is already familiar. In the explanation of the definition of obligation, the concept of the imperative is introduced first, and then that of the categorical imperative.

Kant defines "*obligation*" as "the necessity of a free action under a categorical imperative of reason" (MS 6:222.3 f.). With this definition he apparently begins from the conventional concept of *obligatio*, which describes the relationship of a (practical or moral) law to a (free) action, by which this becomes a duty or a commanded action. In the place of the law Kant puts the imperative of reason, which, as categorical, is a command of pure practical reason. An "imperative is a practical rule by which an action in itself contingent is m a d e necessary" (MS 6:222.5 f.). By a practical rule, an ontologically contingent action, such as free action, becomes practically necessary and thus obligatory, whereby

6   Cf. Achenwall, 1763a.
7   Cf. Achenwall, 1763b.

this ought need not be moral. An imperative is a special kind of practical laws that is distinguished from its genus by a specific difference in those who are subject to the law. A practical law indeed "represents" (MS 6:222.8) the necessity of an action, i.e., it states how an acting subject necessarily acts; but it leaves open whether this necessary action "already inheres by an *inner* necessity in the acting subject (as in a holy being)" (MS 6:222.9 f.), because this way of acting is a consequence of its essence (which also applies to an *automaton spirituale* (cf. KpV 5:97.15)), or whether relative to the acting subject, as in the case of human beings, it is something in itself contingent, i.e., an action that one can omit without ceasing to be a human being. For the actions of human beings cannot be made necessary by a practical law alone, but rather they can also be determined on natural grounds, i.e., they can be necessary under given conditions, but contingent with respect to his being. Imperatives are practical laws for free subjects whose actions are internally contingent. Thus every imperative is a practical law, but not every practical law is an imperative. In other words: It makes no sense to command a subject to perform actions if he already necessarily performs them. Conversely, then, it only makes sense to command a subject who is capable of actions if it is also possible for him not to carry them out. Only for beings free in this sense—whose actions are necessary neither as a consequence of their essence nor as effects of nature—can an action be commanded by an imperative. "Hence an imperative is a rule the representation of which *makes* necessary an action that is subjectively contingent" (MS 6:222.12 f.). Only a subject "that must be *constrained* (necessitated) to conform with the rule" (MS 6:222.14 f.), because he does not perform actions that accord with the rule on his own or for other reasons, can be the addressee of an imperative. Reason thus commands only such acting subjects as do not always fulfill its command already.

Then follows the definition of the categorical imperative as a special case of imperatives: "A categorical (unconditional) imperative is one that represents an action as objectively necessary and makes it necessary not indirectly, through the representation of some end that can be attained by the action, but through the mere representation of this action itself (its form), and hence directly" (MS 6:222.15–19). Thus it is not the case that an action is commanded by a categorical imperative as a necessary means for reaching an end, which every action naturally has; but rather as itself, i.e., according to its maxims (or general form), an action is by reason (1) thought as objective, i.e., as a necessary action for every rational acting subject, and (2) made subjectively necessary, i.e., it is represented to the subject as an action he is to perform. This special consciousness of obligation is specifically moral; moral imperatives prescribe an obligation that can only be grounded in a moral philosophy that stands by itself, i.e., that is independent of all theoretical knowledge and at the same time is universally valid. Their practical prescriptions are distinguished from all that falls outside the scope of morality by the unconditional character and universal validity of the demand to act in a certain way, where the implicit end of the commanded action has no role in grounding this command. "All other imperatives are *technical* and are, one and all, conditional" (MS 6:222.22 f.). The action (*praxis*) that is commanded by them is in the simplest case only a making (*poiesis*), a bringing forth of works for whose production the commanded action is seen as useful; i.e., hypothetical imperatives command actions only as means to given ends. In general one can say that all realization of ends is action conditioned on the given and theoretically recognizable nature of things (including the available means and the capacity of the acting subject himself). In particular so-called happiness, for the attainment of which certain actions and omissions can be commanded, is for Kant an (end or) object of technical-practical reason, to which only (hypothethical) imperatives of prudence conditioned by reason can correspond, which therefore are to be excluded from morality.

If these are the characteristics of categorical imperatives, then there is room to doubt their possibility, and so also the possibility of a doctrine of morals that deals with them. What remains of a possible command for free action, one could ask, if the only thing that can be commanded of the faculty of choice (*Willkür*) is this acting itself, according to its universal form. Kant's answer reads: "The ground of the possibility of categorical imperatives is this: that they refer to no other property of choice (by which some purpose can be ascribed to it) than simply to its *freedom*" (MS 6:222.23–26). Categorical imperatives thus do not only presuppose, like all imperatives, the acting subject's freedom of choice, but they are laws for this freedom of choice as such, by which it determines itself to outer and inner actions. They are laws of freedom in the sense that through them only freedom itself, i.e., the willing and the outer action of choice according to its inner structure, is regulated, independent of all grounds and consequences of the action that may lie in the possible experience of the inner and outer nature of the acting subject. Acting from choice (*das Willkürhandeln*) itself and as such is the only possible addressee that the practical law of a categorical imperative can command.

The second fundamental concept of Kant's *philosophia practica universalis* is that of permissible (and accordingly of impermissible) action. As it will turn out, there are two meanings of permissible action that Kant distinguishes, following Achenwall's *Prolegomena*.[8] The first concerns the "*licitum*" (MS 6:222.27). Kant defines a permissible action in the sense of the *licitum* as an action "which is not contrary to obligation" (MS 6:222.27 f.). Since the obligation of an action is grounded in a law and since laws may command or forbid, there are two kinds of obligation to distinguish and so also two ways of not being contrary to the law: either an action is permissible because it is not contrary to a command not to do something, i. e., because something is done that is not against a prohibition to do it; or an omission is permissible because it is not against a command not to omit it (but to do it), i. e., because something is omitted that is not contrary to a prohibition to omit it. These distinctions are based simply on the distinction between doing and omitting as two kinds of acting. But one can also construe human activity solely in terms of acting and see prohibitions as commands of omission, thus as specific commands for acting. Since a law then simply commands an action (if one disregards two kinds of laws and actions), there is likewise only one obligation grounded in law. Then it appears that there must also be only one kind of permissible actions (namely in the sense of the *licitum*). However, that is *not* the case. For if an action is permissible that is not contrary to obligation, then this is possible in two ways: Either the action is permissible because it is not contrary to law or is not forbidden, or because it is commanded by law. For also in that case the action is "not opposed" (MS 6:222.27 f., trans. K.S.) to obligation or the law. In brief, commanded actions are also permissible. Thus there are two kinds of permissible actions in the sense of the *licitum*, those that are not contrary to law, i. e., those that are in accord with law, and the commanded actions or duties.

Now Kant turns from permissible action to the acting subject. The subject's freedom, in the case of a permissible action, "is not limited by any opposing imperative" (MS 6:222.28 f.). The limitation of freedom by an imperative opposed to it comes about through a prohibition to perform a particular action. Thus the action that is not forbidden by an imperative is permissible, and relative to this imperative the acting subject has retained his freedom or authorization to perform this action that is not forbidden by the imperative. Kant also calls this authorization "*facul-*

---

8   Cf. Hruschka, 1986, p. 46.

tas moralis" (MS 6:222.29) or "*facultas moralis generatim*" (TL 6:383.5 f.), and he distinguishes it later from the "*facultas iuridica*" (TL 6:383.7) that appears in the doctrine of right. The latter is synonymous with the subjective right of a person. One could also understand authorization (*Befugnis*) in its general sense as entitlement or as moral capacity to do something, independently of whether the (unrestrictive) law is a law of right or ethics, or whether the (unrestrictive) moral imperative is juridical or ethical. But it is more important that authorization is a kind of freedom of choice, namely the freedom, unrestricted by a particular imperative, to do both everything that is not forbidden as well as what is commanded by this imperative. The "*illicitum*" (MS 6:222.30) or the impermissible action is accordingly one that is opposed by an obligation (due to a prohibition), or one whose omission is commanded by the imperative.

The concept of duty is defined by Kant as "that action to which someone is bound" (MS 6:222.31). As with the concept of permissible action and later with the concept of deed (*Tat*), the concept of obligation is the basis of the definition of other fundamental moral concepts. The definition of duty is very traditional and accords with the textbooks on natural law that Kant used. That through which I am bound to an action, the basis of obligation, is a law or an imperative. Thus duty is that to which there is an obligation, "the matter of obligation" (MS 6:222.32). This action can be an outer action of choice, also in relation to other acting subjects (as in the doctrine of right), or an inner action of setting an end or of the selection and adoption of a maxim. One and the same action can become a duty through different ways of obliging us to it. So the omission of a lie, i.e., of an outer action regarding other human beings, can be commanded or become obligatory either juridically, i.e., according to a law for outer actions, or ethically, i.e., according to a law for the inner action of setting an end. Thus the various kinds of obligation need not result in various duties "as to the action" (MS 6:222.33). The action that accords with duty, then, is that outer or inner use of the freedom of choice that is determined by obligation or made necessary by a categorical imperative.

In his elucidation of the concept of duty and its definition, Kant specifies a second meaning of permissible actions to be distinguished from the *licitum* (in both its kinds). Kant begins again from the concept of obligation. A categorical imperative, as a moral-practical law, asserts only "an obligation with respect to certain actions" (MS 6:222.35 f.). It says that certain actions must be performed regardless of their ends,

i. e., that they have practical unconditional necessity. But beyond that it contains also the *"necessitation"* (MS 6:223.2 f.) of the acting subject to an action, and indeed by the law that it itself is. Thus this moral-practical law does not merely, like every practical law, make a pronouncement about how one must act, but it itself lays on me the obligation to perform a certain action; it makes the objective practical necessity to act in a certain way into one that is subjectively valid for an agent, which is expressed with an Ought. Therefore the categorical imperative is not only a moral-practical law, but "a law that either commands or prohibits, depending on whether it represents as a duty the commission or omission of an action" (MS 6:223.3–5). The agent is obliged to the commission or omission of an action by a categorical imperative, by which an action becomes obligatory and determinate, and thus commanded or forbidden.

At this point Kant introduces the second kind of the permissibility of an action, which supplements an action's conformity to law or to a command, which exists merely relative to a given practical law and which is the sense of the *licitum*, with the term "merely *permitted*" (MS 6:223.6).[9] "An action that is neither commanded nor forbidden is merely *permitted*" (MS 6:223.5 f.). Joachim Hruschka pointed out that the lack of emphasis on the word "merely" in the printing of the *Metaphysics of Morals* may have contributed to the fact that the distinctions Kant took over from Achenwall were not recognized as such and were soon lost again.[10] The merely permitted action in Kant corresponds to the *actio permissa* in Achenwall, who defines it as an action neither commanded (*praecepta*) nor forbidden (*prohibita*) by the lawgiver.[11] This mere permissibility of an action results from the fact that relative to it or, as Kant says, "with regard to it there is no law limiting one's freedom (one's authorization) and so too no duty" (MS 6:223.6–8, trans. K.S.). One could therefore also describe it as absolutely permitted, which the term 'merely permitted' makes rather unrecognizable. The traditional expressions *indifferens, adiaphoron, res merae facultatis*[12] indicate, then, that Kant regards such an action as a mere matter of discretion (cf. RL 6:266.8 f.), or, as Achenwall also calls it, an *actus meri arbitrii*[13]. In this action the freedom of choice is thus not restricted by laws, and therefore Kant expresses a doubt

---

9 Cf. Hruschka, 1986, p. 46.
10 Cf. Hruschka, 1986, p. 47 f.
11 Cf. Achenwall, 1763b, §63.
12 The last term in Achenwall, *Ius naturae*, §49; cf. Hruschka, 1986, p. 66.
13 Cf. Achenwall, 1763a, §49.

"whether there are such actions" (MS 6:223.9 f.). According to the opinion of the teachers of natural law, an action that is not determined affirmatively or negatively by any law is either *actio implicite (tacite) permissa*—permissibility in this sense then follows from the silence of the laws—or it is a consequence of a particular legal determination, that says one is permitted to perform or omit this action. Such a law would be a permissive law (*lex permittens* or *permissiva*[14]), by which an action becomes an *actio explicite permissa*[15]. According to Kant this leads to the second question, whether special laws, besides laws commanding and forbidding, would be necessary for the determination of merely permitted actions. Here he leaves this question open. On the one hand a permissive law appears to contain a contradiction. For if the permitted in this sense (i. e., absolutely) is defined as that which is neither commanded nor forbidden, and it follows from this that for such actions there is "no law limiting one's freedom (one's authorization)" and thus also no obligation to perform or omit them, then a law that grants such permission is impossible. On the other hand teachers of natural law have adopted such a *lex permissiva*. The problem exhibits itself in the fact that Achenwall and Baumgarten on the one hand describe the *lex permissiva* as a species of the law of prohibition.[16] Accordingly there would be no separate genus of laws that would be *leges permissivae*. But on the other hand, in the seventh edition of his *Ius naturae* Achenwall wants to admit the *leges permittentes* as a separate type of laws after all, and he considers it conceivable that they find their place next to the *leges iubentes*.[17] Kant's question whether there are morally indifferent actions, and whether a separate law is needed in order that someone be free to do or omit something, refers to a problem discussed by Jean Barbeyrac in his critique of Grotius and Pufendorf with regard to this question,[18] without taking a position on it. Kant gives only a hypothetical answer: If such a permissive law is necessary, then the authorization granted by it cannot concern the morally indifferent *adiaphora* or merely permitted actions. For instance, the postulate Kant puts forward in §2 of the *Doctrine of Right* of the possibility to have an external object of one's choice as one's own, which certainly concerns no "morally indifferent" (MS 6:223.8) action, one "can"

---

14 Cf. Achenwall, 1763b, §63; Baumgarten, 1760, §68.
15 Cf. Achenwall, 1763b, §63.
16 Cf. Achenwall, 1763b, §90; Baumgarten, 1760, §68.
17 Cf. Achenwall, 1781, §46.
18 Cf. Mellin, 1799, p. 386.

according to Kant "call" a "permissive law of practical reason" (RL 6:247.1 f.), in spite of the difficulty indicated.

In what follows Kant defines and explains the concepts of deed, person, thing, right and wrong in general, transgression, conflict of duties as well as natural and positive law. Then the discussion of concepts on this list is interrupted and a treatment of the practical law, the universal categorical imperative and the freedom of choice is inserted; following this are definitions of law, imputation, merit and what is owed, as well as the discussion of several individual problems. This unsystematic structure of the section on the "Prior Concepts of the Metaphysics of Morals" allows me here to break off the commentary on these definitions of concepts and turn to the universal categorical imperative and to choice.

First the discussion concerns the differentiation of the practical law and maxims. These two kinds of rules or principles and their relation in the acting subject determine the next five paragraphs (cf. MS 6:225.1–226.11), i.e., including the first paragraph of Kant's critique of Reinhold (cf. MS 6:226.4–227.9). That a practical law is here called a "principle [Grundsatz]" (MS 6:225.1) underscores the logical aspect under which the Kantian expositions are to be read. A practical law is a (practical) proposition (*Satz*) that can serve as a principle (*Grundsatz*) for the derivation of rules for acting. But a practical law is always also a law that commands or forbids, that "makes certain actions [i.e., the doing or omitting, M.B.] a duty" (MS 6:225.1). That is nothing new, but the concept of duty reminds one that the actions of the subject who stands under the law do not follow of themselves in harmony with this law. The concept newly introduced is that of the maxim. It is defined as that "rule that the agent himself makes his principle on subjective grounds" (MS 6:225.2 f.), and indeed also when a sensible inclination underlies its adoption. For its part it serves as a (subjective) principle (*Grundsatz*) or principle of derivation (*Ableitungsprinzip*) for actions, but the agent has "his" maxim only through the fact that he adopted it, i.e., "on subjective grounds" made it into his maxim. Here the subjectivity of these grounds consists in this, that the end—which is the matter of his maxim as a rule of his actions for the attainment of this end—is only his own. That is why "with regard to the same law" in accordance with which different agents should act or in fact act, "the maxims of the agents" can be "very different" (MS 6:225.2–4), according to individual preferences and aversions in their setting of ends.

The concept of obligation in turn underlies the concept of duty. It means, as we know, the subjective and unconditioned necessity of a free action under a categorical imperative of reason. Among these categorical imperatives as grounds of obligation and duty one is the most supreme and universal, "which as such only affirms what obligation is" (MS 6:225.6 f.), and that means: It expresses no particular obligation, as in the sentence 'you should not lie.' Thus while particular categorical imperatives state which particular obligation there is for acting—which in ethics means, which maxims of setting ends it is a duty to have, and in *Ius* means, which outer actions are duties—the "supreme principle" (MS 6:226.1) of the doctrine of duties as "the formal principle of duty" (TL 6:389.1) states only what obligation and duty are in general. That means that from this principle (*Grundsatz*), which at the same time is an imperative, all particular maxims of duty and all particular duties must be able to be derived—not according to their content, it is true, but according to their necessary validity. In the *Groundwork of the Metaphysics of Morals* Kant had said about "the *supreme principle of morality*" (GMS 4:392) as he had formulated it there: "There is [...] only a single categorical imperative and it is this: [...]. Now, if all imperatives of duty can be derived from this single imperative as from their principle, then [...] we shall at least be able to show what we think by it [by the concept of duty, M.B.] and what the concept wants to say" (GMS 4:421.6–13). Thus it is not according to their matter but only according to their form that duties with determinate content are a priori able to be derived from the categorical imperative.

We know that the general concept of duty was defined as that determinate inner or outer action to which someone is bound or obliged, and that it therefore could be called the matter of obligation, i. e., an action with determinate content to which there is a duty. Apparently this matter of obligation is determined by the formal principle of duty, so that it decides what can be a duty and what cannot. The categorical imperative "act upon a maxim that can also hold as a universal law" (MS 6:225.7 f.) does not make a particular action but rather a way of acting (*Handlungsweise*) obligatory or into a duty, namely that way of acting which is determined by a formal feature of this action's maxim, such as underlies all rational actions. This feature is the qualification of my maxim to hold as a universal law, i. e., as a rule of action that holds for all rational agents. This categorical imperative, i. e., this universal law of inner and outer action, as Kant will soon say, is like a mathematical postulate "*indemonstrable*" (MS 6:225.27, trans. K.S.).

By this supreme principle it becomes a duty to subject a maxim to a test prior to its adoption. By testing it, one may objectively ascertain whether my maxim can be followed without contradiction by all rational agents as a maxim of their action in relation to others, to themselves and to me. I thereby ascertain at the same time whether I can be the lawgiver of a universal law by which I make it that all rational agents act according to my maxim. But since an action commanded by law is a duty, in the command that my maxims be suitable to be a law, I am at the same time commanded to choose my maxims in such a way that all rationally acting beings, as subjected to a law which could be given by me, including myself, could perform an action in accordance with law, i.e., in accordance with duty, thus a morally possible or permitted action. By this law, then, no determinate maxim is commanded and especially not the setting of a determinate end or an action determined by it. It is rather my duty to act only according to such a maxim as can function as a universal law; but such a maxim, as being suitable to be a law, is not yet one that makes an action following it already into a duty. An action whose maxim is suitable for universal lawgiving by me is only a morally possible or permissible action, and accordingly its maxim is a permissible maxim, if we transfer the *licitum* from actions to their maxims. But an action, and only such an action, is a duty, whose maxim is morally permissible, while at the same time the maxim of its omission is morally impermissible or forbidden. That is the "test" (MS 6:225.11) to which I must subject my subjective principles of action in order to recognize my duties. The universal categorical imperative is at the same time the formal and objective principle of the derivation of all particular imperatives and all particular duties.

It is known that Kant did not hold his principle of duty to be a new discovery, and that he ascribed to himself only the discovery of a new and surprisingly simple formula for this principle of duty. Therefore he can also refer to the "commanding regard" (MS 6:225.16, trans. K.S.) in which this simple law stands, independent of its new formulation by Kant. But he speaks also of the astonishment (*Befremden*) that this commanding regard produces in that observer of the law who realizes that it does not carry any visible incentive with it. That is due to the purity, formality and unconditionality of this imperative, which is not bound up with any promise of a reward or threat of punishment, but in particular not with the expectation that one will become happy by following it. For those are the usual incentives that, according to conventional moral philosophy, necessitate obedience to the moral law, or recommend such obedience or make it advisable. It should produce "wonder" that our reason has the "capacity [...] to determine choice by the mere idea that a maxim

qualifies for the *universality* of a practical law" (MS 6:225.18–20). This
cannot mean that acting according to this law is a fact of experience, but
only that all human beings, in the consciousness that they should act according to the law, are actually aware of it, and so are also aware of their
capacity to act inwardly and outwardly in accordance with this law.

The mention of this capacity is at the same time an anticipation of
the specification of freedom of choice—directed against Reinhold—as
a capacity to follow the lawgiving of reason in the adoption of its maxims,
since this is commanded by the will as practical reason. It is by the moral-
practical laws or imperatives that the freedom of choice is "first made
known" (MS 6:225.21 f., trans. K.S.), indeed even "shown incontestably"
(MS 6:225.26, trans. K.S.), because in them the lawgiving of pure reason
is expressed, and at the same time, in the consciousness of being obligated
to follow its laws is expressed the resulting positive capacity of choice to
do so.

The definitions of legality and morality that follow tie into what was
said about the *licitum* and appear to belong to the list of "prior concepts
of the metaphysics of morals" (MS 6:221.5, trans. K.S.). An action's accordance with law, its *legalitas*, is its not standing in conflict "with the law
of duty," which Kant here describes as "accord" (MS 6:225.31 f.). It exists, as noted, also in the case of actions that *conformity* with the respective
law of duty. Conformity "of the maxim of an action with the law" is defined as their (the maxim's and the action's) "*morality (moralitas)*" (MS
6:225.33 f., trans. K.S.). If the acting subject adopts a maxim of his action because in its form it can hold as a universal law, then he acts not
merely in conformity with law and duty (legally), but rather out of
duty, i.e., in obedience to the law of reason for his choice of maxims.

Finally Kant adds, concerning every maxim that does not qualify as
universal law, that it is thereby contrary to the supreme principle of
the doctrine of morals and so is also "contrary to morality" (MS
6:226.3, trans. K.S.), i.e., it is contrary to all obligation in *Ius* and ethics.

In the following two paragraphs (which are indented in the printed
text), the new determination of will and choice and their relations to
one another represents a reaction of Kant's to a passage in the second volume of Reinhold's *Letters on the Kantian Philosophy*[19], which Kant interpreted as Reinhold's definition of freedom of choice. Reinhold's text
reads:

---

19 Cf. Reinhold, 1792 [2005], pp. 104–123 ("Eighth Letter").

In this twofold independence [from the demands of the disinterested and the self-interested drive, M.B.] consists the negative freedom of the will, and in choice, or the capacity to determine oneself for one of the two demands, consists the positive freedom of the will, which one can therefore never even conceive without self-determination for or against the practical law.[20]

We are in the fortunate position of having available a preliminary draft of Kant's for the "Introduction to the Metaphysics of Morals," on a loose page from Kant's unpublished works; from this, together with the later printed text, one can gather why Kant wants to see will and choice distinguished as two different practical capacities of human beings, although one does not yet find there the provocative assertion of the printed edition, that "the will [...] cannot be called either free or unfree" (MS 6:226.5–7).

Against Reinhold's conception of the freedom of the will Kant now objects in two ways: First, it cannot be ascribed to the will but rather only to the faculty of choice (*Willkür*), and second, this statement is then no definition ('explanation') of choice, but only a contingently true proposition about it.

In the preliminary draft Kant says right at the beginning: "The will of the human being must be distinguished from the faculty of choice. Only the latter can be called free and it merely concerns appearances, i.e., *actus*, which are determined in the sensible world" (VAMS 23:248.3–5, trans. K.S.). The freedom of choice is accordingly a kind of causality of the human capacity for acting, whose actions are based on concepts of ends and maxims and are performed in the inner and outer "sensible world." As objects of our possible experience these actions are simply *actus*, as based on concepts of ends and maxims they are *facta* that take place in time and so are determined as (subsequent) effects of the choice of human beings as their cause. As such they are subject to the transcendental law of all change in time, its predetermination through preceding causes.

The will, then, must be distinguished from the faculty of choice understood in this way: "For the will is not under the law, but rather it is itself the lawgiver for choice and is absolute practical spontaneity in the determination of choice" (VAMS 23:248.5–8, trans. K.S.). The law under which the will—in contrast to the faculty of choice—does not stand, is first of all the transcendental natural law of predetermination of the actions of a cause. The determination of choice, as the capacity of

---

20 Reinhold, 1792 [2008], p. 205 f., trans. K.S.

maxims, by the will is not an action that takes place under temporal conditions, but rather is only a conceivable act of lawgiving without direct effect in the world of experience. The will is thus the same as practical reason; in both, lawgiving is not based on causes that precede them in time and determine them, but is "absolute practical spontaneity" (VAMS 23:248.7, trans. K.S.) of the indirect determination of human action, that is (1) independent from events that precede in time, and (2) something that proves the capacity of the will (or of practical reason) to act by itself, i.e., to have an unconditional causality as lawgiver first in relation to choice and its maxims, and indirectly in relation to the actions that follow in accordance with these in the sensible world. The 'absolute' spontaneity or the 'transcendental' freedom of the will is thereby distinguished from the mere comparative freedom of the faculty of choice, to determine oneself independently of particular inclinations of the faculty of desire, thus from what Kant in the *Critique of Pure Reason* called 'practical freedom,' which he sees as a fact of experience.

But in the preliminary draft mentioned, Kant is concerned with another difference between will and choice, namely a difference in the kind of freedom, as on the one hand a positive capacity for lawgiving and on the other hand as a natural capacity for choice among maxims. If I ascribe positive freedom to this natural capacity of choice, the human being has it not as *phenomenon* or object of sense, but only as *noumenon* or object of understanding. For in nature as the sum total of *phenomena* in time, there can be no freedom, since this is impossible under the conditions of the possibility of experience. So when I ascribe free choice to a human being, I refer to the human being who is indeed an object of sense, but only *as noumenon*, insofar as he is no object of sense conditioned by time, but rather merely an object of thought. Accordingly, it says in the preliminary draft: "Choice [Willkühr] is the capacity to choose among given objects. [...] The ground of the possibility of choice in general in the concept of the human being as *noumenon* is only that of freedom (independence from determinations by sensibility, therefore merely negative)" (VAMS 23:248.19–25, trans. K.S.). The natural capacity of human choice can have freedom precisely not *as* a natural capacity, but only as a capacity of a *noumenon*. But the assumption that this capacity for choice (*Wahlvermögen*) in its choice (*Wahl*) of maxims is free—from which it would follow that it must be the capacity of a noumenal cause—is based then only on the independence of the adoption of maxims from particular "determinations by sensibility," an independence that one can putatively experience, that we may empirically know as our 'practical freedom,' but which presupposes without justification the possibility of a transcendental freedom, which for its part is not at all possible under conditions of experience.

But the faculty of choice can be called free in still another sense, namely as free with respect to the moral laws given by the will as lawgiver. For the maxims of the faculty of choice, which as subjective rules are based on an act of their adoption by precisely this faculty of choice, can be contrary to law and thus evil, in spite of the lawgiving for this choice of maxims by the will as pure practical reason. Kant says:

> The maxims of the faculty of choice [...], because they concern actions as appearances in the sensible world, can be evil, and choice as a natural capacity is free in respect to those laws (of the concept of duty) by which it [i.e., choice, M.B.] cannot actually be determined immediately [to actions, M.B.], but rather only by means of maxims, to adopt them in accordance with or against that [concept of duty, M.B.] (VAMS 23:248.10–14, trans. K.S.).

The freedom of the faculty of choice in this sense, then, is freedom with respect to the moral laws that command duties. Kant thus assumes that the faculty of choice (*Willkür*) as an empirically known capacity to choose (*Wahlvermögen*) is in this choice (*Wahl*) negatively free to choose and adopt a maxim that cannot be thought of as a universal law for all rational beings, and thus in respect to the moral law that grounds all duties, is contrary to law and so contrary to duty. This kind of freedom to choose (*Wahlfreiheit, liberum arbitrium*) as freedom from being immediately determined by will or pure practical reason is thus indeed an empirical fact, but nonetheless its possibility is inexplicable. The faculty of choice, then, is indeed determinable by the will as lawgiver, yet not immediately, but rather by means of the commanded kind of maxims. With regard to them the will determines only by the general criterion of their form, which one the faculty of choice (*Willkür*) has to choose and adopt, and which it should not choose and adopt without the will's having determined or commanded a particular maxim. That is the reason for the material indeterminability and, in this sense, negative freedom of the faculty of choice (*Willkür*) as an independence of its choice (*Wahl*) with respect to the will as lawgiver.

We cannot positively cognize the character of choice, so that it would also be possible to understand the possibility of this independence of a capacity for choice with respect to the lawgiving will. Nonetheless, the faculty of choice is in its way a capacity for lawgiving, namely insofar as it prescribes to sensibility a "subjective law" (VAMS 23:249.23, trans. K.S.) in the form of the chosen maxim. For action according to

a maxim is rational action, in which the individual represented action is
subsumed as a case of a universal rule of my actions and thereby, and by
the corresponding decision of choice, is taken away from sensibility as a
source of impulses to action (*stimuli*). The faculty of choice must therefore be such a positive capacity for the adoption of maxims as principles
of action, even if we do not understand its inner possibility and way of
functioning. For this capacity implies after all that the agent acting rationally according to maxims or rules cannot deviate according to a law
of nature from that subjective law that he gave himself by adopting his
maxim. "The deviation from law is [also however, M.B.] no supersensible
capacity" (VAMS 23:248.28, trans. K.S.), but rather an incapacity of the
human being to act according to his own practical reason (by following
his maxims), that for its part cannot be understood in its possibility.
This deviation from law, though—be it from the subjective (the
maxim), or from the objective law of pure practical reason for the adoption of maxims by choice—cannot be explained as its action "according
to a law of nature" (VAMS 23:248.27, trans. K.S.), since it then
would be unambiguously determined by this law of nature, the maxim
contrary to law would thus be predetermined and so one could not attribute it to choice itself. It is also for this reason that deviation from law in
the choice (*Wahl*) of maxims by the faculty of choice (*Willkür*) must remain inexplicable.

Kant summarizes his preceding considerations on the necessity of a
distinction between will and choice in this way:

> Freedom of choice [Willkühr] in respect to the actions of the human being
> as *phenomenon* consists indeed in the capacity to choose between two op-
> posed [maxims, M.B.] (conforming to law and contrary to law) and accord-
> ing to this freedom the human being regards himself as *phenomenon*. – The
> human being as *noumenon* is to himself both theoretically and practically
> lawgiving for the objects of the faculty of choice [Willkühr] and in this
> sense free, but without choice [Wahl] (VAMS 23:248.29–34, trans. K.S.).

Accordingly, the freedom of the faculty of choice (*Willkürfreiheit*), as *phenomenon*, is indeed really a mere freedom to choose (*Wahlfreiheit*), which
also includes the possibility to choose maxims contrary to law. On the
other hand, if I ascribe to the human being a will that gives the law to
himself (corresponding to the theoretical lawgiving by pure understanding and determinative judgment), such a self-lawgiving for the ends of the
human being as objects of his choice can only belong to him as a being
that can be thought and not cognized (*noumenon*), whose autonomy
makes him a positively free author of his actions, but only indirectly,

through the determinacy of the form of his maxims; he is the author of his inner actions, in the setting of ends and the adoption of maxims, and of his outer actions, including the ones with respect to other human beings as persons.

But the freedom of lawgiving for the faculty of choice by the will, as that of self-lawgiving, is not that of a free deed, because the will as practical reason cannot omit it. This lawgiving can only be called 'free insofar' as autonomy means self-determination and not foreign determination in lawgiving. But practical reason as lawgiver is only active or practical insofar as it gives the law for the faculty of choice (*Willkür*) and its choice (*Wahl*) of maxims, which are for their part maxims of action, i. e., rational grounds for the determination of action. Thus the will as lawgiver precisely does not have the freedom to choose (*die Freiheit der Wahl*), which is constitutive of the faculty of choice (*Willkür*); indeed the will is not itself an immediately practical capacity, since it does not even determine the contents of the action's maxim, but only prescribes its form as a criterion of its fitness to be chosen. Still less is free will, like the faculty of choice, the cause of individual actions according to maxims. Therefore Kant, in the "Introduction to the Metaphysics of Morals," can say in agreement with his preliminary draft that the will, "which is directed to nothing beyond the law itself," thus as lawgiver which does not itself act, "cannot be called either free or unfree" (MS 6:226.6 f.). That is something that Kant could only say after the terminological and systematic distinction between will and choice that may have been prompted by Reinhold. The will, Kant continues accordingly, which is not directed to actions, but rather as lawgiving practical reason is directed "immediately to giving laws for the maxims of actions," is "therefore also absolutely necessary" (MS 6:226.8–10). The will, which does not itself act, but only gives the law to "act on a maxim which can also hold as a universal law" (MS 6:226.1 f.), has neither freedom to choose (*die Freiheit der Wahl*)—since this law arises from will itself as pure practical reason and therefore is not possible any other way than it actually is—nor is it, like the faculty of choice in its adoption of maxims, even "*capable*" of a "necessitation" (MS 6:226.10, trans. K.S.) which could be expressed by an Ought. For from will itself first comes all moral necessitation that is expressed in the moral law as a categorical imperative, and grounds all moral obligation of actions as duties. The law given to the faculty of choice by the will—as a law for the setting of ends as objects of choice and for the adoption of maxims that accord with them, but also for right action in the outer relation of the human being to himself and other human beings—can for its part be subject to no choice (*Wahl*), but can only be the necessary expression of pure practical reason as lawgiver, of which expression one can say metaphorically at most that the will willed it.

But the faculty of choice stands *under* the law of pure practical reason as a law that concerns the maxims of the actions of the human being, "in which he has a choice [Wahl]" (VAMS 23:249.7, trans. K.S.). The freedom of this choice (*Wahl*) is only that of a limited spontaneity in relation to possible maxims dependent on their ends or incentives. The absolute spontaneity of self-lawgiving thus logically precedes the choice of maxims. To this extent the faculty of choice, in choosing its maxims, is "free to do or to omit what the law orders" (VAMS 23:249.8 f., trans. K.S.), namely to make those maxims that are fit to be laws into his own maxims, at its own discretion. Precisely because of this freedom of the chosen maxim from determination by will and so also of the faculty of choice in relation to the moral law that precedes its decision, this faculty of choice can decide against the command of the law and choose a maxim that is contrary to the moral law because it cannot be willed as a law for all rational beings. Such a choice (*Wahl*) is an act of spontaneous choice (*Willkür*), which experience shows often happens, but which does not belong in a definition (cf. MS 6:226.32–36) of the freedom of the faculty of choice (*Willkür*), since it cannot belong to the necessary properties of free choice (*Willkür*) as such. For nothing would prevent the faculty of choice (*Willkür*) in its free choice (*Wahl*) from always taking up the maxims that conform to law and making them its own, although this decision of choice (*Wahlentscheidung*) would not be made objectively necessary by a natural law nor by the moral law that merely necessitates by an Ought. Thus the decision for a maxim contrary to law remains also a merely contingent if also frequent special case of choosing (*Wahl*) by the faculty of choice (*Willkür*), which should in no way be cited among the necessary and enduring features that are united in the definition of the concept of free choice (*Willkür*).

"But will is free in another sense, because it is *lawgiving*, not obedient to the law of nature or to another, and in this sense freedom is a positive capacity, not indeed to choose, for here there is no choice [Wahl], but rather to determine the subject in regard to the sensible of actions" (VAMS 23:249.9–13, trans. K.S.). Freedom of the will is thus not merely its capacity independent from sensibility, but rather a positive capacity of unconditional (though indirect) causality, insofar as the human being, through the law given by the will, is necessitated with respect to his possible natural ends to carry out only such setting of ends as the maxims of which can hold as universal law. Free will thus, without itself choosing, has the causality of restricting the sensibly conditioned setting of ends to the condition of its maxims' suitability to be law, even without a particular action's being brought about by it. Its causality—and that means its freedom—is recognizable in the consciousness of an Ought, by which the moral law is experienced as necessitating the faculty of choice (*Willkür*) in choosing among its maxims. That means that the will only has freedom as a kind of causality insofar as the faculty of choice, in relation to the maxims that can be chosen by it, is not determined but only necessitated to make a 'form' of actions, more precisely: to make the form of the maxims of such actions the condition of their being carried out by us. The faculty of choice's freedom to choose is thus only the negative freedom of its independence from natural determination; the positive freedom of the will is that of the determination of the human being's faculty of choice—which follows from the will itself—by a law of his own pure practical reason; this law brings about no action, but proves that this pure reason can be practical by itself insofar as it really provides a principle for the selection of the maxims of action. If it is then possible for a human being to take an interest in those actions whose maxims are in accord with the moral law and *therefore* are adopted by the faculty of choice, then pure practical reason or—what is the same thing—the free will of the human being can *indirectly* have an effect in the world of experience, in the form of morally good actions.

In another preliminary draft (LBl 46, OP 21:470.4–437.23) for the passage of the *Metaphysics of Morals* mentioned, which is likewise concerned with the inadmissibility of a definition of the freedom of choice that takes experiential propositions as a basis, Kant did not yet place any value on the distinction between will and the faculty of choice. I quote from it only a few places in which Kant deviates from the first preliminary draft mentioned and from the text of the *Metaphysics of Morals*. About freedom this preliminary draft says that it is "a capacity of choice incomprehensible to us [...] to *withstand* sensible incentives [...], not merely a capacity to choose among them" (OP 21:470.9–11, trans. K.S.). A little later it says that by the concept of freedom of choice one thinks of "a capacity to follow the law, in spite of all inclinations to the contrary" (OP 21:472.7 f., trans. K.S.). Here, beyond the negative determination of the freedom of choice as independence from sensibility with its incentives and inclinations, Kant adopts a capacity for withstanding these, i. e., for a real repugnance (*Realrepugnanz*), and indeed on the

one hand against sensible incentives and on the other hand against inclinations contrary to law, whereby this capacity, as a positive one, is not
newly determined but is merely borrowed from a practical anthropology.
Further, this choice between incentives and inclinations is distinguished
from a choice (*Wahl*) of maxims of actions, to which "absolute spontaneity" and "*libertas noumenon*" (OP 21:470.17 f., trans. K.S.) is here ascribed, which according to the first preliminary draft mentioned seemed to
belong only to the will in distinction from the faculty of choice. Finally
free choice as "self-determining choice (not determined by given objects
(of sense))" (OP 21:470.13 f.) is again negatively defined by its empirically known independence, and at the same time almost as what is elsewhere called will. But Kant then makes a connection between the fact of
reason in the *Critique of Practical Reason*—which likewise does not rely
on the distinction between will and choice—and the conception of the
freedom of choice "as a *negative* characteristic in us, namely to be *necessitated* by no sensible ground of determination" (OP 21:471.5 f., trans.
K.S.). This formulation, like the ones that follow it, is taken over almost
word for word in the *Metaphysics of Morals* (cf. MS 6:226). The freedom
that we first know empirically in ourselves only as a negative characteristic
is the same one that, as positive, "first becomes manifest to us through the
moral law" (MS 6:226.16 f.), insofar as we infer freedom from our consciousness of this law. But already because of the lack of a more precise
analysis of the function of the moral law in relation to will and choice
in this preliminary draft, a positive determination of freedom cannot
be given, but only intimated. Lawgiving and the choice of maxims are
merely mentioned as elements of the *libertas noumenon* of the faculty
of choice, taken as a capacity to will, in contrast to choice as a capacity
to act, whereby only a "respective spontaneity" (OP 21:479.16, trans.
K.S.) is ascribed to this capacity to act, and its indifference with respect
to being in accord with law or contrary to it is conceded. In addition,
Kant speaks here only of *liberum arbitrium* as a capacity "to overcome
the impressions on our sensible faculty of desire" (KrV A802/B830) or
as a "capacity [...] to *withstand* sensible incentives" (OP 21:470.9 f.,
trans. K.S.). He thereby rejects the view of a necessitation by these impressions and incentives, namely if it is not about one or another sensible
ground of determination, but about them all. In spite of all the differences from the first preliminary draft indicated, these passages are compatible with the assertion of the *Metaphysics of Morals:* "Only *choice* [Will-
kür] can [...] be called *free*" (MS 6:226.10 f., trans. K.S.).

References

Achenwall, Gottfried (^{5}1763a), *Ius naturae*, Göttingen: Victor Bossiegel.
Achenwall, Gottfried (^{2}1763b), *Prolegomena iuris naturalis*, Göttingen: Victor Bossiegel.
Achenwall, Gottfried (^{7}1781), *Ius naturae*, Göttingen: Victor Bossiegel.
Baumgarten, Alexander Gottlieb (1760), *Initia Philosophiae Practicae Primae*, Halle/Magdeburg: Hemmerde.
Hruschka, Joachim (1986), *Das deontologische Sechseck bei Gottfried Achenwall im Jahre 1776*, Göttingen: Vandenhoeck & Ruprecht.
Mellin, Georg Samuel Albert (1799), "Erlaubt", in: id., *Encyclopädisches Wörterbuch der kritischen Philosophie*, vol. 2, Jena/Leipzig: Frommann.
Reinhold, Karl Leonhard (1792) [2008], *Briefe über die Kantische Philosophie*, in: Karl Leonhard Reinhold, *Gesammelte Schriften*, vol. 2, Martin Bondeli (ed.), Basel: Schwabe.
Reinhold, Karl Leonhard (1792) [2005], *Letters on the Kantian Philosophy*, Karl Ameriks (ed.), Cambridge: Cambridge University Press.
Wolff, Christian (1738–1739), *Philosophia practica universalis*, Frankfurt/Leipzig: Prostat in Officina Libraria Rengeriana.

The Concept and Necessity of an End in Ethics (TL 6:379–389)

Andreas Trampota

In this text[1] Kant introduces into his moral philosophy a concept that does not appear in any earlier writings: the concept of an end which is also a duty. It is a concept central to the *Doctrine of Virtue*, perhaps even its linchpin, since an adequate understanding of what Kant says in the *Doctrine of Virtue* depends on a correct interpretation of the concept. Thus, in what follows, we intend to define this concept and also, more importantly, reconstruct what prompted Kant to introduce it precisely when he did. What is the 'logic,' the *necessity*, that led to its introduction? In order to answer this question, we must first of all recall what Kant said about the concept of an end in the *Groundwork* and also what various commentators have said about the apparent inconsistency of the theory of ends brought forward there. It is only against this background that we can understand what Kant says about ends which are also duties in the *Doctrine of Virtue*. Hence, we begin by calling to mind what Kant tells us about the concept of an end in his foundational writings on moral philosophy.

I. The Alleged Inconsistency in Kant's Theory of Ends

In the second section of the *Groundwork*, in the context of his reflections on the three ways of representing the supreme moral principle, Kant writes:

> Rational nature is distinguished from the rest of nature by this, that it sets itself an end. This end would be the matter of every good will. But since, in the idea of a will absolutely good without any limiting condition (attainment of this or that end) abstraction must be made altogether from every end to be *effected* (this would make every will only relatively good), the end must here be thought not as an end to be effected but as an *independently*

---

1   I'd like to express my gratitude to Oliver Sensen and Ron Tacelli for their detailed and constructive comments on an earlier version of this text.

existing, and hence thought only negatively, that is, as that which must never be acted against and which must therefore in every volition be estimated never merely as a means but always at the same time as an end. Now, this end can be nothing other than the subject of all possible ends itself, because this subject is also the subject of a possible absolutely good will; for, such a will cannot without contradiction be subordinated to any other object (GMS 4:437.21 – 33).

The point of this text is that all ends to be effected which originate from sensibility and, hence, are merely subjective and relative ends, are precluded from the idea of an absolutely good will. Only the subject of all possible ends which is an independently existing end is admitted as principle of the universal categorical imperative as *merely a negative, restricting condition* of the maxims.[2]

On the other hand, the examples of duty three and four in the *Groundwork* (the examples of imperfect duties) (cf. GMS 4:422.37 – 423.35, 430.10 – 27) suggest that the human being should also be understood as an "end in itself" (GMS 4:430.12) *in a positive sense*. As in the ethical thought of the ancient world certain goals are understood as goals which *should be desired and striven after*, Kant apparently wants to say in this context that one's own perfection and the happiness of others are ends that *ought to be adopted* as one's own *in a positive sense*. If these examples teach us that one should promote humanity in one's own person and in that of another in this two-fold way, by in some way perfecting ourselves and by contributing to the happiness of others, then these positive determinations of ends of the wide (imperfect, meritorious) duties at least *prima facie* appear to contradict the assumption that the idea of an objective end can only be thought of as negative.

At any rate, this is what Herbert J. Paton and Lewis W. Beck held; whereas the former considered the alleged contradiction only an imprecision and thus did not attach importance to it, the latter saw in it the manifestation of a tension which, so he thought, pervades all of Kant's moral philosophy.[3] John Atwell, who takes the credit for the clarification of the

---

2   Cf. Schmucker, 1997, p. 134 f.
3   Paton comments on Kant's thesis that rational nature is to be thought of as a merely negative, restricting condition of the maxims with the remark: "In this negative statement he appears to forget imperfect duties" (Paton, 1963, p. 177, note 5). Beck's assessment is to be found in his article "Kant on Revolution" (Beck, 1971). However, Beck's thesis is stated in the context of his claim that Kant's enthusiasm for the French Revolution is not justified by his formalistic moral system: "Kant's enthusiasm for the French Revolution is based upon his

concept of an end in Kant's moral philosophy, has contradicted both these great Kant interpreters, pointing out that Kant never held anything like a conception of objective ends.[4] Since by this Atwell means merely, in the words of Mary Gregor, "no end in the positive sense of some state of affairs to be brought into being by our action,"[5] we can agree with him. But nevertheless, there *is* an objective theory of ends *of a totally different kind* in Kant's moral philosophy—one that does not have a teleological basis. On this point I can also agree with Atwell. But it is my contention that one does justice to this rational 'matter'[6] in Kant's moral philosophy only if one assumes—with Manfred Baum, Georg Geismann, Georg Römpp and others—that (a) the *Metaphysics of Morals* is Kant's principal work in moral philosophy and that (b) his system of duties of right and virtue in its entirety is only found here.[7] What is crucial for an adequate understanding of Kant's theory of ends which are also duties in the second part of the *Metaphysics of Morals*—ends which for the sake of simplicity I will henceforth call 'obligatory ends' or 'ends of duty'—is their systematic place in the multi-dimensional or multi-level 'edifice' of Kant's moral philosophy.

II. The Multi-dimensional or Multi-level Structure of Kant's Moral Philosophy

This multi-dimensionality which shapes the *Metaphysics of Morals* is clearest in sections I and III of the introduction to the *Metaphysics of Morals*,[8] as well as in sections I, X and XIV of the introduction to the *Doc-*

---

teleological conception of history, which is a forerunner of Hegel's definition of history as 'the progress of the consciousness of freedom.' That the final purpose of the world is moral, not eudaemonistic, makes it possible for Kant to have a moral enthusiasm for the Revolution which his formalistic moral system does not justify. Had Kant's approval of the Revolution been eudaemonistic, the inconsistency would have been greater. But some inconsistency remains because Kantian ethics is not adequate to resolve the painful problems of conflicting duties" (Ibid., p. 421 f.).

4   Cf. Atwell, 1974, p. 161.
5   Gregor, 1971, p. 25.
6   'Matter' is to be understood in this article in the Kantian technical sense of this term being the antonym to 'form.'
7   Cf. Baum, 2005, p. 37; Baum, 2007, p. 213. See also: Geismann, 2006; Römpp, 2006.
8   Cf. MS 6:214.1–30, 218.11–221.3.

trine of Virtue.[9] Kant here differentiates between two domains of human freedom, the external and the internal domain. He does this by distinguishing external (juridical) and internal (ethical) *legislation*, external and internal *acts*, external and internal use of *choice* (*Willkür*) (two aspects of *choice*),[10] external and internal *determining grounds of choice*, and external and internal *duties* (those in accordance with juridical, and those in accordance with ethical legislation).

The two fields of action demarcated from each other in this way may also be described as the field of the *internal determination* of ends and the field of the *external realization* or *achievement* of ends. These two domains can also be thought of in a complementary way as two levels of human action—namely, as the level of (internal) willing and of (external) acting and omitting. Regardless of whether we speak of domains of freedom or levels of human action, it is in any case crucial that the purely formal, merely negative basic law of morality be superordinate to both dimensions of the structure of Kant's moral philosophy. As the supreme, most general categorical imperative, this law simply states what obligation is (what moral duty is), but in its reference to one or the other domain of freedom it is modified.[11] While in his propaedeutic writings on moral

---

9   Cf. TL 6:379.15–382.4, 396.4–31, 406.29–407.2. It is in the *Metaphysics of Morals* that this two-dimensionality first clearly comes to light because this is where the 'system' is dealt with. (See especially the preface and the introduction to the *Metaphysics of Morals*. See also: GMS 4:392.6–16.)

10 Cf. Gregor, 1963, p. 81. See also Baum, 2005, p. 37 f.: "Choice is [...] the faculty of desire as guided by concepts of an end, which previously was also called 'will,' as long as these concepts of an end are able to determine it to bring about the corresponding object by its acting as the means, and this in such a way that he who desires the end considers himself as sufficiently able to achieve his intention. The self-determination of the desire by means of the desiring person's concept of an end makes his faculty of desire a faculty to act as one pleases, i.e. to generate the object of his concept or to refrain from this acting. The willing of the desiring of or refraining from an end-oriented action is thus an internal act of choosing this action. On this basis concerning the theory of action the will is introduced [...]" (trans. A.T.).

11 Cf. MS 6:225.1–226.3; TL 6:388.34–389.11; VATL 23:394.1–34. Similar formulations can be found in the foundational writings on moral philosophy, in the *Groundwork* and in the *Critique of Practical Reason*. Nonetheless, Geismann correctly points out that the variations of the categorical imperative that are found in these writings are for the most part only foundational for ethics because they concern volition, i.e. the internal use of free choice (cf. Geismann, 2006, p. 36, note 202; see also Baum, 2005, p. 35). Thus, Kant speaks, for in-

philosophy,[12] in the *Groundwork* and the second *Critique*, Kant treats the categorical imperative as the undifferentiated supreme principle of any duty, in the *Metaphysics of Morals* it *first* turns into the supreme principle of all duties that can be imposed on us by *external* legislation (cf. RL 6:231.10–18), and *then* into the supreme principle of those duties that are only possible by *ethical* legislation (cf. TL 6:395.15–21).[13] This is why Höffe asserts—rightly, in my opinion—that the categorical imperative at first does not have a normative-ethical significance, but rather a meta-ethical one, because at first it only defines the concept of the moral good.[14] The bifurcation of the "general doctrine of duties" (TL 6:380.16) in the *Metaphysics of Morals* into the doctrine of right and the doctrine of virtue is based on the distinction between the internal and the external use of freedom (cf. e.g. TL 6:380.16–25), and the diversity of legislation which is a consequence of it. It entails two basic principles that are independent of each other and are subordinate to the supreme principle of morality, the supreme principle of right and the supreme principle of virtue.

Analogous to this bifurcation, one can also distinguish two levels of action where the guiding question of Kant's practical philosophy 'What should I do?' arises—namely, the level of volition, which involves the choosing of maxims and the determination of ends, on the basis of which one acts, and the level of action in the more narrow, external sense, which involves the execution of ends determined in accordance with the chosen maxims, i. e. the realization of ends. The basis of this distinction is the insight that *the freedom of willing which is concerned with setting ends* is something totally different from *the freedom of acting which is directed at ends.* This is very clear in the following assertion by Kant:

> Another can indeed *coerce* me *to do* something that is not my end (but only a means to another's end), but not to *make this my end*; and yet I have no end without making it an end for myself. To have an end that I have not myself made an end is self-contradictory, an act of freedom which is yet not free (TL 6:381.30–35).

---

stance, of an end that must be estimated *in every volition* (cf. GMS 4:437.23–30).
12 Cf. Kersting 2004, pp. 198, 219.
13 See also Gregor, 1963, p. 80.
14 Cf. Höffe, 1979, pp. 9 f. See also: Höffe, 1987, p. 89.

Principles of freedom for the one field are quite inappropriate for the other. If ethical principles are supposed to serve to restrict freedom materially in such a way that the specific human faculty for the determination of ends itself dictates the end for all acting persons,[15] then these principles are completely useless as principles of right since the domain of right by definition involves bringing into agreement the external freedom of action of several persons.[16] Admittedly, it is essential to all duties that they imply a constraining of free choice by the idea of a maxim that qualifies for a universal law. But the substantial difference between the doctrine of right and the doctrine of virtue consists in this: The determining ground of choice in the doctrine of right *directly* makes the external action necessary (and external action, of course, also is an acting on maxims)[17], whereas in the doctrine of virtue the necessity is found in adopting and having maxims which make the willing rational. Here the relation to external action is only *indirect*[18]: "Ethics does not give laws for *actions* (*ius* does that), but only for *maxims* of actions" (TL 6:388.32 f.).[19] The doctrine of virtue deals with the internal determining ground of choice, a self-constraint exercised by reason on *willing*, which is the indication of internal freedom.[20] If maxims are adopted because they are in conformity with the law of reason for maxims, for which self-constraint is required, they turn into *internal determining grounds* of choice.[21] Precisely *this* is what no one can be constrained to do by another. As long as this internal determining ground remains restricted to the idea (the representation) of duty as the internal incentive to action, it can also bear on duties of right; it makes *indirect ethical* duties out of them (cf. MS 6:221.1–03). But this internal self-constraint is only the *formal* principle of virtue, which does not constitute any specific duties of virtue. Kant does not speak of 'duties of virtue' until the setting of ends is made obligatory, i. e. once a definite *matter* of choice is represented as necessary (cf. TL 6:394.33–395.1, 398 picture).

---

15 Cf. Baum, 2005, p. 42.
16 Cf. Geismann, 2006, p. 24.
17 The maxim of the action is the ground determining choice to action.
18 Cf. Baum, 2005, p. 39; Geismann, 2006, p. 30.
19 See also VATL 23:379.6–32.
20 Cf. TL 6:379.15–382.1, 394.15–32, 401.33–35.
21 Cf. Baum, 2005, p. 41.

III. The Upward and Downward Movement of Practical Reason and the Ambiguity of the Theory of Ends

The two-level structure of Kant's concept of action, which has been mentioned several times already, makes reference to another significant structural element of Kant's moral philosophy; a correct assessment of the doctrine of objective ends depends on a consideration of this element. It could perhaps be described as the upward and downward movement of practical reason. In the *Groundwork*, what is decisive for "the search for and establishment of the *supreme principle of morality*" (GMS 4:392.3 f.) (the upward movement) is that the will's *material determining grounds* be precluded because they are all categorized as sensible (*sinnlich*). However, it in no way follows that the moral legislation resulting from this process does not have any matter. This has already been pointed out emphatically by Julius Ebbinghaus:

> The categorical imperative *abstracts from all ends* because, in deriving from it an absolute demand as such, I cannot rest my case on any end that I presuppose; but this does not mean that the categorical imperative demands a will *that has no ends at all* and so wills nothing.[22]

Still, at the very summit of the meta-ethical upward movement in the *Groundwork*—which inquires into the concept of the moral good and in the course of this purifies the will from any matter—the matter (the end) can only be thought of as negative. The rational being as the subject of all possible ends is at this level the supreme limiting condition of all relative ends (cf. GMS 4:430.24–431.9). However, in the normative-ethical *downward* movement of reason in the *Metaphysics of Morals*—a movement effected by relating the supreme moral principle to the internal and external use of free choice—the matter is then thought of as *positive*. The following should make this clear.

In terms of the meta-ethical upward movement, which aims at determining the concept of the moral good, the end is understood as "what serves the will as the objective ground of its self-determination" (GMS 4:427.22 f.).[23] As a result, one must abstract from all subjective-sensible ends. Hence, Kant writes in the *Groundwork*: "The [searched-for, A.T.] categorical imperative would be that which represented an action as ob-

---

22 Ebbinghaus, 1954, p. 107.
23 This end of morality has to be distinguished from that of prudence and skill: cf. GMS 4:415.6–416.6.

jectively necessary of itself, without reference to another end" (GMS 4:414.15–17). What remains after this process of abstraction is only the objective end, which as a law is the highest limiting condition of all subjective ends. But in the case of the descent of practical reason to the level of human action—the level at which human beings act as "rational *natural* beings" (TL 6:379.20 f.), the level at which not only the will and its determination is concerned, but also free choice (cf. MS 6:226.4–11)—the matter is the object or the end of *free choice*, the representation of which determines it to an action (by which the object is brought about) (cf. TL 6:381.4–6, 384.33 f.). As a result of this process of descent to the sphere of specific *human* action, the thesis holds: *No determination of choice without an end.* Or: No action without an end (cf. TL 6:385.1). And this is valid both on the level of external action and on the level of willing. What is involved on the level of external action are the "ends the human being *does adopt* in keeping with the sensible impulses of his nature" (TL 6:385.19 f.). Kant calls the doctrine of ends on this level based on empirical principles "the technical (subjective) doctrine of ends" (TL 6:385.22), and adds that "it is really the pragmatic doctrine of ends, containing the rules of prudence in the choice of one's ends" (TL 6:385.22 f.). On the level of willing, however, we have the "objects of free choice under its laws, which he [the human being, A.T.] *ought to make* his ends" (TL 6:385.20 f.). Kant names the doctrine of ends at this level "the moral (objective) doctrine of ends" (TL 6:385.24) because it rests on principles given *a priori* in pure practical reason. Basically, only two possible relations between duty and end are conceivable: either the concept of an end proceeds from that of duty, or vice versa. The doctrine of right takes the first path; the doctrine of virtue, the second (cf. TL 6:382.8–27).

IV. The Doctrine of Virtue is a Treatise on Ends in a Positive Sense

We have only reached the doctrine of virtue when we are dealing with duties of virtue that are commanded, that is, with obligatory ends that are objects of legislation. A doctrine of virtue could also be thought of as a theory which remains restricted to the formal aspect of the moral determination of the will and only requires a certain form of ethical motivation. It might, for example, only demand that any action in conformity with duty should also be done from duty. However, Kant distinguishes clearly between "ethical duties" (TL 6:383.9) that merely concern the form and "duties of virtue" (TL 6:383.10) that also relate to an end, i.e. the matter (the object) of choice (cf. TL 6:383.8–17). Only an end that is also a duty may be called a duty of virtue. Ethics is primarily about ends in a positive sense; it is, as Kant says, "the system of the ends of pure practical reason" (TL 6:381.18f.). And the principle of virtue superordinate to them is an affirmative principle (cf. TL 6:395.15 f.).[24]

This must be emphatically emphasized since the imperfect duties mentioned in the *Groundwork* are only derived indirectly. Here the impossibility that the will can be universally legislative by means of the material determination of the negative maxims on which these duties are based (indifference in principle to one's own talents and the need of other human beings for help) is the reason why the *opposing* maxims become moral necessities (due to the autonomy of freedom) and why it thus becomes a duty to have these opposing maxims, i.e. to determine oneself to action by means of the end-setting implied in them (cf. GMS 6:422.37–423.35). In this derivation, however, the end-oriented nature of human action is tacitly presupposed—something Mary Gregor (among others) has pointed out.[25] And certain natural orientations of human beings—Ebbinghaus has emphasized this point[26]—are also taken for granted. If one reflects about what one can *will* without contradiction, an understanding of the *specific constitution* of the relevant rational being is needed. In the case of human beings, this is their sensible-rational dual nature (human beings are rational *natural* beings). Hence, we can only fully recognize humanity as an end in itself in human beings if we act in accord with humanity not only negatively, but also positively—if, that is to say, we try to promote to a certain degree their subjective ends, too.[27] It is with this in mind that O'Neill writes:

---

24 See also Gregor, 1963, p. 85.

25 Cf. Gregor, 1963, p. 88.

26 It is thus, for instance, a case attested by experience that human beings need mutual assistance for the realization of their happiness (cf. Ebbinghaus, 1959, p. 210 f.).

27 Cf. on this point the following statement from the *Groundwork:* "[…] concerning meritorious duty to others, the natural end that all human beings have is their own happiness. Now, humanity might indeed subsist if no one contributed to the happiness of others but yet did not intentionally withdraw anything from it; but there is still only a negative and not a positive agreement with *humanity as an end* in itself unless everyone also tries, as far as he can, to further the ends of others.

Only by making the ends of others to some extent our own do we recognize others' agency fully, and acknowledge that they are initiators of their projects as well as responders to our projects, and moreover vulnerable and non-self-sufficient initiators of projects. That (I think) is the point of the idea that we should agree 'positively' with humanity as an end-in-itself.[28]

One should also make the humanity of other human beings one's end in a positive way because human beings, as sensible rational beings pursuing their natural end (an end which—just like their rational-moral destiny—represents a *necessity*), are dependent upon this 'external' support. In the *Groundwork*, of course, these imperfect duties are only derived indirectly and are not yet an object of positive legislation (which is understandable given Kant's intention in the *Groundwork*). It is only in the *Doctrine of Virtue*—despite numerous parallels between the *Groundwork* and the *Metaphysics of Morals*—that a positive theory of ends is to be found.

V. The Why and the How of the Positive End

The question then arises: Why precisely are these ends of duty needed in ethics? What grounds the necessity[29] of the determination of positive ends required in this context? Kant's answer to this question is found in the following paragraph:

> The doctrine of right dealt only with the *formal* condition of outer freedom (the consistency of outer freedom with itself if its maxim were made universal law), that is, with **right.** But ethics goes beyond this and provides a *matter* (an object of free choice), an **end** of pure reason which it represents as an end that is also objectively necessary, that is, an end that, as far as human beings are concerned, it is a duty to have. – For since the sensible inclinations of human beings tempt them to ends (the matter of choice) that can be contrary to duty, lawgiving reason can in turn check their influence only by a moral end set up against the ends of inclination, an end that must therefore be given *a priori*, independently of inclinations (TL 6:380.19–381.3).

And a few sentences later, he adds:

> [...] if I am under obligation to make my end something that lies in concepts of practical reason, and so to have, besides the formal determining

For the ends of a subject who is an end in itself must as far as possible be also *my* ends, if that representation is to have its *full* effect in me" (GMS 4:430.18–27).
28 O'Neill, 1989, p. 140.
29 For the central importance which the concept of necessity has in Kant's moral philosophy see e. g. MS 6:221.19–223.5.

ground of choice (such as right contains), a material one as well, an end that could be set against the end arising from sensible impulses, this would be the concept of an *end that is in itself a duty*. But the doctrine of this end would not belong to the doctrine of right but rather to ethics, since *self-constraint* in accordance with (moral) laws belongs to the concept of ethics alone (TL 6:381.9–27).

Hence, the material guiding principle of ethics, which commands the adoption of specific objective ends, is necessary as a complement to the supreme formal principle of morality. These ends are absolutely necessary as a *material* counterweight to the subjective ends based on the sensible impulses that everyone has (cf. TL 6:389.14). Though these ends are not necessarily contrary to duty, they can be so because they arise from spontaneous, unreflected stimuli. For this reason, from the perspective of duty, a force in the form of a *rational matter* is needed which opposes their influence.[30] In the field of internal freedom characteristic of the doctrine of virtue a categorical imperative of pure practical reason is required, "which connects a *concept of duty* with that of an end in general" (TL 6:385.8 f.).

With this, the question concerning the *why* of the positive theory of ends is answered. But what has not yet been dealt with is the additional, closely related question concerning the *how* of this necessity. For according to what we have learned from Kant in the *Groundwork* about ends in moral philosophy, it is uncertain *whether* and—if so—*how* this kind of theory of ends can be integrated consistently into Kant's moral philosophy. We may well stand in need of objective ends as efficacious antagonists to the subjective ends. But this says nothing about whether and how these ends are *possible*.[31] Hence, we need to ask: How does this positive theory of ends come about?

The decisive step on the way to justifying these ends seems to be that the supreme principle of the doctrine of morals (cf. MS 6:226.1) is ap-

---

30   This oppositional function of the obligatory ends is no surprise if one considers that Kant defines virtue as a form of courage (*fortitudo*), namely as "the capacity and considered resolve to withstand a strong but unjust opponent" (TL 6:380.13 f.).

31   This is exactly the question that Kant wants to answer at the very beginning of the introduction to the *Doctrine of Virtue*. Section I ends in the following way: "But how is such an end possible? That is the question now. For that the concept of a thing is possible (not self-contradictory) is not yet sufficient for assuming the possibility of the thing itself (the objective reality of the concept)" (TL 6:382.1–4).

plied to *one's own will*; in contrast to right, ethics requires that we think of the supreme principle of all duty as the principle of *one's own will*, not as a principle of *will in general*:

> The concept of duty stands in immediate relation to a *law* (even if I abstract from all ends, as the matter of the law). The formal principle of duty, in the categorical imperative "So act that the maxim of your action could become a universal *law*," already indicates this. Ethics adds only that this principle is to be thought as the law of *your* own will and not of will in general, which could also be the will of others; in the latter case the law would provide a duty of right, which lies outside the sphere of ethics (TL 6:388.34–389.6).

By relating the general principle of morality to one's own will, it turns into the requirement that one must be able to be the *legislator of every-body's ends* by means of one's maxim: "The supreme principle of the doctrine of virtue is: act in accordance with a maxim of *ends* that it can be a universal law for everyone to have" (TL 6:395.15 f.). Freedom of choice is restricted here, not as in the field of right in a negative way, but rather in a positive, end-setting way.[32] Kant accordingly comments on the distinction between the rightful principle of external freedom and the principle of ends distinctive of the doctrine of virtue in his preliminary drafts for the *Doctrine of Right*:

> The doctrine of right is the doctrine of duties insofar as it is determined by the choice [Willkür] of others in accordance with the principle of freedom – the doctrine of virtue insofar as it is determined by one's own choice in accordance with the principle of ends (VARL 23:269.1–4, trans. A.T.).[33]

And about the fundamental distinction between 'the constraint by means of the choice of another in accordance with laws of freedom' and 'the constraint by means of one's own representation of the law' he says in the preliminary drafts for the *Doctrine of Right*:

> A rational being has duties if the *freedom* of his *choice* [Willkür] is restricted by a law [...] If it is restricted by the *choice* [Willkür] of *another*, then a ra-

---

32 Cf. Baum, 2005, p. 43; Geismann, 2006, p. 40. The *restriction* occurs by *subordinating* the subjective ends to the objective ends: "Only the concept of an *end* that is also a duty, a concept that belongs exclusively to ethics, establishes a [positive, A.T.] law for maxims of actions by subordinating the subjective end (that everyone has) to the objective end (that everyone ought to make his end)" (TL 6:389.12–15).

33 See also VATL 23:376.25–27: "In the first [in the duties of right, A.T.], the choice [Willkür] of others can be determining for my own, in the second [in the duties of virtue, A.T.], only my own choice can contain the determining ground (*ius et ethica*)" (trans A.T.).

tional being has *duties of right*; if, however, it is only restricted by the internal law of the practical reason of the subject itself, it has duties of virtue. [...] that [obligation, A.T.] in which the constraining subject must be another person [is, A.T.] the *rightful* [obligation, A.T.]; that in which it must be the very same person, the *ethical* obligation. In the first case the *obligatus* is constrained by the *choice* of another in accordance with laws of freedom, in the second merely by the representation of the law (VARL 23:344.19 – 23, 345.1 – 5, trans. A.T.).

When the supreme moral principle is related to *one's own will* such that it turns into the principle of an *internal legislation* and the principle of freedom of *internal action* (of the internal freedom of a person, the freedom of his own willing), then a law results for *one's own internal use of choice*, which manifests itself in internal actions of setting ends or adopting maxims. It is, then, a law *for the ends of every rational being*, which prescribes that one must be able to make one's own determination of ends an object of the legislation of everyone (including oneself). The lawful determination of the *internal* use of choice can relate only to *my own* choice. The supreme principle of virtue, which is a law for having maxims concerning ends, is a direct consequence of the supreme principle of the doctrine of morals, if this principle is applied to the determination of ends by means of my own choice.[34]

For this reason, the route from right to virtue which Kant chooses in the *Metaphysics of Morals* implies a 'transition from one order to another'[35]. One might perhaps also speak of a 'change of perspective': Virtue is something which is closely linked to decisively adopting the first-person perspective for practical purposes. This is already made clear at the beginning of the *Doctrine of Virtue*, when the concept of virtue is being introduced. Here (a) the doctrine of morals in general is divided into doctrine of right and doctrine of virtue, (b) the two fields are identified with the 'outside' and 'inside' of freedom, (c) the internal dimension of freedom is defined as free self-constraint and (d) this free self-constraint is identified with virtue in the sense of a *fortitudo moralis* (cf. TL 6:379.5 – 380.18). It is one thing to act according to a maxim that can

---

34 Cf. Geismann, 2006, p. 40; Baum, 2005, p. 39. The law of right differs from the ethical law since, on the one hand, it does not concern internal, but rather external action, and, on the other, it does not concern one's own, but rather the acting of everyone in its external relation to everyone else (cf. Geismann, 2006, p. 83).

35 In the preliminary drafts for the *Doctrine of Right* Kant speaks under the heading "Transition from the doctrine of right to ethics" of a "transition from one order of things to another (*metabasis eis allo genos*)" (VARL 23:353.22 f., trans. A.T.).

function as a universal law of external freedom, but it is quite another to make the idea of the universality of the maxim the principle of *my own will*[36] and, hence, the principle of *my own determination of ends*. In the first case, the question involved is which of the possible maxims of action one *can* have; in the latter, however, the question is which maxims one *should* have. If I make the idea of universal validity the internal principle of my willing, my ends will be restricted to the condition that I must be able to make my own determination of ends the object of the legislation of everyone (including myself). The resulting law for the adoption of maxims reads as follows: "act in accordance with a maxim of *ends* that it can be a universal law for everyone to have" (TL 6:395.15f.). Hence, the duties of virtue are precisely those *a priori* commanded ends that I can have in accordance with a universal law.[37] They are those ends that can be duties in accordance with a universal law of setting ends.[38] In this way, internal freedom is restricted to the conditions of its universal consistency with itself (cf. Refl 7249–7251, 19:294.13–24). In other words, the necessity of this determination of ends is based on the fact that it is the condition for the *consistent* use of internal freedom (cf. VAMS 23:250.7–18).[39]

The necessity of setting ends thus concerns the individual. Moreover, it relates only to his maxims, since this necessity is located on a higher level than his subjective ends (the level of ends one *ought to have*, not merely of ends one *actually has*).[40] It is the answer to the question how

36 On this also see Gregor, 1963, p. 83, note 18. Ethics apprehends the supreme moral law as what it originally and primarily is, namely the law of one's *own will*. For in terms of their origin all moral principles are laws of *one's own pure will*. They originate directly from the self-legislation of practical reason; their authority is grounded in this. And this is valid not only for the laws of virtue, but for the laws of right, too. Admittedly, they are conceived quite deliberately in such a way that they can be enforced by means of external incentives. But their *moral* validity derives from the fact that every person wills them to be enforceable by external coercion—*assuming his own rational will*. Hence, one could say: The *morally-binding* power of the external legislation is rooted in the self-legislation of one's own will, as it is with ethical legislation; this, however, is not true for its *rightfully-binding* power (cf. Tieftrunk, 1798, p. 90).
37 Cf. Baum, 2005, p. 43.
38 Cf. Baum, 1998, p. 49 f.
39 See also Geismann, 2006, p. 30.
40 If it would not be so ambiguous, one might also say: The necessity of the determination of ends concerns only the *intention* of the individual. In the preliminary drafts for the *Metaphysics of Morals*, Kant distinguishes between maxims or laws of *intention* and those of *execution* (cf. VAMS 23:381.34–382.4). However, he

I ought to determine my willing and—since there is no volition without object—which ends I should set in this respect. What is demanded here is that not only the maxims but also the 'maxims for the adoption of maxims' qualify for universal laws; the matter of choice, too, ought to be determined by law. The guiding principle of the doctrine of virtue is a principle of ends for me alone; it is the law of my own will.

VI. One's Own Perfection and the Happiness of Others

Why are the duties of virtue directed at one's own perfection and the happiness of others? A brief answer to this question could be this: Because only these two determinations of ends are concerned with the very capacity for setting ends. For the setting of ends which is commanded by the duties of virtue always has to do with the human capacity for setting ends as the possibility of freedom under the conditions of imperfect beings.[41] In principle, this capacity for setting ends can be promoted in two

---

did not take up this distinction in the *Doctrine of Virtue*. The same thing is also true for the interesting distinction between 'maxim of will' and 'maxim of choice,' which is found in the preliminary drafts for the *Doctrine of Virtue* (cf. VATL 23:376.5–20). That the necessity of setting ends concerns 'only' the maxims, has been clearly explicated by Tieftrunk who wrote: "Now an *obligation* is called *wide* when what one is to do and to omit is not determined for all possible cases with perfect strictness, but only the general rule is provided as an internal principle of the will, whereas the determination of the *cases* (of the individual and the particular [...]) is left to the free judgment and own's own decision: All ethical duties as such only provide the principle of willing; they tell us which maxims one should have, what the 'way of thinking' [Denkungsart] should be attuned to generally, without specifying and determining the particular real-life cases as that which is determinable by them; hence, they are wide duties. – So reason by commanding merely the having of a *maxim*, without as it were listing and exactly determining the *particular actions* which fall under it, thus *extends* the field for practicing virtue, gives a certain *latitude* to it, which is not available at all for the *narrow* duty. For narrow duty determines what one is to do and to omit in a most measured and precise way; thus it determines not only the *maxim* but also the *action*" (Tieftrunk, 1798, p. 97, trans. A.T.). In the footnote we read: "Hence, choice has a latitude (*Latitudinem*) here; but not in view of the maxim, for that is determined unchangeably by the rule of morality, but only in view of the *application* of the law of duty to real-life cases of life" (Tieftrunk, 1798, p. 98, note, trans. A.T.).

41 Cf. Römpp, 2006, p. 173. Kant writes: "[...] since there are free actions there must also be ends to which, as their objects, these actions are directed" (TL 6:385.11 f.).

ways. If *one's own person* is concerned, the only end that one can make one's own with regard to the promotion of the capacity for setting ends is one's own perfection in a teleological and qualitative (formal) sense, understood as "the harmony of a thing's properties with an *end*" (TL 6:386.23 f.). This does not mean that one should become a perfect human being in a *definite* sense, as demanded by a perfectionist account of ethics. Quite the contrary, it implies that one should maintain and cultivate a certain *personal indeterminacy* in which the human being as a being of freedom takes possession of himself, preserves the capacity freely to set ends for himself 'from scratch,' again and again.[42] This is the very heart of Kant's idea of 'perfection.'

Perfection in a sense that is relevant to ethics is not something that is received; it is not the object of some form of receptivity. It is rather an object of spontaneity that has to be brought about self-actively. Hence, if someone wants to become perfect, to do justice to the end of humanity in his own person, that implies, among other things, that he procures and promotes "the *capacity* to realize all sorts of possible ends" (TL 6:392.5 f.). To Kant the "perfection" of a human being is primarily the "fitness of his person for all sorts of possible ends" (VATL 23:391.35–392.2, trans. A.T.).[43] And since ends can only be set by oneself, this is only possible through self-determination. In the case of perfection, only those ends are involved whose possibility of being ends rests on the subject's own *spontaneity*.[44]

If, however, *the person of other human beings* is concerned, the obligatory end can only be their happiness because one cannot make their perfection one's own end:

> For the *perfection* of another human being, as a person, consists just in this: that he *himself* is able to set his end in accordance with his own concepts of duty; and it is self-contradictory to require that I do (make it my duty to do) something that only the other himself can do (TL 6:386.23 f.).

However, *in an indirect way* I can make the capacity of other human beings for setting ends my concern, namely by making their ends—in a

---

42 Cf. Römpp, 2006, p. 279. Accordingly, an essential aspect of Kant's definition of virtue is this: "Virtue is always *in progress* and yet always starts *from the beginning*" (TL 6:409.21 f.).

43 Kant's contemporary Tieftrunk characterizes the internal, moral-practical perfection as the "human fitness to make every particular end which is also a duty one's object" (Tieftrunk, 1798, p. 82, trans. A.T.).

44 Cf. Tieftrunk, 1798, p. 74.

mode and to an extent that I determine myself—a determining factor of my free choice (cf. TL 6:388.5–11)[45] so as thus to support them in the realization of their subjective ends of happiness. For as rational natural beings they are dependent on this kind of external support. Making *own's own* happiness one's end, however, cannot be a duty of virtue, since this is the natural end of every human being and, therefore, does not fall under the concept of duty (cf. TL 6:386.3–6). In other words, the duty to promote the happiness of others involves those ends whose possibility to be ends rests on the *receptivity* of the subjects. It is only these ends of others that I can make my own; not those that they themselves need to make their ends in order to be perfect. The end whose ground is the receptivity of the subject is the end of happiness, the pursuit of which is a natural necessity for all human beings. By helping other human beings realize their (permitted) (cf. TL 6:388.7) subjective ends— thereby contributing to their contentment by helping them to satisfy their inclinations—I fulfill the duty to promote the happiness of others. To the perfection of other human beings, however, I can at best make an indirect and mediate contribution.[46]

VII. Conclusion

The doctrine of virtue is not about which of the ends recommended as objects of choice by nature one *can* reasonably have, but rather about the ends of freedom one *should* have as a rational being. The two obligatory ends—one's own perfection and the happiness of others—are introduced into Kant's moral philosophy as the required matter of choice because they are *the material aspect of internal freedom under the conditions of finite rational beings*. This becomes evident only from the first-person perspective on the level of willing. Duties of virtue, which command that I should have certain practical ends, require only general internal principles of willing—principles which, as such, are supposed to be valid without exception (cf. TL 6:390.9–14). They are wide duties since they only demand general rules which tell me that I should have certain types of ends, and they allow a latitude to judgment in the determination of individual, particular actions which follow from having these maxims in certain specific situations.

---

45 See also Römpp, 2006, p. 82.
46 Cf. Tieftrunk, 1798, p. 74.

References

Allison, Henry E. (1993), "Kant's Doctrine of Obligatory Ends", in: *Annual Review of Law and Ethics*, vol. 1, pp. 7–24. (Reprinted in: id., *Idealism and Freedom: Essays on Kant's Theoretical and Practical Philosophy*, Cambridge: Cambridge University Press 1996, pp. 155–168.)

Anderson, Georg (1921), "Die 'Materie' in Kants Tugendlehre und der Formalismus der kritischen Ethik", in: *Kant-Studien*, vol. 26, pp. 289–317.

Anderson, Georg (1923), "Kants Metaphysik der Sitten – ihre Idee und ihr Verhältnis zur Ethik der Wolffschen Schule", in: *Kant-Studien*, vol. 28, pp. 41–61.

Atwell, John E. (1974), "Objective Ends in Kant's Ethics", in: *Archiv für Geschichte der Philosophie*, vol. 56, pp. 156–171.

Atwell, John E. (1986), *Ends and Principles in Kant's Moral Thought*, Dordrecht: Martin Nijhoff.

Baum, Manfred (1998), "Probleme der Begründung Kantischer Tugendpflichten", in: *Annual Review of Law and Ethics*, vol. 6, pp. 42–56.

Baum, Manfred (2005), "Freiheit und Verbindlichkeit in Kants Moralphilosophie", in: *Annual Review of Law and Ethics*, vol. 13, pp. 31–44.

Baum, Manfred (2007), "Recht und Ethik in Kants praktischer Philosophie", in: Jürgen Stolzenberg (ed.), *Kant in der Gegenwart*, Berlin/New York: Walter de Gruyter, pp. 213–226.

Beck, Lewis W. (1971), "Kant on Revolution", in: *Journal of the History of Ideas*, vol. 32, pp. 411–422.

Ebbinghaus, Julius (1954), "Interpretation and Misinterpretation of the Categorical Imperative", in: *The Philosophical Quarterly*, vol. 4, pp. 97–108. (German Version: "Deutung und Mißdeutung des kategorischen Imperativs", in: id., *Gesammelte Schriften*, vol. 1: *Sittlichkeit und Recht: Praktische Philosophie 1929–1954*, Georg Geismann/Hariolf Oberer (ed.), Bonn: Bouvier 1986, pp. 279–298.)

Ebbinghaus, Julius (1959), "Die Formeln des kategorischen Imperativs und die Ableitung inhaltlich bestimmter Pflichten", in: *Studi e ricerche di storia della filosofia*, vol. 32, pp. 3–23. (Reprinted in: id., *Gesammelte Schriften*, vol. 2: *Philosophie der Freiheit: Praktische Philosophie 1955–1972*, Georg Geismann/Hariolf Oberer (ed.), Bonn: Bouvier 1988, pp. 209–229.)

Geismann, Georg (2006), "Recht und Moral in der Philosophie Kants", in: *Annual Review of Law and Ethics*, vol. 14, pp. 3–124.

Gregor, Mary (1963), *Laws of Freedom: A Study of Kant's Method of Applying the Categorical Imperative in the 'Metaphysik der Sitten'*, Oxford: Blackwell.

Gregor, Mary (1971), "Translator's Introduction", in: Immanuel Kant, *The Doctrine of Virtue* (Part II of *The Metaphysics of Morals*), Philadelphia: University of Pennsylvania Press.

Herman, Barbara (2007), *Moral Literacy*, Cambridge/MA: Harvard University Press, chs. 9–12.

Höffe, Otfried (1979), "Recht und Moral: Ein kantischer Problemaufriss", in: *Neue Hefte für Philosophie*, vol. 17, pp. 1–36.

Höffe, Otfried (1987), "Der kategorische Imperativ als Grundbegriff einer normativen Rechts- und Staatsphilosophie", in: Reinhard Löw (ed.), *Oikeiosis*, Weinheim: Acta humaniora.

Kersting, Wolfgang (2004), "'Das starke Gesetz der Schuldigkeit und das schwächere der Gütigkeit': Kant und die Pflichtenlehre des 18. Jahrhunderts", in: id., *Kant über Recht*, Paderborn: Mentis, pp. 197–232.

Paton, Herbert J. (1963), *The Categorical Imperative*, Philadelphia: University of Pennsylvania Press.

Potter, Nelson (1985), "Kant on Ends that Are at the Same Time Duties", in: *Pacific Philosophical Quarterly*, vol. 66, pp. 78–92.

Römpp, Georg (2006), *Kants Kritik der reinen Freiheit: Eine Erörterung der 'Metaphysik der Sitten'*, Berlin: Duncker & Humblot. (Philosophische Schriften, vol. 65)

Schmucker, Josef (1997), "Der Formalismus und die materialen Zweckprinzipien in der Ethik Kants", in: Hariolf Oberer (ed.), *Kant. Analysen – Probleme – Kritik*, vol. 3, Würzburg: Königshausen & Neumann, pp. 99–156. (First published in: Johannes B. Lotz (ed.), *Kant und die Scholastik heute*, Pullach b. München: Berchmansverlag 1955, pp. 154–205.)

Tieftrunk, Johann Heinrich (1798), *Philosophische Untersuchungen über die Tugendlehre zur Erläuterung und Beurtheilung der metaphysischen Anfangsgründe der Tugendlehre vom Herrn Prof. Imm. Kant*, Halle: Rengersche Buchhandlung.

O'Neill, Onora (1989), "Universal Laws and Ends-in-Themselves", in: id., *Constructions of Reason: Explorations of Kant's Practical Philosophy*, Cambridge: Cambridge University Press, pp. 126–144.

O'Neill, Onora (1996), "Kant's Virtues", in: Roger Crisp (ed.), *How Should One live? Essays on the Virtues*, Oxford: Oxford University Press, pp. 77–97.

Virtue and Its Ends
(TL 6:394–398)

Lara Denis

This essay focuses on Kant's account of virtue, as set forth in the "Introduction to the doctrine of virtue," sections IX, X, XI. Kant characterizes virtue in five intertwined ways in these sections: as strength, self-constraint, moral disposition, volitional conformity to duty, and its own end and reward. I explore each characterization, and the questions it raises, in turn, drawing connections among the various characterizations as I go. A rich picture of Kantian virtue emerges, according to which it is a robust, pervasive realization of the inner freedom of a human being, in which her pure, unwavering, fundamental commitment to the moral law is expressed not only through her resistance to the influence of inclinations contrary to morality, but also through her protection, cultivation, and employment of feelings, predispositions, and other aspects of sensibility conducive to her fulfillment of duty—and thereby also to her moral self-realization. After delineating Kant's claims about virtue (in sections 1–5), I conclude (in sections 6–7) by suggesting some ways in which Kant's account of duties of virtue increases our understanding of Kantian virtue: by indicating key elements of the direction, structure, and content of a morally-governed human life.

1. Strength

"*Virtue* is the strength of a human being's maxims in fulfilling his duty" (TL 6:394.15 f.). Kant identifies the concept of virtue with that of strength (cf. TL 6:392.36), citing etymology for support (cf. V-MS/ Vigil 27:492.8 f.; TL 6:390.22 f.). In what does a maxim's strength consist? A plausible answer is that its strength consists in its motivational power, or more precisely, in the moving power of its corresponding incentive.[1] Virtue as strength, then, could be understood as the effective force of the moral incentive (respect for the law) to move a human being to action on maxims complying with the moral law. Kant often describes virtue as "a moral strength of the will" (e. g. TL 6:405.11). This description can be understood in a manner that is consistent with the proposed analysis of virtue as the strength of a human being's maxims in fulfilling her duty, and that aids refinement of that account. For the moving power of the moral incentive should be understood not only as driving action (within the phenomenal world) on particular moral maxims, but also as reflecting the agent's fundamental (noumenal) commitment to the moral law, and the authority and priority she assigns to the moral law within her supreme maxim. Indeed, another aspect of virtue as moral strength is the firmness, stability, and constancy of the moral commitment as a ground of choice (cf. TL 6:409.8–10).

Kant says that we can grasp strength only relatively: "Strength of any kind can be recognized only by the obstacles it can overcome, and in the case of virtue these obstacles are natural inclinations, which can come into conflict with the human being's moral resolution" (TL 6:394.16–18). At first glance, this passage seems to present a picture of our moral resolution (or moral maxims) as opposed by a wholly external, merely natural force: inclination. But this cannot be correct. In the first place, Kant holds that we are culpable for the very presence of these obstacles: "it is the human being himself who puts these obstacles in the way of his maxims" (TL 6:394.19 f.). Inclinations are *habitual* desires (cf. RL 6:212.20–213.9).[2] So even the natural inclinations—those grounded in animal nature and with 'true natural needs' as their objects—reflect our patterns of choosing and acting. More important, Kant holds that we must regard ourselves and others, *qua* persons, as responsible for our entire empirical characters, and thus for the features of ourselves in virtue of which we are susceptible to influence by particular emotions, impulses, and inclinations.[3]

---

1   For one version of this sort of analysis: see McCarty, 2009, pp. 31–38, 80–82, 182 f. Also relevant are Guyer, 2008, pp. 179–197 and Geiger, 2011, pp. 286–292.

2   Although aspects of sensibility other than inclination (narrowly construed) can also be problematic, deeply rooted inclinations and passions are more pernicious than fleeting impulses and affects (cf. TL 6:408.5–14).

3   See KpV 5:97.21–98.12, 99.19–100.14. There have been attempts to rescue Kant from the most extreme interpretations of his view—according to which, for example, one could never cite powerful inclinations as a mitigating factor

In the second place, maxims and moral resolutions seem to be such different kinds of things than inclinations are that it does not on the face of it make sense to think of them as opponents. They seem to operate in separate spheres: maxims in the realm of freedom, and inclinations in the realm of sensibility.[4] We might therefore conceive of the struggle in which virtue constitutes strength as *fundamentally* between the moral incentive and some other incentive—perhaps self-love—both of which we incorporate into our supreme maxim.[5] Alternatively, we could view the conflict as basically between virtue as the moral disposition, and vice—or perhaps particular vices, "the brood of dispositions opposing the law, [which] are the monsters [...] [the human being, L.D.] has to fight" (TL 6:405.25 f.).[6]

This raises the question: If virtue is moral strength, what is moral weakness, and how does that weakness compare with vice? Moral weakness is a lack of strength in moral maxims, characterized by a susceptibility to temptation and a failure fully to conform one's willing to the moral law—e. g., by doing little to promote obligatory ends. This lack of moral strength "can coexist with the best will" (TL 6:408.4). Vice, by contrast, presupposes immoral maxims: the "distinction between virtue and vice can never be sought in the *degree* to which one follows certain maxims; it must rather be sought only in the specific *quality* of the maxims (their relation to the law)" (TL 6:404.3–6). Kant presents the conceptual relations this way: "Virtue $= +a$ is opposed to *negative lack of virtue* (moral weakness $= 0$) as its *logical opposite* (*contradictorie oppositum*); but it is opposed to vice $= -a$ as its *real opposite* (*contrarie s. realiter oppositum*)" (TL 6:384.5–8).

It would be a mistake, however, to think that moral weakness in human beings is independent of genuine moral evil, or that evil cannot express itself as weakness. Both vice and weakness are expressions of "the radical evil in human nature" (RGV 6:32.31 f.), the propensity to favor incentives of self-love over those of morality. Kant says that 'the human being is evil' means that "he is conscious of the moral law and yet has incorporated into his maxim the (occasional) deviation from it"

---

in moral judgments of others. See Korsgaard, 1996, pp. 209–212. And see V-Mo/Collins 27:295.28–31 on charity in judging others.

4   See Grenberg, 2010, pp. 152 f.

5   The problem is not self-love per se, but self-love as a rival to morality, i.e., as "*self-conceit*," which is self-love when it "makes itself lawgiving and the unconditional practical principle" (KpV 5:74.18 f.).

6   I discuss particular vices and virtues in Denis, 2006, pp. 518–523.

(RGV 6:32.14–16). If we are free, our choice can be determined only by an incentive we have incorporated into our maxim (cf. RGV 6:23 f.).[7] We would have no opportunity for weakness if we had not incorporated self-love into our supreme maxim in such a way as to allow it to compete with morality, which we must take to be an incentive for all of us, "even the worst" (RGV 6:36.1, 46.1–5):

> If the good = a, the opposite contradicting it is the not-good. Now, this not-good is the consequence either of the mere lack of a ground of the good, = 0, or of a positive ground antagonistic to the good, = – a; in the latter case, the not-good can also be called positive evil [...] Now, if the moral law in us were not an incentive of the power of choice, the morally good (the agreement of the power of choice with the law) would be = a, and the not-good = 0; the latter however would just be the consequence of the lack of a moral incentive, = a x 0. In us, however, the law is incentive, = a. Hence the lack of agreement of the power of choice with it (= 0) is possible only as the consequence of real and opposite determination of the power of choice, i. e., of a *resistance* on its part, = – a; or again, it is only possible through an evil power of choice (RGV 6:22n.29–35–23n.4–9, see also 24).

Although we may reasonably associate vice with the highest degree of radical evil, depravity, "the propensity to adopt evil maxims" (RGV 6:29.21 f.), some level of opposition to the moral law must be assumed in all of us—"even the best" (RGV 6:30.20, 32.21, 36.23 f.)—and seems to underlie moral weakness (cf. RGV 6:59.1–15). Kant characterizes the frailty of human nature, the lowest degree of radical evil, as "the general weakness of the human heart in complying with the adopted maxims" (RGV 6:29.17 f.), as when someone "incorporate[s] the good (the law) into the maxim of [...] [his] power of choice[,] but this good, which is an irresistible incentive objectively or ideally [...] is subjectively [...] the weaker (in comparison with inclination) whenever the maxim is to be followed" (RGV 6:29.26–30).

Inclinations, then, are sufficient neither for our acting wrongly, nor even for our being tempted to act wrongly. Kant says that natural inclinations themselves "are good" (RGV 6:58.1), requiring management and discipline, not extirpation. That in us which resists the moral incentive, and which virtue as strength must overcome, is fundamentally our propensity to evil, which "is itself morally evil, since it must ultimately be

---

7   For contrasting analyses of this claim's meaning and significance: see Allison, 1990, pp. 40, 147 f. and McCarty, 2009, pp. 71–81.

sought in a free power of choice, and hence is imputable" (RGV 6:37.9–11).[8]

Finally, note Kant's specification of virtue as the strength of a human being's maxim "in fulfilling his duty" (TL 6:394.15 f.). Kant often specifies that he is talking about a 'moral' strength of a maxim, will, or resolution when he characterizes virtue as strength. The account of a maxim's strength as the moving power of its incentive, however, suggests vice too could be strong. Vice could be understood, for example, as the strength of a human being's maxim in violating his duty (cf. RGV 6:35.20–25). Less diabolically, vice's strength could consist in the effective power of the incentive of self-love (as self-conceit) to overcome obstacles in the way of the satisfaction of inclinations. It seems that vice, no less than virtue, can be motivationally forceful, as well as stable, firm, and constant. Indeed, Kant's positing vice as virtue's "real opposite" (TL 6:384.7 f.) and true opponent seems to support a notion of vice as strength. But although Kant contrasts vice with weakness, he is adamant in the *Doctrine of Virtue* that vice is not properly understood as strength.

> [I]t is not only unnecessary but even improper to ask whether great crimes might not require more strength of soul[9] than do great virtues. For by strength of soul we mean strength of resolution in a human being as a being endowed with freedom, hence his strength insofar as he is in control of himself [...] and so in the state of *health* proper to a human being (TL 6:384.8–14).[10]

In the "Introduction to the metaphysics of morals", Kant explains how we must (and must not) construe freedom:

> [F]reedom can never be located in a rational subject's being able to choose in opposition to his (lawgiving) reason, even though experience proves often enough that this happens [...] Only freedom in relation to the inner lawgiving of reason is really an ability; the possibility of deviating from it is an inability (MS 6:226.29–227.4).

---

8 For further elaboration of this position: see Grenberg, 2010, pp. 155–158.
9 Here "soul" (TL 6:384.19) refers to "the vital principle of man in the free use of his powers" (TL 6:384.19 f.).
10 Cf. Kant on Sulla's strength of soul (Anth 7:293). In this context, Kant reserves "greatness of soul" (Anth 7:293.22) for those with a good and strong character, but allows "strength of soul" (Anth 7:293.19) to those with a bad but firm character. I have room discuss neither these claims, nor Kant's notion of character in general. See Frierson, 2003, pp. 61–64, 111. As Frierson notes, Kant's account of frailty suggests that it is a symptom of lack of character generally, not just lack of morally good character.

The strength of a human being's maxim, or a human being's strength of will, must reflect and realize her freedom; her freedom consists in her ability to conform her choice to the moral law, through the thought of the law; her freedom is realized through, and only through, that conformity. Thus, we cannot understand all motivational efficacy as strength, or the moving power of just any incentive as rendering its maxim strong. Only if a maxim incorporates, springs from, or otherwise reflects the moral incentive can it be strong, for only then is it a realization of the human beings' capacity to comply with the moral law from respect for it.

2. Self-Constraint

Kant says that "the moral capacity to constrain oneself can be called virtue" (TL 6:394.28 – 30). He defines virtue as "a self-constraint in accordance with a principle of inner freedom, and so through the mere representation of one's duty in accordance with its formal law" (TL 6:394.21 – 23, see also 406.26 – 407.25). He proceeds to identify "*inner* freedom" (TL 6:396.19) with "the capacity for self-constraint […] by pure practical reason" (TL 6:396.20 f.). In the second *Critique*, Kant suggests that inner freedom allows a human being "to release himself from the impetuous importunity of inclinations so that none of them, not even the dearest, has any influence on a resolution for which we are now to make use of our reason" (KpV 5:161.4 – 8). The foregoing suggests that inner freedom consists most basically in the volitional power to comply with the moral law through respect for the law.

Kant distinguishes between the bare capacity of moral self-constraint or inner freedom and that capacity realized as strength:

> [W]hile the capacity (*facultas*) to overcome all opposing sensible impulses can and must be simply *presupposed* in man on account of his freedom, yet this capacity as strength (*robur*) is something he must acquire; and the way to acquire it is to enhance the moral incentive (the thought of the law), both by contemplating the dignity of the pure rational law in us (*contemplatione*) and by practicing virtue (*exercitio*) (TL 6:397.12 – 19).

The capacity for moral self-constraint—i. e., constraint of pure practical reason—is essential to our nature as autonomous rational beings lacking holy wills. If we could not follow our rationally self-legislated moral law, we would lack moral personality (cf. TL 6:417.24 – 418.3, 420.16 – 26). If we had holy wills, no constraint would be necessary in order for us to comply with the moral law (cf. GMS 4:439.28 – 30; KpV 5:32.17 – 35).

When the bare capacity for inner freedom is strengthened, it becomes virtue.[11] The stronger one's inner freedom, the more ready is one's morally-
motivated compliance with the moral law. Virtue thus presupposes, engages, and realizes our inner freedom.

Kant further develops his notion of virtue as an acquired strength of
moral self-constraint through the notion of autocracy: the power of pure
practical reason to implement the moral law.[12] "Virtue is [...] the moral
strength of a *human being's* will in fulfilling his *duty*, a moral *constraint*
through his own lawgiving reason, insofar as this constitutes itself an authority *executing* the law" (TL 6:405.15–18). Pure practical reason's autonomy consists in its legislation of the moral law, while its autocracy
consists in its execution of that law. Kant associates the moral incentive
with the latter:

> If reason determines the will through the moral law, it has the force of an
> incentive, and in that case it has, not autonomy merely, but also autocracy.
> It then has both legislative and executive power. The autocracy of reason, to
> determine the will in accordance with moral laws, would then be the moral
> feeling [i.e., inner reverence for the law, L.D.]. Man does really possess the
> force for this, if only he is taught to perceive the strength and necessity of
> virtue (V-Mo/Mron II 29:626.2–9).[13]

Autocracy presupposes our autonomy and our susceptibility to temptation
through inclination. Through autocracy, we exercise a developed capacity for moral self-rule, including rule over our inclinations.

> For finite *holy* beings (who could never be tempted to violate duty) there
> would be no doctrine of virtue but only a doctrine of morals, since the latter
> is autonomy of practical reason whereas the former is also *autocracy* of prac-
> tical reason, that is, it involves consciousness of the *capacity* to master one's
> inclinations when they rebel against the law (TL 6:383.20–27).

---

11 For discussion of inner freedom, its close relation to the positive conception of
    practical freedom, and its realization as virtue: see Engstrom, 2002. Also relevant
    is Korsgaard, 1996, pp. 176–183.
12 For a book-length account of Kantian virtue as autocracy: see Baxley, 2010. In
    the political realm, Kant characterizes an autocrat as the sole sovereign and legis-
    lator, the "*one* in the state [who] has command over all [...] who rules *by himself*
    and has *all* the authority" (RL 6:338.31–339.2).
13 The full paragraph from which this passage is drawn suggests that autocracy may
    be conceived as a feature of our will that must be presupposed as well as culti-
    vated. This ambiguity (or dual usage) is unproblematic; it is in keeping with sim-
    ilar claims about (e.g.) the capacity for moral self-constraint and the moral incen-
    tive, both of which we must somehow presuppose yet also must cultivate.

Although few of us may develop autocracy, its bases in our freedom, and in moral feeling as "a *susceptibility* on the part of free choice to be moved by pure practical reason (and its law)" (TL 6:400.18 f.), must be presupposed in all of human beings.

In light of autocracy's reliance on the strength of the moral incentive, it might seem surprising that Kant's lengthy discussions of autocracy in his lectures on ethics emphasize the importance of disciplining inclinations, resisting affects, and governing passions in the pursuit and maintenance of this condition (see V-Mo/Collins 27:360.4–369.2; TL 6:407.19–408.22). Though conceptually distinct, these negative and positive tasks are closely bound up with each other practically. For example, Kant holds one can strengthen the moral incentive *by* weakening the influence of inclinations, impulses, affects, and passions that may compete with it (see V-Mo/Collins 27:361.25 f.).[14]

The discussion of autocracy takes us back to Kant's claim (at TL 6:397.14–19) that one builds moral strength by enhancing the moral incentive through contemplation and practice. Contemplation of the dignity of the moral law enhances the moral incentive by enlivening our respect for it. The moral law strikes down our self-conceit, simultaneously pointing us toward the realization of our higher, moral vocation (see KpV 5:73.2–27, 78.27–79.19, 160.26–161.24). We recognize—and feel—its authority over us, its supremacy over and independence of our sensibility. Consciousness of our independence from determination by inclination inspires our desire for independence even from its influence. Through our respect for the moral law, our sense of its sublimity, we see the relative triviality and transitivity of our sensible natures' impulses, feelings, and inclinations, weakening their influence over us and thus facilitating our triumph over them.[15] In moral practice, we engage the moral incentive, sometimes through moral struggle. Resisting affects, eradicating damaging passions, avoiding vices, and disciplining inclinations may be seen as negative or corrective aspects of this practice through which we 'get hold of' ourselves and 'gain the upper hand' over temptation (see TL 6:407.19–409.3). Positive or constructive aspects include

---

14 In the Collins lecture notes, Kant often treats autocracy as the provenance of duties to oneself. See V-Mo/Collins 27:360.4–369.2. See also the reference to inner freedom in relation to perfect duties to oneself as a moral being only at TL 6:420.13–26.

15 On contemplation and Kantian virtue: see Engstrom, 2002, pp. 311–315 and Grenberg, 2010, pp. 163–165.

development of particular virtues (see TL 6:446.21–23, 447.6–15), as well as cultivation of "natural predispositions of the mind [...] for being affected by the concepts of duty" (TL 6:399.11 f.) and naturally occurring feelings such as sympathy that can assist us in recognizing and fulfilling our duties (cf. TL 6:399.1–403.6, 406.18–24, 456.20–33).[16]

3. Moral Disposition

In these pages, Kant only fleetingly and ambiguously links the notions of virtue and moral disposition. He seems to identify virtue with the disposition of respect for the moral law—or perhaps the disposition of obedience to the moral law—when he says: "Since the moral capacity to constrain oneself can be called virtue, action springing from such a disposition [Gesinnung] (respect for the law) can be called virtuous (ethical) action" (TL 6:394.28–30). Elsewhere Kant is more sanguine about this characterization of virtue. In the *Groundwork*, he equates virtue with "the morally good disposition" (GMS 4:435.29), and in the *Religion*, with "conformity of the *disposition* to the law of duty" (RGV 6:37.33 f.). In the *Critique of Practical Reason*, Kant defines virtue as "a disposition conformed with the law *from respect* for the law" (KpV 5:128.5).[17] Similarly emphasizing the moral incentive in the *Religion*, he defines virtue as "a constant *disposition* toward [...] actions [conforming to duty, L.D.] from *duty* (because of their morality)" (RGV 6:14.6 f.).[18] Even on the characterization of virtue as the morally good disposition, however, virtue presupposes *inner resistance* to compliance with the law. For example, in the *Critique of Practical Reason*, Kant calls virtue, "moral disposition *in conflict*" (KpV 5:84.33 f.), contrasting it with holiness, which is "a complete purity of dispositions of the will" (KpV 5:84.34 f., see also 122.9 f.).

---

16 See Guyer, 2010, for account of how respect for the moral law engages other feelings.

17 Paul Guyer argues that virtue as strength, persistence, and facility in fulfilling one's duty is the *product* of virtue as motivation by respect for the moral law alone, which reflects the supremacy of the moral law within the agent's supreme maxim. See Guyer, 2000, pp. 303–311.

18 In the passage cited, Kant contrasts phenomenal virtue with noumenal virtue, identifying the former with "a facility in *actions* conforming to duty (according to their legality)" (RGV 6:14.4 f.) and the latter with the pure and constant moral motivation to such actions (RGV 6:14.6 f., see also 47.1–28).

What, though, is a disposition (*Gesinnung*), and what makes it morally good? In the *Critique of Practical Reason*, Kant equates the disposition with "the supreme determining ground of the will" (KpV 5:125.11). He develops this account further in the *Religion*, defining the disposition as "the first subjective ground of the adoption of maxims" (RGV 6:25.5 f.), which "applies to the entire use of freedom universally" (RGV 6:25.6 f.) and can be imputed to us. If a human being has a morally good disposition, the moral law is the supreme determining ground of her will.

According to Kant, however, the radical evil in human nature consists in the fact "that the human being (even the best) [...] reverses the moral order of incentives in incorporating them in his maxims" (RGV 6:36.23–25); "he makes the incentives of self-love and their inclinations the condition of compliance with the moral law" (RGV 6:36.29 f.), or at least a ground for occasional deviation from it (cf. RGV 6:29.4–11, 32.13–15, 37.18–31).[19] It might seem then that no one can become virtuous. After all, we must attribute to ourselves the propensity to evil. Further, we should assume that we begin our moral struggle in depravity, not mere frailty (cf. RGV 6:51.1–6). Even getting onto the path of virtue requires "a *revolution* in the disposition of the human being" (RGV 6:47.24 f.). Worse still, since the propensity to evil "corrupts the ground of all maxims" (RGV 6:37.12) and cannot be extirpated by human efforts, this revolution seems beyond our power.

Nevertheless, Kant assures us, "it must be possible to *overcome* this evil, for it is found in the human being acting freely" (RGV 6:37.16 f.). Our certainty that we ought to justifies our hope that we can (cf. RGV 6:45.7–11 50.19–21).[20] Our life-long moral struggle can be conceived as a prolonged attempt to correct the inversion of incentives, or as a temporal manifestation of that intelligible reversal:

> For the judgment of human beings [...] who can assess themselves and the strength of their maxims only by the upper hand they gain over the senses in time, the change is to be regarded only as an ever-continuing striving for the better, hence as a gradual reformation of the propensity to evil, of the perverted attitude of mind (RGV 6:48.12–16).

19 The relation of the disposition to the supreme maxim is disputed. For two accounts of this issue as it bears on the radical evil in human nature: see Allison, 1990, pp. 136–145, 153–157 and McCarty, 2009, pp. 205–210.
20 For one account of God's assistance in this process: see Hare, 1996, pp. 38–68.

The human being who observes a steady, continuous improvement in her moral conduct over the course of her life may reasonably hope that her disposition has fundamentally improved (see RGV 6:68 f.).

4. Volitional Conformity

Kant provides a *"formal"* (TL 6:395.10) characterization of virtue as "the will's conformity with every duty, based on a firm disposition" (TL 6:395.9 f.). This characterization depends on the previous one, because only if respect for the moral moral law is the supreme ground of all maxim-adoption can all willing fully conform to the moral law. Fulfilling duties is characteristic of virtue. Virtue connotes power and efficacy, not mere good intention and benevolent wish. But complete conformity requires more than facility in performance of necessary actions. It requires not only firmness but also *purity* of disposition.[21]

Complete conformity is an ideal. Kant describes virtue as "an ideal and unattainable, while yet constant approximation to it is a duty" (TL 6:409.23 f.). Yet it is not virtue, but *holiness*, that constitutes "complete conformity of the will with the moral law" (KpV 5:122.9 f.). Although we must strive for it, it will always be beyond our reach—at least during our earthly lives (cf. KpV 5:122.4–123.7; TL 6:446.17–33). After all, if "[t]he greatest perfection of a human being is to do his duty *from duty*" (TL 6:392.20 f.), and to act from duty implies self-constraint and thus inner resistance to the moral law, the greatest perfection of a human being falls incomparably short of holiness. A holy being is one "in whom no hindering impulses would impede the law of its will and who would thus gladly do everything in conformity with the law" (TL 6:405.13–15); she "could never be tempted to violate duty" (TL 6:383.21 f.). The will of such a being "would not be capable of any maxim conflicting with the moral law" (KpV 5:32.20 f.); its "maxims necessarily harmonize with the laws of autonomy" (GMS 4:439.28 f.). So if virtue is the conformity of the human will with the moral law, it is not *complete* conformity.

Kant notes that our struggle to comply to the moral law impresses us in a way that the effortless compliance of a holy will does not: "Virtue so

---

21 Kant divides the duty to perfect oneself into the injunctions "be holy," which concerns "the *purity* [...] of one's disposition to duty" and "be perfect," which requires "fulfilling all one's duties" (TL 6:446.13–20).

shines as an ideal that it seems, by human standards, to eclipse *holiness* itself, which is never tempted to break the law" (TL 6:396.34–397.1). Kant views this assessment as mistaken, however, explaining it as:

> an illusion arising from the fact that, having no way to measure the degree of a strength except by the magnitude of the obstacles it could overcome (in us, these are inclinations), we are led to mistake the *subjective* conditions by which we assess the magnitude for the *objective* conditions of the magnitude itself (TL 6:397.1–6).

Holiness is, objectively, a better moral condition than virtue. Moreover, within human beings, frequent, active struggle against vice is *not* characteristic of virtue. "The rules for practicing virtue [...] aim at a frame of mind that is both *valiant* and *cheerful* in fulfilling its duties" (TL 6:484.20–23). "The true strength of virtue is a *tranquil mind* with a considered and firm resolution to put the law of virtue into practice. That is the state of *health* in the moral life" (TL 6:409.8–10). If a human being properly governs himself he can "prevent any rebellion of the rabble in his soul [i.e., his inclinations, L.D.] [...] no war will arise in him, and where there is no war, no conquest is necessary either. It is therefore far better if a man is so governed that he need gain no victory over himself" (V-Mo/Collins 27:368.34–369.2). Yet in human beings, rational self-government requires constant vigilance and continuing effort: "[V]irtue can never settle down in peace and quiet with its maxims adopted once and for all but, if it is not rising, is unavoidably sinking" (TL 6:409.26–28; see also RGV 6:93.4–13).

5. Its Own End and Reward

"The highest, unconditional end of pure practical reason (which is still a duty) consists in this: that virtue be its own end and, despite the benefits it confers on human beings, also its own reward" (TL 6:396.31–34). Virtue is itself an end we are obligated to have: an end that we are obligated through moral self-constraint to pursue. But what sense or senses of virtue does it make sense to think of as an end for which to strive? On the face of it, it does not make sense to think of us as obliged to adopt the end of virtue as moral self-constraint, for it is only through moral self-constraint that we can be bound to adopt any end (cf. TL 6:405.19–22). Furthermore, "the capacity (*facultas*) to overcome all opposing sensible impulses can and must be simply *presupposed* in man on account of his freedom" (TL 6:397.12–14). Kant seems mainly to have in mind virtue as strength: "It is […] correct to say that the human being is under obligation *to virtue* (as moral strength). […] this capacity as *strength* (*robur*) is something he must acquire" (TL 6:397.11–16) by enhancing the moral incentive. It is fitting to think of moral self-constraint *realized as strength* as an end for which we are bound to strive, for "this constraint is to be irresistible, [so] strength is required" (TL 6:405.22 f.). Additionally, this way of thinking about virtue as a morally necessary end agrees with Kant's characterization of the obligatory end of our moral perfection. We are to promote this end by striving to cultivate the "purest virtuous disposition" (TL 6:387.13), according to which "the *law* becomes also the incentive to […] [one's] actions that conform with duty and […] [one] obeys the law from duty" (TL 6:387.13–15).

What does the claim that virtue ought to be recognized as "its own reward" (TL 6:396.34) add to the claim that it ought to be recognized as "its own end" (TL 6:396.33)? One might think it is just another way of saying that virtue should be sought for itself, not merely as a means; otherwise one's moral commitment is impure. But there is more to it. There are several ways that Kant portrays virtue as its own reward. I will mention four.

The first two are closely related: moral contentment with oneself and one's state. Kant calls contentment with oneself, "a satisfaction with one's existence" that constitutes "an analogue of happiness that must necessarily accompany consciousness of [one's] virtue" (KpV 5:117.26–28). This contentment "*with oneself*" (KpV 5:117.28 f.) gives rise to a moral contentment with one's state. *Self*-contentment involves "consciousness of freedom as an ability to follow the moral law with an unyielding disposition" (KpV 5:117.31–33) and thus an "*independence from the inclinations*" (KpV 5:117.33) as impediments to such obedience. The contentment *with one's state* consequent on this sense of one's "mastery over one's inclinations" (KpV 5:118.26) is an indirect enjoyment of freedom. Kant calls it a "negative satisfaction with one's state" because instead of involving consciousness of the satisfaction of one's inclinations or the achievement of one's discretionary ends, one's consciousness of one's independence from inclinations largely relieves "the discontent that always accompanies them" and the burden they impose on the finite rational being as they shift, fluctuate, "grow with […] indulgence" or become frustrated (cf. KpV 5:118.1–37).

The third is merit. Kant claims that "there is a subjective principle of ethical *reward*, that is, a receptivity to being rewarded in accordance with laws of virtue" (TL 6:391.9–12), which corresponds to ethical duties and facilitates our compliance with them. This "ethical *reward*" (TL 6:391.10) is "a moral pleasure that goes beyond mere contentment with oneself (which can be merely negative) and which is celebrated in the saying that, through consciousness of this pleasure, virtue is its own reward" (TL 6:391.12–15). Kant gives as one example of the sort of ethical reward he has in mind the "moral enjoyment" (TL 6:391.19 f.) one feels when one promotes the happiness of others in such a way as to please them; he calls this "*sweet merit*" (TL 6:391.19). Here Kant attributes our tendency toward such enjoyment in the happiness of others as a consequence of our action to *sympathy* (cf. TL 6:456.24–26). Elsewhere, however, he suggests that it is "[l]ove of human beings" (TL 6:401.23), one of the "natural predispositions of the mind [...] for being affected by concepts of duty" (TL 6:399.11 f.) which leads one to love one's fellow human beings, and thus to enjoy fulfilling one's duties of beneficence toward them (cf. TL 6:399.6 f., 401.24–402.21). This dual attribution is interesting, as Kant generally portrays sympathy as a morally useful but natural feeling (part of our animal nature), and love of one's neighbor as a distinctly "moral endowment[]" (TL 6:399.4), consciousness of which "is not of empirical origin" (TL 6:399.14 f.) but must "follow from consciousness of a moral law, as the effect this has on the mind" (TL 6:399.15 f.). Kant does, however, distinguish sympathy grounded in pure practical reason from merely natural sympathy (or compassion), giving each a role to play (cf. TL 6:456.28–457.5). He claims that "it is a duty to sympathize actively in [others'] fate; and to this end it is therefore an indirect duty to cultivate the compassionate natural [...] feelings in us, and to make use of them as so many means to sympathy based on moral principles and the feeling appropriate to them" (TL 6:457.25–29).[22]

Fourth is moral self-approbation (KpV 5:80.33–81.9). Through the moral strength of virtue, the human being realizes his freedom, 'living up' to his status as a person. Approaching his higher vocation, living in accordance with his dignity, is possible only through his willing, not through the operations of nature or the conduct of others (cf. GMS 4:398.27–37, 440.7–13).[23] Insofar as we take an interest in our rational

---

22 On of the relation among moral incentive or virtue, love of human beings, and sympathy: see Guyer, 2010, pp. 145–149 and Baxley, 2010, pp. 155–170.

23 Any dignity attained through virtue is dependent on the innate dignity of human beings due simply to their freedom (see TL 6:420.21–23, 462.10–15). See Sensen, 2009, pp. 315–318.

freedom, we feel satisfaction in our (hard-earned) moral progress. We are 'elevated' by our free submission to the law (cf. KpV 5:86.8–89.8; RGV 6:183.22–37).[24]

Related to his description of virtue as its own end and own reward, Kant says: "[T]he worth of virtue itself, as its own end, far exceeds the worth of any usefulness and any empirical ends and advantages that virtue may still bring in its wake" (TL 6:397.8–10). There is a strong resemblance between passages like this about the goodness of virtue, and those about the goodness of a good will. For example:

> A good will is not good because of what it effects or accomplishes, because of its fitness to attain some proposed end, but only because of its volition, that is, it is good in itself and, regarded for itself, is to be valued incomparably higher than all that could merely be brought about by it in favor of some inclination and indeed […] of the sum of all inclinations (GMS 4:394.13–18).

This raises the question of whether and how we should distinguish a good will from virtue. This would be an easier question to settle if it were obvious how best to understand a good will. Kant often characterizes a good will as a will committed to and compliant with the moral law out of respect for the law (cf. GMS 4:401n.17–40, 413.1–8). Sometimes he identifies it with a will that has the categorical imperative as its principle (cf. GMS 4:444.28 f.). Sometimes he seems to think of a good will as the predisposition to personality which we must presuppose in all human beings (cf. RGV 6:44.18–24). Sometimes Kant depicts it as an ideal will we each attribute to ourselves when we think of ourselves as subject to moral self-constraint (cf. GMS 4:455.1–9). And sometimes he seems to use the notions of virtue and a good will interchangeably, e. g., as identical with the morally good disposition. Usually, however, virtue seems to involve a fuller realization of *human* morality than does a good will. For example, the notion of a good will does not presuppose inner resistance to the moral law or temptation through inclinations, as virtue does. Furthermore, one might have a good will, and yet lack the apathy and self-mastery essential to virtue. A good will is incompatible with vice, but can be "childish and weak" (TL 6:408.3) in the face of emotions and impulses. Thus, we may conclude that, insofar as they are conceptually distinct, virtue is the fullest actualization of a good will possible in a human being. Kant's account of virtue encompasses much of the more narrow, abstract

---

24 For further discussion of the appeal of virtue as realized inner freedom: see Guyer, 2000, pp. 107–117 and Uleman, 2010, pp. 149–173.

notion of a good will, but builds on it in a manner proper to the speci-
fications of *human* moral agency, thus yielding a far more complete picture of what we should aspire to be like.[25]

6. The Matter of Virtue

The various strands of the preceding account coalesce to depict Kantian
virtue as a moral ideal for human beings. Virtue is a realization of freedom in the form volitional conformity with the moral law through
moral self-constraint. As beings whose inclinations can tempt us to diso-
bey the moral law, virtue is a victory over them. Virtue is a victory more
fundamentally, however, over our tendency to subordinate the moral law
to self-love. Virtue requires the establishment of a morally good disposition. Furthermore, the development and practice of virtue involves the
preservation, cultivation, and utilization of whatever capacities, feelings,
predispositions, mental powers, and rational desires are conductive to
our fulfillment of duty. Our efforts to govern ourselves through the
moral law are critical to our self-realization as free, rational, human beings.

   Duties of virtue figure significantly in this process of moral self-realization. In section IX of the "Introduction to the doctrine of virtue,"
Kant elucidates his notion of a duty of virtue by drawing on the notions
of virtue as self-constraint through respect for the law and as a morally
good disposition, and distinguishing between "what is virtuous to do"
and what is "a *duty of virtue* strictly speaking" (cf. TL 6:394.33–
395.1, see also 383.8–14, 410.21–32): "What it is virtuous to do
may concern only *what is formal* in maxims, whereas a duty of virtue
has to do with their matter, that is to say, with an end that is thought
as also a duty" (TL 6:394.33–395.1). Any duty, including duties of
right, can meet the formal condition of being performed from respect
for the law. Duties of virtue, however, are unique in that they are obligations to have ends.

   I can here explore neither the question of whether the only ends we
are obligated to have in the relevant sense are one's own perfection and

---

25 For further discussion of the good will and virtue: see Hill, 2008, pp. 40–50 and
    Baxley, 2010, pp. 172–179.

the happiness of others[26], nor the question of whether (or how) the negative duties included in the doctrine of virtue constitute duties of virtue. Instead, I will focus on these two points: that the *Doctrine of Virtue* sets forth ends for the sake of which we must act, and that the obligatory ends and imperfect duties pertaining to their promotion are presented as ways of making the human being as such one's end.

The supreme principle of the doctrine of virtue (SPDV) is, "act in accordance with a maxim of *ends* that it can be a universal law for everyone to have" (TL 6:395.15 f.).[27] Kant calls SPDV "a categorical imperative" (TL 6:395.22 f.), and provides it a "deduction from pure practical reason" (TL 6:395.23 f., see also 382.17–22, 385.25–29).[28] SPDV is an application of the requirement of universal validity to our end-setting, which, as an act of freedom, is subject to the laws of pure practical reason. According to Kant, this principle's employment yields not only prohibitions of and permissions for various inclination-based ends, but also prescriptions of some purely rational ends—most obviously, one's own perfection and the happiness of others—which we must adopt and with which our maxims must be congruent.

Roughly, Kant argues that pure practical reason's legislation of ends follows from the unconditioned practical validity of the moral law and the essentially end-directed determination of human choice. Kant takes the moral law's authority over us to establish that we are free: our choice is determinable by reason independently of sensibility. Determination of our choice involves the representation of an end. If reason were not a source of ends a priori, our ends could derive only from sensibility. But then our choice would not be determinable by reason independently of sensibility. So it must be the case that reason sets forth some ends a

---

26 And perhaps also the specific ends individual agents adopt under those general headings as particular instantiations of those ends. According to Allen Wood: "The obligatory ends may be ends of pure reason insofar as they fall under the headings 'my own perfection' and 'others' happiness,' but it is always the particular instances as such that are the ends of reason. Kant's view is *not* that the real ends of reason are only the larger categories [...]" (Wood, 1999, p. 328).

27 Kant calls this a "synthetic" principle (TL 6:396.15; V-MS/Vigil 27:583.34–38, 600.32–38). Although Kant notes that it adds to the analytic principle of right an *end* in relation to which duties are determined, the synthetic nature of SPDV stems from its basis in *human agency* in particular rather than freedom in general. These features are not unrelated, of course (see RGV 6:7n.20–42). See Gregor, 1963, p. 88.

28 For extended reconstructions and discussion of pertinent arguments: see Gregor, 1963, pp. 76–94 and Allison, 1996, pp. 155–164.

priori. Since we tend to set and pursue ends that satisfy sensible inclinations, pure practical reason *constrains* us to adopt these objective ends and
maxims that promote or otherwise accord with them.[29] The whole system
of ends of pure practical reason is the highest good. So we can see SPDV
as demanding the reshaping of our subjective end of our personal happiness so that it can be willed as part of the morally-conditioned, universal
happiness.

Fundamental to the moral reshaping of one's own happiness mandat-
ed by SPDV is making 'the human being as such' one's end. Kant elaborates on SPDV like this:

> In accordance with this principle, a human being is an end for himself as well
> as for others, and it is not enough that he is not authorized to use either him-
> self or others merely as a means (since he could then still be indifferent to
> them); it is in itself his duty to make the human being as such his end
> (TL 6:395.17–21, see also 410.13–20).

This elaboration can be read as saying that SPDV requires human agents
to determine their wills in relation to themselves and other human beings
as objects. This requirement echoes that of the formula of humanity
(FH), which Kant established in the *Groundwork*, but emphasizes its internal and positive aspects. It internalizes FH by saying that humanity—
or 'the human being as such'[30]—must operate within each individual as a
reason for action and omission; she herself must take it as a reason. It emphasizes the positive aspect of FH by indicating that making the human
being one's end is more than (even intentionally) restricting one's use of
means to so as not to degrade humanity, or even intentionally preserving
and protecting humanity; it involves fostering humanity, primarily by
promoting one's own perfection and the happiness of others, which we

---

29 Not all ends of pure practical reason are duties. See Kant's discussions of our own
    happiness and the perfection of others (cf. TL 6:385.30–386.14; V-MS/Vigil
    27:543.30–544.23).

30 Although I do not deny significance to Kant's referring to 'the human being as
    such' rather than to 'humanity' in the elaboration of SPDV, I think it reasonable
    to focus on the continuity with FH. The beings we are to treat as ends are not
    holy, but human, with duties our own reason lays upon us (cf. TL 6:379.17–25,
    435.11–13); our specifically human nature is important to determining which
    duties we have to ourselves and others. But our humanity is fundamental to
    our status as beings capable of active as well as passive obligation (cf. RL
    6:239.23–26, 295.11 f.; TL 6:418.17–20); and the *Groundwork* presentation
    of FH states, "the *human being* and in general every rational being *exists* as an
    end in itself [...] [and] must in all his actions [...] always be regarded *at the
    same time as an end*" (GMS 4:428.7–11, first italics L.D.).

must have as ends. If one accepts this interpretation, one can see SPDV as underlying all duties of virtue, perfect and imperfect alike. Regardless of whether (or how) it grounds all duties enumerated in the doctrine of virtue, however, SPDV undoubtedly requires the adoption and promotion of the obligatory ends of one's own perfection and the happiness of others, duties which Kant portrays as at least partially constitutive of making the human being as such as one's end.

7. Ends, Inner Freedom, and Life's Direction

Through their relation to ends, duties of virtue illuminate the material side of Kantian virtue. They indicate traits, commitments, and attitudes characteristic of a virtuous person—both as manifestations of a morally good disposition, and as tools in cultivating and maintaining autocracy. They also provide a rough blueprint for a morally-structured life through which the agent is able to realize herself as a particular individual.[31]

Duties of virtue are duties to make ends prescribed by pure practical reason our own. Compliance with these duties can be compelled only through moral self-constraint, the coercion of pure practical reason. Since our wills are not holy, the coercive power of pure practical reason is a condition of the capacity of our choice to comply with the moral law. Kant calls the capacity of choice to determine itself independently of inclination's influence 'inner freedom'. Inner freedom involves freedom *to* choose in accordance with the moral law, and freedom *from* the tyranny of inclination. As a bare capacity, inner freedom is a condition of virtue and duties of virtue; as strength, it is virtue. Kant holds that inner freedom both requires and employs objective ends:

> [E]thics [...] provides a *matter* (an object of free choice), an **end** of pure reason which it represents as an end that is also objectively necessary, that is, an end that, as far as human beings are concerned, it is a duty to have. – For since the sensible inclinations of human beings tempt them to ends (the matter of choice) that can be contrary to duty, lawgiving reason can in turn check their influence only by a moral end set up against the ends of inclination, an end that must therefore be given *a priori*, independently of inclinations.
>
> [...] [I]f I am under obligation to make my end something that lies in concepts of pure practical reason, and so to have, besides the formal determining ground of choice (such as right contains), a material one as well,

---

31 See Denis, 2011, for development of this idea.

an end that could be set against the end arising from sensible impulses, this would be the concept of an *end that is in itself a duty* (TL 6:380.22–381.15).

This passage's claim about the necessity of objective ends might give the impression that pure reason cannot determine human choice through the moral law. Obviously such a claim would conflict with Kant's fundamental commitments about morality and freedom. But there is no conflict. The prescription of some ends a priori is an *aspect of* pure reason's determination of our choice through the moral law. The moral constraint that compels our adoption of the unconditionally necessary ends and our maxims' agreement with them is constraint through the moral incentive. The more virtuous the agent, the stronger her moral incentive to adopt these ends and choose more particular ends and maxims in accordance with them.[32]

Obviously, Kant's comments here also reflect his position, discussed in section 2, about strengthening the moral incentive by weakening opposing inclinations. This passage suggests that objective ends play a crucial role in strengthening inner freedom. Unconditionally necessary ends are alternatives to inclination-based ends. The recognition that we can take up these ends as duties demonstrates to us our motivational independence from inclination. This weakens inclination's sway over us and, indirectly and relatively, strengthens the moral incentive. Moreover, this reminder of our motivational independence from inclination intensifies our sense of our sublimity as moral beings, thus strengthening the moral incentive more directly. Furthermore, duties of virtue are not only duties for which inner freedom is required and revealed. Their fulfillment enhances inner freedom in other ways as well, often through the cultivation of particular virtues. For example, Kant claims that actively helping others, as the duty of beneficence requires, "will produce a love of them in you (as an aptitude of the inclination to beneficence in general)" (TL 6:402.20 f.); this aptitude facilitates further compliance with beneficence and other duties of love. Fulfillment of many duties of virtue involves cultivation of predispositions and feelings through which the moral incentive finds expression in human beings. Thus, the promotion of objective ends is a vehicle for our inner freedom's growth not only in strength, but also, as I explain further below, in expression.

---

32 On the relation of the moral incentive to fulfillment of duties of virtue: see Timmons, 2002, Stratton-Lake, 2009, pp. 111–114 and McCarty, 2009, pp. 191–195.

Objective ends—especially the obligatory ends of our own perfection and others' happiness—give rational shape and direction to our lives.[33] The ends we adopt in accordance with SPDV—and especially those prescribed by pure practical reason—are most genuinely our own because they manifest our freedom as moral beings (cf. GMS 4:436.1–7; TL 6:392.1–9, 392.20–23). Since particular ends necessitated through this principle are ways of making the human being as such our end, adherence to maxims of their promotion entails living so as to realize rational nature in ourselves and to support its expression in others. Were there no purely rational ends, all our ends would fall under the rubric of self-love, aiming ultimately at our personal happiness.

Obligatory ends set our lives on a moral trajectory. They present us with a framework in which to build a coherent, distinctive, moral life—a life fundamentally guided and shaped by the ends of reason, but with much flexibility for our own discretionary ends. They give our lives a purpose, meaning, and an integrity it could not have otherwise. These ends guide us in our adoption of more specific ends, and thus reshape our conceptions of happiness. They point us individually and collectively toward the realization of the highest good, the unconditioned totality of the ends of pure practical reason. This is the end in relation to which we all may orient our practical lives, and which provides the answer to the unavoidable human question, "*What is then the result of this right conduct of ours?*" (RGV 6:5.3 f.).

References

Allison, Henry E. (1990), *Kant's Theory of Freedom*, Cambridge: Cambridge University Press.
Allison, Henry E. (1996), *Idealism and Freedom*, Cambridge: Cambridge University Press.
Baxley, Anne Margaret (2010), *Kant's Theory of Virtue: The Value of Autocracy*, Cambridge: Cambridge University Press.
Betzler, Monika (ed.) (2008), *Kant's Ethics of Virtue*, Berlin/New York: Walter de Gruyter.
Denis, Lara (1997), "Kant's Ethics and Duties to Oneself", in: *Pacific Philosophical Quarterly*, vol. 78, pp. 321–348.
Denis, Lara (2001), *Moral Self-Regard: Duties to Oneself in Kant's Moral Theory*, New York: Garland.

---

33 Barbara Herman has written eloquently and extensively on this. See Herman, 2007, pp. 211–215, 254–275, and 2011, pp. 111–114.

Denis, Lara (2006), "Kant's Conception of Virtue", in: Paul Guyer (ed.), *The Cambridge Companion to Kant and Modern Philosophy*, Cambridge: Cambridge University Press, pp. 505–537.

Denis, Lara (ed.) (2010), *Kant's 'Metaphysics of Morals': A Critical Guide*, Cambridge: Cambridge University Press.

Denis, Lara (2010), "Freedom, Primacy, and Perfect Duties to Oneself", in: Denis (ed.) (2010), pp. 170–191.

Denis, Lara (2011), "A Kantian Conception of Human Flourishing", in: Lawrence Jost/Julian Wuerth (eds.), *Perfecting Virtue: New Essays in Kantian Ethics and Virtue Ethics*, Cambridge: Cambridge University Press, pp. 164–193.

Engstrom, Stephen (2002), "The Inner Freedom of Virtue", in: Mark Timmons (ed.), *Kant's 'Metaphysics of Morals': Interpretative Essays*, Oxford: Oxford University Press, pp. 289–316.

Frierson, Patrick R. (2003), *Freedom and Anthropology in Kant's Moral Philosophy*, Cambridge: Cambridge University Press.

Geiger, Ido (2011), "Rational Feelings and Moral Agency", in: *Kantian Review*, vol. 16, pp. 283–308.

Grenberg, Jeanine M. (2010), "What is the Enemy of Virtue?", in: Denis (ed.) (2010), pp. 152–169.

Gregor, Mary J. (1963), *Laws of Freedom*, Oxford: Basil Blackwell.

Guyer, Paul (2000), *Kant on Freedom, Law, and Happiness*, Cambridge: Cambridge University Press.

Guyer, Paul (2008), *Knowledge, Reason, and Taste: Kant's Response to Hume*, Princeton: Princeton University Press.

Guyer, Paul (2010), "Moral Feelings in the 'Metaphysics of Morals'", in: Denis (ed.) (2010), pp. 130–151.

Hare, John E. (1996), *The Moral Gap*, Oxford: Clarendon Press.

Herman, Barbara (2007), *Moral Literacy*, Cambridge/MA: Harvard University Press.

Herman, Barbara (2011), "The Difference that Ends Make", in: Lawrence Jost/Julian Wuerth (eds.), *Perfecting Virtue: New Essays in Kantian Ethics and Virtue Ethics*, Cambridge: Cambridge University Press, pp. 92–115.

Hill, Thomas E. (2008), "Kantian Virtue and 'Virtue Ethics'", in: Betzler (ed.) (2008), pp. 29–59.

Kerstein, Samuel J. (2008), "Treating Oneself Merely as a Means", in: Betzler (ed.) (2008), pp. 201–211.

Korsgaard, Christine M. (1996), *Creating the Kingdom of Ends*, Cambridge: Cambridge University Press.

McCarty, Richard (2009), *Kant's Theory of Action*, Oxford: Oxford University Press.

Sensen, Oliver (2009), "Kant's Conception of Human Dignity", in: *Kant-Studien*, vol. 100, pp. 309–331.

Stratton-Lake, Philip (2008), "Being Virtuous and Duties of Virtue: Two Aspects of Kant's 'Doctrine of Virtue'", in: Betzler (ed.) (2008), pp. 100–121.

Timmons, Mark (2002), "Motive and Rightness in Kant's Ethical System", in: id. (ed.), *Kant's 'Metaphysics of Morals': Interpretative Essays*, Oxford: Oxford University Press, pp. 255–287.

Uleman, Jennifer (2010), *An Introduction to Kant's Moral Philosophy*, Cambridge: Cambridge University Press.
Wood, Allen W. (1999), *Kant's Ethical Thought*, Cambridge: Cambridge University Press.

Virtue and Sensibility
(TL 6:399–409)

Ina Goy

I. On the Systematic Importance of Sections XII–XVI of the "Introduction to the Doctrine of Virtue"

Sections XII–XVI from the last third of the "Introduction to the Doctrine of Virtue" can be subsumed under three thematic units of varying importance. Section XII: In the earlier sections of the "Introduction," Kant argued that the behavior we call virtuous has two a priori conceptual foundations. First, virtuous actions are moral actions that we are obligated to perform on the basis of the categorical imperative of pure practical reason, for virtue is the strength of a person's maxims in "fulfilling his *duty*" (TL 6:394.15 f., italics I.G.). Second, an action can be virtuous only if it tends to the realization of specific aims or ends consistent with the categorical imperative: "Only *an end that is also a duty* can be called a **duty of virtue**" (TL 6:383.13 f.). There are two kinds of ends that satisfy this condition, those that aim at actions serving one's own perfection and those that aim at promoting the happiness of others.

After presenting the a priori conceptual preconditions of virtue—let us call them the 'logic of morals'—Kant turns to the "aesthetic of morals" (TL 6:406.20) in section XII. Here, he treats the question of which if any a priori sensible elements can enter into the foundation of virtue. According to Kant, human beings have four sensible "predispositions of the mind" (TL 6:399.11) that make them susceptible to moral obligation: the predispositions of "*moral feeling*," "*conscience*," "*love* of one's neighbor" and "*respect*" (TL 6:399.6 f.)[1].

The systematic importance of section XII cannot be stressed enough. As is well known, one of the essential if controversial achievements of Kant's philosophy lies in distinguishing empirical from a priori elements

---

1   Quotations for which the reference is not given immediately are covered by the following reference.

184   Ina Goy

of sensibility, thus attributing to its a priori form a potential for ultimate justification and grounding. Accordingly, in the first *Critique*, the sensible principles of space and time, together with the categories in their capacity as concepts and the principles as a priori laws, found the theoretical cognition of objects of experience. Accordingly also, in the second *Critique*, the moral feeling of respect as an a priori sensible element, together with the concept of the good and the a priori practical law, founds the moral action.—Analogously, I claim that in the *Metaphysics of Morals*, the four predispositions of the mind mentioned above are a priori sensible principles founding the virtuous action together with certain conceptual ends which are consistent with the a priori law of the categorical imperative.

In returning to issues already treated, <u>section XIII</u> discusses three 'principles' supposed to guarantee a scientific[2] treatment of the doctrine of virtue. First, there are different duties of virtue but only one ground of obligation that serves as their basis. Second, virtue and vice differ in principle, not just in degree. Third: The concept of virtue must be derived a priori, not empirically. While the systematic weight of section XIII is rather low due to its largely repetitive character, it is interesting from a historical point of view in that its second principle inspires one of the rare Kantian responses to Aristotle's ethics, more precisely, his doctrine of the mean (*mesotes*) which will be discussed again in §10 of the "Doctrine of the Elements of Ethics."

The following subsection entitled "On Virtue in General" contains a shift of focus directed at the remaining foundational questions of virtue in relation to sensibility in sections XIV–XVI. Here, Kant discusses more deeply why "strength" of will is a presupposition of virtuous actions (TL 6:405.11, 405.15 f.; see also TL 6:394.15 f.).

To answer these questions in <u>sections XIV–XVI</u>, Kant resorts to a criterion of distinction between duties of virtue and duties of right that he developed in both introductions (see MS 6:218.24–220.37; TL 6:379.15–381.17). Virtue, in contrast to obedience to legal laws, cannot be externally coerced, but only internally and through the will of the actor. Thus, acting on strength of will according to the "*principle of inner freedom*" (TL 6:407.4) means that one can only force *oneself* to follow a moral command, just as one can only set ends to *oneself* that are consistent with the moral command (section XIV). Ends that are at

---

2   Different from our modern use of the word in the natural sciences, 'scientific' in Kant's approach means a pure and a priori, non-empirical grounding or justification of something.

the same time duties compete with empirical inclinations. Two capacities are required to handle these inclinations properly: self-government in dealing with affects and passions (section XV) and moral apathy (section XVI). It is particularly in sections XV and XVI that Kant incorporates influences of the ethics of the late classic period, for instance the ideal of the stoic sage.

According to the weighted assessment given in this introduction, my commentary will deal most extensively with section XII. For further readings about the issues at hand, I recommend: on moral feelings in the *Metaphysics of Morals* in general Guyer, 2010, on love as a moral disposition of the mind Horn, 2008, and Schönecker, 2010, on the predisposition of conscience Timmermann, 2006, on the predisposition of respect Goy, 2007, on inner freedom Engstrom, 2002, and on moral apathy Denis, 2000.

II. Commentary on Sections XII–XVI

II.1 Section XII: A Priori Sensible Foundations of Virtue

In the extraordinarily dense thirteen-line introductory passage of section XII, Kant's thesis is that the human consciousness possesses four "concepts of what is presupposed on the part of feeling [[ä]sthetische Vorbegriffe]" or "antecedent," "natural predispositions of the mind (*praedispositio*)" that enable it to be "affected by concepts of duty": the predispositions of "*moral feeling*," "*conscience*," "*love* of one's neighbor" and "*respect* for oneself (*self-esteem*)" (TL 6:399.2–12).

II.1.1 General Characteristics of the A Priori Sensible Predispositions to Virtue

Kant describes the predispositions to virtue as aesthetic, prior or preliminary concepts ("[ä]sthetische Vorbegriffe" (TL 6:399.2)). Like in the "Transcendental Aesthetic" of the first *Critique* (see KrV A21n/B35n), the word 'aesthetic' (from Greek *aisthesis*: sensibility, sensory perception) does not apply to the context of art or taste, but to sensible principles, in this case to the sensible principles of virtue insofar as they are a priori.

Kant uses the notion of 'preliminary concepts' not only in the title of section XII but also in the titles of section IV[3] of the "Introduction to the

---

3   Section III in the Cambridge Edition.

Metaphysics of Morals" (TL 6:221.5) and section XVII of the "Introduction to the Doctrine of Virtue" (TL 6:410.2).[4] Kant's use of the notion in these passages strengthens the suggestion that the discussion of preliminary concepts is intended to clarify in principle some important basic concepts of the doctrine of virtue. Thus, section XII would serve to expound the most important a priori sensible concepts of the doctrine of virtue before the actual discussion of the doctrine of virtue starts with the "Doctrine of the Elements of Ethics." A literal reading of the word "Vorbegriffe" (TL 6:399.2), however, according to which the four predispositions of the mind are moral dispositions prior to *all* concepts, seems implausible, because Kant is very clear in saying that the "[c]onsciousness" of the four predispositions can "only follow from consciousness of a moral law, as the effect this has on the mind" (TL 6:399.14–16). If "Vorbegriffe," thirdly, described the preconceptual form in which the consciousness becomes aware of the four predispositions of the mind (aesthetically, as feelings, not logically, as concepts), this would entail a reduplication of the notion 'aesthetic' which would be redundant if factually correct.

A second twofold characterization of the sensible predispositions to virtue is even more decisive: On the one hand, Kant describes the four predispositions as *"antecedent,"* "natural predispositions of the mind (*praedispositio*) for being affected by concepts of duty" (TL 6:399.11 f., first italics I.G.). They are dispositions which "every human being has," and "by virtue of them" can "be put under obligation" (TL 6:399.13 f.). They are an essential component of the moral consciousness of every human being, which is why there can be "no duty to acquire them," as everybody already has them (TL 6:399.4 f.). On the other hand, Kant claims that "[c]onsciousness of them is not of empirical origin" but can only *"follow* from consciousness of a moral law," as the "effect" it has on the mind (cf. TL 6:399.14–16, italics I.G.). This twofold characterization creates one of the fundamental exegetical problems of Kant's treatment of the predispositions of the mind: Kant does not distinguish precisely *predispositions* for a priori sensible feelings from the *feelings* generated by them. For at first glance, it seems hard to reconcile the

---

4   Here we are faced with a problem of Gregor's translation: Translating "[ä]sthetische Vorbegriffe" with "concepts of what is presupposed on the part of feeling" (TL 6:399.2) and "Vorbegriffe" either with "preliminary concepts" (TL 6:221.5) or with "concepts preliminary" (TL 6:410.2), she obscures the exegetical ambiguity of 'Vorbegriffe' in Kant's text.

claim that the four predispositions are *"antecedent"* "predispositions of the mind" (TL 6.399.11, italics I.G.) with the claim that "[c]onsciousness of them" can only *"follow* from consciousness of a moral law," as the "effect" it has on the mind (TL 6.399.14–16, italics I.G.).

What exactly is the sense in which the four phenomena are *antecedent*, and in which sense (less plainly expounded by Kant) are they nevertheless *subsequent?* They are *antecedent* in that they are present in the subject a priori, as preconditions of the possibility of virtue. They are pure, pre-empirical endowments of the moral consciousness like the pure practical reason. The four predispositions are *subsequent* in that they are only able to generate a priori sensible feelings if they have been affected by the moral law of the pure practical reason, for again: *"moral feeling," "conscience," "love* of one's neighbor" and *"respect"* are conscious only "as the effect" of a "moral law" (TL 6:399.6 f., 15 f.). Pure practical reason and pure practical sensibility, both being a priori endowments of the subject, constitute two equally fundamental sources of virtuous actions. Their relation, however, is hierarchical with respect to their function, for the a priori sensible *predispositions* are present inside us even before the pure practical reason ever proclaimed its practical law (and applied it to certain ends). But it is only possible to have the respective a priori sensible *feelings* after we have a consciousness of the practical law.

The four predispositions of the mind dispose to *something.* What is this something? Kant provides two varying answers. On the one hand, he says, they dispose to "the mind's receptivity to concepts of duty as such" (TL 6:399.2 f.), that is, its capacity "for being affected by concepts of duty" (TL 6:399.11 f.). On the other hand, he claims that they are necessary for "receptiveness of the concept of duty" (TL 6:399.9)[5]. For example, he claims that the conscience is "the condition of all duties [Pflicht] as such," but not of "all *duties of virtue [Tugendpflicht[en]]"* (TL 6:406.34–407.1). The use of the plural in "concepts of duty" seems to point to the fact that the a priori sensible predispositions of the mind enable us to incorporate in our moral consciousness a categorical imperative that has already been applied to different ends. Taken in this sense, the a priori sensible predispositions of the mind would be the foundation of duties of virtue, insofar as the a priori feelings signify the presence of ends that are also duties. On the contrary, the use of the singular in "concept of duty," and in "duty as such" seems to say that the a priori sensible predispositions of the mind serve to incorporate into

---

5   Cf. "the law of duty" (TL 6:399.21).

our moral consciousness a categorical imperative that has not yet been applied to specific ends of duties of virtue. In this case, the a priori sensible predispositions of the mind would be the foundation merely of the obligation of virtue, the practical law, but not of duties of virtue, that is, ends which are consistent with the practical law. Only in the first case (the plural, "concepts of duty") would a priori sensible predispositions in a narrow sense be predispositions to virtuous actions.

Kant treats the four a priori sensible predispositions of the mind in the following order: "*a. Moral feeling,*" "*b. Conscience,*" "*c. Love of human beings,*" "*d. Respect*" (TL 6:399.17–403.6).

II.1.2 The Predisposition to Moral Feeling

A first a priori sensible predisposition to duties of virtue which every human being has "in him originally" (TL 6:399.32) is that of moral feeling. Moral feeling is an aesthetic condition (the Cambridge edition has "state of *feeling*") of "pleasure or displeasure" caused "merely from being aware that our actions are consistent with or contrary to the law of duty." While we can experience empirical, or, as Kant calls them, "*pathological*" feelings before and independent from perceiving the practical law inside us, the moral feeling of pleasure can only follow the "representation of the [practical, I.G.] law" (TL 6:399.19–27). Moral feeling is the "*susceptibility* on the part of free choice to be moved by pure practical reason (and its law)" (TL 6:400.18 f.).

Other traditional approaches—here, Kant could have in mind the theories of Shaftesbury, Hutcheson, or Hume[6]—often use the term "moral *sense* [moralische[r] *Sinn*]" (TL 6:400.5) when referring to moral feeling. This expression is misleading from Kant's point of view, because in his doctrine of theoretical cognition, Kant assumes an inner and an outer sense containing the a priori forms of intuition of space and time (cf. KrV A19–49/B33–73). Describing the moral feeling of practical philosophy as a 'sense' as well would introduce an ambiguity into the concept, for, as Kant argues already in the second *Critique*, the a priori sensibility of practical philosophy is not "regarded as a capacity for intuition at all but only as feeling" (KpV 5:90.12–23). This is why Kant prefers to speak of moral feeling rather than moral sense (cf. TL 6:400.5–20).

---

6   Cf. Shaftesbury, 1699, p. 173; Hutcheson, 1728, p. 109; Hume, 1739/40, III.1.2.

II.1.3 The Predisposition to Conscience

A second a priori sensible disposition to virtue lies in the conscience which every human being is "originally" endowed with "as a moral being" (TL 6:400.24 f.). Kant treats of the conscience in two places in the *Doctrine of Virtue:* in the "Introduction to the Doctrine of Virtue" (TL 6:400.21–401.21) and in the "Doctrine of the Elements of Ethics" (TL 6:437.29–440.34). Both the fact that Kant introduces the concept of conscience in both places and that, in the latter place, he calls it an "original[ly] intellectual [...] moral disposition" (TL 6:438.24 f.) (as opposed to an *aesthetic* one), could lead to the assumption that Kant wants to expound the a priori sensible features of the conscience in the "Introduction" and its intellectual features in the "Doctrine of the Elements." This interpretation would be intuitively convincing for a phenomenology of conscience, as it contains traits of both sensible perceptions, for instance the feeling you have when your conscience is clean or guilty, and those of propositional sentences appearing in the form of admonitions like 'you should have done this' or 'if only you hadn't done that.'

This interpretation, however, ignores the fact that the nature of the a priori sensible features of the conscience as expounded in the "Introduction" is unclear. For even though Kant very clearly ranks the predisposition of conscience among the aesthetic phenomena, he defines it as "practical reason holding the human being's duty before him for his acquittal or condemnation in every case that comes under a law" (TL 6:400.27 f.). This definition removes the difference between pure practical reason and the conscience as an a priori sensible predisposition: "[C]onscience *is* practical reason" (TL 6:400.27 f., italics I.G.). Difficulties rather grow when Kant claims in the following sentence, that in the conscience the "moral feeling" (!) is being affected by an act of "practical reason" (TL 6:400.27–30). This in turn removes the distinction between the a priori sensible predisposition of moral feeling and that of the conscience. Timmermann assumes a kind of identification of the conscience with moral feeling to be the reason why, for Kant, conscience falls under the heading of aesthetic moral conditions.[7] But what exactly would, then, be the *differentia specifica* between the predisposition of moral feeling and that of conscience? A genuine description of the conscience both as an a priori sensible predisposition and as a feeling derived from this predisposition, is not given in Kant's text.

---

7   Cf. Timmermann, 2006, p. 297.

190   Ina Goy

The rest of the passage merely provides clarifications of the scientific
as opposed to the colloquial account of conscience. As the predisposition
of conscience is an "unavoidable fact" (TL 6:400.30 f.), two kinds of per-
functory parlance need correcting. First, the statement that someone 'has
no conscience' can only be intended to mean that the respective person
tries (ultimately in vain) to ignore the unavoidable voice of conscience.
In the same vein, there is no real "[u]nconscientiousness" but only a "propensity to pay no heed" to the "judgment" of conscience (cf. TL
6:401.3–18).

II.1.4 The Predisposition to Love of One's Neighbor

A third a priori sensible predisposition to virtue lies in "*love* of one's
neighbor" (TL 6:399.6 f.). An interpretation of this predisposition is
made difficult by the vast ambiguity of the concepts of love Kant mentions in the two short relevant passages introducing it (cf. TL 6:399.4–
16, 401.22–402.26). This ambiguity raised the question as to which of
the forms of love mentioned is the relevant predisposition of the mind.[8]
Schönecker considers it to be "*delight (amor complacentiae)* [Liebe des
Wohlgefallens]" (TL 6:402.22).[9] Horn, however, argues that all forms of
love are emotional, and cannot be enforced, so that every form of love
is inadequate to morality in its strict sense, because all moral actions
rest on constraint. But, he says, we might interpret '*benevolence (amor benevolentiae)* [*Liebe des Wohlwollens*]' as a form of love emerging from the
practice of doing good to others. In this way, it would be possible to claim
that love is adequate to morality, if only indirectly as a habit evolving sub-
sequently.[10] Horn more or less rejects the claim that any sensible predisposition of the mind is given a priori.

First we have to say that there is an a priori conception of love in
Kant's philosophy, and that the only form of love explicitly addressed
as a predisposition by Kant is "*love* of one's neighbor" (TL 6:399.6 f.),
mentioned as one of the four a priori sensible predispositions of the
mind in the introductory paragraph of section XII. *All* other forms and
kinds of love introduced by Kant in his commentary on the predisposition of love in sub-section "*c. Love of human beings*," such as "[*l*]*ove*" as "a
matter of *feeling*," "*benevolence (amor benevolentiae)*," and "*delight (amor*

---

8 Cf. Horn, 2008; Schönecker, 2010.
9 Cf. Schönecker, 2010, pp. 133, 135.
10 Cf. Horn, 2008, p. 154.

complacentiae)" (TL 6:401.22–402.26), are not being referred to as predispositions. Thus, any interpretation of the moral predisposition of love must cope with the fact that Kant calls the a priori sensible predisposition of love that of "*love* of one's neighbor." Taking Kant literally in reading this passage, however, and following his claim that the moral predisposition lies in "*love* of one's neighbor," requires the qualification that Kant is not trying to introduce the denominational Christian contents of charity (neighborly love) into the sensible foundation of virtue (such as the theological motivation for imitating God's love in one's own acts of love), but merely to reconstruct the core of neighborly love that consists in a particular structure of moral motivation, which displays exactly those features that Kant intends an a priori conception of love as a foundation of virtues to have.

How is this structure of moral motivation to be conceived of? What is the predisposition to love one's neighbor a reaction to and what kind of feeling emerges from this predisposition? Kant explains the generation of the *feeling* of love of one's neighbor in the context of an ethical (not a theological) interpretation of the Christian commandment to love one's neighbor:

> So the saying 'you ought to *love* your neighbor as yourself' does not mean that you ought immediately (first) to love him and (afterwards) by means of this love do good to him. It means, rather, *do good* to your fellow human beings, and your beneficence will produce love of them in you (as an aptitude of the inclination to beneficence in general) (TL 6:402.16–21).

As already mentioned, this second passage, unlike the first, does not call love of one's neighbor an a priori predisposition of the mind, but merely describes how the respective feeling is being generated. In the context of said passage I would like to propose the following reconstruction of this sentence:

The a priori sensible predisposition to love one's neighbor is such that it will be stimulated, when the desire of "*benevolence (amor benevolentiae)*" (TL 6:401.27) to another human being has been transformed into a maxim of beneficence which has been tested against the practical law and has become the determining ground of the action.[11] Once such a maxim of beneficence stimulates the *predisposition* of love of one's neighbor in singular cases, the respective form of love is produced as a *feeling* of love of one's neighbor wrought a priori. Frequent repetition

---

11   On the notions of benevolence and beneficence: cf. especially TL 6:452.23–30.

of this process transforms the individual feeling of love of one's neighbor into a general love of human beings which in turn will be reflected in "an aptitude of the inclination to beneficence in general" (TL 6:402.20 f.). Kant later explains "*aptitude* (*habitus*)" to be an acquired "facility of acting and a subjective perfection of *choice*" (TL 6:407.5 f.); it designates an attitude which has become part of a person's character, enabling him to act accordingly without difficulty. Kant claims that we possess an a priori sensible predisposition to love our neighbor which produces a feeling precisely in the case when the desire to act to the benefit of another has been transformed into a moral maxim of beneficence that we act on. The feeling we develop thereby is love of one's neighbor; repetition of the respective behavior turns this feeling into love of human beings (love of all other human beings as our neighbors). Experiencing this feeling in turn makes it easier to choose to act beneficently in the future, thus initiating the development of a character attitude of love of human beings.

Against Horn, I maintain that Kant is not of the opinion that all kinds of love are emotional (read: 'empirical'?) feelings, because both the predisposition of love of one's neighbor and the succeeding feeling of love of one's neighbor are doubtlessly wrought a priori. The sentence that leads Horn to his assumption that all forms of love are emotional, is at the beginning of sub-section "*c. Love of human beings*": "*Love* is a matter of *feeling*, not of willing, and I cannot love because I *will* to, still less because I *ought* to [...]; so a *duty to love* is an absurdity" (TL 6:401.24 – 26). Almost the same wording can be found when Kant characterizes the "*love* of one's neighbor" in the introductory passage of section XII as a moral trait which presupposes "no duty to acquire" it, because it belongs to those predispositions the possession of which "cannot be considered a duty" (cf. TL 6:399.5 – 13). But do both statements mean the same thing, and if so, would the predisposition to love one's neighbor then be emotional/empirical as Horn claims?

It is quite clear that Kant sees two different reasons as to why certain forms of love do not fall under duty: First, one cannot and does not have to be obliged to follow an *a priori* sensible predisposition of love of one's neighbor as it, being a *predisposition*, is always present a priori in every subject's moral consciousness. Still, the development of the *feeling* deriving from this predisposition presupposes the consciousness of a concept of duty. This is because the feeling of love for human beings is only brought about by the impact of the practical law (a concept of duty) on the a priori sensible predisposition for love of one's neighbor.

Concerning love as "a matter of *feeling* [Empfindung]" (TL 6:401.24), it can be said that there is an according a priori predisposition in the subject as well, so that there is no duty to acquire a predisposition for empirical feelings of love either, because everyone already has it! In the case of love as a matter of feeling, however, the feeling deriving from the respective disposition is *independent* from the concept of duty as well, as it is *no* effect of the impact of the practical law, but of empirical stimuli of the senses. It is precisely because of this difference that the love of one's neighbor deriving from the according predisposition is indicative of morality and virtue while love as a matter of feeling is not indicative of morality but rather an empirical feeling.

What seems to argue against Schönecker's thesis that the predisposition we are looking for is that of "*delight (amor complacentiae)* [Liebe des Wohlgefallens]" is Kant's definition of it as "a pleasure joined immediately to the representation of an object's existence" (TL 6:402.22–24), which could be understood as an empirical reference of love to the object. Not only does an *existing* object possess factual reality, but it is also an object of experience. If it causes pleasure, then this love is empirical. Schönecker wants us to understand this "pleasure" in "the representation of an object's existence" as a pleasure of the perfection of others. However, the perfection of another person is precisely the idea of his end, but in a strict sense the *existence* of an idea is hard to comprehend. Besides, speaking loosely of "an object" seems vague in light of the fact that the specific object at hand is the perfection of others.

A further weakness of this interpretation is that "a pleasure joined immediately to the representation of an object's existence" could also be a pleasure one feels about oneself. While the love of one's *neighbor* as a moral predisposition of the mind by definition rules out the self as a permissible object, no such exclusion is given in the definition of delight. Thus, if we take delight to be the moral predisposition to love, then there is no way to preclude the possibility that the person so predisposed is affected by pleasure for the self. Consequently, the moral predisposition of love could be a predisposition to an unmoral self-love and hence be a self-contradiction.

II.1.5 The Predisposition to Respect for Oneself (Self-esteem)

A fourth a priori sensible predisposition to virtue lies in the predisposition of "*respect* for oneself (*self-esteem*)" (TL 6:399.7). Just like the other three predispositions, the feeling of "*self-esteem*" (TL 6:402.35) emerges precisely in the case when the practical law has an impact on the predisposition of the actor and "unavoidably forces from him *respect* for his own being" (TL 6:402.36–403.1). Together with the practical law (or, more precisely, a maxim of ends consistent with the practical law), the feeling of self-esteem of a person "is the basis of certain duties, that is, of certain actions that are consistent with his duty to himself" (TL 6:403.2 f.). Quite correctly, Forkl has pointed out that, in section XII, Kant only speaks of a predisposition to respect for *oneself*, and that this respect is only used to found duties of virtue to *oneself*.[12] The inadequacy of Forkl's comment, however, lies in his uncritical acceptance of Kant's text and the resulting implicit assumption that Kant had sound systematic reasons for restricting the predisposition of respect to respect for oneself and to the grounding of duties to oneself. But doesn't the opposite seem to be the case? Does it not seem strange, considering that the *Doctrine of Virtue* as a whole discusses extensively the concept of respect in the context of duties to others, that Kant conceives of the a priori sensible moral predisposition exclusively as a predisposition to respect oneself? Could he not instead have described it more widely as a predisposition of respect for oneself and for others, thus making it a possible foundation of duties of virtue both to oneself and to others? I can give no explanation for this systematic imbalance.

Before ending my presentation of Kant's account of the a priori sensible predispositions of the mind, I would like to address certain other interpretative problems which I cannot discuss here at length. The a priori sensible predispositions Kant expounds—moral feeling, conscience, love of one's neighbor, and respect for oneself—seem to form a very heterogeneous group of phenomena. What is their relation to each other? Are they of the same rank, are they divided into two pairs of closely related phenomena or is one superior to the rest, moral feeling, for example, as a generic term not describing any particular feeling while love and respect are specific feelings? Why does Kant treat of these four predispositions and feelings and of no others?—It remains equally obscure how the foundation of virtues arising from these predispositions impacts the different duties of virtue developed later in the "Doctrine of the Elements of Ethics." As can be seen with respect to the virtue of gratitude, which is a duty of virtue of *love* of others but which, as Kant says, also presupposes the feeling of *respect* (cf. TL 6:454.33), an all too straightforward correlation is

12 Cf. Forkl, 2001, p. 93 f.

impossible. Furthermore, apart from the short reference in the "Introduction," moral feeling, as opposed to the other three phenomena treated of, has *no* theoretical place of its own within the doctrine of the duties of virtue, even if it could be considered as a generic term for the other three phenomena. Hence, one could ask whether the concept of moral feeling is no more than a terminological 'relic' from earlier stages of Kant's moral philosophy, one that lost its systematic importance for Kant when he discovered that the moral feeling as a sensible grounding of virtue can be replaced by more idiosyncratic phenomena like love of one's neighbor, respect, and conscience.

II.2 Section XIII: The Foundation of Virtue Must Follow from Pure Principles

Section XIII comprises two parts that return to general discussions of the concept of virtue. The first part reconsiders the assumptions that should be made in order to render the concept of virtue scientific and *"pure"* (TL 6:403.9), i.e., independent of empirical conditions. Here, Kant first presents three pure principles [Grundsätze] that he maintains himself (cf. TL 6:403.10–405.2), contrasting them at the end of the section with three opposite assumptions taken from earlier philosophical doctrines (cf. TL 6:405.2–9). Kant's theses are: There are many duties of virtue but only one duty (ground of obligation of virtue); virtue and vice differ in principle, not just in degree; the concept of virtue must be grounded a priori, not empirically.

In the second part of section XIII, entitled "Of Virtue in General," Kant discusses the question, to what extent virtue presupposes strength of will. After having discussed the *a priori* sensible predispositions of virtue in section XII, this passage leads to the final important issue of the "Introduction to the Doctrine of Virtue": How should a person who strives to be virtuous handle *empirical* sensibility adequately (cf. TL 6:405.10–406.25)?

II.2.1 Three Principles (*Grundsätze*) of a Scientific Treatment of a Pure Doctrine of Virtue

Kant's introduction of his three principles of "handling a *pure* doctrine of virtue" (TL 6:403.9) and their opposite principles (cf. TL 6:405.2–9) is systematically imbalanced and cryptic in parts. The respective antitheses do not match well with the theses and are thus particularly in need of discussion. In what follows, T denominates Kant's thesis, while A stands for the antithesis Kant draws from the philosophical tradition and rejects.

The first principle

T 1: "For One duty only one *single* ground of obligation can be found" (TL 6:403.10 f., trans. I.G.).
A 1: "There is only one virtue and one vice" (TL 6:405.5).

Juxtaposing these principles in this manner shows that it does not become instantly clear how these sentences are supposed to be "opposed" (TL 6:405.4). In case of a real opposition T 1 would read: 'There is not only one virtue and not only one vice.' Consider, however, how the text continues from T 1: "and if someone produces two or more proofs for a duty, this is a sure sign either that he has not yet found a valid proof or that he has mistaken two or more duties for [O]ne" (TL 6:403.11–13, emendation I.G.). It seems that the antithesis aims at the singularity and uniqueness of virtue, while Kant's thesis makes a claim about the singularity and unambiguousness of the ground (justification) of obligation of virtue while allowing for a plurality of duties of virtue. Precisely how is the content of T 1 to be reconstructed both to make it match the theory of virtue, argued for up to here in the introduction, and to contradict A 1?

One could read T 1 to mean that it is in the practical law that every single duty of virtue has the same ground of obligation. The opposite of A 1 would then lie in the specification that while there is only one ground of obligation, there can be many different duties of virtue. Alternately, T 1 could be understood to imply that every single duty of virtue also has a specific ground of obligation, each consisting in a particular maxim itself tested against the practical law. The opposite of A 1 would then be that there can be many different duties of virtue that come about through universalization of different respective maxims. Both ways of reconstruction sit well with Kant's account. Their difference lies in putting the emphasis regarding the conceptual aspect of the grounding of virtue either on the practical law or on the maxim of the virtuous action tested against the practical law. In both readings, Kant's criticism of A 1 adds up to the claim that in the account of virtue one has to distinguish between a singular ground of obligation, the practical law, different maxims of duties of virtue—each of which comes about by different material choices of ends—and different duties of virtue resulting from these concepts.

Kant's explanations of T 1 and A 1, however, shift the emphasis of his criticism in yet a different direction:

For here Kant claims that there has to be one singular and unambiguous "ground of obligation" for every single duty of virtue precisely because "moral proof" has to be effected "philosophical[ly]," "drawn only by means of rational knowledge *from concepts*," and is unlike mathematical proof, which, following from a "construction of concepts" in "a priori *intuition*," allows for ambiguity (TL 6:403.10–21). Kant expounds this reasoning in extreme brevity. What does he mean? Having shown a priori sensibility to be a part of the foundation of virtue in section XII, he can't be interpreted to deny it now. All he wants to say here is that the a priori sensibility in the foundation of virtue does not cause the same ambiguity as the a priori sensible moment does in mathematics.

Kant's distinction of the mathematical from the philosophical method of cognition reverts to a subtle theorem Kant expounds in the "Doctrine of Method" of the first *Critique* (cf. KrV A712–738/B740–766): To Kant, mathematical cognition is synthetically a priori, that is, it rests on propositions that include an extension of cognition independent of all experience. This a priori extension is grounded in the construction of mathematical concepts in a priori intuition. The concept of a triangle, for example, must be conceived of as a right, acute, or obtuse triangle as soon as it is constructed in a priori intuition, thus adding to the concept of a triangle the quality of being right, acute, or obtuse (cf. KrV A721 f./B749 f.). Put differently (and emphasizing Kant's actual point), the concept of a triangle becomes ambiguous as soon as it must be exhibited in pure intuition. In the first *Critique*, Kant denies that in philosophical (as opposed to mathematical) cognition, the "transcendental" concepts and propositions could become ambiguous by their representation in intuition. For "transcendental concept[s]" or propositions such as "reality" or "substance" are not related to "intuition[s] that exhibit[] the concept [...] *in concreto*" but rather to the very ability of being intuited, such as to "time-conditions in general" (KrV A722 and note/B750 and note).

Can these explanations be useful for an understanding of this passage in the *Doctrine of Virtue?* A grounding of duties of virtue depends, first, on the practical law, second, on a maxim of the choice of ends consistent with this law, and, third, on a priori sensible elements. How can the latter guarantee a grounding of duties of virtue which is different for different duties, yet unambiguous for each? How is the uniqueness of the grounding of the duties of virtue safeguarded by the a priori sensible aspect of virtue when it allows for ambiguity in the realm of mathematics?

As the a priori sensible elements in the grounding of virtue consist in nothing but non-conceptual representations of maxims of the setting of ends consistent (or inconsistent) with the practical law, the feeling facilitated by the respective sensible predisposition will unambiguously either be generated or not. To Kant, a certain maxim (for instance a maxim of gratitude, beneficence, respect for others) tested against the practical law constitutes a distinct yet unique conceptual ground of obligation for the respective duty of virtue. The a priori sensible elements, however, only indicate whether the maxim of the setting of ends that serves as the ground of obligation is consistent with the practical law or not. Despite the indispensability of a priori sensible representations they do not change anything about either the content or the moral status of the respective maxim of a virtuous action. Even if there are different duties of virtue grounded in an a priori conceptual and an a priori sensible element, it is not the ambiguity of the feeling that causes different duties of virtue but the difference of the maxim which prescribes unambiguously what a duty of virtue requires for each maxim.

The second principle

T 2: "The distinction between virtue and vice can never be sought in the *degree* to which one follows certain maxims; it must rather be sought only in the specific *quality* of the maxims (their relation to the law). In other words, the well-known principle (Aristotle's) which locates virtue in the *mean* between two vices is false" (TL 6:404.3–7).

A 2: "Virtue is the observance of the middle way between opposing opinions" (TL 6:405.6 f., trans. I.G.[13]).

Kant's second principle of a pure and thus scientific treatment of the doctrine of virtue states that there is no way leading from vice to virtue except that which consists in changing the "*principle*" (TL 6:404.33) on which one's disposition is based. This is so, he claims, because virtue lies in the strength of a person's maxim in *observing* the practical law, while vices result from including a principle of the *non-observance* of the practical law into one's maxim of action. Virtue and vice differ in principle, not in degree.

---

13 The editors of the Academy Edition consider replacing 'opinions' in the first edition with 'inclinations,' while the Cambridge edition simply speaks of 'vices.'

If, on the contrary, the antithesis A 2 were valid, virtue and vice would be distinguished only by degrees, and virtue could be attained by a gradual reduction of its opposing vices. One could then, for example, attain an appropriate economic activity by disengaging oneself from avarice and spending more money, or by curbing one's propensity to wastefulness and living a thriftier life (cf. TL 6:404.8–15; see also TL 6:432.19–25).

On the basis of the second principle, Kant disputes the Aristotelian doctrine of the mean and its aphoristic Roman reception (cf. TL 6:404.6–22, 404.27–37, 409.3–5). This passage is of particular historical importance, since Kant is often charged with failing to deal with systematic challenges from classical Greek ethics (especially Aristotle), a charge extended even to the allegation of concealing pertinent Aristotelian (and Platonic) alternatives to his own theory in systematically central passages (such as KpV 5:39.5–41.38).

In the second book of his *Nicomachean Ethics*, Aristotle develops his famous thesis that virtues are those human character dispositions promoting a good life which are preserved by what is "proportionate"[14] while being destroyed by "defect[s] and excess[es]"[15]. The "mean"[16] (*mesotes*) which the virtues consist in does not describe a 'mediocrity' but "in a sense an extreme"[17], an optimum.

Kant's criticism of this position is based on an over-simplification, maybe even a misunderstanding of Aristotle's doctrine of the mean. For Kant seems to interpret Aristotle to consider 'mean' as arithmetical—so that an appropriate economic activity would be a mean between avarice and prodigality attainable by a "diminution" (TL 6:404.10) of prodigality and an "increase of spending" (TL 6:404.11)—, an idea which Aristotle explicitly repudiates. *Mesotes* does not denote an arithmetical mean in Aristotle's philosophy but an "intermediate relatively to us"[18] to be measured against complex normative conceptions of what is good for the actor and the aims of his actions. It neither calls for a halving of defective extremes nor an identical mean for all human beings, but rather for an adequacy of action relative to the individual person and rel-

---

14 Aristotle, *Nicomachean Ethics*, 1104a17.
15 Ibid., 1104a12.
16 Ibid., 1104a26.
17 Ibid., 1107a23.
18 Ibid., 1106a31.

ative also to "the right times"[19], "the right objects, towards the right people, with the right aim, and in the right way"[20].

Kant was intimately acquainted with the multifaceted Roman transformations of the doctrine of the mean, probably already since the many years of his Latin studies at the Fridericianum. This is exemplified by Kant's *impromptu* quotation in the footnote (see TL 6:404.27–37, 409.3–5) of Ovid's *Metamorphoses:* "medio tutissimus ibis"[21] (in the middle is the safest path), of two of Horace's aphorisms from the *Sermons:* "est modus in rebus"[22] (there is measure in all things) and the *Epistles:* "insani sapiens nomen ferat aequus iniqui—ultra quam satis est Virtutem si petat ipsam"[23] (let the wise man bear the name of madman, the just of unjust, should he pursue Virtue herself beyond due bounds). In addition, Kant mentions late classic variations of the *mesotes*-principle, the sources of which are unclear, such as "medium tenuere beati" (happy are those who keep to the mean) or "omne nimium vertitur in vitium" (every excess turns into a vice) (TL 6:404.28 f.). A maxim very similar to the last formula can be found in Seneca's *On tranquillity of mind:* "[v]itiosum est ubique quod, nimium est"[24] (excess in anything becomes a fault). Kant dismisses these adaptations of a theory of the mean like their Aristotelian original as "a superficial wisdom which really has no determinate principles" (TL 6:404.29 f.), because it considers virtue and vice to differ merely in degree.

The third principle

T 3: "[The] moral capacity must be estimated by the law, which commands categorically, and so in accordance with our rational knowledge of what they ought to be in keeping with the idea of humanity, not in accordance with the empirical knowledge we have of them as they are" (TL 6:404.23–26, 405.1 f.).

A 3: "Virtue (like prudence) must be learned from experience" (TL 6:405.8 f.).

Trying to learn virtue from experience according to principle A 3 would necessarily lead to failure, because, according to Kant, experience in many

---

19 Ibid., 1106b21.
20 Ibid.
21 Ovid, *Metamorphoses*, II 137.
22 Horace, *Sermons*, I.1.106.
23 Id., *Epistles*, I.6.15 f.
24 Seneca, *On tranquillity of mind*, IX.6.

concrete cases will show nothing but a human being's imperfection in following his moral duties. A doctrine of virtue both scientific and based on pure principles cannot orientate itself towards human beings as they *are*—for "how could one expect to construct something completely straight from such crooked wood?" (RGV 6:100.26–28; cf. IaG 8:23.22–24)—but has to take for a measure instead the idea of humanity as it *ought* to be conceived as a final end and ideal.

In A 3, Kant implicitly criticizes the identification of virtue with prudence as a knowledge arising from experience. Such an identification can be found again in Aristotle, where prudence (*phronesis*) is one of the six intellectual virtues, and is specified by the fact that it presupposes experience of life, as it is not only "concerned with universals"[25] but also with "the ultimate particular fact"[26] which is an object of "perception"[27], i.e. experience. To Kant, prudence pertains primarily to the realm of hypothetical imperatives, especially pragmatic ones. It is concerned with the skilful choice of means for hypothetical ends (cf. GMS 4:416.2–5, 416.19) and is thus not a concept of moral philosophy.

II.2.2 Transition to the Problem of Strength of Will as a Foundation of Virtue

The second part of section XIII is entitled "Of Virtue in General." This is a quite astonishingly fundamental claim, given that it is in the title of a mere sub-section, and considering that Kant has already expounded virtue's essential aspects in the preceding sections. The only plausible reading of this title seems to be that Kant now does not intend to speak of the a priori (and thus most strictly scientific) foundations of virtue only but also about those preconditions of virtue which every person has to acquire during the development of his character, above all strength of will. While this process is grounded a priori, it unfolds historically, as a part of the moral biography of a person. "Of Virtue in General," then, does not mean 'Of the essence of virtue' but 'Of virtue in a broader sense,' 'Of what is left to say about the preconditions of virtue.'

Already in the second *Critique*, it was Kant's view that virtue is "moral disposition *in conflict*, and not *holiness* in the supposed *possession* of a complete *purity* of dispositions of the will" (KpV 5:84.33–35) which

---

25 Aristotle, *Nicomachean Ethics*, 1141b14.
26 Ibid., 1142a24.
27 Ibid.

is only due to gods and angels. Being non-sensible rational beings, gods and angels are never virtuous in the actual sense of the word (cf. TL 6:405.11–18). The obstacles *for a human being* to acquire a pure will are his empirical inclinations—insofar as they oppose the moral law. To have strength of will in moral matters means to follow the demands of pure practical reason even in the face of empirical inclinations. This is what the moral "*courage (fortitudo moralis)*" of a person's will consists in, which in turn serves to realize "the *final end* of his existence on earth," for it strives "for the ideal of humanity in its moral perfection" and is thus a part of "*wisdom* in the strict sense, namely practical wisdom" (TL 6:405.25–406.1).

II.3 Sections XIV–XVI: Of Strength of Will as a Foundation of Virtue

Let us recall Kant's definition of virtue: Virtue is the "*strength* of a human being's maxims in fulfilling his duty" (TL 6:394.15 f., italics I.G.).

How does a person acquire the strength necessary as the basis of virtue? What is it that is strong about her? What is the respective strength aiming at and what is it aiming against? Can a human being ever be certain of her strength? Kant dedicates the remaining sections XIV–XVI of the "Introduction to the Doctrine of Virtue" to these questions.

According to Kant, strength in following one's duty rests on three components: First, it presupposes inner freedom, that is, an aptitude of the will "to determine oneself to act through the thought of the law" (TL 6:407.13 f.) (section XIV). Second, strength of will implies a capacity of governing oneself. This is necessary when dealing with empirical inclinations in the form of affects and passions (section XV). Third, strength of will presupposes moral apathy, that is, the consciousness of a duty to follow the a priori, not the empirical sensible motivation in situations that require acting ethically (section XVI).

II.3.1 Section XIV: Strength of Will Presupposes Inner Freedom

After referring back to the principal difference between the doctrines of right and virtue respectively (cf. MS 6:214.13–30, 218.9–221.3; TL 6:379.3–12), Kant announces an elucidation of "*inner freedom*" as "the condition of all *duties of virtue*" at the beginning of section XIV (TL 6:406.32–34). Inner freedom is more than just "*aptitude*", that is, a "facility in acting and a subjective perfection of *choice* [Willkür]" (TL

6:407.5 f., cf. TL 6:383.33). After all, this very facility in acting could have been acquired by long practice and uniformity of behavior and thus be based on thoughtless repetition and heteronomy rather than inner freedom. Nor does inner freedom denominate a capacity of subjective "*choice* [Willkür]" to decide between this or that subjective reason for acting. Rather, inner freedom consists in the property of the "*will*" to determine oneself "to act through the thought of the law" (TL 6:407.13–15).[28]

For a human being to act on the basis of a will determined by the notion of the practical law, two subordinate capacities are necessary: First, the command of reason must not be covered by affects and passions; a person must be "*ruling* oneself" (TL 6:407.21). Additionally, her mind should be calm, reflected, and resolved so that she is her "own *master* in a given case" (TL 6:407.20), that is, in a morally relevant situation, thus enabling her to accept the command of reason. Both capacities taken together constitute what Kant calls a "noble," elevated as opposed to a "mean" (TL 6:407.23–25), ignoble, and slavish character.

II.3.2 Section XV: Inner Freedom Entails a Capacity to Govern Oneself

The first component of inner freedom that Kant turns to in more detail is the capacity to govern oneself (cf. TL 6:407.21). This capacity is supposed to keep in check affects and passions. Affects and passions like anger and hatred are two distinct phenomena. Affects are a part of "*feeling*" (TL 6:407.30); they are quick and vehement but never run deep. Parallel passages in the *Anthropology* (§§74 f.) call the "affect" a "surprise through sensation, by means of which the mind's composure" is "suspended." Affects temporarily weaken reason and understanding, and lead to rashness. Passion, however, is deeply rooted and calculating. It "takes its time and reflects, no matter how fierce it may be," it is "deceitful and hidden," and "persistent" to "the point of dementia" in the pursuit of its ends (cf. Anth 7:252.3–36).

Affects are less opposed to virtue than passions because they only temporarily weaken reason and understanding while passions accept evil into the maxim "as something premeditated" (TL 6:408.12 f.) and tend to manifest themselves in vice. Although Kant conspicuously expounds the difference between affect and passion, the two objects of governing oneself, he does not supply an explanation of *how* they can be governed.

---

28 See the subtle remarks in Engstrom, 2002.

For the systematic difference between the two objects should account for a nameable systematic difference of the respective forms of governing oneself, say, whether, as in the case of affects, reason and understanding are only temporarily clouded by sensible excitement, or as in the case of passions, reason has to facilitate a change from immoral to moral maxims in principle.

II.3.3 Section XVI: Inner Freedom Entails the Capacity for Moral Apathy

The second component of inner freedom is *"moral apathy"* (TL 6:408.30). The word *apatheia* is of Greek origin,[29] consisting of the privative prefix *'a'* and the word *'pathos'* (from Greek: passion, affect), and meaning something like insensibility, sedateness or absence of affects. *'Apatheia'* is a fundamental concept of late classic ethics: Introduced into Stoic philosophy via the Cynic Antisthenes[30], it is a presupposition for the attainment of the highest ethical good, the imperturbable soul, which is a sign of the sage for both schools of thought. Differences about the reach of the concept of *apatheia* arose early on. In a moderate sense, it was understood to mean the repelling of and rule over passionate, destructive emotions; in a more radical sense, it was interpreted as a complete extinction of affects and emotions. This radical interpretation of *apatheia* was repudiated by Cicero, among others, who argued that a person without passions resembles a "rock"[31] more than she does a human being.

Kant refers to discussions about the extension of the concept of *apatheia* in the beginning of section XVI, when he writes that the word "has fallen into disrepute, as if it meant lack of feeling and so subjective indifference with respect to objects of choice [Willkür]; it is taken for weakness" (TL 6:408.26–28). Kant agrees with the opinion that indifference against *all* feelings and subjective desires is unnatural and exaggerated. For there are any number of *"adiaphora,"* things that are *"morally indifferent,"* and questions which undoubtedly allow a person to follow her empirical feelings and preferences deriving therefrom without violating ethical commands (cf. TL 6:409.13–17). Kant mentions issues such as "whether I eat meat or fish, drink beer or wine" (TL 6:409.13–17).

---

29 Cf. Aristotle, *De anima*, 429a29.
30 Cf. Diogenes Laertios, *Lives*, I.VI.1, pp. 13 ff.
31 Cicero, *Tusculum*, III.12.

He recommends a purified apathy (cf. Anth 7:253.19–254.25), that is, a behavior aloof of one's own empirical inclinations, *whenever moral decisions are concerned.* It is only this interpretation of the concept as a "strength" that Kant calls *"moral apathy"* (TL 6:408.24, 30). It implies an "absence of affects" concerning "feelings arising from sensible impressions" if and only if another feeling, namely the a priori feeling of "respect for the law is more powerful than all such feelings together" (cf. TL 6:408.29–33)[32].

Besides, Kant remarks that an exaggerated "affect, even one aroused by the thought of *what is good,*" is detrimental to "the state of *health* in the moral life" (TL 6:409.10–12). A pathologically excessive enthusiasm, even if it is directed at virtue, is wrong; on the one hand, because a strong feeling is followed by an according exhaustion, rendering the enthusiast of virtue even more apt to a subsequent non-observance of virtue, on the other hand, because the person who does not acknowledge the existence of morally indifferent things, "would turn the government of virtue into tyranny" (TL 6:409.19). Grounding virtue on inner freedom includes not having oneself enchained by exaggerated virtuousness.

Remark

Kant sums up the double character of virtue in aphoristic acuteness: "Virtue is always *in progress* and yet always starts *from the beginning"* (TL 6:409.21 f.). Virtue's paradoxical features emerge from an interplay of an objective and a subjective trait. When measured against its objective ideal of an unchallenged compliance with duty, virtue is always in progress. When measured against the subjective reality of a compliance with duty, which is permanently challenged by empirical inclinations and personal preferences, virtue starts from the beginning again and again.

References

Aristotle [1995a], *Nicomachean Ethics*, in: *The Complete Works of Aristotle*, vol. 2, Jonathan Barnes (ed.), Princeton: Princeton University Press, pp. 1729–1867.

Aristotle [1995b], *De anima*, in: *The Complete Works of Aristotle*, vol. 1, Jonathan Barnes (ed.), Princeton: Princeton University Press, pp. 641–692.

---

32 Cf. Denis, 2000, pp. 52 f.; Wood, 1999, p. 252.

Betzler, Monika (ed.) (2008), *Kant's Ethics of Virtue*, Berlin/New York: Walter de Gruyter.

Cicero, Marcus Tullius [1971], *Tusculan Disputations*, in: *Works*, vol. 17, Eric Herbert Warmington (ed.), trans. by Justin E. King, Cambridge/MA: Harvard University Press.

Denis, Lara (2000), "Kant's Cold Sage and the Sublimity of Apathy", in: *Kantian Review*, vol. 4, pp. 48–73.

Diogenes Laertius [1972], "Antisthenes", in: *Lives of Eminent Philosophers*, vol. 2, Eric Herbert Warmington (ed.), trans. by Robert D. Hicks, Cambridge/MA: Harvard University Press, pp. 2–23.

Engstrom, Stephen (2002), "The Inner Freedom of Virtue", in: Mark Timmons (ed.), *Kant's 'Metaphysics of Morals': Interpretative Essays*, Oxford: Oxford University Press, pp. 289–315.

Forkl, Markus (2001), "Die Abschnitte XII–XVII. Kants Tugendepistemologie", in: id., *Kants System der Tugendpflichten: Eine Begleitschrift zu den 'Metaphysischen Anfangsgründen der Tugendlehre'*, Frankfurt/M.: Peter Lang, pp. 87–105.

Goy, Ina (2007), "Immanuel Kant über das moralische Gefühl der Achtung", in: *Zeitschrift für philosophische Forschung*, vol. 61, pp. 337–360.

Guyer, Paul (2010), "Moral Feelings in the 'Metaphysics of Morals'", in: Lara Denis (ed.), *Kant's 'Metaphysics of Morals': A Critical Guide*, Cambridge: Cambridge University Press, pp. 130–151.

Horace (Quintus Horatius Flaccus) [1999], *Satires, Epistles, Ars Poetica*, lat.-engl., Eric Herbert Warmington (ed.), trans. by H. Rushton Fairclough, Cambridge/MA: Harvard University Press.

Horn, Christoph (2008), "The Concept of Love in Kant's Virtue Ethics", in: Betzler (ed.) (2008), pp. 147–173.

Hume, David (1739/40) [2000], *A Treatise of Human Nature*, David Fate Norton/Mary J. Norton (eds.), Oxford: Oxford University Press.

Hutcheson, Francis (1728) [1999], "Illustrations upon the Moral Sense", in: *On the Nature and the Conduct of the Passions with Illustrations on the Moral Sense*, Manchester: Clinamen Press, pp. 107–165.

Ovid (Publius Ovidius Naso) [1925], *Metamorphoses*, vol. 1, lat.-engl., Eric Herbert Warmington (ed.), trans. by Frank Justus Miller, New York: G. P. Putnam's Sons.

Seneca, Lucius Annaeus [1965], "On tranquillity of mind", in: *Moral Essays*, vol. 2, lat.-engl., Eric Herbert Warmington (ed.), trans. by John W. Basore, Cambridge/MA: Harvard University Press, pp. 202–285.

Schönecker, Dieter (2010), "Kant über Menschenliebe als moralische Gemütsanlage", in: *Archiv für Geschichte der Philosophie*, vol. 92, pp. 133–175.

Shaftesbury, Anthony Ashley Cooper (1699) [1999], "An Inquiry Concerning Virtue and Merit", in: id., *Characteristics of Men, Manners, Opinions, Times*, Cambridge: Cambridge University Press, pp. 163–230.

Timmermann, Jens (2006), "Kant on Conscience, 'Indirect' Duty, and Moral Error", in: *International Philosophical Quarterly*, vol. 46, pp. 293–308.

Wood, Allen W. (1999), *Kant's Ethical Thought*, Cambridge: Cambridge University Press.

Duties to Oneself as Such
(TL 6:417–420)

Jens Timmermann

The general introduction[1] to the topic of duties to oneself in the *Tugend-lehre* demonstrates some of the usual characteristics of a Kantian antinomy. The first two sections contain arguments in support of two conflicting philosophical claims. The thesis—that human beings have *no* duties to themselves—is the subject matter of §1, where the very concept of such duties is alleged to contain a contradiction. The antithesis—that we *do* have duties to ourselves—is argued for in §2, on the grounds that without such duties there would be no duties at all, a proposition too dreadful for either side of the dispute to contemplate. The arguments for both sides of the controversy remind us of the indirect proofs familiar from the "Dialectic" of the *Critique of Pure Reason*, and once again they were clearly formulated with the solution in mind. In the heading of §3, Kant announces his intention to settle the antinomial conflict. As is customary, the solution draws on the resources of his transcendental idealism. It turns out that the thesis side fails to take account of the critical

---

1   The headings of the original editions, the Academy Edition and the Cambridge translation are corrupt: "Ethical Doctrine of Elements/Part I/On Duties to Oneself as Such/Introduction" (TL 6:417.1–4, trans. J.T.). The topic of Part I is not 'duties to oneself as such' but 'duties to oneself' in general, as opposed to duties (of virtue) to others (cf. TL 6:448.3). Part I is subdivided into two 'Books,' the first of which covers perfect duties to oneself (cf. TL 6:421.5), the second a human being's imperfect duties to oneself 'with regard to his end' (cf. TL 6:444.12). The topic of duties to oneself 'as such' (*überhaupt*) is discussed in the introduction to Part I (cf. TL 6:417.4–420.30), which is the subject of this paper. We should thus expect either 'Ethical Doctrine of Elements/Part I/ On Duties to Oneself/Introduction/On Duties to Oneself as Such' or at least 'Ethical Doctrine of Elements/Part I/Introduction/On Duties to Oneself as Such,' and the text should be amended accordingly. Note that the second edition turns roman numerals into 'parts,' parts into 'books,' whereas a book becomes a 'division' (*Abteilung*), but that does not solve the problem. Mary Gregor's Cambridge translation follows the lead of the Academy Edition, which uses the headings of the first edition.

distinction between human beings as on the one hand sensuous, and on the other as intellectual.[2]

In other respects, however, this new antinomy is quite extraordinary. Many of the attributes of the paradigmatic first *Critique* antinomies are missing. The two sides are not formally labeled 'thesis' and 'antithesis' (in fact, the thesis is never explicitly formulated); they do not feature separate 'proofs' or 'remarks,' presented on facing pages of the book, or in separate columns. The proofs are extremely compressed, not to say cryptic. So is the solution. More significantly, both sides of the conflict are treated unequally, even more so than thesis and antithesis in the "Dialectic" of the *Critique of Practical Reason*. In the second *Critique*, both positions are dismissed as stated, but the antithesis has the edge over the thesis because it is merely conditionally, not unconditionally, wrong; and hence salvageable by transferring the causal link it posits to the world of understanding (cf. KpV 5:114.29–34). In the *Tugendlehre*, by contrast, Kant does not impugn or relativize the antithesis argument at all. In fact, the very persuasiveness of the antithesis helps us to discredit the erroneous assumption that lends the thesis much of its *prima facie* plausibility.

As a result, there is no transcendental illusion. Kant does not argue that reason will continue to produce in us contradictory impressions supporting thesis and antithesis, or that we will continue to be attracted to the thesis that there can be no duties to oneself once the puzzle has been resolved. As the antithesis emerges victorious, the thesis argument is shown to rest on a simple mistake. Therefore, the concept of duties to oneself produces merely the semblance of an antinomy, and only at first sight. That is why Kant uses the language of deceptive appearance (*Anschein, scheinbar*) in the headings of both §1 and §3. On closer inspection, then, there is no antinomy. The apparent conflict disappears when we learn to think of the binding self and the bound self as distinct, whereas in an actual Kantian antinomy both sides retain an appearance of reasonableness even when the conflict has been resolved by critical means.

---

2   Alternatively, one might take "scheinbare[] Antinomie" (TL 6:418.4) to refer to the apparent contradiction in §1, dispelled in §3, not to the clash of a thesis implied by §1 and an antithesis expressly defended in §2. However, in accordance with its etymology, the word 'antinomy' refers to a conflict (*Widerstreit*) of two general propositions everywhere else in Kant's writings, not to a mere contradiction (*Widerspruch*) inherent in a particular philosophical concept. Why should the §3 heading of the *Tugendlehre* depart from this pattern?

§1. At First Appearance, the Concept of a Duty to Oneself Contains a Contradiction

This section contains two distinct parts, separated by a dash. The first part contains the main argument against duties to oneself, to the effect that the concept of such a duty is self-contradictory (cf. TL 6:417.7–16). The second part tries to shed some additional light on this contradiction (cf. TL 6:417.16–22).

Kant first sketches an argument to the effect that the very concept of such a duty contains a contradiction (an argument he does not himself endorse). Self-contradictory concepts cannot be instantiated. If so, human beings have no duties to themselves. This is the thesis of the (seeming) antinomy. Kant does not state it explicitly—the discussion revolves entirely around the question of self-contradiction. It must be supplied in analogy with the heading of §2, which asserts that human beings do have duties to themselves (cf. TL 6:417.23).

The threat of self-contradiction is spelt out as follows. Let us take the expression 'I have a duty to myself' at face value and assume that there is only one self; that the two selves mentioned are one and the same; that the *obligated* self [3] is identical with the *obligating* self [4]; or, as Kant puts it, that the self is in both cases "taken in [one and, J.T.] the same sense [in einerlei Sinn genommen]" (TL 6:417.7).[5] Let us call this the 'identity assumption.' It is a natural assumption to make. As yet, there is no reason to believe that the two selves referred to in the expression are not identical, nor any indication how they could possibly fail to be the same.

Now, the concept of duty contains that of *passive* necessitation, i.e. the notion of *being obligated or bound* to do something. There is no contradiction in that. Yet if the duty in question is a duty *to one's own self*, the argument goes, the self is also thought of as *actively binding*. If A has a duty to B, B is holding A to that duty. But as, *ex hypothesi*, the self is

---

3   i.e. the self that faces the duty, and ought to act accordingly.
4   i.e. the self that effects the binding and to which one consequently has a duty.
5   Kant repeatedly returns to this formulation in his solution in §3: "under two attributes [in zwiefacher Qualität]" (TL 6:418.6), "taken in [...] two different senses" (TL 6:418.20 f.) and "not thought in one and the same sense" (TL 6:418.22). For similar turns of phrase in an antinomial context see e.g. Kant's summary of the resolution of the third antinomy in the second-edition preface to the first *Critique* ("in eben derselben Bedeutung" (KrV B xxvii), as was inevitable in a pre-critical framework) and the resolution of the antinomy of taste in the third ("nicht in einerlei Sinn genommen" (KU 5:339.10)).

one and the same in both roles, a single self is conceived as being both actively and passively involved in the same token obligation, as being acting and acted upon, binding and bound, at the same time and in the same respect, which is a contradiction. We are left to conclude that there can be no duties to oneself.

Unfortunately, Kant now obscures the argument by glossing a duty to oneself in terms of "an obligation to be obligated [eine Verbindlichkeit verbunden zu sein]" (TL 6:417.14, trans. J.T.). That sounds splendidly paradoxical but does little to clarify the point.[6] He presumably means that the self would be confronted with an obligation to generate an obligation by binding itself. In that case, there would be no initial obligation; and no obligation could result. This is reflected in Mary Gregor's less than literal reflexive rendering of the expression. According to Gregor's translation, a duty to myself would amount to "being bound to bind myself" (TL 6:417.14). To account for the obligation incurred one might posit yet another duty (to oneself), but that would only create the need for another one, and so *ad infinitum.* This type of argument is reminiscent of a theme that pervades Kant's earlier discussion of the aesthetic preliminary concepts of morality (cf. TL 6:399.1–403.6). Moral feeling, conscience and respect for the law within us cannot be subject to obligation because they are preconditions of our *recognition*[7] of duty.[8] The similarity is most striking in the case of respect. A duty to have respect, Kant argues, would amount "to being duty-bound to duty [zur Pflicht verpflichtet werden]" (TL 6:402.34, trans. J.T.), which similarly creates an air of paradox at the expense of perspicuity.

---

6 Kant glosses the phrase as "a passive obligation that yet, in the same sense of the relation, would also be an active one" (TL 6:417.15 f., trans. J.T.), merely repeating what has been said before.

7 Kant emphasizes the subjective or epistemic character of these moral qualities throughout. There can be no obligation to have or acquire them because they underpin morality as "*subjective* conditions of receptiveness [Empfänglichkeit] to the concept of duty, not as objective conditions" (TL 6:399.8 f.). In this respect, their foundational status is different from the impossibility of an—objectively paradoxical—"obligation to be obligated."

8 The remaining (third) preliminary concept of 'love of human beings' has deliberately been omitted from the list. Contrary to Kant's initial declaration at TL 6:399.6, *Menschenliebe* appears to be an aesthetic *consequence* of sustained, active benevolence, not a subjective *precondition* of recognizing benevolence as a duty (cf. TL 6:402.14–16). If love of human beings cannot be commanded, it is because it belongs to the sphere of feeling.

The secondary argument is introduced by the phrase "[o]ne can also bring this contradiction to light" at TL 6:417.16. It reads like an afterthought prompted by the insight that the notion of an 'obligation to be obligated' is not very helpful. Duties to oneself are now said to make no sense on the grounds that the agent (in his role as the author of the obligation) could always release himself (as the subject of the obligation) from doing the thing he has a duty to do.[9] If so, the duty would not be binding, and hence be no duty at all. A duty to oneself would be a duty that is not a duty; which constitutes a contraction.[10]

However, why should the identity assumption be taken to imply that the agent can always release himself from an obligation to himself? The text suggests the following reply: Kant is assuming that obligation consists in the active element's free subjection of the passive element.[11] If so, it is reasonable to assume that the active element can equally freely undo or reverse this act of subjection. The passive element is bound by the active element. The active element is not itself bound—if it were it would be passive, and no longer free. If, then, the active self and the passive self are identical, the single self is not permanently bound—; and there is no duty. The identity assumption implies that the self put under an obligation can always release itself from that very obligation, because it is grounded in itself. Under ordinary circumstances the subject of the obligation can only relieve himself from an obligation by discharging it in the proper way, i.e. by doing his duty. On the identity assumption, however, he can actually discharge himself.

§2. Nevertheless, a Human Being Has Duties to Himself

The very brief second section contains the argument in support of duties to oneself. The proof of the antithesis position takes the shape of a conventional *reductio ad absurdum* of the thesis: the chief implication of §1 that there can be, and consequently are, no duties to oneself.

---

9 Note that the secondary argument still relies on the identity assumption.

10 According to Dieter Schönecker, the contradiction consists in the same self's both possessing and lacking the capacity to release itself from an obligation (cf. Schönecker, 2010, p. 248). This is a contradiction, and it can be developed on the basis of the materials provided by §1, but there is no need to stray from Kant's text. The self-contradiction of a duty that is not binding is perfectly sufficient for the purposes of the argument.

11 This theme reappears in the solution in §3 below, see particularly TL 6:418.12.

Assuming the truth of the thesis does not entail a straightforward contradiction, but the consequences are still unacceptable.[12] If there were no duties to oneself, Kant tells us, there would be *no duties whatsoever*,[13] which is a state of affairs neither Kant nor the defender of the thesis is prepared to envisage.[14] As to Kant, there is no reason why he should take global skepticism seriously at this point.[15] What is more relevant in the context of §2, however, is that the proponent of the thesis argument is unlikely to be a radical moral skeptic either. §1 targets the concept of duties to oneself, not the possibility of duty *tout court*. This explains the curious formulation that without duties to oneself there would be no duties, and hence no "external duties,"[16] i.e. duties to others, "either [auch keine äußere Pflichten]" (TL 6:417.25). In short, the existence of duties to oneself is a matter of dispute, whereas the existence of duties to others is common ground. This is the beauty of §2. If the argu-

---

12 Note that Kant now for the first time speaks in his own voice. He obviously endorses the argument of §2.

13 Without duties to oneself, Kant adds, there would not even be "external duties" (TL 6:417.25). What kind of duty does he have in mind? The internal/external distinction is drawn differently at different points in the book. At times it seems to concern the source of legislation, but Kant also argues for external aspects of ethical legislation, which cannot be externally enforced (e.g. duties of benevolence at MS 6:220.29). In a general sense, external duties are therefore simply "obligations to external actions" (MS 6:220.30 f.); or, as he puts it in his notes on the *Metaphysics of Morals*, duties of 'performance' (*Leistungen*) according to their effect (*ihrer Wirkung nach*), as opposed to internal duties, which are associated with 'attitudes' or 'dispositions' (*Gesinnungen*) (cf. VATL 23:251.7, trans. J.T.). At TL 6:417.25, however, Kant has specifically duties of performance *to others* in mind, as the next sentence shows: "For I cannot recognize myself to be under an obligation to others [...]" (trans. J.T.). – There is a further question whether Kant is referring to external *ethical* duties to others only at TL 6:417.25, or whether external *juridical* duties are thought to be threatened by there being no duties to oneself as well.

14 Here Schönecker and I concur: Kant is not trying to emphasize that duties to others specifically are impossible without duties to oneself, conventionally construed (cf. Schönecker, 2010, p. 236). Rather, all duties—duties to oneself and duties to others—are grounded in the same way in an autonomous will. Without the autonomy of the obligating self there would be neither duties to oneself nor duties to others. See Timmermann, 2006, p. 512, fn. 17.

15 As the system of the *Metaphysics of Morals* is intended as a follow-up to the *Critique of Practical Reason* (cf. "Preface," MS 6:205.2 f.), we may assume that Kant is relying on establishing the factual reality of duty in the earlier work.

16 Quotations for which the reference is not given immediately are covered by the following reference.

ment works, Kant's opponent will have to admit that there are duties to oneself, or else embrace amoralism.

So, why should it be the case that there would be no duties at all if there were no duties to oneself, not even otherwise non-controversial external duties to others? Let us return to the text of the *Tugendlehre*:

> For I cannot recognize myself to be under an obligation to others unless [ich kann mich gegen Andere nicht für verbunden erkennen, als nur so fern] I at the same time put myself under an obligation [ich zugleich mich selbst verbinde]: since the law by virtue of which I regard myself as being under an obligation proceeds in every case from my own practical reason; and in being constrained by my own reason, I am also the one constraining myself. (TL 6:417.24–418.3, first part trans. J.T.)

The emphasis on 'recognizing' oneself to be under an obligation may seem to suggest that Kant is talking about an epistemic condition for determining what one has to do. If so, it is not clear what his point would be, or how this is supposed to strengthen the case for duties to oneself. Rather, the gist of the first sentence seems to be that recognition of any specific obligation to do something must result in an act of self-obligation. Whenever I see that I face an obligation—in the sense that I see that here and now some specific action is made necessary by the moral law—I must bind myself to do it (i. e. I must *put* myself under the obligation, I must try to make myself act accordingly). This conception of self-obligation is very close to the thin conceptual notion of a 'duty to oneself' employed throughout in §§1–3.[17] Even duties to others involve self-necessitation and thus consist, at last in part, of a 'duty to oneself' in this sense.[18] In Kant's ethical theory, others cannot obligate me directly. They can bind me only if I bind myself.

---

17 Duties to oneself are spelt out in terms of "I *ought* to bind myself" (TL 6:417.13 f.) both in the thesis, the antithesis and the solution. Substantive duties to oneself, such as the prohibition of suicide and avarice, enter the scene only in §4. Consequently, Kant is not saying that particular duties to oneself (such as the prohibition of suicide or the injunction to develop one's talents) are foundational with regard to duties to others (e. g. beneficence). So far, he is talking about duties to oneself in a literal, 'thin' or formal sense, as the emphasis on the word 'concept' in §1 indicates.

18 For other interpretations of the primacy of duties to oneself—e. g. the idea that duties to oneself must be discharged first, or the thesis that duties to oneself are instrumentally valuable in discharging any duty—see Timmermann, 2006, pp. 510–515.

There are overtones of Kant's ethics of autonomy here, even if the word 'autonomy' is not mentioned.[19] The conceptual 'thin' notion of a duty to oneself is not identical with Kantian autonomy, but it can be seen as a corollary. Indeed, Kant continues to explain the self-binding process in terms reminiscent of the foundations of his ethical theory laid out in the *Groundwork* and the second *Critique*. When I stand under an obligation, the law that binds me "proceeds in every case *from my own practical reason*" (TL 6:417.27–418.1, italics J.T.), which alone possesses this authority. I am constrained by my own reason. I have to obey, but at the same time I am the one who does the constraining. Autonomous self-constraint in this sense is the foundation of all duties, both of duties to oneself in the ordinary, substantive sense—e. g. not to throw away one's life—and of duties to others.[20]

In other words, a duty is owed to the lawgiver. As *my own* rational faculty is the lawgiver, I owe any duty to myself, *qua* autonomous legislator. In this sense, then, any ethical duty is a duty to oneself. This idea does not directly affect duties to others or substantive duties to oneself in the ordinary sense of the term. This can be seen from the analogy of a—by Kant's standards heteronomous—theological system of obligation. Within such a framework, God is the legislator who imposes obligations upon us. We would owe moral action to him, whether obligation affects our conduct towards him, ourselves, others or creation at large etc. In Kant's ethics of autonomy, our own practical reason has taken over from God as moral legislator, so we owe all moral conduct to ourselves. But again, there are still duties to ourselves in a substantive sense, as well as duties to others.

---

19 In the *Metaphysics of Morals*, 'autonomy' (of practical reason) is explicitly mentioned only twice (cf. TL 6:383.23 and 6:480.2).

20 It is the principal message of *Groundwork* II that only this model of obligation can account for the categoricity of moral imperatives. If any authority other than my own practical reason were to try to impose an obligation upon me externally, it would have to be tied to my will by a desire and hence become a conditional (hypothetical) imperative. See Kant's 'paradox of autonomy' at GMS 4:439.3–12.

§3. Unlocking the Apparent Antinomy

In the third section, Kant introduces his key to solving or 'unlocking' ("Aufschluß" (TL 6:418.4)[21]) the apparent antinomy[22] provoked by the seemingly self-contradictory concept of a duty to oneself. The headings of the first two sections indicate that this is done in a somewhat unconventional fashion, by denying the consequent of the thesis on the strength of the manifest truth of the antithesis. The overall argument of §§1–3 proceeds as follows:

1. If the self that imposes an obligation to oneself is the same self as that on which the obligation is imposed, the notion of an obligation to oneself is incoherent, and duties to oneself are impossible (§1).
2. But there are duties to oneself—hence duties to oneself are not impossible—because duties (to others) do exist: for without duties to oneself there would be no duties whatsoever (§2).
3. Therefore, the self that imposes an obligation to oneself must be different from the self upon which the obligation is imposed (§3).

Anyone who accepts the argument of §2 must reject the identity assumption. But that does not mean that he has the wherewithal to identify the two selves involved, or to make sense of how the self can bind the self.[23] Important work remains to be done. That is why, as in his attempts to

---

21 As Adelung, 1811, column 529, notes, *Aufschluß* in the figurative sense of 'solution' was a neologism in the late 18th century. It was particularly associated with clearing up an obscurity or puzzle—Kant uses it to refer to the 'secret' of how synthetic a priori judgments are possible at KrV A10. These connotations are largely absent from various modern idiomatic expressions in use today (*Aufschluß geben, erhalten, sich Aufschluß erwarten* etc.). *Aufschluß* seems to be a more decisive expression than the customary Kantian term, *Auflösung* (resolution, of an antinomy), perhaps chosen to indicate that no residue or transcendental illusion remains once the critical job is done.
22 At this point, the theme of antinomial conflict is made explicit for the first time. TL 6:418.4 is the only occurrence of the word 'antinomy' (*Antinomie*) in the *Tugendlehre*.
23 As Andrews Reath notes, the success of §2 indicates that the apparent inconsistency within the concept of a duty to oneself "should be resolvable, though without showing how" (Reath, 2002, p. 354). The contradiction of §1 has not been resolved in §2, as Schönecker suggests (cf. Schönecker, 2010, p. 259), even if the autonomy model of obligation of §2 points Kant's readers in the right direction. Autonomy would be impossible without the transcendental distinction of phenomena and noumena first introduced in §3.

resolve the antinomies of the *Critiques,* Kant now draws on the resources of his transcendental idealism to defuse the present antinomy.

The first paragraph of §3 contains a number of preparatory reflections. In being conscious of myself as the subject of a duty to myself I am said to ascribe to myself two distinct properties: I regard myself both as a sensuous being ("Sinnenwesen" (TL 6:418.6 f.)) and as an intelligible being ("Vernunftwesen" (TL 6:418.8)).[24] The former is a kind of animal, determined by the senses; the latter cannot be influenced by the senses at all.[25] Summarizing his doctrine of moral awareness as the *ratio cognoscendi* of freedom as put forward in the *Critique of Practical Reason,* Kant adds that we are conscious of our status as intelligible beings only from a moral or practical perspective, as "the incomprehensible property of *freedom* is revealed by the influence of reason on the inner lawgiving will" (TL 6:418.11–13).

The actual solution of the alleged antinomy follows in the second paragraph, at TL 6:418.14. Taking up the above distinction between two ways of regarding oneself when faced with an obligation to oneself, Kant asserts that as a natural being one's choices are susceptible to the power of reason and can cause actions in the world of sense. In describing a human being in these terms, we regard him as a member of the world of sense, as *homo phaenomenon.* As such, he is pre- or non-moral, and the concept of an obligation ("der Begriff einer [sic!] Verbindlichkeit" (TL 6:418.16)) is still irrelevant. However, according to his *"personality,"* i.e. considered as a creature endowed with the gift of inner freedom, as *homo noumenon,* he "is a being that is capable of obligation, namely

---

24 The distinction at TL 6:418.8 between a human being as *Vernunftwesen*—rendered *"intelligible being"* in the Cambridge translation—and as *vernünftiges Wesen*—rendered "a being that has reason"—does not permit of an idiomatic English translation, as Mary Gregor's roundabout choice of terms shows. Luckily, it is just a side-remark. It does not advance the main argument. Kant reminds us that the kind of rational being required to resolve the present difficulty is not just a being endowed with theoretical reason (and possibly, as a consequence, empirical practical reason), but rather a being that can determine its own actions by pure practical reason. The distinction is taken up again when TL 6:418.14 *homo phaenomenon* is the gloss provided for *vernünftiges Naturwesen,* i.e. a natural being capable of rational choices.

25 This point is obscured by Gregor's peculiar translation: "The senses cannot attain this latter aspect of a human being," she writes, starting a new sentence, whereas Kant's relative clause quite straightforwardly speaks of the "intelligible being [...] that no sense reaches [welches kein Sinn erreicht]" (TL 6:418.8–10, trans. J.T.), and that can only be cognized in a practical respect etc.

regarded as directed towards itself [...] [ist ein der Verpflichtung fähiges Wesen und zwar gegen sich selbst [...] betrachtet]" (TL 6:418.17–20, trans. J.T.).[26]

What does this mean? The argument of §2, as well as the skeptical objection formulated in §1, strongly suggest that the obligation *homo noumenon* is capable of is the *active* obligation of *homo phaenomenon*, which results in an obligation to himself (i. e. to *homo noumenon*) glossed as a duty to "the humanity in his own person" (TL 6:418.20). As intellectual beings we are free and can therefore impose obligations upon ourselves as natural beings that can be determined by rational considerations. The 'capacity of obligation' is the capacity actively to obligate, not the capacity to be obligated—if *being* obligated or susceptible to obligation is a capacity (*Fähigkeit*) in Kant's sense at all. If so, Kant's conclusion makes perfect sense: "[...] the human being (taken in these two different senses) can acknowledge a duty to himself without falling into a contradiction (because the concept of a human being is not thought in one and the same sense)" (TL 6:418.20–23).

The solution of the conflict in §3 thus rejects the identity assumption, i. e. the central assumption of §1. What is more, it helps us to make sense of duties to oneself by accounting for the difference in kind between the obligating and the obligated self. Without the identity assumption, the argument for the thesis loses all its philosophical force, while he argument for the antithesis remains intact. But an antithesis without a thesis is no antinomy. Strictly speaking, it is not even an antith-

---

26 Unfortunately, Mary Gregor muddies Kant's central argument in her Cambridge translation by rendering TL 6:418.19 f. "is regarded as *a being that can be put under obligation* and, indeed, under obligation to himself" (italics J.T.). Following Bernd Ludwig, Andrews Reath notes this mistake, but argues that 'obligation' in "a being that is capable of obligation" should be taken to include both perspectives, the act of obligating and the fact of being obligated (cf. Reath, 2002, p. 355). That is a step in the right direction, but Reath does not go far enough. *Qua* intelligible being, a human being is free and precisely *not* bound by laws of obligation. Rather, it is obligating *homo phaenomenon*. I am tempted to translate "a being that is capable of obligating"—Kant adds: "namely regarded as directed towards itself," i. e. a being endowed with personality can create obligations towards itself. Relatedly, Gregor leaves the "noch" in "noch nicht in Betrachtung" at TL 6:418.17 above untranslated: and so far the concept of an obligation "does not [yet, J.T.] come into consideration." In fact, it is difficult to see how on her reconstruction the human being as *homo phaenomenon* can *ever* come into consideration in matters of duties to oneself.

esis. §1 and §2 of the *Tugendlehre* create merely the semblance of an antinomy.

§4. On the Principle of the Division of Duties to Oneself

So far, Kant has been discussing duties to one's own self in a thin conceptual sense. They can be explained as the result of the capacity of *homo noumenon* to obligate *homo phaenomenon*, which is the foundation of all ethical duties. In the last section of the introduction he finally turns to his classification of substantive duties to oneself, which are the subject matter of the remaining pages of Part I (TL 6:421–447).

Kant argues that all duties to oneself are duties to the same subject—the human being—and that body and soul should not be thought of as separate targets of obligation. The classification can therefore only be made with regard to the objects of duty, not the subject, which is a whole. We thus have duties towards *persons*, oneself and others. Yet he proceeds to develop two distinct divisions of duties to oneself. The *objective* division (TL 6:419.15–36) concerns what is formal and what is material in duties to oneself in a manner familiar from the discussion of perfect and imperfect duties in the *Groundwork*. The former negatively limit the agent's actions (*einschränkend*), the second positively propose to expand the ends to be pursued (*erweiternd*). The *subjective* division (TL 6:419.37–420.30) depends on whether the subject of a duty to oneself views himself both as an animal or physical being and as a moral being, or as a moral being only. The books and chapters of "Part I" follow both divisions.

References

Adelung, Johann Christoph (1811), "Aufschluß", in: id., *Grammatisch-kritisches Wörterbuch der hochdeutschen Mundart*, vol. 1, Wien: Bauer, column 529.
Reath, Andrews (2002), "Self-Legislation and Duties to Oneself", in: Mark Timmons (ed.), *Kant's 'Metaphysics of Morals': Interpretative Essays*, Oxford: Oxford University Press, pp. 349–370.
Schönecker, Dieter (2010), "Kant über die Möglichkeit von Pflichten gegen sich selbst (*Tugendlehre*, §§1–3): Eine Skizze", in: Hubertus Busche/Anton Schmitt (eds.), *Kant als Bezugspunkt philosophischen Denkens: Festschrift für Peter Baumanns zum 75. Geburtstag*, Würzburg: Königshausen & Neumann, pp. 235–260.

Timmermann, Jens (2006), "Kantian Duties to the Self, Explained and Defended", in: *Philosophy*, vol. 81, pp. 505–530.

The Perfect Duty to Oneself as an Animal Being (TL 6:421–428)

Mark Timmons

Chapter 1 of the "Doctrine of Elements" in Kant's *Doctrine of Virtue* (*Tugendlehre*) is devoted to perfect duties to oneself as moral being with an animal nature. This short chapter includes three 'articles,' each of which treats what Kant considers to be a fundamental type of duty comprising this category: suicide and self-mutilation, misuse of one's sexual organs, and excess in consumption of food and drink. Kant's *Tugendlehre* discussions of these duties (as well as the other duties discussed in this work) are extremely compressed, and we find various interwoven strands of thought that require some disentangling and elaboration in order to bring Kant's main arguments and associated claims into clear focus. Fortunately, we are helped in this endeavor by consulting some of Kant's other writings (particularly the *Lectures on Ethics*) where we find more detailed discussion of the various duties and related themes that comprise Kant's overall system of duties which, as we shall see, help fill in various gaps that we find in his laconic *Tugendlehre* treatment of them. The aim of my commentary, then, is to examine Kant's arguments and associated claims in the *Tugendlehre*, chapter 1, making some use of these other writings.

Before examining chapter 1 of the *Tugendlehre*, there are some preliminary matters of importance that must be addressed. Kant's arguments for the various duties comprising his grand system of duties appeal (almost without exception) to the humanity formulation of the categorical imperative: "*So act that you use humanity, whether in your own person or in the person of any other, always at the same time as an end and never simply as a means*" (GMS 4:429.10–12)[1]. They also appeal to Kant's view of human nature (or what Kant calls anthropology), and in particular to the relation between what Kant takes to be basic components of

---

1   The exception is Kant's argument for the general duty of beneficence which appeals to the universal law formulation. (See TL 6:393.16–23, 451.4–19 and 453.5–15)

human nature: one's humanity and animality. Given the central role of these components in Kant's arguments, I will begin in the next section with some general and very brief remarks about them, with the aim of highlighting certain themes and theses that play an important role in Kant's discussion of the duties with which we are concerned.

I. Humanity and Animality

According to Kant, humanity[2], or more precisely *personality*, understood as "freedom and independence from the mechanism of the whole of nature, regarded nevertheless as also a capacity of a being subject to special laws—namely pure practical laws given by his own reason" (KpV 5:87.3–6), is the basis or ground of having a certain status—that of being an end-in-oneself, a being with non-relative, absolute worth that Kant calls "dignity" (GMS 4:435.4) To have this sort of status demands that one be treated with respect; such demands constituting unconditional moral demands or duties. Considerations having to do with the bearing of one's actions and attitudes on the preservation and cultivation of one's humanity serve as the grounds or *reasons* that morally favor or disfavor certain actions. Let us use the term 'humanity-based reason' to refer to those morally relevant considerations regarding actions and circumstances that bear on the deontic status of actions. Thus, for instance, the fact that

---

2   Kant seems to use this term in both a broad and a narrow sense. Used broadly, the term refers to those rational capacities, including the capacity to set and act for ends, that (*i*) have to do with the end of happiness (which is set for us by nature), as well as (*ii*) those that have to do with morality, which in turn requires the sort of robust freedom of choice (autonomy) or what Kant calls 'personality' that he associates with the possibility of acting for moral reasons. Used narrowly, 'humanity' refers to those rational capacities other than those distinctive of personality. The humanity/personality distinction is most clearly drawn in *Religion* (RGV 6:27.4–28.7) In the *Tugendlehre*, we find Kant using both terms, though he often seems to use 'humanity' in a broad sense that includes both humanity (narrow) and personality. And this is how I will use it throughout, because as I understand Kant's appeal to the dignity of humanity in his arguments for various duties, some of them seem to require what I'm calling the broad sense of the term 'humanity.' (See Christiano, 2008, for an illuminating discussion of this matter.) Kant's chapter 1 arguments against suicide and unnatural sex make specific reference to one's personality; the arguments against self-mutilation, drunkenness, and gluttony seem to rest upon an appeal to humanity in the broad sense of the term.

a certain action would be an intentional killing of oneself (suicide) constitutes one sort of humanity-based reason against performing that action. Humanity-based reasons for action are to be contrasted with reasons that have their source in what Kant calls "discretionary end[s]" (TL 6:423.4)—ends that pertain to one's happiness or well-being.

I claim the following theses partially characterize Kant's conception of humanity-based reasons:

- *Inescapability thesis:* humanity-based reasons are always in principle applicable to one's choices, actions, and attitudes.
- *Supremacy thesis:* humanity-based reasons that either require or at least justify certain responses of rational agents enjoy normative supremacy over reasons whose basis concerns discretionary ends.[3]

In cases where there are humanity-based (and thus moral) reasons for incompatible courses of action, Kant claims that "practical philosophy says, not that the stronger obligation takes precedence [...], but that the stronger *ground of obligation* prevails [...]" (MS 6:224.23–25).[4] This suggests the following requirement:

- *Authorization requirement:* An action of a type that normally violates one or more duties can be morally justified (authorized), but only if there are humanity-based reasons favoring the action that are at least as strong (normatively) as whatever humanity-based reasons disfavor the action.

All three of these theses obviously deserve detailed discussion, elaboration, and defense that I am not able to provide in this article. I hope they strike readers as commitments characteristic of Kant's moral philosophy. As I shall proceed to explain in section II, they each play important

---

3   Two comments are in order. First, talk of reasons 'requiring or at least justifying' is meant to allow for the fact that some reasons that give rise to perfect duties function to require certain actions or omissions, though other reasons, associated with fulfillment of imperfect duties, while they do not require specific actions, they can serve to justify in the sense of making it rational to perform certain specific actions. In both of these ways, moral reasons enjoy normative supremacy over non-moral reasons for action. Second, talk of 'normative supremacy' is deliberately vague to allow that moral reasons may have supremacy either by *overriding* non-moral reasons, or by *silencing* them. Thanks to Tom Hill and Jens Timmermann for discussion of these issues.
4   For an illuminating discussion of this passage see Jens Timmermann, 2013, ch. 1.

roles in Kant's *Tugendlehre* discussion of the duties to self that we are about to examine.

One's animality has to do with one's physical nature, which includes certain drives that are associated with 'natural ends' that are in turn directed (by nature) toward certain modes of preservation:

> [...] nature [through various impulses operating in humans, M.T.] aims at a) his self-preservation, b) the preservation of the species, and c) the preservation of his capacity to [use his powers purposefully and to, M.T.] enjoy life [...] (TL 6:420.5–7).

At bottom, duties to oneself with respect to one's animal nature concern maintenance of the proper relation of *self-governance*[5] between one's animal nature and one's humanity or rational nature.[6] Failure of such governance through action and attitude reflects bad self-government: a failure to respect the dignity of one's humanity. And it is such lack of self-respect that explains why at bottom certain actions and attitudes are morally wrong; violations of duty to oneself. One aspect of Kantian self-governance has to do with negative duties of omission and concerns the idea that the natural impulses partly constitutive of one's animal nature are to 'serve' the person in the proper exercise of those rational capacities that are constitutive of her humanity. More formally:

- *Moral harm principle:* One has a duty to oneself to subordinate and control one's natural impulses (including those having to do with self-preservation, preservation of the species, and preservation of the capacity to enjoy life) so that these impulses and their associated bodily powers may be of use in the pursuit of non-discretionary ends determined by reason. Unauthorized actions that destroy or harm one's capacity to pursue such ends or interfere with their pursuit manifest a lack of self-respect and thus violate this duty to oneself.

---

5 See, for instance, V-Mo/Collins 27:379.

6 With respect to duties to oneself qua animal, Kant distinguishes between those that have to do with the *preservation* of one's nature (one's "moral **health**" (TL 6:419.24 f.)) and those having to do with its *cultivation* and development (one's "moral *prosperity*" (TL 6:419.29 f.)). The latter are positive duties of commission, while the former are negative duties of omission with which we are here concerned.

This principle expresses the controlling idea in Kant's *Tugendlehre* objections to suicide, drunkenness and gluttony, and (as we shall see) in Kant's objection to masturbation that we find in the *Pedagogy*.[7]

My plan in what follows is to make use of these various theses in attempting to understand and evaluate the various arguments in chapter 1 of the *Tugendlehre*. But I should first mention what I consider to be an important methodological point. In defending claims about actions being in violation of duty, one would like (if possible) an explanation of *why* the action in question violates the dignity of humanity, and thereby constitutes a lack of self-respect. Perhaps for some actions it is self-evident that they dishonor the dignity of humanity because they stand as exemplars of the very concept of morally dishonorable behavior. But for any action that is supposed to violate a person's dignity, it is preferable to be able to *explain why* it is a violation. Call this the *explanatory burden*. Meeting this burden is, I think, particularly problematic for Kant's attempt in the *Tugendlehre* to argue against forms of unnatural and non-procreative sex.

II. Perfect Duties to Oneself qua Animal (and Moral) Being

Kant begins the chapter on duties to self qua animal (§5) with the remark that the most general negative duty of self-preservation[8] is the *"first, though not the principal"* (TL 6:421.10) duty to oneself qua animal, which implies that the positive duty to cultivate one's (non-moral) powers and capacities is the principal duty to oneself as an animal being. He then goes on to claim (in effect) that each of the more specific perfect (nega-

---

7   In addition to the moral harm principle, Kant's conception of self-governance also includes what I call the *moral degradation principle:* One has an obligation to refrain from acting in ways that are inherently degrading in relation to one's own worth or dignity—degrading either because they directly express a lack of self-respect or because they are expressions of a morally defective character. This principle is most clearly operative in Kant's objection to servility—a duty to oneself as a moral being only. I would also argue that this principle could be used as a basis for mounting distinct, non-harm based arguments against the duties to oneself qua animal being, although in the *Tugendlehre* Kant does not do so. However, limitations of space do not allow examining the matter.

8   By 'self-preservation' Kant is not just referring to the duty to refrain from suicide, rather he is referring to all of the duties that have to do with maintenance of one's physical being.

tive) duties to oneself qua animal being have to do with types of action, the performance of which deprives oneself of some physical power or capacity (or the use of such powers and capacities) that are essential to the preservation and maintenance of one's humanity. Suicide, of course, results in a total deprivation of one's powers and capacities; partial deprivation results from physical mutilation and from misuse of one's sexual and nutritive powers.

In taking up questions about the morality of these types of action, each of Kant's three articles feature his reasoning in defense of the duty under consideration—the 'core' of the article—followed by casuistical questions about what are arguably 'hard' cases that he does not propose to answer in a book whose aim is to set forth the general principles of duty comprising a metaphysic of morals. The core passages contain Kant's arguments for the various claims about duties to oneself, and they sometimes contain remarks about the comparative degree of violation of duties to oneself that the various condemned actions represent. Let us now examine these passages. For reasons I will later make clear, I will comment on Articles II and III in reverse order.

Article I: On killing oneself (§6)

The core of this article has five paragraphs. The first four of them concern suicide, the fifth concerns mutilation. Kant begins in § 1 with the remark that willfully killing oneself constitutes murdering oneself (and is thus wrongful killing) *only if* it can be shown either that such killing violates a duty to oneself or a duty to others.[9] He then proceeds in the next paragraph to explain that although this act can be regarded as a violation of one's duty to others (e. g. to one's spouse, family, fellow citizens,

---

9   In *Lectures on Ethics* Kant gives what I take to be the core of his definition of suicide: "It is the intention to destroy oneself that constitutes suicide" (V-Mo/Collins 27:371.8 f.). In these passages, Kant distinguishes suicide from self-sacrifice, the difference being that the latter does not involve the intention to actively kill oneself. Rather, cases of self-sacrifice involve knowingly giving up one's life at the hands of another. He also (in these same passages) condemns all suicide, including the case of Cato (which, in the *Tugendlehre*, is mentioned in the section on casuistry), but claims that self-sacrifice can be justified: "if I cannot preserve [my life, M.T.] other than by violating the duties to myself, then I am bound to sacrifice it, rather than violate those duties; yet on the other hand, suicide is not permitted under any condition" (V-Mo/Collins 27:372.27–31).

God), the present concern is whether, apart from all such relations, "a human being is still bound to preserve his life simply by virtue of his quality as a person and whether he must acknowledge in this a duty (and indeed a strict duty) to himself" (TL 6:422.17–19). What is note-worthy about Kant's paragraph 1 claim is that because some cases of will-ful killing of oneself may not violate either a duty to others or to oneself, such cases would not be violations of duty; there might be morally jus-tified cases of suicide. If there are such cases, the authorization require-ment would have to be satisfied. Given some of Kant's remarks in the associated section on casuistry, this possibility is apparently left open. On the other hand, the remark in the second paragraph about preserva-tion of one's life being a *strict* duty might seem to block the possibility of morally justified cases of suicide. This would follow if by talk of strict duty Kant means *exceptionless* duty, and in addition the duty not to com-mit suicide is not qualified in some way that would specify some subclass of cases of suicide that are absolutely prohibited. Let us temporarily put aside this issue about the strictness of the prohibition and proceed to the third and fourth paragraphs in which Kant makes his case for his main claim that (possible exceptions aside) suicide is a violation of a duty to oneself.

In paragraph 3, Kant raises what is perhaps the most persistent worry about duties to oneself, namely that wrongful action requires there to be a subject who is wronged, and to be wronged requires the performance of an action against one's will. Since willfully killing oneself does not satisfy the requirement in question, one has a moral prerogative (as some Stoic philosophers held) "to depart from life at [...] [one's] discretion (as from a smoked-filled room)" (TL 6:422.22–24), at least in cases where one judges of one's continued existence that it would be on balance useless, or perhaps filled with misery, sickness, or some debilitating malady. Re-garding this alleged prerogative, Kant (in effect) remarks that those who take this position fail to recognize a source of reasons whose normative authority is greater than any degree of normative authority one's desires and aversions (those "sensible incentives" (TL 6:422.29)) might possess. This remark is followed in the fourth paragraph by Kant's main argument for the claim that suicide is a violation of duty to oneself that cannot be overridden by considerations of self-interest. Here is the paragraph in full with bracketed numbers inserted:

> [1] A human being cannot renounce his personality as long as he is a subject of duty, hence as long as he lives; and [2] it is a contradiction that he should

be authorized to withdraw from all obligation, that is, [3] freely to act as if no authorization were needed for this action. [4] To annihilate the subject of morality in one's own person is to root out the existence of morality itself from the world, as far as one can, even though [5] morality is an end in itself. Consequently, [6] disposing of oneself as a mere means to some discretionary end is debasing humanity in one's person (*homo noumenon*), [7] to which the human being (*homo phenomenon*) was nevertheless entrusted for preservation (TL 6:422.31–423.7).

As I understand this passage, it may be usefully divided into two parts. Claims 1–3 represent quite general remarks about moral obligation intended to address a fundamental misconception implicit in the Stoic prerogative stance toward suicide. Claims 4–7 express the core of Kant's main anti-suicide argument. Let us consider the two parts in more detail.

To "renounce" (TL 6:422.31) one's personality (humanity) would seem to refer to all forms of violation of duties to oneself though, of course, killing oneself is an obvious way renouncing one's humanity. Kant's inescapability thesis directly implies that one is subject to the requirements of duty as long as one is alive—at least as long as one is alive and possesses those rational capacities that constitute one's humanity. Claim 1 calls attention to these ideas as a basis for claiming [in 2 and 3] that the Stoic prerogative position on suicide contradicts the authorization thesis.

Kant's main anti-suicide argument contained in claims 4–7 is a fairly straightforward application of the humanity formulation of the categorical imperative, but requires some reconstruction and comment. Claim 5 expresses the central idea of the humanity formulation of the categorical imperative: humanity (the subject of morality) is an end in itself—something of supreme value. And [4] certainly one way of failing to respect one's humanity is to cause its annihilation by intentionally putting an end to the continuation of one's animal powers that realize or sustain one's humanity. But note that the conclusion of the argument, expressed in 6, only refers to killing oneself as a means to some "discretionary end" (TL 6:423.4). Now if the only sorts of reasons one could have for taking one's own life have to do with discretionary ends, then the implication is that suicide is always wrong; no authorization is possible. But what I think is the more charitable reading (especially in light of Kant's casuistical questions) is the more restricted claim that suicide for reasons that concern discretionary ends is always morally wrong. Suicide so qualified is what I think should be understood as the sort of strict, exceptionless duty Kant has in mind in paragraph 2 of this article. This leaves open the question of whether cases in which non-discretionary (moral) ends favor killing oneself, suicide may be authorized.

Note also, that 6 does not include the intended conclusion of the argument, viz., that suicide for reasons grounded in discretionary ends is a violation of a duty to oneself. Rather, it claims that such suicides constitute treating oneself as a *mere* means with the implication (given the humanity formulation) that such acts are violations of duty. The very idea of treating oneself as a mere means is perhaps somewhat puzzling here, since its clearest application is in interpersonal contexts where, for example, one party manipulates another party by deception or coercion. Self-manipulation (if it even makes sense) is not characteristic of suicides. So, in the present context, it isn't clear to me that there is any more to treating oneself as a mere means than simply sacrificing what has absolute and supreme value for normatively inferior reasons—to accomplish some end whose value and reason-providing authority is far inferior to the end of one's humanity. I thus leave out reference to the idea of treating oneself as a mere means in my reconstruction of Kant's argument.

Here, then, is Kant's main anti-suicide argument—stated without specification of the range of reasons grounded in discretionary ends, and thus somewhat abstractly:

Kant's humanity-based anti-suicide argument[10]

1. Actions that fail to treat one's own humanity as an end in itself are morally wrong, violations of a duty to oneself. (From the humanity formulation of the categorical imperative.)
2. Intentionally killing oneself (suicide) involves (*a*) the destruction of (and thus harm to) one's humanity and thereby, (*b*) unless authorized, represents a case of failing to treat one's humanity as an end in itself. (Part *a* is allegedly true in virtue of fundamental anthropological facts about human beings, while part *b* is from the moral harm principle.)
3. Reasons for killing oneself that are grounded in discretionary ends do not authorize one to kill oneself. (From the authorization requirement.)

   Thus,

---

10 A somewhat similar argument can be found in *Lectures on Ethics* (V-Mo/Collins 27:343), though Kant does not mention discretionary ends and so the argument draws what seems to be an absolutist conclusion about suicide—a conclusion consistent with Kant's stance in the *Lectures*. (See the previous note.)

4. intentionally killing oneself for some discretionary end (reason) constitutes failing to treat one's own humanity as an end in itself.
   (From 2 and 3.)

   Thus,

5. to commit suicide for some discretionary end (reason) is morally
   wrong; a violation of a duty to oneself. (From 1 and 4.)[11]

I find the argument reasonably compelling. For those who (like me) think
that there are duties to oneself and that suicide is (at least prima facie) a
violation of duty to self, the main bone of contention will be over what
does and does not count as a discretionary end—an end that grounds reasons that are never strong enough to outweigh humanity-based reasons.[12]
Now in accord with the authorization thesis Kant writes that "Misery
gives no man the right to take his life" (V-Mo/Collins 27:373.33 f.).
But it is sometimes argued (in Kantian spirit) that, for instance, terminal-
ly ill patients, whose remaining short life is now filled and will continue
to be filled with unremitting agony, would be morally justified in deciding to commit suicide on grounds that such an existence is degrading or
dehumanizing. Such decisions (I would argue), which might be made in
advance of the onset of debilitating agony, need not be frivolous, ill-con-
sidered, or incompatible with properly valuing the dignity of humanity.[13]
In such cases, one certainly is not frivolously "throwing oneself away" (TL
6:425.30). Here is one place in which what does and does not constitute
respect for humanity seems to be open to a more fine-grained treatment
than Kant officially allows. Furthermore, as we shall see in a moment,

---

11 Claim 7 from the quoted passage does not seem essential to the humanity-based
    argument for the conclusion that suicide is a violation of duty to oneself; rather,
    it seemingly explains why suicide counts as a debasement of one's person. Unau-
    thorized suicide debases one's humanity because it represents an inversion of the
    proper relationship between one's sensible and rational natures. The idea of view-
    ing one's life as something that has been "entrusted" (TL 6:423.6) to one's care is
    also featured in Kant's theological arguments against suicide. (See, for example,
    V-Mo/Collins 27:375.36 f. and TL 6:422.13)

12 Or, if one embraces Kant's notion of a discretionary end, the main bone of con-
    tention will be whether one may sometimes be morally authorized to commit
    suicide for some such end.

13 The point has been well argued by Thomas E. Hill Jr. who proposes the follow-
    ing modified Kantian principle regarding suicide: "A morally ideal person will
    value life as a rational, autonomous agent for its own sake, at least provided
    that the life not fall below a certain threshold of gross, irremediable, and uncom-
    pensated pain and suffering" (Hill, 1991, p. 95).

given his stance on self-sacrifice, it would seem that Kant provides some reason to allow such cases of suicide, on pain of inconsistency.

Having given his main anti-suicide argument, Kant proceeds in the fifth paragraph to remark on what he calls "material" (TL 6:421.17) deprivation of one's physical nature which he claims are "ways of partially murdering oneself" (TL 6:423.10 f.) because of the usefulness of various body parts in exercising one's powers and capacities. As examples, he mentions giving away or selling a tooth to be transplanted into another person and castration as a way of increasing one's chances to make singing a profession. Not all instances of material deprivation are morally wrong; cases in which one must undergo the amputation of an arm or a leg in order to save one's life are, of course, justified exceptions to the general prohibition. In such cases, the justification (authorization) of such deprivation derives from the requirement to preserve one's own life.

Kant's examples of wrongful material deprivation are puzzling. Giving away or selling a tooth (assuming one has plenty of others) does not fit the mold of the sort of causal argument Kant uses in objecting to suicide and to drunkenness and gluttony. Those arguments claim that such and so action has negative causal consequences bearing on the possession and exercise of one's rational capacities and thus (according to the moral harm principle) manifest a lack of self respect. Rather, if Kant has a basis in his moral theory for any objection to such actions, it would seem to be grounded in the idea that in performing them either one somehow *expresses* disrespect for one's humanity, or their performance is an *expression of* such disrespect—apart from any harmful effects upon one's humanity.[14] Moreover, with regard to giving away a tooth, for instance, it isn't enough to merely say that the action is intrinsically degrading; the explanatory burden puts pressure on one to offer an explanation (in terms of respecting humanity) of why such actions are intrinsically degrading. I doubt that Kant's moral theory can rise to this particular challenge regarding the cases he mentions.

Turning now to Kant's casuistical remarks, he considers five cases.[15] Two of them have to do with being in a position of responsibility for one's country and killing oneself (or being prepared to do so) for the

---

14   This kind of argument would appeal to what I referred to in note 7 as the moral degradation principle.
15   For a detailed discussion of Kant's casuistical questions about suicide, see James, 1999, who calls attention to potentially morally relevant differences among these cases.

sake of one's people.[16] In such cases, the fact that one would be committing suicide is one ground of obligation that favors refraining from that act, while the fact that in so doing one would be saving one's people from some sort of harm (together with facts about one's role vis-à-vis one's country) provide grounds for committing suicide. In a third case, Kant considers someone who, suffering from hydrophobia (rabies) as a result of a dog bite, commits suicide for fear of going mad and thereby becoming a danger to the well-being of others. All three cases involve conflicting grounds of obligation, and although in his casuistical remarks on suicide, Kant leaves open which of the competing grounds is strongest, it is arguable that the authorization requirement can, in these or perhaps other cases, be met on behalf of committing suicide.[17]

In a fourth case, Kant refers to Seneca who, being unjustly sentenced to death by Nero, was permitted by the latter to commit suicide. Here the two considerations—being unjustly sentenced to death and one's suicide being 'officially' permitted—are the grounds that Kant puts forth as possibly justifying one killing oneself. In *Anthropology* (at Anth 7:259) Kant explains that execution under the law is disgraceful to the one executed, and that killing oneself rather than being unjustly executed can be (and presumably in Seneca's case was) choosing a death with some honor over a means of death that is not only otherwise disgraceful but in such cases not deserved. Kant's stance on suicide in his *Lectures on Ethics* is (as indicated above in note 9) absolutist. However, he also claims that self-sacrifice for the sake of one's honor can be morally justified.

> If somebody, for example, can preserve his life no longer save by surrendering their person to the will of another, they are bound rather to sacrifice their life, than to dishonor the dignity of humanity in their person, which is what they do by giving themselves up as a thing to the will of another (V-Mo/Collins 27:377.34–39).

---

16 Kant mentions Marcus Curtius a legendary Roman figure who apparently sacrificed his life to save Rome by riding his horse into an open fissure, and also Frederick the Great who, as Kant notes, carried a fast-acting poison with him so that if caught by enemy forces he could end his life rather than allow his state to be held to ransom.

17 Yvonne Unna, 2003, points to passages in the *Anthropology, Lectures on Ethics,* and *Reflexionen* in which Kant takes a stand against the permissibility of the cases he considers in his casuistical questions. If so, and if what I'm calling Kant's humanity-based anti-suicide argument properly represents his *Tugendlehre* view, then there is a mismatch between Kant's theory and his personal convictions.

The humanity-based argument presented above leaves room for justified suicides, contrary to Kant's official *Lectures* stance. But if self-sacrifice for the sake of honor may in some cases be justified, then it would seem to follow by parity of reasoning that opting for suicide rather than dishonoring the dignity of humanity is sometimes permissible. Perhaps Kant would want to lean on the intention/mere foresight distinction in morally distinguishing suicide from self-sacrifice. I won't pursue this possibility further.

Kant's fifth case concerns smallpox vaccination which involves some risk to one's life.[18] Kant compares this risk to the risk a sailor undertakes of being caught in a storm. He claims that the former "is in a far more doubtful situation" (TL 6:424.5) with respect to duty, since the vaccinated person is causally responsible for inducing or permitting (what is hoped to be) a mild form of the disease, while the sailor is not causally responsible for bringing on the storm. Kant does not say that death from the vaccination would be a case of intentionally bringing about one's death; that seems implausible. Thus, one's death in this kind of case is not suicide. Both the vaccination and the sailor case involve someone knowingly risking death. It would therefore seem that the reasons for taking the risk (which in the vaccination case clearly do constitute a putative moral justification) together with the degree of risk of death or serious injury involved (if any) in refraining from the risky action, ought to be the chief factors that guide one's moral deliberation. In any case, as with the other hard cases featured in Kant's discussion of suicide, the putative justifying moral reason concerns preserving humanity and thus may be an authorized case of risking one's life.

Let us sum up. Kant's humanity-based argument against suicide only justifies a prohibition on killing oneself for reasons grounded in what Kant considers to be discretionary ends. Moreover, although the argument—stated abstractly as I have—is reasonably plausible, there is room for dispute about Kant's dismissal of certain considerations relating to one's well-being as justifying suicide and hence room for disputing Kant's particular authorization requirement. Finally, it is somewhat puz-

---

18 The practice of exposing a healthy person to infected material from a person with smallpox is called 'variolation' and was common among European physicians in the 1700s. According to sources, 2–3 % of those who were variolated died of the disease; however, variolation presumably decreased the smallpox fatalities tenfold. What is called 'vaccination' involves exposing the patient to cowpox (less serious than smallpox). Vaccination was introduced in 1797 by English physician, Edward Jenner.

zling that Kant is willing to allow (indeed require) self-sacrifice rather than surrender to the will of another person and thus dishonor one's dignity, but does not seem to allow suicide in such cases, or in cases where natural causes produced by disease put one in a state of severe mental and physical incapacity that arguably threatens to seriously and permanently undermine the ground of one's dignity.

Article III: On stupefying oneself by the excessive use of food or drink (§8)

Drunkenness and gluttony are forms of vicious behavior which, in contrast to the sorts of 'material' deprivation of one's animal nature discussed in §6, are condemned on grounds that they temporarily or permanently deprive one of the use of his or her powers. In Kant-speak, such deprivations are (or at least tend to be) 'formal.' As Kant points out in the first of the two paragraphs comprising the core section of this article, such vices can be condemned on grounds of prudence—owing simply to any bodily harm or other setback to one's interests (that Kant classifies as considerations of personal well-being or happiness) that may result from such actions. In articulating specifically moral (in contrast to prudential) reasons that explain the viciousness of these types of intemperance, in paragraph 2 Kant writes:

> [1] Brutish excess in the use of food and drink is misuse of the means of nourishment that restricts or exhausts our capacity to use them intelligently. *Drunkenness* and *gluttony* are vices that come under this heading. [2] A human being who is drunk is like a mere animal, not to be treated as a human being. [3] When stuffed with food he is in a condition in which he is incapacitated, for a time, for actions that would require him to use his powers of skill and deliberation. [4] – It is obvious that putting oneself in such a state violates a duty to oneself (TL 6:427).

Claims 1 and 3 are clearly being used in support of 4 and constitute a causal argument: the premises point to the *negative causal impact* of being drunk or of overeating on the use of one's powers, including one's capacity for their intelligent and effective use. Barring authorization, such activities are ruled out by the moral harm principle.[19]

---

19 Claim 2 does not, so far as I can tell, play an essential role in Kant's argument, so I will set it aside.

In claim 1, Kant refers specifically to one's powers of nourishment, while in 3 he refers more generally to powers of skill and deliberation. It is not clear how excess in food or drink 'restricts' or 'exhausts' our capacity to use the powers of nourishment intelligently. It does make sense to say that being in such states *constitutes* a non-intelligent use of the powers of nourishment. But then this is a claim to be argued for, not a premise in an argument against being in such states. Of course, one way to argue for this claim (and what I take to be Kant's main line of argument in this passage) is suggested by the claim in 3 that such excesses hinder, at least temporarily, one's capacity to make intelligent use of various powers and skills that could be put to good effect in, for example, a state of sobriety. And at least drunkenness tends to impair one's deliberative capacity. So, the claim being made in 3 carries the main argumentative burden of what I'm calling Kant's moral harm argument against drunkenness and gluttony. Of course, drunkenness and gluttony, by restricting, exhausting, or incapacitating one in the intelligent use of one's powers may negatively affect one's well-being. So, insofar as there is a distinctive non-prudential moral consideration having to do with the negative causal impact of these excesses which also provides a moral reason for refraining from them, it must have to do with how such activities affect the powers constituting one's rational nature. And here it is important to distinguish drunkenness and gluttony as habits from non-habitual, and thus occasional, instances of being in one or both of these states. Someone who is an alcoholic or a glutton has acquired habits that are contrary to the morally prescribed end of preserving one's humanity, let alone cultivating it—such habits have a likely negative causal impact on one's humanity.

Given the causal claim about the effects of alcoholism and of gluttony, Kant's argument strikes me as fairly persuasive. Certainly habitual *brutish* excess in alcohol consumption as well as habitual use of certain drugs (Kant mentions opium) are very likely to lead to the kind of impairment of one's powers constituting one's humanity—the basis of Kant's argument. It is perhaps less clear that brutish habitual overeating has the same negative bearing on one's cognitive powers—powers of mind and spirit. But because gluttony is likely to lead to physical maladies and thus weaken one's physical powers and perhaps cut short one's life, the argument seems to hold good for gluttony as well as alcoholism.

What about particular instances of drunkenness and gluttony, apart from their being part of some acquired habit—*occasional* overindulgence? Kant says [in 3] that being incapacitated *for a time* is morally objectionable. There are various ways in which being in such states on an occasion is morally culpable. First, particular occasions of getting drunk or overeating make it somewhat likely that one will eventually come to acquire the associated habit. (As we shall see, Kant raises concerns about such things as accepting invitations to banquets, since such events entice one to overindulge in eating and drinking and are thus morally risky.) Second, one's incapacitation owing to overindulgence may negatively affect one's capacity to fulfill some positive duty that is called for on that occasion. Third, such incapacitation (especially drunkenness) might also affect one's resistance to temptation of one sort or another. Gluttony and drunkenness are sometimes referred to as 'gateway' sins. These considerations have to do with taking certain risks. But in addition, while drunk (and perhaps while overstuffed), one has intentionally forfeited full control over one's rational powers—one is the cause of this loss. What of these concerns?

As with risk-taking generally (which we considered briefly in connection with smallpox inoculation), such considerations do not seem to generate a sweeping condemnation of all instances of overindulgence; details will matter, including how risky such behavior is for this or that individual in that or that circumstance.[20] As for temporarily forfeiting full control over one's powers for the sake of pleasure, one might wonder whether this consideration, if sufficient to morally rule out an action, will rule out such fun activities as thrill rides at an amusement park. After all, such all-consuming experiences no doubt interfere (as least for some) with exercising some if not all of their powers except screaming.

There are two further claims Kant makes in this article that are worth noting. First, he claims that drunkenness and gluttony are debasements of one's humanity that put one "below even the nature of an animal" (TL 6:427.22)[21] and that "[g]luttony is even lower than [...] [drunkenness,

---

20 Kant does condemn certain forms of risky behavior engaged in for self-interest where the risk is to one's life. In the *Lectures*, he writes that "we ought not to risk our life, and hazard it from mere interest or private aims, for in that case we not only act imprudently, but also ignobly, e. g., if we wanted to wager a considerable sum on swimming across a lake" (V-Mo/Collins 27:376.37–377.2).

21 With regard to all of the beastly vices, Kant claims that such actions are not only degrading, in the sense that they express something about one's character that is beneath one's dignity, but that such actions are so degrading that one "degrades himself lower than a beast" (V-Mo/Collins 27:391.16). This is because such actions are contrary to one's animal nature, while the "devilish" (V-Mo/Collins 27:380.29) vices (including envy, ingratitude, and malice) are only contrary to one's humanity considered as a being with a moral nature. (See, for instance, V-Mo/Collins 27:380.23–35 and V-Mo/Collins 27:390.9–392.23)

M.T.] since it only lulls the senses into a passive condition and, unlike drunkenness, does not even arouse imagination to an *active* play of representations; so it approaches even more closely the enjoyment of cattle" (TL 6:427.29–33). In the *Anthropology*, Kant expresses some sympathy for overindulgence in drink—particularly wine—in the fact that social drinking helps promote the good of sociability because although "drink loosens the tongue (*in vino disertus*)."[22] But it also opens the heart wide, and is an instrumental vehicle of a moral quality, namely frankness" (Anth 7:171.18–20). Kant considers solitary drunkenness to be a moral par with gluttony.

Second, because of its utility in promoting sociability, Kant's casuistical questions concern whether social drinking (he mentions wine specifically) bordering on intoxication can be justified and (relatedly) whether accepting invitations to banquets which, Kant claims, are formal invitations to overindulgence, may be accepted in good conscience. Elsewhere, I have argued that for Kant motives (other than the motive of duty) can be deontically relevant in determining whether an action is a violation of a duty of virtue.[23] Here we find that the motive of sociability can perhaps mitigate at least somewhat the degree of violation of the duty regarding intemperance, if not entirely justify intemperate acts.

Article II: On defiling oneself by lust (§7)

The *Tugendlehre* arguments against suicide, self-mutilation, drunkenness and gluttony are all based on the moral harm principle. Not so with Kant's arguments in this article, which is why I've taken articles II and III out of order. The three paragraphs constituting this article seem to focus primarily on what Kant considers to be types of *"unnatural"* (TL 6:424.33 f.) sex. In *Lectures on Ethics* (V-Mo/Collins 27:390.9–392.23), Kant distinguishes two general categories of wrongful sex (*crimina carnis*). First, certain kinds of sexual activity including prostitution, fornication, and adultery, are all types of action that are *"secundum naturam"* (V-Mo/Collins 27:390.14), that is, according to nature, and thus not contrary to the natural end of one's sexual organs, namely procreation. Such actions, according to Kant, are nevertheless "contrary to sound reason" (V-Mo/Collins 27:390.16) and morally wrong for this reason. By

---

22 Trans.: "Wine makes eloquent."
23 Timmons, 2002.

contrast, masturbation, homosexuality, and bestiality are inherently "contrary to" (V-Mo/Collins 27:390.17) procreation—an aspect of one's animal nature. The members of the latter group are forms of unnatural sex, *crimina carnis contra naturam*, whose moral wrongness is explained by appeal to the (alleged) fact that they are contrary to nature. Although in article II Kant does not mention any types of unnatural sex by name, masturbation seems to be the main focus of the article.[24] In any case, if engaging in unnatural sex violates a duty to oneself, one would think it would be most apparent in cases that do not involve the complexities of homosexuality and bestiality. So, let us focus just on masturbation, about which Kant makes two claims. First, it is a violation of a duty to oneself and, second, the degree of violation is even greater than the degree of violation in acts of wrongful suicide. Let us take these claims in order.

Kant begins the article by calling attention to what he takes to be the *"natural end"* (TL 6:424.14) of sexual love, namely, procreation, noting that talk of natural ends is to be understood as referring to "that connection of a cause with an effect in which, although no understanding is ascribed to the cause, it is still thought by analogy with an intelligent cause, and so as if it produced human beings on purpose" (TL 6:424.15–18). Having introduced this teleological perspective into the discussion, Kant writes:

> What is now in question is whether a person's use of his sexual capacity is subject to a limiting law of duty with regard to the person himself or whether he is authorized to direct the use of his sexual attributes to mere animal pleasure, without having in view the preservation of the species, and would not thereby be acting contrary to a duty to himself (TL 6:424.18–23).

---

24 Kant distinguishes *"unnatural"* (TL 6:424.33 f.) lust from natural lust, the latter presumably being what Kant calls sexual love or what we might refer to as sexual attraction. Lust itself is unnatural if one's arousal is the product of one's imagination rather than a "real object" (TL 6:424.34–425.1) The idea seems to be that masturbation (typically?) involves being stimulated by the mere thought of a desirable sexual partner which "brings forth a desire contrary to nature's end" (TL 6:425.2 f.). Kant's remarks about the imagination, unnatural lust, and unnatural desire are fairly opaque and I will not try to delve into their significance owing to lack of space. For a fairly sympathetic discussion of Kant's appeal to imagination in this context, see Kielkopf, 1997. But see also Sobel, 2003, for a (scathing) critique of Kant's sexual ethics, including some discussion of Kant's appeal to imagination in connection with sex.

So, the question about natural ends and morality that Kant is raising about masturbation is this: If we view sexual attraction (or what Kant also calls "carnal lust" (TL 6:424.30)) as functioning (as if it were an intelligence) to bring about offspring by motivating one to use one's sexual organs, is one permitted to engage in sexual activity for the sole purpose of the sort of enjoyment that comes from such activity and thus without "having in view" (TL 6:424.23) procreation. This expresses Kant's general moral question about all forms of sexual activity. And from the passage just quoted, Kant seems committed to the claim that there is something morally wrong with acting "contrary to" (TL 6:424.23) the natural end of sexual love. Of course, given the explanatory requirement, what he must do is characterize the notion of acting contrary to the natural end of procreation that makes clear *why* such acting involves a lack of respect for the dignity of persons. Since we are here concerned with masturbation, what is needed, in addition to this characterization, is an explanation of why masturbation in particular, because it is contrary to procreation, expresses lack of respect for one's own dignity.

After calling attention in the second paragraph to the alleged fact that the mere thought of masturbation strikes "everyone immediately" (TL 6:424.8) as a violation of duty in the highest degree in response to which shame is the appropriate reaction, Kant proceeds in the third paragraph to defend his two central claims of the article. In defense of the claim that masturbation is a violation of a duty to oneself, he writes:

> But it is not so easy to produce a rational proof that unnatural, and even merely unpurposive, use of one's sexual attribute is inadmissible as being a violation of duty to oneself (and indeed, as far as its unnatural use is concerned, a violation in the highest degree). – The *ground of proof* is, indeed, that by it the human being surrenders his personality (throwing it away), since he uses himself merely as a means to satisfy an animal impulse (TL 6:425.20–26).

Here we have an attempt at a direct application of the humanity formulation to the case (we are assuming) of masturbation. What is left unexplained is why this kind of sexual act, even if engaged in merely for sexual pleasure, involves treating oneself as a mere means. The explanation can't merely be that one's primary aim is to satisfy an animal impulse. One eats and drinks to satisfy animal impulses, but such actions are not thereby wrong. I may eat a donut *merely* for the sake of pleasure, not because I'm hungry and in light of my knowledge that such food items lack nutritional value. Of course, Kant is arguing against unnatural or mere unpurposive sex. But what follows? Notice that Kant does not argue that because masturbation is non-procreative or unnatural that it is *thereby* wrong; he claims that it is not easy to find a proof that such sex is wrong.[25] So, if the wrongness of masturbation has anything to do with its being non-procreative or unnatural (i. e., by its very nature non-procreative) it must be because there is an appropriate connection between the non-procreative nature of these acts and failing to treat humanity as an end in itself—an implication of the explanatory burden. This burden is brought into sharp relief when, in the section on casuistry, Kant raises worries about what does and does not constitute acting contrary to procreation. So let us proceed to Kant's casuistical remarks, before turning to his claim about the degree of viciousness expressed by unnatural sex.

Kant poses only one question of casuistry in this article. After stating what he takes himself to have established, namely that in engaging in sexual activity, "one may not, at least, act contrary to" (TL 6:426.3 f.) the end of procreation,[26] he poses the sole casuistical question of the section: "is it permitted to engage in this practice (even within marriage) *without taking this end into consideration*" (TL 6:426.4–6). As examples of sex within marriage that do not take procreation into consideration, he mentions cases in which the wife cannot become pregnant (owing to her already being pregnant or to sterility).[27] However, Kant leaves unexplained just what the distinction is supposed to be between sex that is "contrary to" (TL 6:426.4) procreation and sex where the couple omits or perhaps refrains from taking procreation into consideration. But supposing that sexual intercourse between married partners during what they know to be an infertile period is not contrary to procreation, Kant's explanatory burden in connection with non-procreative sex is thereby sharpened. Perhaps (again) the intention/mere foresight distinction could be put to use in characterizing non-procreative sex that is also not contrary to procre-

---

25 This is a point stressed by Lara Denis, 1999. Both Denis and Mary Gregor, 1963, p. 144, argue that teleological considerations play a legitimate, but limited role in Kant's moral arguments generally and his arguments regarding sex in particular.

26 Here, Kant perhaps seems to draw a moral conclusion directly from a claim about nature's end, contrary to his earlier remark about the difficulty of providing a rational proof that such sex is a violation of a duty to oneself. In any case, he is not entitled to the move here without first satisfying the explanatory requirement which he does not do in these passages.

27 He also mentions cases in which the wife "feels no desire for intercourse" (TL 6:426.8 f.). This case is strikingly different from the case of sex during non-fertile periods, but I won't pause here to discuss this further.

ation. But in any case, I am doubtful that the explanatory burden can be satisfied on the basis of Kant's moral theory. Any such attempt will, I believe, meet the same unhappy fate as the so-called unnaturalness argument for the wrongness of certain forms of sexual behavior including masturbation and homosexuality.[28]

We have been considering Kant's appeal to teleology and the role of natural ends in his discussion of unnatural sex. Let us now consider a straightforward causal argument grounded in the moral harm principle. A single act of masturbation does not have the incapacitating effects vis-à-vis one's rational powers as does being very drunk. However, in his *On Pedagogy*, Kant makes the following suggestion about the education of young people who have reached the age of sexual maturity:

> Nothing weakens the mind as well as the body of the human being more than the kind of lust which is directed towards oneself, and it is entirely contrary to the nature of the human being. But this lust also must not be concealed from the young man. It must be placed before him in all its atrocity, he must be told that he thereby makes himself useless for the reproduction of the species, that through it his bodily powers are ruined the most, that it brings on premature old age and that his mind will suffer a great deal in the process, and so forth. [...] one must put the thoughts about it [sex, M.T.] out of one's mind. For even if the object only remains in the imagination, it still corrodes the vital power. If one directs one's inclinations toward the other sex, one always still finds some resistance, but if one directs it towards oneself, then one can satisfy it at any time. The physical effect is extremely harmful, but the consequences as regards morality are far worse. Here one transgresses the boundaries of nature, and inclination rages without arrest because no real satisfaction takes place (Päd 9:497f.).

Presumably, such claims about the negative effects of masturbation on one's mind and body were common in Kant's day, common even among professionals.[29] The causal claims being made in this passage are brought forth on behalf of prudence and morality. And they would enable Kant to argue against masturbation in the same manner in which he argues against habitual drunkenness and gluttony: such habits interfere with the health of one's rational powers and thus with the obligatory end of preserving and cultivating them. So, even if Kant's appeal

---

28   See for example the Catholic Church arguments as expressed in the 1976 *Vatican Declaration on Some Questions of Sexual Ethics.*

29   See Kerstein, 2008, for defense of this point. Kerstein does not cite the *Pedagogy* passage, but it makes credible his claim that Kant's view about the morality of masturbation was likely influenced by what at the time were beliefs about the harmful effects of masturbation.

to the teleology of sexual love cannot be made to work, he can and does appeal to negative causal consequences in objecting to masturbation. Of course, the problem with the argument is that it rests on extremely dubious if not outright false causal claims. So, Kant's causal argument against masturbation does not have nearly the force of his causal arguments regarding intemperance.

Finally, let us turn to Kant's second main claim, viz., that unnatural sex is not only degrading to humanity, but expresses something worse: "*a defiling* [eine Schändung]" (TL 6:424.28) of one's humanity. To defile something is to make it dirty, to stain or taint it. Disgust is an appropriate response to what is dirty or tainted—a type of reaction that is often felt toward certain bodily functions.[30] But apart from the particular moral reaction that the thought of, or engagement in, unnatural sex prompts, Kant's reason for ranking unnatural sex as a greater violation of one's dignity over suicide is that it involves "complete abandonment of oneself to animal inclination[] [and] makes the human being not only an object of enjoyment but, still further, a thing that is contrary to nature, that is a *loathsome* object, and so deprives him of all respect for himself" (TL 6:425.33–36). This may strike many contemporary readers as over the top. But the basis of Kant's comparison of unnatural sex with suicide is, as he makes clear, in terms of what unnatural sex reveals about one's character. Suicide (at least in many cases) requires a kind of courage, which masturbation does not. And so acts of suicide result from something analogous to the sort of moral self-governance that constitutes virtue. Even if we don't agree with Kant's overall comparative assessment here, he has a point.

III. Conclusion

I have argued that Kant's various moral harm arguments meet with mixed success, depending on the plausibility of the causal claims they rest upon. I have also argued that none of these arguments establishes absolutist conclusions about the general types of action under consideration. Kant's use of teleology in his discussion of carnal self-defilement fails (so far as I can tell) to meet the relevant explanatory burden that would require saying how non-procreative sexual activity constitutes a degradation of the dig-

---

30 See V-Mo/Collins 27:392.4 f. where Kant claims that unnatural sex "occasions a disgust that does not occur with suicide."

nity of humanity. It won't do to just insist that it does, or to point to the disgust reactions of Kant and other like-minded individuals. Those reactions only have probative force if they are responsive to wrong-making features that are possessed by the actions that prompt them.[31]

References

Christiano, Thomas (2008), "Two Conceptions of the Dignity of Persons", in: *Annual Review of Law and Ethics*, vol. 16, pp. 101–127.

Denis, Lara (1999), "Kant on the Wrongness of 'Unnatural' Sex", in: *History of Philosophy Quarterly*, vol. 16, pp. 225–47.

Gregor, Mary J. (1963), *Laws of Freedom*, New York: Barnes & Noble.

Hill, Thomas E. (1991), "Self-Regarding Suicide: A Modified Kantian View", in: id., *Autonomy and Self-Respect*, Cambridge: Cambridge University Press, pp. 85–103. (First published in: *Suicide and Life-Threatening Behavior*, vol. 13, 1983, pp. 254–275.)

James, David N. (1999), "Suicide and Stoic Ethics in the 'Doctrine of Virtue'", in: *Kant-Studien*, vol. 90, pp. 40–58.

Kerstein, Samuel J. (2008), "Treating Oneself Merely as a Means", in: Monika Betzler (ed.), *Kant's Ethics of Virtue*, Berlin/New York: Walter de Gruyter, pp. 201–218.

Kielkopf, Charles (1997), "Masturbation: A Kantian Condemnation", in: *Philosophia*, vol. 25, pp. 223–46.

Seidler, Michael J. (1983), "Kant and the Stoics on Suicide", in: *Journal of the History of Ideas*, vol. 44, pp. 429–53.

Sobel, Alan (2003), "Kant and Sexual Perversion", in: *The Monist*, vol. 86, pp. 55–90.

Timmermann, Jens (2013), "Kantian Dilemmas? Moral Conflict in Kant's Ethical Theory", in: *Archiv für Geschichte der Philosophie*, vol. 95, *forthcoming*.

Timmons, Mark (2002), "Motive and Rightness in Kant's Ethical System", in: id. (ed.), *Kant's 'Metaphysics of Morals': Interpretative Essays*, Oxford: Oxford University Press, pp. 255–88.

Unna, Yvonne (2003), "Kant's Answers to the Casuistical Questions Concerning Self-Disembodiment", in: *Kant-Studien*, vol. 94, pp. 454–73.

---

31 I wish to thank the participants at the conference on Kant on duties to oneself that took place in Munich on February 14 and 15, 2009 for a stimulating discussion of an earlier version of this paper.

The Perfect Duty to Oneself Merely as a Moral Being (TL 6:428–437)

Stefano Bacin

1. Explaining a Duty Through Three Vices

Some of the most innovative aspects of Kant's account of duties to the self, which he presents as crucial to his ethics and as fundamentally different from the picture given of them by previous accounts,[1] are expounded in the chapter of the *Doctrine of Virtue* on the "Human Being's Duty to Himself merely as a Moral Being." The *idea* of a duty to oneself merely as a moral being is itself an innovation, since it does not appear in the traditional subdivisions of duties, which Kant rejects as inappropriate.[2] This chapter also significantly extends the *scope* of duties to oneself, discussing topics which had previously been treated primarily as other-regarding acts. The innovations of the chapter become more evident when it is compared with the significant example of the previous approach provided by Baumgarten's *Ethica philosophica* (along with Georg Friedrich Meier's extended development), which was not only the textbook for Kant's lectures, but also a main target of his critical remarks.

Before analyzing Kant's main points concerning one's duty to oneself as a moral being, however, his approach to this subject requires some attention. The chapter simply provides an examination of three vices and says surprisingly little about the duty mentioned in the title. Indeed, Kant expounds this duty *per negativum*, examining its three most relevant violations. As with the issues addressed in the previous chapter (cf. TL 6:421.6–428.26), this duty can be examined negatively, because it is a perfect duty, which does not command any positive end, but requires omissions (cf. TL 6:419.23). An analysis of the corresponding violations thus puts us in a position to grasp the complex meaning of this duty to

---

1 Cf. e.g. V-Mo/Mron 27:1479.13–34; V-Mo/Kaehler(Stark), p. 169; V-MS/Vigil 27:604.26–32.
2 Cf. TL 6:418 ff.; see also e.g. V-MS/Vigil 27:607.13–15.

oneself. As Kant remarks in the ethics lectures about duties to oneself in general, "the better to appreciate such duties, if we picture to ourselves the evil consequences of violating them," as they "help [...] to provide better insight into the principium" (V-Mo/Collins 27:347.27–31; cf. also V-Mo/Kaehler(Stark), p. 182).

In the present case, different ways of acting share a common feature: all of them deprive the agent "of the *prerogative* of a moral being, that of acting in accordance with principles" (TL 6:420.17 f.). Paradoxically, "they make it one's basic principle to have no basic principle" (TL 6:420.24 f.). All such vices are grounded in choices that affect one's capacity to make moral choices. An important innovation of the whole *Metaphysics of Morals* is that ethics should deal with the *maxims* of our conduct, not with the resulting actions.[3] As we shall see, this also provides the key to Kant's position on the issues of this chapter. Furthermore, in the present case, the analysis must focus specifically on the *formal* features of the corresponding maxims (cf. TL 6:420.13)—that is, it must focus on the structural implications rather than the intended objectives of one's choice.[4] In each of these cases, the decision involves a violation or a rejection of the status in virtue of which a human being is capable of moral choices. In Kant's language, these are ways in which a human being violates his dignity (cf. TL 6:420.22 f.), and thus the topic of the chapter is properly a "duty with reference to the dignity of humanity within us, and so to ourselves" (§12, TL 6:436.15 f.; cf. Päd 9:488.30–37). Kant's analysis thus provides us with elements for a better understanding of his notion of dignity.[5]

The novel idea of a duty to ourselves merely as moral beings adds a further dimension to the traditional basic obligation of self-preservation, which, in Kant's view, is not limited to our properties as living beings. After having examined the vices of physical self-destruction or mutilation, Kant here abstracts from such properties ("without taking his animality into consideration" (TL 6:420.14)) and considers the main ways in which we can violate our moral nature and commit a sort of a "moral suicide"[6]. The analogy with the traditional emphasis on self-preservation is also suggested by his vocabulary: Kant speaks of "moral *self-preservation*"

---

3   Cf. TL 6:388 f. On this general feature, see Esser, 2004, and Bacin, 2006, pp. 240 f.
4   See e.g. the use of "formal" in Refl 8096 HN 19:641.1–7.
5   On the general features of Kant's notion of dignity: see Sensen, 2009.
6   Atwell, 1986, p. 133.

(TL 6:419.20) and "moral health" (TL 6:419.25 f., cf. also TL 6:384.11–14).

This is the general issue underlying the apparently divergent topics of the chapter. Although they yield different kind of acts, these vices share such implications. Hence, they should not be examined separately, like prior moral philosophy did, but together, insofar as they concern one fundamental obligation, whose conceptual unity Kant also emphasizes by always referring to it in the singular. The sections of the chapter deal with its most representative violations: lying (§9), avarice (§10), and servility (§11), while other examples are alluded to in the lectures (see the list in V-MS/Vigil 27:605–607) and, here, in §12.[7]

2. "On Lying"

Here, for the first time (albeit quite briefly), Kant develops his idea that lying must be regarded foremost as a violation of a duty to oneself. While in the *Groundwork* he, quite close to previous ethical theories, considered lying merely as a way of acting towards others, using it as an example of how to deal with duties to others from the perspective of the categorical imperative (cf. GMS 4:429.29–430.9), in his lectures (including those given prior to the *Groundwork*) he had suggested that a different point of view should be adopted.[8] Yet such a point of view was never developed until the *Doctrine of Virtue*.[9] As they focus on this new perspective, his remarks in this section must be distinguished from the essay *On a Supposed Right to Lie from Philanthropy*: as Kant points out in the latter text, "what is under discussion here is a duty of right" (VRML 8:426n.34), and, in that context Kant does not consider lying as a violation of a duty to oneself. In order to see the peculiar features of the *Doctrine of Virtue* clearly, these two perspectives should not be confused. A novelty of Kant's approach in this work lies precisely in the fact that

---

7   Since the further examples in §12 cannot be entirely subsumed under servility, but concern the "duty with reference to the dignity of humanity within us" (TL 6:436.15.f.) in general, the section seems to belong not before, but *after* the casuistical remarks on servility. (On the grounds of some uncertainty about the text of the *Metaphysics of Morals*: see Parma, 2000.)

8   Cf. V-PP/Herder 27:59 f.; V-Mo/Collins 27:341.28–32; V-MS/Vigil 27:604.35–37; see also Br 11:332.31–36.

9   Accordingly, Kant gradually abandons the analysis of lying as an other-regarding violation: see Mahon, 2006.

the act of lying is not examined from the traditional standpoint of natural law, but as a self-regarding act that is ethically wrong.

Kant introduces his view by excluding the usual accounts. Firstly, he insists that ethics must not examine lying with regard to its effects and the possible damage it causes to other people: "the harm that can come to others from lying is not what distinguishes this vice (for if it were, the vice would consist only in violating one's duty to others)" (TL 6:429.17–19).[10] Rather than as lying, the damage to others caused by a false declaration should be considered as a juridical violation of their freedom (cf. RL 6:238.29–32),[11] or as a violation of one's ethical duty of benevolence toward them (cf. TL 6:403.21–27). Indeed, the moral quality of lying is not determined by the consequences of the act. If we tell a lie, we can still be properly blamed for it if the addressee is not damaged by it, and even if the lie turns out to be favorable to him (cf. V-MS/Vigil 27:605.2–17). Thus, "in ethics […] no authorization [Befugniß] is derived from harmlessness" (TL 6:429.9 f.). The same applies with regard to ourselves. While previous moral philosophers regarded the act of lying as a violation of our duty to ourselves only in consideration of the possible harm to ourselves and our reputation,[12] for Kant this is no real moral matter: such consequences make lying "a mere error in prudence" (TL 6:429.21), not a vice. Finally, the relationship between our words and the state of affairs we are talking about is not essential to lying either, since it is obviously possible that we intend to hide a *false* belief we have (or even that we declare something that is true, but which we do not believe). Kant stresses this point by distinguishing between truth and truthfulness, a distinction that is already present in the philosophical vocabulary, but with a different connotation.[13]

---

10 Cf. TL 6:430.2 and 403.21–25; V-MS/Vigil 27:700.22–25. See also KpV 5:87.37: "an otherwise harmless lie".

11 Juridically, a lie "always harms another, even if not another individual, nevertheless humanity generally, inasmuch as it makes the source of right unusable" (VRML 8:426.28–30). On the distinction between the ethical and the juridical standpoint on lying: see also V-MS/Vigil 27:604.35–605.4, 700.19–25, 701.3–5.

12 Cf. e.g. Baumgarten, 1763, §342, and Meier, 1762–1774, IV, §863, p. 276. The other common way to relate lying with the duties to oneself in previous moral philosophy was to consider *lying* as a duty to oneself, in the cases where a *Notlüge* is necessary to save the own life: see e.g. Baumgarten, 1763, §344.

13 Truth concerns the content of the discourse, while truthfulness only is to be understood as a virtue: cf. Wolff, 1740–1748, III, §181; Wolff, 1750–1753, V, §522; Pufendorf, 1673, X, §VII. See also Annen, 1997, p. 27.

What is morally essential to lying, then, is the relation between the declaration and the belief,[14] namely the truthfulness of the *subject*. Ethics should thus define lying as the "contrary of truthfulness" (TL 6:429.6).[15] Therefore Kant's analysis does not rely on the presupposition that truth is an independent value that should always be respected, as is often alleged.[16] On the contrary, because the morally determinant feature of lying is the intentional lack of truthfulness, lying affects the agent first of all, who thereby causes "dishonor [Ehrlosigkeit]" (TL 6:429.11) to himself. Thus, ethics must focus on the self-regarding features of lying. Kant develops this insight through two quite different lines of reasoning: on the one hand, he refers to the purpose of language, and on the other he refers to the notion of an 'inner lie'.[17]

Kant's first point recasts a well-known argument against lying (maybe *the* most traditional argument, since it already occurs in Augustine, had a preeminent role in the modern natural law tradition,[18] and is still endorsed by some authors),[19] namely the argument according to which lying is condemnable because it perverts the natural function of language (cf. TL 6:429.31 f.). This has generally been regarded as a weak and unsatisfying argument, mainly because such teleological considerations seem particularly out of place in Kant's moral theory.[20] Nevertheless, this remark does not really seem to be Kant's crucial argument. Kant might rather intend to show at this point that the most traditional account of lying also implicitly construes it as a fundamentally self-regarding act, in a way that can easily be rephrased using his notions of *homo phaenomenon* and *homo noumenon* (cf. TL 6:430.15–19). Kant's transition from the traditional perspective to the new one thereby goes a step further; as the re-interpretation of the language argument can show that the perver-

---

14 Cf. TL 6:429.24 f.; MpVT 8:267.27–33; and e.g. Refl 6309 HN 18:603.
15 Cf. TL 6:433.19. See also VNAEF 8:421.30 f. and VRML 8:426.2–4.
16 See e.g. MacIntyre, 1995, pp. 315, 337 (repr. 2006, pp. 106,123 f.), who thus associates Kant with Aquinas.
17 In the edited text, these two issues seem to run parallel through the section, without merging. Yet, given the textual issues concerning the *Metaphysics of Morals*, it is possible to propose a change of the text order which, among other advantages, provides a more plausible distribution of the two main points: see Bacin/Schönecker, 2010. However, the present analysis is independent from that conjecture.
18 See e.g. Pufendorf, 1673, X, §1; Wolff, 1750–1753, V, §533.
19 See the examples mentioned in MacIntyre, 1995, pp. 311 ff. (repr. 2006, pp. 103 f.).
20 See e.g. Gregor, 1963, p. 150; Atwell, 1986, p. 133; Denis, 2001, p. 94; Timmermann, 2000, p. 280; Dietz, 2002, pp. 98 f.; Kerstein, 2008, pp. 215 f.

sion of the communicative function of language is grounded on a misuse of the *subject's* capacities, it can show that lying is a violation of ourselves, not of language in general.[21]

However, this first approximation is not yet sufficient to provide a direct justification of any duty to oneself merely as a moral being. If we refer to the use of a natural capacity, we can at best discern an obligation towards the physical being (the *animal rationale*), but not towards the moral being, which is what should be at issue here.[22] Towards himself as a moral being, man is rather "under obligation [...] to *truthfulness* [zur Wahrhaftigkeit verpflichtet]" (TL 6:430.19). The ethically relevant point is not that the purpose of language is disrespected, but the *decision* to breach "the condition of the agreement with the declaration [die Bedingung der Übereinstimmung mit der Erklärung]" (TL 6:430.17 f., translation slightly modified S.B.) delivered through that capacity,[23] namely the decision to hide one's own thoughts. The alleged language argument shows only what is (mis)used as the organ of lying, in every case.[24] What is special about language is not that its function has a higher value than other natural capacities, which can give rise to an ethical prohibition, but merely the fact that it happens to be the crucial instrument of insincerity. Insincerity is the ethically relevant issue.

Thus, in order to understand the conscious lack of sincerity—which is the proper definition of the "contrary of truthfulness" (cf. TL 6:429.33–36; RGV 6:190.22–23)—it is not sufficient to refer to language. Kant's analysis has to go a step further. He does this by his second

---

21 See also V-PP/Powalski 27:231.22–24; V-MS/Vigil 27:605.7–11; Refl 7082 HN 19:245.5–6.

22 Notice that in §11 Kant underscores that all rational capacities as such belong merely to the set of properties of man as a living being, and do not possess *per se* a moral relevance. See below, §4.

23 Cf. VAMS 23:267.18–22: "Speech is the capacity to communicate one's thoughts, *with the will* at the same time that the communication fully accords with what one thinks. Thus, at the same time promise of this agreement. Sincerity is the condition without which speech would involve a usefulness without any possible use" (italics S.B.). See also Esser, 2004, p. 262.

24 This applies also to the lies told to ourselves, as "declarations, which a human being perpetrates upon himself [Erklärungen, die man gegen sich selbst verübt]" (TL 6:430.36; cf. also MpVT 8:270.33), since Kant understands thinking as "speaking with oneself" (Anth 7:192.31 f.; cf. also Refl 3444 HN 16:839.10–12). Such cases are already included as Kant refers to what is told "another (even if the other is a merely ideal person)" (TL 6:429.25). On the contrary, Esser holds that lying is not bound to a use of language (cf. Esser, 2008, p. 294).

point, which proceeds from the distinction between an external lie and an inner lie (cf. TL 6:429.13–23; cf. also VNAEF 8:421.30–33), which is a significant innovation of the *Doctrine of Virtue,* compared to the lectures. While the terminological distinction was not Kant's invention, he gives it a very different meaning and a much more important role than earlier philosophers do. Thereby he further emphasizes the relevance of the dishonor which lying causes to the agent. According to the previous version of the distinction, *both* kinds of lies offend *other* people: what can be external or internal is precisely the offense, and the external is taken to be the worst one.[25] By contrast, Kant differentiates the two cases with regard to the scope of the liar's dishonor: by lying a man "makes himself an object of contempt *in the eyes of others*" or "*in his own eyes*" and thus he "violates the dignity of humanity in *his* own person" (TL 6:429.14–17, italics S.B.). An external lie and an inner lie are not different because of their addressees, as if the former were a technical term for a lie told to others and the latter were a technical term for a lie told to oneself, or for self-deception, as the text is usually understood.[26] Since it dishonors the liar in front of others, the external lie is the kind of lie which one has to avoid in order to protect one's own reputation. Because this is a matter of prudence (cf. TL 6:429.21–23), it should not be examined here, and this explains why the external lie is not mentioned again after the distinction. The morally relevant case is rather that of the "inner lie," which makes the agent dishonorable regardless of any consequences of his conduct, such as damage to his reputa-

---

25 See Baumgarten, 1763, §344: "falsiloquium morale alios homines laedens est mendacium externum, externe, internum interne laedens". See also Meier, 1762–1774, §863, IV, pp. 273 f.: "alle Lügen sind entweder äusserliche, oder innerliche Lügen. Durch jene wird ein anderer Mensch äusserlich beleidiget, indem er dadurch entweder um seinen ehrlichen Namen, oder um seine äusserliches Eigenthum, oder um sein Leben u.s.w. gebracht wird. Solche Lügen sind die allerschändlichsten Lügen. [...] Durch innerliche Lügen werden andere Menschen nur innerlich beleidiget, indem dadurch die Ehre anderer Leute geschmälert, oder irgend eine Liebespflicht gegen sie übertreten wird". On the notion of inner lie prior to Kant: see Annen, 1997, pp. 236 f.
26 Some interpreters claim that, speaking of inner and external lie, Kant simply discusses *two* different problems: see e.g. Denis, 2001, p. 91 f. But the external lie is not really an issue here. Schleiermacher, 1803, p. 227, remarked that Kant, "*at odds with everyone else*" as well as "*doing violence to the language*", here employs "*two entirely different concepts*" (italics S.B.).

tion.[27] Insofar as ethics understands lying as a way of acting which "*by its mere form*" amounts to a "worthlessness that must make him contemptible *in his own eyes*" (TL 6:430.6–8, italics S.B; cf. V-MS/Vigil 27:700.30 f.), every lie has to be reduced to an inner lie. This is why this notion becomes the central issue.[28]

This turns out to be Kant's main argument to construe lying as a self-regarding vice, and his real attempt to explain why lying involves self-disrespect. Lying makes the liar dishonorable in his own eyes since it is grounded on insincerity, which involves the deliberate choice to adopt a maxim that he cannot declare even to himself and to his own conscience. By lying, the agent wants to display an intention that does not correspond to his real one, and projects a fictive identity ("a mere deceptive appearance of a human being" (TL 6:429.33 f.)), which is an expression of a different maxim than the one he actually adopted, under the assumption that the real maxim would not be judged a good one.

This central point is clarified by Kant's examples, which may be somewhat unexpected, but deserve special attention. Both concern a profession of faith that is not founded on genuine belief or conviction, but on prudential reasoning. The first example concerns someone who brings himself to believe in "a future judge of the world" because he thinks that it might be useful and prudent to do so (cf. TL 6:430.19–23). The second concerns someone who makes himself believe that his fear of God's punishment is in fact genuine faith (cf. TL 6:430.23–26).[29] As Kant observes in the *Religion* with regard to corresponding examples, we may have "truth in what is believed, yet at the same time untruthfulness in the belief" (RGV 6:187.35 f.), as when someone tells (himself) something true that he does not believe.

An inner lie involves, therefore, faking a persuasion (cf. MpVT 8:268n). However, this fictive identity is not merely useful for pragmatic purposes. Its deeper function is, in Kant's analysis, to deceive the agent's conscience. This crucial point is also expressed in Kant's examples. Indeed, he does not mention ordinary private convictions, but cases which, in earlier ethical doctrines, belong specifically to one's duties to

27 On the non-correspondence between inner and external lie see VNAEF 8:421.32 f.: "both may occur united together, or also in contradiction to one another".
28 The priority of the inner lie (understood, however, as a self-lie) has been stressed also by Esser, 2004, p. 263, and Esser, 2008, p. 295. See also Gamberini, 2006.
29 Cf. MpVT 8:268.22 ff. See also OP 22:64.12–16; HN 17:188.6–9.

God.[30] While Kant excludes such duties from the scope of proper moral obligations because we cannot interact with God, he re-interprets them as duties to oneself concerning our inner moral disposition, that is, as a duty that is "not objective, an obligation to perform certain services for another, but only subjective, for the sake of strengthening the moral incentive in our own lawgiving reason" (TL 6:487.22–25; cf. also V-MS/Vigil 27:713). The examples are meant to stress how lying affects one's disposition to recognize the authority of a superior moral verdict, since Kant equates religion (in the subjective or 'inner' sense) and conscientiousness (*Gewissenhaftigkeit*; cf. V-MS/Vigil 27:574 f., 718 f.; cf. RGV 6:190.19 f.). Since the insincerity towards God is a "*violation of conscience* [Verletzung des Gewissens]" (RGV 6:188.18 f.), the sincerity of our faith in a judge of the world, and of our conduct, is, in the perspective of the agent, equivalent to his acceptance of the scrutiny of conscience, which is at the same time an authority we take part in. In any ethically relevant lie we therefore violate our conscientiousness, because we decide to deny the "subjective conviction [subjectives Fürwahrhalten]" (V-MS/Vigil 27:719.5) that it consists in: we know our belief or purpose, but we express another—maybe even in our own thoughts—in order to elude the condemnation, even though we are at the same time aware that the judging authority is *our own* conscience. Insofar as untruthfulness is a falsification of a *Fürwahrhalten*, it always affects the subject and his conscience first (cf. MpVT 8:267.32 f.). What the previous moral philosophers improperly called *conscientia erronea* (cf. TL 6:401.3 ff.)—that is the application of an inappropriate moral norm, or the application of the law to the wrong act[31]—must rather be understood as an inner lie (cf. MpVT 8:268.10–269.2): its alleged error follows from a deliberate deception, as the agent manipulates the inner judge and its verdict. But by regarding the conscience as "an other person" (TL 6:430.28 f.; cf. the "merely ideal person" in TL 6:429.25 with 439.3), the liar rejects both the authority of the moral law and his moral identity as a person.

Thus, Kant, who has often stressed that man has a tendency to try to escape his own moral judgment through captious reasoning (see e.g. GMS 4:405.12–19), here presents lying as one distinctive (though not the only) outcome of such a tendency, and at the same time clarifies why he considers lying the most evident manifestation of an original

---

30 See e.g. Baumgarten, 1763, §§115, 119 and 141, and the remarks in V-MS/Vigil 27:724.31 ff.
31 See Baumgarten, 1763, §177.

bad propensity in man (cf. 6:430.37–431.1; MpVT 8:270.16–31).[32]
Every lie is grounded on the decision to be untruthful in front of the
own conscience in the first place. Deciding to be untruthful towards others means that the agent chooses to deceive his own conscience, namely
himself as a moral being, as he does not recognize himself as involved
in the self-legislation underlying the verdict of conscience. For this reason
Kant understands sincerity as "the ground of every virtuous intention"
(MpVT 8:269.1 f.). The conscious rejection of both one's own identity
and the basis of one's own moral status explains Kant's special insistence
on the gravity of lying, as the first and worst vice; it affects the basic
structures of the endorsement of moral principles, in a way that also
seems to spread through other people, so that this fundamentally self-regarding vice undermines the collective fulfillment of moral demands.[33]
Furthermore, the combination of the rejection of one's own moral status
and the rejection of the moral law is the fundamental similarity that lying
has with the other vices examined here.

While we deceive our conscience by using cases to make room for acting notwithstanding moral principles (cf. e. g. V-MS/Vigil 27:620.2 ff.),
Kant's analysis of lying focuses entirely on principles, without taking
into consideration if we could make any distinction between lying and
alleged morally permissible lies. In an earlier note Kant remarks:
"When I ask, Should I lie or not? what is at stake is not a motivating
ground, but a rule" (Refl 7019 HN 19:228, trans. S.B.). This section
of the *Doctrine of Virtue* develops that thought, as it examines merely
how lying affects the genuine adoption of maxims (cf. TL 6:420.24 f.).
Precisely because this is the proper level of the issue, the prohibition of
lying must not leave any room for exceptions (cf. e. g. V-PP/Powalski
27:231.34 f.; V-MS/Vigil 27:701.5 f.). If an act is permissible it is not

---

32 Therefore, I believe that it is right (and necessary) to stress the connection be-
    tween the inner lie and radical evil, but without identifying them, as some inter-
    preters do (see Allison, 1990, pp. 271 f.; Gamberini, 2006). See on this also HN
    19:640.1–641.10 and 646.19.

33 Therefore the inner lie is the fundamental vice (the "rotten spot" (TL 6:430.37);
    cf. VNAEF 8:422.3 f.; MpVT 8:269.5 f.) from which "the ill of untruthfulness
    spreads *into his* [sc.: a human being's, S.B.] *relations with* other human beings"
    (TL 6:431.1 f., italics S.B.; cf. RGV 6:38.25 f.). It is noteworthy that, in
    Kant's view, lying has also a specific relevance in philosophy: The key for the
    "perpetual peace in philosophy" would be provided by the command, not to
    lie (cf. VNAEF 8:422.8–12; see also Refl 8096 HN 19:641.10, and the quota-
    tion of the Latin definition mentioned in the *Doctrine of Virtue* also used in the
    Erklärung in Beziehung auf Fichtes Wissenschaftslehre, Br 12:371.22 f.).

to be understood as lying, as it relies on a different maxim. Kant does not analyze lying in such a general and strict way in order to be pedagogically or rhetorically efficacious,[34] but because his theory does not focus on the diversity of acts but on the underlying maxim. Providing a detailed classification of morally permissible acts that do not contradict the prohibition of lying remains extraneous to his aims. Even his casuistical remarks add little much and refer to rather unproblematic cases.[35] The novelty of Kant's approach also lies in the fact that, while the other accounts lead to discussions about the admissibility or excusability of the different possible kinds of alleged lies, he focuses entirely on the matter of principle which lying is all about.

3. "On Avarice"

The section on avarice seems to be the least original part of the chapter. Unlike lying and servility, avarice was already treated in the context of duties to oneself, as we can see in Baumgarten's *Ethica philosophica* (§§285–289). However, Kant contradicts the usual account and develops a divergent interpretation of the vice of avarice, drawing implications closely connected with his general position about the features of virtue. Maybe Kant's intention to stress his opposition to then current accounts explains the peculiar structure of this section: the bulk of the text concerns the unsuitableness of gradual distinctions between virtue and vice, while Kant's remarks about why avarice must be considered a violation of a duty to oneself are quite brief and appear last, in the subsection on casuistical questions (which, in this case, puts forth no cases for consideration). For clarity's sake I shall first examine Kant's definition of the topic, then examine his argument for including it among the duties to oneself, and then examine his observations against the idea of a qualitative difference between avarice and the corresponding virtue.

In the first place, Kant tries to define the kind of avarice that must be seen as a self-regarding vice. On this matter, the text of the *Doctrine of Virtue* is perhaps not as clear as it could be. At the beginning of the section, Kant remarks that the topic to be discussed is not "*greedy avarice* [habsüchtiger Geiz]," that is, the "acquiring the means to good living in excess of one's true needs," since this is to be construed as a violation of

---

34   This is suggested by Wood, 2008, p. 252.
35   See Annen, 1997, pp. 238 ff. on the debate about the *Höflichkeitslüge*.

a duty to other people; but, he adds, also *"miserly avarice* [karge[r] Geiz]" violates our obligations to others when it becomes *"stinginess* or niggardliness [Knickerei oder Knauserei]" (cf. TL 6:432.4–10).[36] By contrast, a violation of a duty to oneself is the kind of avarice which consists in "restricting *one's own* enjoyment of the means to good living so narrowly as to leave one's own true needs unsatisfied" (TL 6:432.10–12), which is genuine miserly avarice, and which could have no negative consequences for other people. So, when Kant later refers to *karger Geiz* or *Kargheit* (miserliness) generally (cf. TL 6:432.31–433.5)—which, at first sight, Kant seems suddenly to reintroduce, after having put miserly avarice explicitly aside—, he means the third kind of avarice of the initial distinction, which he also calls *Filzigkeit* or *filziger Geiz.*[37] The miserly avarice examined here as a vice towards ourselves, therefore, is a way of acting which consists merely in striving to possess money, forgetful of any possible intention to use it.

Some of Kant's early critics already objected that his analysis of avarice must follow from undeclared eudaemonistic presuppositions, nothwithstanding his claims concerning the foundations of ethics.[38] If avarice is wrong, it must be because it hinders our pursuit of well-being, which then turns out to be a positive moral value after all. Accordingly, this vice should be understood, at best, as a violation of a duty to ourselves as *animal* beings. Kant addresses this predictable objection in the casuistical section: "it may be asked whether either prodigality or miserliness should be called a vice at all, or whether both are not mere imprudence" (TL 6:434.4–6). Here again, what must be examined, and what makes this way of acting morally reproachable, is not its consequence (the fact that eventually we are not able to live a decent life), but the maxim that this way of acting is grounded upon (cf. TL 6:433.1–3).[39] If we take the maxim into consideration, we can see

---

36 This very brief comment on stinginess (*Knickerei*) should also be seen as Kant's correction of Baumgarten's definition, since Baumgarten connects *Knickerei* with *Filzigkeit*—which for Kant is the self-regarding miserly avarice—as different grades of "intemperantia in servandis opibus" (Baumgarten, 1763, §288; see also Meier, 1762–1774, §746, III, p. 614). Kant's opposition to the idea of quantitative distinctions in moral worth, which he discusses in what follows, seems then to be implicitly present since the opening of the section.

37 See e.g. V-MS/Vigil 27:606.9. On the different sorts of avarice: see also V-PP/Powalski 27:220.31–38 and V-MS/Vigil 27:659.9–15.

38 See Schwab, 1800, p. 80; Schleiermacher, 1803, p. 226.

39 See also Esser, 2004, p. 365.

that miserly avarice precludes us from living according to "the principle of independence from everything except the law" (TL 6:434.13). Therefore, Kant's point is that avarice leads to "slavish subjection of oneself to the goods that contribute to happiness" (TL 6:434.8 f., cf. §29, TL 6:452.19). If we descend into miserly avarice, Kant claims, this is because we have completely forgotten the genuine moral order of ends and means and take what should be merely a means (although a means to every-thing)[40] as the end we have to lead our life according to (cf. V-MS/Vigil 27:659.20–28; V-Anth/Mron 25:1306.17 f.). Miserly avarice, therefore, is grounded on a perversion of the moral practical use of rea-son, which is, at the same time, a profound injury to our status as moral beings.[41] The morally relevant implication of avarice, therefore, is not that we cannot enjoy life's pleasures, but that we eventually forget to be moral beings and treat ourselves as something worth less than a thing like money. Such perversion is so deep, in Kant's view, that here "one enjoys the power in thought" (V-Mo/Collins 27:399.28 f.)[42], with-out using money as a means to some real pleasure. In order to emphasize the significance of this reversal of the structure of morality and its con-nection with our moral integrity, Kant even claims in his lectures that the moral damage caused by avarice is "incorrigible," since "the miser is [...] a stranger to himself; he does not know his own nature," so that "he can in no way be persuaded of his fault" (V-Mo/Collins 27:402.6–8)[43].

Miserly avarice represents for Kant the most appropriate occasion to make clear, with regard to a precise aspect of moral life, why no gradual differentiation should be applied to virtue. The issue was already dis-cussed in the "Introduction to the Doctrine of Virtue," and avarice was mentioned there as well (cf. TL 6:404.8–22 and 31–37; see also

---

40 See V-MS/Vigil 27:658.37–39: "Among all means of acquisition, none has a value so predominant as money, since it is taken as *a sign for everything open to acquisition*" (italics S.B.). See also V-PP/Powalski 27:220.22 f. Equivalently, the following §11 states that money has a *"pretium eminens"* (TL 6:434.31) and therefore is worth more than other things.

41 Taylor, 2006, p. 34, argues that miserly avarice cannot be interpreted in the light of this logical fallacy, which, she claims, should be seen rather as its consequence and not as its cause. But Kant's point is that this is not just a logical fallacy, but a real reversal of our thinking about ends and means.

42 Cf. V-PP/Herder 27:87.4–8; V-MS/Vigil 27:606.24; V-Anth/Mron 25:1261.36–1262.2, 1358.32–35.

43 Cf. V-Mo/Kaehler(Stark), p. 264; cf. also V-Anth/Mron 25:1358.32–35.

VAMS 23:397.7–11). The target of Kant's criticism is what he calls the *"Aristotelian* principle": "that virtue consists in the middle way between two vices" (TL 6:432.16–18), which was also endorsed by Baumgarten, among others.[44] Kant did probably not suspect that this traditional principle cannot be identified with Aristotle's actual position; however, his aim was to criticize the modern ethicists and to eradicate a sort of philosophical commonplace, which, in his view, involves an improper understanding of morality.[45] Indeed, Kant's criticism of the quantitative idea of virtue also concerns a more general point, namely that the traditional idea of moderation and temperance, which was usually the outcome of the analyses of avarice, and which was often considered the main issue of duties to oneself in general,[46] has no crucial role to play in his account of morality. The inner strength of virtue does not consist in mediating opposite extremes, but in reaching, maintaining and consolidating a fundamental recognition of ourselves (and others) as moral beings.

Kant's objections against the common version of the *mesotes* doctrine are a further development of the fundamental point that the moral worth of our conduct depends on the maxim that it is grounded on, not on our specific acts in the physical world ("If a vice is to be distinguished from a virtue, the difference one must cognize and explain is not a difference in the *degree* of practicing moral maxims but rather in the objective *principle* of the maxims" (TL 6:432.26–28)). Thus, the moral evaluation of a way of acting does not consider any quantifiable aspect of this way of acting. While there is a quantitative distinction between the amount of money that we can acquire, spare, or spend, the moral wrongness of the maxim of denying ourselves everything else in order to enjoy the mere possession of money is not determined by such details, and this maxim is thus fully incomparable with any maxim that justly regards our money as a means to morally pursuable ends. Analogously, Kant underscores (cf. TL 6:433n.10–38), that there are no degrees in the corresponding virtue: our conduct is not worth more if we make proper use of a greater amount of money. The alleged Aristotelian principle, then, is useless (or "a tautology" (TL 6:433.11)), since it cannot tell us any-

---

44 See Baumgarten, 1763, §170. For Kant's criticism of the alleged Aristotelian principle, beside TL 6:404.3–22, see e.g. V-PP/Powalski 27:195.36–39; V-MS/Vigil 27:611.23–612.35, 654.9–15.
45 On the limits of Kant's knowledge of Aristotle's practical philosophy: see Ferrarin, 2004, pp. 64 ff.
46 See e.g. Walch, 1727, §XLIX, p. 424; Eberhard, 1786, §157, p. 186.

thing about the moral worth of our possible actions. Ethics cannot tell us exactly which acts we ought to perform (here, how much we ought to spend or spare), since it can only explain to us which maxim we ought to act on and must then leave us and our capacity to judge to determine how the principle should be applied (cf. TL 6:433n.23 – 27). Thus like the (pseudo-)Aristotelian principle, Kant also rejects the result of its application to avarice, which leads us to regard thrift as the corresponding virtue.[47] In the *Doctrine of Virtue* Kant only alludes to this common view through a question at the end of the casuistical section, which he leaves unanswered (as he often does in the casuistical remarks in this work): "Or is thrift as such a virtue?" (TL 6:434.17 f.). But his position on the matter is explicit in other texts: thrift "is not a virtue" (V-Mo/Collins 27:405.18 f.)[48]. Since thrift relates to the quantity of money it is advisable for us to spend, it is not a virtue, but belongs merely to prudence. Kant observes that sometimes thrift could even be combined with avarice (cf. V-MS/Vigil 27:660.14 – 17; V-PP/Powalski 27:220.29 – 31), which implies that it cannot be regarded as a virtue.

4. "On Servility"

Kant's further broadening of the scope of the duties to oneself in §11 shows that he does not conceive of them as merely private obligations.[49] In presenting what he calls servility or false humility as a violation of the moral self, he proposes a double correction to the prior accounts. On the one hand, he rectifies the traditional inclusion of humility among duties to oneself and, on the other hand, interprets flattery, which was understood as a violation of others, as a self-regarding vice. In doing so, Kant unifies issues that were previously considered separately and divergently: humility was presented as duty to oneself, while flattery was seen as a violation of a duty to others.

---

47 See Baumgarten, 1763, §289. Meier sees the obligation to thrift as an implication of the more general obligation to moderation (cf. Meier 1762–1774, §743, III, pp. 601 f., §748, pp. 620 f.).

48 Cf. V-Mo/Mron 27:1531.17; see also V-MS/Vigil 27:613.19 f..

49 See Hill, 1973. While Hill holds that, from the standpoint of a conceptual analysis, "if there are duties to oneself, it is natural to expect that a duty to avoid being servile would have a prominent place among them" (p. 87), Kant is in fact the first to deal with the issue from this perspective.

As to the first point, humility was traditionally prescribed as the demand not to overestimate our moral perfection in comparison with that of others. Accordingly, Baumgarten defines it as "habitus de imperfectionibus suis recte iudicandi [a habit of assessing correctly ones' own imperfections] Also: … iudicandi [a habit of assessing correctly ones' own imperfections]" (Baumgarten, 1763, §168, trans. S.B.; cf. §169).[50] Kant develops a contrasting view. According to his analysis of moral motivation, humility is a core aspect of our moral self-knowledge insofar as it arises from our consciousness of morality, its authority, and our status in front of it (cf. KpV 5:73.18–34, 154.5–8). This inescapable humility relies on the fact that, as moral beings, we have to compare ourselves with the moral law itself (cf. TL 6:435.23–25). Even if we feel and express genuine humility in front of a virtuous person, this is not because we are led to feel the limits of our moral strength in comparison with that person as a paragon of virtue, but because we see the moral law embodied in that good example (cf. KpV 5:77.1–15; cf. also GMS 4:401n.35 f.). Thus, humility is an underlying feature of moral life, but not a specific duty.

The crucial failure of the traditional account of humility is that it requires us to evaluate ourselves according to the improper standard represented by other people (cf. V-PP/Powalski 27:194.36–195.4; V-Mo/Collins 27:349.11–16). This is one of the cases where, in Kant's view, the inadequacy of a moral philosophy has negative consequences on the common understanding of morality and on conduct. Therefore, he proposes specific corrections to previous accounts of morality. The traditional conception of humility, which overlooks its essential connection with the moral law, leads to a morally inconsistent practice of humility in our interaction with others, so that we tend to see only the limit of our 'moral perfection' and not our dignity as moral beings.[51] Thus, this merely interpersonal conception of humility eventually leads to consequences in one's moral life that are contrary to genuine moral humility, since the latter involves the equality of all persons as such (cf. TL 6:435.3–5), who share the same dignity as moral beings. For these reasons, Kant can claim that what moralists usually mean by humility is only an apparent virtue, a

---

50 See also Meier, 1762–1774, §444, II, p. 488.

51 An analogous violation of ourselves as moral beings is involved in humiliating ourselves in front of religious symbols, if this does not express our awareness of our inferiority to an ideal, but the devotion to an idol: cf. §12, TL 6:436.28–437.2; cf. RGV 6:185.4–8; V-MS/Vigil 27:607.4–9.

"monkish virtue" (V-Mo/Collins 27:349.14)[52] (while he also confirms his point through a biblical quote: "Be no man's lackey" (TL 6:436.18; cf. 1 Corinthians 7:23.).

As to the second aspect, if we construe flattery as an other-regarding violation (hence, not just as servile behavior), we cannot really see why it is a vice, since we cannot see that it is grounded on adopting the comparison with others as one's moral standard. Like other authors before him, Kant remarks that this kind of humility can be false in a twofold way, since it can be not only morally wrong, but also deceptive towards others;[53] nevertheless, this is not his main point. Whether or not we act this way in order to achieve some purpose, the relevant fact is that we adopt the judgment of others as our moral standard (even if only functionally). We thereby compromise our dignity as persons, not just because we adopt an inferior standpoint,[54] but because our dignity rests only on the genuine standard given by the moral law. Deceiving others involves, therefore, a deeper self-deception about our status as persons.[55] The connection with false humility lets us see that servile conduct does not amount to any wrong done to others, but to an inadequate appreciation of ourselves as persons.[56] A "parasite," or a beggar, who behaves in a servile manner without deceiving others, is guilty of the same vice (cf. TL 6:436.20–23).[57] The same applies, interestingly, to the apparently opposite case of a "conviction of the greatness of one's moral worth," which can be called "*moral arrogance* [Tugendstolz]," as it derives "from failure to compare it with the law" as well (cf. TL 6:435.25–27; cf. also V-Mo/Collins 27:349.10 f.). This is an analogous violation, because it breaches the condition of our moral status (comparing ourselves with the moral law) for some individual purpose. Thus like in the case of avarice, this vice does not consist in a quantitative defect which can be recti-

52 Cf. V-Mo/Kaehler(Stark), p. 185 and V-MS/Vigil 27:703.31; see also TL 6:485.10–19. On Kant's position on humility: see Louden, 2007.
53 See e.g. Wolff, 1750–1753, III, §213; Baumgarten, 1763, §352.
54 Eylon/Heyd, 2008, p. 688, remark that "flattery is made from a position of inferiority or need—material or psychological." However, they refer mainly to Plato and Aristotle, separating flattery from servility, and do not mention Kant, even if they eventually see in servility "the lack of self-respect" (ibid., p. 696).
55 Cf. VAMS 23:403.25 f.: "Anything that crawls is at the same time false. For every human being is aware of the inalienable right of equality" (trans. S.B.).
56 See also Durán Casas, 1996, pp. 294 f.
57 Cf. also V-MS/Vigil 27:605.27–38 and 606.30–33

fied by increasing the self-respect or moral self-awareness expressed in our conduct.[58] This vice also consists in its underlying maxim, which is fundamentally incompatible with our 'moral health.'

Both false humility and flattery (as well as arrogance), thus, involve discarding our status as moral beings, as well as the genuine moral standard it relies on. Kant emphasizes that we have to consider these issues from this new perspective by introducing §11 with a recapitulation of the axiological status of human beings, which recalls and further develops the distinction between price and dignity drawn in the *Groundwork* (cf. GMS 4:434.31–435.4). Here, Kant draws a conceptual distinction not only between animal and human beings, but also between human and moral beings, in a way that parallels the trichotomy of the predispositions characterizing the human condition in the *Religion* (cf. RGV 6:26–28). If, as a living being, man has only "an ordinary value (*pretium vulgare*)" like any other "offspring of the earth," whose worth depends only on their physical properties, even as a rational being man has only "*extrinsic* value" (a "*pretium usus*"), depending on how his pragmatic abilities can serve as means to possible ends (cf. TL 6:434.22–27).[59] In contrast to the traditional priority given to the *animal rationale*, in Kant's view rationality as such is merely functional and does not provide any special worth (cf. TL 6:418.4–23).[60] Indeed, man has a superior value, that is, "dignity (an absolute inner worth)," only since he is capable to recognize and set himself obligatory ends, in virtue of his moral practical reason (TL 6:434.32–435.5).[61] The normative implications developed in §11 result from this fundamental distinction.

The special emphasis Kant adds here to his view on the status of moral beings lies in the remark that a person in the full sense of the notion "exacts *respect* for himself from all other rational beings in the world"

---

58 Cf. Dillon, 2003, p. 201. The quantitative pattern of the mean between two opposite vices is applied to humility and arrogance by Baumgarten (cf. Baumgarten, 1763, §382, see also §§171 and 173).

59 The notions of *pretium vulgare* and *pretium usus* might amount to Pufendorf's doctrine: Pufendorf, 1673, ch. XIV.

60 The contrast with the traditional view becomes very clear in Schwab's reaction: see Schwab, 1800, p. 81.

61 Correspondingly, in the same period, Kant insists that the fulfillment of rationality is to be seen only in its moral practical use, in opposition to mere technical practical reason (see e. g. OP 21:12.15–19). On technical vs. practical: see KpV 5:26n.34–40; KU 5:172.14–17 and 455.25; EEKU 20:199 ff.; VAZeF 23:163.

and "can measure himself with every other being of this kind and value himself on a footing of equality with them" (TL 6:435.2–5).[62] While considering rationality, or other abilities, as the source of value would not allow any equality (cf. TL 6:434.27–31), the status of moral being involves a direct demand for respect and an assertion of equality with any person, since moral considerations rule out every other comparison.[63] The analysis of an interpersonal way of acting like servility requires us to focus on this aspect of our moral status. Nevertheless, this statement on the dignity of persons is meant to explain why servility must be seen as a *self*-regarding vice. Foremost, that restatement about our moral status should show that our way of acting undermines our entitlement to exact respect. If in acting, we reject the genuine moral standard, we also lose the equal status granted by that standard. Correspondingly, the duty to respect others is ultimately grounded on the self-respect which *they* owe *themselves*.[64] An offense, and our reaction to it (a demand for apologies, or an offer of forgiveness), are conceptually possible only if we respect ourselves as moral beings.[65] Therefore, unlike in prior moral philosophy, "how I ought to let others treat me" is a matter of one's duties to oneself (cf. Br 11:307.23 f., 11:399.5–9).

5. A Human Being's Virtue Towards Oneself as a Moral Being

Through the examination of these three vices, the reader should grasp the content and relevance of the duty everyone has towards oneself merely as a moral being. In the *Doctrine of Virtue*, only a few words are devoted to the fulfillment of this duty: "[t]he virtue that is opposed to all these vices could be called *love of honor* [Ehrliebe] (*honestas interna, iustum sui aestimium*)" (TL 6:420.26–28; cf. VAMS 23:403.3 f.). The phrase "*could be called*" (italics S.B.) does not express some hesitation, but the necessity

---

62 On this aspect: see Darwall, 2008, pp. 188 ff. See also Darwall, 2006, pp. 120 ff.

63 Cf. e.g. KpV 5:73.18–24.

64 Cf. TL 6:462.26–29: "But just as he cannot give himself away for any price (this would conflict with his duty to self-esteem), so neither can he act contrary to *the equally necessary self-esteem of others*, as human beings" (italics S.B.).

65 Cf. V-MS/Vigil 27:606 f.: if one "wishes [will] others to have respect for his person, he must likewise hold fast to it, and show that he respects himself. He must at least bring the offending party to the point of an apology, so that he may be forgiven".

to carefully distinguish *Ehrliebe* from other related notions.[66] While Baumgarten equates *Ehrliebe* with the Greco-latin notion of *philotimia* and mentions it as an aspect of our duties to ourselves concerning the *cura existimationis*, the care for the reputation we enjoy as individuals,[67] Kant understands it as a virtue that does not at all concern an individual's standing and thus distinguishes it from the *honestas externa*.[68] The genuine love of honor, in his view, does not depend on merit, like in Baumgarten, but on the esteem of oneself as a moral being, as it is expressed by the connection between *honestas interna* and *iustum sui aestimium*, which were previously separated notions.[69]

The distinction between *Ehrliebe* ("*love of honor*") and *Ehrbegierde* ("*ambition*") (TL 6:420.27 f.; cf. TL 6:465.10–22), which is almost all the *Doctrine of Virtue* says about it,[70] points in the same direction, and recalls the distinction between valuation according to the law and valuation according to the moral views of others: while *Ehrbegierde* pursues merely the esteem of others and is essentially a social passion, which leads us to violate our duties to others, the *Ehrliebe* is an inner disposition concerning the own moral stance. So, "he who is ambitious cannot be alone, because he wants always to be honored by someone. He who loves honor seeks to be alone and unknown" (V-PP/Powalski 27:222.6–8; trans. S.B.).[71] Kant also draws a corresponding distinction between two kinds of pride: *Ehrliebe* should be understood as "**pride**" (TL 6:465.16; cf. TL 6:459.23), that is, as the right way to be affected from the awareness of the own worth as a person.

Kant's normative concern in this chapter is to explain how some ways of acting involve a lack of *Ehrliebe*, that is a fundamental failure to appreciate one's own status as a moral being. To sum-up the main examples, by

---

66 From a completely different perspective, Kant's use of this notion is stressed by Anderson, 2008. Interesting critical remarks (which cannot be discussed here) on the underlying role of honor in Kant's ethical thought can be found in Skorupski, 2005, pp. 341 ff.

67 Baumgarten, 1763, §293: "habitus existimationem appetendi". In his *Metaphysica* (§684) *Ehrliebe* (*gloria*) is defined, from the standpoint of psychology, as "gaudium ex honore."

68 See V-Mo/Collins 27:408.38–409.1: "we might call the love of honour *honestas*, though it would then need to be distinguished from respectability [Ehrbarkeit]."

69 Compare Baumgarten, 1763, §168 (where "*iustum sui aestimium*" is translated as "gehörige Selbstschätzung") and §300.

70 See e.g. V-Mo/Kaehler(Stark), p. 272 f. (and Werner Stark's note on Kant's use of these terms), and V-MS/Vigil 27:664.23–26.

71 Cf. also V-Mo/Collins 27:409.1–7; V-Anth/Parow 25:424.11–14.

lying I hide my principles from myself in the first place; through avarice and servility I assume false moral standards and make my participation in morality impossible. Thus, while it is common to equate the 'inner lie' with the phenomenon of self-deception,[72] in Kant's view *all* these vices are construed as forms of self-deception about the own moral status. Of course, every vice makes the agent unworthy insofar as it causes *demerit*, but what is distinctive about the vices regarding ourselves as moral beings is that they *directly* affect the capacity to act on good maxims and jeopardize the *dignity* he has as a being capable of morality.[73] Most importantly, such dignity turns out to be endangered foremost by *our* own decisions, not by the conduct of others, whose disrespect for us does not obliterate our moral status. Only self-regarding vices can directly injure our dignity.

A vice towards oneself as a moral being is thus a way of acting which deprives the agent of his access to morality. Therefore it is particularly important to underscore their implications, showing that such vices deprive the agent of the recognition owed to moral beings. This chapter thus expounds what is probably the most crucial aspect of the priority which Kant ascribes to duties to oneself: they express some fundamental conditions of morality, whose violation deprives our conduct of a moral relevance.[74] The reason why our actions "*must* spring from a love of honor [aus der Ehrliebe]" (V-Mo/Collins 27:412.4 f., italics S.B.) seems to be that only an agent who, in acting, maintains his awareness of his moral status can be recognized as a moral agent.

---

72 See e.g. Denis, 2001, p. 92; Potter, 2002; Gamberini, 2006; Wood, 2008, p. 255.

73 It seems questionable, then, that the duty to bear physical pain should apply "especially" if we know that we deserve it, as in the case of the death penalty, where Kant believes that "a criminal's death *may be* ennobled [...] by the resoluteness with which he dies" (TL 6:436.25–27). Accordingly, Kant holds that, if the condemned could choose between death penalty and "convict labor" (RL 6:333.37), the proper awareness of his dignity, namely love of honour, should lead him to choose death. For he "is acquainted with something that he values even more highly than life, namely *honor*" (RL 6:334.2 f.).

74 See e.g. V-MS/Vigil 27:604.14–26; V-Mo/Mron 27:1482.10–21; V-Mo/Kaehler(Stark), p. 202; V-Mo/Collins 27:360.5–10. On this issue, see also Reath, 2002, p. 352; Timmermann, 2006, pp. 512 ff.; Louden, 2006, p. 83; Bacin, 2008, pp. 206 ff.

References

Allison, Henry E. (1990), *Kant's Theory of Freedom*, Cambridge: Cambridge University Press.
Anderson, Elisabeth (2008), "Emotions in Kant's Later Moral Philosophy: Honour and the Phenomenology of Moral Value", in: Betzler (ed.) (2008), pp. 123–145.
Annen, Martin (1997), *Das Problem der Wahrhaftigkeit in der Philosophie der deutschen Aufklärung: Ein Beitrag zur Ethik und zum Naturrecht des 18. Jahrhunderts*, Würzburg: Königshausen & Neumann.
Atwell, John E. (1986), *Ends and Principles in Kant's Moral Thought*, Dordrecht: Martin Nijhoff.
Bacin, Stefano (2006), *Il senso dell'etica: Kant e la costruzione di una teoria morale*, Bologna: Il Mulino.
Bacin, Stefano (2008), "Una nuova dottrina dei doveri: Sull'etica della 'Metafisica dei costumi' e il significato dei doveri verso se stessi", in: Luca Fonnesu (ed.), *Etica e mondo in Kant*, Bologna: Il Mulino, pp. 189–208.
Bacin, Stefano/Schönecker, Dieter (2010), "Zwei Konjekturvorschläge zur 'Tugendlehre,' §9", in: *Kant-Studien*, vol. 101, pp. 247–252.
Baumgarten, Alexander Gottlieb (^{3}1763), *Ethica philosophica*, Halle: Hemmerde. (Reprint: Hildesheim: Olms [1969].)
Baumgarten, Alexander Gottlieb (^{7}1779), *Metaphysica*, Halle: Hemmerde. (Reprint: Hildesheim: Olms [1982].)
Betzler, Monika (ed.) (2008), *Kant's Ethics of Virtue*, Berlin/New York: Walter de Gruyter.
Darwall, Stephen (2006), *The Second-Person Standpoint: Morality, Respect, and Accountability*, Cambridge/MA: Harvard University Press.
Darwall, Stephen (2008), "Kant on Respect, Dignity, and Duty", in: Betzler (ed.) (2008), pp. 175–199.
Denis, Lara (2001), *Moral Self-Regard: Duties to Oneself in Kant's Moral Theory*, New York: Garland Press.
Dietz, Simone (2002), "Immanuel Kants Begründungen des Lügenverbots", in: Rochus Leonhardt/Martin Rösel (eds.), *Dürfen wir lügen? Beiträge zu einem aktuellen Thema*, Neukirchen-Vluyn: Neukirchener Verlagsgesellschaft, pp. 91–115.
Dillon, Robin S. (2003), "Kant on Arrogance and Self-Respect", in: Cheshire Calhoun (ed.), *Setting the Moral Compass: Essays by Women Philosophers*, Oxford: Oxford University Press, pp. 191–216.
Durán Casas, Vicente (1996), *Die Pflichten gegen sich selbst in Kants 'Metaphysik der Sitten'*, Frankfurt/M.: Peter Lang.
Eberhard, Johann August (^{2}1786), *Sittenlehre der Vernunft*, Berlin: Nicolai.
Esser, Andrea (2004), *Eine Ethik für Endliche: Kants Tugendlehre in der Gegenwart*, Stuttgart-Bad Cannstatt: Frommann-Holzboog.
Esser, Andrea (2008), "Kant on Solving Moral Conflicts", in: Betzler (ed.) (2008), pp. 279–302.
Eylon, Yuval/Heyd, David (2008), "Flattery", in: *Philosophy and Phenomenological Research*, vol. 77, pp. 685–704.

Ferrarin, Alfredo (2004), *Saggezza, immaginazione, giudizio pratico. Studio su Aristotele e Kant*, Pisa: ETS.

Gamberini, Paola (2006), "Mentire a se stessi: Kant e il problema della menzogna interiore", in: *Dianoia*, vol. 11, pp. 205–242.

Gregor, Mary (1963), *Laws of Freedom: A Study of Kant's Method of Applying the Categorical Imperative in the 'Metaphysik der Sitten'*, Oxford: Blackwell.

Hill, Thomas E. (1973), "Servility and Self-Respect", in: *The Monist*, vol. 57, pp. 87–104. (Reprinted in: id., *Autonomy and Self-Respect*, Cambridge: Cambridge University Press 1991).

Kerstein, Samuel J. (2008), "Treating Oneself Merely as a Means", in: Betzler (ed.) (2008), pp. 197–214.

Louden, Robert B. (2006), "Moralische Stärke: Tugend als eine Pflicht gegen sich selbst", in: Heiner F. Klemme/Manfred Kühn/Dieter Schönecker (eds.), *Moralische Motivation: Kant und die Alternativen*, Hamburg: Meiner, pp. 79–95.

Louden, Robert B. (2007), "Kantian Moral Humility: Between Aristotle and Paul", in: *Philosophy and Phenomenological Research*, vol. 75, pp. 632–639.

MacIntyre, Alasdair (1995), "Truthfulness, Lies, and Moral Philosophers: What can we Learn from Mill and Kant?", in: *Tanner Lectures on Human Values*, vol. 16, Grethe B. Peterson (ed.), Salt Lake City: University of Utah Press, pp. 309–361. (Reprinted in: id., *Ethics and Politics: Selected Essays*, vol. 2, Cambridge: Cambridge University Press 2006, pp. 101–142.)

Mahon, James E. (2006), "Kant and the Perfect Duty to Others not to Lie", in: *British Journal for the History of Philosophy*, vol. 14, pp. 653–685.

Meier, Georg Friedrich ([2]1762–1774), *Philosophische Sittenlehre*, Halle: Hemmerde. (Reprint: Hildesheim: Olms [2007].)

Parma, Vinicio (2000): "Es war einmal eine Metaphysik der Sitten...", in: *Kant-Studien*, vol. 91 (Sonderheft), pp. 42–65.

Potter, Nelson (2002), "Duties to Oneself, Motivational Internalism, and Self-Deception", in: Mark Timmons (ed.), *Kant's 'Metaphysics of Morals': Interpretative Essays*, Oxford: Oxford University Press, pp. 371–390.

Pufendorf, Samuel ([1]1673) [1997], *De officio hominis et civis juxta legem naturalem* (Londini Scanorum), in: id., *Gesammelte Werke*, vol. 2, Gerald Hartung (ed.), Berlin: Akademie Verlag.

Reath, Andrews (2002), "Self-Legislation and Duties to Oneself", in: Mark Timmons (ed.), *Kant's 'Metaphysics of Morals': Interpretative Essays*, Oxford: Oxford University Press, pp. 349–370. (Reprinted in: Andrews Reath, *Agency and Autonomy in Kant's Moral Theory: Selected Essays*, Oxford: Oxford University Press [2006], pp. 231–249.)

Schleiermacher, Friedrich Daniel Ernst ([1]1803) [2002], *Grundlinien einer Kritik der bisherigen Sittenlehre*, in: id., *Kritische Gesamtausgabe*, sect. I, vol. 4, Eilert Herms/Günter Meckenstock/Michael Pietsch (eds.), Berlin/New York: Walter de Gruyter.

Schwab, Johann Christoph (1800), *Vergleichung des Kantischen Moralprincips mit dem Leibnitzisch-Wolffischen*, Berlin: Nicolai. (Reprint: Bruxelles: Culture et Civilisation [1973].)

Sensen, Oliver (2009), "Kant's Conception of Human Dignity", in: *Kant-Studien*, vol. 100, pp. 309–331.

Stefano Bacin

Skorupski, John (2005), "Blame, Respect and Recognition: A Reply to Theo van Willigenburg", in: *Utilitas*, vol. 17, pp. 333–347.

Timmermann, Jens (2000), "Kant und die Lüge aus Pflicht: Zur Auflösung moralischer Dilemmata in einer kantischen Ethik", in: *Philosophisches Jahrbuch*, vol. 107, pp. 267–283.

Timmermann, Jens (2006), "Kant's Duties to the Self, Explained and Defended", in: *Philosophy*, vol. 81, pp. 505–530.

Taylor, Gabriele (2006), *Deadly Vices*, Oxford: Clarendon Press.

Walch, Johann Georg (1727), *Einleitung in die Philosophie*, Leipzig: Gleditsch. (Reprint: Hildesheim: Olms [2007].)

Wolff, Christian (1740–1748), *Jus Naturae, methodo scientifica pertractatum*, Frankfurt/Leipzig/Halle: Renger. (Reprinted in: id., *Gesammelte Werke*, vols. II.17–24 , Hildesheim: Olms [1968–1972].)

Wolff, Christian (1750–1753), *Philosophia moralis sive Ethica, methodo scientifica pertractata*, Halle: Renger. (Reprinted in: id., *Gesammelte Werke*, vols. II.12–16, Hildesheim: Olms [1970–1973].)

Wood, Allen W. (2008), *Kantian Ethics*, Cambridge: Cambridge University Press.

The Inner Court of Conscience, Moral Self-Knowledge, and the Proper Object of Duty (TL 6:437–444)

Andrea M. EsserEsser; translated by Eva Schestag

A. Positioning of §§13–18 of the *Doctrine of Virtue*—Note on the Structure and Edition of the Text

Kant's *Doctrine of Virtue* is considered a 'brittle' work in view of the organization of the text, the unbalanced ratio between the length of the "Introduction," which comprises almost half of the work, and the length of the main part of the text. Some editors assume that the *Doctrine of Virtue* was "assembled from various parts that Kant had long had at hand" without "letting these pieces undergo a process of adaptation so as to create a unified composition."[1] In particular "Chapter II" that is to be discussed here, or rather its "First" and "Second Section," as well as the subsequent "Episodic Section" (TL 6:437.27–444.8)[2] give rise to this supposition, inasmuch as:

§13 of "Section I" is devoted to conscience, characterizing it as an "inner court of justice" (TL 6:438.11, trans. A.E.), despite the fact that Kant has already devoted a section to conscience in section XII of the "Introduction to the doctrine of virtue."

The three sections of "Chapter II" were not announced in §4 of the *Doctrine of Elements* ("On the principle of the division of the duties toward ourselves" (trans. A.E.)), which is meant to structure the subsequent parts of the text. §4 divides the 'duties to ourselves' into 'perfect' and 'imperfect' duties and further differentiates between 'duties toward ourselves as animal being' and as 'moral being.' *This* division can in fact be found again in the subsequent text of the first and the second book. However, the duties of §§13–18—at least at first glance—do not fall into the cat-

---

1 See, for instance, Ludwig, 1990, p. XXIII.
2 Quotations for which the reference is not given immediately are covered by the following reference.

egory of 'perfect duties': for 'perfect duties' are introduced as 'negative duties' while §13 articulates no 'duty of omission' and §14 deals with a *command* (!), namely the command to moral self-knowledge (cf. TL 6:441.4). It should probably be called "the *first command* of all [!] duties to oneself" (TL 6:441.2), because it comprises even the imperfect duties.[3] Equally, the "Episodic Section" does not seem to fit without some friction into the range of 'perfect duties toward ourselves,' since it explains merely the error of confusing the 'duties toward ourselves' with the 'duties toward others.' Once again the situation gets more complicated as this section discusses duties toward 'superhuman' and 'subhuman' beings and traces them back to 'duties toward ourselves,' even though the duties toward 'superhuman' and 'subhuman' beings appear in the first outline of section XIX of the "Introduction" where they are contrasted with the 'duties of man toward man' (and thereby also with the 'duties toward ourselves'); in the main text, however, they are not mentioned at all.

One could conclude from these considerations that the three sections "have not been integrated appropriately within the architecture of the work" and may have been only "externally attached to the First Chapter."[4] On the other hand, there is no other place in which they could occur that would be more convincing. Regarding this question Bernd Ludwig's edition takes §4 as a point of reference and suggests that one should simply read these three sections separately. Such a separation would also be consistent with the change of the title in the second edition of the *Doctrine of Virtue*—which was probably done by a corrector: here the three sections are untitled as part of a 'Third Chapter' without any further ado.[5] The

---

3   Cf. Ludwig, 1990, p. XIX.
4   Ludwig, 1990, p. XIX, trans. A.E. If you take a look at the "Preliminary Notes" to the "Metaphysical Foundations of the Doctrine of Virtue" (VATL 23:371), you encounter yet again other divisions into sections, namely "Doctrine of Elements I: duties to oneself, trans. A.E." (VATL 23:399.2 f.) and "Doctrine of Elements II: duties to others, trans. A.E." (VATL 23:406.22). In terms of content Kant arrives already in the first part of the "Doctrine of Elements I: duties to oneself" at the topic of §14 (moral self-knowledge) as well as at the considerations of the "Episodic Section," §§16–18. This indicates that from the very beginning Kant had considered the topics of the problematic sections as important and intended to publish them in the printed edition. Hence the "Preliminary Works" counter Ludwig's thought that §§13–18 were only added retroactively.
5   Forkl sees §§13–18 as an "epistemological" reflection and considers them as systematically related but subordinate to the preceding ones, because they do not deal with the system of material duties, a topic that is dealt with predominantly

confusion created by the differing accounts of this book's structure is now largely removed. Moreover, the position of these three sections can be accounted for in terms of their content. Each of the three sections presents general considerations, which can be related to all of the duties discussed in the previous sections. For they reflect on the conditions in which the hitherto developed specific "perfect duties to oneself" (TL 6:421–437) can be incorporated into acting. Accordingly, they deal with the authorities and methods of moral self-examination necessary for the implementation of these duties (the 'inner court of conscience,' 'moral self-knowledge' and the correct attribution of obligation discussed in the "Episodic Section" and in Kant's repeated clarification of one's relationship to God and to religion).[6] In this respect, they form a meaningful unit that is both homogenous and coherent, whose contents address the acting subject with commands that are prior to specific duties but which, nonetheless, pronounce a 'perfect' obligation and must consequently be formulated after the discussion of 'perfect duties toward oneself.'

B. Overview of the Content in §§13–18

In §13 Kant develops the concept of conscience and attributes to it the status of a "moral predisposition" (TL 6:438.25), which all human beings bear within themselves. This predisposition enables us to become immediately conscious of the "inner court of justice" (TL 6:438.11, trans. A.E.) in ourselves through a feeling. However, the proceedings of the trial, occasioned by a specific case and ultimately leading to a "verdict of conscience" (TL 6:440.25), are also characterized as a "business of a human being with himself" (TL 6:438.26) and are presented as a cooperative achievement of different faculties: practical understanding, the faculty of judgment, and reason. Kant's use of the image of an "*internal court* in the human being" "before which his thoughts accuse or excuse one another" (TL 6:438.11 f.) draws upon the traditional image of the

---

in the *Metaphysics of Morals* (cf. Forkl, 2001, p. 175). In my opinion there is no indication for the assumption that 'subordination' is at work in the text.

6   The topic of moral self-knowledge is once more taken up with similar wording in the subsequent "Book II" (TL 6:444.10) and its "Section II" (TL 6:446.9) ("On a human being's duty to himself to increase his **moral** perfection, that is, for a moral purpose only" (TL 6:446.10 f.)). However, there Kant looks at it from a different angle—asking the question: to what extent does 'moral self-knowledge' contribute to moral perfection?

conscience as *forum internum*[7] and integrates this concept into his critically founded ethics. However, by treating conscience as one of the "aesthetic preliminary concepts [[ä]sthetische Vorbegriffe]" (TL 6:399.2, trans. A.E.) and defining it as a feeling that arises involuntarily, Kant assigns to conscience a role that is subordinate to moral reflection. Conscience does not directly contribute to moral orientation, but merely exhorts us to always subject our actions to moral reflection and criticism, and to appeal to the 'inner court of justice.' We need to strictly separate Kant's subsequent explanations of the command to 'moral self-knowledge' in §§14 and 15 from this concept of 'conscience.' Unlike the section on conscience, these sections do not deal with the question of whether, in a specific case, one has pronounced a practical judgment at all, and whether one can attribute moral value to a specific action. Rather, they merely address the problem of a correct moral self-description and a correct moral self-criticism. In the subsequent "Episodic Section" of §16, Kant deals with the concept of 'duty' in a quite general fashion but makes it clear that relationships of obligation are *only* possible to persons from the world of experience. Following this stipulation (see the subsequent §§17 and 18) he states that a) lifeless nature and b) living but unreasoning nature (plants and animals) as well as c) God and divine beings can never directly become addressees or partners within a relationship of obligation. Towards such beings one can only articulate moral obligations in an indirect way—i.e. through a duty of a human being towards himself. Therefore, duties are only conceivable *"with regard to,"* but not *"to"* these objects or subjects (cf. TL 6:443.25). At the end of the Chapter (§18) Kant returns to his original thought in §13, in which a human being imagines the verdict of conscience to be the voice of another person—be it "either real or merely ideal" (TL 6:438.36–439.2, trans. A.E.)—and thereby personifies the verdict of conscience "by analogy" (TL 6:440.2, trans. A.E.) as the voice of God. This personification represents merely an analogical means of presentation, which is once more clearly brought out in §18. Thus the relationship between the *Doctrine of Virtue* and religion is elaborated on a critical foundation, and the achievement of religion is restricted to conveying the implementation of morality in terms of analogous sensuous schematizations of basic practical concepts.

---

7   On the history of ideas of the conscience as a *forum internum:* see Kittsteiner, 1995.

C. Interpretative Aspects of the Doctrine of Conscience and Their Relation to Religion

First Section of the Second Chapter
"On the Human Being's Duty to Himself as His Own Innate Judge"

a) The Relation Between §13 and section XII of the "Introduction to the doctrine of virtue"

At first glance there is some tension between the considerations in §13 and section XIIb of the "Introduction." For we can read in the "Introduction" that there is no duty to provide ourselves with a conscience (cf. TL 6:400.23–25); §13, however, is about a "human being's duty to himself as his own innate judge" (TL 6:437.29 f.) and does not seem quite compatible with the definition of conscience as an "aesthetic preliminary concept" (TL 6:399.2, trans. A.E.).[8] It is possible to resolve this tension if we read the introductory reflections as a fundamental status determination and phenomenology of conscience. The fact that conscience is dealt with under "aesthetic preliminary concepts" clearly underlines its subordinate status, which Kant generally ascribes to conscience in his moral philosophy. For already in these short introductory remarks, it does become clear that conscience is not meant to be a separate faculty of judgment, but rather a "*subjective* condition of receptiveness to the concept of duty" (TL 6:399.8 f.). As a matter of fact, the main text invariably returns to and complements these determinations of the introductory section. The introduction, for instance, characterizes conscience as a "fact" (TL 6:400.6) and §13 further specifies this "fact" as a "predisposition" (TL 6:438.25) of a human being which requires development and cultivation. The introduction states that conscience does not deal with an object but is "merely [directed, A.E.] to the subject" (TL 6:400.29 f.) so that §13 can speak about "a business of a human being with himself" (TL 6:438.26). Both sections make the following clear: conscience does not pronounce what duty is objectively; nor does it direct human acting. Rather, it directs the attention of the agent to his moral responsibility and the related "duty to acquit or to condemn" (6:400), in every individual case (see also TL 6:438.15, 440.2 f.). Conscience "involuntarily" (TL 6:401.16) exhorts me to examine whether I have in fact compared my actions with my (here judicially acting) "practical reason" (TL

---

8   Cf. e.g. Lehmann, 1980, p. 30.

6:400.28). As Kant emphasizes in the introductory section, with regard to this "subjective judgment" (TL 6:401.7) of conscience, it is impossible to err, since the agent surely knows whether or not he has made a practical judgment in a particular case, i. e. on the basis of the categorical imperative. This is why Kant also rejects the possibility of an "*erring* conscience" (TL 6:401.5), a possibility that was conceded by others such as Baumgarten. Even though §13 no longer speaks about the impossibility of an 'erring conscience,' the explanations there are still compatible with the stipulations in the introductory section, because, even in §13, conscience is not considered to be the result of a fallible conclusion but the involuntary 'awareness of an inner court of justice.' At first the introduction rejects the idea of the existence of a 'direct' duty to provide ourselves with conscience; but at the end of the same section, Kant reminds us of the indirect duty to cultivate our predisposition to conscience in order to obtain a hearing for the voice of the inner judge (cf. TL 6:401.19–21). It is exactly this duty to cultivate our predisposition to conscience that Kant addresses in §13. The only difference here is that the image of the "inner judge" (TL 6:401.20) and the authorities of the court of justice, for which he seeks to obtain a hearing, are explained in more detail. In this respect there is no friction between §13 and the introductory section, but the former may be regarded as an extension of the introductory passages.

Certainly, it remains to be clarified how Kant's characterizations of the conscience within §13, as a "predisposition" (TL 6:438.25) (or even as an "instinct" (V-Mo/Collins 27:351.22, 353.25)) as Kant calls it in his lectures on the one hand, and as an "inner court of justice" (TL 6:438.11, trans. A.E.) on the other hand, are related to each other. Conscience, as a predisposition, seems to be a sensibility capable of cultivation and is therefore clearly distinguished from Baumgarten's logicized concept of conscience. Conversely, in his description of conscience as an 'inner court of justice,' Kant uses characterizations derived from the traditional understanding of conscience as "*syllogismus practicus*" (HN 19:12.9) and particularly from Baumgarten's conception of this syllogism. This syllogism consists in: the norm (*lex aeterna*), (Kant's "practical reason" (6:395.25 f.) which provides the rule), the examination of the things that occurred and their relation to the norm by means of 'joint knowledge' (*Mitwissen*), (*conscientia*), (Kant's subjective imputation of the deed by the 'faculty of judgment'), and the sentence (*conclusio*) (Kant's 'conclusion of reason'). The image of an 'inner court of justice' (in the footnote, for instance, and at the end of the paragraph) presents the activity of conscience as a lawsuit in which a number of authorities fighting a case appear (the prosecutor, the accused, the attorney). Kant further explains this image with reference to the *Second Epistle to the Romans* by the Apostle Paul[9], in which it is not the effect of an immediate disposition or sensibility that is being described. Rather, conscience thereby seems to be some kind of knowledge that is obtained and conveyed on the basis of concept, judgment, conclusion, i.e. through subsumption; this is very close to Baumgarten's view and therefore perplexing, because Kant expressly distances himself from Baumgarten in other passages (cf. TL 6:401.3). Of course, one could try to explain the inconsistency in Kant's representation of conscience by stating that Kant has adopted two conceptions of conscience that were present in the tradition, i.e. the moral-sense-theory and the Wolff-Baumgarten tradition, and incorporated them—obviously with questionable success—into his theory. However, his explanations of conscience in the *Doctrine of Virtue* are so brief that they cannot serve as a basis on which to decide which of the two conceptions Kant used as a foundation to integrate the two traditional conceptions. Therefore, all we can do is draw on further sources in order to reconstruct the Kantian doctrine of conscience.

b) The Doctrine of Conscience in §13 Within the Context of Kant's Lectures and his Other Writings

In his foundational works on morality, Kant hardly mentions conscience (only in GMS 4:404.20, 422.19; KpV 5:98.14). However, the lecture notes, particularly those taken by Vigilantius (see V-MS/Vigil 27:...) provide extensive material on conscience. Further significant passages on conscience, where even the wording is consistent with the *Doctrine of Virtue*, are contained in *On the Miscarriage of All Philosophical Trials in the Theodicy* (MpVT 8:267.15–271.18) and *Religion within the Boundaries of Mere Reason* (in particular RGV 6:185.12–190.8).

Some authors have concluded from the existence of extensive explanations on conscience, in particular, in the lecture notes and in his work on

---

9 According to this passage we must imagine the court as a place where "their thoughts now accusing now even defending them." (Romans 2,15, New International Version (UK)). Insofar as in the Epistle to the Romans conscience is represented as an authority that is equally ascribed to pagans, Kant certainly shares this view. However, in the *Doctrine of Virtue* the citation from Paul's Epistle (Romans 2,15) does not include the reference to the Last Judgment, which directly follows the passage cited above.

religion, that Kant did, in fact, attribute a significant meaning to the concept of conscience in his practical philosophy at the end of his career.[10] According to them, the lecture notes should not be regarded as merely a secondary source in this context, but they do, in fact, provide the crucial material for Kant's doctrine of conscience. Furthermore, they help create a coherent context for the doctrine of conscience that also serves an important systematic function: it is supposed to close a gap left by the ethics of Kant's foundational works insofar as conscience builds a bridge between the "time-transcendent formal personal identity"[11] and the acting of a specific person in reality. Following this train of thought, conscience can be seen as a "real reflection of the practical existence of the individual"[12] and can be assigned the status of a rich and therefore important component of the moral process of judgment. Another interpretation, which also makes ample use of the lecture notes, assigns a systematically supportive function to the *Doctrine of Virtue*, i. e. the function of solving the incentive problem.[13]

Kant's lectures on morals, to which many commentators refer, certainly offer ample material for the further development of his doctrine of conscience. However, it is problematic to consult them in order to illuminate the explanations in Kant's printed publications. The lecture notes are merely transcripts of his lectures, and we must not attach the same importance to them as to the printed publications.[14] Moreover, Lehmann has convincingly pointed out that between 1775 and 1791 Kant presented the same material in his lectures—that is, practical philosophy and ethics according to Baumgarten—despite the fact that the critical works of his moral philosophy had been published in the meantime.[15] Insofar as we have to proceed from the assumption that the most advanced and elaborate version of the doctrine of conscience can only be found in the printed publications, they are the benchmark against which the material in the transcripts must be evaluated.

If, on this assumption, we take a closer look at the other sources of Kant's doctrine of conscience, we can clearly see that Kant has adopted traditional and religious concepts. However, with this material we can

---

10 E.g. Hoffmann, 2002, p. 426.
11 Hoffmann, 2002, p. 433, trans. A.E.
12 Ibid., trans. A.E.
13 Cf. Kittsteiner, 1995, p. 283.
14 On the status of the lecture notes see Stark, 1991, pp. 90–99. See also: Stark, 1988, pp. 7–29.
15 See Lehmann, 1980, p. 28.

also clearly elaborate on how the concept of conscience, through its integration into his critical ethics, has obtained a distinctly critical nature and is therefore of only very limited importance. In his own doctrine of conscience, Kant clearly separates, on the one hand, the concept of 'conscience' from the logicizing variants of the Wolff-Baumgarten-Tradition, and, on the other hand, tries to detach it from the religious context. Within his critical ethics conscience is characterized as a directly felt awareness of the question as to whether or not, in a particular case, the agent has striven to undertake a serious moral examination *at all*, and thereby it is merely assigned a marginal function in the process of moral reflection. Insofar as this characterization of conscience introduces an element of subjective immediacy into Kant's critical ethics, the conception of conscience remains problematic.

When examining the transcript of Vigilantius and Kant's work on religion, we can primarily identify passages which, just like §13 of the *Doctrine of Virtue*, deny our conscience any legitimizing power or legislative competency (cf. V-MS/Vigil 27:616) and which can be fully reconciled with the stipulations of the *Doctrine of Virtue*. Conscience should neither be equated with the faculty of judgment[16] (cf. V-MS/Vigil 27:615), nor

---

16 That conscience must *not* be identified with the faculty of judgment becomes clear from Kant's rejection of an "erring conscience" (TL 6:401.5), for the faculty of judgment can err. Another argument against this identification is Kant's continual emphasis on the fact that conscience speaks involuntarily and immediately. This fact notwithstanding, many commentators have misinterpreted the definition of conscience as "moral faculty of judgment, passing judgment upon itself" (RGV 6:186.10 f.) in Kant's *Religion within the Boundaries of Mere Reason* (e. g. Simon, 2003, p. 433; Hoffman, 2002, pp. 424–443, fn. 425; Wieland, 2001, p. 166). Kant introduces the alleged definition as follows: "Conscience could also be defined as *the moral faculty of judgment, passing judgment upon itself* " (RGV 6:186.10 f.). In the subsequent phrase he immediately points out the problem involved in such definition: "except that this definition would be much in need of prior clarification of the concepts contained in it" (RGV 6:186.11 f.). In my view it seems clear that Kant rejects this definition of conscience as problematic. Kant knew that it was not sufficient to refer to the faculty of judgment in this context, because the question of conscience would thereby be answered with only an empty phrase. Thomas Sören Hoffmann elaborates in minute detail Kant's doctrine of conscience and argues convincingly against Nietzsche's criticism that the Kantian model of conscience does not follow a mechanic but rather a reflexively structured conception. He assumes that conscience plays a "central role" (Hoffmann, 2001, p. 426, trans. A.E.) in the philosophy of late Kant. However, in my opinion he fails to show clearly why a conflict between

misconceived as a legislative power—for that is incumbent on "practical reason" alone (cf. V-MS/Vigil 27:616) to judge the lawfulness or unlaw-fulness of an action (cf. V-MS/Vigil 27:613). Furthermore, Kant did not see conscience as a naturally given or even innate 'faculty of judgment.' Just as the passages in the *Doctrine of* Virtue, the lecture notes consistently point out the necessity of the cultivation and 'awakening' of a predisposition, which Kant, in his *Doctrine of Virtue*, later calls an "intellectual and [...] moral" (TL 6:438.24 f.) predisposition. Thus, conscience neither emerges through internalization of an 'external' or a moral authority nor is it 'made' by and for ourselves, but "[e]very human being *has* a conscience" (an internal judge) (cf. 6:438.13) in himself, provided he has practical reason. In exactly this sense—i.e. conditional on the competence of practical reason—conscience is to be regarded as a "fact" (TL 6:400.31).

Additionally, the two different working modes of conscience—on the one hand, as a scrutinizing and warning conscience that insists on a practical examination in every anticipated case, and on the other hand, as a judging conscience that conducts an evaluation after the executed actions *ex post*—can be found, not only in the lecture transcripts, but also in an identical characterization in §13.

When evaluating Kant's writing on religion and the small study *On the Miscarriage of All Philosophical Trials in Theodicy* we need to take into account that, in these writings, he treats the role of conscience in the context of religious questions and its application to specific cases (i.e. "matters of faith," (MpVT 8:267.17)). However, the original ethical function, which Kant tries to assign to conscience in his *Doctrine of Virtue*, clearly emerges in these contexts as well. Kant not only regards the religious attitude throughout the above-mentioned writings as subordinate to their moral attitude,[17] but also emphasizes that, in the context of "matters of faith," conscience is neither a legislative nor a judicial authority that can be traced back to divine law. He thus continues to characterize conscience as a kind of 'inner business' that only raises our awareness as to "whether it [i.e. reason, A.E.] has actually undertaken, with all diligence, that examination of actions (whether they are right or wrong)" (RGV 6:186.16–18). Conscience calls upon the human being himself

---

the moral law and a "decision of conscience" in this case should be unimaginable (cf. Hoffmann, 2001, p. 425, trans. A.E.)).

17 Cf. Kant, MpVT 8:267.10 f.: "For with this disposition he proved that he did not found his morality on faith, but his faith on morality."

"to witness *for* or *against* himself whether *this* has taken place or not" (RGV 6:186.18–20; third emphasis A.E.). One can indeed err in the judgment on what is objectively right, but in the judgment "whether I in fact believe to be right (or merely pretend it)" (MpVT 8:268.16, trans. A.E.) one can absolutely not be mistaken.

The examples quoted in the writing on religion and in *The Conflict of the Faculties*, the inquisitor (RGV 6:186.21–36) and Abraham's sacrifice of Isaac (SF 7:63n.32–38), are meant to clarify this point. Both cases do, in fact, deal with "matters of faith" and this is exactly why they highlight the ethical significance and impact of conscience, which is independent from all religious authorities and—at least in Kant's view—noticeable by every human being. Both the ideologically blinded inquisitor, who tortures people of different religious convictions, and Abraham, who is to slaughter his own son like a sheep, possess practical reason and therefore could have, and should have, refrained from their deeds, had they only listened to the warning voice of their conscience. Their conscience could not have given them any explanation as to whether the principles of their actions were objectively right or wrong, but it would have called for their "diligence" (RGV 6:185.23 f.) and sincerity and would have thereby suggested that there was always the possibility "of coming across an error" (RGV 6:187.12 f., trans. A.E.). They would have thus understood that it was unscrupulous to act upon these principles "at the risk of violating a human duty in itself certain" (RGV 6:187.14 f.). Even in cases where high authorities (such as in the examples taken from the writing on religion mentioned above: the church or even God) have commanded the action one should, according to the wording in the *Doctrine of Virtue*, act with "utmost scrupulosity (*scrupulositas*)" (TL 6:440.12, trans. A.E.) and ask oneself whether or not one can err in the judgment on the rightness of the action and whether or not one should rather refrain from acting, because that possibility cannot be excluded.

In retrospect the question of conscience—whether or not after serious examination one could have known that an action was morally wrong—is treated as a process of self-examination, which we usually imagine to be analogous to an 'inner court of justice.' It is conscience that initiates this process of examination by somehow appealing to the 'inner court of justice,' where the human being plays the part of the prosecutor and reminds himself of the duty to verify by all means whether he, as the agent, can be absolved of any guilt or whether he is to be sentenced or condemned for his conscious negligence of a particular duty. Therefore, this hearing is about nothing less than the question of the practical im-

putation, i. e. imputation undertaken through the application of the categorical imperative. In the end the very same person, now playing the
part of the judge, pronounces a judgment on the question of whether
in the case now under scrutiny one has acted according to ones moral
duty, or whether one has actually absolved oneself from a well-understood
duty without any permission and declared oneself, unlawfully, not responsible. The trial of the 'inner court of justice' in its imaginary and personalized form is a self-examination of the question: "whether I in fact
believe to be right (or merely pretend it)" (MpVT 8:268.16, trans.
A.E.). Unlike in the external court of justice, the principle of the
Roman Law "*minima non curat praetor*" (TL 6:440.12)—"the praetor
is not concerned about trifles" (trans. A.E.)—is not to be applied; 'utmost
diligence' should prevail. Kant articulates this 'diligence' in other writings
as a principle, the application of which is recommended by conscience
along the following lines: "*we ought to venture nothing where there is danger that it might be wrong*"[18] (RGV 6:185.23 f.). On the same grounds,
but from a linguistic point of view, Kant rejects the usage of wrong metaphors such as "*wide* conscience" (TL 6:440.18), calling it a glorifying,
conciliatory representation of an actually existing unconscientiousness.
Thus, a dispute before the "inner court of justice" (TL 6:438.11,
trans. A.E.) cannot be settled "amicably (*per amicabilem compositionem*),"
but must be decided "with all the rigor of right" and therefore unambiguously and in view of the distinction between "*acquitting*" and "*condemning*" (cf. TL 6:440.22–26).

Kant confers on conscience the status of a predisposition, which is
given to us along with the faculty to determine ourselves reasonably in
practical respect, and which is therefore considered an "intellectual and
[…] moral" (TL 6:438.24 f.) predisposition. It designates an emotional
sensibility for our moral claims, which indicates that we are aware of
our moral duty. Since it is merely a predisposition, conscience requires
further cultivation. Through techniques of self-persuasion, through systematic distraction and continuous blunting, it can certainly deteriorate
so that the receptiveness for moral claims then gradually decreases. In
contrast, when fully developed conscience initiates a "subjective judgment" (TL 6:401.7) of the person as to whether or not she has pronounced a practical judgment at all, i.e. whether or not she has actually

---

18 And Kant continues: "Quod dubitas, ne feceris! Plin. […] Now it is understanding, not conscience, which judges whether an action is in general right or wrong"
(RGV 6:185.24–186.3, trans. A.E.).

contemplated the question of the universalizability of her maxim. Even if the agent may be mistaken about her objective duties, the verdict of her conscience—in terms of a determination regarding the existence or non-existence of practical responsibility—cannot err. Kant thus restricts the accomplishments of conscience and tries to prevent the erection of an 'unverifiable' authority through conscience, which could enter into competition with practical reason. Therefore, in Kant's moral philosophy conscience is assigned neither a causal role nor a leading role in terms of content, nor a generally or systematically important role, but only a marginal one. This determination of conscience is distinctly different from the traditional concept of conscience as well as from the modern notion of conscience.[19] The fact that the *Doctrine of Virtue* deals with conscience at all cannot provide evidence for a revaluation of conscience, but is proof of Kant's ambition to find a place in his ethics even for this concept—of course, a place corresponding to its marginal position: the phenomenon 'conscience' is only relevant in connection with questions regarding the application of moral principles. It is a matter of no particular interest, unless the purpose of its examination is to further specify and elaborate the claims of the general moral law in consideration of the concrete conditions of human existence or to explore the concrete human conditions of the application of the moral law.

c) The Personification of Conscience as Inner Judge and God
(§13 and §18)

The metaphorical representation of conscience as a trial with prosecutor, accused, advocate and judge already personalizes the moral process of self-

---

19 On the modern concept of conscience cf. e. g. Schwemmer, 2008, pp. 133–135. With regard to the central significance of conscience in the moral process of judgment, in the affirmative, cf. Spaemann, 2004, p. 75; the suggestion to return to Kant's concept of conscience comes from: Funke, 1971, pp. 226–251. Funke puts emphasis on the difference between the modern concept of conscience and the Kantian one: "Der Garant für das Gelingen der moralphilosophischen Untersuchung ist nicht ein ‚Spruch des Gewissens‘ und nicht die Überzeugung eines ‚wahren Bewusstseins‘, sondern das Faktum, dass die Menschen Pflichten kennen und anerkennen, bzw. sittliche Gesetze hinnehmen und fordern" (Funke, 1971, p. 246). According to him the Kantian concept of conscience, which makes sure that the principle "*quod dubitas, ne feceris!*" (RGV 6:185.24 f.) is applied, should be opposed to all irrational, pre-rational conceptions promoting a "good conscience" and a "true consciousness" (Funke, 1971, p. 251).

examination. However, this sensualization of the examination of the conscience is peculiar because apart from the personalization of conscience, this "business of a human being with himself" (TL 6:438.26, trans. A.E.) is represented as if the voice of another person—of a real or merely ideal person—pronounced the verdict. This projection of the voice of conscience into an imaginary other is necessary, according to Kant, to dispel the contradiction, which seems to arise from the self-reflexive structure of conscience, even in the analogous representation of the court of justice (where one and the same person is to play the part of the prosecutor and the accused). The transcendental explanation of the possibility to impose a duty to oneself (cf. §§1–3 (TL 6:417.5–418.23)) has already made it necessary that a human being views himself "under two attributes: first as a *sensible being* and secondly as an intelligible being and that through practical reflection a human being somehow creates a "doubled self," and yet remains the self of that same human being (*numero idem*) (cf. TL 6:439n. 23–30, trans. A.E.). Similarly, the defendant and the innate judge are introduced as different persons within the metaphor of the 'court of justice.' If the judge of the trial is an imaginary person separate from the agent, he must still be a "scrutinizer of hearts," (TL 6:439.4) in order to perform his office correctly. However, this can only be an omnipotent person who imposes all obligation, and thus "conscience must be thought of as the subjective principle of being accountable to God for all one's deeds" (TL 6:439.13–15)—and therefore, by analogy the judge at the court of justice cannot but be defined as a divine "lawgiver for all rational beings" (TL 6:440.2 f.). Hence, the will that was in evidence in moral philosophical theory as 'practical reason in itself' does not seem to be the agent's own lawgiving will, but is imagined— "following out the analogy" (TL 6:440.2, trans. A.E.)—as the will of God.[20] This sensualization of conscience by analogy does not, of course, have the status of a proof of God's existence nor does it give a human being an obligation "to *assume* that such a supreme being *actually exists* outside himself" (TL 6:439.19–20). In addition, it is not conceivable at all, as distinctly pointed out in §18 at the end of the "Episodic Section," to be under obligation to any 'superhuman beings' (cf. TL 6:444.1 f.), which cannot be encountered within the limits of our experience. This is just simply not possible, because the idea of God "proceeds

---

20 Therefore, J. Simon's view is absolutely convincing: "Der Glaube (als der für das eigene Handeln als hinreichend erachtete Modus der Weltorientierung) ist und bleibt für Kant etwas Ästhetisches" (Simon, 2003, p. 436).

entirely from our own reason and we ourselves make it" (TL 6:443.32–444.1), as shown in §13. Yet Kant confers the status of a duty upon the aesthetic projection of moral obligation and self-examination to a divine being, and emphatically states: "to have religion is a duty of the human being to himself" (TL 6:444.7 f.): for if we view the moral duty to ourselves as an obligation towards a divine will and his commands, this could give at least some stability to the abstract and causal relation of the intelligible to the sensible (which cannot be explained by "any theory" (TL 6:439n.32 f., trans. A.E.), and thus it is "of the greatest moral fruitfulness" (TL 6:444.5 f.).

d) The Relation of the Doctrine of Conscience to Critical Ethics

By integrating the concept of conscience into the *Doctrine of Virtue*, an element of immediacy enters Kant's critical ethics: conscience speaks immediately and therefore infallibly. Its voice does not give the agent any certainty concerning whether or not a particular action was or is morally right or wrong. However, the sentence of conscience makes us unmistakably aware of the fact that the person has actually subjected his action to the moral claim of the Categorical Imperative and examined it accordingly. From this point of view the voice of conscience at least conveys some subjective moral certainty.

According to Kant's works on the foundation of ethics, the agent is "immediately" certain merely of the awareness of duty. Moreover, the moral law "cannot prescribe the internal act of the determination of the will by the concept of duty, but only the maxim to seek the pureness of the incentive"[21]. We are, however, indirectly required to explain to ourselves critically our own true motivation for acting; but we cannot say with certainty whether or not our actions or the actions of others are morally good. If we want to discover the true *motivation* for our actions we must not only 'attend to ourselves' but also look critically at our actions by forming hypotheses on their 'moral meaning.'[22] In such a process of examination, we make ourselves and our actions the object of empirical examination, the results of which are—like all empirical knowledge—fallible.[23] A fundamental uncertainty with respect to the real *motives* of the subjective moral consciousness must therefore always be conceded. We

---

21 Gregor, 1990, p. LV, trans. A.E.
22 On the problem of establishing maxims: cf. Esser, 2008, pp. 279–302.
23 On the distinction between maxim and motive of an action: cf. Esser, 2004, pp. 273 ff.

can obtain certainty only with regard to the 'aptitude' or 'inaptitude' of a *maxim* for the universal legislation, if and because it is the result of a deliberate and consciously conducted process of examination. However, whether, after examining a maxim in this fashion, we have actually adopted it as a maxim for our actions and acted upon it, must always remain in question, and shall ultimately make us continuously submit our actions to moral critique. Such fundamental uncertainty and the concomitant subjective doubt concerning whether one can rightfully claim a moral attitude for oneself, are in no way detrimental to the development of good character. Rather, they make an attitude stand out as moral, by keeping the process of self-examination open for further reflection. The subjective certainty that one's actions or the maxims of one's actions fully accord with one's own moral principles, coupled with the subjective certainty of having sincerely examined all aspects of one's own actions, which a 'good conscience' would ensure, even holds the danger of detaching oneself from the critical process of examination and thereby abandoning further self-criticism.

The situation in the *Doctrine of Virtue* is entirely different. The introduction of the concept of conscience makes it difficult to differentiate between the consciousness of an objective duty and the moral self-consciousness of a subject, and gives the agent another source of certainty: the self-certainty of moral 'self-consciousness.' However, by introducing this concept, the *Doctrine of Virtue* promotes the danger that this self-consciousness enters into competition with the claims of duty. The agent could be inclined to think that conscience "is at this point already true conscience in and for itself"[24] because "it has its truth in the immediate certainty of itself"[25] as Hegel points out in his critique of the concept of conscience.[26] Hegel, for instance, provides the diagnosis that in this "independent self-certainty, with its independence of knowledge and decision, both morality and evil have their common root"[27]. According to him, the recourse to conscience already expresses "the majesty of its elevation above specific law and every content of duty"[28]. Kant may also have been aware of the potential consequences of a subject's appropriating

---

24 Hegel, 1952 [1821], §137.
25 Hegel, 1977 [1807], §387.
26 On the dialectics of conscience in Hegel and its reference to Kant: see Köhler, 2006, pp. 211 ff.
27 Hegel, 1952 [1821], §139.
28 Hegel, 1977 [1807], §397.

morality because he considers himself to be sure about the verdict of conscience. He may have tried to prevent this appropriation by reducing the certainty, which was to ensue from the verdict, to the alternative "acquitting or condemning" (TL 6:400.28). The examination of one's conscience is not meant to lead to self-contented blessedness, but at best "relief from preceding anxiety" (TL 6:440.31 f.). Even a conscience that merely exonerates the agent, can enter into competition with the claim of duty to normative objectivity insofar as its judgment claims to be infallible. But even a conviction sincerely grounded in conscience can be *objectively* wrong; therefore even conscience can be mistaken about its own sincerity. The fact that conscience occurs as an unspecific feeling of displeasure would seem to rule out the immediate certainty it allegedly conveys. Even if this feeling of displeasure immediately enters our awareness, it would be a mediated and fallible act of interpretation to take it as a sign of a bad conscience, and we should seek to reflect on the emergence-conditions of this feeling. Only through such a reflection, involving the examination of the moral valence of these conditions, may we conclude with certainty that we are dealing with a moral feeling—i.e. conscience rather than a feeling of displeasure resulting from a presumed moral obligation. Thus conscience can at best represent an aspect of the comprehensive process of self-examination, which will never achieve infallibility, but it can never lead to certainty itself. Hermann Cohen went further and pointed out the problematic possibility of confusing conscience with the moral incentive, and took a problematic example from Kant's brief essay *On a Presumed Right to Lie* to illustrate that, in this case, the retreat to moral inwardness and the erection of a further moral authority may have highly problematic effects:

> [...] if the decision had to be that, in spite of the most serious concerns, I have to give my friend up to the murderer, because otherwise I would tarnish my self-awareness with a lie, it seems as if this self-awareness was conceived egoistically and naturalistically, in isolation from the larger totality. It is not self-awareness in the ethical sense, which would be threatened by this attack. Such ethical self-awareness does not even empathize with the soul of the other whose life is at risk; it does not even need this intermediation [...] Such ethically trained self-awareness does not need any private control as to whether conscience's shield of honour remained blank and immaculate.[29]

The individualistic understanding of morality that was criticized by Cohen and to which the doctrine of conscience leads, cannot avoid the

---

29 Cohen, 1981, p. 527, trans. A.E.

fatal consequence that a person who claims to have acted by the sincerity of her conscience would have to be absolved of her responsibility, even if she acted on a morally wrong maxim. On the basis of these considerations, it seems questionable whether Kant's *Doctrine of Virtue* is systematically necessary in this form. It is far more obvious that Kant's conviction that he needed to integrate the concept of conscience into his ethics at all results from his conciliatoriness towards the religious tradition of this concept.[30] Within his ethics one can find another conception that is more appropriate for the examination of subjective morality and can also be better systematically combined with the insights of critical ethics. This conception ensues from the demand of self-knowledge, which Kant describes as a toilsome process of examining oneself and avoiding self-deception. In the text it directly follows the section on conscience. In contrast to the doctrine of conscience, the implementation of the command to self-knowledge is a *task* which cannot and must not be completed, for otherwise it would be suggested that there was a 'self,' ready and complete with respect to its moral determination, which, moreover, could be entirely known.[31]

---

30 Kittsteiner's consideration that Kant's concept of conscience could solve the problem of the incentives (*Triebfederproblem*) is countered by the fact that conscience is merely an aesthetic preliminary concept without taking on the role as motive for an action. Even §13 does not change this status, since also there conscience continues to act merely as a subjective reiterated self-control. The incentive of a moral action is the 'respect for the law' and not the verdict of conscience and even less so, as Hill points out, the fear of the tortures of a bad conscience. He may be right in saying: "being motivated by conscience may be (and one hopes often is) fundamentally a matter of being motivated by respect for morality, and so ultimately by respect for the legitimate claims of others and our owns better nature" (Hill, 2002, p. 249). However, it remains to be verified whether this is true in every individual case.

31 Simon attributes to conscience the function of casting doubt on the certitude of an ethical reflection, and of rendering "a certitude reached at a particular point uncertain through new questions and doubts" (Simon, 2003, p. 437). It surely is one of the functions of conscience to initiate the 'lawsuit before the court.' In my view, one might still critically get back to this consideration with the question whether or not conscience speaks to us invariably and at the right point in time. 'Moral self-awareness' or con-science, as conscience is understood by many commentators, is not 'given,' but must be actively created through practical self-determination of a person. Therefore, we cannot exclude that a person's conscience fails insofar as it does not speak at all.

Second Section of the Second Chapter
"On the **First Command** of All Duties To Oneself" (§§14 and 15)

The "Second Section" deals with 'moral self-knowledge' which unlike the self-examination of conscience, does not only ask whether or not I have in fact subjected my actions to demands of practical obligation and the critique ensuing from it. It verifies whether or not the maxims on which I act are actually moral and whether or not I only present my actions through euphemistic self-descriptions as morally good. The faculty of judgment contributes to this self-examination insofar as it must critically judge the imputations of the acts. The picture we have of ourselves can thereby be critically changed: this examination may reveal that some good attitude, which a person uncritically regards as a moral act and credit himself with it, is actually mere moral luck, the result of a merely accidentally good pre-disposition or the privilege of his circumstances. Conversely, immoral action, the cause of which allegedly lies in our reality's pressures to adapt, may, after critical self-examination, ultimately have to be evaluated as pertaining to the moral status of the person. This relentless self-scrutiny, to which Kant refers as "descent into the hell of self-cognition" (TL 6:441.19) by using a quotation from Hamann[32], is conditional on the relentless examination not of one's psychological motivation—even though Kant's reference to the "depths (the abyss) of one's heart which are quite difficult to fathom" (TL 6:441.12 f.) may seem to suggest this from a linguistic point of view—but rather of the maxim that one has actually adopted.

This toilsome, critical moral self-cognition is the beginning of all "human wisdom" (TL 6:441.13 f.) and it is the precondition of that radical, moral revolution which Kant considered to be possible for every human being at any time. In his preliminary drafts for the *Doctrine of Virtue* Kant dedicates a separate section (VATL 23:402.6 ff.) to that "human wisdom" and recognizes in it the sincerity necessary to this end (VATL 23:400.17–19): "a formal duty to oneself" which, however, is not "virtue, but subjective precondition of all virtues." Therefore, it has found the right position in this 'Third Chapter.'

The subsequent brief §15 emphasizes that moral self-cognition always includes valuing this specific faculty and thus excludes an "enthusiastic" (TL 6:443.21) contempt of oneself or of the entire human species, which ultimately provides relief from the serious endeavor of self-correc-

---

32 Cf. Hamann, 1950 [1761], p. 164; cf. also SF 7:55.29 f.

tion and moral perfection. Such 'flight into the general' with an attitude
of resignation is detrimental to the improvement of one's own morality
and to righting the wrongs that exist, just like the empty commitment
to the good, be it in form of a mere declaration of intent or of 'wishes
and prayers,' all of which Kant has often denounced. Instead, in his ethics
Kant demands distinctly pragmatic and active proofs of the presumably
good attitude, which are to be reflected in observable acts of will. The
meaning of these demands is revealed as soon as they are seen in the context of Kant's concept of will and his conception of maxims. We should
talk about 'will' as opposed to 'wish' only if the agent has, in fact, made
efforts (mustered all his resources) in order to realize the presumably intended purpose. Against this background Kant's conception of a maxim
takes on a less individualistic dimension, for as a subjective principle of
the will, it does not express the psychological intention, but it rather *represents* the end that the agent really pursues with his will. Since this *representation* may be wrong and distorted because it may have fallen for an
inner lie, a critical self-examination—which in turn is conditional on the
internal judge—is indispensable (cf. the close connection to TL
6:430.27–431.3).

Episodic Section
"On an **amphiboly in moral concepts of reflection,** taking what is a human being's duty to himself for a duty to other beings"

As its title announces, the "Episodic Section" is an 'interpolated,' append-
ed section, which does not serve the function of a proof but merely the
task of an explanation—just as in other writings by Kant (cf. KU
5:401 f., note §76; or RL 6:291 f., §32). At this point in the preliminary
notes of the *Doctrine of Virtue*, we have already come across some matters
from the "Episodic Section" (§§16–18)—specifically in the draft of the
"Doctrine of Elements I: duties to oneself" (VATL 23:399.2 f.). Even
there, great importance is attached to the discussion of the question: towards what kinds of beings is a relationship of duty possible at all? The
paragraph on the "duties to oneself" (VATL 23:399.3) even begins with
the "duty of religion" (VATL 23:399.6), which is discussed only in §18 in
the printed edition, and clearly states entirely in line with the amphiboly-
section: "We have no direct duties to God and to living organisms in the
world, but it is all direct duties to ourselves" (VATL 23:400.24–26,
trans. A.E.). A problematic amphiboly or ambiguity may arise in the pres-

ent case with regard to the concept of 'duty.' For if it is only taken as a
concept without critically reflecting its possible objects, it will lead to a
confusion ("amphiboly" (TL 6:442.4)) of objects when wrongly applied
to objects to which we cannot develop a relationship of obligation. Then
we believe that we have duties to objects "*other than persons*," to "*nonhu-
man*" (plants, minerals or animals) or "*superhuman*" objects and beings
(angels, God) (cf. TL 6:442.26–32). The 'transcendental reflection' is
meant to explain this error for it shows, as in the amphiboly-chapter in
the *Critique of Pure Reason*, "for which cognitive power" the objects are
objects (cf. KrV A261/B317) and explains "the cognitive power in
which they [the concepts, A.E.] subjectively belong to each other"
(KrV A261/B317). With regard to the concept of duty, it can be
shown clearly that the object of this concept can only be a will because
a relationship of obligation is conditional on the relationship between
persons who are able to relate to themselves consciously and normatively
by virtue of the will. This condition of mutually connecting wills necessitates that these wills pertain to persons who really, i. e. by experience,
exist; otherwise we would not notice any expression of their will and
therefore not be aware of it. Since our experience so far could only account for men as beings who are capable of a personal will, relationships
of obligation are therefore only possible among human beings.

However, nature can neither be a self-committing contractual partner
nor the addressee of duties to nature itself or to us, just because nature has
no will in this practical sense. Therefore, attributing volition to nature is
merely a projection or an illegitimate subreption.[33] We cannot commit
nature, which has no will, to any actions, but we can commit ourselves
to handling nature in a certain way. As a result, our relationship to living
and to lifeless nature can only be designed as a relationship of self-com-
mitment. Once this is understood in the transcendental reflection (by
pure reason), we must exclude a relationship of duty with regard to the
objects mentioned in the text—be it nature, the realm of animals or
the realm of plants. That it is impossible to enter into a direct relationship of duty with nature does not imply, of course, that we can deal with
nature as we please: senseless destruction of nature or cruelty to animals,
even unnecessary research based on vague speculations are morally inad-
missible, because they destroy the moral feelings of man and (this, however, would be a duty toward others) jeopardize the foundation of exis-

---

33 On the concept of subreption see KU 5:257.22 f.: "substitution of a respect for
     the object instead of for the idea of humanity in our subject."

tence of free beings in the future. Even gratitude toward 'useful animals' (cf. TL 6:443.22–25) is indirectly part of the duty of man. However, such gratitude is merely a duty he must impose upon himself, because only he can assign himself to it. The often-criticized 'anthropomorphism,' which is apparently connected with this insight, has its systematic conceptual rationale in the concept of duty rather than in any anthropological requirements or human needs.

References

Cohen, Hermann (1904) [⁵1981], *Ethik des reinen Willens*, Hildesheim: Olms.

Donagan, Alan (1977), *The Theory of Morality*, Chicago/London: University of Chicago Press.

Esser, Andrea Marlen (2004), *Eine Ethik für Endliche*, Stuttgart-Bad Cannstatt: Frommann-Holzboog.

Esser, Andrea Marlen (2008), "Kant on Solving Moral Conflicts", in: Monika Betzler (ed.), *Kant's Ethics of Virtue*, Berlin/New York: Walter de Gruyter, pp. 279–302.

Fischer, Norbert (2004), *Kants Metaphysik und Religionsphilosophie*, Hamburg: Meiner.

Forkl, Markus (2001), *Kants System der Tugendpflichten: Eine Begleitschrift zu den Metaphysischen Anfangsgründen der Tugendlehre*, Frankfurt/M.: Peter Lang.

Funke, Gerhard (1971), "Gutes Gewissen, falsches Bewusstsein, richtende Vernunft", in: *Zeitschrift für philosophische Forschung*, vol. 25, pp. 226–251.

Gregor, Mary (1990), "Kants System der Pflichten in der Metaphysik der Sitten", in: Immanuel Kant, *Metaphysische Anfangsgründe der Tugendlehre*, Bernd Ludwig (ed.), Hamburg: Meiner, pp. XXIX–LXVI.

Hamann, Johann Georg (1761) [1950], "Abaelardi Virbii: Chimärische Einfälle über den zehnten Theil der Briefe die Neueste Litteratur betreffend", in: id., *Sämtliche Werke*, vol. 2: *Schriften über Philosophie/Philologie/Kritik 1758–1763*, Josef Nadler (ed.), Wien: Herder, pp. 157–164.

Hegel, Georg Wilhelm Friedrich (1807) [1977], *Phenomenology of Spirit*, trans. by Arnold V. Miller, Oxford: Clarendon Press.

Hegel, Georg Wilhelm Friedrich (1821) [1952], *Philosophy of Right*, trans. by Thomas M. Knox, Oxford: Oxford University Press.

Hill, Thomas E. (2002), "Punishment, Conscience, and Moral Worth", in: Mark Timmons (ed.), *Kant's 'Metaphysics of Morals': Interpretative Essays*, Oxford: Oxford University Press, pp. 233–255.

Hoffmann, Thomas Sören (2002), "Gewissen als praktische Apperzeption: Zur Lehre vom Gewissen in Kants Ethik-Vorlesungen", in: *Kant-Studien*, vol. 93, pp. 424–443.

Kittsteiner, Heinz Dieter (1995), *Die Entstehung des modernen Gewissens*, Frankfurt/M.: Suhrkamp.

Köhler, Dietmar (2006), "Hegels Gewissensdialektik", in: Dietmar Köhler/Otto Pöggeler (eds.), *G.W.F. Hegel. Phänomenologie des Geistes*, Berlin: Akademie Verlag, pp. 211–228. (Klassiker Auslegen, vol. 16.)

Langthaler, Rudolf (1991), *Kants Ethik als System der Zwecke*, Berlin/New York: Walter de Gruyter.

Lehmann, Gerhard (1980), *Kants Tugenden: Neue Beiträge zur Geschichte und Interpretation der Philosophie Kants*, Berlin/New York: Walter de Gruyter.

Ludwig, Bernd (1990), "Einleitung", in: Immanuel Kant, *Metaphysische Anfangsgründe der Tugendlehre: Metaphysik der Sitten. Zweiter Teil*, Bernd Ludwig (ed.), Hamburg: Meiner, pp. XIII–LXX.

Schwemmer, Oswald (^{2}2008), "Gewissen", in: Jürgen Mittelstraß (ed.), *Enzyklopädie Philosophie und Wissenschaftstheorie*, vol. 3, Stuttgart/Weimar: Metzler, pp. 133–135.

Simon, Josef (2003), *Die fremde Vernunft und die Sprache der Philosophie*, Berlin/New York: Walter de Gruyter.

Spaemann, Robert (2004), *Moralische Grundbegriffe*, München: Beck.

Stark, Werner (1988), "Zu Kants Mitwirkung an der Drucklegung seiner Schriften", in: Bernd Ludwig (ed.), *Kants Rechtslehre*, Hamburg: Meiner, pp. 7–29.

Stark, Werner (1991), "quaestiones in terminis: Überlegungen und Fakten zum Nachschreibewesen im universitären Lehrbetrieb des 18. Jahrhunderts. Aus den Präliminarien einer Untersuchung zu Kants Vorlesungen", in: Martin Stern (ed.), *Textkonstitution bei mündlicher und schriftlicher Überlieferung*, vol.1 (editio suppl.), Tübingen: Niemeyer, pp. 90–99.

Velleman, David James (1999), "The Voice of Conscience", in: *Proceedings of the Aristotelian Society*, vol. 99, pp. 57–76.

Wieland, Wolfgang (2001), *Urteil und Gefühl: Kants Theorie der Urteilskraft*, Göttingen: Vandenhoeck & Ruprecht.

Imperfect Duties to Oneself
(TL 6:444–447)

Thomas Hill

The text at TL 6:444.9–447.17 concludes Kant's discussion of ethical duties to oneself with Book II entitled "On a Human Being's Imperfect Duties to Himself (with Regard to His End)" (TL 6:444.11 f.). The discussion is divided into two sections with descriptive titles: "On a Human Being's Duty to Himself to Develop and Increase His **Natural Perfection**, That Is, for a Pragmatic Purpose" (TL 6:444.14–16) and "On a Human Being's Duty to Himself to Increase His **Moral** Perfection, That Is, for a Moral Purpose Only" (TL 6:446.10 f.).

My comments will be divided as follows. *First*, as background I review some general points about *ethical* duties, duties *to oneself*, and *imperfect* duties. *Second*, I summarize and comment briefly on the text regarding the duty to develop and increase one's natural perfection, book II, section I, §19 and §20 (TL 6:444.13–446.8). Here the main questions are: what is required, and why? We need also to consider the significance of "for a Pragmatic Purpose" (TL 6:444.15–16). *Third*, I review and comment briefly on the text regarding the duty to increase one's moral perfection, section II, §21 and §22 (TL 6:446.9–447.17). Again, the main questions are: what is required, and why? Here we must consider the significance of "the *frailty* (*fragilitas*) of human nature" (TL 6:446.27) and the 'unfathomable depths' (cf. TL 6:447.1) of the human heart. The answer should help to see why the duty to increase one's moral perfection is "imperfect" (TL 6:446.26) even though it does not allow the same kinds of latitude as the imperfect duties of beneficence and cultivation of one's natural powers.

I. Background: Some Basic Distinctions

The main concepts employed in TL 6:444–446 have been presented in previous sections. A brief review of some points, however, may be useful for subsequent discussion.

Ethical Duties

The imperfect duties to oneself are *ethical* duties, belonging to the *Doctrine of Virtue*, as opposed to *juridical* duties as discussed in the *Doctrine of Right*. Among other things, this implies that they are not duties that can be externally legislated (e. g. by Parliament or Congress) or enforced (e. g. by police) in a legal system. Further, rather than prescribing specific actions, *ethics* (in the narrow sense relevant here) basically prescribes *ends*. Kant's explanation of the supreme principle of the *Doctrine of Virtue* has elements of the universal law formula and the humanity formula of the categorical imperative. Most generally, it says "act in accordance with a maxim of *ends* that it can be a universal law for everyone to have" (TL 6:395.15 f.). Kant explains: "In accordance with this principle a human being is an end for himself as well as for others" (TL 6:395.17). Thus, beyond merely avoiding using himself (or his humanity) as a mere means, it is "his duty to make the human being as such his end" (TL 6:395.20 f.). On this basis, presumably, Kant proposes that the two main 'ends that are duties' are the perfection of oneself and the happiness of others (cf. TL 6:385.30–388.30, 391.26–394.12).

It should be noted that Kant seems to use two different ideas of an *end*. Perfection and happiness are ends of a kind that can be developed and promoted to various degrees, but at least in the *Groundwork* humanity as an end in itself seems to be a status or value, ascribed by reason, to be respected and honored in various ways rather than itself an end literally to be promoted (like the happiness of others) or increased (like the degree of perfection of our natural and moral powers).[1] There need be no inconsistency here. 'Treating humanity in each person as an *end in itself*' in the *Groundwork* may not mean quite the same as 'making the human being as such one's *end*' in the *Doctrine of Virtue*. In the *Doctrine of Virtue*, for example, Kant primarily focuses on how a proper regard for humanity requires more than refraining from specific acts that treat per-

---

1   At GMS 4:430, Kant does suggest that by developing "the capacities for greater perfection" (GMS 4:430.13 f.) that are "in humanity" (GMS 4:430.13) we not only "harmonize" (GMS 4:430.22) with humanity as an end in itself but "promote" (GMS 4:430.24) it. At GMS 4:437, however, Kant says the end in itself is not "an end to be produced" (GMS 4:437.27) but "self-sufficient" (GMS 4:437.27), "conceived only negatively" (GMS 4:437.28), "an end we should never act against" (GMS 4:437.28) in contrast to "every end that has to be *brought about*" (GMS 4:437.24).

sons as mere means.[2] If so, then the *Groundwork* principle that we must treat humanity as an *end-in-itself* rather than a mere means can be consistently regarded as a *ground* for making perfection and happiness *ends* (in a narrower sense) to pursue and promote (cf. GMS 4:430.10–27). Whether or not there is a shift in the sense in which humanity is an 'end' from the *Groundwork* to the *Doctrine of Virtue*, the crucial question is how one's own perfection and the happiness of others are the two fundamental ends required by proper regard for humanity as an end. And here we are concerned with the *Doctrine of Virtue*.

If we were to treat the requirement to *make the human being as such our end* as different from the humanity formula of the *Groundwork*, the former would be a more specific principle suitable for the *Doctrine of Virtue* whereas another aspect of the humanity formula (i. e. do not treat persons as mere means) would remain especially appropriate to the *Doctrine of Right*.[3] On this view, one might suppose that the human being as such is an *end* in the same way that perfection and happiness are ends. The expression "a human being as such" (TL 6:395.20) would refer to an abstract ideal of a person who realized as fully as possible the distinctive

---

2   This is especially, or at least most obviously, true with regard to the imperfect duties. Regarding perfect duties to oneself, note that "unnatural use [...] of one's sexual attribute" (TL 6:425.6 f.) is said to "use himself merely as a means to satisfy an animal impulse" (TL 6:425.25 f.), but what Kant emphasizes as its special wrong-making feature is that it "deprives him of all respect for himself" (TL 6:425.36). Again, suicide that amounts to "disposing of oneself as a mere means to some discretionary end" (TL 6:423.3 f.) is condemned not because it "wrong[s] [one]self" (TL 6:422.20) but simply "by virtue of [one's] quality as a person" (TL 6:422.17–18), i.e. because it "debas[es] humanity in one's person" (TL 6:423.4 f.). These passages fit with the idea that the *special* prescription of these duties *as duties of virtue* is an attitude of respect or proper valuing of humanity that is more than avoiding acts that use persons as mere means. It is not clear to me, however, whether this is just a matter of emphasis or indicates a shift in meaning between the *Groundwork*'s 'treating humanity as an end (in itself)' and the *Doctrine of Virtue*'s 'making the human being as such one's end.'

3   The *Doctrine of Virtue* is concerned primarily with our reason-sensitive attitudes (and acts assessed in terms of these) rather than with hindrances of 'eternal liberty.' So, for example, respect, a motive of duty, (practical) love, and many vicious attitudes are primarily the focus. But to suppose that the prohibition on treating persons merely as means applies only to the *Doctrine of Right* and the prescription to promote humanity as an end applies only to the *Doctrine of Virtue* is too neat a division to account for either Kant's own discussions or a sensible reconstruction. Perfect duties to oneself and duties of respect for others especially seem to depend in part on the assumption that the attitude of regarding someone as a mere means, and so also the corresponding maxims and acts, are forbidden.

human capacities for morality and the cultivation and use of theoretical and practical reason. It is an obligatory end in the sense that we should strive to make ourselves more like the ideal. As others have noted, there is textual support for this use of the idea of humanity—or a human being as such—as an ideal to strive for.

Duties to Oneself

Kant's classification of imperfect duties of self-perfection as *duties to one-self* has implications regarding their object, source, and appropriate sanctions. Their *object*—what they are about—is how we treat ourselves especially regarding important natural and moral capacities, dispositions, and powers, such as survival, sex, food and drink, speech, socially useful talents, memory, imagination, conscience, and ability to do what is right from duty despite temptations. Perfect duties to oneself are typically about whether we abuse, damage, or disrespect our basic human powers and capacities, whereas the imperfect duties to oneself are about developing these and improving them. Lying is contrary to a duty to oneself because it is an abuse of the power of speech. Servility violates a duty to oneself because it fails to respect one's own value or status as a human being.

The *source* of *all* ethical duties, in a sense, is that humanity in each person is an end in itself, but we can think of the source of duties *to one-self* in particular as that value or status of humanity *in one's own person*. We must preserve, develop, and respect ourselves as human beings and not simply to enable us to fulfill our responsibilities to others. Kant does not develop in detail the arguments from one's humanity as an end to particular duties to oneself, but to say that the former is the *source* of the latter (as I understand it) is just to say that there are good arguments of this sort, not that there is a metaphysical brute fact from which normative conclusions flow.

With regard to appropriate *sanctions* for non-compliance, the expression 'a duty to (someone)' is commonly used to identify the person who has the primary claim and right to complain if the duty is not fulfilled. Accordingly if I have a duty to myself, I would be the person who has the primary responsibility to fulfill the duty and the right to complain and pass judgment (on myself) for failures.[4] This seems to be Kant's position. Not only are these duties to oneself unenforceable by law, they are generally not the business of others.[5] The only basic end obligatory to promote regarding others is their happiness, not their perfection. Conscience serves as an inner court in which we accuse and pass judgment on ourselves but not, of course, on others. Even our duty not to lead others into temptation, Kant argues, depends on concern not for their moral well-being, but for the happiness they might lose because of pangs of conscience (cf. TL 6:394.1–12).

Imperfect Duties

Kant's distinctions between perfect and imperfect and between wide and narrow are controversial, but some points are clear enough. The principles that express imperfect duties in the *Doctrine of Virtue* are fundamentally requirements to adopt the obligatory ends whole-heartedly and so have these ends shape one's plans and pursuits in an appropriate way.

4　This seems especially common in close relationships on matters beyond the law. Although sometimes others may need to intervene on behalf of the person *to whom* better treatment or respect was owed, the offense is primarily against that person and intervention by others usually needs to be authorized by that person explicitly or implicitly.

5　This by itself leaves it open that we might *permissibly* try to help promote others' perfection even though doing so is not per se obligatory. On other grounds, of course, Kant would take a dim view of invasive attempts to promote other adults' natural or moral perfection without their invitation or permission. Kant's argument that it cannot be obligatory to make others' perfection one's end is that it is something that "only the other himself can do" (TL 6:386.13 f.). This is initially puzzling but does not, I think, deny that we can and may help others promote their natural and even moral capacities with their permission. We cannot, of course, make anyone set his own perfection an end, but neither can we make him set the happiness of others as an end. No one can fulfill someone else's fundamental duty to adopt obligatory ends, whatever these are, but this by itself does not explain why pursuing the perfection of one's natural and moral powers is only a duty to oneself. For that, further assumptions about the content of the end seem to be required, for example, the impossibility of anyone else directly cultivating one's natural powers and increasing one's moral purity and virtue. Even if others cannot directly pursue one's ends as described in these terms, this does not rule out that others can, may and even should help others in their pursuits and promote social conditions that encourage and aid their development.

To adopt the ends is a strict duty, a categorical imperative, but the principles do not specify completely what one must do, when, and how much.[6] As ethical duties, the principles of imperfect duty "leave[] a playroom (*latitudo*) for free choice in following (complying with) the law, that is, [...] the law cannot specify precisely in what way one is to act and how much one is to do by the action for an end that is also a duty" (TL 6:390.6–9). We must make it our maxim to pursue the obligatory ends, but the principles do not specify particular acts that must be done or exactly how much latitude we have in promoting the ends. Judgment is required, and the kind and amount of latitude varies with the end in question. Our duty to ourselves to promote our natural perfection, Kant says, is "*wide* and imperfect" (TL 6:446.5) because "it determines nothing about the kind and extent of actions themselves but allows latitude for free choice" (TL 6:446.6–8). The classification of the duty to promote one's moral perfection is more complex and harder to understand. Kant says, "[t]his duty to oneself is a *narrow* and perfect one in terms of [...] quality [...] and imperfect in terms of [...] degree, because of the *frailty* (*fragilitas*) of human nature" (TL 6:446.25–27). We need to consider what this means after reviewing the content of the duty.

II. One's Duty to Oneself to Develop One's Natural Powers

The general topic is in the heading "On a Human Being's Imperfect Duties to Himself (with Regard to His End)." (TL 6:444:11 f.) The ideas of imperfect duties and duties to oneself have been reviewed briefly above, and "with Regard to His End" indicates that the duties in question are about the end referred to in the supreme principle of the *Doctrine of Virtue*. This is an end that "can be a universal law for everyone to have" (TL 6:395.16)—humanity or "man as such" (TL 6:395.20). At least regarding the imperfect duties, this seems to be an abstract ideal of a human being that has fully realized certain distinctive natural and moral capacities. And the duty, beyond not treating these as mere means, is to strive to approximate more closely this ideal and to do so on principle. The duty,

---

6 Arnulf Zweig commented in conversation that the term '*unvollkommen*' as applied to duties might be translated 'incomplete,' indicating that the principles articulating the duties do not completely specify the content of what must be *done* to satisfy them even though making it one's maxim to adopt the obligatory ends (and to act accordingly) is strictly required.

like all duties of virtue, can be fulfilled only if one adopts the end from duty or respect for the moral law rather than, for example, to promote one's happiness. Moreover, because it is a duty *to oneself* the requirement cannot be met if one's motive is simply to acquire the means to satisfy one's duties to others. Self-improvement is a requirement of self-respect, not just prudence or service to others.

The Content and Latitude of the Duty to Develop Natural Powers

The first derivative imperfect duty to oneself regarding one's end is described in the heading to Section I: "On a Human Being's Duty to Himself to Develop and Increase His **Natural Perfection**, That Is, for a Pragmatic Purpose" (TL 6:444.14–16). Natural perfection, Kant has said, is "the *cultivation* of any capacities whatever [überhaupt] for furthering ends set forth by reason" (TL 6:391.30 f.). These capacities are divided into *powers of spirit* (for example, creative use of reason in mathematics, logic, and theoretical philosophy), *powers of soul* (for example, memory, imagination), and *powers of the body* (aspects of our animality needed to realize our ends) (cf. TL 6:445.8–26). Kant suggests that the powers of spirit especially serve the purposes of reason (such as science and wisdom), the powers of soul especially serve the purposes of understanding, but they and the powers of the body are needed for all sorts of unspecified purposes that reason endorses in various contexts.

This requirement, then, is to develop and improve (more closely approximate perfection of) our natural powers of body and mind (broadly construed). There are many ways of doing this, of course. Our time is limited and we have other competing responsibilities. Moreover, opportunities to develop various powers vary with one's circumstances, and whether it is more useful to develop one power or another varies with one's occupation and commitments. Quite reasonably, Kant acknowledges these variations and accordingly grants that the general duty to improve one's natural powers leaves much room for judgment and choice:

> Which of these natural perfections should take *precedence*, and in what proportion one against the other it may be a human being's duty to himself to make these natural perfections his end, are matters left for him to choose in accordance with his own rational reflection about what sort of life he would like to lead and whether he has the powers necessary for it (e. g., whether it should be a trade, commerce, or a learned profession) (TL 6:445.28–34).

The choice of "what sort of life" to lead, however, is not wide open, for "a human being has a duty to himself to be a useful member of the world" (TL 6:446.1 f.). Presumably improving one's strength in order to be a more effective bully and studying mathematics in order better to cheat stock holders are not among the ways of fulfilling the duty. I will return to questions about latitude later.

The Reason for the Duty

Why should we try to improve our natural powers? Kant's qualification "for a Pragmatic Purpose" (TL 6:444.15 f.) seems to provide a clue, but it may be misleading. In saying that we must develop our natural powers "for a Pragmatic Purpose" Kant obviously meant to contrast this duty with the duty to increase our moral perfection "for a Moral Purpose Only" (TL 6:446.11). At least part of the point of "for a Pragmatic Purpose" must be that, as Kant often says, the powers to be developed are those useful for various purposes. It might be tempting to suppose that Kant also means that we *have a duty* to develop the natural powers *simply because* they are useful, but we need to be careful here. That the powers are useful for various purposes must be a premise in any argument for the duty, but there must be more to the argument to warrant the conclusion that it is a *moral duty* to develop the natural powers. There are many instrumentally valuable things that we could increase, such as wealth and fame, but we do not in general have a moral duty to do so. What more is there to Kant's argument?

Earlier Kant describes the capacities that need to be developed as capacities "for furthering *ends set forth by reason*" (TL 6:391.30 f., italics T.H.). This eliminates crazy and immoral ends from consideration, but from Kant's discussion we can also infer that he is not referring only to the basic *ends that are duties* here. As human beings we set ourselves permissible ends of all kinds, varying according to our preferences and circumstances. Prudence, a reasonable pursuit of one's own happiness, gives us good reason to develop multi-purpose ends, but Kant cannot take this as sufficient to make it a moral duty. In both the *Groundwork* and later in the *Doctrine of Virtue*, Kant argues that we have a general duty to promote others' happiness, to make the ends of others our own. This might suggest that the moral justification for developing one's useful capacities is to promote happiness in general. In fact this may be suggested by Kant's remark that "apart from the need to maintain himself, which [...] cannot establish a duty, a human being has a duty to himself to be a useful member of the world [...]" (TL 6:445.34–446.2). A duty to oneself, however, cannot be derivative from duties to others.

So, insofar as it is a duty to oneself, the 'duty to make oneself a useful member of the world' must have a special source in the humanity in one's own person. This is suggested by the rest of the sentence just quoted: "[...] make himself a useful member of the world, *since this also belongs to the worth of humanity in his own person, which he ought not to degrade*" (TL 6:446.2 f., italics T.H.). To neglect altogether those human capacities that can enable one to live among others as a reciprocating, cooperative member is to degrade oneself. It devalues the human resources in oneself that make one fit to live in a world of reason-governed persons in human circumstances. The conclusion is that one must make oneself a useful member of the world, but insofar as this is a duty to oneself the basic premise cannot be that one owes it to others or that general happiness is an intrinsically valuable end. This interpretation fits well Kant's description of the duty as "to be in a pragmatic respect a human being *equal to the end of his existence* (TL 6:445.6 f., italics T.H.), for the "end of his existence" is not to make himself or others happy.

As a rational autonomous person, Kant suggests in many works, one is disposed to set oneself all sorts of ends beyond immediate animal needs—for one's own projects, for improving reciprocal reason-governed relations with others, and for the improvement of the species in culture and enlightenment.[7] Developing some of one's natural powers useful for all sorts of (often still unforeseen) purposes is a necessary means to these ends, and we cannot rationally will the ends without willing the means. Thus, arguably, we have a duty to make ourselves more fit and ready to pursue these various ends that we have and will develop as rational persons, even if the particular ends are not all obligatory or adopted in order to satisfy our duties to others. Developing our natural powers may of course also have other sources, such as our obligations in various social roles. But the reason it is a duty to oneself to develop useful natural powers, it seems, is to make oneself worthy of one's humanity by becoming more fit and ready to live as rational autonomous person in a reciprocating world community of such persons. This may be regarded a duty to oneself regardless of the extent to which we will actually be able to live and serve in such a world because the duty is not based on a duty to aid

---

7   See, for example, the reference to Rousseau and "the end of his existence" at TL 6:444.30–445.7. The theme is evident also in the works on history.

others—or oneself. By making oneself closer to the ideal of perfected humanity, one is respecting humanity in oneself, but one's humanity cannot be understood apart from its rational concern for self-development, rational relations with others, and perfection of reason in the human species.

The Role of Natural Teleology

Do Kant's reasons for the duty to develop our natural powers depend on assumptions about natural teleology that seem outmoded today? This raises issues beyond the texts that are our immediate concern, but a few remarks may be in order.[8] First, it is undeniably true that Kant thought there are good reasons to try to see the world as if ordered in a hierarchy of natural purposes and that his discussions in the *Doctrine of Virtue* often make use of this idea. The crucial question, however, is to what extent does his case for the various duties of virtue rest on the assumption that our powers have a purpose as a part of a teleological system of nature? The answer to an analogous question regarding divine purposes seems clear: morality does not depend on religion even though, once our duties are identified and their rational ground is established, we can and should see our duties as if commanded by God.[9] On one major point, it seems that the situation should be similar regarding natural teleology. That is, although we may usefully see our duties as if they are ways of fulfilling nature's purposes for our various powers and for us as human beings, we cannot identify or establish those duties by first identifying those purposes in a neutral, non-circular way.[10] To conceive of them as

---

8   It should perhaps be noted that in our text TL 6:444.10–447.17 Kant does not appeal explicitly to the idea that the various natural powers of spirit, soul, and body that he identifies have given purposes in the system of nature. This claim is more prominent in the third example in the *Groundwork* and at various other places in the *Doctrine of Virtue*. Reference to 'perfecting natural powers,' of course, in the context seems implicitly to invoke the idea of a teleological system of nature, but not necessarily as the basic ground or reason for moral conclusions.

9   Cf. RGV 6:144.14–145.5; TL 6:443.27–444.8.

10   Suppose we were normatively neutral in listing the capacities, dispositions, and powers that human beings have, as we find them 'in nature.' We would be looking for traits more or less common to the species even without various sorts of training, socialization, and cultural conditioning—traits like dispositions to drink when deprived of water, to scratch when itching, to remember what was terrifying, etc. There may be evolutionary explanations why many salient capaci-

moral duties is to regard them as required ultimately by principles of pure practical reason that cannot be discovered or extrapolated from the study of nature. To be sure, these rational principles need to be applied to the empirical world that we live in, but a system of natural teleology—for Kant as well as the ancients—is not a normatively neutral description of how the world in fact is. It is a set of ideas that in large part arise from and serve to express presuppositions about what is good to aim for and worth developing. (A similar point could be made about the values inherent in Kant's idea of God when he says we should see duties as if commanded by God.) If this is right, Kant can consistently make use of the idea of natural purposes in his 'more popular' sequel to his major works on the foundations of morality (vg. TL 6:391.34–37), using this idea so familiar to his readers to organize and express various duties of virtue without serving as their ultimate justification.

---

ties and dispositions that come to mind tend to be beneficial to the possessor or the species, at least *good* for their survival long enough to reproduce; and what is 'good' in this sense can be regarded as a normatively neutral matter of what happens to serve as a means to prolonging life. Ancient philosophers typically had a thicker conception of natural capacities, dispositions, and powers, however, for they were regarded as tendencies that were *good* for the possessor in that they contributed to its *thriving* and *living* as *well* as possible for a member of the species. The natural traits were good and beneficial in the sense that they provided a good reason, for those capable of following reason, to protect, develop, and use them. (For Aristotle, for example, the notion of human thriving was inseparable from the idea of living the sort of life one had good reason to pursue.) To return, then, if we were normatively neutral in our attempt to list natural traits of human beings, there is no guarantee or compelling reason to expect that the traits on our list of natural capacities and dispositions will be ones that we have good reason to develop. Some may be harmful, and some may be indifferent. Even those that tend to prolong life of the individual or species may not be traits that would be endorsed and encouraged by a common practical reason that attributes an equal basic worth to each human being. In short, we cannot assume that we have good reasons to develop the neutrally identified list of natural capacities and dispositions. It is only when we look for a list of capacities and dispositions that we have prior good reason to develop that we can identify those that are part of a system of nature in a normatively relevant sense. And if this is how the list is drawn up, then it is front-loaded with value judgments that may be used to express moral conclusions but not to justify them.

III. One's Duty to Oneself to Increase One's Moral Perfection

Kant describes the content of this duty at TL 6:446.9–447.17 (Section II, §21 f.). He also comments on the "quality" (TL 6:446.25) and "degree" (TL 6:446.26) of the duty and reasons why it is only "wide and imperfect" (TL 6:446.26) in its degree and with regard to its subject. As before, previous sections are relevant, especially TL 6:391.26–393.10 (section VIII of the "Introduction": "One's Own Perfection as an End That Is Also a Duty").

The Content of the Duty

In Kant's words, the first moral imperative is "'be holy'" (TL 6:446.17) or perfect in the "*purity* […] of one's disposition to duty" (TL 6:446.13 f.) and "in actions being done not only in conformity with duty but also *from duty*" (TL 6:446.16 f.). In a morally pure disposition "the law" (TL 6:446.15) is "by itself alone the incentive, without admixture of aims derived from sensibility" (TL 6:446.14–16). This contrasts with impurity in one's basic life-governing maxim as described in *Religion* (cf. RGV 6:29.31–30.8). Moral purity, I take it, is a firm over-riding commitment to do what is right, come what may, because it is right. A pure disposition counts duty as a sufficient and over-riding reason to act or refrain, independently of any competing or cooperating reasons of self-interest or other-regarding compassion. Regarding purity in action, that one is morally required to conform to first order duties (e. g. to refrain from lying) is not at issue here; that is obvious. It is also obvious that one should never fail to will as one's maxim and end to promote one's natural perfection and the happiness of others. The perfection of moral *purity* in action would be always to make duty, or respect for the moral law, a sufficient incentive in conforming to such first order duties. As Kant repeatedly acknowledges, we cannot achieve perfect purity in disposition and action even though we must continue to strive for it.

Second, Kant describes a moral imperative "having to do with one's entire moral end" (TL 6:446.18) (beyond just purity in disposition and moral action) as urging us to perfection that "consists objectively in fulfilling all one's duties and in attaining completely one's moral end with regard to oneself." (TL 6:446.17–20) Here the command is "be perfect" (TL 6:446.20) even though our "striving after this end always remains only a progress from *one* perfection to another" (TL

6:446.21 f.). Setting aside for now the 'objectively vs. subjectively' distinction (cf. TL 6:446.13–23), the moral aim here is to fulfill all one's duties, presumably including the duty to seek purity in one's moral disposition and reasons for conformity to duty, but also something more—"attaining completely one's moral end with regard to oneself" (TL 6:446.19 f.). As previous discussion suggests, this further perfection might be the attainment (impossible for us) of complete realization in ourselves of the ideal of humanity, which includes rational human capacities realized perfectly in all respects. Conceivably, this would involve developing and using to the highest possible level our capacities for a reason-governed life, respecting the priorities of duty without neglecting prudence and theoretical understanding. This is one way of thinking of the ideal of realizing our humanity as an end.

More obviously, however, Kant seems to have meant the development of perfect *virtue*—the strength of moral will to overcome all inclinations contrary to duty (cf. TL 6:447.8). A good will is a basic commitment to doing what is right for the right reasons, but due to the frailty of human nature a person of good will sometimes fails to act on the commitment.[11] To develop virtue is an on-going struggle, taking time, practice, and attentiveness to the moral law and what is needed to implement it.[12] It is a duty to oneself to strive continually for virtue as a core feature of what it would be to perfect our humanity.

---

11 Kant implies in §22 (TL 6:446.24–447.15) that the depravity of human nature, a kind of weakness of moral will that requires virtue to be overcome, is the reason why "be perfect" (TL 6:446.20) is only wide and imperfect in terms of "degree" (TL 6:446.26) and "*with regard to* the subject" (TL 6:446.32–33). "[B]e holy" (TL 6:446.17) and "be perfect" (TL 6:446.20), as Mary Gregor notes are from Peter 1:16, Matthew 5:48, and Philippians 4:8. Kant discusses the natural human 'propensities' to impurity and frailty in *Religion within the Limits of Mere Reason* (cf. RGV 6:28.25–31.32), contrasting these with several 'predispositions' to what is basically good (cf. RGV 6:26.1–28.24). I extend the terms to characterize those who have voluntarily incorporated these propensities into their basic, life-governing maxims. In Kant's view as I understand it, a person who shows frailty or moral weakness does not literally suffer from an *inability* to do what is right for the right reasons but nevertheless tends to fail to carry out her basic moral commitment when under great temptation. Someone who is 'impure' also has a basically good will but at times requires cooperating motives of sensibility in order to do what is right.

12 The relevant passages regarding virtue and interpretations are many. I try to explain my understanding in an earlier essay: Hill, 2008a. Frailty and purity are also discussed in Hill, 2008b.

Perhaps understandably, Kant does not bother to elaborate at TL
6:444.10–447.17 the reasons why moral perfection should be a morally
obligatory end. Instead he devotes his brief remarks to explaining how
and why the duty is "wide and imperfect" (TL 6:446.5) in some respects
and yet narrow and perfect in other respects. He says that the duty is narrow and perfect in quality and *"with regard to* its object (the Idea that one
should make it one's end to realize)" (TL 6:446.30–32). The point, I
take it, is that we *must* aim for purity and perfect virtue—giving up
the effort is not an option. *Persistently striving to improve one's motivation
and strength of moral will* characterizes the *object* of the duty—the quality
of will we absolutely must aim for. The exact "degree" (TL 6:446.26) of
purity or virtue (or improvement in these respects), however, cannot be
specified as what we human beings, the 'subjects' of the duty, must achieve. This apparently is because of the human propensity to frailty (or
weakness of moral will) and inability to tell with any confidence whether
one's motives are pure and how virtuous we are (cf. TL 6:446.28–
447.15). How are these relevant? The frailty of human nature does not
justify compromising our idea of the ideal—the object we are to aim
for—but it is relevant to whether our conscience should hold us subject
to blame for failing to achieve a definite degree of purity and virtue, assuming that we continue sincerely to try to improve.[13] We should not use
frailty as an excuse, as if it made further improvement impossible, but at
least it means the task is hard and we never know how much is possible
over any given period of time. Kant clearly acknowledged that perfect virtue cannot be achieved overnight—in fact not even in this life time. We
do not know what is possible in the short run, or even exactly what we
can do to improve.

In §22 Kant also suggests that the wideness in the "degree" (TL
6:446.26) of the duty of moral self-perfection also stems from 'the unfathomable depths of the human heart' (cf. TL 6:447.1) and even our in-

---

13 Conscience, as I understand it, cannot judge what is objectively right (*that* is the
role of moral reason and reason-guided judgment), but it is a forum in which we
accuse, defend, and judge ourselves for having not even lived up to our own best
judgments as to what is right. It judges 'subjective rightness,' as some use the
term, not 'objective rightness.' Kant says conscience cannot 'err' not because
he thinks we cannot make mistakes in judging what is really ('objectively')
right, but (apparently) because he thought that *when we reflect appropriately*
(take ourselves to trial before conscience) we cannot help but realize our failure
to live by the moral judgments and principles that we readily apply to others. For
some comparisons, see Hill, 2002, pp. 277–309.

ability to know for sure whether having any particular cluster of particular "virtues" (TL 6:447.12) is sufficient for having virtue. Why is this relevant, one may wonder? The idea, perhaps, is that to be obligated (and to expect oneself in good conscience) to meet an exact standard, one must be able to measure or judge reliably when we are meeting the standard and when we are not. It is a natural thought but questionable as a general claim. If I am perfectly capable of doing a job well to a definite degree, assuming a proper effort and instruction, but I am a very poor judge of whether or not I have succeeded and even of whether I am 'trying hard enough,' should this require us to concede that I have no obligation to do it well to a definite degree? In any case, it seems at least plausible to say that my conscience should not hold me to a definite *degree* of moral improvement in a given period if it is unknowable whether that amount of success is possible. And if we cannot know with confidence what kind of striving can be effective or even whether one is really striving as hard as one thinks, then again a definite degree of obligatory striving cannot reasonably be demanded.

Although Kant did not think that becoming virtuous is a matter of developing habits in the way that Aristotle did, he grants that it takes time and practice. A basically good will is not yet virtue. This raises the question of *how* one is to strive. Obviously, doing what one sees clearly to be one's first-order duty on each occasion is necessary and, we must presume, possible for us to do. Keeping one's eye on the moral law is recommended, but surely not consciously and explicitly at every moment. If I am tempted to commit suicide and know this is wrong, then perhaps keeping my focus on my fundamental moral commitment is a good idea. But is it necessary if, loving life, I simply turn down an unfriendly suggestion that I commit suicide? It hardly seems necessary as a means to achieving virtue, and my disposition towards morality seems no less pure if, being ready to refuse from duty if necessary, I refuse now because dying today does not fit with my (permissible) plans.

These comments raise questions beyond the text at TL 6:444.10– 447.17. My main point is just that 'degree of striving' is not a simple concept. Thinking carefully before undertaking to do something that causes great harm to others is obviously a way of *trying hard* to be virtuous, but obsessive deliberation over trivia is not. Doing Stoic exercises in self-mastery (e. g. spitting out the cold water when you are thirsty, as Epictetus recommends) may have its place, but for proper striving there is a limit to this sort of thing.

References

Hill, Thomas E. (2002), "Four Conceptions of Conscience", in: id., *Human Welfare and Moral Worth*, Oxford: Oxford University Press, pp. 277–309.

Hill, Thomas E. (2008a), "Kantian Virtue and 'Virtue Ethics'", in: Monika Betzler (ed.), *Kant's Ethics of Virtue*, Berlin/New York: Walter de Gruyter, pp. 29–60.

Hill, Thomas E. (2008b), "Kant on Weakness of Will", in: Tobias Hoffmann (ed.), *Weakness of Will from Plato to the Present*, Washington, D.C.: Catholic University of America Press, pp. 210–230.

Duties to Others from Love
(TL 6:448–461)

Dieter Schönecker

Make no mistake: It is impossible to interpret Kant's account of duties of love in §§23–26 of the *Tugendlehre* in just twenty pages or so. I will not even try to provide such an interpretation. I will provide, however, a partial interpretation that shall demonstrate *why* it is impossible to interpret Kant's theory in only a few pages. At the same time, I will sketch a research program to show what kind of work needs to be done.

A preliminary though superficial understanding of the overall structure will be necessary; thus I begin with a very brief overview (1.); I will then analyse §23 in detail (2.); I conclude with a sketch of a research program concerning some other sections (3.).

Anyone familiar with reading texts in the original language that they are written in knows that one cannot do serious research on a text without a very solid knowledge of its language; this should go without saying (though, I am afraid, this commonplace has lost its wide acceptance, mostly because of the 'analytic' approach to the history of philosphy). Even if there were a translation of Kant's *Tugendlehre* that were as good as its gets it would still be unable to bring across all the nuances and connotations, not to mention that some words simply cannot be translated (say, '*accessorisch*') and that others have, for grammatical reasons, possible references that cannot be brought across. Again, all that's trivially true. In reality, of course, translations are far from being perfect. That they are not, indeed, I will demonstrate in passing by reference to Mary Gregor's translation of the *Tugendlehre*[1]. This is not to say that translations are not useful in certain contexts, e. g. for introductory classes on Kant (as a matter of fact, a new translation of the *Tugendlehre* would be very worthwhile); but it is to say that serious research can only be done using the original text, and with an excellent facility in the language in which it was written.

---

1   In: Kant (1797) [1999].

1. The Structure of §§23–36 and Two Central Concepts— an Overview

The Structure of §§23–36

§§23–36 constitute the first section (*Abschnitt*) ("On the Duty of Love to Other Human Beings" (TL 6:448.7)) of chapter I ("On Duties to Others Merely as Human Beings" (TL 6:448.5)) of part II ("Duties of Virtue to Others" (TL 6:448.3)) of the "Doctrine of the Elements of Ethics" (TL 6:448.1) §§23–36 can quite clearly be divided into four parts:

1. In §23, Kant begins with a "division" (TL 6:448.8) into the duties of love and respect. He briefly introduces duties of love as wide (meritorious) duties and duties of respect as narrow (owed). For the most part (as I will show), he discusses how these duties are connected accessorily.[2] In §§24 and 25, both kinds of duties are further elaborated upon in quite a general manner.[3]

2. §§26–28 deal with "the duty of love in particular" (TL 6:450.14), and although these sections already focus on duty (or duties) of love they do so by discussing these duties still quite generally. §26 once more puts emphasis on the practical character of love for human beings and introduces some concepts relevant to this practical concept of philanthropy (friend of humanity, enemy of humanity, selfishness, misanthropy). §§27–28 discuss problems that arise from the maxim of love of one's neighbor: first, the problem that this love must also somehow be directed towards oneself (§27); sec-

---

2   Let me make the preliminary remark that 'accessoric' and 'accessoric connection' might not be acceptable expressions in English. As we will see, Kant says that duties of love are "accessorisch geknüpft" (TL 6:448.22) with duties of respect, and vice versa; note that 'accessorisch' is an adverb here, and this I translate as 'connected accessorily.' The German expression ("accessorisch geknüpft" (TL 6:448.22)) is translated by Gregor as "joined to it as accessory." I will explain what Kant means by this; in any event, if those expressions are not standard English, take them as a neologism (the term 'accessoric' is derived from the Latin '*accedere*').

3   On the distinction between duties of love and duties of respect in §25, cf. Sensen's contribution to this volume as well as Bacin, forthcoming. – It is, by the way, remarkable that Kant treats duties of love first and only then duties of respect, but it is not obvious why that is so; thanks to Stefano Bacin who pointed this out to me.

ond, the problem that despite the universality of the required love of human beings certain degrees of obligation must be allowed, partly because one human being can be closer to oneself than another (§28).

3. In what follows, Kant presents the "division of duties of love" (TL 6:452.10) and their treatment: beneficence (§§29–31), gratitude (§§32–33), and sympathetic feeling (*Teilnehmung*) (§§34–35).[4]

4. Section I concludes with §36 on several vices stemming from hatred for human beings (envy, ingratitude, malice).

Two Central Concepts in §§23–36: Love and Benevolence

Kant's use of the concept 'love' is extraordinarily complex—in Kant's philosophy, one has to distinguish four different contexts or basic meanings of love and twelve or so aspects or connotations.[5] With regard to §§23–36 the following distinctions are crucial: The most important concept in this context is, of course, 'duty of love' (*Liebespflicht*); as a matter of fact, it is only in the heading of section I of the *Tugendlehre* that this concept is used in a systematic manner for the very first time.[6] Of duties of love, though not only of them,[7] Kant claims that they are "usually called duties

---

4   Note that the discussion of the duty of beneficence concludes with casuistical questions (cf. TL 6:454) as does the discussion of sympathetic feeling (*teilnehmende Empfindung*) (cf. TL 6:458); the treatment of gratitude, however, has no casuistical questions.

5   Cf. Schönecker, 2010.

6   Kant mentions "duties [...] of love for one's neighbor" (TL 6:410.16 f.) in the "Introduction;" only in passing, Kant uses "duties of love" (TL 6:432.10) in the chapter on avarice; see also TL 6:448: "On the Duty of Love to Other Human Beings." Both in TL 6:450.1 ("duty of love") as well as in TL 6:450.3 ("duty of love") Kant uses the singular. – All in all, Kant makes a rather sparse use of the term 'duty of love' in his writings; note, however, that the concept shows up in the *Grundlegung* (cf. GMS 4:430, note). In *Erläuterungen Kants zu A.G. Baumgartens Initia philosophiae practicae primae* (Acadamy Edition, vol. 19) the concept of '*Liebespflicht*' appears several times. In Kant's *Physischer Geographie* one finds an interessting example: "Dagegen wird es in Lappland für eine ausgezeichnete Liebespflicht gehalten, wenn der Sohn seinen auf der Jagd verwundeten Vater mit einer Sehne vom Rennthiere tödtet, daher sie derselbe auch allezeit seinem geliebtesten Sohne anvertraut" (PG 9:164.20–23).

7   According to this passage (cf. section XVIII of the "Einleitung" (TL 6:410)), Kant distinguishes between "duties of self-love and of love for one's neighbor" (TL 6:410.16 f.), such that the latter would also include duties of respect (at least as far as the content of the duties is concerned, their 'material').

312   Dieter Schönecker

[...] of love for one's neighbor" (TL 6:410.16 f.). Accordingly, in §25
Kant speaks again of the "duty of love for one's neighbor" (TL
6:450.3), and in §36 he mentions "love for our neighbor, which is incumbent on us as a duty" (TL 6:460.11); however, Kant emphasizes,
this expression ('love for one's neighbor,' (*Nächstenliebe*)) is an expression
"used inappropriately [in uneigentlicher Bedeutung], since there can be
no direct duty to love, but instead to do that by which a human being
[der Mensch] makes himself and other human beings [andere] his end"
(TL 6:410.17–20, trans. D.S.).[8] Thus, the love which duties of love
are about, is taken to be "the *maxim* of benevolence (practical love)"
(TL 6:449.20 f., italics D.S., emphasis in the original erased); this
love, which in the context of duties Kant understands as "practical"
(TL 6:450.16), he also calls "love of human beings [Menschenliebe] (philanthropy)" (TL 6:450.16) or "practical love of human beings" (TL
6:450.31). In §§25–26, this practical love of human beings is twice
and clearly distinguished from "love that is delight [Liebe des Wohlgefal-
lens]" (TL 6:449.18, 450.17). It is thus distinguished from the "love that
is *delight* (*amor complacentiae*)" (TL 6:402.22), which in section XII of
the "Introduction" is identified as that very love of human beings
which is one of the four "natural predispositions of the mind [natürliche
Gemüthsanlagen]" (TL 6:399.11) that enable human beings to be affected by the moral law and concepts of duty in the first place.[9] Also, Kant
discusses love in the context of friendship (§26 and §47).

It is obvious that next to the concept of love the concept of benevolence (*Wohlwollen*) plays a crucial role in Kant's theory of duties of love.
Remarkably, love of human beings as a duty (generally speaking) is introduced as "the maxim of *benevolence*" (TL 6:449.20 f.) and "the law making *benevolence* a duty [Pflichtgesetz des *Wohlwollens*]" (TL 6:451.8 f.,
italics D.S.) although only one of the three basic kinds of duties of
love is "beneficence" (TL 6:452.14) (§29 ff.). Maybe this suggests that
the three basic duties of love (beneficence, gratitude, sympathetic feeling)
are not on the same level; maybe Kant understands beneficence as the
grounding duty upon which the others are somehow based (but that is

8   Gregor translates: "[...] by which *one* makes oneself and others one's end" (TL
     6:410.19 f., italics D.S.).
9   "[*A*]*mor complacentiae*" (TL 6:402.22) is thus opposed both to "*benevolence
     (amor benevolentiae)*" (TL 6:401.27) and to "love of human beings (as an apti-
     tude of the inclination to beneficence in general)" (TL 6:402.20 f., trans. D.S.).
     For a detailed interpretation of these moral predispositions see Schönecker,
     2010; see also in this volume Goy.

a topic for another paper). In any event, the concepts of benevolence and beneficence are not easy to grasp. For there is, first, *active* benevolence (*tätiges Wohlwollen*) (cf. e. g. TL 6:401.27, 452.4); there is, second, benevolence in wishes (*Wohlwollen des Wunsches*) (cf. TL 6:452.1, 452.23) which is *not* a duty; there is, thirdly, mere heartfelt benevolence (*bloß herzliches Wohlwollen*) (cf. TL 6:455.1–22) which *is* a duty; and possibly there is, fourth, benevolence in the general love for all human beings (*Wohlwollen in der allgemeinen Menschenliebe*) (cf. TL 6:451.21) which might be identical with benevolence in wishes.

2. A *kommentarische Interpretation* of §23

The Division of Duties at the Beginning of §23

The "chief division" (TL 6:448.10) refers to the duties to others merely as human beings mentioned in the title of chapter I. This chief division of duties to others is the division of such duties to others by which others (i) are put under obligation towards oneself and (ii) those duties by which others are not obligated. The latter Kant calls "*owed*" (TL 6:448.14), the former "*meritorious*" (TL 6:448.13). Of course, this meritoriousness must not be understood as supererogatoriness, but in terms of wide or perfect duties; thus, in §25 Kant remarks that duties of love are "*wide*" (TL 6:450.2) whereas duties of "free respect toward others" (TL 6:449.31) are "*narrow*" (TL 6:450.1).[10] Roughly, meritorious duties "result in obligation on the part of others" (TL 6:448.12) because one is not obliged to perform a (*this* very) specific action that would be considered a wide duty (though of course a wide duty remains a *duty*) and so, if I do it, the recipient of my action is indebted to me for that specific action. Narrow duties, on the contrary, I must perform under all circumstances anyway. – I will not comment on this further; to the present day, there is no detailed and satisfying account of the basic distinction between wide and narrow duties on the one hand and duties of virtue and duties of right on the other.

---

10 See, for instance, the meaning of "wide [weit]" in the *Grundlegung* (GMS 4:424.11, 430.10).

What Is §23 About?

Right after the "chief division" (TL 6:448.10), Kant continues: "*Love* and *respect* are the feelings that accompany [begleiten] the carrying out of these duties" (TL 6:448.14 f.). '*These* duties' are the 'meritorious' and 'owed' duties mentioned before. In the first few lines, Kant does not use the terms 'duties of love' or 'duties of respect,' but of course, they are what is talked about. Thus, it is quite natural to think that love accompanies the carrying out of the duty of love, whereas respect accompanies the carrying out of the duty of respect; however, this is *not* the case.[11] That indeed a duty of love is *not* necessarily accompanied by a feeling of love becomes evident in Kant's analysis of the duty of gratitude. There, Kant writes very clearly that it is *not* the feeling of love that is connected with the duty of gratitude (which is a duty of love), but the feeling of "respect" (TL 6:454.33, 458.13): "Gratitude consists in honoring a person because of a benefit he has rendered us. The *feeling* connected with this judgment is *respect* for the benefactor (who puts one under obligation), whereas the benefactor is viewed as only in relation of love toward the recipient" (TL 6:454.31–455.1, italics D.S., emphasis in the original erased).[12] Thus a duty of love can be accompanied by a feeling of respect (and vice versa, one would think). But why then does Kant call wide duties duties of *love* and narrow duties duties of *respect*? There is, I believe, no strict philosophical justification; probably it simply is a reference to the Christian tradition. I will return to this question in due course.[13]

Love and respect, says Kant, are the feelings that accompany the carrying out of the duties of love and respect. As demonstrated, this can easily be misunderstood. In what follows, Kant is even more confusing:

---

11   Cf. Gregor, 1963, p. 182: "Kant mentions that the duties are called duties of love and respect because of the feelings which accompany our observance of them" – but where does Kant 'mention' this? Nowhere, really. Forkl, 2001, p. 206, claims that love always accompanies the carrying out of duties of love and respect the carrying out of duties of respect: "Die Liebe begleitet stets die Ausübung der verdienstlichen Pflichten, die Achtung stets die Ausübung der schuldigen Pflichten."

12   See also TL 6:458.12: "Gratitude is not, strictly speaking, love [Gegenliebe] toward a benefactor on the part of someone he has put under obligation, but rather *respect* for him." Still gratitude is a duty of love.

13   Beck even claims that Kant regards practical love "as equivalent to the love commaneded by Christianity" (Beck ³1963, p. 233).

"They [Sie] can be considered separately (each by itself) and can also exist in this way [i.e. separately, D.S.]" (TL 6:448.15 f., trans. D.S.).

One very tempting interpretation is to take the demonstrative pronoun 'they' to refer to those feelings of love and respect, so that Kant's claim would be that the feeling of love and the feeling of respect "can be considered separately (each by itself) and can also exist separately" (TL 6:448.15 f.). Yet again, this is *not* the case. My central claim is this: Beginning with that sentence ('They can be considered separately …'), *the whole section (§23) is on the accessoric connection of duties, and not about the feelings of love and respect.* To see this, we have to take a closer look. First, the German original:

> Liebe und Achtung sind die Gefühle, welche die Ausübung dieser Pflichten begleiten. **Sie** können abgesondert (jede für sich allein) erwogen werden und auch so bestehen (Liebe des Nächsten, ob dieser gleich wenig Achtung verdienen möchte; imgleichen nothwendige Achtung für jeden Menschen, unerachtet er kaum der Liebe werth zu sein beurtheilt würde). **Sie** sind aber im Grunde dem Gesetze nach jederzeit mit einander in einer Pflicht zusammen verbunden; nur so, daß bald die eine Pflicht, bald die andere das Prinzip im Subject ausmacht, an welche die andere accessorisch geknüpft ist. – So werden wir gegen einen Armen wohlthätig zu uns für verpflichtet erkennen; aber weil diese Gunst doch auch Abhängigkeit seines Wohls von meiner Großmut enthält, die doch den Anderen erniedrigt, so ist es Pflicht, dem Empfänger durch ein Betragen, welches diese Wohltätigkeit entweder als bloße Schuldigkeit oder geringen Liebesdienst vorstellt, die Demüthigung zu ersparen und ihm seine Achtung für sich selbst zu erhalten (TL 6:448.14–449.2, bold D.S.).

Here's Gregor's translation:

> *Love* and *respect* are the feelings that accompany the carrying out of these duties. **They** [Sie] can be considered separately (each by itself) and can also exist separately (one can *love* one's neighbor though he might deserve but little *respect*, and can show him the respect necessary for every human being regardless of the fact that he would hardly be judged worthy of love). But **they** [Sie] are basically always united by the law into one duty, only in such a way that now one duty and now the other is the subject's principle, with the other joined to it as accessory. – So we shall acknowledge that we are under obligation to help someone poor; but since the favor we do implies that his well-being depends on our generosity, and this humbles him, it is our duty to behave as if our help is either merely what is due him [sic!] or but a slight service of love, and to spare him humiliation and maintain his respect for himself (TL 6:448.14–449.2, bold D.S.).

316   Dieter Schönecker

Here's my translation:[14]

> Love and respect are the feelings that accompany the carrying out of these
> duties. **They** [Sie] can be considered separately (each by itself) and can
> also exist in this way [i.e. separately, D.S.] (love of one's neighbor though
> he might deserve but little respect; likewise necessary respect for every
> human being regardless of the fact that he would be judged hardly worthy
> of love). But **they** [Sie] are really always united with each other according
> to the law in a single duty, yet only in such a way that now one duty,
> now the other constitutes the principle in the subject, such that one duty
> is joined to the other accessorily. – So we shall recognize ourselves as
> being obligated to be beneficent to someone poor; but because this favour
> also implies the dependence of his well-being on my generosity, which
> does humble the other, it is a duty to spare the recipient humiliation and
> to maintain for him his respect for himself, by means of a conduct that pres-
> ents this beneficence either as something simply due to him or as a small
> service of love (TL 6:448.14–449.2, trans. and bold D.S.).

The crucial question simply is this: What do the two demonstrative pro-
nouns "[t]hey [Sie]" (TL 6:448.15, 448.19) refer to? Depending on the
answer, the meaning of the text changes completely (a very rare phenomenon when it comes to philosophical texts). This is not only a matter of
how to interpret *this* passage; a correct understanding of this passage
might have far reaching consequences for the interpretation of other passages as well (I will give an example in support of this claim later). It is a
widespread misunderstanding to believe that close reading will at best disclose details that are, however, irrelevant to the philosophical argument or
thesis. Arguments are not simply 'there;' they must be reconstructed by a
detailed, interpretative effort, and numerous examples can be given that
demonstrate how paying attention to (so-called) details can entirely

---

14 Let me point out the main differences: Gregor translates "Liebe des Nächsten"
    (TL 6:448.16 f.) with "one can *love* one's neighbor" instead of "love of one's
    neighbor" (more on this below); she misplaces "hardly" (TL 6:448.18), making
    it an adverb which it is not; she leaves "mit einander [with each other]" (TL
    6:448.20, trans. D.S.) untranslated; "accessorisch" (TL 6:448.22) is an adverb
    to "geknüpft" (TL 6:448.22); she translates "to *help* someone poor" where it
    says "gegen einen Armen *wohltätig* zu sein [to be *beneficent* to someone poor]"
    (TL 6:448.23, trans. and italics D.S.); and the latter part of the last sentence con-
    tains some more minor flaws. Let me point out that I have the greatest respect for
    her translation of Kant's *Metaphysik der Sitten*; this is hard and tedious work. I
    hope that one can see, however, that serious research on Kant's text cannot be
    done without the ability to read German. – Many thanks to Richard Capobianco
    for helping with my translation and many thanks as well to Marcia Baron for
    checking the whole paper.

change our understanding of an argument.[15] In any event, even if there were no far reaching consequences with regard to §23, a correct interpretation is still at order.

Just looking at the first "They" (TL 6:448.15) (for short: They$_1$), there will be a strong tendency to think that it refers to "[l]ove and respect" (TL 6:448.14) (and thus indirectly to the "feelings" (TL 6:448.14)).[16] This yields the following proposition:

(F1) The feelings of love and respect "can be considered separately (each by itself) and can also exist separately" (TL 6:448.15 f.).

Once this is assumed, the second "They" (TL 6:448.19) (for short: They$_2$) must also refer to those feelings because it clearly relates to the first noun which is They$_1$. Hence we get:

(F2) The feelings of love and respect "are really always united with each other according to the law in a single duty, yet only in such a way that now one duty, now the other constitutes the principle in the subject, such that one duty is joined to the other accessorily" (TL 6:448.19–22, trans. D.S.).

This is the *prima facie* way of reading those sentences. This reading cannot possibly be correct, though. In order to see this, it is important to read the whole section with the end of the section in mind. At the conclusion of this section, there is an example which certainly is *not* about the feelings of love and respect but about the *accessoric* connection of one duty to another.[17] I will go into the details later, but the basic idea seems simple: One duty, which in the example is the duty of love to help as a specified duty of beneficence, entails—if that is not too strong a term (read: brings along)—another duty (which in the example is the narrow duty of not humiliating the recipient of one's help). Having to carry out a duty of love involves having to carry out a duty of respect; if I am to help a poor man, doing so brings along the duty not to humiliate that poor man (the recipient of my beneficence).[18] In any event, the

---

15 For a recent example, cf. Schönecker, 2010b.
16 For grammatical reasons (because of "(*jede* für sich allein)" (TL 6:448.16, italics D.S.)), the reference can, if at all, only be to "[l]ove and respect" (TL 6:448.14, emphasis in the original erased, D.S.); I will get back to this later. In any event, love and respect *are* the feelings talked about.
17 Again, in German: "accessorisch geknüpft" (TL 6:448.22).
18 The same idea one can find in §31 of the *Tugendlehre*. Note, however, that in §31 Kant refers explicitly to "him [er]" (TL 6:453.22), which goes back to

"So" (TL 6:448.22) (both in German and English) clearly expresses that we are provided with an *example*. Now if the example is about this accessoric connection of one duty with another ("such that one duty is joined to the other accessorily" (TL 6:448.21 f., trans. and italics D.S.)), and if the example ("So" (TL 6:448.22)) exemplifies a thesis in the preceding sentence, then this sentence must be about the accessoric connection of one duty with another. Referring They$_2$ to duties rather than to feelings of love and respect, the meaning of that sentence then is:

(D2) Duties of love and duties of respect "are really always united with each other according to the law in a single duty, yet only in such a way that now one duty, now the other constitutes the principle in the subject, such that one duty is joined to the other accessorily" (TL 6:448.19–22, trans. D.S.).

If, however, They$_2$ does refer to *duties* of love and respect, and not to the *feelings* of love and respect, then They$_1$ also must refer to these duties (again, because They$_2$ picks up the noun They$_1$). Thus we get:

(D1) Duties of love and respect "can be considered separately (each by itself) and can also exist separately" (TL 6:448.15 f.).

But then the *whole* passage beginning with They$_1$ is about *duties* of love and respect, not about the *feelings* of love and respect that accompany these duties, and thus the *prima facie* interpretation must be given up.

Marcia Baron shares the *prima facie* reading and yet cannot help but note: "It is hard to believe that Kant really means that as *feelings* love and respect are 'united by the law into one duty.' So, although he says he is speaking of them as feelings at this point, I am not convinced that he is."[19] But Baron *does* believe *that* Kant 'says' so, and so do Forkl, 2001, p. 206 and Burggraf, 2005, p. 159. Koch, 2003, pp. 147 f., on the other hand, simply assumes that D2 is the correct interpretation, not F2; but he says next to nothing about it. Horn, 2008, p. 166 mentions §23 only in passing, without seeing the interpretative problem; the same is true for Anderson, 2008, p. 141, Malibabo, 2000, pp. 208 ff., Moors, 2005, pp. 64 f., Römpp, 2006, p. 225, Steigleder, 2002, pp. 260 f., and Witschen, 2006, p. 628. Esser, 2004, pp. 371 f., discusses §24, but not §23 (in a similar fashion, but very brief cf. Mairhofer, 1975, p. 47 and Murphy, 1994, p. 83 f.); Streich, 1924, pp. 36 ff., and Guyer, 2010, dis-

the beginning of the section where Kant introduces someone who is "*rich*" (TL 6:453.17).

19 Baron, 2004, p. 395.

cusses love in the *Metaphysik der Sitten*, but do not discuss §23. Gregor, 1963, p. 182, footnote 4, has a somewhat mixed interpretation: "The feelings of love and respect for others can occur separately, but practical love and respect are always united in a duty of virtue to others;" but she just states this without any interpretation. As far as I can tell, there is to the present day no detailed analysis of §23 (not even by non-*kommentarische* standards), and very little on the other sections on duties of love as well. (I will not discuss the literature regarding the other sections.)

Let us now have a closer look at the text of §23. Not only do the grammatical reasons just provided speak for the claim that most of it is about duties, not about feelings; read this way, it also makes much more philosophical sense.

Duties of Love and Respect as Accessorily Connected

No doubt, the example ('*So* we shall recognize ourselves …') is about duties and their accessoric connection. Once this is recognized, it will come as no surprise that the preceding sentence (to which the example refers) is also clearly about duties and their accessoric connection. Let us look again: "[T]hey are really always united with each other according to the law in a single duty, yet only in such a way that now one duty, now the other constitutes the principle in the subject, such that one duty is joined to the other accessorily" (TL 6:448.19–22, trans. D.S.). On close reading, it is very hard to see how this can be read as a statement about feelings (in terms of F2). The latter part of this sentence is about duties ('now one duty, now the other (duty),' 'such that one duty is joined to the other (duty) accessorily'). The former part of the sentence *could*, just at its semantic surface, be read as referring to feelings in terms of F2, maybe saying that the feelings of love and respect are "really always united with each other according to the law in a single duty yet *only in* […] *a way*" (TL 6:448.19–21, trans. and italics D.S.) that sometimes the duty of love, sometimes the duty of respect "constitutes the principle in the subject" (TL 6:448.21 f., trans. D.S.). So on this reading the idea would be that because those duties are 'accessorily connected,' the feelings that accompany these duties are also 'united,' to wit, united 'in a *single* duty,' that is, a single (one) duty inasmuch it connects two duties one of which is accessoric. – But this reading is highly implausible. First of all, if the real theme of that sentence were the connection of feelings, then that theme would, quite confusingly, receive no treatment in the ex-

ample; the example simply is *not* about such a connection of feelings but
about the connection of duties (which the latter part of that sentence
speaks very clearly about). Second, even if that charitable reading is assumed, it remains opaque what exactly it would mean that the feelings
of love and respect are "really always *united* with each other according
to the law *in a single duty*" (TL 6:448.19 f., trans. and italics D.S.).
Third, the new reading also fits much better with the rest of the sentence,
because the claim then is that really (*im Grunde*) duties of love and of
respect are 'united with each other,' '*only*' in such way' that one is joined
to the other as accessory. Kant's formulation that the duties are 'accessorily connected' is a specification of the preceding formulation that they
are 'united with each other'.

What then does Kant say about the accessoric connection expressed
in D1 and D2? Let us try to look at the details of Kant's theory of the
accessoric connection of duties of love and respect; this will further
strengthen our alternative (*secunda facie*) reading.[20]

(i) Kant: Duties of love and duties of respect "are really *always* united
with each other according to the law in a single duty" (TL 6:448.19 f.,
trans. and italics D.S.). – This is a strong claim: Every duty to beneficence, gratitude and sympathy is always (*jederzeit*) connected accessorily
with a duty of respect; whenever I (have to) carry out a duty of love, I
(have to) carry out a duty of respect, and *vice versa*. But is this really
true for all duties of love and respect, and is it true in both directions
such that all duties of love are connected with duties of respect, and
vice versa, one of them constituting "the principle in the subject" (TL
6:448.21, trans. D.S.)? As for the duty of beneficence, its accessoric connection with the duty of respect seems to make sense right away. For if I
carry out such a wide, meritorious duty, the recipient of my beneficence is
put under obligation, and this humbles him and can be detrimental to his
self-respect. Hence, I must follow the duty of respect not to humiliate
him. However, what exactly is this duty of respect? If the duty of respect
is a negative duty (avoid arrogance, defamation, ridicule),[21] what exactly
is then the connection with the duty of love? Kant says very little about
this; as a matter of fact, all he says about the accessoric connection of duties of love with duties of respect is in §23.[22] How about this: When it

---

20 For further interpretations see Bacin, forthcoming.
21 Cf. §§42–44.
22 The term 'accessorisch' (as such) appears only once in Kant's opus (to wit, in
     §23).

comes to beneficence, arrogance (entailing humiliation) must be avoided; as for gratitude, defamation is the lurking vice; and concerning sympathy (*teilnehmende Empfindung*) all three vices must be actively avoided. One can easily see that this is far from obvious; as often with Kant, the example works fine, but the general claim behind it is much less convincing. Even less striking is Kant's thesis that duties of respect are accessorily connected with duties of love—what could that possibly mean with regard to the *specific* duties of love and respect?

(ii) Kant: Duties of love and duties of respect "are really always united with each other *according to the law* in a single duty" (TL 6:448.19 f., trans. and italics D.S.). – What does 'according to the law' (*dem Gesetze nach*) mean? It can not mean that the accessoric conncetion between duties is always the case; this is true, says Kant, but this aspect is already expressed by 'always.' Rather, the idea must be that duties of love and respect are founded on a general law, i.e. the moral law or the categorical imperative. This is a well known claim of Kant's; what *exactly* it means, I cannot discuss here.

(iii) Kant: Duties of love and duties of respect "are really always united with each other according to the law *in a single* duty" (TL 6:448.19 f., trans. and italics D.S.). – This is just the claim that duties of love and duties of respect are connected, such that they build a *conjunctive* duty, and in that sense a 'single' (or 'one') duty. However, Kant is eager to stress in the latter part of D2 that they are one duty, but "*only in such a way* that now one duty, now the other constitutes the principle in the subject, such that one duty is joined to the other accessorily" (TL 6:448.21 f., trans. and italics D.S.). Recall that D2 in the original formulation says: "*But* they[$_2$] [duties of love and respect, D.S.] are really always united with each other according to the law in a single duty" (TL 6:448.19 f., trans. and italics D.S.). The 'but' refers to D1 in opposition to which D2 is stated: "They[$_1$] [duties of love and respect, D.S.] can be considered separately (each by itself) and can also exist in this way [i.e. separately, D.S.]" (TL 6:448.15 f., trans. D.S.). So these duties are separate (*abgesondert*) duties, *but* on the other hand they are accessorily connected and in this respect 'a single' duty. Note that the 'but' provides additional evidence that D1 is about duties, not about feelings; the general topic in these sentences is the separateness and connection of those duties.

(iv) Kant: In accessorily connected duties there is one duty that "constitutes the *principle in the subject*" (TL 6:448.21 f., trans. and italics D.S.). – Let us again look at the example: Note that it says: "we shall recognize ourselves as being obligated to be beneficent to *someone* poor [gegen *einen* Armen]" (TL 6:448.22 f., trans. and italics D.S.), not 'to *the* poor.' Thus, there is an actualized duty to beneficence, 'actualized' in the sense that a wide duty must be fulfilled specifically given a specific situation. This duty is what I recognize (*erkennen*) and which moves me; contrary to this duty, the duty "to spare the recipient humiliation and to maintain for him his respect for himself" (TL 6:448.25–449.2, trans. D.S.) is a secondary duty which only applies because the wide duty to beneficence is actualized. If in a given case I do not recognize myself as obligated to be beneficent to this particular poor person, then I am not obligated 'to spare that person humiliation and to maintain for him his respect for himself' simply because I cannot behave in a way that presents my beneficence "either as something simply due to him or as a small service of love" (TL 6.448.26–449.1, trans. D.S.) (still I must not humiliate him in other ways, of course). Thus in the example the duty of beneficence constitutes "the principle in the subject" (TL 6:448.21, trans. D.S.) inasmuch it is the primary duty that entails the secondary.[23]

(v) Kant: Duties of love and duties of respect are *accessorily* connected. – This has been accounted for: The connection is accessoric because one duty (in the example the duty of respect not to humiliate) accedes, as it were, to another, (in the example: to the duty of love to be beneficent); the former would not apply without the latter.

(vi) Kant: Although duties of love and respect are accessorily connected, "[t]hey can be *considered separately* (each by itself) and can also *exist separately*" (TL 6:448.15 f., italics D.S.). – It is to be expected that Kant will put forward such a claim, if only for the reason that indeed he *does* treat duties of love and duties of respect separately in different chapters. There is a certain tension, though, between this claim and the central claim that duties of love and respect are accessorily connected. Once more, let us look at the example: Certainly, there is no difficulty to consider the duty of beneficence and the duty not to humiliate "separately" (TL 6:448.15), i.e. "each by itself [jede für sich allein]" (TL

---

23 In *Der Streit der Fakultäten* there is a passage in wich Kants distinguishes between what belongs "zum Wesentlichen (*principale*)" (SF 7:64.9 f.) and "zum Beigesellten (*accessorium*)" (SF 7:64.10). – The term 'accessoric' is often used in juridical contexts. In *Pierer's Universal-Lexikon*, vol. 12, Altenburg, 1861, pp. 188–189, I find (online) the following note: "Jede Obligation ist ferner entweder eine selbständige, für sich bestehende, od. accessorische, welche erst einer anderen O. hinzutritt, z. B. eine Bürgschaft." In (German) jurisprudence, there is still a 'Prinzip der Akzessorietät'; for this juridical context see RL 6:268.

6:448.16).[24] However, how shall the duty not to humiliate also 'exist like this,' i.e. exist separately, if "exist [bestehen]" (TL 6:448.16) means something like 'apply,' 'to be in force' or 'to be valid'? There is, it seems, a dilemma: Either a duty of love (likewise, a duty of respect) "can [...] exist separately" (TL 6:448.15 f.), in which case it is neither "accessori[c]" (TL 6:448.22) nor the "principle in the subject" (TL 6:448.21, trans. D.S.); or it is part of such an accessoric connection of duties, in which case it can*not* "exist separately" (TL 6:448.15 f.).

(vii) Kant: They (duties of love and respect) can be considered separately (each by itself) and can also exist like this ("love of one's neighbor though he might deserve but little respect; likewise necessary respect for every human being regardless of the fact that he would be judged hardly worthy of love" (TL 6:448.16–19, trans. D.S., emphasis in the original erased)). – I would now like to analyze what is said in parenthesis about love and respect. Again, it all depends on how one reads the 'They' (i.e. They$_1$). If it refers to the feelings of love and respect, then what is said about love and respect in parenthesis is also about those feelings. Here, it is worthwhile to take a closer look at Gregor's translation of the passage: "[...] (one can *love* one's neighbor though he might deserve but little *respect*, and can show him the respect necessary for every human being regardless of the fact that he would hardly be judged worthy of love)" (TL 6:448.16–19). In German, there is no hint that"one can love one's neighbor" (TL 6:448.16); it simply says "Liebe des Nächsten" (TL 6:448.16) which should therefore be translated with 'love of one's neighbor.' (The term is no less strange in German than it is in English.) Gregor's translation strongly suggests that it is the feeling of love that one can bring up against someone who deserves not even respect ("one can love" (TL 6:448.16)), and "likewise" (TL 6:448.17 f.) the other way round. However, on the assumption that "They" (TL 6:448.15) at the beginning

---

24 I already pointed out that the grammatical form of the parenthesis "(jede für sich allein)" (TL 6:448.16) only allows the reference to "Liebe and Achtung" (TL 6:448.14), provided that one refers They$_1$ to the feelings of love and respect at all. If the reference were "Gefühle" (TL 6:448.14), it would need to say 'jedes für sich allein'; note, by the way, that this is a grammatical point that gets lost, and must get lost, in the translation. Still, the reference of "jede" to "love and respect" would be awkward, for then one must read (in German; again, that's not translatable): 'jede, sowohl die Liebe wie auch die Achtung, für sich allein ...' If, however, one refers They$_1$ to the duties of love and respect and, accordingly, "jede für sich allein" to these duties as well, the reference is easy and smooth.

of that sentence refers to the duties rather than to the feelings of love and
respect, there must be another interpretation of that sentence. A closer
look reveals that this is not only possible, but obvious.[25] First of all,
note that 'love of one's neighbor' is an expression that in the context of
§§23–36 Kant uses (as he does elsewhere)[26] to refer to the duty of
love of one's neighbor. Just two sections later (in §2) Kant speaks of
the "*duty* of love for one's neighbor" (TL 6:450.3, italics D.S.); and
again a bit later (in §§27 and 28) he twice mentions the Christian
duty to love one's neighbor (cf. TL 6:450.33, 451.29). There is no
doubt that in the wider context of §§23 ff. Kant explicitly understands
love as a normative concept, not as a feeling: "In this context [hier], however, love is not to be understood as feeling [...] It must rather be thought
as the maxim of benevolence (practical love), which results in beneficence" (TL 6:449.17–22, emphasis in the original erased, D.S.); and a
few lines later: "Since the love of human beings (philanthropy) we are
thinking of here is practical love [...]" (TL 6:450.16 f.). By the same
token, there is a "duty of respect for one's neighbor" (TL 6:450.5). Of
course, in §23 love and respect are first introduced as feelings ('Love
and respect are the feelings that accompany the carrying out of these duties'). But as we have seen, right after that Kant (with They₁) moves on to
love and respect as duties,[27] so that 'love of one's neighbor' in that parenthetical clause of §23 can and must indeed be understood as the 'practical
love' (of beneficence) that is a duty. The same is true for the "respect [...]
for every human being" (TL 6:448.18). Kant qualifies this respect as
"necessary [nothwendige]" (TL 6:448.18),[28] as something that ought to
be and thus as a duty; feelings are not 'necessary,' and so if Kant referred
to respect as a feeling he could not call it necessary. Secondly, it is important to see that the sentence in parentheses is obviously meant as a com-

---

25 It is therefore potentially misleading that Bernd Ludwig edits that parenthesis as a
    separate sentence (Kant (1797) [¹1990]); this is different in the Academy Edi-
    tion.
26 See, for instance, KpV 5:81–86.
27 Things would have been easier, if Kant had written '*Diese*' (These) rather than
    "Sie [They]" (TL 6:448.15). In TL 6:483.26–31 one finds another example
    of a sentence in which Kant uses "sie" (TL 6:483.31) where '*diese*' would have
    been appropriate ("sie" (TL 6:483.31) there refers to "Pflicht" (TL 6:483.30)).
28 The "necessary" (TL 6:448.18) really is an attribute to "respect" (TL 6:448.18),
    so the claim is that respect is necessary, but not that it is (as in Gregor's transla-
    tion) "necessary *for* every human being" (TL 6:448.18, italics D.S.) (whatever
    that means).

ment on the main clause which is about the separateness of the duties of love and respect; thus it further elaborates upon that separateness. Note, however, that love and respect are not entirely separated: One shall love one's neighbor though she "might deserve but little respect" (TL 6:448.17); and one shall respect one's neighbor though she "would be judged hardly worthy of love" (TL 6:448.18 f., trans. D.S.). It is hard to see what Kant's point is, but maybe it can be formulated as follows: The wide duty of love must be fulfilled even if someone seems not even worthy of the narrow duty of respect that we owe him; and we owe every human being respect regardless of how much (or rather little) actions of love it deserves. The sentence in parentheses remains somewhat enigmatic; but it does so on any reading of its context. It would be much easier to understand if Kant meant to say that one must love one's neighbor whether she's worthy of love or not; and that one must respect one's neighbor whether she's worthy of respect or not.[29]

Finally, one more note on love and respect as the accompanying feelings.[30] We have already seen that it is *not* Kant's claim that the feeling of love accompanies duties of love and that the feeling of respect accompanies duties of respect. But it is also not his claim that the only feelings that *specifically*[31] accompany these duties are love and respect. Once more it is important not to discuss duties of love just generally, but to specify these duties as Kant does himself (duties of beneficence, gratitude, sympathy):

(i) When it comes to beneficence, there is the "*satisfaction* [*Vergnügen*] in the happiness (well-being) of others" (TL 6:452.27, italics D.S.). In section XII of the "Introduction" Kant mentions "love of [...] [human beings, D.S.] [*Menschenliebe*] (as an aptitude [*Fertigkeit*] of the inclination to beneficence in general)" (TL 6:402.20 f.,) that results from beneficence; in *Vorarbeiten zur Tugendlehre* Kant understands love of human beings as the "*Freude* über das physische und moralische Wohlseyn eines Anderen" (VATL 23:407.34 f., italics D.S.).

(ii) As already mentioned, the duty of gratitude as a duty of love is not accompanied by the feeling of love but by the feeling of respect; another term Kant avails himself of in this context is "*honoring* [Vereh-

---

29 See §27 where Kant says that practical love "is a duty of all human beings toward one another, whether or not one finds them worthy of love" (TL 6:450.31–33).

30 See, once more, TL 6:454.32 f.: "The feeling *connected* with this judgment [...]" (italics D.S.).

31 Of course, all kinds of context-relative and subject-relative emotions and feelings can be involved in a concrete carrying out of a duty.

rung]" (TL 6:454.31), since gratitude (as *"active"* (TL 6:455.3) gratitude) is maybe defined as *"honoring* a person because of a benefit he has rendered us" (TL 6:454.31 f.).[32] Next to this Kant also knows of another form of gratitude which very clearly is something like a feeling, sc. *"affective* [affectionellen] gratitude" (TL 6:455.3 f.).

(iii) The duty of sympathetic feeling is the one most clearly accompanied by specific feelings; these are the feelings of *"[s]ympathetic joy* and *sadness* [Mitfreude und Mitleid]" (TL 6:456.20).

(iv) Last but not least, one has to ask whether what Kant means by "carrying out [Ausübung]" (TL 6:448.15) duties of love and respect is just a *successful* carrying out of these duties (such that one really *is* beneficent, grateful, and sympathetic) or a *failing* of carrying out of these duties. In the latter case, *"envy, ingratitude,* and *malice"* (TL 6:458.23 f.) (§36) need to be considered.

A Possible Consequence: Accessoric vs. Intimate Union of Love and Respect

According to §23, the connection of the duties of love with the duties of respect is accessoric. Kant goes on to discuss the duties of respect (up to §36); part II (§§37–44), then, is about the duties of respect. Both these kinds of duties to others are duties to others merely as human beings; later, there is a very brief chapter (only one section, i.e. §45) on ethical duties of human beings toward one another with regard to their condition. But that's not the end of part II of the doctrine of virtues to others; there is a "conclusion of the elements of ethics" (TL 6:469.13) which is about the "most intimate union of love with respect in **friendship**" (TL 6:469.14 f.), laid out in §46–47.

These two sections are difficult and require an analysis no less detailed (or *kommentarisch*[33]) then the one I tried for §23. I cannot do this here, but I would like to draw attention to the following point. To begin with, friendship in this context (moral friendship anyway, "as dis-

---

32   I say 'maybe,' because active gratitude—similar to practical philanthropy—might not be an actual feeling in any proper sense (actual *"honoring"* (TL 6:454.31)), but just a maxim, whatever the feeling would be connected with it (or its effected action). Thus one could be gratitious without having the feeling of gratitude.
33   On the idea of *'kommentarische'* interpretations cf. Schönecker, ²2004, and Damschen/Schönecker, 2012, pp. 203–272.

tinguished from aesthetic friendship" (TL 6:471.26, trans. D.S.)[34]) is understood as a "duty" (TL 6:469.23). Therefore, love and respect as the ingredients of friendship are *not* understood as feelings either; for instance, pointing out one's friend's faults to him or her is interpreted by Kant as a duty of friendship (which is a "duty of love" (TL 6:470.23)). He also describes love as "attraction" (TL 6:470.5) and respect as "repulsion" (TL 6:470.5), two concepts easily misunderstood as feelings too; but Kant explicitly says that "the *principle* of the former [i.e. of attraction resp. love, D.S.][35] *commands* approach, the [principle, D.S.] of the second [i.e. of repulsion resp. respect, D.S.] *requires* to keep each other at a proper distance" (TL 6:470.5–7, trans. and italics D.S.). This "analogy" (TL 6:449.7) is already used in §24. There too, Kant speaks of "*attraction* and *repulsion*" (TL 6:449.8), and there too he means that we are "*commanded*" (TL 6:449.9, trans. and italics D.S.) by the "principle of **mutual love [Wechselliebe]**" (TL 6:449.9),[36] and that respect is something which we "*owe*" (TL 6:449.10, italics D.S.) to each other; all of this cannot be true of feelings, but only of duties.[37] Whereas duties of love and respect are only *accessorily* connected such that in a given case there is one duty that "constitutes the principle in the subject" (TL 6:448.21 f., trans. D.S.), in friendship this accessoric union of duties is replaced by a "*most intimate* union [innigsten Vereinigung]" (TL 6:469.14, italics D.S.). This is how Kant describes the union of the duty of love and the duty of respect in friendship. In friendship, this union is not accessoric, rather it is essential to friend-

34 Gregor translates "ästhetischen [*Freundschaft*, D.S.]" (TL 6:471.26) with "friendship based on feeling;" this is probably what it means to say that a friendship is 'aesthetic', still it is not what the text says.
35 Gregor's translation is faulty: "For love [jene] can be regarded as attraction and respect [diese] as repulsion, and if the principle of love [der ersteren] bids friends [there's no talk of 'friends' in German, D.S.] to draw closer, the principle of respect [der zweiten] requires them to stay [halten] at a proper distance from each other" (TL 6:470.4–7). Especially the replacement of "der ersteren" by "love" and "der zweiten" by "respect" is problematic; Kant might very well mean 'Prinzip der Annäherung' and 'Prinzip der Abstoßung' such that the principle of attraction is the principle of love and the principle of repulsion is the principle of respect (though §23 suggests another reading). Here, this might only be a minor point; but again, one can see that translations are not trustworthy and potentially misleading.
36 Cf. TL 6:471.15 and 473.6.
37 Kant begins §24 like this: "In speaking of *laws* of duty [...]" (TL 6:449.4, italics D.S.).

ship that love and respect are in an *"Ebenmaß des Gleichgewichts"* (TL 6:470.3, italics D.S.), in *"equal* balance required for friendship" (TL 6:470.3 f., italics D.S.). In §§26–36 duties of love are treated 'separately,' and in §§37–44 the same is done with duties of respect; they are treated 'separately' although they "are really always united with each other according to the law in a single duty, yet only in such a way that now one duty, now the other constitutes the principle in the subject, such that one duty is joined to the other accessorily" (TL 6:448.19–22, trans. D.S.) (D2). When it comes to friendship, however, there is no separateness, and there is no accessoric connection; there is an *'innigste Vereinigung'*.[38]

3. A Sketch of a Research Program

In what follows I will try to sketch a *research program* for some of the other sections in the chapter on duties of love; this is a sketch only, because there are simply too many questions to be raised and too many observations to be made. By 'research program' I mean (in this specific context) that there is a certain text highly in need of interpretation—up to the present day, there's practically no detailed analysis of those sections—, and that one can make *textual observations* that call for a coherent interpretation whatever eventually the actual interpretation will be. Such a textual observation is (at least to some extent) interpretatively neutral, i.e. it does not necessarily imply a certain interpretation; still, it is an observation to be made, to be paid attention to and to be taken into account. For instance, pointing out that those occurrences of the demonstrative pronoun "They" in §23 (TL 6:448.15, 448.19) are, at least at first sight, ambiguous, is a textual observation (along with further observations related to this). An interpretation of the whole section that accounts for They$_1$ and They$_2$ was offered too, and, of course, one may very well find this (my) interpretation false. The crucial point, however, is that one has to provide reasons *why* one finds it false and *why* an alternative interpretation is better, *that is*, the alternative interpretation must *pay attention* to and *explicitly account for* the textual observations *that have been* made already. So anyone who writes an (interpretative) paper on

---

38 Burggraf, 2005, p. 159, thus gets it quite wrong when he claims that love and respect are "really always united with each other according to the law in a single duty" (TL 6:448.19–21, trans. D.S.) and then calls this very same union on the basis of §46 'friendship'.

§23³⁹ must be aware of the literature written on this and must take into account, and account for, the textual observations that have been made in this literature; and then must offer a coherent interpretation that is true to the text, possibly accounting for even more textual details. If someone writes on §23 and does not refer to the problem of They₁/They₂ at all, or refers to it, but rejects the suggested interpretation without giving reasons, or refers to it, providing an alternative reading without accounting for the other textual observations related to the problem of They₁/They₂, then no progress in our Kant research has been made.⁴⁰ 'Research' like this, and there are numerous examples for it, can go on forever and ever without making any demonstrable progress in better understanding Kant.

So let me draw your attention to some crucial questions to which I can only, if at all, sketch an answer. All questions refer to the introductory remarks on the duties of love; needless to say, Kant's discussion of these duties proper is no less difficult and no less in need of interpretation.

What Is the Maxim of the Duty of Love?

In §25, Kant mentions the "maxim of *benevolence*" (TL 6:449.20 f.), and this again shows up, with exactly the same wording, in §27 (cf. TL 6:450.31) and also, slightly changed, as the "maxim (of beneficence)" (again in §27) (TL 6:451.18; see also TL 6:451.7). But what exactly is the maxim when it comes to duties of love?⁴¹ There are three possibilities: There could be (i) a general maxim of the duties of virtue toward others, (ii) a general maxim of all duties of love, and there could be (iii) specified maxims for each duty of love (a maxim of benevolence, a maxim of gratitude, and a maxim of sympathetic feeling). Let us have a brief look.

---

39 If someone does not want to interpret the text of §23, one wonders why he or she refers to it.

40 Next to the central question of the reference of They₁/They₂, future research on §23, I submit, should be in a position to account for the role of the example and its relation to the preceding sentences (and thus for the "So" (TL 6:448.22)); for "(*jede* für sich allein)" (TL 6:448.16, italics D.S.); for the sentence in parenthesis ("love of one's neighbor though [...]" (TL 6:448.16 f., trans. D.S.), noting the 'necessary' quality of love and respect); and to account for all the other details observed in (i)–(vii).

41 Here I cannot discuss the question of what a maxim is; but it would have an effect on the interpretation.

Ad (i) A general maxim of the duties of virtue toward others: In §§23 – 25, which are about duties of love *and* respect, Kant does not mention a general maxim of (all) these duties of virtue toward others; rather, Kant distinguishes between a maxim of duties of love and a maxim of duties of respect. In the *Vorarbeiten zur Tugendlehre*, this is different. There it says: "Das allgemeine Princip der Tugendpflicht gegen andere Menschen ist: trage gegen jedermann Liebe und Achtung" (VATL 23:407.19 f.). ("The general principle of the duty of virtue toward other human beings is: have [trage] love and respect toward everyone" (VATL 23:407.19 f., trans. D.S.).)

Not much is said herewith; for what does it mean to "have love and respect toward everyone"? Incidentally, in those *Vorarbeiten* (as in §25), Kant also puts much emphasis on his claim that love and respect in this context are not treated as feelings, but as duties.

Ad (ii) A general maxim of all duties of love: It is somewhat confusing or misleading that in §§25 and 27 Kant speaks of a 'maxim of *benevolence*' (or beneficence); after all, benevolence is only *one* of the three duties of love, and up to §27, the text is about duties of love in general (up to §25 it is even about respect). As a matter of fact, Kant speaks repeatedly about duties of love as if these duties consisted only in duties of benevolence. Thus, in §26 (a section still about duties of love in general) he says that 'practical philanthropy'—which earlier he had called "love of one's neighbor" (TL 6:448.16 f., trans. D.S.)[42] and "duty of love for one's neighbor" (TL 6:450.3)—"must be taken as active benevolence" (TL 6:450.16 – 18), almost as if *Menschenliebe* as a duty is nothing but such (active) benevolence.[43] Yet, something like a general maxim of all duties of love can be found in §25:

First, the German original:

> Die Pflicht der Nächstenliebe kann also auch so ausgedrückt werden: sie ist die Pflicht, Anderer ihre Zwecke (sofern diese nur nicht unsittlich sind) zu den meinen zu machen; die Pflicht der Achtung meines Nächsten ist in der Maxime enthalten, keinen anderen Menschen bloß als Mittel zu meinen

---

42 On my interpretation, 'love of one's neighbor' in TL 6:448.16 (i.e. in §23) is about practical love, not about the feeling; here too it shows how important a close reading of §23 is for other contexts as well.

43 It is therefore remarkable that Kant in one place of the *Vorarbeiten zur Tugendlehre* (VATL 23:410) discusses duties of love in general, but notes in parentheses after "Liebespflichten" (VATL 23:410.28): "(eigentlich die des Wohlwollens) [(actually the [duty, D.S.] of benevolence)]" (VATL 23:410.28).

Zwecken abzuwürdigen (nicht zu verlangen, der Andere solle sich selbst weg-
werfen, um meinem Zwecke zu fröhnen) (TL 6:450.3–8).

Here's my translation:

> Thus the duty of love for one's neighbor can also be expressed like this: It is
> the duty to make the other's *ends* my own (provided only that these are not
> immoral); the duty of respect for my neighbor is contained in the maxim not
> to devalue any other human being to a mere means to my ends (not to de-
> mand that the other cast away himself in order to indulge my end) (TL
> 6:450.3–8, trans. D.S.).

The "maxim" (TL 6:450.6) of the "duty of respect for my neighbor" (TL
6:450.5, trans. D.S.) shall be of no interest to us here.[44] However, note
that Kant does speak of a '*maxim*' here, and that he does so in a way
that emphasizes the parallel of the maxim of duties of respect with the
maxim of duties of love although the first part of the sentence does
not make use of the term 'maxim' with regard to duties of love; clearly,
however, Kant has a maxim of the duties of love in mind. Based on the
first part of that sentence ("Thus the duty of love for one's neighbor can
also be expressed like this: It is the duty to make the other's *ends* my own
(provided only that these are not immoral)" (TL 6:450.3–5, trans.
D.S.)), this maxim can be expressed as follows: *Make other's ends your
own!*[45] Further passages confirm this: Thus, beneficence as practical benevolence, i.a. a benevolence based on a maxim, is defined as "making the
other's well-being and good one's end [sich das Wohl und Heil des Anderen zum Zweck zu machen, (das Wohlthun)]" (TL 6:452.4 f., trans.

---

44 See also TL 6:488.14–19: "All moral relations of rational beings, which involve
    a principle of the harmony of the will of one with that of another, can be reduced
    to *love* and *respect*; and, insofar as this principle is practical, in the case of love the
    basis for determining one's will can be reduced to another's *end*, and in the case of
    respect, to another's *right*." – On duties of respect, see Sensen's contribution to
    this volume.

45 Accordingly, the maxim of respect would be: *Do not degrade any other human
    being to a mere means to your ends!* (The proviso regarding the morality of the
    ends goes without saying.) – Note that Kant says that the duty of love of one's
    neighbor (*Nächstenliebe*) can "*also*" (TL 6:450.3, italics D.S.) be expressed as
    'making the other's ends my own.' But why 'also'? Maybe because the maxim
    to make the other's ends my own is an explication of 'benevolence;' but
    maybe this formulation (to make the other's ends my own) is a *replacement* of
    the Biblical command (and formulation) that is usually connected with the con-
    cept of 'Nächstenliebe' sc., 'love your neighbor as yourself' which, however, is
    only manifest in §§27–28. – Many thanks to Christian Hamm for a very fruitful
    discussion on this.

and italics D.S.); again, for Kant beneficence often stands for duties of love in general. Further, in section XVIII of the "Introduction" it says that duties of love for one's neigbor are duties to perform actions "by which one makes [...] others an end" (TL 6:410.19 f.)[46]. Finally, this interpretation is confirmed by *Vorarbeiten zur Tugendlehre*. For there the maxim of the duties of love is expressed as follows: "den Zweck Anderer auch zu dem Meinen zu machen" ("to make other's ends also my own") (VATL 23:407.28, trans. D.S.). Duties of love, says Kant in those *Vorarbeiten*, "gehen auf die Zusammenstimmung des Zwecks der Menschen zu den Zwecken aller Anderen" (roughly: "are directed toward the harmony between the ends of all human beings") (VATL 23:406.29–407.1, trans. D.S.).[47]

Ad (iii) Specified maxims for each duty of love:

(a) *The maxim of benevolence:* As already mentioned, in § 28 Kant speaks of a 'maxim of benevolence.' In the following sections, there are further formulations that narrow the circle of the adressees of one's beneficence.[48] Beneficence, says Kant in §29, is practical benevolence "with regard to those *in need* [in Ansehung der *Bedürftigen*]" (TL 6:452.25, italics D.S.).[49] Formulated as a duty[50] (§30), Kant says: "To be beneficent, that is, to promote according to one's means the happiness of others [anderen Menschen] in need [in Nöthen], without hoping for something in return, is everyone's [jedes Menschen] duty" (TL 6:453.2–4); in his comments on this, Kant uses "Noth" three times (TL 6:453.5, 453.7, 453.9), but replaces this term by the one (and somewhat weaker) term used in §30, to wit, "Bedürftige" (TL 6:453.13) resp. "bedürftige" (TL 6:453.14).[51] Fi-

---

46 Gregor's translation might be misleading: "[...] by which one makes [...] others *one's* end" (italics D.S.); but "one's" has no equivalent in German. It just says: "[...] durch die der Mensch [...] andere.*zum* Zweck macht" (italics D.S.) (it does *not* say: 'zu *seinem* Zweck macht').

47 Cf. VATL 23:411.6 f.: "Liebe ist Zusammenstimmung mit dem Zweck Anderer."

48 With regard to gratitude, Kant calls this "E x t e n s i o n" (TL 6:455.26) of a duty (Gregor translates "*extent*").

49 The whole passage is only loosely translated by Gregor; I will not get into details.

50 In §29 it says that we have the duty "to adopt this maxim [of beneficence, D.S.] as a universal law" (TL 6:452.29 f.).

51 Gregor translates *both* terms (*Not, Bedürftige*) and their variants with 'need.' That's noteworthy, because one can be '*bedürftig*' without being '*in Not*;' after all, it is a crucial question how much latitude one has in carrying out the duty of beneficence.

nally, note one more difficult formulation in §29: "Wohlwollen ist das Vergnügen an der Glückseligkeit (dem Wohlsein) Anderer; Wohlthun aber die Maxime, sich *dasselbe* zum Zweck zu machen" (in Gregor's translation: "Benevolence is satisfaction in the happiness (well-being) of others; but beneficence is the maxim of making others' happiness one's end") (TL 6:452.26–28, italics D.S.). What does "dasselbe" (TL 6:452.28) refer to? For grammatical reasons, it cannot refer to "Glückseligkeit [happiness]" (TL 6:452.27), since "dasselbe" (TL 6:452.28) requires a neuter, "Glückseligkeit" (TL 6:452.27), however, is feminine.[52] As for the gender, one could refer it to "dem Wohlsein" (TL 6:452.27) (in parentheses, the "well-being [Wohlsein]" (TL 6:452.27) is neuter), with the result that the maxim is to make the well-being of others one's end, which makes sense, of course. Strictly speaking, however, "dasselbe" (TL 6:452.28) can only refer to "Vergnügen" (TL 6:452.27) (satisfaction or fun), and then the proposition is to make that "*Vergnügen*" (TL 6:452.27, italics D.S.) one's end. Given that "Vergnügen an der Glückseligkeit (dem Wohlsein) Anderer" ("satisfaction in the happiness (well-being) of others") (TL 6:452.27) is the definition of "[b]enevolence" (TL 6:452.26), Kant's claim would be that beneficence is the maxim to make benevolence one's end; and that does not sound so absurd, does it?[53]

---

52 Gregor replaces "dasselbe" (TL 6:452.28) with "happiness." – Note another problem with §29 as well: Kant begins this section (§29) with a paragraph on the "Pflicht des Menschen *gegen sich selbst* [duty of man *to himself*]" (TL 6:452.22, trans. and italics D.S.). That is strange because Kant is about to write on the duty of beneficence as a duty to *others*. Even more remarkable is that the first sentence of the next paragraph (in the English translation) begins as follows: "*But* beyond benevolence in our wishes [...]" (TL 6:452.23, italics D.S., emphasis in the original erased), and then in this paragraph there is absolutely no reference to what is said in the first paragraph of §29; this "[b]ut" cannot be explained. Suppose we consider a conjecture: The first paragraph of §29 as it is edited (TL 6:452.16–22) does not belong to that §29 at all; rather, the second paragraph of §29 (as it is now: TL 6:452.23–30) should be the first paragraph of §29. This would make for a very fitting connection with the last paragraph in the proceeding §28 where Kant does talk about "benevolence in *wishes*" (TL 6:452.1). The question, of course, then is where TL 6:452.16–22 belongs—maybe to §27 where Kant discusses the duty of benevolence to oneself (which is the topic of TL 6:452.16–22)? I cannot get into further details here; note, however, that editorial problems of the *Metaphysik der Sitten* are common. For a recent example, see Bacin/Schönecker, 2010.
53 This "Vergnügen" is mentioned again in §31 (TL 6:453.20).

(b) *The maxim of gratitude:* There is no direct or indirect formulation of a 'maxim' of gratitude. It all depends on what 'gratitude' is, and that is not a question easy to answer because it involves, generally speaking, both a feeling (honoring) and an act of service.

(c) *The maxim of sympathy:* The same is (possibly) true for "[t]heilnehmende Empfindung" (TL 6:456.18): There seems to be no direct or indirect formulation of a 'maxim' of this sympathy; but it is not entirely clear because the relevant sections (§§32–33) are very hard to understand.

Is There a Duty to Be Benevolent To Oneself? (§27)

Kant often puts his ethical maxims or precepts in the context of Christian ethics.[54] In §§27–28 too he relates the duty and maxim of benevolence to the "formula [Formel][55]: Love your *neighbor* [Nächsten][56] (your fellow human being) as yourself" (TL 6:451.28 f., trans. D.S.).[57] I have already noted that §27 is about the question of whether, and how, benevolence can be directed towards oneself (given that the Christian precept commands love of one's neighbor *as oneself*); §28 discussses the problem that benevolence (or philanthropy), despite the universality of the required love of one's neighbors, must allow for degrees. These sections, in particular §28, are very hard to understand. Let me pose some questions, first on §27.

(1) §27 begins as follows: "In accordance with the ethical law of perfection 'love your neighbor as yourself,' the maxim of benevolence (practical love of human beings) is a duty of all human beings toward one another, whether or not one finds them worthy of love" (TL 6:450.31–34). Is it really beyond doubt (as Gregor's translation suggests) that the "ethical law of perfection" (TL 6:450.33), rather than the "maxim of benevolence" (TL 6:450.31), is to be identified with that Christian precept (to love your neighbor as yourself)? Maybe the "maxim of benevolence" (TL

---

54 An important passage is KpV 5:81 ff.
55 Gregor translates "Formel" (TL 6:451.28) as "precept."
56 The literal meaning of '*Nächster*' is: someone who is near (close) to you.
57 The opposite maxim, as it were, is this: "everyone for himself, God for us all" (TL 6:452.3), and: "Everyone for himself, God (fortune) for us all" (TL 6:452.32 f.).

6:450.31) (at the beginning of the first sentence)[58] is to be identified with that precept; after all, in §25 the duty of love is called the "duty of love for one's neighbor" (TL 6:450.3). And then the claim would be this: 'The maxim of benevolence is a duty of all human beings towards one another, whether or not one finds them worthy of love, according to the ethical law of perfection (which is *not* formulated), and the maxim is this: Love your neighbor as yourself.' In what follows, Kant does speak about love of one's neighbor and then again twice about a maxim, so that would fit.

(2) The main argument of §27, I believe, is as follows:

1. The maxim of benevolence is a universal duty for all human beings regarding all human beings.
2. I am a human being.

Therefore, the maxim of benevolence is a duty for me regarding myself as well.

The main problem is this: Since everyone loves himself or herself anyway, there can be, so it seems, no *duty* to love oneself. How is this reconcilable with that argument? Despite the fact that "the law making benevolence a duty will include myself, as an object of benevolence" (TL 6:451.8 f.), Kant says very clearly that there can be "no obligation" (TL 6:451.12) to love oneself. Rather, he says, the maxim "*permits* you to be benevolent to yourself" (TL 6:451.16 f.). But how is this a solution to the problem? Of course, everything that is obligatory is permitted; not everything that is permitted, however, is obligatory. But the maxim does not say that it is permissible to love all human beings (including oneself); it says that one *ought* to love all human beings (including oneself). Adding the condition that one may only be benevolent to oneself provided one is "benevolent to every other as well" (TL 6:451.17) does not, it seems to me, change that; still the question remains whether benevolence to oneself is permissible or obligatory.

---

58 Gregor restructures the sentence. In German, it says: "Die Maxime des Wohlwollens (die praktische Menschenliebe) ist aller Menschen Pflicht gegen einander, man mag diese nun liebenswürdig finden oder nicht, nach dem ethischen Gesetz der Vollkommenheit: Liebe deinen Nebenmenschen als dich selbst" (TL 6:450.31–34). I cannot pursue this but note that there is an important difference in the punctuation between the Meiner Edition and the Academy Edition; the Meiner Edition, but not the Academy Edition, supports the Gregor-reading.

May There Be Different Degrees of Benevolence? (§28)

This section is one of the most difficult sections of the entire book, I would maintain. Again, I can only sketch some observations and questions.

1) What is the main topic? Setting aside (for the time being) the first paragraph and looking only at the second (and final) paragraph, there seems to be a clear structure. Kant formulates a problem up to the hyphen (cf. TL 6:451.35); after the hyphen, the problem is solved. What is the problem? At first sight, things seem to be fairly easy; it's about the 'fitting' of the evangelical command[59] with certain facts about me and my neighbors: "Yet one human being is closer [näher] to me than the other, and in benevolence I am to myself the closest [der Nächste]. How does this fit with the formula: Love your *neighbor* [deinen Nächsten] (your fellow human being)[60] as yourself?" (TL 6:451.27–29, trans. D.S.)[61] So Kant sees a contradiction: "I cannot, without contradicting myself, say that I ought to love every human being as myself" (TL 6:451.33 f.). Why not? The evangelical command says "that I ought to love every human being as myself" (TL 6:451.34), i.e. love everyone with that degree x of love with which I love myself. This, however, appears not to be compatible with Kant's assumption that different degrees of obligatory benevolence are permissible. For if it is permissible to show *different* degrees of benevolence to *different* people, how then shall I show the *same* degree x of benevolence to *all* people ('love everyone with that degree x of love')?

2) In the second paragraph, Kant uses several variants of '*Nähe*' (closeness) six times.[62] One would think that what he means by this '*Nähe*' is something like, say, personal closeness on grounds of social, spiritual, family relations or whatever. This is certainly true for some of these occurrences of '*Nähe*,' but not true for at least two of them. For in (at

59 This is how Kant calls it, for instance, in the second *Critique* (cf. KpV 5:81 f.).

60 In German, it says "*Mit*menschen" (TL 6:451.29, italics D.S.); in the earlier formulation of the evangelical command in §27, Kant says "*Neben*menschen" (TL 6:450.34, italics D.S.); Gregor translates the latter with "neighbor," the former with "fellow-human being."

61 Kants construes the problem around the German words '*näher*,' '*der Nächste*,' '*deinen Nächsten*;' this is an important connotation that gets lost if one only reads the translation: 'Love your neighbor' should literally be translated as 'love the one that is next to you,' or: 'that is close to you.'

62 Cf. TL 6:451.27, 451.28, 451.29, 451.30, 451.32, 452.7.

least) two cases, this closeness is not understood descriptively (I *am* close to someone), but prescriptively (I *ought* to be close to someone). Kant writes: "If one is closer to me than another (*in the duty of benevolence*), [and, D.S.][63] I am thus [also][64] *obliged* to greater benevolence to one than to the other but am admittedly closer to myself (*even in terms of duty* [*selbst der Pflicht nach*])[65] than to any other [...]" (TL 6:451.29–33, trans. and italics D.S.). So one can be 'closer' to some person than to another 'in the duty of benevolence,' i.e. one can be obliged to more or to less benevolence ('greater benevolence' or less) depending on the person to whom my benevolence will be directed. Of course, here the second meaning of 'closeness' kicks in: *Whether* I am under obligation to more or to less benevolence, will (among other things, none of them mentioned in §28) depend on my personal closeness. This meaning of 'closeness' (i.e. personal closeness), I believe, is what Kant has in mind when at the end of the paragraph he says that "in acting the degree [of obligation, D.S.] can vary quite greatly, according to the variety among those who are loved [Verschiedenheit der Geliebten] (one of whom concerns me more *closely* than the other [deren Einer mich *näher* angeht als der Andere])" (TL 6:452.6–9, trans. and italics D.S.).[66]

3) What is Kant's solution to that alleged 'contradiction'? In the last sentence just discussed, the problem is described as running the risk of "violating the universality of the maxim" (TL 6:452.8) by allowing different degrees of benevolence to which one is obligated. But that, it seems to me, is *not* the problem introduced before the hyphen. Rather, the problem is that "the measure of self-love would allow for no difference in degree" (TL 6:451.34 f.). Kant does not discuss, let alone justify, the claim that due to personal closeness different degrees of closeness 'in the duty of benevolence' are real and permissible. His claim is, I believe, true yet far from self-evident. Moreover, he has no solution to the real problem: If I am to love everyone as I love myself, then I am to love everyone with the

---

63 There's no '*und*' in German (as Gregor's translation suggests); though it's hard in English to omit it.

64 Gregor translates '*also*' with 'therefore;' but that's misleading, because the '*also*' is only explicative (in terms of 'that is ...').

65 Gregor translates: "even in accordance with duty".

66 Again, Gregor's translation is much looser: "[...] in acting I can [...] vary the degree greatly in accordance with the different objects of my love (one of whom concerns me more closely than another)." The "Geliebten" (TL 6:452.7), however, are not 'objects' of my love, but persons; in German, 'Geliebte' is never a word used for objects but for persons.

one, and only one, degree of love I love myself; but then there can be no differences in degree when it comes to my love toward others.

4) In the first paragraph of §28, Kant talks about "the benevolence in the general love for human beings [allgemeine[] Menschenliebe]" (TL 6:451.21, trans. D.S.).[67] It is far from clear, though, what this '*allgemeine Menschenliebe*' is. '*Menschenliebe*' is certainly equivalent to, or even identical with, benevolence. However, since benevolence has both an aesthetic and a practical meaning, that '*allgemeine Menschenliebe*' could be two different things.

In one interpretation, it would be a "*feeling*" (TL 6:449.17), or maybe "benevolence in *wishes*" (TL 6:452.1), or an inclination, possibly based on the definition of philanthropy in §28 where a friend of humanity is understood as someone who finds pleasure in the well-being of human beings as such. In any event, '*allgemein*' (general, universal) is this '*Menschenliebe*' inasmuch as every human being is loved by those who possess '*Menschenliebe*'.

Another interpretation takes '*allgemeine Menschenliebe*' to be that benevolence that to have and to actively perform (beneficence) is a wide *duty* (of love). This interpretation is supported by the following consideration: The second paragraph in §28 is connected with the first by a "Yet [Aber]" (TL 6:451.27).[68] Later in that paragraph, Kant explicitly distinguishes "benevolence in *wishes*" (TL 6:452.1) from "active, practical benevolence" (TL 6:452.4), which consists in "making the well-being and happiness of others my *end*" (TL 6:452.4 f.), and the latter is certainly benevolence as a duty. If one reads the proviso "what is meant *here*" (TL 6:452.1, italics D.S.) back to what is said before the hyphen, this suggests that '*allgemeine Menschenliebe*' is that practical benevolence. If so, the idea expressed in the first paragraph of §28 is just the same as

---

67 Gregor translates: "the benevolence present in love for all human beings" (TL 6:451.21). There's no equivalent for 'present' in the German text. The most important (and difficult) term in that formulation, to wit, "allgemeinen [general]" (TL 6:451.21) is rendered with "*all* human beings" (italics D.S.), but that is already an interpretation. A bit later, Kant speaks again about "allgemeinen Menschenliebe" (TL 6:451.23 f.), and that too is translated with "love for all human beings." In §35, however, Kant also speaks of an "allgemeinen Nächstenliebe" (TL 6:458.13 f.) which Gregor does not translate with 'love for all one's neighbors' (or so), but (correctly) with "*universal* love for one's neighbor" (italics D.S.). Incidentally, in that translation 'present' has no equivalence in the German text.

68 Also, the first sentence of §28 picks up what was said before (with the "now" (TL 6:451.21)), and in the predeceding section practical benevolence was discussed.

what Kant already pointed out in §27: Benevolence is "a duty of *all* human beings toward one another" (TL 6:450.31 f., italics D.S.); everyone is obligated, and everyone is the object of one's obligation. This being said, the question now is … (and then Kant continues with his analysis of closeness and different degrees). Thus, the generality of the love for human beings (*'allgemeine Menschenliebe'*) would be taken up again in the "universality of the maxim [Allgemeinheit der Maxime]" (TL 6:452.8).[69]

But the other interpretation, according to which *'allgemeine Menschenliebe'* is not understood as a duty, has something to be said for it as well: It says that "I *take* an interest in this human being's well-being" (TL 6:451.23, italics D.S.), rather than 'I *ought* to take' such an interest; and that "I *am* only not indifferent with regard to him" (TL 6:451.25 f., italics D.S.), rather than 'I *ought* only not to be indifferent with regard to him.' Also, if practical benevolence is what Kant has in mind in the first paragraph of §28, then this practical benevolence would be "the smallest in its *degree*" (TL 6:451.22). But would this make sense? Practical benevolence, i.e. the required action (beneficence) as a wide duty has no degree whatsoever before its specified (unless all Kant wants to say is that there is a general and *prima facie* duty to be benevolent).[70]

References

Anderson, Elizabeth (2008), "Emotions in Kant's Later Moral Philosophy: Honour and the Phenomenology of Moral Value", in: Betzler (ed.) (2008), pp. 123–145.
Bacin, Stefano/Schönecker, Dieter (2010), "Zwei Konjekturvorschläge zur 'Tugendlehre,' §9", in: *Kant-Studien*, vol. 101, pp. 247–252.
Bacin, Stefano (forthcoming), "Kant on the Relation between Duties of Love and Duties of Respect", in: Claudio La Rocca/Alfredo Ferrarin/Stefano Bacin/Margit Ruffing (eds.), *Kant und die Philosophie in weltbürgerlicher Absicht.*

---

69 One cannot (as easily) note this in Gregor's translation because she translates "*allgemeine*[] Menschenliebe" (TL 6:451.21 and 451.23) with "love for *all* human beings" (italics D.S.) whereas "*Allgemeinheit* der Maxime" (TL 6:452.8, italics D.S.) she translates with "*universality* of the maxim" (italics D.S.).
70 I'm very grateful to the participants of the 4. *Siegener Kant-Tagung* (Sept. 2009) for very fruitful discussions on the topic of my paper: Stefano Bacin, Bernd Dörflinger, Ina Goy, Christian Hamm, Thomas Höwing, Eva Oggionni, Friedo Ricken, Jens Timmermann, Andreas Trampota.

Akten des XI. Internationalen Kant-Kongresses 2010, Berlin/New York: Walter de Gruyter.

Baron, Marcia (2004), "Love and Respect in the Doctrine of Virtue", in: Mark Timmons (ed.), *Kant's 'Metaphysics of Morals': Interpretative Essays*, Oxford: Oxford University Press, pp. 391–407.

Beck, Lewis White ([3]1963), *A Commentary on Kant's 'Critique of Practical Reason'*, Chicago: University of Chicago Press.

Betzler, Monika (ed.) (2008), *Kant's Ethics of Virtue*, Berlin/New York: Walter de Gruyter.

Burggraf, Volker-Herbert (2005), *Interessen und Imperative bei Kant*, Bonn, Rheinische Friedrich-Wilhelms-Universität, Diss. (http://hss.ulb.uni-bonn.de/2005/0450/0450.pdf, 6/23/2010).

Damschen, Gregor/Schönecker, Dieter (2012), *Selbst philosophieren: Ein Methodenbuch*, Berlin/Boston: Walter de Gruyter.

Esser, Andrea (2004), *Eine Ethik für Endliche: Kants Tugendlehre in der Gegenwart*, Stuttgart: Frommann-Holzboog.

Forkl, Markus (2001), *Kants System der Tugendpflichten: Eine Begleitschrift zu den Metaphysischen Anfangsgründen der Tugendlehre*, Frankfurt/M.: Peter Lang.

Gregor, Mary (1963), *Laws of Freedom: A Study of Kant's Method of Applying the Categorcial Imperative in the 'Metaphysik der Sitten'*, New York: Barnes & Noble.

Guyer, Paul (2010), "Moral Feelings in the 'Metaphysics of Morals'", in: Lara Denis (ed.), *Kant's 'Metaphysics of Morals': A Critical Guide*, Cambridge: Cambridge University Press, pp. 130–151.

Horn, Christoph (2008): "The Concept of Love in Kant's Virtue Ethics", in: Betzler (ed.) (2008), pp. 147–173.

Kant, Immanuel (1797) [[1]1990], *Metaphysische Anfangsgründe der Tugendlehre*, Bernd Ludwig (ed.), Hamburg: Meiner.

Kant, Immanuel (1797) [1999], *Metaphysics of Morals*, in: *Practical Philosophy* (The Cambridge Edition of the Works of Immanuel Kant), Mary J. Gregor (ed.), Cambridge: Cambridge University Press, pp. 353–603.

Koch, Lutz (2003): *Kants ethische Didaktik*, Würzburg: Königshausen & Neumann.

Mairhofer, Heinrich (1975), "Kants Entwurf einer inhaltlichen Ethik in der 'Metaphysik der Sitten'", in: *Wiener Jahrbuch für Philosophie*, vol. 8, pp. 39–53.

Malibabo, Balimbanga (2000), *Kants Konzept einer kritischen Metaphysik der Sitten*, Würzburg: Königshausen & Neumann.

Moors, Martin (2006), "Kant on 'Love god above all, and your neighbour as yourself'", in: Gabor Boros (ed.), *Moral Theories of Emotions and Passions: The Concept of Love in Modern Philosophy*, Brussels: KVAB, pp. 63–80.

Murphy, S. J., Séamus (1994), "Kant and Moral Motivation: Why Love is not enough", in: *Milltown Studies*, vol. 33, pp. 65–88.

Nikolaus, Wolfgang (1986), "Moralität – Sittlichkeit – Liebe: Zum Konkretisierungsproblem des 'kategorischen Imperativs'", in: *Wiener Jahrbuch für Philosophie*, vol. 18, pp. 135–148.

Römpp, Georg (2006), *Kants Kritik der reinen Freiheit: Eine Erörterung der Metaphysik der Sitten*, Berlin: Duncker & Humblot.

Schönecker, Dieter (²2004), "Textvergessenheit in der Philosophiehistorie", in: Dieter Schönecker/Thomas Zwenger (eds.), *Kant verstehen/Understanding Kant: Über die Interpretation philosophischer Texte*, Darmstadt: Wissenschaftliche Buchgesellschaft, pp. 159–181.

Schönecker, Dieter (2010), "Kant über Menschenliebe als moralische Gemütsanlage", in: *Archiv für Geschichte der Philosophie*, vol. 92, pp. 133–175. (Unter Mitarbeit von Alexander Cotter, Magdalena Eckes, Sebastian Maly.)

Schönecker, Dieter (2010b): "Kant über die Möglichkeit von Pflichten gegen sich selbst (*Tugendlehre* §§1–3)", in: Hubertus Busche/Anton Schmitt (eds.), *Kant als Bezugspunkt philosophischen Denkens*, Würzburg: Königshausen & Neumann, pp. 235–260.

Steigleder, Klaus (2002), *Kants Moralphilosophie: Die Selbstbezüglichkeit reiner praktischer Vernunft*, Stuttgart/Weimar: Metzler.

Streich, Detlev (1924), *Der Begriff der Liebe bei Kant*, Greifswald, Ernst Moritz Arndt Universität, Diss. (Kopie der maschinenschriftlichen Dissertation aus der Akte UAG, Phil.Diss. II – 274).

Witschen, Dieter (2006), "Achtung und Nächstenliebe: Zu einer Unterscheidung in Kants 'Metaphysik der Sitten'", in: *Freiburger Zeitschrift für Theologie und Philosophie*, vol. 53, pp. 617–634.

Duties to Others From Respect
(TL 6:462–468)

Oliver Sensen

As part of his treatment of duties in the *Doctrine of Virtue*, Kant outlines duties that are owed to *others* from respect due to them (cf. TL 6:462.1 – 468.13). He discusses them in the second section of a chapter on duties towards other human beings, the first section of which dealt with duties of love.[1] Duties of respect emphasize a negative aspect of one's duty. They are limiting conditions, admonishing to keep oneself at a distance from others. Everyone owes these duties to everyone else without putting the other person under a further obligation (of gratitude etc.). They are analogous to duties of right as presented in Kant's *Doctrine of Right*, "not to encroach upon what belongs to anyone" (TL 6:449.33; cf. TL 6:449 f.).

The section on duties toward others from respect is divided into eight sub-sections (§§37–44). The first five are general remarks, containing definitions (§37), the justification for why one should respect others (§38), clarifications of what should be respected (§39), a contrast to the feeling of respect (§40), and a clarification of the nature of the vices of disrespect (§41). Kant then elucidates the three vices of disrespect: arrogance (§42), defamation (§43), and ridicule (§44). These eight sub-sections should be of prime interest to moral philosophy. Since this *Doctrine of Virtue* passage is the main place where Kant discusses negative duties towards others, one would expect a substantive and thorough account of those duties in these paragraphs.

This makes it more puzzling which particular vices Kant discusses, and how little room he devotes to duties from respect. Among negative duties towards others one would expect the prohibition of much more serious offences (such as murder, rape, deception). One would also expect a longer discussion, maybe even divided into duties towards others as natural beings (e. g. the prohibition of murder, mutilation, intoxication), and as moral beings (e. g. the prohibition of deception, the use of others as

---

1 For the relation between the two sections see Baron, 2002, pp. 393–400; Esser, 2004, pp. 370–374; and Gregor, 1963, pp. 182–188.

mere means, and contempt for others)—corresponding to the division
Kant gives for negative duties towards self (cf. TL 6:421.1–437.26; cf.
V-MS/Vigil 27:594.33–596.9). Why does Kant merely put forth arro-
gance, defamation, and ridicule as vices of disrespect?

On the other hand, why does he bring up negative duties at all?[2] The
introduction to the *Doctrine of Virtue* gave the impression that ethics is
about ends that are also duties (cf. TL 6:380.22–382.1). These ends
are said to be one's own perfection and the happiness of others (cf. TL
6:385.31 f.). Kant discusses these in the sections on one's imperfect
duty to increase one's natural and moral perfection (cf. TL 6:444.9–
447.17), and in the section on the imperfect duty of love towards others
(cf. TL 6:448.1–461.31).[3] These duties correspond to the examples three
and four given in the *Groundwork* under the description of positive duties
(cf. GMS 4:422.37–423.35). What then is the justification for negative
duties?

There are therefore at least three puzzles that come up in reading the
section on duties towards others from respect:

1.) Why does Kant put forth only these particular three vices of arrogance, defamation, and ridicule?
2.) Why does he not put forth other violations of negative duties towards
others (e. g. murder, rape, deception)?
3.) What is the justification for duties towards others from respect?

In this commentary I shall try to answer these questions. I shall treat them
in reverse order, since the third seems to hold the key for answering the
other two.

1. The Justification for Duties Toward Others from Respect

Why exactly should one respect others? What is the justification for the
negative duty not to encroach upon them? At first glance one might
think that it is something about the others that generates the requirement.
Does Kant not say that others have an absolute value, called 'dignity,' and
that this value grounds the obligation to respect them? In the first sub-
section (§37), for instance, Kant says the following:

2   Cf. Gregor, 1963, p. 181; Esser, 2004, p. 344; and V-MS/Vigil 27:600.12–22.
3   Cf. the contributions to this volume by Thomas Hill and Dieter Schönecker re-
    spectively.

The *respect* that I have for others or that another can require from me (*observantia aliis praestanda*) is therefore recognition of a *dignity* (*dignitas*) in other human beings, that is, of a worth that has no price (TL 6:462.10–13).

If one reads this passage in isolation, it suggests the following picture: Every human being has within himself an incomparable value which commands respect from every other rational being. This view is nowadays commonly attributed to Kant.[4] However, in this section I shall argue that this popular view—despite the appearance of a few well-known passages—is not actually Kant's view.

To argue for this claim, I shall first go beyond the *Doctrine of Virtue* to present Kant's views on value (section 1.1), the reason why one should respect others (1.2), and dignity (1.3). I shall then come back to the §§37–41 to show that the alternative reading is actually in the *Doctrine of Virtue* as well (1.4). In short my claim will be that the justification for why one should respect others does not rest on a recognition of a value inherent in others, but is grounded on an initial command of one's own reason. The passage just quoted states *what* should be respected in others, but is not meant as a justification of *why* others should be respected. The alternative justification allows one to explain why Kant talks about these three particular vices of disrespect. I shall start my argument with Kant's conception of value.

1.1 Kant's Account of Absolute Inner Value

Why would one think that Kant does *not* ground the requirement to respect others on a value of human beings? The reason is that he directly argues against such a justification of moral requirements in the *Critique of Practical Reason*. His argument is a *reductio ad absurdum*. He starts out in assuming that there is a value that could ground laws that are necessary and a priori (as moral laws must be). He goes on to argue that under that assumption there would not be any moral law: "Suppose that we wanted to begin with the concept of the good in order to derive from it laws of the will [...] the possibility of a priori practical laws would be at once excluded" (KpV 5:63.11–25). How does he reach that conclusion?[5]

---

4 See e. g. Wood, 2009. For complications with this popular view see Darwall, 2008. For an exception to this interpretation see Esser, 2004, esp. pp. 372, 389, 198–202.

5 For a fuller discussion of the following see Sensen, 2011.

Kant's argument is that if value should be the foundation of the moral claim, then one first would need an account of how one can discern this value (and why one should be motivated to follow it). For Kant this could only be via a feeling of pleasure:

> If the concept of the good is not to be derived from an antecedent practical law, but, instead, is to serve as its basis, it can be only the concept of something whose existence promises pleasure and thus determines the causality of the subject, that is, the faculty of desire, to produce it (KpV 5:58.10–14).

One could know the value (and be motivated by it) only via pleasure, because anything that would be 'out there' (like a value of other human beings) would have to be cognized by sensibility and not the faculty of understanding:

> Pleasure [...], insofar it is to be a determining ground of desire for this thing, is based on the *receptivity* of the subject, since it *depends* upon the existence of an object; hence it belongs to sense (feeling) and not to the understanding, [...] (KpV 5:22.9–13).

If a value of human beings were to be the ground of moral requirements to respect them, one could only cognize this value (and be motivated by it) via sensibility. If it is not given in any of the five senses, then the sense would have to be a feeling of pleasure. However, pleasure is relative and contingent: "[...] pleasure or displeasure [...] can never be assumed to be universally directed to the same objects" (KpV 5:26.5 f.). It therefore cannot ground a necessary and universal law (as moral laws must be (cf. GMS 4:389.11–23)).

A modern-day intuitionist or moral realist would not think that Kant's alternatives exhaust all the options. Why could there not be a sixth sense for discerning a value of human beings, and why could one not be motivated by the same feeling of respect Kant puts forth for the moral law? However, what the argument shows is that this was not Kant's view. It could even be argued that Kant did not even know of or envision the realist view of value as a non-natural property.[6]

Kant's usage of 'value' therefore does not commit him to the existence of a metaphysical value entity. Instead, Kant structures moral notions

---

6   Kant envisions the good to be either pleasure, a moral feeling, perfection or divine will (cf. GMS 4:441.32–442.5; KpV 5:39.5–40, 64.15–17; V-Mo/Mron II 29:620.38–629.12). In the second *Critique* Kant adds education and civil constitution and calls them all "all previous" (KpV 5:39.6) and "all possible" (KpV 5:39.11) material grounds of morality. He does not envision value to be a non-natural property.

around the faculty of reason. If reason deems something necessary as a means to something else, Kant can say that the action (or object) has conditional or relative value (cf. GMS 4:428.11–14). What, on the other hand, "reason independently of inclinations cognizes as practically necessary, that is, as good" (GMS 4:412.33f.) has absolute or inner value. In this respect 'absolute' and 'inner' specify that reason prescribes it in "every respect and without any further condition" (KpV 5:60.21 f.; cf. KrV A324/B381). The grammatical form 'x has value' is therefore only a shorthand for saying that x *should* be valued. Kant conceives of value as a *prescription* of reason.[7] In comparison to popular Kant interpretations one could describe Kant's views on value as—so to speak—another Copernican Revolution:[8] Moral claims do not derive from an existing value, but claims of (absolute) value derive from the moral law: "[...] nothing can have a worth other than that which the law determines for it" (GMS 4:436.1 f.; cf. V-MS/Vigil 27:513.4 f.).[9]

It is important to note that Kant's views on the grounding of moral laws have not changed in the *Doctrine of Virtue*. In the "Introduction" he does discuss ends that are a duty to have (cf. TL 6:380.22–381.24). However, these ends do not ground the requirement to respect others. They are not humanity, but one's own perfection and the happiness of others. More importantly, these ends are not said to be the foundation of the moral law, but explicitly said to *follow* from it:

> One can think of the relation of end to duty in two ways: one can begin with the end and seek out the *maxim* of actions in conformity with duty or, on the other hand, one can begin with the maxim of actions in conformity with duty and seek out the end that is also a duty. – The *doctrine of right* takes the first way. [...] But *ethics* takes the opposite way (TL 6:382.8–17).

The *Doctrine of Virtue* does not introduce a new ultimate *justification* for moral duties: Ends that are duties follow from the moral law. Nor is this contradicted by the supreme principle of the *Doctrine of Virtue*. The supreme law reads: "act in accordance with a maxim of *ends* that it can be a universal law for everyone to have" (TL 6:395.15 f.). Since these ends

---

7 Cf. Hill, 2003, p. 19; Wood, 2008, p. 91.
8 See Engstrom, 2009, pp. 13 f.
9 In my view, value is a secondary notion for Kant, cf. also Schneewind, 1998, pp. 285–288. It is not only secondary for questions of justification, but also for the derivation of concrete duties. Kant's views on value sketched above also rule out any independent value (in addition to anthropological knowledge) that would be needed to apply the Categorical Imperative. I thank Marcia Baron, Joshua Glasgow and Sally Sedgwick for pressing me on this point.

that it is a duty to have follow from the moral law, the emphasis on ends marks no departure from the Categorical Imperative (as formulated at GMS 4:421.6–8).[10]

1.2 The Justification for Respect Owed to Others

If Kant does not justify the requirement to respect others in reference to a value they possess, what is the reason for the requirement? Kant explains it in the following way: "The duty of respect for my neighbor is contained in the maxim not to degrade any other to a mere means to my ends" (TL 6:450.5–7). To have the maxim not to treat others as mere means is a requirement of Kant's Categorical Imperative in the Formula of Humanity: "*So act that you use humanity, whether in your own person or in the person of any other, always at the same time as an end, never merely as a means*" (GMS 4:429.10–12). If the requirement to respect others is expressed by the Formula of Humanity, how is that formula itself justified?[11]

The justification cannot refer to a prior value. The Formula of Humanity is also a categorical imperative, valid necessarily and universally. The argument sketched above in section 1.1 therefore equally applies here. Instead, Kant says the requirement not to treat others as mere means is already contained in the main formula of the Categorical Imperative: "*act only in accordance with that maxim through which you can at the same time will that it become a universal law*" (GMS 4:421.7 f.). Kant explains that containment in the following way: The main formulation of the Categorical Imperative requires that one can universalize one's maxim. This means that one should not act on maxims that could not also be adopted by others or spring from the will of others. However, this also means that in not acting on the improper maxim one already respects others as equals and as limiting conditions for one's maxims:

> [...] every will [...] is restricted to the condition of agreement with the *autonomy* of the rational being, that is to say, such a being is not to be subjected to any purpose that is not possible in accordance with a law that could arise from the will of the affected subject himself; hence this subject is to be used

---

10 For a fuller discussion of TL 6:380–382 see Andreas Trampota's contribution to this volume.
11 I defend the following more fully in Sensen, 2009b.

never merely as a means but as at the same time an end (KpV 5:87.21 – 27).[12]

One would treat others as mere means if one acted on a maxim that could not be adopted by them. The requirement to respect others is already contained in the main formulation of the Categorical Imperative, which is "the principle of equality" (TL 6:451.15).[13]

To complete the argument that value is not the foundation of Kant's moral philosophy, it is important to note that the Categorical Imperative itself is not justified in reference to a prior and independent value (see again section 1.1). Instead Kant conceives of the imperative as the causal law of freedom. Freedom is in the first instance not a normative property for Kant, but a form of causality (cf. GMS 4:446.13–447.7)[14]. Every causality needs a law, and the moral law would describe the actions of a purely free being. The moral law only appears as an imperative to beings that are not completely free. But the imperative is not derived from a normative fact (e.g. a value), but follows from freedom in a descriptive sense.[15]

Kant justifies the requirement to respect others as a direct command of reason. In this sense Kant's ethics is not second-personal—he does not ground the requirement in the recognition of another's authority to demand respect, despite the advantages of such an approach.[16] Rather for him every duty towards others is subordinate to a duty to oneself to follow the Categorical Imperative: "since the law by virtue of which I regard myself as being under obligation proceeds in every case from my own practical reason" (TL 6:417.27–418.1).[17] Accordingly, another can

---

12 Cf. GMS 4:437.21–438.7. See also Hill, 2000, pp. 201–209.
13 The justification outlined here does not conflict with the *Groundwork* passage leading up to the Formula of Humanity (GMS 4:427.19–429.13). There Kant had asked the question whether the main formulation of the Categorical Imperative is a necessary law for all rational beings (cf. GMS 4:426.22–25). He answers this question by saying that the ground of the imperative is rational nature in virtue of freedom (i.e. as an end in itself). Since everyone has to regard himself as free, the Categorical Imperative is an objective principle for all. This foreshadows the justification Kant gives in the third Section of the *Groundwork* to which he refers explicitly (see GMS 4:429n.35 f.). For a fuller defense of this reading see Sensen, 2009b.
14 See also V-MS/Vigil 27:481.26–29.
15 See Timmermann, 2007, pp. 122, 130 f.; and Johnson, 2009.
16 See Darwall, 2009.
17 On this point see Jens Timmermann's contribution to this volume; Schönecker, 2010; and Denis, 2010.

claim what is owed to him in reminding the agent of *his duty*, expressed in the imperative (cf. RL 6:239.13–21)[18]. For Kant obligations arise from the first-personal standpoint, not the second-personal. However, since the requirement of the Categorical Imperative can also be expressed in the Formula of Humanity, Kant can make free use of the formula throughout the *Doctrine of Virtue* without introducing a new justification.

1.3 Kant's Conception of Dignity

The final concept that has to be addressed for a full understanding of the *Doctrine of Virtue* passage is Kant's concept of dignity. Kant's usage of 'dignity' is far more complex than it is often said to be.[19] It cannot be a foundational value for Kant's moral philosophy, since he does not set forth such a value (see again Section 1.1). Instead he uses 'dignity' in three slightly different but related ways. What these have in common is that 'dignity' expresses a rank or elevated position. Kant uses 'dignity' to say that one thing x is higher or elevated over something else y. Most often he specifies dignity as a form of sublimity (*Erhabenheit*)[20], which is something that is absolutely great or great without comparison (cf. KU 5:248.5–10).

In a first and non-moral sense, Kant uses 'dignity' to express the higher rank of one person or entity over another. In this sense he talks about a "kingly dignity" (Anth 7:131.9), the dignity of a regent or minister (cf. ZeF 8:344.6–8), the dignity of philosophy (cf. KrV A62/B86, A319/B375, A463/B491), mathematics (cf. KrV A464/B492), the dignity of a teacher (cf. RGV 6:162.19) or of a philosopher (cf. Log 9:26.14). These are not moral usages, but they express the higher rank of a king in the state, or a teacher in the classroom. These are also not isolated usages, but have a direct relevance for the passage in the *Doctrine of Virtue* (cf. §§37–44). For there Kant talks about the respect that should be shown to differences in "rank and dignity" (TL 6:468.9) (*Stand und Würde*) that someone contingently occupies in society, and about mere customs that are falsely "raised to the dignity of a law" (TL 6:464.18 f.), and he says that against mockery it is right "either to put

---

18   See also TL 6:467.33–468.5; V-MS/Vigil 27:580.37–581.8.
19   For a fuller account of the following, see Sensen, 2009a.
20   Cf. BDG 2:117.35; GSE 2:212.1, 215.20, 241.18; GMS 4:425.28, 440.1; KpV 5:71.21; TL 6:435.20; Log 9:30.12.

up no defense [...] or to conduct it with dignity and seriousness" (TL 6:467.26 f.). In these instances Kant is not talking about morality (nor a foundational moral value), but about a higher rank one entity occupies over another (and the conduct befitting one's higher position).

In a second but related way Kant talks about the 'dignity of humanity.' The idea is that *all* human beings are elevated over the rest of nature in virtue of being free. This is still a descriptive or pre-moral sense. It describes the fact that human beings are not mere playthings of external forces, but are special in nature in that they are free and can act independently of natural causality.[21] By itself this fact does not generate a duty. Rather freedom comes with the moral law that commands duties. The second usage of 'dignity' will be important for understanding one aspect of the *Doctrine of Virtue* passage (cf. §38), where Kant refers to: "his dignity [...], by which he raises himself above all other beings in the world that are not human beings" (TL 6:462.24–26). Here Kant uses 'dignity' to describe human beings as special in nature.

The main usage of 'dignity' that is important for the *Doctrine of Virtue* passage is a third one. Kant often uses 'dignity' in connection with morality to express that moral worth is raised above other forms of value ("raised above all price" (GMS 4:434.33; cf. TL 6:462.21–32, 436.5–13)). This usage of 'dignity' is closely related to the second: Human beings are special in nature in virtue of possessing freedom. However, only if one makes proper usage of one's freedom (in accordance with the Categorical Imperative) does one fully realize one's initial inborn dignity: "The dignity of human nature lies only in its freedom [...]. But the dignity of one human being (worthiness) rests on the use of his freedom" (Refl 6856 19:181.4–9, trans. O.S.).[22] In this third sense 'dignity' is not the name for a moral value, but rather expresses that moral value is higher than other value, in that only morality should be pursued unconditionally. This sense will be important because Kant often uses it in the *Doctrine of Virtue* passage—not to *justify* why others should be respected (even the vicious person deserves respect (cf. TL 6:463.12–15))—but to clarify *what* should be respected in others.

---

21 Cf. RGV 6:57n.27–58n.16, 183.19–37; TL 6:420.13–19; V-NR/Feyerabend 27:1319.2–1322.29.

22 Cf. Päd 9:488. At this point Kant's usage of 'dignity' is reminiscent of an ethics of honor, cf. Baron, 2002, p. 399, note 12; and Anderson, 2008.

So in the *Doctrine of Virtue* passage (§§37–41) Kant uses 'dignity' in three different ways. Having distinguished these, I shall now turn to the commentary of this passage.

1.4 The Justification of Duties of Respect in §§37–41

§37 contains definitions regarding the respect due to others. In the introduction to duties towards others in general (§25) Kant had characterized duties of respect as "not exalting oneself above others" (TL 6:449.32). In respecting others one does not "detract anything from the worth that the other, as a human being, is authorized to put upon himself" (TL 6:450.12 f.). Accordingly, in §37 Kant defines modesty as the "willing restriction of one's self-love in view of the self-love of others" (TL 6:462.5 f.). If one does not restrict one's self-love, but exalts it over the self-love of others, the attitude would be "*self-conceit (arrogantia)* [Eigendünkel]" (TL 6:462.10). The most extreme vice of disrespect is to deny the other any worth: "Judging something to be worthless is contempt" (TL 6:462.15 f.).

Respect for others is therefore "recognition of a *dignity (dignitas)* in other human beings" (TL 6:462.12 f.). In respecting others one does not place oneself above them, but recognizes a certain rank or standing (i.e. dignity). One leaves intact the worth that the other is justified placing upon himself. This worth is not the *justification* for why one should respect others—'worth' here merely refers to self-esteem—but it explains *what* should be respected in others. One should acknowledge the self-respect the other is justified in placing on himself. But why does Kant say that recognition of a dignity in others is recognition "of a worth that has no price, no equivalent for which the object evaluated (*aestimii*) could be exchanged" (TL 6:462.13–15)? He explains this in §38.

§38 contains the justification for the requirement to respect others. It is a dense passage that relies on Kant's fuller treatment elsewhere. It begins: "Every human being has a legitimate claim to respect from his fellow human beings and is *in turn* bound to respect every other" (TL 6:462.18–20). At first this just reads as the thesis to be proven. However, it already contains a reference to the justification. One can make a claim for respect on others, but it could only be binding if one "*in turn*" grants it to others. The moral bindingness enters through the universality of the

Categorical Imperative.[23] However, Kant also spells the justification out as he proceeds.

He goes on: "Humanity itself is a dignity" (TL 6:462.21). I have argued that this should be read as saying: 'Humanity is elevated over the rest of nature.' Why is it elevated? "[F]or a human being cannot be used merely as a means [...] but must always be used at the same time as an end" (TL 6:462.21–23). Human beings have a dignity *because* ("for") the moral law, as articulated in the Formula of Humanity, demands respect for human beings. Dignity is not the ground of that requirement (similarly: TL 6:434.32–435.2). In this context Kant uses 'dignity' to express that human beings are special in nature because they are protected by the requirement to respect others, as expressed in the Formula of Humanity: "It is just in this that his dignity (personality[24]) consists, by which he raises himself above all other beings in the world that are not human beings and yet can be used, and so over all *things*[25]" (TL 6:462.24–26). The Formula of Humanity is the justification for why one should respect others, confirming what Kant had said earlier (cf. §25), that the requirement to respect others is already contained in the requirement not to degrade others to mere means (cf. TL 6:450.5–8).

The rest of §38 specifies *what* should be respected in others. Kant goes on:

> But just as he cannot give himself away for any price (this would conflict with his duty of self-esteem), so neither can he act contrary to the equally necessary self-esteem of others, as human beings, that is, he is under obligation to acknowledge, in a practical way, the dignity of humanity in every other human beings (TL 6:462.26–31).

What one should respect in others is their self-esteem. As one is under a duty to esteem oneself, so everyone else is under this duty also. The self-esteem is said to be necessary and linked to dignity. In which sense is self-esteem necessary, and what is its link to dignity? In order to answer these questions, I shall have a brief look at where Kant explains these ideas in

---

23 Cf. TL 6:393.19–22: "we [...] make ourselves an end for others; and the only way this maxim can be binding is through its qualification as a universal law". Cf. TL 6:451; and V-MS/Vigil 27:580.

24 Kant's use of "personality" here indicates that it is being under the moral law, i.e. freedom, that elevates one over the rest of nature and that is to be respected. This will come out as §38 continues.

25 On Kant's views about duties towards animals, cf. O'Neill, 1998; and Sensen, 2009b.

§11.[26] The answer will explain why Kant had said in §37 that respecting others means respecting their dignity and a worth that has no price.

Kant explains the duty of self-esteem in connection with the vice of servility or false humility (cf. TL 6:434.20–437.26). The vice would be "belittling one's own moral worth merely as a means to acquiring the favor of another" (TL 6:435.37–436.2). Instead true humility relates to the Categorical Imperative: "True humility follows unavoidably from our sincere and exact comparison of ourselves with the moral law" (TL 6:436.5–7). The idea is that everyone is subject to the Categorical Imperative. In following it, one is capable of achieving a good will, and with it a worth that is beyond price (in the sense specified in Section 1.1 above). As this is the only worth that is of prime importance, one does not have to lower oneself to anyone, but one should "revere the (moral) human being within his own person" (TL 6:436.8 f.). Therefore one has a duty of self-esteem, and a duty not to fall into servility or false humility. For "as the subject of a morally practical reason" (TL 6:434.32 f.) the human being "can measure himself with every other being of this kind and value himself on a footing of equality with them" (TL 6:435.3–5; cf. V-MS/Vigil 27:609.35–610.3).

Kant uses 'dignity' to express the *same* claims in terms of higher and lower. The duty of self-esteem is based on the thought that one can attain what is of prime importance: a good will as commanded by the moral law. This aspect of oneself is therefore higher: It is sublime in its importance and can exalt oneself over the rest of nature. This is how Kant puts it in §11: "In the system of nature, a human being […] is a being of slight importance […]" (TL 6:434.22 f.). However, "his insignificance as a *human animal* may not infringe upon the consciousness of his dignity as a *rational human being*" (TL 6:434.14 f.). A human being therefore "should not disavow the moral self-esteem of such a being" (TL 6:434.15 f.), and should maintain this esteem "with consciousness of his sublime moral predisposition" (TL 6:434.19 f.). This means that "from our capacity for internal lawgiving and from the (natural) human being's feeling himself compelled to revere the (moral) human being within his own person, at the same time there comes *exaltation* of the highest self-esteem" (TL 6:436.7–10). The moral aspect of human beings is connected with a "feeling of his inner worth (*valor*),

---

26 For a full commentary on that section see Stefano Bacin's contribution to this volume.

in terms of which he is above any price (*pretium*) and possesses an inalienable dignity" (TL 6:434.10–12).

Self-esteem is therefore pride in the dignity of one's moral "vocation" (TL 6:437.4). Kant uses 'dignity' to express that something is 'sublime', 'exalted' or 'above any price.' In this context what is exalted is the *moral* vocation (which alone should be pursued unconditionally), or the idea of oneself as morally good.[27] In this context dignity is clearly connected to morality. It is not itself a value, but is used to express a higher standing of moral value over other forms of behavior. This gives a fuller picture of why Kant says that respecting others is recognition of a dignity, or a worth that has no price (cf. §37): As one is oneself under the duty of moral self-esteem to realize one's initial dignity and form a morally good will, so everyone else is under the same duty. If one should respect others—as is commanded by the Formula of Humanity—then one should respect them in their striving to realize their dignity and form a morally good will.

In §39 Kant makes clear that the duty to respect the moral striving in others does not mean that one should only respect morally worthy people: "To be *contemptuous* of others (*contemnere*), that is, to deny them the respect owed to human beings in general, is in every case contrary to duty; for they are human beings" (TL 6:463.2–4). One does not owe respect only to human beings that are morally good, and does not just owe it because they might be good after all (even though they do not show any sign of it). Moral worth is not the justification for respecting others. The Formula of Humanity commands that one respect all human beings as such: Even a vicious man deserves respect "as a human being, even though by his deeds he makes himself unworthy of it" (TL 6:463.13–5). Kant does not say that a vicious human being really is good deep down, or that his striving gives him worth, or that the capacity for morality has worth. Even if one could judge that a vicious being has no moral worth, one still should not treat him as if he were a thing or with complete contempt. He remains a human being and is to be respected. Neither moral vice nor faulty reasoning justifies contempt: "for on this supposition he could never be improved, and this is not consistent with the idea of a *human being*, who as such (as a moral being) can never lose entirely his predisposition for the good" (TL 6:463.36–464.3). One should respect all human beings as such. What one should respect in them is their moral capacity (freedom and

---

27 Cf. TL 4:436.7–10; V-MS/Vigil 27:593.5–9; GMS 4:434.29 f.

the Categorical Imperative), but the degree to which the other is moral—
and his corresponding moral worth—do not justify a lack of respect.

Kant grants that one often cannot help but *feel* contempt (e.g. for a
villain), however, the respect owed to others is not a feeling, but the
maxim of limiting one's self-esteem by the equal high rank or dignity
of others:

> [...] **respect** to be shown to others [...] is not to be understood as the mere
> *feeling* that comes from comparing our own *worth* with another's (such as a
> child feels merely from habit toward his parents, a pupil toward his teacher,
> or any subordinate toward his superior). It is rather to be understood as the
> *maxim* of limiting our self-esteem by the dignity of humanity in another per-
> son, and so as respect in a practical sense (TL 6:449.23–30).

So Kant seems to use 'respect' in three different ways: the esteem one
might have for the other's appearance or non-moral achievements (cf.
TL 6:449.24–27), the moral feeling of respect for the law (cf. KpV
5:71.26–89.8), and a commanded maxim of not exalting oneself
above others (cf. TL 6:449.28–30). In the *Doctrine of Virtue* passage
on respect (§§37–44) Kant is talking about the last of the three senses.[28]
Even if one cannot help but feel contempt for a villain in the first sense of
respect, "the outward manifestation of this is, nevertheless, an offense"
(TL 6:463.5 f.).

In §40 Kant unfolds connections between several concepts. Although
the respect owed to others is not a feeling, there is a way in which it is
connected to the moral feeling of respect for the moral law. What one
should respect in others and in oneself is the moral law. On the motivational or subjective side this duty is connected to the feeling of respect
(*Achtung*), and since feeling respect is awareness of one's duty in Kant's
framework, feeling respect for the moral aspect of others is awareness
of one's duty to others:

> Respect for the law, which in its subjective aspect is called moral feeling, is
> identical with consciousness of one's duty. This is why showing respect for a
> human being as a moral being (holding his duty in highest esteem) is also a
> duty that others have toward him (TL 6:464.5–9).

---

28 On the other hand, in TL 6:435.2 f.—where Kant says that a human being "pos-
    sesses a *dignity* [...] by which he exacts *respect* for himself"—he talks about re-
    spect in the second sense: It is the moral law in others that exacts a feeling of
    respect from an observer (cf. GMS 4:401n.27 f.). I thank Dieter Schönecker
    for pressing me on this point.

The reconciliation of the respect owed to others with feeling is not a justification for why one should respect others. A feeling cannot be commanded (cf. TL 6:401.24–26), and one cannot be bound to revere others, only to revere the moral law (cf. TL 6:467.33–468.5). In §40 Kant merely gives a fuller picture of what is involved in respecting others. He goes on to specify the claim to respect from others as "*love of honor*" (TL 6:464.10), the manifestation of this claim in one's conduct "*respectability*" (TL 6:464.11), and the offence against respectability a "*scandal*" (TL 6:464.12). Real scandal is therefore not tied to someone being merely unconventional (as violating customs of one's society), but in violating the duty of equal respect (TL 6:464.10–20).

§41 likewise does not contain any new claim about the justification to respect others. Kant merely points out that the failure to respect others is not merely the lack of virtue but a vice, since it infringes upon a lawful claim. He will now elaborate the vices that violate duties of respect for other human beings, which are: a) arrogance (*Hochmut*), b) defamation (*Afterreden*), and c) ridicule (*Verhöhnung*) (cf. TL 6:465.5f.).

This answers the question of justification of duties of respect: One should respect other human beings because it is commanded by the Categorical Imperative, brought closer to intuition by the Formula of Humanity. But why does the imperative only prohibit the vices of arrogance, defamation, and ridicule? Why not others (like murder, mutilation, deception)? To this question I shall now turn.

2. The Particular Duties: Why Not Others?

In order to answer in the next section the question why Kant puts forth these particular three vices, one first has to see why he does not propose other more obvious duties (e. g. the prohibition of murder etc.). This can be explained by looking at the particular level to which the imperative is applied at this stage of the *Metaphysics of Morals*. There are at least four different aspects one could evaluate in regard to any given action.[29]

1.) One could merely test whether the type of action, as observable by an outsider, could be universalized. In this connection Kant says that "ethics does not give laws for *actions* (*ius* does that), but only for *maxims* of actions" (TL 6:388.32 f.; cf. 6:410.8–10).

---

29 Cf. Baron, 2002, pp. 401–405.

2.) Instead of the outer behavior the imperative could evaluate the motivation from which one acts. This is the second half of Kant's famous distinction between the *legality* and *morality* of actions (cf. KpV 5:71.28–72.11; MS 6:214.13–19): "in the case of what is to be morally good it is not enough that it *conform* with the moral law but it must also be done *for the sake of the law*" (GMS 4:390.4–6). This is a requirement about the proper motivation for moral actions, "of doing such actions not from inclination but *from duty*" (GMS 4:398.19 f.; cf. 432).

3.) However, one might distinguish further aspects of maxims. The imperative can command that one adopt a maxim with a certain end: one's own perfection and the happiness of others. This seems to be different from the requirement of moral motivation: If one adopts the end to help others pursue their happiness, one could do it from different motivations: e. g. for one's reputation, out of love, or simply out of duty.[30]

4.) Duties of respect do not seem to fit into any of the three previous categories. They are not one of the ends that it is a duty to have (cf. TL 6:385 f.), nor are they in the first instance a requirement of the right motivation. Duties of respect are similar to duties of right in that they are negative, stricter, and concerned with not encroaching upon others. However, they differ from duties of right in that for the latter only an external lawgiving is possible—one can coerce someone to the outward fulfillment of the duty, but not to the inner free adoption of the maxim of respect. The lawgiving for duties of respect is "an inner one [...], since they are derived from the concept of freedom through the law of non-contradiction" (V-MS/Vigil 27:587; cf. TL 6:380). So, duties of respect concern the internal determination of one's will to adopt a maxim of respect (cf. TL 6:449).

This answers the second question posed at the outset. Kant does not talk about particular types of action (e. g. murder, mutilation, deception) since these are already dealt with in the *Doctrine of Right* (e. g. under civil independence and contract laws). These would be outer violations of one's innate right to freedom (cf. RL 6:230), and coercion can be used to prevent violations (ibid. 230–2). However, it is important to note that the prohibition of holding maxims of disrespect will rule out any action that would be used to express that inner disrespect. A maxim of con-

---

30 I am side-stepping the question whether helping others for one's own self-interest or simply out of duty are the same end pursued out of different motivations, or two different ends (cf. Baron, 2002, p. 402). I am merely distinguishing different aspects to clarify what exactly duties of respect require.

tempt would "contain a general determination of the will, having under it several practical rules" (KpV 5:19.7 f.). The prohibition of maxims of disrespect rules out any means of implementing these vices, as well as any "outward manifestation" or action on these maxims (TL 6:463.6). But even if one can explain why Kant confines himself to *maxims* of disrespect at this point, why does he put forth the particular three of arrogance, defamation and ridicule?

3. Arrogance, Defamation, and Ridicule: Why these three?

As far as I can see, this particular classification of three vices of respect is Kant's own. It is not in Baumgarten's *Introduction to Practical First Philosophy* or his *Philosophical Ethics,* the textbooks for Kant's lectures on moral philosophy.[31] Is there a good reason why Kant should list these particular three?

The answer—I think—lies in the justification for duties of respect. I have argued that the ultimate justification for why one should respect others is the Categorical Imperative. Kant explains the imperative as follows:

> If we now attend to ourselves in any transgression of duty, we find that we do not really will that our maxim should become a universal law, since that is impossible for us, but that the opposite of our maxim should instead remain a universal law, only we take the liberty of making an *exception* to it for ourselves (or just for this once) to the advantage of our inclination (GMS 4:424.15–20).

The central idea behind the Categorical Imperative in its main formulation is that one should not make an exception for oneself (or in the case of duties towards self: not this once). The central idea behind duties of respect as described in the *Doctrine of Virtue* is that one should not exalt oneself above others: "[...] a duty of free respect toward others is, strictly speaking only a negative one (of not exalting oneself above others)" (TL 6:449.31 f.). For Kant the Categorical Imperative in its main

---

31   Accordingly the classification is not in the Collins notes on Kant's lectures on practical philosophy and Baumgarten (1784/85). Comments on arrogance, defamation, and ridicule are scattered throughout the Vigilantius notes on Kant's lecture on the metaphysics of morals (1793/94), but Kant does not treat duties of respect as a separate category (cf. V-MS/Vigil 27:600, 611, 666, 687, 705, 708 f.).

formulation and the Formula of Humanity are "at bottom the same" (GMS 4:438.1, cf. 436.9). One can see why. If one makes an exception for oneself, one thereby exalts oneself over others who do have to follow the law. And if one thinks of oneself as being above others, one considers oneself to be an exception, and is likely to act accordingly. The Categorical Imperative and the Formula of Humanity are one command put in different ways.[32]

It also explains why Kant puts forth the particular maxims of arrogance, defamation, and ridicule. They can be read as a *progression* on the vice of disrespecting others. Regarding arrogance as "an inclination to be always *on top* [...] we demand that others think little of themselves in comparison with us" (TL 6:465.10–13). "By defamation [...] I mean only the immediate inclination, with no particular aim in view, to bring into the open something prejudicial to respect for others" (TL 6:466.10–14). "But holding up to ridicule a person's real faults [...], in order to deprive him of the respect he deserves [...] has something of fiendish joy in it; and this makes it an even more serious violation of one's duty of respect for other human beings" (TL 6:467.10–15).

There is a progression in the forms of contempt the three vices display. Arrogance makes one *regard* others as lower. Defamation intends to lower the other *in public* or in the open. Ridicule attaches to this a *joy* in the lowering of others. Kant cites three vices and these three vices because they are the possible expressions of the vice of disrespecting others.[33]

Kant lists vices and not corresponding virtues because the duty is only a negative one: "I am not bound to *revere* others [...]. The only reverence to which I am bound by nature is reverence for law as such" (TL 6:467.33–468.1). The ultimate reason for respect is the moral law or Categorical Imperative: "[...] to revere the law [...] is a human being's universal and unconditional duty toward others" (TL 6:467.35–468.4). The imperative also explains why Kant regards arrogance, defamation, and ridicule as the vices concerning the respect owed to others.

---

32 This is why in the second *Critique* Kant can use the main formulation of the imperative to rule out self-conceit (as an inflated self-esteem or *Eigendünkel*) (cf. KpV 5:73 f.; see also Darwall, 2008, pp. 184–187).

33 In discussing defamation Kant also cites the indirect bad consequences defamation has. However, the real reason is that it would make "contempt the prevalent cast of mind" (TL 6:466.23), and contempt is ruled out by the Categorical Imperative.

Concluding Remarks

I have argued that for Kant duties of respect are already contained in the Categorical Imperative. However, can the imperative carry the weight that is placed upon it? Can the formal principle deliver the content that one wants for a moral theory?[34]

I think that this worry misunderstands the aim of Kant's moral philosophy. His aim is not to give a full moral theory, laying down once and for all generations what exactly should and should not be done.[35] Even in the *Doctrine of Virtue*, in which he presents the fullest account of ethical duties in his published writings, the list he gives is quite minimal (of not undermining one's freedom, but perfecting oneself, of not thinking of others as worthless, but helping them in their pursuit of happiness). Kant's aim is to give a very general framework in which a more particular moral system would have to be worked out according to the specifics of the situation:

> The different forms of respect to be shown to others in accordance with differences in their qualities or contingent relations – differences of age, sex, birth, strength or weakness, or even rank and dignity, which depend in part on arbitrary arrangements—cannot be set forth in detail and classified in the *metaphysical* first principles of a doctrine of virtue, since this has to do only with its pure rational principles (TL 6:468.6–13).

Even in the *Doctrine of Virtue* Kant deliberately stays at a very general level. His account leaves a lot of freedom for individuals and individual societies to pursue their conception of a good life. Different accounts of the good life are permitted, as long as one's freedom "can coexist with everyone's freedom in accordance with a universal law" (RL 6:231.11 f.), and does not violate duties towards self. In a diverse world, where different traditions coexist, Kant's moral framework does not prescribe one uniform way of life, but merely demands respect for humanity in all of its manifestations. I regard this as a strength, rather than a weakness.[36]

---

34 This echoes Hegel's charge that the imperative is empty and unable to derive specific duties (cf. Hegel, 1821/2008, §135).

35 Similarly Esser, 2004, pp. 389 f.

36 For their helpful comments I would like to thank Kathryn Sensen, Andreas Trampota, Marcia Baron, Stefano Bacin, and the participants of the conference at which I presented this essay.

References

Anderson, Elizabeth (2008), "Emotions in Kant's Later Moral Philosophy: Honour and the Phenomenology of Moral Value", in: Betzler (ed.) (2008), pp. 123–145.

Baron, Marcia (2002), "Love and Respect in the *Doctrine of Virtue*", in: Mark Timmons (ed.), *Kant's 'Metaphysics of Morals': Interpretative Essays*, Oxford: Oxford University Press, pp. 391–407.

Betzler, Monika (ed.) (2008), *Kant's Ethics of Virtue*, Berlin/New York: Walter de Gruyter.

Darwall, Stephen (2008), "Kant on Respect, Dignity, and the Duty of Respect", in: Betzler (ed.) (2008), pp. 175–199.

Darwall, Stephen (2009), "Why Kant Needs the Second-Person Standpoint", in: Hill (ed.) (2009), pp. 138–158.

Denis, Lara (2010), "Freedom, Primacy, and Perfect Duties to Oneself", in: Lara Denis (ed.), *Kant's 'Metaphysics of Morals': A Critical Guide*, Cambridge: Cambridge University Press.

Engstrom, Stephen (2009), *The Form of Practical Knowledge*, Cambridge/MA: Harvard University Press.

Esser, Andrea (2004), *Eine Ethik für Endliche: Kants Tugendlehre in der Gegenwart*, Stuttgart-Bad Cannstatt: Frommann-Holzboog.

Gregor, Mary (1963), *Laws of Freedom*, Oxford: Basil Blackwell.

Hegel, Georg Wilhelm Friedrich (1821) [2008], *Outlines of the Philosophy of Right*, trans. T.M. Knox, Oxford: Oxford University Press.

Hill, Thomas E. (2000), *Respect, Pluralism, and Justice*, Oxford: Oxford University Press.

Hill, Thomas E. (2003), "Treating Criminals as Ends in Themselves", in: *Annual Review of Law and Ethics*, vol. 11, pp. 17–36.

Hill, Thomas E. (ed.) (2009), *The Blackwell Guide to Kant's Ethics*, Oxford: Wiley-Blackwell.

Johnson, Robert (2009), "The Moral Law as Causal Law", in: Timmermann (ed.) (2009), pp. 82–101.

O'Neill, Onora (1998), "Kant on Duties Regarding Nonrational Nature II", in: *Aristotelian Society Supplement*, vol. 72, pp. 211–228.

Schneewind, Jerome B. (1998), "Kant and Stoic Ethics", in: Stephen Engstrom/ Jennifer Whiting (eds.), *Aristotle, Kant, and the Stoics*, Cambridge: Cambridge University Press, pp. 285–301.

Schönecker, Dieter (2010), "Kant über die Möglichkeit von Pflichten gegen sich selbst (*Tugendlehre* §§ 1–3): Eine Skizze", in: Hubertus Busche/Anton Schmitt (eds.), *Kant als Bezugspunkt philosophischen Denkens*, Würzburg: Königshausen & Neumann, pp. 235–260.

Sensen, Oliver (2009a), "Kant's Conception of Human Dignity", in: *Kant-Studien*, vol. 100, pp. 309–331.

Sensen, Oliver (2009b), "Dignity and the Formula of Humanity", in: Timmermann (ed.) (2009), pp. 102–118.

Sensen, Oliver (2011), "Kant's Conception of Inner Value", in: *European Journal of Philosophy*, vol. 19, pp. 262–280.

Timmermann, Jens (2007), *Kant's 'Groundwork of the Metaphysics of Morals'*, Cambridge: Cambridge University Press.
Timmermann, Jens (ed.) (2009), *Kant's 'Groundwork of the Metaphysics of Morals': A Critical Guide*, Cambridge: Cambridge University Press.
Wood, Allen (2008), *Kantian Ethics*, Cambridge: Cambridge University Press.
Wood, Allen (2009), "Duties to Oneself, Duties of Respect to Others", in: Hill (ed.) (2009), pp. 229–251.

Friendship, Duties Regarding Specific Conditions of Persons, and the Virtues of Social Intercourse (TL 6:468–474)

Marcia Baron

I. Introduction

My portion of the *Tugendlehre* consists of three parts: the very short second (and final) chapter of Part II of the "Doctrine of the Elements of Ethics" (Part II being "Duties of Virtue to Others"); the longer and much more complex "Conclusion of the Elements of Ethics"; and a short "Appendix" on "The Virtues of Social Intercourse." Most of my discussion—sections III–VIII—will concern "Conclusion of the Elements of Ethics."

II. Ethical Duties of Men Toward One Another with Regard to Their Condition

It is sometimes claimed that according to Kant, all of our duties to persons are simply duties to persons as such, without regard to differences either in the persons themselves, or in their situations. Brief reflection discloses one error in that claim: we can hardly fulfill our duty to promote others' happiness without attending to the situations of the persons whose happiness we aim to promote.[1] After all, to promote their happiness we need to take into account what their happiness consists in and what hindrances they face. TL 6:468.14–469.12 brings out another way in which that claim is in error.[2] Although it is true that our duties to others are in-

---

1 Likewise, to develop our talents we need to take into account what talents we have, or could come to have, and what it takes to develop them.
2 So does TL 6:452.6–8 where, speaking of beneficence, Kant writes that "in acting I can, without violating the universality of the maxim, vary the degree greatly

deed duties to persons qua persons, rather than to persons qua wealthy, or especially virtuous, or very learned, that someone is wealthy, or poor, or depraved, or virtuous, or ignorant, or learned has a bearing on how our duties are to be fulfilled. What sort of bearing? It is not that it is more important to fulfill our duties vis-à-vis the virtuous than the morally depraved, or vis-à-vis the learned than the ignorant; rather, the idea is that just what it is to show another respect is shaped by the other's situation, and the same is true, albeit for slightly different reasons, of the duty to promote another's happiness. As Kant observes in the moral catechism, we are not to "give a lazy fellow soft cushions so that he [can] pass his life away in sweet idleness" (TL 6:480.32–481.1). Thus in applying the general principles of duties of virtue to others, we are to take into account the differences in persons themselves and in their situations, even though the duties are themselves not based on (or eroded by) such differences.

III. *Menschenfreundschaft*

Friendship, on Kant's view, properly takes the following forms: (1) "the union of two persons through equal mutual love and respect" (TL 6:469.17f.), and (2) being a *"friend of human beings* as such" (TL 6:472.33) (hereafter '*Menschenfreund*'). The idea in (2) is that one takes an "affective interest in the well-being of all human beings," rejoicing with them (TL 6:472.34 f.).[3] Although most of my discussion will, mirroring Kant's, be directed to (1), (2) is also of importance and merits attention. I begin with (2) and then turn to the more complex (1).

Critical to being a *Menschenfreund* is the *Menschenfreund*'s "thought and consideration for the *equality*" (TL 6:473.1) among human beings. Earlier in the *Tugendlehre*, Kant remarked that a benefactor should "carefully avoid any appearance of intending to bind the other" by his beneficence, and instead "must show that he is himself put under obligation by the other's acceptance or honored by it" (cf. TL 6:453.22–28; see also

---

in accordance with the different objects of my love (one of whom concerns me
more closely than another)."

3   In using 'affective' I break with the 1996 Cambridge edition and instead follow
Gregor's 1991 translation, judging the former's translation of 'ästhetisch' as 'effective' to be a typo.

TL 6:448.24–449.2)[4]. Kant returns to this point in his discussion of friendship: "Taking to heart the duty of being benevolent as a friend of human beings (a necessary humbling of oneself) serves to guard against the pride that usually comes over those fortunate enough to have the means of beneficence" (TL 6:473.8–11; see also TL 6:454.22–28). Thus being a *Menschenfreund* is important for practicing beneficence in a way that does not "humble[] the other in his own eyes" (TL 6:453.25–26). Indeed, it is a duty to be benevolent *as a friend of man*.

IV. Friendship as the Union of Two Persons Through Equal Mutual Love and Respect

Significant though *Menschenfreundschaft* is, particularly in connection with beneficence, Kant's real interest in his "Conclusion" is in friendship as the union of two persons through equal mutual love and respect. This, he holds, is friendship in its perfection (cf. TL 6:469.17–18).[5] In such a union, each participates and shares sympathetically in the other's well-being through the moral good will that unites them. Kant also indicates in these two sentences that the adoption of this ideal makes one[6] deserving of happiness, and that in virtue of this fact, human friendship is a duty.

These lofty, inspiring remarks are immediately followed by a claim that friendship is "unattainable in practice" (TL 6:469.25) as well as a clarification that the duty is a duty to strive for friendship. Both call for discussion. I begin with the latter. Just what is the content of that duty? This much is easy: we can see that the duty is not to be a friend, or to have such-and-such a friendship, but rather to strive for friendship;

---

4   Quotations for which the reference is not given immediately are covered by the following reference.

5   As I explain below, the idea here is that the love is supposed to be equal in both persons, and the respect is supposed to be equal in both persons; in addition, the love and respect are to be perfectly balanced.

6   Or should we say 'the mutual adoption of this ideal makes them'? Is it significant that Kant says that "die Aufnahme desselben in *ihre beiderseitige* Gesinnung die Würdigkeit enthalte" (TL 6:469.22f., italics M.B.)? That is, is it that the mutual adoption of this ideal makes them deserving of happiness? Or do I make myself deserving of happiness if I adopt this ideal towards my friend, even though he does not do likewise?

"striving for friendship (as a maximum of good disposition toward each other) is a duty set by reason" (TL 6:469.25 – 28). Now things get harder. First of all, it is not clear how much weight to put on the parenthetical part. Is Kant saying that the object of the duty is merely to strive for a maximum of good disposition toward each other? The rest of the paragraph suggests that the object of the duty is more than just that. Supposing that is right, what might the object be? Is it to strive to ensure that within any such union we have with another—any such union that purports to be a friendship—we not only love and respect each other but also do so as equally as possible? Although Kant is not explicit about this, it is reasonably clear that the duty is not so limited; that is, it is not just that if we have any friends, we should see to it that the friendship is of such-and-such a sort. Rather, we are to resist any temptation we may have to isolate ourselves (cf. TL 6:473.16 – 18). We are to strive to be friends to someone (one or more people), and not merely to be *Menschenfreunde* but to unite with someone in friendship. (I take it that Kant is picturing friendship as a one-to-one relationship, but at the same time, does not hold that one can have such a relationship with only one person, or with only one person at a time.)[7]

The content of the duty is thus to strive to be a friend (i.e., not to isolate oneself from others), and also to strive for a certain sort of relationship with one's friend. What sort of relationship? A union of two persons through equal mutual love and respect, but what that means is not clear. In particular, how seriously, or literally, are we to take the suggestion that the friends are supposed to have the same amount of love for each other and the same amount of respect? It might be tempting to downplay "equal [gleiche]" (TL 6:469.18), since a focus on whether I love and re-

---

7   In the *Tugendlehre* he speaks as if it is just one. In the Collins lectures he speaks of more than one, saying that we can "unbosom ourselves and be wholly companionate [...] only in the company of one or two friends" (V-Mo/Collins 27:427.19 – 21), thus leaving room for having not only more than one friend, but more than two (since perhaps one could unbosom oneself with one or two good friends on one occasion, and with another one or two at a different time). In the Vigilantius lectures he says that it is "almost impossible to have many friends," given how important it is "to engage in a reciprocal development of our principles, and above all to track down those on which we have a need to decide with our friend whether there may be any misunderstandings that hinder agreement; to clear up errors and come together as much as possible, e.g., in religious opinions" (V-MS/Vigil 27:685.30 – 35). In the Herder lectures, as in the *Tugendlehre*, the picture of friendship is that one has at most one true friend (cf. V-PP/Herder 27:54.16 – 18).

spect my friend just as much as (and no more than) he or she loves and respects me seems rather unhealthy. One might therefore be tempted to read Kant as saying not that we are to strive to ensure that the mutual love and respect are (respectively) equal but that we are to strive to ensure that the relationship is one in which we each participate and share sympathetically in the other's well-being.

And yet, obsessive and silly though the requirement of equal mutual love and respect may seem, we should be careful not to downplay "equal" to the point of ignoring it. Kant is onto something here: a friendship is indeed flawed to the extent that the fondness A has for B is considerably greater than the fondness B has for A, and the same is true of respect. At any rate, although there is some textual support to be found in TL 6:469.19–21 for downplaying "equal" (since there is no mention there of equal participation or equal sympathetic sharing, or equal anything else) it is clear from the reasons that Kant puts forward in explaining and defending his claim that friendship is unattainable in practice that he indeed does mean for "equal" to be taken seriously.

In support of his claim that friendship is unattainable in practice, Kant asks how one can "ascertain whether one of the elements requisite to this duty," e. g. benevolence, "is *equal* in the disposition of each of the friends" (TL 6:469.28–32), and implies that it cannot be ascertained. It is evident from his rhetorical question that he does indeed believe that the elements requisite to this duty need to be equal in the disposition of each of the friends, and moreover, the friends need to be confident that they are equal.

There is another unclarity in the claim that friendship is the union of two persons through equal mutual love and respect. This unclarity concerns just what has to be equal: A's love and B's love (and A's respect and B's respect)? Or also A's love and A's respect? It is clear from Kant's rhetorical question that he believes that A's love for B must be equal to B's love for A (and A's respect for B must equal B's respect for A). But does he hold that in addition, A's love for B must equal A's respect for B (and B's love for A must equal B's respect for A)? This is not evident, but also is not, I think, terribly important to settle. Gregor's translation of "das Ebenmaß des Gleichgewichts" (TL 6:470.3) as "equal balance" in the passage below, in which Kant is putting forward a second reason why perfect friendship is unattainable, may suggest equality when in fact the German need not be read that way:

[E]ven more difficult, how can he tell what relation there is in the same person between the feeling from one duty and that from the other (the feeling from benevolence and that from respect)? And how can he be sure that if the *love* of one is stronger, he may not, just because of this, forfeit something of the other's *respect*, so that it will be difficult for both to bring love and respect subjectively into that equal balance required for friendship? (TL 6:469.32–470.4)

Once again the questions are rhetorical, Kant's point being that one *cannot* tell. My friend may love me more than she respects me (or may respect me more than she loves me). As I suggested above, whether Kant really means that in a perfect friendship my friend respects me just as much as (and no more than) she loves me is not entirely clear, but he clearly holds that respect and love need to be in proper balance within each individual. Whether that proper balance is a 1:1 ratio is not evident.

V. Love, Respect, and our Unsociable Sociability

Kant's discussion of an "Ebenmaß" between love and respect builds on a striking passage at TL 6:449.8–11, where respect and love are presented as providing counterweights to each other. The "principle of mutual love" admonishes us "to *come closer* to one another"; that of respect, to keep ourselves "*at a distance* from one another"; and "should one of these great moral forces fail, 'then nothingness (immorality), with gaping throat, would drink up the whole kingdom of (moral) beings like a drop of water'" (TL 6:449.8–14). At TL 6:470.4–7 he develops this theme in relation to friendship: "For love can be regarded as attraction and respect as repulsion, and if the principle of love bids friends to draw closer, the principle of respect requires them to stay at a proper distance from each other." It is one source of objections to Kant's ethics—and especially to how he views persons in relation to other persons—that he places more emphasis on the principle of respect than on the principle of love. To that shortly.

Is this "limitation on intimacy" (TL 6:470.7) merely a safeguard against smothering another with attention, concern, and a desire constantly to be with him or her? No. If it were, the tension between the principles of love and respect would not be as deep, nor the obstacles to attaining perfect friendship as formidable, as Kant thinks they are.

The problem is deeply rooted, a facet of our "unsociable sociability" (IaG 8:20.30)[8]: we are "meant for society" (TL 6:471.30 f.) yet are also "unsociable."[9] In connection with friendship, a particularly troublesome difficulty is that we badly want to reveal ourselves to others, yet "hemmed in [...] by fear of the misuse others may make" of the thoughts we have disclosed, we feel "constrained *to lock up*" in ourselves a "good part" of our judgments (cf. TL 6:471.33–472.1).

The need to share our thoughts and sentiments is both strongly felt and a matter of objective importance. Such communication is indeed vital for reason itself, since reason "must subject itself to critique in all its undertakings" (KrV A738/B766).[10] Those who do not share thoughts and feelings are liable to become like—or at least suffer the same failures of judgment as—the logical egoist and the aesthetic egoist, described in *Anthropology:*

> The *logical egoist* considers it unnecessary [...] to test his judgment by the understanding of others; as if he had no need at all for this touchstone [...] (Anth 7:128.31–33).

---

8 Although 'unsocial sociability' is more mellifluous than 'unsociable sociability,' Allen Wood has convinced me that 'unsociable' is a better choice than 'unsocial.' As he put it to me in an e-mail, "'Unsocial' suggests withdrawal from society, what Kant calls '*anthropophobia*' or '*Menschenscheu*' (and is a form of the vice of misanthropy), while 'unsociable' suggests positive engagement with others, not flight from them, but engagement in a way that involves conflict or anti-social behavior—rivalry, competition, one-up-manship [and the like]."

9 In *Idea of a Human History with a Cosmopolitan Aim*, where Kant offers his most complete account of "unsociable sociability," he says the predisposition for it "obviously lies in human nature" (IaG 8:20.33 f.). He explains "unsociable sociability" as the "propensity to enter into society, which, however, is combined with a thoroughgoing resistance that constantly threatens to break up this society" (IaG 8:20.31–33). In more detail: "The human being has an inclination to become *socialized*, since in such a condition he feels himself as more a human being, i.e. feels the development of his natural predispositions. But he also has a great propensity to *individualize* (isolate) himself, because he simultaneously encounters in himself the unsociable property of willing to direct everything so as to get his own way, and hence expects resistance everywhere because he knows of himself that he is inclined on his side toward resistance against others" (IaG 8:20.34–21.5). For discussions of "unsociable sociability," see Wood, 2008, as well as Wood, 1991.

10 Recall too the second of the three "unalterable commands" (Anth 7:228.29) for thinkers: "to think ourselves into the place of *every other man* (with whom we are communicating)" (Anth 7:228.32f.). Thinking ourselves into the place of others requires open communication with them, and specifically listening to them, and in a context in which they feel very free to express themselves.

The *aesthetic egoist* is satisfied with his own taste, even if others find his vers-
es, paintings, music, and similar things ever so bad, and criticize or even
laugh at them. He deprives himself of progress toward that which is better
when he isolates himself with his own judgment; he applauds himself and
seeks the touchstone of artistic beauty only in himself (Anth 7:129.34–
130.2).[11]

Self-revelation, together with listening to the revelations of others, is thus
of vital importance, both objectively and subjectively. Reason requires it,
and we badly want this exchange with others (and in particular, it seems,
we want to air our views). Egoists excepted, humans do not want to be
"completely alone with" their "thoughts, as in a prison […]" (TL
6:472.12 f.).

Why, then, is there such anxiety about self-disclosure? One might
think that the barrier to sharing our thoughts and feelings with others
is simply fear—our fear that our friend, particularly if the friendship
ends, will abuse our trust, and perhaps also a fear of our friend's disap-
proval if we express our thoughts and feelings freely. If so, the solution
would seem to be just to conquer the fear, and learn to trust our friends.
But in fact Kant generally regards such caution about self-disclosure as
warranted and salutary (cf. TL 6:470.7–15, 472.3–17).[12] That he sees
it as salutary is another source of dissatisfaction with his account of
friendship.[13]

This tension between the risks of self-disclosure and the importance
of very open conversation between friends is not a problem that Kant
treats as having a clear solution, and he is probably right, apart from exaggerating the severity of the problem. It is part of the human condition
that we long to bare our souls to others yet also fear being laughed at or

---

11 Cf. V-Mo/Collins 27:427.23–25: "If I possess such a friend, of whom I know
    that his disposition is upright and kindly, neither malicious nor false, he will […]
    be helpful in rectifying my judgement." See also V-MS/Vigil 27:683.26–33:
    "Only that pure interest which is the end of this inclination converted to a
    need, determining them through the judgement of others, is the one pure goal
    that must lead us to friendship. This is all the more beneficial, in that we cannot
    rectify circumscribed ideas and thoughts in any other way than by sharing them,
    and should this not occur, we are never secured against errors […]."
12 See also RL 6:33, though it is not altogether clear that he is endorsing the dark
    view he reports there. For a striking exception, see his letter to Maria von Herbert
    (Br 11:331.15–334.25), where he says that this "reticence" (Br 11:332.16; cf. Br
    11.332.4, 8) or "want of candor" (Br 11:332.16 f.) is "one of the limitations of
    our nature" (Br 11:332.22)
13 See below, sections VIII and IX.

silently criticized. Moreover, it is a facet of something that is not about to go away, and indeed is, at least on Kant's view, not lamentable: unsociable sociability is the source of human progress.[14]

Although he is particularly concerned with self-disclosure, since it is both important and yet risky, Kant also notes another difficulty (another of the "difficulties in perfect friendship" (TL 6:470.20)), one which also concerns the question of how open and frank to be with one's friend. While it is "a duty for one of the friends to point out the other's faults to him," Kant writes, "the latter sees in this a lack of the respect he expected from his friend and thinks that he has either already lost or is in constant danger of losing something of his friend's respect" (TL 6:470.21–27). This difficulty, like the last, reflects the tension between love and respect. It is a "duty of love" (TL 6:470.23) to point out to one's friend her flaws,[15] yet at the same time the recipient of this well-intentioned criticism feels then that she has lost, or is in danger of losing, her friend's respect. Once again love bids us to be open with one another, while respect, it seems, advises us to maintain a distance. Moreover, what is prompted by love may undermine respect. When A points out B's faults, B is likely to think she has already lost or is in danger of losing A's respect; likewise, if A conceals from B hers own faults while B openly discloses hers to A, B may "lose something" of A's respect (TL 6:472.6f.).

Yet another difficulty for friendship that Kant raises likewise reflects the tension between love and respect, though it does not concern openness in expressing one's thoughts and feelings. Here the difficulty is feeling (or being) burdened by one's friends. One "wishes for a friend in need" (TL 6:470.29); one wants, as Seneca wrote, to "have someone by whose sick-bed he [...] may sit"[16]. Yet "it is also a heavy burden to feel chained to another's fate and encumbered with his needs" (TL 6:470.31f.). This is curious: is it a heavy burden when the friendship is between friends who are roughly comparable in their neediness and in their ability to help each other? Kant has signaled that he is not speaking of a case where there is no reciprocity: the complete sentence from which the quotation from TL 6:470.29 is taken is "How one wishes

14 *The means nature employs in order to bring about the development of all its predispositions is their **antagonism** in society* [...]. Here I understand by 'antagonism' the *unsociable sociability* of human beings [...]" (IaG 8:20.26–31).
15 But see footnote 26, below.
16 Seneca, Epistle IX, "On Philosophy and Friendship," in: *Epistulae Morales*, vol. 1, p. 47.

for a friend in need (one who is, of course, an active friend, ready to help at his own expense)!" (TL 6:470.29–31). Be that as it may, Kant sees this problem to have a solution: we must take care not to view friendship as a "union aimed at mutual advantage" (TL 6:470.33) and although we know we can count on the other in case of need, we try to avoid even letting on that we are in need, and try to avoid accepting any favor from our friend. We shall consider this further in section VIII.

VI. What Does Kant Mean in Saying that Friendship is Unattainable in Practice?

Does Kant mean by "unattainable in practice [in der Ausübung zwar unerreichbar]" (TL 6:469.25) literally unattainable? Or does "in practice" offer a qualification, suggesting only that it is very difficult to obtain, and only rarely obtained? The question arises in part because of his remarks about moral friendship, remarks that, if we treat moral friendship as equivalent to perfect friendship, would contradict the claim that friendship is unattainable in practice, unless we read 'unattainable' loosely. The apparent contradiction is between Kant's claim that moral friendship "actually exists here and there in its perfection" (TL 6:472.26 f.) and that perfect friendship ("Freundschaft (in ihrer Vollkommenheit betrachtet)" (TL 6:469.17)) is unattainable in practice. The contradiction evaporates if moral friendship and perfect friendship are not identical. But if they are, it would make sense to understand 'in practice' as qualifying 'unattainable.'

The text does not decide the matter, but it seems unlikely that Kant intends 'moral friendship' and 'perfect friendship' to be interchangeable terms. His view seems to be this: moral friendship is as good as it gets—as perfect a friendship as one can have—and though rare, is not non-existent. Some evidence for this understanding of moral friendship lies in Kant's otherwise mysterious use of 'merely' in front of 'moral friendship.' (How often do we find the word 'merely' in front of 'moral' in Kant's writings?) The only fact about moral friendship that could warrant the use of 'merely' would be that it does not qualify as perfect friendship. I take Kant's view to be that moral friendship and perfect friendship are not identical. There is thus no barrier to taking him at his word when he says that it is unattainable in practice (rather than thinking that he might mean only that it is very difficult to obtain).[17]

VII. Moral Friendship

Kant introduces the idea of moral friendship after enumerating what he speaks of as "difficulties in perfect friendship" (TL 6:470.20). Although these might be read as additional reasons offered in support of his claim that perfect friendship is unattainable, the location of the enumerated difficulties, together with the fact that he introduces them as "difficulties in perfect friendship," suggests that they are not best viewed as a continuation of his list of reasons why perfect friendship is unattainable. Instead, he is indicating why friendship is so difficult, and then introducing moral friendship as the type of friendship that can best avoid these difficulties.

Moral friendship is "the complete confidence of two persons in revealing their secret judgments and feelings to each other, as far as such disclosures are consistent with mutual respect" (TL 6:471.27–29). This addresses the chief difficulty in friendship: we so want to share our thoughts and feelings with others, and yet there is—and we know there is—a danger that the disclosure will undermine our mutual respect. To this end we are to aim at complete confidence, but with the constraint indicated. Moreover, we are to be very careful about whom we confide in. The friend with whom one can speak freely has "Verstand" (TL 6:472.8)[18] and shares one's "general outlook on things" (TL

---

17   Another relevant—and complicating—detail is that Kant says that "merely moral friendship" (TL 6:472.25) is "not just an ideal [kein Ideal]" (TL 6:472.25) and that perfect friendship is "only an idea [eine bloße [...] Idee]" (TL 6:469.24 f.). If 'ideal' and 'idea' are intended to be interchangeable in this context, this lends further support to my claim that moral friendship and perfect friendship are non-identical (since otherwise he would be contradicting himself, in claiming that moral friendship is "kein Ideal" but that perfect friendship is "eine bloße [...] Idee"). Whether he intends them to be understood as interchangeable is unclear. Elsewhere he does differentiate between them, but the usual distinction between them does not very clearly apply here. Moreover, he speaks of perfect friendship as an "Ideal" (TL 6:469.19) in the second sentence of §46, and then in the next sentence speaks of it as an "Idee" (TL 6:469.25).

18   Gregor translates "der Verstand hat" as "someone intelligent" (TL 6:472.8). While this is certainly not incorrect, it is important not to think of having *Verstand* simply as being *klug*. "Verstand" carries a suggestion of having a cool head, good powers of judgment, good sense.

6:472.10 f.) (in addition, of course, to being trustworthy, someone who
will not "share the secrets entrusted to him with anyone else, no matter
how reliable he thinks him, without explicit permission to do so" (TL
6:472.22–24)). The idea is not that one's friend is someone who will
not disagree with one; if so, one would not reap some of the most valuable benefits of communicating one's thoughts with another. It is, rather,
that the friends have the same general outlook, while very likely disagree-
ing on (possibly many) particular matters.[19]

Nothing is said in the description of moral friendship to address the
second difficulty in friendship that Kant mentioned: friends have a duty
to point out the other's faults, and yet this may be perceived by the recipient of the helpful pointers as reflecting a lack of respect. Perhaps Kant
has in mind that a friend who has *Verstand* is not very likely to take offense at the critical remarks because he is not small-minded, and understands that it is a duty of friends to point out each others' mistakes and
even character flaws, as this will aid the other both in the specific matter
at hand (about which the friend is arguably mistaken) and in the ongoing
process of self-improvement.

A further noteworthy feature of moral friendship is that it stands in
contrast to that "(pragmatic) friendship, which burdens itself with the
ends of others" (TL 6:472.27 f.).[20] Thus the burden problem is addressed
simply by stipulating that moral friendship is not about sharing burdens.
Rather, it is about sharing thoughts and feelings with another.

VIII. Worries About Kant's Account of Friendship

As I noted above, one source of objections to Kant's account of friendship
is that Kant places more emphasis on respect than on love. Although he is
concerned that they be in balance, the concern seems to be to give respect
its due. Related to this, the requirements for respect, as he conceives
them, seem excessive.

---

19 Cf. V-Mo/Collins 27:428f. and V-MS/Vigil 27:683f..
20 Kant's debt to Aristotle's discussion of friendship is evident at a number of points
    in his discussion, one being in his differentiation of moral friendship from both
    pragmatic friendship and friendship based on feeling. Although not identical to
    it, it parallels Aristotle's differentiation of complete friendships from friendships
    for utility and friendships for pleasure. (See Aristotle, *Nicomachean Ethics*, Book
    VIII.)

Kant's endorsement of caution about divulging one's secret judgments and feelings is to my mind not the main concern, though I shall say more about it in section IX. More worrisome is his view on accepting favors from friends. Why is each "generously concerned," in a moral friendship, "with sparing the other his burden and bearing it all by himself, even concealing it altogether from his friend" (TL 6:471.3–5)? This is troubling on two counts. First, even if friendship should not be mainly about burden-sharing, shouldn't friends be able to turn to each other for solace? Second, if Kant endorses concealing his burden from his friend, that has implications for what he means by the qualification in the following (cited above): "*Moral friendship* [...] is the complete confidence of two persons in revealing their secret judgments and feelings to each other, as far as such disclosures are consistent with mutual respect" (TL 6:471.26–29). If respect calls for concealing my burden from my friend, am I then not to share with my friend the fact that (for example) I've been diagnosed with a life-threatening illness?

Perhaps. But Kant's lectures on ethics suggest that when he speaks of "sparing the other his burden and bearing it all by himself," he has in mind first and foremost financial burdens, and not such burdens as a diagnosis of cancer. Consider the following, from Vigilantius:

> Friends do indeed undertake to support one another in their needs with all their powers and means; and it is in itself reassuring to be able to count on such assistance, on the resources, pledges and favourable influence in case of need; yet it is prudent, and a sign of much greater and purer friendship, to abstain from those needs which make it necessary to call upon our friend for help. For to demand such support in the way of funds, or the attainment of specific ends, really lies beyond the essential limits of friendship; it can become burdensome to the other, to meet my needs, and may be accompanied by a sacrifice of resources or by unwelcome conditions; our intercourse is tempered by the fear that such services may be called for more frequently; that engenders reserve, and the supported party loses in the freedom of his judgement, the purity of his maxims; he becomes in a certain respect dependent in his conduct, and must acknowledge the superior powers of the other to whom he is beholden, and forfeits his self-possession (V-MS/Vigil 27:684.12–29).[21]

It is noteworthy here that Kant does not say that we should not turn to our friend when in need; rather, we are to moderate our activities so as to avoid creating a situation where we will need to call upon our friend for help. Thus, don't buy a new horse if you are unsure whether you can

---

21 See also V-Mo/Collins 27:425.18–426.21.

cover your debts yet are confident that in case of a shortfall, your dear friend would help you out; it is better not to create a situation in which you will need to call upon him for help.

Loans are not the only sort of request that would be covered by this passage. We all know people who volunteer for much more than they can take on, but then turn to their friends to provide rides to their children or themselves, to babysit so that they can go to their meetings, to pick them up from the airport (for although there is a shuttle service, they are so busy that they do not want to wait for the shuttle). We all know the strain it puts on a friendship when one's friend often turns to one for help rather than absorb the inconveniences himself or cut back on the activities that give rise to the need for constant help. Kant may also be thinking of instances where one counts on another to put in a word to have a debt forgiven, or to extricate him from some other scrape. Here too, the advice that one should avoid creating situations where one will need the other's aid—aid that it might be uncomfortable for the friend to provide—seems wise.

Thus there is no need to read Kant as holding that friends should not accept help from their friends in the form of, say, meals brought to them while recovering from childbirth, much less as maintaining that friends should conceal from each other such 'burdens' as disturbing personal medical news.[22] That said, it would have been nice if Kant had recognized more than he does that it is part of a good friendship that one gladly helps the other—as long, that is, as the other does not exploit one's generosity, asking for too many favors, paying too little attention to the intrusion on the other's time, and perhaps exaggerating to oneself the pleasantness of (say) giving a friend a ride to the airport. Likewise, it is part of a good friendship that one can comfortably accept one's friend's assistance—while also taking care not to exploit his or her kind-

---

22 On the other hand, the Collins lectures report Kant as saying: "Hence no man will cause trouble to a friend with his affairs, and each will prefer to endure his woes alone, rather than burden his friend with them" (V-Mo/Collins 27:425.21–24). Although it is not entirely clear what kinds of woes Kant has in mind, it is unfortunate that he did not indicate that his claim holds only for certain kinds of woes and did not observe that it is part of a good friendship that we share some of our woes with our friends. Indeed, given the duty to cultivate our compassionate natural feelings (cf. TL 6:457.26 f.), it would be surprising if Kant did not think it a part of friendship (including moral friendship) both to "sympathize actively in [the friend's] fate" (TL 6:457.25 f.) and to offer emotional support.

ness, and to find opportunities to return the favor or provide help of a different sort to one's friend.[23]

IX. The Virtues of Social Intercourse

We are to see ourselves as "citizens of the world" (TL 6:473.21), people united, in their disposition, by a commitment to cultivating the ideals that lead indirectly to what is best for the world. These ideals are "a disposition of reciprocity – agreeableness, tolerance, mutual love and respect (affability and propriety, *humanitas aesthetica et decorum*)" (TL 6:473.23–25).[24]

Kant's "Appendix" thus suggests another reason for his endorsement of the "rule that even the best of friends should not make themselves too familiar with each other" (TL 6:470.8f.). In addition to the concern that one's friend will slip up and disclose to another person what one told him in confidence, there is the consideration that preservation of *decorum* is necessary.

> The question arises, whether in such friendship,[25] there is still a need for reserve? Yes, but not so much for one's own sake, as for that of the other; for everyone has his weaknesses, and these must be kept hidden even from our friends. Intimacy relates only to dispositions and sentiment, not to decorum; that must be observed, indeed, and one's weaknesses in that respect concealed, so that humanity should not be offended thereby. Even to our best friend, we must not discover ourselves as we naturally are and know ourselves to be, for that would be a nasty business (V-Mo/Collins 27:427.27– 35).

This position seems rather more extreme than anything Kant said in the *Tugendlehre*. Indeed, it would be odd if he endorsed this position in the *Tugendlehre*, since it does not sit well with the claim that it is a friend's

---

23 See also V-Mo/Collins 27:442.25–443.14 and V-MS/Vigil 27:696.18–697.16 for (arguably) exaggerated worries about the risks of accepting benefits from a friend.

24 Because the dash raises questions about scope, it might be helpful to have the German before us, even though that requires quoting more German than just the part translated in the quotation above: "[…] nicht eben um das Weltbeste als Zweck zu befördern, sondern nur die wechselseitige Zusammenkunft, die indirect dahin führt, die Annehmlichkeit in derselben, die Verträglichkeit, die wechselseitige Liebe und Achtung (Leutseligkeit und Wohlanständigkeit, *humanitas aesthetica et decorum*) zu cultiviren" (TL 6:473.22–25).

25 I take Kant to mean moral friendship.

duty to point out the other's flaws.[26] Nonetheless, an attenuated form of the position in Collins may underlie Kant's remarks at TL 6:470.8f.. These remarks may reflect a view that some weaknesses are best hidden even from one's close friends, lest (and here I bring in his remarks at TL 6:473.22–25) tolerance be undermined, and misanthropy fueled. If revealing certain hankerings or fantasies is likely to give rise to cynicism or even disgust in one's confidante, such revelations are a hindrance to the cultivation of the ideals of agreeableness, tolerance, and mutual love and respect. Hence the need for caution in what we reveal about ourselves.

The virtues of social intercourse, despite being *"externals"* (TL 6:473.28), help promote the feeling of virtue; and, I have suggested, maintaining *decorum* by limiting intimacy to dispositions and sentiment and understanding intimacy to be properly restrained by the need for *decorum* help to promote the enumerated ideals by not providing sustenance to their enemy: misanthropy.

In the final paragraph of "Appendix," Kant raises the interesting question of whether one may keep company with those who are vicious. On this matter, the need to maintain *decorum* is in tension with the value of both friendship and a reluctance to judge others. On the one hand "our judgment about them is not competent" (TL 6:474.6f.); moreover, although Kant does not say this, we may learn something from bouncing ideas off people who do not follow all the social conventions we follow and perhaps are very unconventional indeed, even positively shocking. But we should try to have little to do with those who openly show "contempt for the strict laws of duty," since "continued association with such a person deprives virtue of its honor and puts it up for sale to anyone who is rich enough to bribe parasites with the pleasures of luxury" (TL 6:474.

---

26 In the Collins lectures, he does not take the view that it is a duty to point out our friend's faults to him. Indeed, he states that "we must be blind to the other's faults" (V-Mo/Collins 27:452.22 f.). He makes a point of criticizing the view that he later takes in the *Tugendlehre:* "Just as I am not entitled to spy upon another, so I also have no right to tell him his faults; for even if he should ask for this, the other never hears of it without offence; he knows better than I that he has such faults. [...] It is not good, therefore, for people to say: Friends must tell each other their faults, because the other can know them better; nobody, after all, can know my faults better than I do; the other, admittedly, can know better than I, whether or not I stand and walk upright; but who is to know better than I do myself, if only I choose to examine myself?" (V-Mo/Collins 27:452.9–20). See also the Vigilantius lectures, where he says "a friend has no duty to reprove the other's moral faults, and point them out to him" (V-MS/Vigil 27:685.11 f.) but is less firmly opposed to doing so than in the Collins lectures.

8–14). Kant apparently thinks that onlookers will assume that the person who chooses to associate with the scandalous person does so because he has decided that virtue is worth less than some benefits he receives from the scandalous person.

X. Conclusion

One might wonder why Kant chose his conclusion to the "Elements of Ethics" as the place for a complex discussion of the nature of friendship. Why introduce that in the conclusion? But in fact there is good reason for it. It is fitting that a discussion of the harmony of love and respect be placed at the conclusion of a work which discussed throughout duties of love and duties of respect, separating the discussions into two distinct sections within "On Duties to Others Merely as Human Beings." The conclusion brings into harmony—and explains the complexity and fragility of that harmony—love and respect, and proclaims that the two are most intimately united in friendship. Friendship, considered in its perfection, brings love and respect into a proper balance.[27]

References

Aristotle [1995], *Nicomachean Ethics*, in: *The Complete Works of Aristotle*, vol. 2, Jonathan Barnes (ed.), Princeton: Princeton University Press.

Denis, Lara (2001), "From Friendship to Marriage: Revising Kant", in: *Philosophy and Phenomenological Research*, vol. 63, pp. 1–28.

Fasching, Maria (1990), *Zum Begriff der Freundschaft bei Aristoteles und Kant*, Würzburg: Königshausen & Neumann.

James, David (1995), "Kant on Ideal Friendship in the Doctrine of Virtue", in: Hoke Robinson (ed.), *Proceedings of the Eighth International Kant Congress*, II.2.557, Milwaukee: Marquette University Press.

Marcucci, Silvestro (1999), "Moral Friendship in Kant", in: *Kant-Studien*, vol. 90, pp. 434–441.

Paton, Herbert J. (1956), "Kant on Friendship", in: *Proceedings of the British Academy*, vol. 42, pp. 46–66. (Reprinted in: Neera Kapur Badhwar (ed.),

---

27 I am grateful to Oliver Sensen, Andreas Trampota, and Allen Wood for their comments on an earlier version of this paper, to discussants at the Oct. 2009 Conference on Kant's *Tugendlehre* (Hochschule für Philosophie, München) for their helpful and stimulating discussion, and to both the College Arts and Humanities Institute of Indiana University and the National Endowment for the Humanities for fellowship support.

Friendship: A Philosophical Reader, Ithaca/NY: Cornell University Press 1993, pp. 133–154.)

Seneca [1970], Epistle IX, "On Philosophy and Friendship", in: *Epistulae Morales*, vol. 1, trans. by Richard M. Gummere, London: William Heinemann and Cambridge/MA: Harvard University Press.

Trampota, Andreas (forthcoming), "Freundschaft", in: Georg Mohr/Jürgen Stolzenberg/Marcus Willaschek (eds.), *Kant-Lexikon*, Berlin/New York: Walter de Gruyter.

Wood, Allen W. (2008), *Kantian Ethics*, New York: Cambridge University Press.

Wood, Allen W. (1991), "Unsociable Sociability: The Anthropological Basis of Kantian Ethics", in: *Philosophical Topics*, vol. 19, pp. 325–351.

Ethische Methodenlehre: Didaktik und Asketik (TL 6:477–485)

Bernd Dörflinger

Im Abschnitt „Vorbegriffe zur Eintheilung der Tugendlehre" (TL 6:410.1–412.11) begründet Kant das Erfordernis einer ethischen Methodenlehre. Eine solche sei nötig – anders als im Fall der Rechtslehre, deren Pflichten „strenge (präcis) bestimmend" (TL 6:411.7) seien[1] –, weil die Tugendpflichten weite Pflichten seien, d. h. „wegen des Spielraums, den sie [die Ethik, B.D.] ihren unvollkommenen Pflichten verstattet" (TL 6:411.10 f.). In diesem Fall sei nach einer „Vorschrift (Methode)" (TL 6:411.8) zu fragen, „wie im Urtheilen verfahren werden soll" (TL 6:411.8 f.). Anders ausgedrückt, stellten sich „Fragen, welche die Urtheilskraft auffordern auszumachen, wie eine Maxime in besonderen Fällen anzuwenden sei" (TL 6:411.11–13).

Nach dieser Problembeschreibung handelt es sich bei der ethischen Methodenlehre um eine Theorie der bestimmenden Urteilskraft auf dem Spezialgebiet der Tugendlehre. Nach der allgemeinen Definition der bestimmenden Urteilskraft aus der dritten *Kritik* ist dieses Vermögen „das Vermögen, das Besondere als enthalten unter dem Allgemeinen zu denken" (KU 5:179.19 f.), d. h. es darunter zu subsumieren, wobei „das Allgemeine (die Regel, das Princip, das Gesetz) gegeben" (KU 5:179.20 f.) ist. Unter dem vorausgesetzten Allgemeinen ist auf dem Gebiet der Tugendlehre eine Tugendpflicht zu verstehen und unter dem Besonderen ein ethisch relevanter Einzelfall. In ihrer Absicht auf Subsumtion sieht sich bestimmende Urteilskraft allerdings vor einem Problem, das sich etwa so beschreiben lässt: Sie verfügt zwar über eine gegebene Regel, also etwa über das Bewusstsein einer Tugendpflicht, doch über keine Regel zur Anwendung dieser Regel. Aus diesem Grund, eine Subsumtionsaufgabe ohne eine Regel zu ihrer Bewältigung erfüllen zu müssen, nennt Kant die Urteilskraft schon in der ersten *Kritik* „ein

---

1 Ob die Rechtspflichten streng präzise bestimmend sind, könnte problematisiert werden; wenn nicht, wäre auch für die Rechtslehre eine Methodenlehre zu fordern. Die Frage liegt allerdings außerhalb der hier zu behandelnden Thematik.

besonderes Talent [...], welches gar nicht belehrt, sondern nur geübt sein will" (KrV A133/B172). Es will am Einzelfall geübt sein, der auch dann, wenn es zu Regeln noch untergeordnete, spezifizierende Regeln gibt, nie nach einer Anwendungsregel subsumiert werden kann und also eine eigene Dignität behält. Diesem Umstand Rechnung tragend, wird die ethische Methodenlehre als Anwendungstheorie die Bedeutung der Kasuistik betonen. Im Abschnitt über die „Vorbegriffe zur Eintheilung der Tugendlehre" ist „Casuistik" schon vorweg bestimmt als „Übung, wie die Wahrheit" (TL 6:411.20) – auf dem thematischen Gebiet also die angemessene Subsumtion eines Falls unter einen Pflichtbegriff – „solle gesucht werden" (TL 6:411.20 f.).

Der durch das Vorige bereits akzentuierte Aspekt des Übens ist auch in den vorausweisenden Angaben Kants zu den beiden Teilen der ethischen Methodenlehre enthalten, wobei eine Verschiebung hinsichtlich des Vermögens, das durch Übung auszubilden ist, zu erklären sein wird. Es heißt im Blick auf diese beiden Teile: „[N]icht sowohl die Urtheilskraft, als vielmehr die Vernunft und zwar in der Theorie seiner Pflichten sowohl als in der Praxis zu üben, das gehört besonders zur Ethik, als Methodenlehre der moralisch-praktischen Vernunft" (TL 6:411.24–27). Die Einteilung der ethischen Methodenlehre richtet sich demnach nach der Unterscheidung: Vernunft in der Theorie der Pflichten üben; Vernunft in der Praxis der Pflichten üben. Wie zu sehen sein wird, werden in der ethischen Didaktik, dem ersten Teil dieser Methodenlehre, mit einem „Lehrling" (TL 6:478.17) Entwicklung und Anwendung von Pflichtbegriffen geübt. Vernunft in der *Theorie* der Pflichten zu üben und nicht etwa Pflichten selbst auszuüben bzw. zu erfüllen, bedeutet, dass es sich um ein Üben in Gedanken handeln wird. Das trägt dem Umstand Rechnung, dass das in der didaktischen Situation unter den Beteiligten Verhandelte für diese nicht der moralische Ernstfall selbst ist, sondern nur der simulierte Ernstfall zum Zweck der Vorbereitung auf den tatsächlichen. Von daher mag sich auch die Verschiebung in der Angabe des in der Übung auszubildenden Vermögens von der Urteilskraft zur Vernunft erklären, denn das originäre Feld der Betätigung der praktischen bestimmenden Urteilskraft ist das tatsächlicher moralischer Praxis im Leben, nicht das des Übens in der Theorie der Pflichten im Kontext der Lehre von Tugend.

Im zweiten Teil der ethischen Methodenlehre, der ethischen Asketik, wird zwar kein Üben in der Theorie, sondern ein Üben in der Praxis thematisch sein, doch als ein Üben überhaupt ist auch Askese nicht selbst moralischer Ernst, sondern erst Vorbereitung darauf. Obwohl bloß vorbereitend, verlangt aber auch die Asketik, wie noch zu sehen sein wird, Subsumtion von Besonderem unter ein Allgemeines, also Urteilskraft, nämlich in der Beurteilung von Neigungen entweder als zuzulassende oder aber als zu disziplinierende.

Zum ersten Abschnitt der ethischen Methodenlehre: „Die ethische Didaktik" (TL 6:477.1–480.13)

Zum § 49

Der erste Paragraph der ethischen Methodenlehre (§ 49) hat einleitenden und vorausweisenden Charakter in Hinsicht auf alle folgenden Paragraphen (§§ 50–53) ihrer beiden Abschnitte und in Hinsicht auf eine längere Anmerkung zum ersten Abschnitt. Indem er auch das Thema des zweiten Abschnitts (§ 53), der ethischen Asketik, d. h. das Thema der Kultur der Tugend, vorbereitet, hätte dieser Paragraph nicht in den ersten Abschnitt integriert werden müssen, sondern hätte auch beiden Abschnitten vorangestellt werden können. Zum Thema des ersten Abschnitts, der ethischen Didaktik, das das Thema der Lehre der Tugend ist, enthält er zwei, vorerst nur ansatzweise erläuterte Thesen: 1. Tugend muss erworben werden und ist nicht angeboren; 2. Tugend kann und muss gelehrt werden. (Vgl. TL 6:477.5–14) Auch der Vorverweis auf die ethische Asketik lässt sich komprimiert durch eine These formulieren: Durch bloße Lehre wird die Kraft zur Tugend noch nicht erworben; sie muss durch Versuche der Bekämpfung der Neigungen kultiviert werden.

Indem Kant die erste These, dass Tugend notwendig erworbene Tugend ist, als „schon in dem Begriffe" (TL 6:477.7) der Tugend enthalten erachtet, ist sie nach seiner sonstigen Terminologie als ein analytisches Urteil zu kennzeichnen, als ein Erläuterungsurteil also, das ein den Begriff konstituierendes Merkmal verdeutlicht. Man darf sich zu diesem Urteil nicht „auf anthropologische Kenntnisse aus der Erfahrung berufen" (TL 6:477.6), in welchem Fall es bloß Erläuterung einer a posteriori gewonnenen Einsicht wäre. Es wäre dann bloß mit dem Anspruch auf Faktizität zu sagen, dass es Fälle der Erwerbung von Tugend gegeben hat, vielleicht alle bisherigen, nicht aber, dass Tugend *notwendigerweise* erworbene Tugend ist. (Vgl. 6:477.13–20)

Kant fährt mit einer Erläuterung fort, die ihrerseits weiterer Klärungen bedarf: „Denn das sittliche Vermögen des Menschen wäre nicht
Tugend, wenn es nicht durch die Stärke des Vorsatzes in dem Streit mit
so mächtigen entgegenstehenden Neigungen hervorgebracht wäre." (TL
6:477.7–10) Tugend ist hier offenbar als das Resultat aus einem Widerstreit zweier Kräfte verstanden, wovon die eine durch den starken
Vorsatz und die andere durch die entgegenstehenden Neigungen angesprochen ist. Der Vorsatz kann dabei nicht bloß Vorsatz geblieben,
sondern er muss wirksam geworden sein, d.h. den Streit für sich entschieden haben. Im anderen Fall eines bloßen Entgegenstehens der Kräfte
würde nichts „hervorgebracht" (TL 6:477.10). Zugleich können, um den
verwirklichten Vorsatz als Fall erworbener *Tugend* betrachten zu können,
die beteiligten Kräfte nicht bloß indifferente Kräfte nach der Art von
Kräften der Natur sein, sondern der einen Kraft, nämlich der Kraft des
Vorsatzes, muss ein Vorzug zukommen. Dieser Vorzug kann nicht schon
darin bestehen, überhaupt Vorsatz oder auch verwirklichter Vorsatz zu
sein, sondern es muss sich um einen *qualifizierten* Vorsatz handeln.
Welche Qualifikation das ist, nämlich die moralische, drückt Kant dann
eigens aus: „Sie [die Tugend, B.D.] ist das Product aus der reinen
praktischen Vernunft, so fern diese im Bewußtsein ihrer Überlegenheit
(aus Freiheit) über jene [die Neigungen, B.D.] die Obermacht gewinnt."
(TL 6:477.10–12) Ohne die in reiner praktischer Vernunft durch ihre
freie Verpflichtung zur Moralität gründende Auszeichnung eines Vorsatzes bewiese seine Verwirklichung gegen einen Widerstand bloß größere
Stärke, nicht aber, dass durch diese Verwirklichung eine Auszeichnung
erworben ist. Mit dem Begriff der Tugend aber ist eben dies gedacht, dass
durch sie ein Wert erworben ist. Unter der Voraussetzung einer angeborenen Tugend könnte diese bloß als etwas im Grunde indifferent
Faktisches, nicht aber als etwas erworbenes Auszeichnendes verstanden
werden.

In Kants Darstellung des Konflikts der Kräfte kommt die zweite
Seite, angesprochen durch die „entgegenstehenden Neigungen" (TL
6:477.9 f.), in allzu großer Verkürzung vor. Es ist nahegelegt, sie, da der
Tugend entgegengesetzt, dem Laster zuzuordnen. Das ist, verglichen mit
Kants Theorie des Bösen, wie sie in seiner *Religionsschrift* ausgeführt ist,
eine Simplifizierung. Nach dieser Theorie liegt der Grund des Bösen
„nicht […] in der Sinnlichkeit […] und den daraus entspringenden
natürlichen Neigungen" (RGV 6:34.18–20); die Neigungen haben danach „keine gerade Beziehung aufs Böse" (RGV 6:34.21), sondern sind
per se unschuldig; sie spielen bloß eine Rolle im Konflikt um das Böse.

Der eigentliche Konflikt ist hier beschrieben als der Konflikt zwischen zwei möglichen intellektuellen Akten, dem Akt der moralischen Willensbestimmung einerseits und dem Akt der Zustimmung zur Überordnung der Neigungen über die moralische Triebfeder andererseits. (Vgl. RGV 6:36.)

Für Kants These, Tugend „könne und müsse gelehrt werden" (TL 6:477.13), findet sich im § 49 nur eine sehr problematische Begründung. Die These folge „schon daraus" (TL 6:477.13), dass Tugend „nicht angeboren" (TL 6:477.14) sei. Dem scheint zu widersprechen, was wenige Zeilen zuvor gesagt wurde, nämlich dass sie „Product aus der reinen praktischen Vernunft" (TL 6:477.10 f.) sei. Als ein solches Produkt aus der Selbstgesetzgebung reiner praktischer Vernunft (Autonomie) ist sie zum einen nicht angeboren, zum anderen aber auch nicht von Lehre abhängig. Die Autonomie-These ernst genommen und vorausgesetzt, wird zwar nicht schlechthin ausgeschlossen werden müssen, dass Tugend gelehrt werden kann, doch ein solches Lehrverhältnis wird gleichwohl mit ihr nicht verträglich sein, in dem etwa ein Lehrer in einem kausal nezessitierenden Verhältnis zu einem ganz passiven Adressaten stünde bzw. Tugend auf die Weise der Informationsübermittlung mitgeteilt würde.

Auch dazu, dass Tugend gelehrt werden *müsse*, wodurch hinzukommend zu ihrer Möglichkeit, gelehrt zu werden, noch die Notwendigkeit einer Pflicht formuliert ist, ist einschränkend zu bemerken, dass unter der Voraussetzung eines autonomen moralischen Subjekts eine bestimmte Deutung dieser Notwendigkeit auszuschließen ist; die Deutung nämlich, dass die zur Tugend erforderliche Überwindung von Neigungen anders nicht möglich sei, als dass ein Lehrer der Tugend seinen Adressaten mit der Fähigkeit zu dieser Überwindung erst ausstatten müsste, wodurch die äußerlich herangetragene Lehre zur notwendigen Bedingung seiner Fähigkeit zur Überwindung von Neigungen würde.

Die Frage, wie unter Wahrung des autonomen moralischen Subjekts die Notwendigkeit der Lehre und die Pflicht dazu noch zu begründen sein mag, lässt sich anhand einer von Kant zuvor eingeführten Unterscheidung beantworten. Es ist die Unterscheidung zwischen dem „Vermögen (*facultas*) der Überwindung aller sinnlich entgegenwirkenden Antriebe" (TL 6:397.12 f.) und diesem „Vermögen als Stärke (*robur*)" (TL 6:397.15). Während nach Kant das erste Vermögen im Menschen „seiner Freiheit halber schlechthin vorausgesetzt werden kann und muß" (TL 6:397.13 f.), ist das zweite etwas, was dadurch erworben werden muss, „daß die moralische Triebfeder (die Vorstellung des Gesetzes) durch Betrachtung (*contemplatione*) der Würde des reinen

Vernunftgesetzes in uns, zugleich aber auch durch Übung (*exercitio*) erhoben wird" (TL 6:397.14–19). Was im Prinzip im Menschen „seiner Freiheit halber" (TL 6:397.13 f.) auch ohne diese Übung, von der die Methodenlehre sowohl im didaktischen Teil als auch im Teil zur Askese durchgängig spricht, vorausgesetzt werden muss und auch dazu hinreichend sein muss, sinnliche Motive zu überwinden, ist doch der Erhebung bzw. der Stärkung fähig, so dass im Fall der durch Übung gestärkten moralischen Triebfeder die Zusatzbedingungen dafür günstiger sind, dass sie sich Geltung verschafft. Notwendige Bedingung für das „Vermögen (*facultas*) der Überwindung aller sinnlich entgegenwirkenden Antriebe" (TL 6:397.12 f.) sind solche etwa durch Lehre verbesserten Umstände aber nicht, eben der „Freiheit halber" (TL 6:397.14). Gleichwohl wird die Pflicht, erleichternde Rahmenbedingungen herzustellen, dadurch nicht gegenstandslos, denn das moralische Interesse muss sich auch darauf erstrecken, was die Moralausübung bloß begünstigt, ohne notwendige Bedingung zu sein.

Im verbleibenden Text des § 49 weist Kant auf den zweiten Abschnitt der ethischen Methodenlehre, die ethische Asketik, voraus. Zu ihrer Rechtfertigung führt er, darin den Stoikern zustimmend, ein Defizit der bloßen Lehre der Tugend an. Es genüge nicht, um dem Tugendbegriff zu entsprechen, d. h. dem Begriff des moralischen Vermögens als Stärke, bloß zu wissen, „wie man sich verhalten solle" (TL 6:477.15) bzw. „bloße Vorstellungen der Pflicht" (TL 6:477.18) zu haben. Es genüge auch nicht, wenn der Wille schon bestimmt sei, wenn also erst Absichten gefasst sind, „denn man kann nicht Alles sofort, was man will" (TL 6:477.20 f.). Es müsse auch „die Kraft zur Ausübung der Regeln […] erworben" (TL 6:477.16 f.) werden. Es müsse, so die Aussage zum Mittel, diese Kraft zu erwerben, die Tugend „durch Versuche der Bekämpfung des inneren Feindes im Menschen (ascetisch) cultiviert, geübt werden" (TL 6:477.19 f.). Abgesehen davon, dass hier noch einmal mit Kant selbst die Charakteristik der Neigungen als Feinde in Frage gestellt werden könnte, kann schon vorweggenommen werden, dass die Ausführung der ethischen Asketik auch den martialischen Ausdruck der Bekämpfung nicht rechtfertigen wird. Ein propädeutisches Üben der Tugend im Einschränken von Neigungen allerdings wird verbleiben.

Den Paragraphen abschließend, hält Kant es noch für nötig, eine Bedingung für den Entschluss zum Üben der Tugend zu formulieren, die erst recht für die Tugendausübung selbst gilt. Die „Entschließung" (TL 6:477.22) müsse „auf einmal vollständig genommen" (TL 6:477.23) werden, weil die Tugend „auf einem einzigen Princip" (TL 6:477.26) beruhe. Damit spricht er sich gegen eine etwaige Gesinnung aus, das Laster bloß „allmählich zu verlassen" (TL 6:477.24). Eine Gesinnung, in der dem Laster noch ein Anteil neben einem Anteil an Tugend zugestanden werden sollte, wäre „unlauter" (TL 6:477.25). Sie ginge auf zwei heterogene Prinzipien zurück und wäre damit nicht etwa teilweise tugendhaft, sondern ganz und gar nicht. Es widerspricht diesem Gedanken nicht, dass Kant selbst andernorts in Hinsicht auf die Erfüllung der Tugendpflichten ein Mehr oder Weniger an Graden annimmt. Grade sind nicht Anteile an etwas Gemischtem, sondern Anteile an einer gleichförmigen intensiven Größe; fehlende Grade also ein bloßer Mangel, im gegebenen Fall also kein Laster.

Zum § 50

Im Paragraphen 50 trifft Kant nach dem allgemeinen Hinweis darauf, dass die Methode der Lehre der Tugend wie im Fall jeder wissenschaftlichen Lehre systematisch sein müsse und nicht fragmentarisch oder tumultuarisch sein dürfe, terminologische Bestimmungen und Einteilungen zum „Vortrag" (TL 6:478.3) dieser Lehre, die sich allerdings als problematisch herausstellen werden. Der Gesichtspunkt der Einteilung ist die jeweilige Rolle, die Lehrer und Schüler bei diesem Vortrag spielen. Der Vortrag, so die oberste Einteilung, kann entweder „akroamatisch" (TL 6:478.6) oder „erotematisch" (TL 6:478.7) sein. Im Fall des akroamatischen Vortrags ist allein der Lehrer aktiv, während die, „welchen er geschieht, bloße Zuhörer sind" (TL 6:478.6 f.). Der erotematische Fall, im Allgemeinen bestimmt, ist der, „wo der Lehrer das, was er seine Jünger lehren will, ihnen abfrägt" (TL 6:478.7 f.), wo diesen also die aktive Rolle des Antwortens zukommt. Die dann folgende Unterteilung der erotematischen Methode bemisst sich daran, ob das Abgefragte „ihrer Vernunft" (TL 6:478.9) oder „blos ihrem Gedächtnisse" (TL 6:478.10) abgefragt ist. Das letzte nennt Kant die „katechetische Lehrart" (TL 6:478.10 f.), das erste die „dialogische" (TL 6:478.10). Die dialogische Lehrart, so erläutert Kant an einer früheren Stelle, an der er sie noch erweiternd „dialogische (Sokratische) Methode" (TL 6:411.34) nennt, setzt voraus, dass das Erfragte, im gegebenen Fall also etwa Pflichtbegriffe, schon in der Vernunft des Schülers „natürlicherweise enthalten sei und es nur daraus entwickelt zu werden brauche" (TL 6:411.33 f.). In unserem Paragraphen der Methodenlehre ist noch ergänzt, dass der Lehrer im Schüler „durch vorgelegte Fälle" (TL

6.478.16) die „Anlage zu gewissen Begriffen [...] entwickelt" (TL
6:478.15 f.). Die sokratisch-dialogische Lehrart ist hier noch des Näheren
dadurch charakterisiert, dass „Lehrer und Schüler einander wechselseitig fragen und antworten" (TL 6:478.13 f.), so dass es sogar zu einem
partiellen Tausch ihrer Rollen kommt. Der Schüler nämlich, dessen inne
geworden, „daß er selbst zu denken vermöge, veranlaßt durch seine
Gegenfragen (über Dunkelheit, oder den eingeräumten Sätzen entge-
genstehende Zweifel), daß der Lehrer nach dem docendo discimus selbst
lernt, wie er gut fragen müsse" (TL 6:478.17–20).
    Nach all dem ist nahegelegt, dass die beschriebene Lehrart, in der ein
Vernünftiger durch Fragen die Spontaneität des Selbstdenkens eines anderen Vernünftigen anregt (nicht verursacht) und umgekehrt von diesem
zur weiteren Klärung seiner Begriffe veranlasst wird, in der also eine Art
von auf verschiedene Individuen verteilte Selbstaufklärung der Vernunft
stattfindet, als musterhaft zu betrachten sein wird, als die durch die
ethische Methodenlehre propagierte Lehrart. Um so mehr muss erstau-
nen, dass die im nächsten Paragraphen tatsächlich geforderte und dann in
einer Anmerkung ansatzweise ausgeführte Lehrart eine abweichende ist.

Zum § 51

Der Punkt der Abweichung lässt sich mittels einer von Kant hier neu
eingeführten Art des Gesprächs bezeichnen, die er ausdrücklich vom
sokratischen Dialog unterscheidet und die er gar nicht Dialog nennen
möchte. In der dialogischen Lehrart seien eben immer „beide Theile
einander fragend und antwortend" (TL 6:479.17). Die neue Art des
Gesprächs soll zwar weiterhin dadurch charakterisiert sein, dass ein fra-
gender Lehrer die Antwort „aus der Vernunft des Lehrlings methodisch
auslockt" (TL 6:479.12 f.), doch ist der Lehrling hier als einer unterstellt,
der „nicht einmal weiß, wie er fragen soll" (TL 6:479.11). Im Vorgriff auf
Kants fragmentarische Ausführung eines solchen Gesprächs lässt sich
feststellen, dass der Lehrling darin zwar immer nur antwortet, ohne zu
fragen, die Art seiner Antworten ist allerdings zum Teil so elaboriert, dass
nicht ersichtlich ist, warum er nicht fragen können sollte. Die zum
Muster erklärte Gesprächsart erscheint von daher künstlich.
    Abgesehen von der Merkwürdigkeit, ein Gespräch ohne beiderseitiges
Fragen nicht Dialog zu nennen, stiftet der Paragraph 51 auch dadurch
terminologische Verwirrung, dass er die Lehrart, die der neuen Gesprächsart entsprechen soll, die „katechetische Lehrart" (TL

6:479.15) nennt und das Instrument der Lehre „moralische[n] Katechism" (TL 6:478.2). Die Kennzeichnung der katechetischen Lehrart aus dem vorangegangenen Paragraphen lautete, dass der Lehrer „blos" dem „Gedächtnisse" der Lehrlinge etwas „abfrägt" (TL 6:478.10). Die jetzt gegebene andere Begründung für die Benennung der Lehrart als katechetisch ist, dass er seine Lehre damit abschließt, dass er das Gelehrte „seinem Gedächtniß anvertraut" (TL 6:479.14 f.), eben nachdem er es „aus der Vernunft des Lehrlings methodisch" (TL 6:478.12 f.) entlockt hat.

In der Sache bleibt trotz der terminologischen Irritationen festzuhalten, dass für Kant das Gespräch im Zentrum der Lehre der Tugend steht, und zwar zwischen als autonom vorausgesetzten moralischen Subjekten. Dem Lehrer in diesem Gespräch ist bloß ein entwickelteres moralisches Bewusstsein zugeschrieben, so dass er aus dieser Position Hilfestellung leisten kann, damit der selbstdenkende Schüler seinerseits sein moralisches Bewusstsein entfalte.

Der diskutierte Paragraph enthält noch eine These, die der Erläuterung bedarf: dass nämlich das nun also „moralischer Katechism" zu nennende „Instrument der Tugendlehre" „vor dem Religionskatechism hergehen" muss (TL 6:478.28–30) und nicht mit diesem vermischt vorgetragen werden soll. Der moralische Katechismus müsse „abgesondert, als ein für sich bestehendes Ganze, vorgetragen werden" (TL 6:478.31 f.). Die Begründung dafür lautet, dass „nur durch rein moralische Grundsätze [...] der Überschritt [...] zur Religion gethan werden" (TL 6:478.32–34) kann. Wie man sich dies vorzustellen hat, erläutert Kant hier nicht; er hätte aber etwa auf die Vorrede zu seiner *Religionsschrift* verweisen können, in der ein Begründungszusammenhang entwickelt wird, durch den gezeigt sein soll: „Moral führt unausbleiblich zur Religion" (RGV 6:8.37, Anm.). Der hier als erzielt behauptete Religionsbegriff (im Ausgang vom moralischen Bewusstsein über den Begriff der Glückswürdigkeit des moralischen Menschen und über die Reflexion, dass ein Gott gedacht werden muss, der allein diesem das verdiente Glück verschaffen kann) ist der Begriff einer Vernunftreligion, nicht der einer historischen Offenbarungsreligion, die von einer empirisch faktischen Selbstmitteilung Gottes ausgeht. In historischen Religionen können, wie Kant etwa dem Christentum zugesteht, moralische Gesetze enthalten sein, aber auch sogenannte statutarische, moralindifferente, aus Vernunft nicht zu entwickelnde, z. B. Vorschriften für einen Ritus. Auch der Gott der Vernunftreligion wird schließlich als moralischer Gesetzgeber gedacht und entsprechend die moralischen Gesetze zugleich als göttliche Gesetze,

doch eben *nach* dem skizzierten Gedankengang im Ausgang vom origi-
nären moralischen Bewusstsein des Menschen, worin dieser sich als durch
das Vermögen reiner praktischer Vernunft selbstgesetzgebend (autonom)
weiß.

Die Frage ist nun, was so schädlich an einem dem moralischen Katechismus vorausgehenden Religionskatechismus wäre, das das harte
Urteil Kants rechtfertigte, dass die daraus gezogenen „Bekenntnisse [...]
unlauter sein würden" (TL 6:478.34). Kant wiederholt am Ende des
Anhangs zum moralischen Katechismus dieses Urteil mit den Worten, es
könne „nichts als Heuchelei" (TL 6:484.14) daraus resultieren, nämlich
„sich aus Furcht zu Pflichten zu bekennen und eine Theilnahme [...], die
nicht im Herzen ist, zu lügen" (TL 6:484.15 f.). Dem Urteil liegt offenbar die Ansicht zugrunde, dass einem nicht im Bewusstsein autonomer
Selbstverpflichtung stehenden Menschen ein sich als göttlich ankündi-
gender, also ein von außen ergehender Befehl zur Moralität als ein
fremdes und unverständliches Ansinnen vorkommen muss. Eine derart
äußerlich befohlene und deshalb unverstandene Moralität dennoch als die
eigene Sache zu bekennen, bedeutete in der Tat, „eine Theilnahme [...],
die nicht im Herzen ist, zu lügen" (TL 6:484.15 f.).

Zum § 52

Die „Autonomie der praktischen Vernunft eines jeden Menschen" (TL
6:480.2 f.) ist auch der Hauptgesichtspunkt dieses Paragraphen, der vor
der Fortsetzung der Katechismus-Thematik eingefügt ist. Aus diesem
Gesichtspunkt wird hier beurteilt, welcher Stellenwert dem guten oder
schlechten Beispiel im Kontext der Lehre einzuräumen ist. Kant gesteht
dem Beispiel zunächst eine eingeschränkte Rolle, nämlich als das „e x -
p e r i m e n t a l e (technische) Mittel" (TL 6:479.20), in dieser Lehre zu,
zuvörderst dem guten Beispiel „an dem Lehrer selbst (von exemplarischer
Führung zu sein)" (TL 6:479.21 f.). Für wirksam hält er das Beispiel
deshalb, weil „Nachahmung [...] dem noch ungebildeten Menschen die
erste Willensbestimmung zu Annehmung von Maximen" (TL 6:479.22–
24) sei. Der Lehrling in der Tugend, worunter hier besonders ein Kind
vorzustellen ist, ist demnach geneigt, nachahmend solche subjektiven
Handlungsgrundsätze zu übernehmen, die es vom Verhalten eines Vor-
bilds her kennt; es will so sein wie dieser oder jener. Bei aller Anerkennung als technisches Mittel verortet Kant ein solches Nachahmen doch
vollständig im Bereich des Vormoralischen. Das Beispiel, „was uns An-

dere geben" (TL 6:480.1), kann „keine Tugendmaxime begründen" (TL 6:478.1). Bloß nachahmend übernommene Maximen können nicht wirklich eigene und also auch keine moralischen sein. Entscheidend im Hinblick auf zunächst von einem Beispiel abgelernte Handlungsgrundsätze ist, dass der Lehrling sie sich „in der Folge" allererst zu wirklich eigenen Maximen „macht". (Vgl. TL 6:479.24) Erst sein freier Akt der Zustimmung und nicht das Nachahmen ist ein Akt der „Autonomie der praktischen Vernunft", für die „nicht Anderer Menschen Verhalten, sondern das Gesetz" die „Triebfeder" ist. (Vgl. TL 6:480.2–4) Kant schließt den Paragraphen mit der Formulierung einer Regel, die dem Beispiel nur noch eine minimale Funktion belässt:

> [...] nicht die Vergleichung mit irgend einem andern Menschen (wie er ist), sondern mit der Idee (der Menschheit), wie er sein soll, also mit dem Gesetz, muß dem Lehrer das nie fehlende Richtmaß seiner Erziehung an die Hand geben. (TL 6:480.10–13)

Der andere Mensch ist so allenfalls noch Anlass für eine sich von ihm lösende Reflexion darauf, wie Menschen sein sollen.

Zur Anmerkung: „Bruchstück eines moralischen Katechismus" (TL 6:480.14–484.16)

Diese Anmerkung schließt ersichtlich an das Thema des vorletzten Paragraphen (§ 51) an. Sie führt zunächst vor, wie Kant sich das Lehrgespräch zur Lehre der Tugend nach der katechetischen Lehrart näherhin vorstellt. In diesem Gespräch werden dem Inhalt nach zentrale Begriffe der praktischen Philosophie Kants behandelt: Glückseligkeit, Glückswürdigkeit, praktische Vernunft, freier Wille, Pflicht, bis hin zum Gottesglauben. Im kommentierenden Nachvollzug soll sowohl auf die Lehrart als auch auf die thematischen Inhalte eingegangen werden.

Der Lehrer entwickelt zunächst *allein* (weil der Schüler auf die entsprechende Frage nicht antwortet), dass das ganze Verlangen im Leben die Glückseligkeit sei, und er gibt zugleich eine Erklärung des Glückseligkeitsverlangens. Es sei das Verlangen des Individuums, dass ihm „Alles und immer nach Wunsch und Willen gehe" (TL 6:480.21 f.). Wenig später paraphrasiert der Lehrer das angestrebte Ziel noch durch die Wendungen „das beständige Wohlergehen", „vergnügtes Leben" und „völlige Zufriedenheit mit seinem Zustande" (TL 6:480.26 f.). Diese Passage mit der Anfangseinsicht in das Wesen der Glückseligkeit entspricht dem von Kant mit der katechetischen Lehrart ausdrücklich für verträglich erklärten Vorgehen, dass dem Schüler etwas „in den Mund" (TL 6:480.19) gelegt werden kann. Dieses Vorgehen steht allerdings unter der einschränkenden Bedingung, dass es auf eine „seine Vernunft leitend[e]" (TL 6:480.18 f.) Weise geschieht, d. h. nicht auf eine ihn okkupierende Weise. Dass der Schüler keinen Widerspruch erhebt, sondern im Gegenteil bereit ist zur gedanklichen Weiterentwicklung auf der Basis der angebotenen Erklärungen, zeigt seine implizite Zustimmung.

Durch die erste Antwort des Schülers auf die weitergehende Frage, ob er wohl im Falle der Verfügungsmacht über alle Glücksgüter der Welt diese auch an andere austeilte, gibt er zu erkennen, dass es ihm in der Tat auch um das Glück anderer zu tun ist. Der Lehrer interpretiert diese Antwort so, dass das „nun wohl" beweise, dass er „noch so ziemlich ein gutes Herz" (TL 6:480.30) habe. Er interpretiert sie also im Sinne eines Indizes dafür, dass der Schüler, wenn auch vielleicht ohne explizites Bewusstsein davon, doch der Tugendpflicht nachkäme, sich das Glück der anderen zum Zweck zu machen. (Vgl. TL 6:385.32) Die merkwürdigen Einschränkungen des Lehrers („nun wohl"; „noch so ziemlich" (TL: 480.30)) mögen den Rest an Unsicherheit ausdrücken, der mit jeder moralischen Beurteilung verbunden ist. Im Prinzip nämlich wäre ein Austeilen von Glücksgütern auch um des eigenen Glücks willen denkbar, insofern man es im Kreis von Unglücklichen für eingeschränkt oder gefährdet halten könnte. Solche außermoralischen Motive sollen aber offenbar, was vom Wohlwollen des Lehrers zeugt, dem Schüler nicht unterstellt werden, sondern eben das „gute[] Herz" (TL 6:480.30).

Im dritten Schritt seiner katechetischen Lehre problematisiert der Lehrer den Glücksbegriff, indem er auf die Diversität individueller Glücksvorstellungen hinweist, insbesondere aber darauf, dass es fragwürdige Zwecksetzungen gibt, z. B. das „süße[] Nichtsthun" (TL 6:481.1), die auch die Mittel zu solchen Zwecken zweifelhaft machen, z. B. das „weiche Polster" (TL 6:480.32). In der Reaktion darauf soll der Schüler zum guten Herzen nun auch noch „guten Verstand" (TL 6:480.31) beweisen, ein intellektuelles Beurteilungsvermögen also. Seine dezidierte Stellungnahme, dass er zum Erfolg der besagten Glücksvorstellungen nichts beitragen würde, bringt sein Bewusstsein zum Ausdruck, wiewohl noch nicht deutlich bezeichnet, dass Glücksvorstellungen qualifiziert und unter Bedingungen gestellt werden müssen, so dass sie sich nach legitimen und illegitimen unterscheiden. Der Lehrer erst drückt es dann auf bestimmte Weise aus, was es in Absicht auf diese Unterscheidung zu untersuchen gilt, nämlich ob das Individuum mit seinen Glücksvorstellungen als „der Glückseligkeit würdig" (TL 6:481.11) erachtet werden kann. Die Erfüllung des Moralkriteriums der Glückswürdigkeit ist demnach die Bedingung, der die Glücksvorstellungen genügen müssen, um legitim zu sein.

Die Art, wie der Lehrer die Bedingung erläutert, nämlich dass durch sie die „Neigung", d.i. das, „was nur nach Glückseligkeit strebt" (TL 6:481.16 f.), allgemein darauf eingeschränkt sei, der „Glückseligkeit zuvor würdig zu sein" (TL 6:481.18), und dass zu untersuchen sei, „wie fern ein jeder der Glückseligkeit würdig wäre" (TL 6:481.11), hinterlässt allerdings eine Schwierigkeit, die der Text des Bruchstücks des Katechismus nicht eindeutig löst. Dieser Text scheint nämlich nahezulegen, dass um der Legitimität der Neigungen willen eine positive moralische Vorleistung erbracht sein muss. Eine solche Deutung erzeugte ein Spannungsverhältnis zu anderen Aussagen Kants zu den Neigungen, die diesen ein Eigenrecht zusprechen, wenn sie nur *nicht gegen* die Moral verstoßen. Per se sind Neigungen diesen Aussagen zufolge natürliche Gegebenheiten und aufgrund ihrer unvermeidlichen Faktizität einer Legitimation weder bedürftig noch fähig. Der nach der Versuchsanordnung Kants im Fragment des Katechismus zur Verteilung von Glücksgütern befähigte Schüler hätte, wenn Neigungen auf diese Weise als natürlich und mithin als unschuldig gelten könnten, nicht erst einen Würdigkeitstest durchzuführen, um das Glück anderer zu befördern. In der *Religionsschrift* sind Neigungen in der skizzierten Art bewertet:

> Natürliche Neigungen sind, an sich selbst betrachtet, gut, d. i. unverwerflich, und es ist nicht allein vergeblich, sondern es wäre auch schädlich und tadelhaft, sie ausrotten zu wollen; man muß sie vielmehr nur bezähmen, damit sie sich untereinander *nicht* selbst aufreiben, sondern zur Zusammenstimmung in einem Ganzen, Glückseligkeit genannt, gebracht werden können. Die Vernunft aber, die dieses ausrichtet, heißt Klugheit. (RGV 6:58.1–7)

Nach dieser Aussage gibt es zwar ein Problem innerhalb der Sphäre der Neigungen in ihrem Verhältnis untereinander, nämlich ihren potentiellen wechselseitigen Konflikt, so dass sie durch Klugheit zur harmonischen „Zusammenstimmung in einem Ganzen" gebracht werden müssen; dieses Problem ist aber nicht das Problem einer etwaigen fraglichen Legitimität der Neigung als solcher vor der Moral, sondern bloß ein Organisationsproblem für Vernunft als Klugheit. Als solche ist die Neigung nach der Stelle der *Religionsschrift* eine unverwerfliche natürliche Gegebenheit, die ausrotten zu wollen unsinnig und sogar „tadelhaft", d. h. moralisch disqualifizierend, wäre. Nach dieser Schrift verlangt reine praktische Vernunft nur für den Fall, dass die Glücksziele der Neigungen und moralisch gebotene Zwecke divergieren, die Unterordnung der Neigungen (vgl. RGV 6:36.19–33), also etwa ihre Suspendierung um der vorrangig gebotenen Erfüllung einer moralischen Anforderung willen.

Kants Beispiele im thematischen Stück der *Metaphysik der Sitten* sind mit dieser Auffassung von den per se unverdächtigen Neigungen eher verträglich als die allgemeine Aussage, dass „zuvor" (TL 6:481.18) eine moralische Würdigkeit erzielt sein muss, damit Glücksziele hernach erst als berechtigt angesehen werden können. In diesen Beispielen sind nämlich nicht die Glücksmittel als solche disqualifiziert, nicht also das weiche Polster, der Wein oder die „einnehmende Gestalt" (TL 6:481.3), sondern es ist disqualifiziert, dass diese Mittel in den Dienst der amoralischen Zwecke Unwürdiger gestellt sind, also dass das weiche Polster dem „Faullenzer" (TL 6:480.32), der Wein dem „Trunkenbold[]" (TL 6:481.1 f.) und die einnehmende Gestalt dem „Betrüger" (TL 6:481.3) dienen sollen. Dem entsprechend müsste dem Schüler nicht gelehrt werden, die Neigungen seien auf die Bedingung einzuschränken, der „Glückseligkeit zuvor würdig zu sein" (TL 6:481.18), sondern die den natürlichen und damit unverwerflichen Status der sinnlichen Neigungen wahrende Lehre müsste lauten, dass die Neigungen auf die Bedingung eingeschränkt seien, nicht zu unwürdigen Zwecken eingesetzt zu werden. In diesem Sinne unwürdig können sie aber nicht durch sich selbst werden, sondern, so wieder die Lehre der *Religionsschrift*, nur durch den intellektuellen Akt der Freiheit einer Person, wodurch diese ihr Glücksstreben der moralischen Triebfeder überordnet. (Vgl. RGV 6:36.29 f.) Was aus dieser Verortung des Unwürdigen in einem freien intellektuellen Akt verkehrten Über- bzw. Unterordnens für die Sinnlichkeit folgt, formuliert Kant hier so: „Mithin kann in keinem die Willkür durch Neigung **bestimmenden** Objecte, in keinem Naturtriebe […] der Grund des Bösen liegen." (RGV 6:21.9–12) Sinnlichkeit und ihre Neigungen lassen demnach nie per se eine Unwürdigkeit begründen. – Die diskutierte Stelle ist die zweite innerhalb der Methodenlehre, an der Kant in der Qualifikation der Sinnlichkeit hinter eigenen elaborierteren Theoriestücken zurückbleibt.

Die nächsten Schritte im Fortgang des Katechismus-Fragments betreffen zum einen die Universalität der Würdigkeitsbedingung, der die Neigungen zu unterwerfen seien, und zum anderen die Frage der Verortung des Ursprungs dieser Bedingung im Ensemble der Gemütsvermögen. Ihrer Universalität stimmt der Schüler nach anfänglichem Unverständnis schließlich dadurch zu, dass er sich selbst wie alle anderen dem Moralkriterium der Glückswürdigkeit unterworfen erklärt. Als Ursprung der Bedingung, die in diesem Kontext auch in der Variante der Nicht-Unwürdigkeit auftritt, wodurch auch durch moralische Indifferenz der Neigungen die Bedingung erfüllt ist und nicht erst durch eine positive Würdigkeit, benennt der Lehrer die Vernunft. Indem er sie ausdrücklich als die Vernunft des Schülers anspricht („deine Vernunft" (TL 6:481.19)), ist seine Anrede als Appell an diesen zu verstehen, das Gesagte durch Selbstdenken zu verifizieren. Was der Lehrer dem Schüler näherhin zur Zustimmung anträgt, ist die Freiheit des Willens, denn diese ist vorauszusetzen, wo Neigungen einzuschränken sind. Indem Neigungen als solche bloß den faktischen Charakter natürlicher Gegebenheiten haben, die sich weder selbst moralischen Anforderungen überordnen, noch sich diesen von selbst unterordnen bzw. sich selbst einschränken, ist zu solcher Unterordnung bzw. Einschränkung eine freie Distanzierung von ihnen nötig; und die „Regel und Anweisung" (TL 6:481.24) zu ihrer Einschränkung aus dem Gesichtspunkt der Moralität setzt einen kontrafaktischen, nicht-natürlichen Akt der Freiheit aus der Distanz zum Gegebenen voraus, einen Akt „ganz allein" (TL 6:481.24) aus „Vernunft" (TL 6:481.24). Indem also die „eigene Vernunft" (TL 6:481.27) unbedingt „lehrt und gebietet" (TL 6:481.27) bzw. durch „unbedingte Nöthigung" (TL 6:481.34) eine „Pflicht" (TL 6:482.2) statuiert – zum Beispiel, dass das Lügen um keines Vorteils für die Neigungen willen erlaubt ist und den „Menschen unwürdig" macht, „glücklich zu sein" (TL 6:481.33 f.), wie der Schüler schließlich eigenständig entwickelt – ist es „nicht nöthig" (TL 6:481.25), moralische Verpflichtung „von der Erfahrung, oder von Anderen durch ihre Unterweisung abzulernen" (TL 6:481.25–27). Speziell durch diese letzte Bemerkung relativiert der Lehrer seine eigene Rolle derart, dass danach moralische Lehre zwar nützlich sein und Anlass für die Reflexion eines Schülers bieten mag, dass sie aber keine notwendige Bedingung für die Entwicklung moralischen Bewusstseins ist. Der eigene Vollzug dieser Reflexion also auch ohne den äußeren Anlass einer Unterweisung durch andere hinreichend zur Erzeugung des Bewusstseins moralischer Verpflichtung ist.

Seine Katechese um einen Aspekt erweiternd, thematisiert der Lehrer im Anschluss an die Entwicklung der „Bedingung der Würdigkeit glücklich zu sein" (TL 6:482.3 f.), die allein in der „Beobachtung seiner Pflicht" (TL 6:482.2 f.) besteht, ob sich auf die Erfüllung dieser Bedingung die „sichere Hoffnung gründen" (TL 6:482.7 f.) könne, das

verdiente Glück auch tatsächlich zu erlangen. Der Schüler verneint zunächst eine solche sichere Hoffnung. Er begründet seine Skepsis mit der
Indifferenz des „Lauf[s] der Natur" (TL 6:482.10), der kein Lebensglück
als notwendiges Korrelat moralischen Verdienstes garantiert, und mit den
„Umständen" (TL 6:482.12) des Lebens, „die bei weitem nicht alle in des
Menschen Gewalt sind" (TL 6:482.12 f). Die schon angeführte Vernunft
als Klugheit (vgl. RGV 6:58.6 f.), die Kant durchaus als probates Mittel
des Glückserwerbs betrachtet, muss im Licht dieser Einsicht als ein sehr
eingeschränktes Mittel erscheinen, das den Lauf der Natur und die
Umstände des Lebens nie ganz beherrschen kann, und zwar „bei weitem
nicht" (TL 6:482.13). Das vorläufige Fazit des Schülers, das er allerdings
nach Einführung des letzten Gedankens des Katechismus-Fragments
noch modifizieren wird, lautet dem entsprechend, dass Glückseligkeit
auch im Fall der Erfüllung der moralischen Pflichten, d. h. im Fall der
Glückswürdigkeit, „immer nur ein Wunsch" (TL 6:482.14) bleibe, es sei
denn, dass das, was nicht in der Macht des Menschen steht, nämlich das
offensichtliche Rationalitätsdefizit einer durch Moralität erworbenen,
aber unerfüllten Glückswürdigkeit zu überwinden, doch im Vermögen
einer „andere[n] Macht" (TL 6:482.15) steht. Wenn diese „andere Macht
hinzukommt" (TL 6:482.15), kann aus dem bloßen Wunsch „Hoffnung
werden" (TL 6:482.15 f.). – Dieses Zwischenergebnis des Schülers entspricht ersichtlich Kants Lehrstück von der Idee des höchsten Guts[2],
worin die gedachte Vereinigung der Sittlichkeit mit der Glückseligkeit
durch ein höheres Wesen ausdrücklich als eine notwendige Vernunftidee
bezeichnet ist.

Der letzte durch den Lehrer in unserem Fragment eingeführte Gedanke thematisiert das Dasein des höheren Wesens, d. h. er wirft die
Frage auf, ob es nicht bloß gedacht und erwünscht werden muss, sondern
ob „Vernunft wohl Gründe für sich" (TL 6:482.17) hat, es „als wirklich
anzunehmen, d. i. an Gott zu glauben" (TL 6:482.20). Der Schüler
antwortet daraufhin mit „Ja" (TL 6:482.21) und verstärkt so seine zuvor
noch hypothetische Gotteserwägung zu einer Assertion. Als Grund führt
er zunächst die „Werke[] der Natur" (TL 6:482.21) ins Feld, an denen
„ausgebreitete und tiefe Weisheit" (TL 6:482.22) sichtbar werde, die
nicht anders erklärbar sei als „durch eine unaussprechlich große Kunst
eines Weltschöpfers" (TL 6:482.23 f.). Mit der Angabe dieses Grundes

---

2   Dieses Lehrstück findet sich zuerst ausgeführt in der *Kritik der reinen Vernunft*
     (vgl. KrV A804/B832–A819/B847), dann aber auch in der *Kritik der praktischen
     Vernunft* (vgl. KpV 5:110–119) und in der *Religionsschrift* (vgl. RGV 6:3–9).

hält er aber offenbar die verlangte Begründung für noch nicht vollendet. Es bedarf ihm zufolge eines Grundes „auch" hinsichtlich dessen, „was die sittliche Ordnung betrifft" (TL 6:482.24 f.), denn der Aspekt der sittlichen Weltordnung ist mit der Beziehung der Naturprodukte bloß auf die Kunstfertigkeit eines Weltschöpfers noch keineswegs thematisch. Die sittliche Weltordnung muss also eigens und zusätzlich thematisiert werden, was der Schüler auch tut, indem er sie als etwas zu den Naturprodukten Hinzukommendes durch eine ästhetisierende Wendung als „höchste Zierde der Welt" (TL 6:482.25) anspricht. Wir hätten uns hinsichtlich der sittlichen Weltordnung als Korrelat „eine nicht minder weise Regierung zu versprechen Ursache" (TL 6:482.26). Als diese Ursache ist, nahegelegt durch einen Doppelpunkt und ein einleitendes „nämlich" (TL 6:482.27), der schon bekannte Gedanke genannt (diesmal in der Variante, dass als Bedingung der Konsequenz der Glückseligkeit bloß die Nicht-Unwürdigkeit auftritt): „daß, wenn wir uns nicht selbst der Glückseligkeit unwürdig machen, welches durch Übertretung unserer Pflicht geschieht, wir auch hoffen können, ihrer theilhaftig zu werden" (TL 6:482.27–29).

An dem hier wiedergegebenen Begründungszusammenhang, durch den nicht weniger als die Assertion des Gottesglaubens begründet werden soll, ist mehreres problematisch, und zwar nach von Kant selbst andernorts detailliert entwickelten Maßstäben. Er kann anders als der vorherige gedankliche Zusammenhang des Katechismus-Fragments bis zur Entwicklung der Idee des höchsten Guts nicht als ein einigermaßen adäquates Entsprechungsstück seiner sonstigen Lehre verstanden werden. Bereits der Anfang der Begründung, dass an den Werken der Natur die Kunst eines weisen Weltschöpfers abzulesen sei, fällt nach Kant selbst als Grund für den Gottesglauben aus, ebenso als Grundlage für die Bildung einer (ohnehin problematischen) Analogie mit der sittlichen Ordnung. Schon die *Kritik der reinen Vernunft* erklärt das physikotheologische Argument für das Dasein Gottes in aller Ausführlichkeit für ungültig. (Vgl. KrV A620/B648–A630/B658) Eine besonders eindringliche Kritik daran findet sich dann noch einmal im § 85 der *Kritik der Urteilskraft*. Hier wird ausgeführt, dass in der Reflexion über Natur zu den Produkten der Natur bloß eine Intelligenz als „Kunstverstand" (KU 5:441.3) hinzuzudenken sei, die den „Begriff von einer Gottheit" (KU 5:438.18) nicht erfülle, weil ihr – anders als der Katechumene in der thematischen Passage meint – gerade „keine Weisheit" (KU 5:441.3) zugeschrieben werden könne. Weisheit ist in der dritten *Kritik* erläutert durch „Güte und Gerechtigkeit" (KU 5:444.26), also durch „moralische Eigenschaften"

(KU 5:444.26). Bloße Naturprodukte aber bieten keinen Anhalt dafür, der sie als erzeugend gedachten Intelligenz moralische Eigenschaften zuzuschreiben; und dieser Intelligenz mehr Eigenschaften zuzuschreiben, als uns „an den Wirkungen derselben offenbart" (KU 5:438.8 f.) ist, also etwa zusätzlich noch Weisheit, wäre willkürlich und also unzulässig.

Von der dargebotenen Begründung für den Gottesglauben des Schülers verbleibt also allein der zweite, auf die sittliche Weltordnung bezogene Teil. Doch auch dieser Teil erscheint problematisch. Zum einen ist nicht ganz klar, ob das genannte Ergebnis des Arguments, nämlich dass wir im Fall der Nicht-Unwürdigkeit auf die von Gott ausgeteilte Glückseligkeit „hoffen können" (TL 6:482.29), mit dem zuvor angegebenen Ziel der Begründung übereinstimmt, nämlich dem Gottes*glauben*. Zum anderen ist nicht ersichtlich, in welchem Punkt die wiederholte Berufung darauf, dass das Teilhaftig-Werden des Glücks, das der moralische Mensch verdient, das er sich aber nicht selbst verschaffen kann, und das die Verhältnisse erst vollständig rational sein ließe, über die bloße Idee des höchsten Guts hinausführen könnte. Es ist also nicht ersichtlich, durch welchen Grund die Denknotwendigkeit des das verdiente Glück austeilenden Gottes daraufhin gesteigert werden könnte, ihn „als wirklich anzunehmen" (TL 6:482.20).

Wenn Kant sein *Bruchstück eines moralischen Katechismus* überzeugender hätte enden lassen wollen, hätte er den Schüler durchaus etwas sagen lassen können, was seiner elaborierten Lehre vom moralischen Glauben besser entsprochen hätte. Er hätte, wie es etwa in der *Kritik der praktischen Vernunft* ausgeführt ist, die moralische Notwendigkeit, „das Dasein Gottes anzunehmen" (KpV 5:125.30), über die „Pflicht [...] zu Hervorbringung und Beförderung des höchsten Guts" (KpV 5:126.1 f.) begründen können, die ihren Pflichtcharakter verlöre, wenn es nicht hervorgebracht werden *könnte*; dass es aber hervorgebracht werden kann, steht nicht in der Macht des Menschen. Der „höchsten Intelligenz [...] Dasein anzunehmen [ist] also" (KpV 5:126.4 f.), so Kant hier, „mit dem Bewußtsein unserer Pflicht verbunden" (KpV 5:126.5 f.). Ein derart begründeter moralischer Glaube ist ganz unabhängig von der Unterstützung durch das ansonsten verworfene physikotheologische Argument. Dass Kant seinen Dialog im „Bruchstück" (TL 6:480.14) anders enden lässt, nämlich ohne Rekurs auf die Pflicht zur Verwirklichung des höchsten Guts, dafür aber mit Bezug auf das haltlose physikotheologische Argument, mag mit dem explizit fragmentarischen Charakter des Lehrgesprächs zu tun haben. Nach dieser Erklärung müsste man sich seine

Fortsetzung mit den nötigen Ergänzungen und Richtigstellungen vorstellen. Zugleich wäre dadurch vorausgesetzt, dass Kants Konzept eines
moralischen Katechismus ein zetetisches ist, wonach der Weg zu vollständigen Einsichten über vorläufige Positionen geht, die sogar irrtümlich
sein können, wie im Fall des für Vernunft zwar attraktiven, ihrer
Selbstkritik aber nicht standhaltenden physikotheologischen Arguments.

Auf das Katechismus-Fragment folgend, hält Kant es noch für nötig,
einige allgemeine Richtlinien für die Ausführung des Projekts eines
moralischen Katechismus zu formulieren. Im ersten der vier Abschnitte
spricht er eine Warnung aus, deren Nichtbeachtung den Pflichtbegriff
zum Verschwinden brächte, was für ein Lehrbuch einer Ethik der
Pflichten aus reiner praktischer Vernunft desaströs wäre. Im zweiten
Abschnitt fordert er, dass der Katechismus am Schluss auch eine bestimmte Gefühlswirkung entfalten soll. Der dritte Abschnitt handelt vom
Nutzen der Behandlung kasuistischer Fragen; der vierte wiederholt die
These von der Priorität des moralischen Katechismus vor dem Religionskatechismus. Außerdem lässt sich über die Abschnitte verstreut einiges
dazu erkennen, wie Kant den Katechismus bis in Einzelheiten hinein
ausgeführt sehen will.

Um mit diesen Spezifikationen zu beginnen, ist etwa gefordert, die
Katechese „durch alle Artikel der Tugend und des Lasters" (TL
6:482.30 f.) durchzuführen und „beim Schlusse" (TL 6:483.16 f.) die
„Pflichten in ihrer Ordnung noch einmal summarisch" (TL 6:483.17 f.)
zu rekapitulieren. Eine über das Bisherige hinausgehende Auskunft über
das didaktische Konzept gibt die nähere Beschreibung der Lehre als
orientiert an der „Verschiedenheit der Stufen des Alters, des Geschlechts
und des Standes, die der Mensch nach und nach betritt" (TL 6:482.9–
11). Dadurch ist den zufälligen empirischen Lebensbedingungen der
Adressaten der Lehre ein großes Gewicht gegeben und von einer angemessenen Lehre also verlangt, dass sie sich diesen Bedingungen gegenüber
variabel zeige. Dass diese Flexibilität aber nur die Lehrart betrifft und dass
also nicht etwa der Inhalt der Lehre von den empirisch zufälligen Umständen hergenommen sein soll, drückt Kant noch in demselben Satz aus,
in dem er auf die Relevanz dieser Umstände hinweist; bei all den genannten Verschiedenheiten nämlich sei die Lehre doch „aus der eigenen
Vernunft des Menschen" (TL 6:483.11 f.) zu entwickeln.

Die angesprochene Warnung, deren Missachtung den moralischen
Katechismus ganz wertlos machte, ist die, dass „das Pflichtgebot ja nicht
auf […] Vorteile oder Nachteile […] gegründet werde" (TL 6:482.32–
35), sondern „ganz rein auf das sittliche Princip" (TL 6:482.35). Das

dieser Warnung zugrunde liegende Argument wird bei Kant vielerorts vorgetragen, wobei die Stoßrichtung die gegen den Empirismus eines Hutcheson oder Hume ist. Wo die Glücksziele des Nutzens oder des zu vermeidenden Schadens zu Bedingungen von Pflichten gemacht werden, da verwandeln sich unbedingt gebietende Imperative, kategorische Imperative also, in bloß hypothetische Imperative, in „bloße pragmatische Vorschriften" (TL 6:483.5), wie Kant im gegebenen Kontext sagt. Wo nur empirisch bedingte Pflichten gelten, d. h. Pflichten nur unter der Bedingung der Befriedigung sinnlicher Bedürfnisse, da „verschwindet der Pflichtbegriff" (TL 6:483.4) im strikten und uneingeschränkten Verständnis einer aus der Freiheit reiner praktischer Vernunft erzeugten Pflicht, wodurch, so Kant, „der Adel des Menschen in seinem eigenen Bewußtsein verschwindet und er für einen Preis feil ist" (TL 6:483.5–7).

Angesichts solch klarer Positionierung und begrifflicher Bestimmung ist es zunächst irritierend, dass Kant es dennoch zulassen will, dass im moralischen Katechismus den aus der Pflichterfüllung resultierenden „Vortheile[n] oder Nachtheile[n]" (TL 6:482.34) doch „Erwähnung" (TL 6:482.37–483.1) geschehe, wenn auch „nur beiläufig, als an sich […] entbehrlicher […] Zusätze" (TL 6:482.34 f.); diese sollen „für den Gaumen der von Natur Schwachen zu bloßen Vehikeln" (TL 6:482.36 f.) dienen. Es wird unmöglich sein, einen in Aussicht gestellten Nutzen aus der Pflichterfüllung auf die Art als Hilfsmittel zu verstehen (vorausgesagte Nachteile daraus werden sich übrigens zu nichts als Hilfsmittel eignen), dass dadurch die moralische Motivation der genannten Schwachen komplettiert würde, denn dieses Mittels zu bedürfen, verhinderte gerade, dass die Motivation eine moralische sein könnte. Eine unvollständige Motivation, die zur moralischen Wirksamkeit nicht hinreicht und die dazu der Ergänzung durch ein sinnliches Element bedarf, ist nicht etwa zum Teil, sondern gar nicht moralisch. Moralische Motivation muss also, wie Kant oftmals betont, immer allein aus reiner praktischer Vernunft stammen, d. h. sie muss nur aus Pflicht erfolgen, um überhaupt eine solche zu sein. Allerdings gibt es nach Kant durchaus empirische Rahmenbedingungen, die moralisches Handeln erleichtern oder erschweren können. Den in Aussicht gestellten Nutzen zu den erleichternden Bedingungen zu zählen, die Aussicht also als hinzukommend zu einer bereits vollständigen und (weil vollständig) auch wirksamen moralischen Motivation zu verstehen, bedeutete keine Aufhebung ihres moralischen Charakters.

Das Gefühl, das zum „Beschluß" (TL 6:483.12) eines moralischen Katechismus im Adressaten erregt werden soll, ist dessen Selbstbewunderung ob „der ihm beiwohnenden ursprünglichen Anlagen" (TL 6:483.15) zur Moralität. Dieses Gefühl, wovon, wenn erzeugt, „der Eindruck nie erlischt" (TL 6:483.16), gibt nach Kant „der Seele eine Erhebung [...], die sie zum Heilighalten der Pflicht nur desto stärker belebt, je mehr sie angefochten wird" (TL 6:483.29–31). Um es hervorzubringen, müsse der Zögling darauf aufmerksam gemacht werden, „daß alle Übel, Drangsale und Leiden des Lebens, selbst Bedrohung mit dem Tode, die ihn darüber, daß er seiner Pflicht treu gehorcht, treffen mögen, ihm doch das Bewußtsein, über sie alle erhoben und Meister zu sein, nicht rauben können" (TL 6:483.19–23).

Schon die Ausdrücke „Erhebung" (TL 6:483.30) und „erhoben" (TL 6:483.22), besonders aber die näheren Angaben zu den Komponenten der Konstitution des Gefühls, lassen es gemäß der von Kant in der *Kritik der Urteilskraft* entfalteten Theorie der ästhetischen Urteile und der durch diese erzeugten Gefühle als ein Gefühl der Erhabenheit identifizieren. Noch darüber hinaus lässt es sich gemäß Kants Untersuchung der Gefühlswirkung aus der Selbstgesetzgebung reiner praktischer Vernunft in der zweiten *Kritik* als das spezielle Erhabenheitsgefühl der „Achtung fürs moralische Gesetz" (KpV 5:78.20) in uns erkennen. „Erhaben" ist nach der *Kritik der Urteilskraft* das, „was durch seinen Widerstand gegen das Interesse der Sinne unmittelbar gefällt" (KU 5:267.28 f.); die Gefühlsqualität der Erhabenheit ist hier näher bestimmt als Zustand einer überwiegenden Lust, die im Durchgang durch eine Unlust erzielt ist. (Vgl. KU 5:260) Eben dies trifft auf die „Achtung fürs moralische Gesetz" (KpV 5:78.20) zu, das zunächst demütigt und „Unlust" (KpV 5:78.26) hervorruft, weil es die „Neigungen [...] einschränkt" (KpV 5:78.25–27), das dann aber das diese Unlust hinter sich lassende Lustgefühl einer „grenzenlosen Hochschätzung" (KpV 5:79.36) seiner selbst erzeugt, d.h. „des reinen, von allem Vorteil entblößten moralischen Gesetzes" (KpV 5:79.36 f.). Alle diese Aspekte werden sich im Bewusstsein des Zöglings finden, der durch den moralischen Katechismus darauf aufmerksam gemacht wird, dass ihn in Erfüllung seiner moralischen Pflichten die Übel des Lebens treffen mögen, dass er darüber aber kraft seines moralischen Selbstverständnisses erhoben ist.

Zum Gefühl der Erhebung über das vom sinnlichen Interesse regierte Leben trägt nach Kant noch zusätzlich bei, dass spekulative Vernunft, also theoretische, Erkenntnis intendierende Vernunft, es *nicht* begreifen kann, was im Menschen es ist, das ihm ermöglicht, die Kräfte der Natur im Fall des Konflikts mit sittlichen Grundsätzen zu besiegen. Eine Erklärung dafür, wodurch – auf den ersten Blick irritierend – eine Dunkelheit und ein Nicht-Wissen eine Auszeichnung erlangen, gibt Kant in der diskutierten Passage nicht. Sie lässt sich aber in seinem Sinne geben, nämlich unter Rückgriff auf ein Hauptergebnis der ersten *Kritik*. Danach ist der Gegenstandsbereich der Erklärungsmöglichkeiten theoretischer Vernunft der Bereich der Kräfte der Natur, als Erscheinungen betrachtet, d. h. in ihrer Relation auf Sinnlichkeit als Anschauungsvermögen, nicht als irrelational unbedingte Dinge an sich. Dieser Gegenstandsbereich ist also restringiert und nicht koextensiv mit der Sphäre aller Dinge überhaupt; er enthält nicht die Gegenstände der Ideen, die Gedankendinge, z. B. nicht das durch die Idee der Freiheit Gedachte, welches eine Voraussetzung ist für Moralität. Der Gegenstandsbereich des für theoretische Vernunft Erklärbaren steht im Gegenteil unter der Herrschaft determinierender Naturgesetze, durch die die Verhältnisse der Erscheinungen untereinander bestimmt sind. In dieser Sphäre ist, etwa durch empirische Forschung, weder Freiheit erweislich, noch ist durch sie, da eben restringiert, die Unmöglichkeit von Freiheit zu beweisen. Freiheit erweist sich nach Kant nicht für theoretische Vernunft, sondern nur durch reine praktische Vernunft, insofern sie aus moralischen Gründen den genannten Sieg über die Kräfte der Natur davontragen und dadurch *praktische Realität* erlangen kann. Die Unerklärbarkeit moralischer Freiheit für theoretische Vernunft, die eine prinzipielle ist und keine bloß faktische Unerklärtheit, ist für das Gefühl der Erhabenheit über die Kräfte der Natur geradezu vorauszusetzen, denn könnte theoretische Vernunft sie erklären, wäre sie mit dieser Erklärung in den Determinationszusammenhang der Kräfte der Natur hineingezogen, als eine Naturkraft unter mehreren. Es resultierte also der Widersinn, dass eine durch theoretische Vernunft erklärte Freiheit sofort aufhörte, Freiheit zu sein; in eins damit müsste das Gefühl der Erhabenheit kollabieren.

Im Fortgang seiner Ausführungsbestimmungen für die katechetische Moralunterweisung empfiehlt Kant nachdrücklich die Behandlung kasuistischer Fragen. Hinsichtlich konkret situierter problematischer Einzelfälle also sollen die Adressaten des Katechismus „ihren Verstand versuchen" (TL 6:483.35). Diese Adressaten sind hier ausdrücklich als „die versammelten Kinder" (TL 6:483.34) angesprochen, so dass man sich demnach die Situation der Lehre (mindestens eine der möglichen Situationen) so vorzustellen hat, dass auf der Basis des Katechismus unter Anleitung eines Lehrers ein gemeinsames Deliberieren über Problemfälle stattfindet. Zwei Ziele sollen dadurch erreicht werden, die von Kant allerdings sehr verschieden gewichtet werden. Das erste Ziel, ein allgemeines, woraufhin die Behandlung jeglicher Art von Problemen dienlich

sein könnte, die die Subsumtion von Einzelnem unter Allgemeines betreffen, ist das, „den Verstand der Jugend überhaupt zu schärfen" (TL
6:484.3), also im Allgemeinen die „Cultur der Vernunft" (TL 6:484.1)
zu befördern. Das ist ein moralindifferentes Ziel, denn nach dem Kul-
turbegriff Kants, wie er etwa in der *Kritik der Urteilskraft* entfaltet ist, ist
Kultur ein vormoralischer Begriff; es ist „Cultur der letzte Zweck [...],
den man der Natur in Ansehung der Menschengattung beizulegen Ursache hat" (KU 5:431.31 f.). In Absicht auf eine allgemeine Kultur der
Vernunft sind sogar spezifisch moralische Einzelfallerwägungen nicht
einmal die geeignetsten, weil Vernunft „in Fragen, die, was Pflicht ist,
betreffen, weit leichter entscheiden kann, als in Ansehung der specula-
tiven" (TL 6:484.1 f.). – Das zweite, gewichtigere Ziel kasuistischer
moralischer Erwägungen ist nach Kant, den „Lehrling durch dergleichen
Übungen unvermerkt in das Interesse der Sittlichkeit" (TL 6:484.7 f.)
zu ziehen. Das könne geschehen, „weil es in der Natur des Menschen
liegt, das zu lieben, worin und in dessen Bearbeitung er es bis zu einer
Wissenschaft (mit der er nun Bescheid weiß) gebracht hat" (TL
6:484.4–7). Trotz der betonten stärkeren Gewichtung des zweiten Ziels
ist auffallend, dass ein so begründetes Interesse an der Sittlichkeit nicht
aus reiner praktischer Vernunft stammt, nicht also aus dem reinen Bewusstsein unbedingter Verpflichtung, das vielleicht aus Anlass kasuistischer Fragen entwickelt werden könnte, sondern daraus, dass, wie im Fall
jeder Befähigung auf dem Gebiet einer Wissenschaft, so auch im Fall
einer Könnerschaft auf dem Gebiet moralischer Einzelfallerwägungen,
eine Zuneigung zum thematischen Gegenstand erwächst. Insofern dieser
Zuneigung eine Lust am eigenen Können vorausgeht, ist ihr ein sinnliches Moment befriedigter Selbstliebe vorausgesetzt. Insgesamt erzeugen
nach Kants Begründung für den Nutzen kasuistischer Erwägungen diese
Erwägungen keine moralische Qualität, sondern ihr Nutzen liegt auf dem
Gebiet der empirischen Rahmenbedingungen für die Ausübung von
Moralität. Diese Bedingungen sind dann günstiger, wenn moralische
Fragestellungen nicht für gleichgültig, sondern für interessant gehalten
werden.

Zum zweiten Abschnitt der ethischen Methodenlehre: „Die ethische Asketik"
(TL 6:484.17–485.31)

Zum § 53

Die beiden zentralen Angaben Kants zur ethischen Asketik sind, dass sie „Übung in der Tugend" (TL 6:484.20) bzw. „Cultur der Tugend" (TL 6:484.30) sei. Ziel solcher Übung in der Tugend sei die Erzeugung zweier „Gemüthsstimmungen" (TL 6:484.21), nämlich „wackeren und fröhlichen Gemüths […] in Befolgung ihrer Pflichten zu sein" (TL 6:484.21–23). Im folgenden Text treten diese Bestimmungen noch in leicht abgewandelter Gestalt auf, wonach es darum geht, dass die Pflicht „rüstig[]" (TL 6:484.31) und „muthig[]" (TL 6:484.31) und „mit Lust" (TL 6:484.26) erfüllt, ja dass sie „geliebt" (TL 6:484.28) wird. Besonders durch die Kennzeichnung als Kultur der Tugend wird deutlich, dass es sich bei der ethischen Asketik zwar nicht um etwas handelt, das wie in der katechetischen Lehrsituation bloß in Gedanken vollzogen werden könnte (wie etwa das Erwägen kasuistischer Fragen, das zu einer Kultur der Vernunft führen sollte), aber um eine Art von praktischer Übung. Doch auch diese kann bloß vorbereitend sein und nicht schon selbst als Erfüllung von Tugendpflichten betrachtet werden. Kultur ist nach der allgemeinen Bestimmung dieses Begriffs in der *Kritik der Urteilskraft* „Hervorbringung der Tauglichkeit eines vernünftigen Wesens zu beliebigen Zwecken" (KU 5:431.28–30). Für die beliebigen Zwecke kann im gegebenen Kontext zwar der Zweck der Tugend eingesetzt werden, doch Kultur der Tugend bleibt nach der Definition immer noch erst Hervorbringung einer Befähigung.

Das Erfordernis, sich zur Tugend durch Erzeugung eines wackeren und fröhlichen Gemüts zu befähigen, begründet Kant damit, dass in der Pflichterfüllung „mit Hindernissen zu kämpfen" (TL 6:484.23) ist, wozu Kraft aufzuwenden ist, und dass um ihretwillen „manche Lebensfreuden zu opfern" (TL 6:484.24 f.) sind, „deren Verlust das Gemüth wohl bisweilen finster und mürrisch machen kann" (TL 6:484.25 f.). Das fröhliche Gemüt erleichtert offenbar nach Kant den Kraftaufwand zur Pflichterfüllung, während die „als Frohndienst" (TL 6:484.26 f.) erfüllte Pflicht die Gefahr heraufbeschwört, der „Gelegenheit ihrer Ausübung so viel [als] möglich" (TL 6:484.28 f.) aus dem Weg zu gehen.

Wenn nun die Frage ist, welche Art von Bedingung für die Tauglichkeit zur Pflichterfüllung das fröhliche Herz ist, so ist zunächst zu antworten: keine notwendige Bedingung. Nach dem Text ist auch die „als Frohndienst" (TL 6:484.26 f.) erfüllte Pflicht nicht ausgeschlossen, und ihre Erfüllung ist auch dem mürrischen Charakter nicht definitiv abgesprochen. Wäre es so, dann wäre das zentrale Lehrstück Kants konterkariert, dass aus reiner praktischer Vernunft unter Vermittlung des rein intellektuell bewirkten Gefühls der Achtung moralisch gehandelt werden kann, wobei alle empirischen Bestimmungen der Sinnlichkeit außer Acht bleiben. Zu diesen empirischen Bestimmungen zählen auch die Lust- und Unlustgefühle des inneren Sinnes, also auch die freudige oder finstere Stimmung. Das fröhliche Gemüt im Interesse der Pflichterfüllung dennoch für wichtig zu erklären, bedeutet demnach, es den empirischen Rahmenbedingungen zuzuordnen, die sie erleichtern. Von diesen Bedingungen gibt es noch andere, z. B. Gesundheit. Dass Kant die moralische Asketik auf dieser Ebene ansiedelt, ist auch daran abzulesen, dass er sie ausdrücklich als „eine Art von Diätetik für den Menschen, sich moralisch gesund zu erhalten" (TL 6:484.34–385.1), bezeichnet, einmal sogar als „ethische Gymnastik" (TL 6:484.19).

Kants Angaben dazu, was zu tun ist, um in die Stimmung des wackeren und fröhlichen Gemüts zu gelangen, sind nicht sehr ausführlich und zudem problembehaftet. Die erste von zwei zu erfüllenden Bedingungen ist als Regel formuliert und als „Wahlspruch der Stoiker" (TL 6:484.32) bezeichnet: „gewöhne dich die zufälligen Lebensübel zu ertragen und die eben so überflüssigen Ergötzlichkeiten zu entbehren" (TL 6:484.32 f.). Diese Forderung geht auf die Erzeugung der Gewohnheiten, auf die nicht unserer Macht unterworfenen Lebensübel affektiv maßvoll zu reagieren, d. h. vom Leid nicht überwältigt zu werden (und damit die Tauglichkeit zur Pflichterfüllung zu schwächen), und ebenso den Annehmlichkeiten, die die Gegenstände sinnlicher Neigungen versprechen, ein Maß zu setzen. Dieses Maß zwischen dem Überflüssigen und dem Zugestandenen ist wenig später als dasjenige „Maß" (TL 6:485.20) in der „Bekämpfung der Naturtriebe" (TL 6:485.20) bestimmt, das so viel von den Naturtrieben belässt, dass es möglich ist, über sie „bei vorkommenden, der Moralität Gefahr drohenden Fällen Meister [zu] werden" (TL 6:485.20 f.). Sich auf diese (trotz des Ausdrucks „Bekämpfung" (TL 6:484.20)) moderate, bloß ein Übermaß an „Ergötzlichkeiten" (TL 6:484.33) vermeidende Weise auf den moralischen Ernstfall vorzubereiten, bedeutet nach Kant, „sich moralisch gesund zu erhalten" (TL 6:485.1).

Dass in Absicht auf das fröhliche Gemüt die Erfüllung einer zweiten Bedingung nötig ist, begründet Kant damit, dass „Gesundheit […] nur ein negatives Wohlbefinden" (TL 6:485.2) ist, bloß eine Abwesenheit von Unlust also, und „selber […] nicht gefühlt werden" (TL 6:495.2 f.) kann. Um über diesen Nullpunkt auf der Skala von Lust und Unlust hinauszukommen, müsse es einen hinzukommenden „angenehmen Lebensgenuß" (TL 6.485.3 f.) geben, der „doch bloß moralisch ist" (TL 6:485.4). Kant nennt dieses Hinzukommende „das jederzeit fröhliche Herz in der Idee des tugendhaften Epikurs" (TL 6:485.4 f.). Zur Erläuterung dieser Anspielung soll dienen:

> Denn wer sollte wohl mehr Ursache haben frohen Muts zu sein und nicht darin selbst eine Pflicht finden, sich in eine fröhliche Gemüthsstimmung zu versetzen und sie sich habituell zu machen, als der, welcher sich keiner vorsetzlichen Übertretung bewußt und wegen des Verfalls in eine solche gesichert ist […]. (TL 6:485.5–10)

Diese Erläuterung erscheint problematisch, denn auf das Wesentliche verkürzt lautet sie: Der Tugendhafte hat Ursache, frohen Muts zu sein. Es mag nun zwar so sein, dass Tugend eine fröhliche Gemütsstimmung erzeugt und sich so selbst stärkt, doch es ist fraglich, ob in der moralischen Asketik, die als Propädeutik die außermoralischen Bedingungen erwägt, die die Ausübung der Moralität begünstigen, mit der Voraussetzung des bereits Tugendhaften operiert werden kann. Merkwürdig ist auch, dass dieser vorausgesetzte Tugendhafte zusätzlich zu seinem aufgrund seiner Tugend schon frohen Mut noch das Bewusstsein der Verpflichtung entwickelt, „sich in eine fröhliche Gemüthsstimmung zu versetzen und sie sich habituell zu machen" (TL 6:485.7 f.). Eine solche eigenständige Pflicht zu erfüllen verlangte die freie Selbsterzeugung gewohnheitsmäßiger innerer Fröhlichkeit. Zur Möglichkeit der Erfüllung einer solchen Pflicht wären weitere Ausführungen Kants wünschenswert gewesen.

Demgegenüber ist es überzeugender, wenn Kant gegen Ende des Paragraphen zur ethischen Asketik die Erfüllung allein der erstgenannten Bedingung, d.i. die Mäßigung der Naturtriebe, als hinreichend dafür darstellt, „wacker und […] fröhlich" (TL 6:485.22 f.) zu werden, wenn er diese Mäßigung also doch nicht bloß so auffasst, dass sie zu einem nicht fühlbaren negativen Wohlgefallen bzw. zu einer Lust-Unlust-Indifferenz führt. Nach der Darstellung hier macht nur die Mäßigung der Naturtriebe schon fröhlich, weil der sich Mäßigende nach der Mäßigung „im Bewußtsein seiner wiedererworbenen Freiheit" (TL 6:485.22 f.) steht.

Verwoben mit der Darstellung seiner moralischen Asketik distanziert Kant sich scharf von einer anderen Asketik, die er „Mönchsascetik" (TL 6:485.10) nennt. Diese zwecke „nicht auf Tugend" (TL 6:485.13) ab, sondern mittels „Selbstpeinigung und Fleischeskreuzigung" (TL 6:485.12) auf „Entsündigung" (TL 6:485.13), d.h. darauf, schließlich ohne Makel dazustehen. Zu dieser Entsündigung wolle der Asket mittels selbst auferlegter Strafe büßen und nicht, was Kant dem Büßen als ein Positives entgegenhält, mit dem Ziel der Besserung bereuen. Abgesehen von dem Widerspruch, den er im Begriff der Selbstbestrafung erkennt, weil Strafe „immer ein Anderer auflegen" (TL 6:485.16 f.) müsse, schreibt er dem Mönchsasketen schwerwiegende moralische Verfehlungen zu, zum einen einen bloß „geheuchelte[n] Abscheu an sich selbst" (TL 6:485.11) und zum anderen einen „geheimen Haß gegen das Tugendgebot" (TL 6:485.18 f.). Die Gefühlswirkung einer solchen Asketik könne nur ein „freudenlos[es], finster[es] und mürrisch[es]" (TL 6:485.28) Gemüt sein.

Die moralischen Vorhaltungen sind nicht explizit erläutert, sind aber wohl aus dem kritisierten Religionsbegriff der Entsündigung zu entwickeln. Der Zweck der Entsündigung als ein Abbüßen von Schuld scheint Motive der Selbstliebe vorauszusetzen, nämlich das Leiden an der Sünde loszuwerden und sich in einen schuldlosen Zustand zurückzuversetzen, der das Wohlgefallen an sich selbst und das Wohlgefallen Gottes wieder erlaubt. Die Unterstellung des Hasses gegen das Tugendgebot könnte entsprechend dadurch begründet werden, dass das dem Mönchsasketen doch gegenwärtige Gebot es ist, dessen Geltung den Zustand unangefochtener Selbstliebe gefährdet und dessen Übertretung diese Selbstliebe lädiert und auch die Gunst Gottes entzieht.

Das von Kant dem Abbüßen entgegengehaltene Bereuen ist nicht der notwendigerweise misslingende Versuch, eine moralische Verfehlung ungeschehen zu machen und in einen schuldlosen Zustand zurückzufinden, der Selbstliebe wieder ermöglicht. Bereuen ist nach Kant bei der „Rückerinnerung ehemaliger Übertretungen unvermeidlich" (TL 6:485.23 f.) und diese Rückerinnerung „sogar Pflicht" (TL 6:485.25). An eine solche Rückerinnerung lässt sich, so der positive Aspekt des Bereuens, die „Absicht auf die Besserung" (TL 6:485.14 f.) anschließen. Aufgrund dieses positiven Aspekts ist auch die Gemütsstimmung der Freude nicht verunmöglicht. Kants Mittel, diese Gemütsstimmung zu bewirken, die ethische Asketik, ist, wie gesehen, nicht exzentrische Selbstpeinigung, sondern eine – übrigens in den Lebensvollzug integriert zu denkende und nicht eigens und isoliert zu praktizierende maßvolle

Disziplin hinsichtlich sinnlicher Neigungen, die das freudige Bewusstsein erweckt, von diesen nicht beherrscht und so auf moralische Anforderungen vorbereitet zu sein.

Die Religionslehre als Lehre der Pflichten gegen Gott liegt außerhalb der Grenzen der reinen Moralphilosophie
(TL 6:486–491)

Friedo Ricken

Der Abschnitt gibt eine Begründung dafür, dass die *Metaphysik der Sitten* in der vorliegenden Form vollständig ist, obwohl ihr Verfasser „nicht, wie es sonst wohl gewöhnlich war, die Religion […] in die Ethik mit hinein gezogen hat" (TL 6:488.3 f.). Religion, so die These, „als Lehre der Pflichten gegen Gott, liegt jenseit aller Grenzen der rein-philosophischen Ethik hinaus" (TL 6:487.37–488.1). Die „Schlußanmerkung" (TL 6:488.13) „bestätigt" (TL 6:491.10) die These dadurch, dass sie zeigt, dass in der Ethik „nur die moralischen Verhältnisse des Menschen gegen den Menschen für uns begreiflich sind" (TL 6:491.6 f.).

I

Prominente Beispiele dafür, „wie es sonst wohl gewöhnlich war" (TL 6:488.3), sind Wolff und Baumgarten. Christian Wolffs *Vernünfftige Gedancken von der Menschen Thun und Lassen*[1] umfasst vier Teile: I. Von dem Tun und Lassen der Menschen überhaupt; II. Von den Pflichten des Menschen gegen sich selbst; III. Von den Pflichten des Menschen gegen Gott; IV. Von den Pflichten des Menschen gegen andere. „Durch die Pflichten gegen Gott verstehe ich diejenigen Handlungen, welche der Mensch vermöge des Gesetzes (und also wo wir bloß von natürlichen Pflichten reden, vermöge des Gesetzes der Natur) in Ansehung Gottes vorzunehmen hat." (§ 650) Alexander Gottlieb Baumgartens *Ethica Philosophica*[2] behandelt im ersten, allgemeinen Teil die allen Menschen gemeinsamen Pflichten und im zweiten Teil die besonderen Pflichten bestimmter Stände. Die allen gemeinsamen Pflichten sind die „erga

---

1 Wolff, [4]1733.
2 Baumgarten, [2]1751/[3]1763.

Deum ad religionem" (§§ 11–149); gegen sich selbst; gegen anderes
(„erga alia") (§ 9). Baumgartens Imperativ lautet: „Perfice te" (§ 10).
Am Beginn des Kapitels „Religio" steht, mit den entsprechenden Verweisen auf Baumgartens *Metaphysica*, das Argument: „Ens perfectissi-
mum uberius, dignius, verius, clarius, certius, ardentius nosse est realitas
[...] Ergo gloria dei in te ponit realitatem [...] Illustratio gloriae divinae
etiam in te ponit realitatem [...] Ergo religio te perficit, ut finem, [...]
adeoque obligaris ad religionem" (§ 11).

In der *Praktischen Philosophie Herder,* die Kant im Sommersemester
1764 nach Baumgarten gelesen hat, ist die kritische Auseinandersetzung
mit dem Kapitel „Religio" bis zu § 126 einschließlich erhalten. Kant
beginnt mit einer grundsätzlichen Kritik: Der Begriff der Religion, wie
Baumgarten ihn bestimmt, sei kein philosophischer Begriff; die Religion
als Lehre von den Pflichten gegenüber Gott habe deshalb in einer philosophischen Ethik, die nach Baumgarten eine Ethik ist „quatenus sine
fide cognsoci potest" (§ 1), keinen Platz. Anhand von § 11 argumentiert
Kant: „Der Begriff der Religion wird in der Metaphysik vorausgesetzt:
als illustratio gloriae Diuinae ist sie die Verbindung der Erkenntnis von
Gottes Eigenschaften als Beweggrund mit unseren Handlungen: – Das
Wort Verherrlichung ist blos ein Wort der geoffenbarten Religion und
also nicht vorauszusetzen" (V-PP/Herder 27:16.36–17.2). Dem stellt
Kant seine Definition entgegen: „Religio est cognitio practica relationis
moralis entis creati ad voluntatem Dei" (V-PP/Herder 27:17.3 f.).

In den Ausführungen der *Praktischen Philosophie Powalski* (Sommersemester 1777 [?]) über die Religion erinnert nur noch die Unterscheidung zwischen der inneren und der äußeren Religion an Baumgarten. „Die moralischen Gesezze sind nicht Sazzungen, sondern sie sind nur
solche Gesezze, die in der Natur liegen. Sie sind keine Statuta des
Göttlichen Willens, sondern sie liegen in dem Begriffe der Freyheit. Gott
ist wohl ein Gesezgeber, aber nicht ein Urheber." (V-PP/Powalski
27:168.37–169.2) „Die Religion ist nichts anderes als die moralitaet die
auf die Theologie angewandt ist [...] Die Religionsobservanzen sind sehr
beschwerlich, obwohl sie moralisch gleichgültig sind. Die observanzen
erfordern gar keine moralische Reinigkeit." (V-PP/Powalski 27:169.14–
16, 169.24–26) „Alle Religion ist innerlich, denn sie dient, die Gesinnungen unsers Willens dem Willen Gottes conform zu machen. Die
Gesinnungen werden als Mittel angesehen, so müssen sie rechtschaffen
und auch practisch sein. Die äußere Religion ist eine contradictio in
adjecto." (V-PP/Powalski 27:185.18–21)

Die natürliche Religion, so heißt es in der *Moralphilosophie Collins* (Wintersemester 1784 und 1785, „über Baumgarten" (V-Mo/Collins 27:241)), sollte

> in der Moral den Schluß machen, und das Siegel der Moralität seyn [...] Allein es hat unserm Autor gefallen, sie vorher abzuhandeln, und weil es eben nicht viel darauf ankommt, so folgen wir ihm [...] Die natürliche Religion ist keine Regel der Moralität, sondern die Religion ist die Moralität auf Gott angewandt [...] Die natürliche Religion ist praktisch und enthält natürliche Erkenntniße unserer Pflichten in Ansehung des höchsten Wesens. (V-Mo/Collins 27:305.10–22)

Kant unterscheidet die religiösen Handlungen in „Gottesfürchtige und Gottesdienstliche Handlungen" (V-Mo/Collins 27:327.37). Der Anthropomorphismus ist Ursache dafür, „daß man sich die Pflichten gegen Gott nach der Analogie mit Pflichten der Menschen vorstellt" (V-Mo/Collins 27:328.1 f.). Wir können einem Menschen durch bestimmte „Dienste[]" (V-Mo/Collins 27:328.6) zeigen, dass wir ihm zu allen beliebigen Diensten bereitwillig zur Verfügung stehen, etwa indem wir einem Fürsten die Cour machen.

> Nun aber sind die Menschen geneigt, solche Dienstleistungen auf Gott anzuwenden und ihm Dienste zu erzeigen und Cour bey ihm zu machen [...] Daher ist der Einfall entstanden, daß die Gottheit, um die Menschen in Uebung zu erhalten, Befehle gegeben habe, die an sich leer sind, wodurch die Menschen auf die Befehle zu merken geübt wurden, und wodurch sie immer dienstbar erhalten wurden [...] Man nennt den Inbegrif der Handlungen, die keine andre Absicht haben, als die Dienstbeflißenheit, den Befehlen Gottes ein Genüge zu leisten, den Gottesdienst. (V-Mo/Collins 27:328.11–328.24)

Die abschließenden Paragrafen (§§ 138–148) der *Metaphysik der Sitten Vigilantius* (Wintersemester 1793/94) handeln über „Pflichten gegen Gott" (V-MS/Vigil 27:712.28). Religion ist „die practische Erkenntniß von Gott" (V-MS/Vigil 27:712.31). Die genauere Bestimmung zeigt, dass sich aus dem Begriff der Religion ergibt, dass es keine Pflichten gegen Gott geben kann. „Religion ist der Inbegriff aller Menschenpflichten als göttlicher Gebote, und mithin kann sie nicht ein Inbegriff der Pflichten der Menschen gegen Gott seyn." (V-MS/Vigil 27:713.3–5) Pflichten, so die erläuternde Argumentation, sind Handlungen, die aus Verbindlichkeit entspringen; Handlungen sind Wirkungen; „nun ist es unmöglich, daß man da Pflichten sich denken kann, wo man nicht wirken kann: alle Pflichten sind wechselseitig [...] Es sind daher nur Pflichten der Menschen gegen sich und gegen einander denkbar, die Pflichten selbst aber werden unter der Vorstellung von Geboten Gottes gedacht." (V-MS/Vigil 27:713.16–28) Kant unterscheidet zwischen Vernunftreligion, „die man natürliche Religion nennt, rationalis, weil sie von aller Erfahrung abstrahirt" (V-MS/Vigil 27:714.21 f.) und geoffenbarter Religion, „die auf empirischen principiis beruht, sie mögen oraliter mitgetheilt, oder durch indicia naturae dargestellt seyn" (V-MS/Vigil 27:714.24–26). Daraus ergibt sich die Unterscheidung zwischen Pflichten der natürlichen und der geoffenbarten Religion. „Wir werden also eher erkennen können und müssen, daß etwas Pflicht sey, ehe wir wissen, daß es göttliches Gebot ist, und dies sind die Pflichten der natürlichen Religion, wogegen man Pflichten, die man dafür nur erkennt, weil sie uns als göttliche Gebote zuvor bekannt geworden, Pflichten der geoffenbarten Religion nennt." (V-MS/Vigil 27:714.37–715.3)

II

TL 6:486.2–13

Die Überschrift formuliert die These, die im Folgenden begründet werden soll, und Kant beginnt mit einem Fall, der anscheinend gegen diese These spricht. Die hohe Obrigkeit von Athen befiehlt, „daß es Götter gebe" (TL 6:486.13). In einer minimalen Auslegung verbietet dieser Befehl, öffentlich die Existenz der Götter zu bestreiten. Das Verbot ist dadurch gerechtfertigt, dass es die Voraussetzung der für die Rechtsordnung unentbehrlichen Institution des Eides sichert. Es gibt also zumindest, so der Einwand, die Pflicht, an Gott oder die Götter zu glauben.

Kant antwortet zunächst mit einer Unterscheidung. Die Richter, die Protagoras verurteilten, weil er gegen dieses Verbot verstoßen hat, haben nach dem geltenden Recht entschieden; dennoch haben sie „als Menschen" (TL 6:486.9) dem Protagoras Unrecht getan. Die Rechtsordnung sieht den Eid vor; die „gesetzgebende Gewalt handelt aber im Grunde unrecht, diese Befugniß der richterlichen zu ertheilen: weil selbst im bürgerlichen Zustande ein Zwang zu Eidesleistungen der unverlierbaren menschlichen Freiheit zuwider ist" (RL 6:304.36–305.2). Der Eid ist eine „*tortura spiritualis*" (RL 6:304.33 f.), ein „Erpressungsmittel der Wahrhaftigkeit in äußern Aussagen" (MpVT 8:268.27). Er rechnet mit dem blinden Aberglauben. Man traut einem Menschen nicht zu, er werde in einer feierlichen Aussage vor Gericht, wo es um das Recht der Menschen, das Heiligste, was es unter Menschen gibt, geht, die Wahrheit sagen, aber man nimmt an, er werde durch eine Formel dazu bewegt, durch welche er die göttlichen Strafen auf sich herabruft, denen er ohnehin, wenn er lügt, nicht entgehen kann.[3]

TL 6:486.15–31

Auch das Christentum hat das Dilemma, das im Prozess des Protagoras deutlich wird, nicht gelöst. Kant verweist auf die Bergpredigt,[4] wo das Verbot des Schwörens damit begründet wird, dass alle Dinge, bei denen man schwört, eine Beziehung zu Gott haben. Das Schwören, so seine Auslegung der Stelle, wird als „beinahe an Blasphemie grenzend" (TL 6:486.16) verboten; es verstößt gegen die Gott geschuldete Ehrfurcht; Gott wird zu einem Mittel, das der Verwaltung der öffentlichen Gerechtigkeit dienen soll. „In der angeführten Schriftstelle", so die Auslegung in der Religionsschrift, „wird diese Art der Betheurung als eine ungereimte Vermessenheit vorgestellt, Dinge gleichsam durch Zauberworte wirklich zu machen, die doch nicht in unserer Gewalt sind" (RGV 6:159.33–35). Dennoch glaubt man „noch immer" (TL 6:486.17), auf dieses Mittel zur Verwaltung der öffentlichen Gerechtigkeit nicht verzichten zu können. Kant spricht von einem „mechanischen" (TL 6:486.17) Mittel: Der Eid arbeitet mit dem psychischen Mechanismus der Furcht, und er wird mit den mechanischen Foltervorrichtungen verglichen.

Wer schwört, ruft Gott zum Zeugen an; er setzt also voraus, dass ein Gott existiert. Der Schwur bringt also zum Ausdruck, dass der Schwörende von der Wahrheit zweier Aussagen überzeugt ist: der Aussage ‚Es existiert ein Gott' und der Aussage, deren Wahrheit er beschwört. Da im Schwur Gott als Zeuge dafür angerufen wird, dass der Schwörende von dem überzeugt ist, was er zum Ausdruck bringt, wird also Gott auch als Zeuge dafür angerufen, dass der Schwörende davon überzeugt ist, dass Gott existiert. Dass man „im Ernst" (TL 6:486.20) Gott zum Zeugen dafür anruft, dass man von seiner Existenz überzeugt ist, hält Kant für eine „Ungereimtheit" (TL 6:486.20). Die für den Akt des Schwörens notwendige und in ihm gemachte Voraussetzung wird zu dessen Inhalt; ich kann den Akt nicht vollziehen, ohne implizit zu versichern, dass ich

---

3 Vgl. RGV 6:159.22–33; RL 6:303.30–304.20; MpVT 8:268.27–269.18.
4 Vgl. Mt 5,34–37.

von der Voraussetzung, die gemacht werden muss, damit dieser Akt
möglich sei, überzeugt bin. Kant fragt deshalb, ob ein Eid möglich sei, in
dem die Frage nach der Existenz Gottes offen gelassen wird, d.h. in dem
der Schwörende seine Bereitschaft ausdrückt, seine Aussage vor Gott zu
verantworten, *wenn* dieser existiert.

> Von einem menschlichen Gerichtshofe wird dem Gewissen des Schwörenden
> nichts weiter zugemuthet, als die Anheischigmachung: daß, wenn es einen
> künftigen Weltrichter […] giebt, er ihm für die Wahrheit seines äußern
> Bekenntnisses verantwortlich sein wolle; daß es einen solchen Welt-
> trichter gebe, davon hat er nicht nöthig ihm ein Bekenntniß abzufordern,
> weil, wenn die erstere Betheurung die Lüge nicht abhalten kann, das zweite
> falsche Bekenntniß eben so wenig Bedenken erregen würde. (MpVT
> 8:269.18–25)

In den folgenden Zeilen (TL 6:486.25–31) geht es wieder um den Eid in
der nicht-hypothetischen Form, in dem implizit die Existenz Gottes
behauptet wird, und zwar um den Fall, dass jemand diesen Eid schwört,
der nicht an die Existenz Gottes glaubt („der Betrüger" (TL 6:486.27)).
Der Betrüger hat keine Bedenken dagegen, einen Eid in der nicht-hypothetischen Form zu schwören, also implizit zu schwören, dass ein Gott
sei. Denn, so argumentiert er, wenn es einen Gott gibt, dann ist die von
mir beschworene Aussage, dass ein Gott ist, wahr; wenn es keinen Gott
gibt, dann kann mich auch kein Gott zur Verantwortung ziehen. Kant
kritisiert, dass die erste Alternative nicht zu Ende gedacht ist. Wenn ein
Gott ist, dann wird er den, der feierlich behauptet, er sei überzeugt, dass
ein Gott ist, ohne jedoch davon überzeugt zu sein, zur Rechenschaft
ziehen. Der Betrüger hat es darauf angelegt, „selbst […] Gott zu täu-
schen" (TL 6:486.30). Die Täuschung besteht darin, dass er vorgibt, es
beständen keinerlei Bedenken dagegen, dass jemand, der von der Existenz
Gottes nicht überzeugt ist, diese in einem Eid implizit beschwört.

TL 6:487.1–7

Kant macht zunächst ein Zugeständnis. Der Eid ist ein unverzichtbares
Mittel zur Verwaltung der öffentlichen Gerechtigkeit; der Eid setzt den
Glauben an die Götter voraus; folglich ist der Gesetzgeber berechtigt zu
befehlen, „daß es Götter gebe" (TL 6:486.13). Daraus folgt, dass der
Glaube an die Götter Pflicht ist und dass „Religionslehre ein inte-
grirender Theil der allgemeinen Pflichtenlehre" (TL 6:487.1 f.) ist.
Beide Termini sind hier in einem weiten Sinn gebraucht. Die „Religi-

onslehre" (TL 6:487.1) umfasst die geoffenbarte und die natürliche Theologie, also die „biblische[] Theologie" (RGV 6:10.22) und die „reine philosophische Religionslehre" (RGV 6:10.23 f.; siehe auch RGV 6:11.1), und die „allgemeine Pflichtenlehre" die „Pflichten der natürlichen Religion" (V-MS/Vigil 27:714.39) und die „Pflichten der geoffenbarten Religion" (V-MS/Vigil 27:715.2 f.). Dass die Pflicht zum Glauben an Gott unter diese weiten Begriffe fällt, wird „zugestanden" (TL 6:487.1) und „eingeräumt" (TL 6:487.2); die Frage, um die es geht, ist die genauere Bestimmung der „Wissenschaft" (TL 6:487.3), zu der die Religionslehre als Pflichtenlehre gehört. Wissenschaft ist „ein System, d. i. ein nach Principien geordnetes Ganze der Erkenntniß" (MAN 4:467.18 f.), und alle Erkenntnis ist „entweder historisch oder rational. Die historische Erkenntnis ist *cognitio ex datis*, die rationale aber *cognitio ex principiis*" (KrV A836/B864). Gehört die Religionslehre als Lehre von den Pflichten gegen Gott zur Ethik, d. h. zur philosophischen Lehre von den Pflichten, die keiner äußeren Gesetzgebung fähig sind, oder handelt es sich um eine historische Erkenntnis? Dass sie nicht zur Rechtslehre gehört, bedarf keiner Begründung. In seiner Antwort unterscheidet Kant zwischen dem Formalen und dem Materialen der Religion.

TL 6:487.8–25

Der Abschnitt[5] unterscheidet zwischen Pflichten *gegen* Gott und einer Pflicht *in Ansehung* Gottes. Es gibt keine Pflichten *gegen* Gott, sondern nur eine Pflicht *in Ansehung* Gottes, und diese Pflicht ist eine Pflicht des Menschen gegen sich selbst und gehört zur philosophischen Moral.

Die Argumentation geht aus von der Definition, Religion sei „der Inbegriff aller Pflichten a l s (*instar*) göttlicher Gebote" (TL 6:487.8 f.). Die Formulierung der zweiten *Kritik* lautet: Religion ist die „Erkenntniß aller Pflichten als göttlicher Gebote" (KpV 5:129.18 f.). Das lateinische „*instar*" (TL 6:487.9) bedeutet ‚einer Sache gleich oder gleich zu achten'. Das „a l s" (TL 6:487.9) ist also nicht im Sinne eines ‚als ob' zu verstehen; vielmehr sollen die Pflichten als das betrachtet werden, was sie tatsächlich sind; es geht, wie es die zweite *Kritik* formuliert, um die *Erkenntnis* dessen, was die Pflichten tatsächlich sind. Die Definition gibt das „F o r m a l e aller Religion" (TL 6:487.8) an, d. h. sie charakterisiert die Religion als eine neue Sicht unserer Pflichten,

---

5   Für hilfreiche Kritik und Hinweise danke ich Dieter Schönecker.

die darin besteht, dass die Vernunft sie auf die „Idee von Gott, welche sie sich selber macht" (TL 6:487.11), bezieht. „Religionspflicht" (TL 6:443.30) wurde in § 18 definiert als „Erkenntniß aller unserer Pflichten *als* (instar) göttlicher Gebote" (TL 6:443.30 f.). ‚Religion' und „Religionspflicht" (TL 6:443.30) bezeichnen also denselben Begriff; Religion ist Pflicht; da sie sich jedoch nur auf die *Idee* von Gott bezieht und von seiner Existenz abstrahiert, ist eine Religionspflicht keine Pflicht „gegen (*erga*) Gott als ein außer unserer Idee existierendes Wesen" (TL 6:487.12 f.).

Die folgenden Zeilen (TL 6:487.14–20) heben nochmals hervor, dass Religion Pflicht ist, und sie begründen diese Pflicht. Die Religionspflicht besteht darin, alle Pflichten, die wir als Menschen haben, als göttliche Gebote anzusehen, und zwar nicht als willkürliche, für sich selbst zufällige Verordnungen eines fremden Willens, sondern als wesentliche Gesetze „eines jeden freien Willens für sich selbst, die aber dennoch als Gebote des höchsten Wesens angesehen werden müssen" (KpV 5:129.21 f.). Sie ist in dem Sinn eine Pflicht zweiter Ordnung, dass sie vorschreibt, wie alle anderen Pflichten „gedacht werden sollen" (TL 6:487.16). Die Sicht aller unserer Pflichten als göttlicher Gebote, so lässt die Begründung sich zusammenfassen, stärkt die moralische Triebfeder in unserer eigenen gesetzgebenden Vernunft, und diese Triebfeder zu stärken ist Pflicht des Menschen gegen sich selbst. Wenden wir uns nun den einzelnen Schritten der Begründung zu.

Der Grund für diese Pflicht ist „nur subjectiv-logisch" (TL 6:487.17). Was das bedeutet, wird im Folgenden näher ausgeführt; diese Pflicht, das soll gezeigt werden, ist ausschließlich durch die Eigenart unseres Erkenntnisvermögens bedingt. Die unausgesprochene Voraussetzung des Folgenden ist, dass wir uns „Verpflichtung (moralische Nöthigung)" (TL 6:487.17 f.) anschaulich machen *müssen*; das sei, so führt der Text dann aus, nicht möglich, ohne Gott dabei zu denken. Dass wir uns Verpflichtung anschaulich machen, ist notwendig „zur Stärkung der moralischen Triebfeder in unserer eigenen gesetzgebenden Vernunft" (TL 6:487.24 f.). „Verpflichtung […] anschaulich machen" (TL 487.17 f.) kann nur als verkürzte Ausdrucksweise eines differenzierteren Zusammenhangs verstanden werden. Inhalt der „Verpflichtung" (TL 487.17) ist, mir das höchste Gut zum letzten Zweck zu machen. „Das moralische Gesetz gebietet, das höchste mögliche Gut in einer Welt mir zum letzten Gegenstande alles Verhaltens zu machen." (KpV 5:129.30–32) Das setzt voraus, dass das höchste Gut möglich ist, was nur dann der Fall ist, wenn Gott existiert; die Einsicht in die Verpflichtung impliziert die ‚Erkenntnis' eines Welturhebers von höchster Vollkommenheit, der allein die Übereinstimmung von Tugend und Glückseligkeit im höchsten Gut bewirken kann. Diese ‚Erkenntnis' ist nicht möglich, ohne der Idee Gottes eine Anschauung zu unterlegen. Bei den Anschauungen, die man Begriffen a priori unterlegt, unterscheidet Kant zwischen „Schemate und Symbole, wovon die erstern directe, die zweiten indirecte Darstellungen des Begriffs enthalten" (KU 5:352.9 f.). In einer symbolischen Darstellung unterlegen wir einem Begriff mittels einer Analogie eine Anschauung; so wird z. B. ein despotischer Staat durch eine Handmühle „symbolisch vorgestellt" (KU 5:352.20). Weil den Ideen keine Anschauung angemessen gegeben werden kann, vermitteln sie keine theoretische Erkenntnis. Dagegen dürfen wir, wenn es um die praktische Bestimmung einer Idee geht, d. h. was die Idee für uns bedeutet und um ihren zweckmäßigen Gebrauch, die symbolische Vorstellung „Erkenntniß nennen" (KU 5:353.3). Alle unsere Erkenntnis von Gott ist bloß symbolisch, und nur als symbolische Erkenntnis kann sie praktisch sein. Nur dann, wenn wir Gott als ein Wesen mit Verstand und Willen denken, hat diese Idee für uns praktische Bedeutung. Die Eigenschaften Verstand und Wille beweisen „allein an Weltwesen ihre objective Realität" (KU 5:353.8 f.). Wer sie „für schematisch nimmt, geräth in den Anthropomorphism" (KU 5:353.9 f.). Wer dagegen alles „Intuitive wegläßt" (KU 5:353.10), d. h. wer sie Gott nicht symbolisch zuspricht, gerät „in den Deism, wodurch überall nichts, *auch nicht in praktischer Absicht*, erkannt wird" (KU 5:353.11 f., kursiv F.R.).

Wir können die sittliche Verpflichtung, uns das höchste Gut zum letzten Zweck zu machen, nur in der Weise anschaulich machen, dass wir sie uns als Gebote des höchsten Wesens vorstellen. Das ist wiederum nur dann möglich, wenn wir in einer symbolischen Erkenntnis dem höchsten Wesen einen Willen zuschreiben. Nur dadurch, dass wir die sittliche Forderung in dieser Weise anschaulich machen, können wir sie verstehen, d. h. einsehen, dass das höchste Gut möglich ist.

„Allein diese Pflicht in Ansehung Gottes [...] ist Pflicht des Menschen gegen sich selbst [...]" (TL 6:487.20–22). Worauf bezieht sich „diese Pflicht" (TL 6:487.20)? Es gibt zwei mögliche Antworten, die sich der Sache nach nicht unterscheiden. (a) Es bezieht sich auf die Forderung, dass „alle Menschenpflichten diesem Formalen [...] gemäß gedacht werden *sollen*" (TL 6:487.14–16, kursiv F.R.). (b) Es bezieht sich auf „Religionspflicht" (TL 6:487.12). Dieser Begriff wird in § 18 erläutert: Es „ist Pflicht des Menschen gegen sich selbst, diese unumgänglich der Vernunft sich selbst darbietende Idee auf das moralische

Gesetz in uns, wo sie[6] von der größten sittlichen Fruchtbarkeit ist, anzuwenden" (TL 6:444.4–6). Die Religionspflicht ist eine Pflicht zweiter Ordnung; es ist die Pflicht, alle Pflichten, die der Mensch hat, unter einer bestimmten Rücksicht zu sehen, weil diese Sicht die moralische Triebfeder in unserer eigenen gesetzgebenden Vernunft stärkt.

„Es kann Pflichten in Ansehung gewisser blos möglicher Wesen geben die doch nicht Pflichten gegen diese Wesen sind." (VAMS 23:416.12 f.) Solche Pflichten liegen vor, wenn diese Wesen als so beschaffen gedacht werden, dass wir auf sie entweder, wie bei übermenschlichen Wesen, gar nicht, oder, wie bei untermenschlichen Wesen, nicht moralisch einwirken können. Wir haben die Pflicht, unsere Pflichten als Gebote Gottes zu betrachten. Werden dadurch aber nicht alle unsere Pflichten zu Pflichten gegen Gott, dessen Gebote wir erfüllen sollen? Dieser Schritt beruht darauf, dass wir „die von uns selbst gemachte Idee von gewissen […] möglichen Wesen als außer uns existirenden Wesen denken würden, d. i. sie personificirten" (VAMS 23:416.20–22). *Gegen* eine Idee können wir keine Pflichten haben, sondern nur in Ansehung einer Idee. *Angesichts* der Idee Gottes entsteht die Pflicht, unsere Pflichten als Gebote Gottes zu erkennen, denn nur so wird deutlich, dass der Endzweck unseres sittlichen Handelns das höchste Gut ist.

Diese „Pflicht in *Ansehung* Gottes" (TL 6:487.20 f.) ist keine „objective" (TL 6:487.23), sondern nur eine „subjective" (TL 6:487.24) Pflicht. ‚Objektive Pflicht' bedeutet hier: Pflicht gegen andere, und ‚subjektive Pflicht' bedeutet: Pflicht gegen sich selbst. Diese „subjective" (TL 6:487.24) Pflicht, d. h. diese Pflicht gegen sich selbst, ist die Pflicht „zur Stärkung der moralischen Triebfeder in unserer eigenen gesetzgebenden Vernunft" (TL 6:487.24 f.).

TL 6:487.26–36

Wird Religion verstanden als Inbegriff der Pflichten *gegen* Gott, dann ist sie, so die These, kein Teil der „reinen philosophischen Moral" (TL 6:487.36).

Dem formalen Begriff der Religion wird ein materialer entgegengestellt: Religion nicht als Perspektive, unter der alle Pflichten gesehen werden müssen, sondern als eine besondere Klasse der Pflichten, die

---

6 B; A und AA: „es".

Pflichten *gegen* Gott, die Kant bestimmt als „den ihm zu leistenden Dienst" (TL 6:487.27). Damit wird vom Begriff „einer reinen moralischen Religion" (RGV 6:103.35) der einer „gottesdienstlichen" (RGV 6:103.34 f.) Religion unterschieden. Die gottesdienstliche Religion entspringt einer Schwäche der menschlichen Natur. Die Menschen sind nicht leicht davon zu überzeugen, dass der moralisch gute Lebenswandel alles ist, was Gott von ihnen fordert. „Sie können sich ihre Verpflichtung nicht wohl anders, als zu irgend einem Dienst denken, den sie Gott zu leisten haben; wo es nicht sowohl auf den innern moralischen Werth der Handlungen, als vielmehr darauf ankommt, daß sie Gott geleistet werden, um, so moralisch indifferent auch an sich selbst sein mögen, doch wenigstens durch passiven Gehorsam Gott zu gefallen." (RGV 6:103.14–19)

Wird Religion in dieser Weise verstanden, so Kants außerordentlich vorsichtig formulierte Argumentation, so könnte sie *„nur* empirisch erkennbare, mithin *nur* zur geoffenbarten Religion gehörende Pflichten als göttliche Gebote enthalten" (TL 6:487.29–31, kursiv F.R.). Kant unterscheidet zwischen natürlicher und geoffenbarter Religion. „Diejenige, in welcher ich vorher wissen muß, daß etwas ein göttliches Gebot sei, um es als meine Pflicht anzuerkennen, ist die geoffenbarte (oder einer Offenbarung benöthigte) Religion: dagegen diejenige, in der ich zuvor wissen muß, daß etwas Pflicht sei, ehe ich es als göttliches Gebot anerkennen kann, ist die natürliche Religion." (RGV 6:153.29–154.5) Eine Religion kann eine natürliche und zugleich geoffenbart sein, „wenn sie so beschaffen ist, daß die Menschen durch den bloßen Gebrauch ihrer Vernunft auf sie von selbst hätten kommen können und sollen" (RGV 6:155.31–33), wenn sie auch ohne Offenbarung „nicht so früh, oder in so weiter Ausbreitung, als verlangt wird, auf dieselbe gekommen sein würden" (RGV 6:155.33 f.). Pflichten, die *nur* zur geoffenbarten Religion gehören, sind also solche, auf die die Menschen durch den Gebrauch ihrer Vernunft nicht hätten kommen können, d.h. Pflichten der „gottesdienstlichen" (RGV 6:103.34 f.) Religion, die keinen inneren moralischen Wert haben.

Diese Pflichten („die" (TL 6:487.31)) setzen das Dasein und nicht nur die Idee Gottes „nicht willkürlich" (TL 6:487.33) voraus. Das folgende Satzglied ist syntaktisch unklar: „sondern als unmittelbar (oder mittelbar) in der Erfahrung gegeben dargelegt werden könnte" (TL 6:487.33 f.). Was wird vorausgesetzt als etwas, das unmittelbar in der Erfahrung gegeben dargelegt werden könnte? Obwohl das Satzglied Teil des Relativsatzes ist, der sich auf „Pflichten" bezieht („Pflichten [...]; die"

(TL 6:487.31)), sind es offensichtlich nicht diese Pflichten, sondern „das Dasein dieses Wesens" (TL 6:487.31 f.); dafür spricht auch der Singular „könnte" (TL 6:487.34). Die nur zur geoffenbarten Religion gehörenden Pflichten setzen das Dasein Gottes als in der Erfahrung gegeben voraus. Bei der geoffenbarten Religion muss ich, um etwas als meine Pflicht anerkennen zu können, wissen, dass es von Gott geboten ist. Der Glaube an eine Offenbarung setzt also den Glauben an die Existenz Gottes voraus. Die „Erfahrung" (TL 6:487.34), in der in der geoffenbarten Religion das Dasein Gottes gegeben ist, dürfte vor allem die Erfahrung von Wundern sein, welche die geoffenbarte Religion beglaubigen; sie wird vermittelt durch die Nachricht von diesen Wundern (vgl. RGV 6:163.10–21). Damit ist die Frage nach der „Grenzbestimmung der Wissenschaft" (TL 6:487.3), zu der die Religion gehört, beantwortet. Die Religion als Inbegriff der Pflichten *gegen* Gott könnte nur empirisch erkennbare Pflichten enthalten; deshalb ist sie kein Teil der „reinen Moralphilosophie" (TL 6:486.3).

TL 6:488.5–12

In der Vorrede zur zweiten Auflage der Religionsschrift verdeutlicht Kant das Verhältnis von Offenbarung und Vernunftreligion durch das Bild von zwei konzentrischen Kreisen; der weitere Kreis der Offenbarung kann den engeren Kreis der reinen Vernunftreligion in sich enthalten. Die Aufgabe der Religionsschrift besteht darin, ausgehend von der historischen Offenbarung den in ihr enthaltenen engeren Kreis der Vernunftreligion zu ermitteln. Dabei soll von dem in der Dialektik der zweiten *Kritik* entworfenen System der Vernunftreligion abstrahiert werden. Die Methode, mit welcher der engere Kreis gefunden werden soll, besteht vielmehr darin, „die Offenbarung als historisches System an moralische Begriffe bloß fragmentarisch [zu] halten" (RGV 6:12.18–20), um zu sehen, ob das Vernunftsystem, das sich auf diese Weise ergibt, „in moralisch-praktischer Absicht selbständig und für eigentliche Religion […] hinreichend sei. Wenn dieses zutrifft, so wird man sagen können, daß zwischen Vernunft und Schrift nicht bloß Verträglichkeit, sondern auch Einigkeit anzutreffen sei, so daß, wer der einen (unter Leitung der moralischen Begriffe) folgt, nicht ermangeln wird auch mit der anderen zusammen zu treffen" (RGV 6:12.23–13.4).

Eine Religion innerhalb der Grenzen der bloßen Vernunft ist die in einer Offenbarung als historischem System enthaltene Vernunftreligion.

Eine Religion innerhalb der Grenzen der bloßen Vernunft ist „nicht aus bloßer Vernunft abgeleitet, sondern zugleich auf Geschichts- und Offenbarungslehren gegründet" (TL 6:488.6 f.). Sie hat also einen zweifachen („zugleich" (TL 6:488.7)) Ausgangspunkt und ein zweifaches Fundament. Sie geht aus „von irgend einer dafür gehaltenen Offenbarung" (RGV 6:12.16), und sie geht aus von der Vernunft, weil sie diese Offenbarung fragmentarisch „an moralische Begriffe" (RGV 6:12.19) hält. Als ein Beispiel für dieses Vorgehen sei auf den Schluss des „Ersten Stück[s]" (RGV 6:19) der Religionsschrift verwiesen. Die Analyse der moralischen Begriffe führt zu dem Ergebnis, dass der Vernunfturprung des Hanges zum Bösen „uns unerforschlich" (RGV 6:43.14) bleibt. „Diese Unbegreiflichkeit [...] drückt die Schrift in der Geschichtserzählung dadurch aus, daß sie das Böse [...] nicht im Menschen, sondern in einem Geiste von ursprünglich erhabnerer Bestimmung voranschickt: wodurch also der erste Anfang alles Bösen überhaupt als für uns unbegreiflich" (RGV 6:43.22–44.2) vorgestellt wird.

Eine Religion innerhalb der Grenzen der bloßen Vernunft „enthält" (TL 6:488.9) „nur die Übereinstimmung der reinen praktischen Vernunft" (TL 6:488.8 f.) mit der historischen Offenbarung; sie ist eine „Vereinigung" (RGV 6:13.12) von Vernunft und Schrift. Die „Offenbarung als historisches System" (RGV 6:12.18 f.) führt zum „reinen Vernunftsystem der Religion zurück" (RGV 6:12.20 f.), so dass die richtig verstandene Offenbarung und das reine Vernunftsystem der Religion identisch sind. Eine Religion innerhalb der Grenzen bloßer Vernunft ist die „unter Leitung der moralischen Begriffe" (RGV 6:13.2 f.) interpretierte Schrift. Sie ist, und darauf kommt es Kant im vorliegenden Zusammenhang an, nicht „reine" (TL 6:488.10) Religionslehre, die den „reine[n] Religionsglaube[n]" (RGV 6:102.34), der „ein bloßer Vernunftglaube ist" (RGV 6:102.35), zum Inhalt hat, sondern auf die historische Offenbarung „angewandte Religionslehre" (TL 6:488.10 f.), und als solche gehört sie nicht zur Ethik als „reiner praktischer Philosophie" (TL 6:488.11 f.), d.h. als „System der Zwecke der reinen praktischen Vernunft" (TL 6:381.18 f.).

TL 6:488.14–25

Der Begriff der moralischen Verhältnisse vernünftiger Wesen, d.h. der Pflichtgesetze (vgl. TL 6:488.14), wird durch den Relativsatz eingeschränkt. Es geht nicht um die Gesetze, die „das äußere und zwar praktische Verhältniß einer Person gegen eine andere, sofern ihre Handlungen als Facta aufeinander […] Einfluß haben können" (RL 6:230.9–11), regeln, sondern um die „Übereinstimmung des Willens" (TL 6:488.15) vernünftiger Wesen. Der Plural „moralische Verhältnisse" (TL 6:488.14) wird durch den Singular „dies Princip" (TL 6:488.17) aufgegriffen. Die Pflicht der Liebe und die Pflicht der Achtung „sind […] im Grunde dem Gesetze nach jederzeit miteinander in *einer* Pflicht zusammen verbunden" (TL 6:448.19 f., kursiv F.R.). Von diesem Prinzip als solchem wird dieses Prinzip unterschieden, sofern es praktisch ist, d. h. hinreichend ist, den Willen zu bestimmen. (Vgl. KpV 5:19.14 f.) Der Bestimmungsgrund der Pflicht der Liebe ist der Zweck des Anderen, d. h. ich handle so, weil ich dadurch den Zweck eines anderen Vernunftwesens erfülle; der Bestimmungsgrund der Pflicht der Achtung ist das Recht des Anderen, d. h. ich unterlasse eine Handlung, weil ich durch sie den Anderen bloß als Mittel für meine Zwecke gebrauchen würde. (Vgl. TL 6:450.3–8)

Bei diesem Prinzip des moralischen Verhältnisses zwischen vernünftigen Wesen sind zwei Formen zu unterscheiden. Es kann sich einmal um das Prinzip des moralischen Verhältnisses zwischen Menschen handeln, die „wechselseitig" (TL 6:488.24) zu gegenseitiger Liebe und Achtung verpflichtet sind. „Ein jeder Mensch hat rechtmäßigen Anspruch auf Achtung von seinen Nebenmenschen, und w e c h s e l s e i t i g ist er dazu auch gegen jeden Anderen verbunden" (TL 6:462.18–20); entsprechend gilt das Prinzip „der **Wechselliebe**" (TL 6:449.9). Dieses Prinzip ist „ein i m m a n e n t e s Princip" (TL 6:488.24 f.), d. h. es ist „für uns begreiflich" (TL 6:491.7). Dem wird das Prinzip des moralischen Verhältnisses zwischen zwei Vernunftwesen gegenüber gestellt, von denen das eine nur Rechte und das andere nur Pflichten hat; der Wille dieser Vernunftwesen ist nicht „gegen einander wechselseitig einschränkend" (TL 6:488.24). Dieses Prinzip, so die These, ist „t r a n s c e n d e n t" (TL 6:488.23), d. h. es „übersteigt" (TL 6:491.9) gänzlich die Grenzen unserer Vernunft und ist „uns schlechterdings unbegreiflich" (TL 6:491.9 f.).

TL 6:488.26–35

Der Aufweis der These geht von einem Einwand aus. Auch die moralischen Verhältnisse zwischen Gott und Mensch sind vom Prinzip der Liebe und Achtung bestimmt und insofern nicht schlechterdings unbegreiflich. Dass sie von der Liebe bestimmt sind, geht daraus hervor, dass der Zweck der Schöpfung die Glückseligkeit der Menschen ist, und das könnte man „nach Menschenart" (TL 6:488.32) auch so ausdrücken: Gott hat vernünftige Wesen geschaffen, um etwas zu haben, „was er lieben könne, oder auch von dem er geliebt werde" (TL 6:488.34 f.). Die Formulierung ist nicht klar. Ist das „oder auch" im Sinne einer Alternative zu verstehen, die offen gelassen werden soll, oder geht es um einen zweifachen Zweck Gottes: Er schafft vernünftige Wesen, damit er sie lieben und damit er von ihnen geliebt werden kann? Nach der zweiten Interpretation gilt auch für das Verhältnis zwischen Gott und Mensch das Prinzip der wechselseitigen Liebe.

Darauf geht der Text nicht weiter ein; Gegenstand der folgenden Ausführungen ist vielmehr das Prinzip der Achtung. Hier ist ausschließlich von der Achtung die Rede, die der Mensch Gott schuldet. Die Rede vom „Princip des Willens Gottes in Ansehung der schuldigen Achtung" (TL 6:499.29 f.) könnte zu der Annahme verleiten, es gehe auch um die Achtung Gottes gegenüber dem Menschen; diese Deutung wird jedoch dadurch ausgeschlossen, dass es die *schuldige* Achtung ist und diese durch den Begriff der „Ehrfurcht" (TL 6:488.30) erläutert wird. Es geht um das Prinzip des Willens Gottes, das der Grund dafür ist, dass der Mensch Gott nicht nur Liebe, sondern auch Achtung schuldet. Die Achtung bezieht sich auf „das Recht des Anderen" (TL 6:488.19), und das Prinzip des göttlichen Rechts kann kein anderes sein als das der Gerechtigkeit, d. h. die Gerechtigkeit bestimmt, worauf Gott einen „rechtmäßigen Anspruch" (TL 6:462.18) hat.

Schwierigkeiten bereitet der Relativsatz „welche die Wirkungen der ersteren einschränkt" (TL 6:488.30 f.). Vom Wortlaut her kann er nur folgendermaßen verstanden werden: Die Achtung (Ehrfurcht) schränkt die Wirkungen der Liebe Gottes ein. Aber wie kann die Achtung des Menschen vor Gott die Wirkungen der Liebe Gottes einschränken? Im folgenden Absatz (TL 6:489.2 f.) ist davon die Rede, dass die Gerechtigkeit Gottes die Liebe Gottes einschränkt. Der Relativsatz würde verständlich, wenn das Relativpronomen sich nicht auf „Achtung (Ehrfurcht)" (TL 6:488.30), sondern auf „Princip" (TL 6:488.29) bezöge; aber dann müsste es jedoch ‚welches' und nicht ‚welche' lauten. Dann wäre die Rede von einem Prinzip, der Gerechtigkeit, das die Wirkungen der Liebe Gottes einschränkt.

TL 6:489.1–10

Gott hat vernünftige Wesen geschaffen, um etwas zu haben, das er lieben könne und „von dem er geliebt werde" (TL 6:488.35). Damit ist ein „Anspruch" (TL 6:489.2) gegeben, den die Liebe Gottes an uns stellt. Er wird verglichen mit dem Anspruch, den die göttliche Gerechtigkeit an uns stellt. Der Anspruch der Gerechtigkeit ist größer als der Anspruch der Liebe, denn die Gerechtigkeit schränkt die Liebe ein, nicht aber die Liebe die Gerechtigkeit. Diese Aussage wird jedoch eingeschränkt. Größer „ist der Anspruch, den die göttliche Gerechtigkeit *im Urtheile unserer eigenen Vernunft* [...] an uns macht" (TL 6:489.2–4, kursiv F.R.). Dieses Urteil führt jedoch, wie in TL 6:490.20–491.4 gezeigt wird, in einen Widerspruch. „Den göttlichen Zweck in Ansehung des menschlichen Geschlechts [...] kann man sich nicht anders denken, als nur aus Liebe" (TL 6:488.26–28). Wäre der Anspruch, den die Gerechtigkeit Gottes an uns macht, größer als der Anspruch seiner Liebe, dann wäre jedoch der „Zweck der Schöpfung nicht in der Liebe des Welturhebers [...], sondern in der strengen Befolgung des Rechts" (TL 6:490.22–24) zu setzen.

Durch den Ausschluss anderer Formen der Gerechtigkeit wird die göttliche Gerechtigkeit näher als strafende Gerechtigkeit bestimmt. Die Strafe ist der „rechtliche Effect einer Verschuldung" (RL 6:227.34). Belohnung ist der rechtliche Effekt „einer verdienstlichen That [...] vorausgesetzt daß sie, im Gesetz verheißen, die Bewegursache war" (RL 6:227.35 f.). Ein Wesen zu belohnen, das nur Pflichten und keine Rechte hat, kann keine Pflicht der Gerechtigkeit, sondern nur eine Pflicht der Wohltätigkeit sein, denn ein Wesen, das gegenüber einem anderen keinerlei Rechte hat, kann auch kein Recht auf Lohn haben. Es ist ein Widerspruch zu sagen, die Gerechtigkeit fordere, dass Gott den Menschen, der ihm gegenüber keinerlei Rechte hat, belohnt.

TL 6:489.11–33

Es werden zwei Begriffe der Strafgerechtigkeit unterschieden; Gesichtspunkt der Unterscheidung ist die Frage: Welche Rechtsverletzung ist Gegenstand der göttlichen Strafgerechtigkeit? (a) Es ist die Verletzung, die Gott selbst und seinem Recht widerfahren ist. Dieser Begriff der Strafgerechtigkeit ist „transcendent" (TL 6:489.19 f.), denn Gott ist „über allen Abbruch an seinen Zwecken erhaben" (TL 6:489.12). Er liegt

„ganz hinaus" (TL 6:489.22) über den Begriff der Strafgerechtigkeit unter Menschen, für den allein wir Beispiele bringen können. (b) Es sind die „Rechtsverletzungen, die Menschen gegen einander verüben und worüber Gott als strafender Richter entscheide[t]" (TL 6:489.16–18). Diese Vorstellung von Gott als strafendem Richter, so der nächste Schritt, ist eine Personifizierung. „Die Idee einer göttlichen Strafgerechtigkeit wird hier personificirt; es ist nicht ein besonderes richtendes Wesen, was sie ausübt" (TL 6:489.26 f.). Die Begründung dafür lautet: Würde sie von einem richtenden Wesen ausgeübt, so „würden Widersprüche desselben mit Rechtsprincipien vorkommen" (TL 6:489.28). Warum, so ist zu fragen, würde Gott, wenn er als Richter die Rechtsverletzungen bestraft, welche die Menschen gegeneinander verüben, Rechtsprinzipien widersprechen? Die Gerechtigkeit, so die Schritte der Personifizierung, wird als Substanz gedacht, und diese Substanz als Person, die nach einer für uns unerforschlichen Notwendigkeit Recht spricht. Das soll durch einige Beispiele verdeutlicht werden.

TL 6:489.34–491.4

Die Stelle aus Horaz, auf die Kant sich bezieht, lautet: „Raro antecedentem scelestum / Deseruit pede Poena claudo"[7] (Selten hat die Strafe einen Frevler, der vor ihr herlief, lahmen Fußes verschont). Stellen aus der Bibel, die Kant bei seinen Beispielen im Auge gehabt haben könnte, sind Gen 4,10; Ex 34,7; Jes 53,11 f. Der wohldenkende Landesherr ist von der Vorstellung bestimmt, dass die Blutschuld eine subsistierende Größe ist, die nur durch Blut getilgt werden kann; wenn er den Mörder begnadigt, geht sie vom Mörder auf das Land über, das sie dann sühnen muss. Die Beispiele sollen zeigen: Wenn wir uns Gott als strafenden Richter vorstellen, dann denken wir ihn nicht als eine Person, die ein gerechtes Urteil fällt; vielmehr ist es die hypostasierte Gerechtigkeit, die hier Recht spricht. Denn, so die Begründung, die Person „würde nicht so sprechen können, ohne Anderen unrecht zu thun" (TL 6:490.14 f.). Dass die Person anderen unrecht tun würde, geht aus den Beispielen hervor: Die Nachkommen müssen für ein Verbrechen büßen, das sie nicht begangen haben; die Gerechtigkeit fordert unbedingt, dass die Sündenschuld bezahlt wird, selbst um den Preis, dass ein Unschuldiger dafür sein Leben hingeben muss.

---

7   Horaz, *Oden*, III 2,31 f.

Wenn wir uns an den Beispielen orientieren, dann leuchtet es ein, dass bei einem richtenden Wesen, das *diese* Strafgerechtigkeit ausübt, „Widersprüche desselben mit Rechtsprincipien" (TL 6:489.28) vorkommen würden. Aber ist *diese* Form die einzig mögliche Form der göttlichen Strafgerechtigkeit? Wie verträgt der Einwand der Personifizierung sich mit dem Gottesbegriff der zweiten *Kritik*, dem Welturheber von höchster Vollkommenheit, der mein Verhalten bis zum Innersten meiner Gesinnung erkennen kann, „um ihm die angemessenen Folgen zu ertheilen" (KpV 5:140.6 f.), oder mit der Rede vom „Weltrichter als Herzenskündiger" (SF 7:9.37 – 10.1)?

Gott als strafender Richter, so Kants Antwort, ist die Hypostasierung der *bloßen* Gerechtigkeit. Es ist die „bloße Gerechtigkeit" (TL 6:490.15), die „das Recht dieses Wesens" (TL 6:490.17), d.h. Gottes als des strafenden Richters, bestimmt. Kant unterscheidet zwischen dem „Formalen" und dem „Materialen" des Prinzips der Gerechtigkeit (vgl. TL 6:490.17 ff.). Das Formale der Gerechtigkeit, so kann man interpretieren, ist die Gleichheit, die bei einer Verteilung zu beachten oder die, wenn sie verletzt wurde, wiederherzustellen ist, das Materiale ist der Zweck, dem die Gerechtigkeit dient, „welcher immer die Glückseligkeit der Menschen ist" (TL 6:490.19). „Jede potestas legislatoria", so formuliert die *Metaphysik der Sitten Vigilantius* diesen Zusammenhang, „setzt nun voraus, daß der Gesetzgeber für seine Unterthanen wohlwollend sey, daß er also, vermöge dieses Wohlwollens, ihr Wohl zur Absicht habe; denn nur durch diese Absicht ist er imstande, uns zu verbinden." (V-MS/Vigil 27:720.26 – 29)

Der Zweck der Schöpfung ist nach der zweiten *Kritik* die Ehre Gottes, und sie besteht im höchsten Gut. „Denn nichts ehrt Gott mehr als das, was das Schätzbarste in der Welt ist, die Achtung für sein Gebot, die Beobachtung der heiligen Pflicht, die uns sein Gesetz auferlegt, wenn seine herrliche Anstalt dazu kommt, eine solche schöne Ordnung mit angemessener Glückseligkeit zu krönen." (KpV 5:131.10 – 14) Wäre Gott die personifizierte Strafgerechtigkeit, so wäre die Ehre Gottes und damit der Zweck der Schöpfung in die strenge Befolgung des Rechts zu setzen. Das widerspräche der Annahme, dass die Liebe Gottes zur Schöpfung der Zweck der Schöpfung ist; diese Annahme ist ausgezeichnet durch den Zusatz „wie man sich doch denken muß" (TL 6:490.23); die Absicht des Urhebers der Welt kann „nur Liebe zum Grunde haben" (TL 6:491.2 f.). Die Gerechtigkeit ist nur die einschränkende Bedingung der Gütigkeit; Gott fügt dem Wunsch der vernünftigen Wesen nach Glückseligkeit „noch eine Bedingung, nämlich die der Glückseligkeit würdig zu sein" (KpV 5:130.32 f.), hinzu. Gott schafft vernünftige Wesen, damit er sie lieben kann und damit sie ihn lieben können. Dieser Zweck könnte vereitelt werden, wenn Gott die subsistierende Strafgerechtigkeit wäre. Denn dann müsste man mit der Möglichkeit rechnen, dass angesichts einer großen Zahl von Verbrechern Gott seine Ehre in die Wahrung des Rechtes setzen müsste und die vernünftigen Wesen nicht lieben, sondern sie für ihr Unrecht bestrafen würde. In diesem Fall hätte die Weltschöpfung unterbleiben müssen, weil sie ein Produkt geliefert hätte, das der Absicht ihres Schöpfers widerspricht.

TL 6:490.28–37

„Das Verbrechen kann nicht ungerächt bleiben" (TL 6:489.37); trifft die Strafe den Verbrecher nicht in seinem Leben, „so muß es in einem Leben nach dem Tode geschehen" (TL 6:490.2 f.). Die These der Fußnote ist: Es bedarf nicht der Hypothese von einem Leben nach dem Tod, um sich vorzustellen, dass die Strafe für ein Verbrechen vollständig vollzogen ist. Kant unterscheidet zwischen dem Dasein des Menschen in der Erscheinung und dem Menschen als übersinnlichem Gegenstand. Auch die Strafe ist kein Prozess, der unter den Bedingungen der Zeit steht; ihre vollständige Vollstreckung setzt deshalb nicht ein Leben nach dem Tod voraus. Die Strafe wird in der übersinnlichen Ordnung vollständig vollzogen, so dass die Gerechtigkeit nicht in Frage gestellt ist.

Kant stellt zwei Möglichkeiten einander gegenüber, wie der Zusammenhang zwischen der Strafgerechtigkeit und dem Glauben an ein Leben nach dem Tod gesehen werden kann. (a) Wir sind von einem Leben nach dem Tod überzeugt und schließen daraus auf eine Strafe im Jenseits. Wenn den Verbrecher die Strafe in diesem Leben nicht erreicht hat, wird sie ihn in seinem Leben nach dem Tod erreichen, *denn* es gibt ein Leben nach dem Tod. (b) Wir sind überzeugt von der Notwendigkeit der Bestrafung und schließen aus ihr auf ein Leben nach dem Tod. Ein Verbrechen muss bestraft werden; geschieht das nicht in diesem Leben, dann muss es in einem anderen Leben geschehen; *also* gibt es ein Leben nach dem Tod.

Literaturverzeichnis

Baumgarten, Alexander Gottlieb (^{2}1751) (^{3}1763), *Ethica Philosophica*, Halle/ Saale: Hemmerde.
Wolff, Christian (^{4}1733), *Vernünfftige Gedancken von der Menschen Thun und Lassen*, Frankfurt/Leipzig. (Wiederabgedruckt in: id., *Gesammelte Werke*, Abt. 1: Deutsche Schriften, Bd. 4, Hildesheim: Olms [1976].)

Notes on Contributors

Stefano Bacin is Marie Curie Fellow at the University of Frankfurt. His publications include *Il senso dell'etica: Kant e la costruzione di una teoria morale* (Il Mulino, 2006), a monograph on the development of Kant's practical philosophy between the 1760s and the *Metaphysics of Morals,* and a volume entitled *Fichte a Schulpforta* (Guerini, 2003; German edition: Frommann-Holzboog, 2007). He is the editor of *Etiche antiche, etiche moderne: Temi di discussione,* a collection of essays on themes in ancient and modern ethical theory (Il Mulino, 2010).

Marcia Baron is Rudy Professor of Philosophy at Indiana University in Bloomington and Professor of Moral Philosophy at the University of St Andrews. She is the author of *Kantian Ethics Almost without Apology* (Cornell University Press, 1995) and co-author (with Philip Pettit and Michael Slote) of *Three Methods of Ethics: A Debate* (Blackwell, 1998). She has written articles on (among other topics) Kant's ethics, Hume's ethics, remorse and agent-regret, friendship and impartiality, patriotism, justifications and excuses, rape, the heat of passion defense, and self-defense.

Manfred Baum is Professor emeritus at the University of Wuppertal. He is an editor of *Kant-Studien* and a former chairman of the Kant-Gesellschaft. He is the author of *Deduktion und Beweis in Kants Transzendentalphilosophie* (Hain, 1986) and *Die Entstehung der Hegelschen Dialektik* (Bouvier, 1986). He has written over 90 articles on matters of theoretical and practical reason in modern philosophy.

Lara Denis is Professor of Philosophy at Agnes Scott College in Decatur, Georgia. She is the author of *Moral Self-Regard: Duties to Oneself in Kant's Moral Theory* (Routledge, 2001), the editor of *Kant's 'Metaphysics of Morals': A Critical Guide* (Cambridge University Press, 2010), and the editor of a supplemented edition of Kant's *Groundwork for the Metaphysics of Morals* (Broadview Press, 2005). She has written numerous articles on Kant's moral philosophy.

Bernd Dörflinger is Professor of Philosophy at the University of Trier. He is chairman of the Kant-Gesellschaft and one of the editors of *Kant-Studien*. His publications include a monograph on Kant's aesthetics, *Die Realität des Schönen in Kants Theorie rein ästhetischer Urteilskraft* (Bouvier, 1988), and a book on his theoretical philosophy in its teleological and practical applications, *Das Leben theoretischer Vernunft* (De Gruyter, 2000), as well as several edited volumes. His articles cover various aspects of Kant's philosophy and its reception up to the present. His current work mainly focuses on Kant's philosophy of religion.

Andrea Esser is Professor of Practical Philosophy at the University of Marburg. She is co-editor of *Deutsche Zeitschrift für Philosophie*. She is the author of *Kunst als Symbol: Die Struktur ästhetischer Reflexion in Kants Theorie des Schönen* (Fink, 1997), of *Eine Ethik für Endliche: Kants Tugendlehre in der Gegenwart* (Frommann-Holzboog, 2004), and of several articles on Kant's ethics and aesthetics.

Ina Goy is a Post-Doctoral Fellow at the University of Tübingen. As a visiting scholar, she spent some time at Stanford University, at the University of California, Berkeley, and at the University of California, San Diego, and she held an appointment as Visiting Professor at the University of Munich. She is co-editor (with Eric Watkins) of *Kant's Theory of Biology* (De Gruyter, forthcoming) and is currently working on a monograph on the same topic.

Thomas Hill is Kenan Professor at the University of North Carolina, Chapel Hill, where he has been teaching since 1984. He previously taught at UCLA (1969–84), Pomona College (1966–68), The Johns Hopkins University (1965–66) and, on visiting appointments, at Stanford University (1980), and the University of Minnesota (1994). His essays on moral and political philosophy are collected in *Autonomy and Self-Respect* (Cambridge University Press, 1991), *Dignity and Practical Reason in Kant's Moral Theory* (Cornell University Press, 1992), *Respect, Pluralism, and Justice: Kantian Perspectives* (Oxford University Press, 2000), and *Human Welfare and Moral Worth: Kantian Perspectives* (Oxford University Press, 2002). He co-edited (with Arnulf Zweig) a translation of Kant's *Groundwork for the Metaphysics of Morals* (Oxford University Press, 2002) and edited *A Blackwell Guide to Kant's Ethics* (2009). Recent essays concern Kantian constructivism, duties to oneself, virtue, revolution, humanitarian interventions, and the treatment of criminals.

Thomas Höwing is a Post-Doctoral Fellow at the University of Frankfurt. He is the author of *Praktische Lust: Kant über das Verhältnis von Fühlen, Begehren und praktischer Vernunft* (De Gruyter, forthcoming), an article entitled „Kant über den Unterschied zwischen Willkür und Wunsch" in *Akten des XI. Internationalen Kant-Kongresses* (ed. by Stefano Bacin et al., De Gruyter, forthcoming), as well as the entries „Träume eines Geistersehers", „Immaterialität", „Geistersehen", and „Geisterwelt" in the forthcoming *Kant-Lexikon* (ed. by Georg Mohr et al., De Gruyter).

Bernd Ludwig is Professor of Philosophy at the University of Göttingen. He is the author of *Kants Rechtslehre* (Meiner 1988, ²2005) and *Die Wiederentdeckung des Epikureischen Naturrechts: Zu Hobbes' philosophischer Entwicklung von 'De Cive' zum 'Leviathan' im Pariser Exil* (Klostermann, 1998). He is also the editor of Kant's *Metaphysische Anfangsgründe der Tugendlehre* (Meiner, 1990) and Kant's *Metaphysische Anfangsgründe der Rechtslehre* (Meiner, ³2009), and co-author (with Andreas Eckl) of *Was ist Eigentum?* (Beck, 2005). His articles concern the history of modern philosophy, legal and moral philosophy, as well as the problem of causality.

Friedo Ricken is Professor emeritus at the Munich School of Philosophy (Hochschule für Philosophie). He was a Visiting Scholar at Oxford University and at Harvard University. He was also a Visiting Professor at the Hochschule St. Georgen in Frankfurt, at the Universities of Innsbruck, Salzburg, and St. Louis, at Georgetown University in Washington, at Pontificia Universidad Javeriana in Bogotá, and at the Sophia University in Tokyo. He is the author of *Der Lustbegriff in der Nikomachischen Ethik des Aristoteles* (Vandenhoeck & Ruprecht, 1976), *Allgemeine Ethik* (Kohlhammer, 1983, ⁴2003), *Philosophie der Antike* (Kohlhammer, 1988, ⁴2007; English translation: *Philosophy of the Ancients*, University of Notre Dame Press, 1991), *Antike Skeptiker* (Beck, 1994), *Religionsphilosophie* (Kohlhammer, 2003), *Gemeinschaft, Tugend, Glück* (Kohlhammer, 2004), *Platon: Politikos* (Vandenhoeck & Ruprecht, 2008), *Warum moralisch sein?* (Kohlhammer, 2010).

Steffi Schadow is a Post-Doctoral Fellow at the University of Bremen. She is the author of *Achtung für das Gesetz: Moral und Motivation bei*

Kant (De Gruyter, 2012), as well as (inter alia) the entries „Handlung", „Handlung, gute/böse", „Handlung, moralische", and „Handlung, innere/äußere" in the forthcoming *Kant-Lexikon* (ed. by Georg Mohr et al., De Gruyter).

Dieter Schönecker is Professor of Practical Philosophy at the University of Siegen. He has previously taught at Stonehill College and the University of Halle-Wittenberg. He was a Visiting Fellow at Yale for two years. He is the author of *Kant: Grundlegung III* (Alber, 1999) and *Kants Begriff transzendentaler und praktischer Freiheit* (De Gruyter, 2005), co-author (with Allen Wood) of *Kants 'Grundlegung zur Metaphysik der Sitten'* (UTB, ³2007), co-editor (with Gregor Damschen) of *Der moralische Status menschlicher Embryonen* (De Gruyter, 2005), and has written several articles on epistemology and ethics.

Oliver Sensen is Associate Professor of Philosophy at Tulane University in New Orleans. He is the author of *Kant on Human Dignity* (De Gruyter, 2011) and the editor of *Kant on Moral Autonomy* (Cambridge University Press, 2012). In addition, he has published articles on Kant and autonomy, constructivism, the formula of humanity, feelings, freedom, human dignity, political philosophy, and value.

Jens Timmermann is Reader in Moral Philosophy at the University of St Andrews. He is the author of *Sittengesetz und Freiheit* (De Gruyter, 2003) and of *Kant's 'Groundwork of the Metaphysics of Morals': A Commentary* (Cambridge University Press, 2007); the editor of *Kant's 'Groundwork of the Metaphysics of Morals': A Critical Guide* (Cambridge University Press, 2009); and co-editor (with Andrews Reath) of *Kant's 'Critique of Practical Reason': A Critical Guide* (Cambridge University Press, 2010). He recently published the first German-English facing-page edition of Kant's *Groundwork of the Metaphysics of Morals* (Cambridge University Press, 2011).

Mark Timmons is Professor of Philosophy at the University of Arizona. He previously taught at Illinois State University and at the University of Memphis. He is the author of *Morality without Foundations* (Oxford University Press, 1999) and *Moral Theory: An Introduction* (Rowman & Littlefield, 2002). He is the editor of *Kant's 'Metaphysics of Morals': Interpretative Essays* (Oxford University Press, 2002) and co-editor of *Metaethics after Moore* (Oxford University Press, 2006).

Andreas Trampota is Lecturer in Ethics and History of Philosophy at the Munich School of Philosophy (Hochschule für Philosophie). He was a Visiting Scholar at Fordham University in New York. His publications include a monograph on the epistemic foundation of ethics in Immanuel Kant and Iris Murdoch entitled *Autonome Vernunft oder moralische Sehkraft? Das epistemische Fundament der Ethik bei Immanuel Kant und Iris Murdoch* (Kohlhammer, 2003) and several articles mainly on practical philosophy.

Günter Zöller is Professor of Philosophy at the University of Munich. He held visiting positions at Princeton University, Emory University, and Seoul National University. He is a member of the Fichte Commission of the Bavarian Academy of Sciences and co-editor of the *J. G. Fichte Edition of the Bavarian Academy of Sciences*. His books include *Theoretische Gegenstandsbeziehung bei Kant* (De Gruyter, 1984) and *Fichte's Transcendental Philosophy* (Cambridge University Press, 1998). As editor he also published *Immanuel Kant: Prolegomena to Any Future Metaphysics* (Oxford University Press, 2004), and as co-editor (with Robert Louden) *Immanuel Kant: Anthropology, History, and Education* (Cambridge University Press, 2007).

Index of Names

Index of Subjects

www.ingramcontent.com/pod-product-compliance
Lightning Source LLC
Chambersburg PA
CBHW030811100426
42814CB00002B/85